D1879676

# A DICTIONARY
OF THE
# BURMAN LANGUAGE.

# A DICTIONARY

OF THE

# BURMAN LANGUAGE,

## WITH EXPLANATIONS IN ENGLISH.

A. JUDSON, D. D.

GYAN

*Published by*

Gyan Publishing House
5, Ansari Road
Daryaganj, New Delhi-110002
Phone: 011-47034999, 9811692060
E-mail: books@gyanbooks.com

*Distribution Network*
gyanbooks.com
India, USA, Canada, UK, Australia, France

**© Publisher**

All rights reserved. No part of this work may be reproduced, stored, adapted, or transmitted in any form or by any means, electronic, mechanical, photocopying, micro-filming, recording or otherwise, or translated in any language, without the prior written permission of the copyright owner and the publisher.

ISBN: 978-81-212-8384-7 (PB)
First Published, 1826

2nd Impression 2023

*Printed at:* Gyan Press, Delhi.

The book is sold subject to the condition that it shall not, by way of trade or otherwise, be lent, resold, hired out, or otherwise circulated without the prior publisher's written consent.

**A DICTIONARY OF THE BURMAN LANGUAGE**
Author: A. JUDSON

# A DICTIONARY

OF THE

# BURMAN LANGUAGE.

## *Final Consonants.*

When a consonant ends a syllable, or is final, it is distinguished by the mark (် ) placed over it, thus တ်; or by another consonant subjoined, thus တ္တ.

N. B. It sometimes happens that two consonants, one placed under the other, are both initials, and therefore an exception to the preceding rule; thus သွာ is equivalent to သဝါ: this is to be regarded as a mere abbreviation.

A double ဉ is written ည, the same as one form of the single.

ဉ, with ဇ subjoined, is written ဉ္ဇ, or simply ဇ. A double သ is written ဿ or သသ.

Final consonants generally assume a new and peculiar power, and also modify the preceding vowel.

These permutations are exhibited in the following table.

### *Table of Finals.*

| အ | | ဣ | ဥ | ဧ | | ဪ | အို |
|---|---|---|---|---|---|---|---|
| အက် | *et.* | အိက် *ik.* | အုက် *oke.* | ေအက် | *eet.* | ေအာက် *ouk.* | အိုက် *aik.* |
| အင် | *eng.* | အိင် *ing.* | အုင် *ong.* | — | | ေအာင် *oung.* | အိုင် *aing.* |
| အစ် | *eet.* | အိစ် *ik.* | အုစ် *oke.* | ေအစ် | *eet.* | ေအာစ် *oot.* | — |
| အဉ် | *een,* | အိဉ် *ing.* | အုဉ် *ong.* | ေအဉ် | *een,* | ေအာဉ် *oon.* | — |
| | *ee.* | — | — | — | *ee.* | — | — |
| အတ် | *at.* | အိတ် *ik.* | အုတ် *oke.* | ေအတ် | *eet.* | ေအာတ် *oot.* | အိုတ် *aik.* |
| အန် | *an.* | အိန် *ing.* | အုန် *ong.* | ေအန် | *een.* | ေအာန် *oon.* | အိုန် *aing.* |
| အပ် | *at.* | အိပ် *ik.* | အုပ် *oke.* | ေအပ် | *eet.* | ေအာပ် *oot.* | အိုပ် *aik.* |
| အမ် | *an.* | အိမ် *ing.* | အုမ် *ong.* | ေအမ် | *een.* | ေအာမ် *oon.* | အိုမ် *aing.* |
| အယ် | *ay.* | — | — | — | | — | အိုယ် *o.* |
| — | | — | — | ေအရ် | *ee.* | — | အိုရ် *o.* |
| အလ် | *an.* | အိလ် *ing.* | အုလ် *ong.* | ေအလ် | *een.* | ေအာလ် *oon.* | အိုလ် *o.* |
| အသ် | *at.* | အိသ် *ik.* | အုသ် *oke.* | ေအသ် | *eet.* | ေအာသ် *oot.* | — |
| အံ | *an.* | အိံ *ing.* | အုံ *ong.* | — | | — | — |

As an appendix to the foregoing table, note :—

1st. Linguals, when final, are the same as dentals.

2nd. The third letter of each class is the same as the first.

3rd. The 2nd and 4th letters of each class never occur as finals, except in some words derived from the Magadha, where they are mute; as, မိုဃ်း (from မေဃ, a cloud,) is pronounced as မိုး.

4th. ဏ် is the same as န် throughout.

5th. ဝ် and ဟ် are mute.

6th. အာ before a final, gives the syllable the same sound as အ; thus အာန် is pronounced *an*.

7th. The final syllables, as exhibited above, are combined with any consonant simple or compound, as ကက် *ket*; ကျင် *kyen*, &c. without any change in their pronunciation, except in two cases, viz. ဝ, before ဋ်, တ်, ပ်, and သ်, is pronounced *woot*, not *wat*; and before ဏ်, န်, မ်, ယ်, or ံ, is pronounced *woon* and *won*, not *wan*; also, consonants compounded with ဝ, as ကွ, စွ, &c. before ဋ်, တ်, ပ်, or သ်, are pronounced *kooat*, *tsooat*, &c. and before ဏ်, န်, မ်, ယ်, and ံ, are pronounced *koo-an*, *tsooan*, &c.; but the latter exception is not sanctioned by court usage.

8th. The sound of a final consonant is frequently lost or absorbed, in the initial consonant of the following syllable or word, as ဧက္ကရာ is pronounced *ekara*, not *etkara*; and sometimes it is modified thereby, as သင်္ဘော is pronounced *thembau*, not *thengbau*; but these permutations, being dictates of nature, will be naturally acquired without rule.

### *Accents.*

There are two accents, namely, the short and the heavy.

The short accent, ( ့ ) called အောက်မြစ်, is placed under the letter thus, ကန့်. It is used with the vowels ဧ, အဲ, ဪ, and အို့, and the nasal consonants.

The heavy accent ( း ) called ဝစ္စပေါက်, is placed after the letter thus, ကန်း. It is used with the vowels အာ, ဦ, ဤ, ဧ, and အိုး, and the nasal consonants.

The heavy accent is considered as inherent in the vowel အဲ, (unless superseded by the short accent ;) also in the final consonant ဉ, when combined with the vowel အ. It is therefore omitted in these cases, as superfluous, by correct writers.

## *Numerical Figures.*

၁, ၂, ၃, ၄, ၅, ၆, ၇, ၈, ၉, ၁၀.
1, 2, 3, 4, 5, 6, 7, 8, 9, 10.

## *Punctuation.*

The mark (၊) is used to separate sentences, and sometimes the clauses of a sentence.

(၊ ၊) Is used to divide paragraphs.

## *Abbreviations.*

| | | |
|---|---|---|
| မ္ည is used .. .. | for .. .. | မည် |
| လ္ည .. .. .. | for .. .. | လည် |
| သ္ည .. .. .. | for .. .. | သည် |
| ငြ္ည .. .. .. | for .. .. | ငြည် |
| ၌ .. .. .. | for .. .. | နှိုက် |
| ၍ .. .. .. | for .. .. | ရွေ့ |
| င်း .. .. .. | for .. .. | ကောင်း |
| င့် .. .. .. | for .. .. | ကြောင့် |
| ၎င *or* ၎ .. .. | for .. .. | လည်းကောင်း |
| ဧ *or* ေဧ .. .. | for .. .. | သော |
| ˙ *(over a letter)* | for .. .. | တ် |
| ကျွှုပ် .. .. | for .. .. | ကျွန်နှုပ် |
| လက္န .. .. .. | for .. .. | လက်နက် |
| လုင် .. .. .. | for .. .. | လုလင် |
| သွေ့ .. .. .. | for .. .. | သွေသောက် |

ယ is sometimes represented by its symbol ျ, after က်, as ယောက်ျား for ယောက်ယား ; ထက်ျာ for ထက်ယာ, &c.

င is frequently removed from its natural situation in the line, and placed over the following letter, as သင်္ဘော, for သင်ဘော.

# BURMAN DICTIONARY.

အ

အ, the first vowel in the Burman alphabet.

အ, *v.* to be dumb, speechless; to stammer, stutter, be imperfect in speech.

အအိမ်, (from အိမ်, a house,) *n.* a sheath.

အအုပ်, *n.* see အကြီး.

အအူ, (see အူ,) the intestines.

အအောင်, *n.* a fee; see အောင်.

အဥ, *n.* an egg.

အဦး, *num. affix*; chief, first.

အဦး, *n.* a beginning.

အကလေး, *adj.* small, little; *n.* a child, an infant.

အက်, *v.* to widen, gape, crack open—less than ကွဲ;—အာ. Hence

အအက်, *n.* an opening, gap, fissure.

အကင်း, *n.* fruit in its first stage after the blossom.

အကန့်, *n.* a line drawn across another line; the spokes of a wheel.

အကယ်အားဖြင့်ဆောင်ချင်, *n.* see ဥဒါဟရုဏ်.

အကယ်, *adj.* right, certain, true; ထကယ် ၊ အမှန်; အကယ်ထင်တင်, do.

အကယ်၍, *adv.* certainly, verily.

အကယ်ပြု, *v.* to assume an appearance of truth or right, make false pretences.

အကာ, *n.* the soft, unsubstantial part of a thing, opposed to အနှစ်, the solid substance; as the soft part of a tree, either the inner rind, or, in some trees, the pithy part, as distinguished from the solid wood; the white of an egg, &c.

အကာလ, *n.* an improper, inconvenient time, unseasonable; အချိန်မဟုတ်သောအခါ.

အကုန်, *adv.* completely, fully.

အကုဋေ, see ကုဋေ.

အကုသိုလ်, *n.* demerit, the punishment of demerit, မကောင်းမှု၊ မကောင်းသောအကျိုး။

အကဲ, *n.* see အကြီး။

အကဲ့, *adv.* by degrees.

အကောက်, *n.* duties, custom.

အကောက်, *n.* see အခွန်.

အကောင်, *numeral affix, (see Grammar.)*

အကောင်, a term affixed to the names of brute animals, as နှံကောင်, a grasshopper.

အကောင်, *n.* a dead body, corpse ; အလောင်းကောင်.

အကောင်းအကန်, *adj.* poor, worthless, of no use.

အကိုင်အလုပ်, *n.* work, business.

အကိုင်း, *n.* a handle.

အကိုင်း, *n.* see အခက်.

အက္ခရာ, *n.* a character or letter of the alphabet, vowel or consonant.

အကျက်, *n.* custom, habit, &c.

အကျင်, *n.* a pin, bolt, that which is used to fasten any thing.

အကျင့်, *n.* a deed, action, custom.

အကျင့်ပါ, *v.* to be natural, habitual.

အကျင့်အထုံပါ, *v.* do.

အကျန်, *n.* a remainder.

အကျဉ်, *n.* an aperture, an opening, hole, the aperture of a door or window ; a door, stopper, cover ; *(figuratively,)* property, abilities.

အကျဉ်းအခဲ, *n.* an induration, hardness ; အကျိတ်အခဲ.

အကျဉ်း, *n.* an abridgment, compilation.

အကျပ်, *n.* a kyat or tickal, weight equal to four mats, (မတ်.)

အကျယ်, *n.* an open part ; more extensive than အကျဉ်—which see.

အကျိတ်အခဲ, *n.* see အကျဉ်းအခဲ.

အကျိတ်, *n.* in a finished, complete, unalterable manner ; difficulty.

အကျိန်ရဲ, *v.* to dare to.

အကြေး, *n.* scales (of fish or other animals); ငါးကြေး။ အချပ်.

အကျောင်း, *n.* a keeper, a herdsman; see ကျောင်း.

အကျော, *n.* a kind of tree.

အကျော်, *n.* an odoriferous substance.

အကျိုး, *n.* a consequence, result; an effect, opposed to အကြောင်း, a cause; a good result, profit, advantage.

အကျိုးနည်း, or နဲ, *v.* to be of little profit; to be ruined, totally lost.

အကျိုးမဲ့စွာ, *ad.* fruitlessly, i. e. without profit.

အကြင်, *pron. adj.* whatever; အကြင်သူ, whoever.

အကြင်ကို, အကြင်သို့, to which.

အကြင်က, အကြင်မှ, အကြင်ကြောင့်, from which, because of which.

အကြင်မှာ, အကြင်မှုကား, among which.

အကြင်သို့, of whatever sort.

အကြင်သို့က, အကြင်သို့မှ, from which sort.

အကြင်သို့ကြောင့်, အသို့သောကြောင့်, because of which sort.

အကြည်း, *n.* appearance; အဆင်း။ အရုပ်.

အကြည်းတန်, *v.* to be homely, ugly, odious, အရုပ်ဆိုး.

အကြည်တော်, *n.* a royal friend, (used by kings in speaking to, or of one another.)

အကြပ်, *n.* a subordinate officer.

အကြား, *adj.* between, betwixt.

အကြား, *n.* a crack, opening, intermediate space; a lane, pathway.

အကြားအသိအမြင်အဆော်, *v.* to know, receive instruction.

အကြိမ်, *n.* time, turn, as တကြိမ် once, နှစ်ကြိမ်, twice; အပန်၊ အသီ.

အကြိမ်ကြိမ် *adj.* again, repeatedly; အပန်ပန်.

အကြီး, *n.* a cover, a chief, a head-man; အကဲ၊ အမှူး၊ အချုပ်၊ အဆုပ်၊ အခေါင်း.

အကြေ, *n.* a lower part (of a river, country, &c.) opposed to အညာ.

အကြေး, *n.* filth, dirt, rust; (2) *n.* the scales of fish; အချပ်.

အကြေးအညစ်, *n.* do.

အကြေးအညော်, *n.* do.

အကြော, *n.* a tubular vessel of the body; a sinew, nerve, tendon; a vein, artery.

အကြောမ, *n.* a large principal do.

အကြောင်း, *n.* an antecedent or cause, opposed to အကျိုး, an effect, an occasion; materials of which a thing is made; a circumstance, business, affair. အရင်း၊ အချင်းအရာ do. အခင်းအရာ၊ အနှင့်၊ အရေး၊ အမှု.

အကြောင်းအချာ, do. အကြောင်းအရာ, do. အကြောင်းအလင်း, do. အကြောင်းအလျှာ, do.

အကြောင်းတရားလေးပါး, the four prime causes, viz. ကံ၊ စိတ်၊ ဥတု၊ အဟာရ.

အကြောင်းကြောင်း, *adv.* variously, in sundry ways, affairs, &c.

အကြောင်း, *num. affix*, (see Gram.)

အကြောင်းမတန်, *adv.* unreasonably, unaccountably.

အကြောင်း, *n.* a line, mark; any thing drawn out, a line, a furrow, road, &c.

အကြိုအကြား, *n.* an interstice, intermediate space; အကြား.

အကြိုနေ့, or ရက်, *n.* the day before worship day.

အကွင်, *n.* the act of encompassing, &c. see ကွင်း.

အကွ, with, or together with; see နှင့်အကွ.

အကွင်း, *num. affix*, (see Gram.) (2) *n.* a remainder.

အကွက်, *n.* a spot, place; see ကွက်.

အကွေ, *n.* a ring put round the end of a handle, to keep it from splitting.

အကွေ့, *n.* a curve, bend, corner, bay. အခွေ; *n.* do.

အကွပ်, *n.* a hoop.

အကျွတ်, see under နိဗ္ဗာန်, *n.* annihilation.

အကျွန်, *pers. n. I*; ကျွန်မ, *fem.*

အကျွန်နှုပ်, see ကျွန်နှုပ်.

အကျွန်, *n.* a feigned appearance; see ကျွန်.

အကျွင်း, *n.* an acquaintance.

အကြွေး, (from ကြွေး, a debt,) *adv.* on credit.

အကြွေးအငင်း, (from ငင်း, to wait,) *adv.* in expectance of the payment of a debt.

အကြွင်းမဲ့, *adv.* wholly, without leaving any part.

အခ, *n.* wages; အခစား, *n.* one who lives on wages.

အခက်, *n.* a branch of a tree; အကိုင်း. အခက်မ, *n.* a main branch.

အခင်, *num. affix*, (see Gram.)

အခင်, *n.* thread wound on a weaver's quill, a skein or bank of thread; ချည်ခင်. (2) *n.* the uvula, လျှာခင်. (3) *n.* the mouth-piece of a musical instrument, as ငြွေခင်၊ တပိုးခင်.

အခင်း, (1) *n.* a portion, division of the day, as ညခင်း, the evening; (2) business, affair, subject, matter, circumstance; အင်္ဂါ၊ အမှု၊ အရာ၊ အရေး။ အခင်း. See ခင်း.

အခင်း, *n.* any thing spread out, or laid out in order; see ခင်း.

အခန့်, *n.* an estimate, measurement, limit, extent.

အခန့်အတာ, *n.* do.

အခန့်အရှည်, *n.* do.

အခန့်သင့်, *v.* to be convenient.

အခစား, *n.* a hired servant; ပေါင်ကျွန်.

အခန်း, *n.* an apartment, room; အခန်းမ, *n.* the principal room.

အခင်းအနား, *n.* equipage; what is carried about a person, utensils, furniture; အဆောင်အရွက်. the business of keeping a festival, performing ceremonies, rites, &c.

အခရာ, *n.* a kara, a certain measure of time.

အငယ်, *adj.* small, little; *n.* a little thing, a child, infant.

အငုံ့အခု, *n.* see အငုံ့အခံ.

အခါ, *n.* time; ကာလ. အခါခါ, *adv.* repeatedly; အခါခါဖန်ဖန်, do. သွားသည့်အခါ, the time of going.

အခါလည်, *v.* to turn a year, be above a year; နှစ်လည်.

အခါဝေးမြင့်, *v.* to delay, be distant in time, be a long time.

အခါမဲ့, *v.* to be out of season, unseasonable.

အခု, *n.* an individual thing, (used as a numeral auxiliary.)

အခု, *n.* wedge, prop, cushion, any thing that gives support, whether a thing or person.

အခုအနှိုး, *n.* do. } also suppressed anger, or malice.
အငုံ့အခံ, *n.* do. }

အခဲ, *n.* an induration, hardness; see ခဲ.

အခေါက်, *n.* a fold, &c. see ခေါက်.

အခေါင်, *n.* summit, top, highest part, chief; အထွဋ်၊ ထိပ်.

အခေါ်ဘဏ်, *n.* an immense number.

အခိုက်, *n.* the time being.

အခိုက်အတန့်, *n.* do.

အခိုင်, *n.* a stock, or branch (of fruit;) see ခိုင်.

အခိုး, *n.* smoke, vapour, အငွေ့ ;—အထုံ့, *n.* perfume.

အချက်, (1) *n.* a middle, central point, where several objects meet, a centre ; အချက်အချာ, *n.* do. (2) *n.* a subject, matter, business ; a mark, sign, as ဗွေ, a mark, impression, stroke. အချက်အလက်၊ အချက် အရာ, do.

အချက်ကျ, *v.* to fall in place, hit the mark or object, be to purpose, be right ; အမှန်ကျ၊ အရာကျ. Hence တချက်တီး, one beat (of a gong) denoting the time, 9 o'clock ; နှစ်ချက်တီး, two beats, denoting 12 o'clock, &c. by which the day and night are divided into four equal periods each. Hence also, တချက်ထည်, *adv.* instantly, at once.

အချက်အချာ, *n.* a point of union ; see အချာ.

အချင်, *n.* the rafters, or ribs of a roof.

အချင်း, (1) *n.* an action, deed, business, affair ; အခွင်၊ အဆင်း.

အချင်းအရာ, *n.* do. conduct, circumstance ; အကြောင်း ; အချင်းများ, *v.* to quarrel, ခုန်တွေ့ ; (2) *n.* an appearance, အရည် ; (3) *n.* a kind of verse ; အဖျားဆို ; *v.* to sing verses. (4) *n.* the secundine, afterbirth. (5) *n.* one who belongs to, or is connected with another ; a friend (used vocatively.)

အချင်းချင်း, *adv.* mutually, one with another ; *sometimes* ချင်း.

အချင့်, *n.* a diameter.

အချည်းစည်း, *adv.* nakedly, without clothes.

အချည်းနှီး, *adv.* in vain, uselessly, to no purpose ; အလကား၊ အကျိုးမနှင်း

အချည်းသက်သက်, *adv.* do.

အချပ်, *n.* the scales of fish, or other animals.

အခြံအရံ, *n.* (1) fence ; (2) *n.* guards, attendants.

အခြား, *pr. adj.* other, another.

အချာ, *n.* that which unites several parts, a point of union.

အချာအချုပ်, *n.* do.

အခါးမဲ့, *n.* in that time.

အချား, *n.* a crack, opening, lane ; (see အကြား.)

အချိန်, *n.* a time, period, season.

အချုပ်, *n.* see အကြိုး.

အချုပ် အချာ, *n.* see အချာ.

အချုပ်သမား, *n.* a tailor.

အချောင်း, *n.* a bar, long piece; အတန်.

အချို့, *pron. adj.* some; တချို့.

အခြံအရံ, *n.* attendants, guards.

အခြေ, *n.* a foundation, bottom, root; အရင်း၊ အမြစ်. See ခြေ.

အချေး, *n.* dirt, rust, (*pron.* အချိ.)

အခွ, *n.* the crotch of a tree, the place of branching out of a river, a fork.

အခွက်အကျင်း, *n.* a capacity (of a vessel).

အခွက်, *n.* a kwet, a weight equal to a piktha, (ပိဿာ,) or viss; it supersedes the latter word in all *capital* numbers, as အခွက်တဆယ် instead of ပိဿာတဆယ်, ten viss.

အခွင့်, *n.* permission, commission, opportunity; အခွင့်အရာ၊ အခွင့် အရေး၊ အမှု, a business, affair.

အခွန်, *n.* revenue accruing from regular assessments on real or personal property, as distinguished from အကောက်, duties on merchandize, and ငွေတော်, arbitrary taxes.

အခွန်အလုပ်, *n.* do.

အခွန်ဝန်, *n.* a head-collector of revenue.

အခွန်း, *n.* a voice, (seldom used but as a numeral auxiliary.)

အခွံ, *n.* bark, rind, peel, shell, skin (of fruit,) &c.

အခြွေအရွေ, see အခြွေအရံ.

အခြွေအရံ, *n.* guards, attendants.

အချွဲ, *n.* any-slimy, mucous matter.

အချွဲ့ငင်ဖြီ, *v.* to keep putting off; to feign both willingness and unwillingness.

အစာရိ, (from အ, priv. and စာရိ, conduct, *Pali*;) *n.* unsuitable carriage, behaviour.

အဂ္ဂသာဝက, (*Pali,*) *n.* a chief, disciple.

အဂ္ဂိရတ်, (from အဂ္ဂိ fire, *Pali,* and ဗျုဂ္ဂရ, a book on pyrology,) *n.* alchymy.

အဂ္ဂိရတ်လုပ် or ထိုး, *v.* to practise alchymy.

အင်, (1) *n.* a kind of tree; အင်ကြင်း, *n.* one species of do. စွဲ (from စွဲ to hang adhesively,) *n.* the gum of do. ပွတ်ရက်; (2) *n.* an earthen cup, bowl, basin. အင်ကွက်, *n.* an earthen cup

အင်တုံ, *n.* a deep earthen pan; (3) *n.* number, quantity, force, strength, abilities of any kind.

အင်သတ္တိ၊ ခွန်အား၊ အင်ခွင်, do.

အင်အား, *n.* military force, troops.

အင်တန်, *adv.* in a middling degree.

အင်မတန်, *adv.* exceedingly, very.

အင်တွဲ, *n.* the gum of a certain tree; or, the tree itself.

အင်း, (1) *n.* a natural pond, lake, smaller than အိုင်; (2) *n.* the space on plates of metal, or other surfaces, inclosed by lines, and commonly subdivided into squares, or other compartments, for entering certain records; အင်းဆိုင်, do.

အင်းစာရင်း, *n.* an account, or register written on do.

အငင်း, see ငင်.

အငန်း, *n.* that which is the peculiar business of a person, a part, portion, allotment; အငန်းအသာ, do. အစု, do.

အင်ကျီ or အင်္ကျီ, *n.* a coat, jacket; အင်္ကျီဒုရင်, do.

အင်္ကျီကိုယ်ကျပ်, *n.* a tight body-jacket.

အင်္ကျီခါးတို, *n.* a short coat, a jacket.

အင်္ကျီနို, *n.* a jacket-tie, a string.

အင်္ကျီလက်ကျပ်, *n.* a tight-sleeved coat or jacket.

အင်္ကျီလက်ဖြိုး, *n.* a loose flowing coat.

အင်္ကျီလည်စွပ်, *n.* a frock, shirt.

အင်ဆန်ပြု, *v.* to make a tumult, or uproar.

အင်ဂတေ, *n.* mortar, plaister; ထကန်စေးအင်္ဂတေ, do.

အင်္ဂါ, (1) *n.* the planet Mars; the third day of the week, Tuesday.

အင်္ဂါ, (2) *n.* a component part or member; အစိတ်; a part of the body, member, limb.

အင်္ဂါဇာတ် or ဇစ်, (from ဇာတ်, to produce, *Pali;)* *n.* organs of generation, whether male or female; နိမိတ်၊ သော၊ လိင်.

အင်္ဂါကိုးပါး, nine parts, into which the Boodhist scriptures are divided, according to a certain distribution, viz. သုတ်၊ ဂေယျ၊ ဂါထာ၊ ဝေယျာကရဏ၊ ဥဒါန၊ ဣတိဝုတ်၊ ဇာတ်၊ အဗ္ဘုတဓမ္မ၊ ဝေဒလ္လ၊

အင်္ဂမကိယျတာက, *n.* domestic or family affairs, အိမ်ထောင်အမှု.

အင်္ဂသမကိယ, do.

အင်္ဂုတ္တရ, *n.* one division of the Boodhist scriptures.

အင်္ဃါ, *n.* see အင်္ဂါ.

အင်ပျဉ်, *n.* a kind of blister.

အင်းပျဉ်, *n.* a kind of bedstead; any flat surface raised on low legs.

အင်ဝ, or အင်ယ; see အဝ.

အငုတ်, *n.* the remainder of a thing, as သစ်ငုတ်, the remainder, that is, the stump, of a tree; ဘုရားငုတ်, the ruins of a pagoda; (see ငုတ်.)

အငူ, *n.* a cape, promontory.

အငူအငေါ, *n.* do.

အငွေ့, *n.* vapour, exhalations, steam, smoke; အခိုး.

အစ, *n.* beginning; အစအဦး.

အစသတ်, *v.* to make an end.

အစ, and so forth, &c. အစသည်.

အစက်, *n.* (from စက်, to make a dot, &c.) a dot, a drop.

အစ်, (1) *n.* a cylindrical box (of any size;) (2) *v.* to be tense, straitened, (applied to the throat.)

အစစ်, *adj.* clean, pure, genuine.

အစဉ်, *n.* some part of the viscera; see စဉ်ဖောင်း.

အစဉ်, *adv.* while, as သွားသည်အစဉ်, during the time of going, or while he goes.

အစဉ်, *adv.* continually, permanently, immutably.

အစဉ်အဆက်, *n.* a lineal succession.

အစဉ်းအဝါး, *adv.* accurately, minutely.

အစပ်, *n.* a joint, or seam, a union of two or more, (applied to things.)

အစာ, (perhaps from စား, to eat;) *n.* food.

အစာတင်, *v.* to dress thread by an application of boiled rice, to size.

အစား, *n.* stead, place, room; *adv.* instead of; ရိုက်, ကိုယ်စား.

အစား, *n.* a price, value; အဖိုး.

အစိမ်းစား, *n.* any thing which does not require to be cooked in order to be eaten.

အစိတ်, *n.* a division, a quarter of any thing.

အစု, *n.* see အစုံး ; (2) *n.* a collection, assemblage.

အစုမဲ့ကျွန်, *n.* a slave that is redeemable, but has no other rights.

အစေအပါ, *n.* a servant, or slave ; ကျွန်.

အစေခံ, *n.* do.

အစေ့, (1) *n.* a seed ; (2) an ancestor of the seventh degree of ascent from one's self.

အစေး, *n.* gum, any glutinous matter.

အစော, *(Siamese,)* *n.* a lord, master, mistress, madam, (used as a term of compellation ;) အရှင်၊ ရှင်မ ; see စော.

အစော, *adv.* early ; အစောကြီး, very early.

အစောက်, *n.* steepness, depth, height.

အစောင်, *a numeral auxiliary, applied to writings.*

အစောင်း, *n.* a sharp edge, a side ; nearness.

အစိုးရ, *v.* (see under ချုပ်). အစိုး, *n.* do.

အစိုင်, *n.* a lump, any adhesive mass.

အစု, *n.* a company, band, (applied to certain people in government service ;) အသင်း.

အစ်ကို, *n.* an elder brother of a brother ; နောင်.

အစ်မ, *n.* an elder sister of a sister.

အစွတ်, *n.* moisture.

အစွန်, *v.* to be strong, powerful, able.

အစွန်, or အစွန်း, *n.* an edge, side, border, end, extremity ; အစွန်အနား၊ အစွန်အမြိတ်.

အစွမ်, *v.* see အစွန် ; အားရှိ.

အစွယ်, *n.* a tusk, fang.

အဆ, *n.* a quantity, portion ; ဆို့, *with numerals,* fold, as သုံးဆ three-fold, အဆသုံးဆယ် thirty-fold.

အဆက်, *n.* any thing thrown into a bargain.

အဆက်, *n.* a junction, union, a joint.

အဆက်ဆက်, *adv.* connectively, successively, one after another.

အဆက်ဆက်ဥပဒေသ, traditionary precepts.

အဆင့်ဆင့်, *adv.* one above another, day after day, or daily.

အဆင်း, *n.* appearance အရုပ်၊ အရောင်၊ အဝါ၊ အရည်.

အဆင်းအပြင်, do. အဆင်းအလှ, do.

အဆင်းတန်, *v.* to appear old, homely; see ဆို.

အဆင်ပြေ, *v.* to be convenient.

အဆင်သင့်, *v.* do.

အဆစ်, *n.* a joint, &c. see ဆစ်.

အဆယ် or အဆဲ, *n.* a ten, the number of ten, (combined with the nine digits to form numerals, as တဆယ်, one ten, or ten; နှစ်ဆယ်, two tens, or twenty, &c.)

အဆန်, *n.* the kernel of a seed of grain, or fruit-stone, (hence ဆန်, husked rice;) the inside or kernel of any thing, as the tongue or clapper of a bell, the pebble in a rattle, the marrow in a bone, &c.

အဆာ, *n.* the unfinished end of wove cloth; ပြိတ်ဆာ.

အဆိတ်, *n.* a small quantity, a pinch.

အဆိပ်, *n.* poison, venom.

အဆိပ်အတောက်, do. (*figurat.*) passion, lust, inebriation.

အဆီ, see ဆီ, oil.

အဆီအပြား, *n.* relishing savoury food.

အဆုတ်, *n.* the lungs, lights.

အဆုံအမ, *n.* instruction, doctrine; see သာသနာ.

အဆုံ, *n.* an end.

အဆုံစွန်, *adj.* last, final; *n.* an end, a conclusion.

အဆုံစွန်ဦ, *n.* the end of life.

အဆုန်အဖြတ်, *n.* a decision, or judgment.

အဆုန်မဲ့, *adj.* infinite, boundless.

အဆုံးသတ်, *v.* to finish, make an end.

အဆူ, *n.* a numeral auxiliary, applied to duties, and some other objects.

အဆူး, see ဆူး, a thorn.

အဆောတလျင်, *adv.* quickly.

အဆော, *adv.* do.

အဆောက်အဆုံ, *n.* utensils, appendages, materials; အဆုံအဆောင်.

အဆောင်အရောင်, *n.* see အခင်းအနား.

အခိုင်း, *n.* a bunch, cluster (of flowers, fruit, &c.)

အဆွေ, *n.* an acquaintance, friend.

အဆွေခင်ပွန်း, *n.* a friend. အဆွေအမျိုးစစ်, *n.* an own relation.

အဆွေဉာတကာ, see အဆွေခင်ပွန်း.

အဆွေဖွဲ့, *v.* to form acquaintance.

အဆွေအမျိုး, *n.* a relation, kinsman, one of the same stock.

အဆွေသားချင်း, do.

အဇ္ဈတ္တိကာယတန်, *n.* the six senses, viz. seeing, hearing, tasting, smelling, feeling, and thinking.

အဉ်, *adv.* yes ; ဆိမ်း.

အဉ့်, *v.* to feign unwillingness, hold off.

အညစ်, *n.* dirt, filth, rust.

အညစ်အကြေး, *n.* do.

အညာ, *n.* a higher part of a river, country, &c. opposed to အကြေ.

အညာသား, *n.* a native of an upper province.

အညိမ့်, *n.* a musical instrument ; အညိမ့်ထိုးရိုယ်၊ အညိမ့်တံဆ.

အညိမ့်သမား, *n.* a player on musical instruments.

အညီ, *n.* evenness, agreement ; *prep.* according to, as အလိုကြိုက်အညီ, according to his pleasure.

အညီး, *adv.* accordingly, like, similar.

အညှာ, *n.* a pedicle, footstalk, stem by which a leaf or fruit is connected with the limb.

အညှိ, *n.* slime, filth.

အညှော်, *n.* see အကြေးအညှော်.

အညှောက်, (1) *n.* a germ, sprout, from a seed ; *figurat.* the protuberance on the root of a creature's tail, (sometimes pron. အညှောင် ;) (2) *n.* an ancestor of the sixth degree of ascent from one's self.

အညှို့, *n.* some part of the viscera.

အဉ်း, see ဆိမ်း.

အဋ္ဌမ, (from အဋ္ဌ, eight, *Pali*,) *adj.* eighth.

အဋ္ဌကထာ, *n.* a commentary on the original Pali text ; see ဋီကာ.

အဋ္ဌာရသ, (a corruption of အဋ္ဌ, eight, and ဒသ, ten ;) *n.* the eighteen sciences ; အဋ္ဌာရသသိပ္ပ.

အဏ္ဍဇာ, *n.* one of the four ways of transition from one body to another.

အတက်, *n.* the shoot of a tree; the spur of a cock.

အထင်း, *n.* a ten, a measure of capacity equal to sixteen pyees; ဖြည်.

အထင့်, *adv.* appearing well, but being otherwise.

အထည်, *n.* a kind, sort, (used as a numeral auxiliary;) အမျိုး၊ အဝ.

အထည်ထည်, *adv.* of several kinds, variously; အသီးသီး၊ အသွယ်သွယ်.

အထည့်အထင်း, truly; အမှန်မှန်.

အတစ်, *n.* a piece, a bit.

အတတ်, *adv.* verily, certainly, truly.

အထန်, *n.* intervening space, distance, extent, length (of time or place;) အတန်ငယ်, *n.* a little while; a little (in quantity.)

အထန်ထန်, *adv.* at intervals, in several places, repeatedly; အတန်ထန်အထည်ထည်, do.

အတန်း, *n.* an extended line, a row, duration.

အတ္တ, *n.* the body; ကိုယ်.

အတ္တဝါဒုပါဒါန်, *n.* one of four evil passions or affections.

အထန့်, *n.* a mark drawn across, a limit, a stop.

အထန့်ထန့်, *adv.* one after another, successively.

အတန်ငယ်, *adj.* small (distance).

အတပ်, *adv.* verily, truly.

အတံ, *n.* a straight long piece, a bar; အချောင်း, (used in composition,) as လှံတံ၊ ဆေးတံ၊ ခဲတံ, &c.

အတန်း, *n.* way, manner, custom; ထုံးစံ.

အတာ, *n.* a measure of distance.

အတိ, (1) *pron. adj.* what; အဘယ် (pron. အဒိ.) (2) *adj.* clear, without mixture, genuine.

အတိဇာတ, *(Pali,) adj.* excellent, (applied to a son who excels his parents.)

အတိတ်, *n.* the past.

အထုတ်အနွန်, see အနွန်အထုတ်.

အထုန်း, *n.* time being, (construed with simple participials, as ရှိထုန်းခါ or ရှိထုန်းတွင်, while he was.)

အတူတကွ, with, together with.

အတူအကွ, do.

အတေကိစ္ဆ, (*Pali,*) *adj.* incurable.

အတောင်, *n.* a feather, a wing.

အတောင်, *n.* a measure of distance equal to two spans.

အတိုင်, (1) *n.* a warp; ရက်ကန်းချည်း (2) *n.* taing, a measure of distance, equal to 1000 tahs; (အတာ) about two miles.

အတိုင်, *adv.* accordingly.

အတိုင်း, according to, as အမှာတော်အတိုင်း, according to the order.

အတိုင်းအရှည်, *n.* an estimate, measurement.

အတိုး, *n.* interest.

အတ္တဘော, (from အတ္တ, body, &c. ဘဝ, being, *Pali*;) *n.* the body; ကိုယ်ကြီးဖြစ်ခြင်း.

အတွင်း, *n.* inside, inner part; အထဲ။ အတွင်းဝန်, *n.* a private minister of state.

အတွင်းနံ့တိုင်မြင်း, *n.* a horse that takes his place near the king in marching.

အတွင်းဘဝါး, see စနည်း.

အတွေ့, *n.* an object of sense.

အထက်, *n.* an upper part; prior time; without; အထက်, *a term of comparison,* as အိမ်ထက်ကြီး၏, it is greater than the house; အပေါ်.

အထစ်ထစ်အရစ်ရစ်, *adv.* unevenly.

အထည်, (1) *n.* a piece of cloth; (2) see အထဲ.

အထပ်တရာ, (1) *n.* kind of a tree; (2) one thing upon another, as the leaves of a book.

အထံ, *n.* nearness, presence; ဆီ၊ ထံပါး၊ ထံရင်း.

အထိန်း, *n.* a muse, guardian, &c.

အထီ, *n.* a male; *adj.* masculine (combined with names of animals, to mark the gender.)

အထီး, *adj.* alone, single.

အထု, (sometimes *pron.* ဒု) *n.* depth, thickness, strength, ability; အထုအား, do.

အထုပ်, *n.* a bundle.

အထုပ္ပတ္တိ, (*Pali,*) *n.* events, circumstances, adventures; ဖြစ်ရာ.

အထုံ, *n.* any fragrant preparative.

အထူးသဖြင့်, *adv.* exceedingly.

အထူးသဖြင့်, an abbreviation of အထူးဖြစ်သဖြင့်.

အထဲ, *n.* an inside, an inner part ; အတွင်း.

အထဲစကား, *n.* candid, undissembling language.

အထောင်, *n.* the number of a thousand (combined with the nine digits to form numerals).

အထောင်း, *n.* a cubit.

အထောင့်, *n.* a curve, bend, corner, bay.

အထွက်နေ့, *n.* the day after worship.

အထွင်း, *n.* a mortice.

အထွဋ်, *n.* a top, summit, pinnacle ; အထျား, the best, most excellent part.

အထွာ, *n.* a span, a measure of length equal to twelve fingers breadth.

အဒရ, *n.* a certain star ; see နက္ခတ်.

အဒိမျှ, how much ; အဘယ်မျှ.

အဓမ္မ, (from အ, *priv.* and ဓမ္မ, right, *Pali,*) transgression, sin, မတရားသောအမှု.

အဓလေ့, *n.* manner, custom, way ; အလေ့.

အဓိကရ, (from အဓိက, excelling, *Pali,* and ရ, to get ;) *v.* to obtain celebrity, be distinguished, extraordinary.

အဓိဋ္ဌာန်, (*Pali,*) *v.* to establish, be steady, constant.

အဓိဋ္ဌာန်, *n.* steadiness, constancy, perseverance.

အဓိပ္ပာယ်, *n.* meaning, explanation, comment ; အဓိပ္ပာယတ္တ, do.

အဓွန့်, *n.* distance of time or place, length, duration.

အန်, (1) *n.* a vomit, an emetic ; အော့၊ အန်ပြိ၊ အန်ဆေး ; (2) *n.* strength, (seldom used alone ;) အန်အား, *n.* strength, force, valour ; အားအန်၊ အန်တု, *v.* to try strength with another, compare strength ; အန်အားသင့်, *v.* to be astounded, stupefied through fear ; (3) *n.* any game in which pieces are moved in different compartments, according to rule, as checkers, chess, backgammon, &c. ; အန်ကစား, *v.* to play do. ; အန်ခဝ်၊ အန်ကြွ *v.* to game to excess, to be a gambler ; အန်ကွက်, *n.* a compartment, square ; အန်စာ, *n.* a piece ; ကျား ရိုလ်၊ အန်ရေအန်စာ, *n.* the squares and pieces collectively.

အန်ဝတ်, *n.* amber, (because supposed to be vomited by a fish.)

အနိုး, *v.* to be a little swelled; ဖော.

အနက် (1) *n.* an interpretation of a word, an explication, translation, version; (2) *n.* a collection, mass, quantity taken altogether; a whole, (seldom used as a simple noun, but combined with some other words to form adverbs, as ထက္ကနက်၊ ထပ္ပြင်နက်, &c.)

အနင်, *n.* fine dust; မှုန့်ညက်.

အနည်, *n.* sediment, dregs.

အနည့် (*pro. adj.*) that, (used when a thing is pointed at, or designated by some outward sign.)

အနည်ငယ်း, *adv.* little, small.

အနတ္တ, (from အ, *priv.* and အတ္တ, substance, *Pali ;*) *adj.* unsubstantial; အနှစ်မဲ့.

အနနိုး, *n.* a kind of tree.

အနန္တ, *adj.* infinite, boundless; အဆုံးမဲ့.

အနန္တရိယကံ, (from အ, *priv.* အန္တရ, an interval, and ကမ္မ, a deed, *Pali ;*) *n.* a deed, which brings upon the perpetrator instant and uninterrnpted misery; of which there are five kinds, viz. killing a father, killing a mother, killing a Rahandah, wounding a Boodh, and making a schism among the disciples of a Boodh.

အန္တ, (*Pali,*) *n.* an end.

အန္တရကပ်, *n.* an intermediate period of time.

အန္တရာယ်, *n.* evil, calamity, misery.

အနံ, (1) *n.* breadth, width; အနံအပြန့် do. (2) see နံ, the side of a body.

အနံ့, *n.* smell, scent.

အနာရွတ်, *n.* a scar.

အနား, *n.* an edge, a side, a near part, nearness; အစောင်း။ အပါး။ အနီး။ အရင်း.

အနားဝတ်, *n.* the border of a petticoat.

အနားပတ်, *n.* an outer facing, encircling the border of clothes; see ကပ္ပတ်.

အနာဂတ်, *n.* futurity, the future.

အနာဂံ, see အနာဂါမိပုဂ္ဂိုလ်.

အနာဂါမိ, *n.* the third state attained by an Areeyah, အရိယာ.

အနာဂါမိမဂ်, *n.* the duties of do.

အနာဂါမိဖိုလ်, *n.* the reward of do.

အနာဂါမိမဂ္ဂဋ္ဌာန်, *n.* one who has performed the duties of do.

အနာဂါမိဖလဋ္ဌာန်, *n.* one who has attained the reward of do. အနာဂါန်.

အနာထူပြား, *v.* to be full of sores, diseased; see မျှငြှာ.

အနာဒရ, (from အ, *priv.* and အာဒရ, respect, *Pali,*) *n.* disrespect.

အနာလယ, (from အ, *priv.* and အာလယ, passion, *Pali,*) *n.* an exemption from passion.

အနိစ္စ, (from အ, *priv.* and နိစ္စ, permanent, *Pali,*) *adj.* transitory, mortal, အမြဲမရှိ; *n.* mortality, death.

အနိစ္စရောက်, *v.* to die, (applied to mankind, commonly to kings.)

အနိဋ္ဌ, (from အ, *priv.* and ဣဋ္ဌ, desire, *Pali,*) *n.* an undesirable object.

အနု, *n.* medicine to excite love, မျက်ချစ်.

အနုထုပ်, *n.* a certain preparation of parched rice.

အနုဇာတ, (*Pali,*) *adj.* like, equal (applied to a son, who neither excels, nor is inferior to his parents.)

အနုမောဒနာ, *n.* (from အနု, much, and မောဒါ, joy, *Pali,*) happiness.

အနုမောဒနာပြု, *v.* to rejoice, be happy, (applied to certain ceremonies on giving to a priest.)

အနုမြူ, (from အနု, small, *Pali,* and မြူ, a grain of dust,) *n.* a very small particle.

အနုသယ, see ထမ္ဗွာန်.

အနုသယခုနစ်ပါး, (from အနုသယ, *Pali,* အစဉ်လိုက်ချင်,) seven accidents common to all beings that have not attained the state of an Areeyah, viz. ကာမရာဂါနုသယ၊ ဘဝရာဂါနုသယ၊ ပဋိဃာနုသယ၊ မာနာနုသယ၊ ဒိဋ္ဌာနုသယ၊ ဝိစိကိစ္ဆာနုသယ၊ အဝိဇ္ဇာနုသယ.

အနုပြင်း, *adv.* at first gently, then forcibly.

အနုဒီ, or အနုထက်, *v.* to act thus.

အနေကျ, *n.* continuance, uniformity.

အနောတ္တပ္ပ, (from အ, *priv.* and ဩတ္တပ္ပ, *Pali,*) *n.* boldness in sin, searedness of conscience, hardness of heart, မထိတ်လန့်ချင်.

အနို., (1) a corruption of အညို; (2) see နို, milk.

အနိုင်အထက်, (from နိုင်, to be able, and ထက်, to be sharp;) *adv.* forcibly, contrary to one's will, အနိုင်အရှိုင်.

အနိုင်အရှိုင်, *adv.* forcibly, contrary to one's will.

အန္တရ, *n.* an intervening space.

အန္တရကပ်, (from အန္တရ, an intervening space, and ကပ္ပ, a period of time,) a subdivision of one of the four grand periods; see မဟာကပ်.

အန္တရာယ်, *n.* a calamity, evil, ဘေး.

အနှစ်, *n.* solidity, substance, opposed to အကာ, which see; consequence, worth, weight.

အနှစ်, *n.* a year.

အနှစ်မဲ့, *adj.* unsubstantial.

အနှံ, *n.* a spike or ear of grain, with or without the stalk.

အနှီး, *n.* a sheet or any thing spread out, a child's cloth; also a capital, or stock in trade.

အနှီးအထောင်း, do.

အနှီးအထု, *n.* a capital, or stock in trade.

အနှောင်, *n.* the back of a knife or other instrument, the head of a punch or wedge; opposed to အသွား.

အနှောင်အဖွဲ့, *n.* a connection, junction, စပ်.

အနွယ်, *n.* a lineal succession, descent.

အနိုး, *v.* to pay to boot; အနိုးရ, *v.* do.

အပ်, (1) *v.* to commit, deliver up, give in charge, နှံ; အပ်နှင်း, *v.* to give; အပ်ပေး, do.; (2) to suit, be suitable, fit, proper, တန်၊ တော်၊ ထိုက်၊ သင့်; (3) *n.* a needle; အပ်ချုပ်သမား, *n.* a tailor.

အပ်ကျည်, *n.* a needle-case.

အပ်နှင်း, *v.* see အပ်.

အပ်သည်ကိုဖြု, see ကဗ္ဗိ.

အပ, *n.* an outside, an outer part, အပြင်.

အပရဂေါယာန်, *n.* the West Island; see ကျွန်း.

အပင်, *n.* a tree, or plant.

အပင်စည်, (dropping အ,) *n.* the trunk, main stock.

အပင်း, *n.* a combination of men, a society, အသင်း.

အပင်းအသင်း, see အသင်းအပင်း.

အပတ် *n.* a circuit, or circle, အဝန်း.

အပတ်ထကျုတ်, a corruption of အပန်းထကျုတ်; *see* ပန်းကျုတ်.

အပန်း, *n.* a fatiguing business, a difficulty.

အပန်းကြီး, *v.* to be of great consequence, requiring great exertion.

အပန်းတကြီး, *adv.* earnestly, indefatigably.

အပ္ပမညာတရားလေးပါး, four principles, viz. မေတ္တာ, ကရုဏာ, မုဒိတာ, and ဥပေက္ခာ; see ကမ္မဋ္ဌာန်း.

အပယ်, *a term of compellation,* used by a husband in addressing his wife, sometimes in addressing other women in a friendly manner.

အပါ, *n,* presence of, nearness to.

အပါး, *n. a numeral auxiliary,* applied to respectable characters, and things immaterial.

အပါယ်, *n.* a state of punishment, of which there are four, viz. ငရဲဘုံ၊ ပြိတ္တာဘုံ၊ တိရစ္ဆာန်ဘုံ၊ အသုရကာယ်ဘုံ.

အပိတ်, *n.* day before worship day.

အပိတ်, *n.* the cover of any vessel.

အပိန့်, *n.* (from ပိန့်,) a rising of the skin, a blister.

အပေါ့, *n.* urine, ကျင်ငယ်၊ ရေဟောင်း၊ သေး.

အပေါင်, *n.* a thigh, (commonly applied to the hind quarters after a creature is killed;) see ပေါင်; the side of a door, a bedstead, a chair, &c. to which the hinges or legs are fixed; see တံခါးပေါင်.

အပေါင်းဖက်, *n.* a partner.

အပေါင်းအပါ, *n.* a companion, associate.

အပေါ်, *n.* an upper part, အထက်.

အပေါ်ပြု, *v.* to act a false, hypocritical part.

အပေါ်စကား, *n.* false language, opposed to အထဲစကား.

အပေါ်မှာ, *prep.* above.

အပိုဒ်, *n.* (from ပိုဒ်, to make stops, &c. which see.)

အပိုင်းအခြား, *n.* a division, distinct part, a section.

အပိုနေ့, *n.* (from ပို, to heap up,) a day kept after worship day, as a work of supererogation.

အပိုင်းသေ, *n.* to be executed in a correct, regular manner, သေချာ.

အပျို, *n.* from ပျို, to be young, &c. which see.

အပြင်, *n.* an outside, outer part, what is beyond or beside, အပ.

အပြင်အလျှာ, *n.* the external or outside appearance of a person or thing.

အပြင်, *n.* a surface, an open vacant surface.

အပြစ်, *n.* result, consequence; evil result or consequence, punishment; guilt, demerit, sin.

အပြစ်တင်, *v.* to criminate, find fault with.

အပြည်ပြည်, (from ပြည်, a country,) *adv.* from country to country, pertaining to various countries.

အပြန်, *n.* a pyan, a certain measure of time.

အပြား, *n.* (from ပြား, to be divided,) breadth, width.

အပြားပြား, *adv.* variously, differently, distinctly.

အပြားအားဖြင့်, *n.* breadth, width; *adv.* numerously; very.

အပြိုနေ့, *n.* a worship day.

အဖြေ, *n.* a reply, an answer, ဖြေဆို.

အပြောက်, *n.* figured, carved, or embroidered work.

အပြောက်အပြွန်း, *n.* do.

အပွင့်, *n.* a flower, blossom.

အပြွပ်, *n.* froth, scum, အမြှုပ်.

အပြွတ်, *n.* a cluster, bunch.

အဖ or အဖထ, *n.* a father, ဖခင်။ ဖထေး။ ဖခင်; *adj.* masculine, (used to designate the gender of certain birds.)

အဖက်, *n.* see under ဖက်, to embrace, &c.

အဖင်, *n.* an ancestor of the fifth degee of ascent from one's self.

အဖတ်, *n.* what remains of a thing after the liquor or juice is extracted, (opposed to အရည်, the liquid part;) any thing rejected from the mouth, after the juice is extracted by chewing; see ဖယ်ဖတ်။ ဖွဲဖတ်, &c.

အဖတ်အရည်, *n.* any substance composed of solid and liquid, အရည်အဖတ်.

အဖန်, *n.* a time, turn, ကြိမ်။ ခါ; *adv.* again.

အဖန်ဖန်, *adv.* repeatedly.

အဘီ or အဘိ, *n.* the father of a great-grandfather, the fourth in ascent from one's self.

အဘိမ, *n.* the mother of a great-grandfather.

အဖုတ်, *n.* the mons veneris.

အဖုံး, *n.* the cover of any vessel.

အဖုး, *n.* a bud, pimple, small boil.

အဘ, *n.* a father, ဘ၊ ဖေဘ.

အဘေး or အဘေး, *n.* a great-grandfather, ဘေး.

အဘေးမ, *n.* a great-grandmother, ဘေးမ.

အဖောက်, *n.* a woof.

အပေါင်း, *n.* see ပေါင်း, to associate, &c.

အဘိုး, (1) *n.* price, value; အဘိုးအခ, do.; အဘိုးအစား, do. အဘိုးအနှုန်း, do. (2) a grandfather, ဘိုးဘေး.

အဘို့ or အဘို့, *n.* a part, portion, share, what is for, အတွက်.

အဘိုသ်, *n.* a wife who has not borne children; the male of certain animals.

အဖြစ်, *n.* (from ဖြစ်, to be,) being, a state of being.

အဖြစ်အပျက်, *n.* events, adventures, affairs.

အဖြစ်အဆန်း, *n.* do. do. do.

အဖျဉ်း, *n.* the spleen, part of the viscera.

အဖြော် or အဖျော်, *n.* a sweet liquor.

အဖျား, *n.* an extremity, point, end; a top, summit, (opposed to အရင်း, a bottom, foundation;) အထွဋ်၊ ထိပ်.

အဖျားအထွဋ်, *n.* see ဖျား.

အဖျော်, *n.* sweet liquor.

အဘွား or အဘွား, *n.* a grandmother, ဘွားဘေး.

အဖြူကျောက်, *n.* a kind of stone, (used in medicine.)

အဘယ် or အဘဲ, *pron. adj.* what, (used interrogatively,) ဘယ်.

အဘယ်၌, do. (occasionally used with words of time.)

အဘယ်သို့, *pron. adj.* of what sort; *adv.* how, အသို့.

အဘယ်နှစ်, *pron. adj.* how many? (combined with numeral auxiliaries, or words denoting a part or quantity, in asking questions; see Grammar.)

အဘိ, *adj.* exceeding.

အဘိညာဉ်, (from အဘိ, exceeding, and ဉာဏ, wisdom, or mental attainment,) *n.* certain excellent attainments, viz. ဒိဗ္ဗစက္ခု, the eye of a Nat, or faculty of seeing like a Nat; ဒိဗ္ဗသောတ, the ear of a Nat; ဣဒ္ဓိဝိဓ, creative power; အဘိညာဉ်စေတောပရိယ,

knowledge of others' thoughts; အနာဂတံသဉာဏ်, prescience; ပုဗ္ဗေနိဝါသာနုဿတိ, knowledge of one's own past existences.

အဘိဓမ္မာ, *n.* one grand division of the Boodhist scriptures, comprising seven books, viz. ဓမ္မသင်္ဂဏီ၊ ဝိဘင်၊ ဓာတုကထာ၊ ပုဂ္ဂလပညတ်၊ ကထာဝတ္ထု၊ ယမိုက်၊ ပဋ္ဌာန်း.

အဘိသင်္ခါရ, *v.* to be subject to the operations of the four causes, (အကြောင်းတရားလေးပါး).

အဘိဓာန်, *n.* a vocabulary.

အဘိသိက်, *pron.* အဘိသိက်သိက်, (from အဘိ, excellent, and သေက, pouring, *Pali,*) *n.* a pouring of water, a ceremony of inauguration, equivalent to that of anointing with oil.

အဘိသိက်သွန်း, *v.* to perform the ceremony of do.

အဘိသိက်ခံ, *v.* to be the subject of do.

အဘဲ, see အဘယ်.

အမ, *n.* a female; the body of a vessel, as distinguished from အဖုံး, the cover; *adj.* feminine, of the female gender.

အမ, *n.* an elder sister of a sister.

အမှံ, *n.* see အမှုံ.

အမင်း, (1) *n.* the hollow head of a tool which receives the handle; (2) *See* မင်း, thou, or you.

အမည်, *n.* a name, နာမ; အမည်အရည်, do.

အမည်း, *n.* flesh (of beasts;) အမည်းသား, do. အမဲ.

အမည်း, *v.* to be dark, black, dark in mind, ignorant, foolish.

အမတ်, *n.* a person of rank, a nobleman, အမှူး.

အမတေ, *see* အမြဲတေ.

အမယ်, (1) *n.* a mother, အမိ၊ အမေ၊ မအေ၊ မိခင်; (2) *an interjection* denoting wonder or distress.

အမရပူရ, *n.* *Ahmerapoora,* the former capital of Burmah.

အမာရွတ်, see အနာရွတ်.

အမိ, *n.* a mother, အမယ်၊ အမေ၊ မအေ၊ မိခင်; *vocatively,* a daughter, wife, or any woman younger than the speaker, (indicative of affection or friendship.)

အမိသားချင်း, *n.* children born of the same mother.

အမှုတ်, *n.* a measure of length equal to five finger breadths.

အမုန်, *n.* the temporal juice, which at certain seasons exudes from an elephant's temples.

အမုံ, *n.* an incipient bud.

အမှုံ, *adv.* again.

အမှု, *n.* a deed, action.

အမှုအကျင့်, *n.* do.

အမှုသည်, *n.* a claimant.

အမှူး, *n.* a person of rank, a nobleman, အမတ် ၊ အမှူးအမတ် ၊ မှူးမတ် ၊ မှူးတော်မတ်တော်.

အမေ, *n.* a mother, အမိ; &c.

အမယ်, *see* အမည်း.

အမောက်, *n.* a cock's comb.

အမောင်, *n.* *see* မောင်, a brother.

အမေန်, *n.* see under မေန်.

အမိုး, *n.* (1) a cover, a roof; (2) a chief.

အမိုးစွန်, *n.* the eaves of a roof.

အမိုက်, *n.* a measure of distance equal to 8 finger breadths.

အမ္ဗဏ, *(Pali,)* *n.* a measure of capacity, equal to a ten, (တင်း.)

အမျက်, *n.* the point in the joint of a bamboo, whence the sprout proceeds; the point in a ring where the stone is set, and such like; see မျက်, a gem.

အမျက်, *n.* anger, resentment, ill temper.

အမျက်ထွက်, *v.* to show anger, be angry.

အမျက်ဝင်, *v.* to be angry.

အမျက်ရှိ, *v.* to be angrily disposed.

အမျက်ဟန်, *v.* to pretend to be angry.

အမျက်ဖိ, *v.* to restrain anger.

အမျှား, *n.* a kind of verse; (2) *v.* to sing verses.

အမျိုး, *n.* a sort, kind, အထည် ၊ အဖြည် ၊ အစ; a race.

အမျိုးအနွယ်, *n.* relationship, kindred.

အမျိုးအဆွေ, *n.* a relation, one of the same race.

အမျိုးတော်ကြိတ်, *n.* a relative, အရင်းအချာ.

အမျိုးအရိုး, *n.* hereditary stock.

အမျိုးသား, *n.* one of the same race, a fellow countryman.

အမျိုးသားချင်း, *n*, one of the same race or country.

အမျိုးသမီး, *n.* a fellow countrywoman.

အမျိုးခုနစ်ဆက်, seven degrees of ancestry, reckoning upwards, viz. အဘ၊ အဘိုး၊ အဘေး၊ အဘီ၊ အဘင်၊ အကြို့ကြား၊ အဘော့; *also* seven degrees of posterity, viz. သား၊ မြေး၊ မြစ်၊ တီ၊ ကျွတ်၊ ဆတ်၊ ဆက်.

အမြစ်, *n.* a root, bottom, origin, source, မူလ၊ အရင်း; the gizzard of birds.

အမြစ်, *n.* a motive, (root of action.)

အမြစ်ဥ, *n.* a bulbous root; အမြစ်မ, *n.* a main root.

အမြည်, *n.* a kind, sort, variety, အထည်၊ အမျိုး.

အမြတ်, *n.* increase, profit, advantage, အကျိုး.

အမြိတ်, *n.* an end, extremity, edge, border, အစွန်း.

အမြိန်အရသာ, *n.* see အမြိုက်.

အမြီး, *n.* a tail.

အမြီးတုံး, *n.* the root of a tail.

အမြီးရင်း, do.

အမြုတေ, *n.* a petrifaction found in the body of an animal, and used as a charm.

အမြုံ့, *n.* (from မြုံ့, to chew,) the cud.

အမြု, *n.* a brood, litter, &c. including the mother.

အမြဲ, *n.* (from မြဲ, to continue,) permanency. အမြဲတည်, do.

အမြဲစေ, *v.* to establish, make permanent.

အမြောက်, *n.* a great gun, a cannon.

အမြိုက်, *n.* any thing relishing, delicious, အမြိန်အရသာ.

အမွေ, *n.* an inheritance, permanent estate.

အမွေအနှစ်, do. အမွေအငွေ, do. အမွေရိဝ, *n.* an heir.

အမွေခံ, *v.* to inherit.

အမွေး, *n.* hair (of the body), wool.

အမွေးညှင်း, *n.* fine, short hair on the hands, arms, &c.

အမွေးထ, *v.* to be subject to horripilation, or to a rising of the hair, through a sudden emotion, ကြက်သီးထ.

အမွေးညှင်းထ, *v.* do.

အမှင်, *n.* stiff hair, bristles, mustaches, whiskers, နှုတ်ခမ်းမွေး; *figuratively* fringe.

အမှန်, *adj.* right, true.

အမှန်အကန်, *adv.* verily, truly.

အမှန်ကျ, *v.* to hit right, get the truth, &c. to be adapted to a case, as language to a person deserving reproof.

အမှိတ်, *n.* see အစွန်.

အမှီပြု, *v.* to trust in, put confidence in.

အမှု, *n.* business, work, affair ; a process in law.

အမှုအခင်း do. အမှုအရာ, do. အမှုအရေး, do.

အမှုသည်, *n.* one who has business ; a party in a suit.

အမှုထမ်း, *n.* a person on service, *commonly* government service.

အမှုထား, *v.* to care for, pay regard to.

အမှုန်, *n.* dirt, dust, an atom, အမှိုက်.

အမှော်, *n.* refuse, what is useless, as sea-weed or slush, the shells of beans, the chaff of grain, &c.

အမှိုက်, *n.* dirt, filth.

အမျှ, *n.* a portion, distribution ; အမျှဝေ, *v.* to divide, apportion.

အမျှ, *adv.* as, as much as, like as, နှင့်အမျှ.

အမျှင်, *n.* any stringy substance.

အမြှုပ်, *n.* (1) froth, scum, အမြှုပ် ; (2) the fœtus, in the second stage of existence ; *see* ကလလ၊ ရေကြည်, and သားတစ်.

အမွေအနှစ်, *n.* an inheritance.

အမွှေး, *n.* an odoriferous substance.

အမ်း, *v.* (1) to be swelled—less than ရောင် ; (2) to be fearful of engaging in any thing.

အယ်, *v.* to be full, puffed up, swollen, (applied to the bowels,) ပေါ့၊ ဖောင်း.

အယ်စာ, what (provincial.)

အယဉ်, *adv.* quickly, မြန်မြန်.

အယံ, (1) *n.* a time, season (of day or night,) အချိန်; (2) *n.* place above, upper part, as မိုးယံ, above or about the clouds ; အပေါ်ယံတွင်, above.

အယာ, *n.* betel-leaf, with the contents made up for chewing.

အယူ, (1) *n.* (*Pali,*) life ; (2) *n.* doctrine, opinion.

အယူယူ, *v.* to embrace, or receive a doctrine.

အရက်, (1) *n.* a natural day ; (2) *n.* spirituous liquor.

အရင်, *n.* a beginning, commencement, အစ၊ အဦး ; *used adverbially*, before, antecedently, first.

**အရင်း**, *n.* see အနှုံး; also stock in trade, a capital.

အရင်း, *n.* a root, bottom, origin, အမြစ် မူလ; opposed to အဖျား; *adj.* original, own, (applied to relatives,) as သားရင်း, an own son, as distinguished from သားမြီး, or သားတော်, an adopted son.

အရင်းအချာ, *n.* do.

အရင်းအချာသူ, *n.* a relative, အမျိုးပေါက်ဖော်; *figurat.* a familiar, a confident.

အရည်, *n.* a name; see အမည်.

အရည်, *n.* (1) appearance, good appearance; ability, faculty, skill; အချင်း၊ အထင်း၊ အရုပ်၊ အရောင်၊ အဝါ၊ အသွင်၊ အသွား၊ အသွေး. အရည်အဖြင်, do.; အရည်အချာ, do.; (2) *n.* liquor, or liquid.

အရည်အပတ်, *see* အပတ်အရည်.

အရည်, *n.* a certain kind of heretical priests of Boodh.

အရပ်, *n.* a place, situation, country; သွားသည်အရပ်, the place of going.

အရပ်ရပ်, *adv.* pertaining to various places.

အရပ်အရာ, *n.* circumstances, appearances.

အရဟ္တ *n.* see အရဟတ္တ.

အရမနီ, *n.* Armenia.

အရသာ, (from ရသ, *Pali,*) *n.* taste, flavour, whether pleasant or unpleasant, the quality in matter which affects the sense of taste. Six are enumerated, viz. အချို, sweet; အချဉ်, sour; အခါး, bitter; အစပ်, hot, pungent; အဖန်, astringent; အငန်, salt. *Figuratively* applied to the ear also.

အရဟန္တာ, *see* ရဟန္တာ.

အရဟတ္တ, (by contraction အရဟ္တ,) *n.* the fourth state attained by an Areeyah, (အရိယာ.)

အရဟတ္တမဂ်, *n.* the duties of one who has attained the state of an Areeyah.

အရဟတ္တဖိုလ်, *n.* the rewards of do.

အရဟတ္တမဂ္ဂဋ္ဌာန်, *n.* one who has performed the duties of do.

အရဟတ္တဖလဋ္ဌာန်, *n.* one who has attained the rewards of do.

အရဟံ, *see* ရဟန္တာ.

**အရံ**, (1) *n.* a time, season, (not used alone, but combined with other words of time,) အခါ၊ အချိန် ; (2) *n.* a pair (applied to certain inanimate things.) (3) *n.* an enclosure, (from အာရာမ, *Pali.*)

**အရာ**, *n.* the number of a hundred, (combined with the nine digits to form numerals.)

**အရာ**, *n.* a thing, subject, matter, ဥစ္စာ၊ ပစ္စည်း၊ အချက်၊ အခင်း၊ အမှု ; a place, situation, office, အရပ်၊ အရိုက်အရာ, a mark, impression, အချက်.

**အရာကျ**, *v.* to be in the right, hit the subject, hit right.

**အရာရှိ**, (*pron.* အရာရှိ,) *n.* one that has an office.

**အရာရာ**, *adv.* pertaining to sundry matters, &c.

**အရိပ်**, *n.* a shadow, shade, shelter, place of rest.

**အရိပ်အရာ**, *n.* a place, situation, office.

**အရိပ်မထွက်**, *n.* a kind of plant.

**အရိမေတ္တေယျ**, *n.* the fifth Boodh, or deity destined to succeed Gaudama.

**အရိယာ**, *n.* an Areeyah, one who has undergone a certain great change, by which he becomes independent of the common destinies of nature, opposed to ပုထုဇ္ဇန်. Areeyahs are distinguished into four grand orders, each subdivided into two classes, thus making in all eight kinds, (အရိယာ ရှစ်ယောက်,) viz. သောတာပတ္တိမဂ္ဂဋ္ဌာန်၊ သောတာပတ္တိဖလဋ္ဌာန်၊ သကဒါဂါမိမဂ္ဂဋ္ဌာန်၊ သကဒါဂါမိဖလဋ္ဌာန်၊ အနာဂါမိမဂ္ဂဋ္ဌာန်၊ အနာဂါမိဖလဋ္ဌာန်၊ အရဟတ္တမဂ္ဂဋ္ဌာန်၊ အရဟတ္တဖလဋ္ဌာန် ; အရိယာမဂ္ဂင် ; see မဂ္ဂင်ရှစ်ပါး.

**အရီ**, *n.* an aunt, a father's sister, or a maternal uncle's wife.

**အရုဏ်**, see အာရုဏ်.

**အရုပ်**, (from ရူပ, *Pali,*) *n.* appearance, အဆင်း၊ အသွင်၊ အရောင်၊ အဝါ ; a representation, resemblance, likeness, figure, image, ဆင်းတု, see ရုပ်.

**အရုံ**, *n.* see အာရုံ, an object of sense, &c.

**အရုံ**, *n.* just so much, and no more, (commonly constructed with simple participles,) as ပြောရုံရှိ၏, (he) just speaks, (i. e. he does no more.)

အရူပ, (from အ, *priv.* and ရူပ, appearance, *Pali,*) *n.* invisibility.

အရူပဗြဟ္မာ, see လဗ္ဗြဟ္မာ.

အရေ, *n.* skin, leather, သားရေ.

အရေး, *n.* an affair, business, work, အကြောင်း၊ အခင်းအကျင်း၊ အခွင့်အမှု.

အရေးပုံ, *n.* a representation of affairs, account, history.

အရောင်, *n.* appearance, brightness, lustre; အရောင်အဝါ, do.

အရိုး, *n.* a handle; အရိုးအိုး, *n.* a monument, urn.

အရိုး, *n.* a bone, a stalk, a ridge of earth, mound, a range of hills; a lineage, line, race; အမျိုးအရိုး, hereditary property or place; အရိုးအရာ, custom, ထုံးနှိုးထုံးစံ.

အရွက်, *n.* a leaf, ဖက်; အရွက်ချပ်, do.

အရွယ်, *n.* age, age of puberty.

အလေ့, *adv.* (by contraction ရှ,) as much as, အမျှ; *adv.* even, *see* မျှ.

အရှက်, *n.* modesty, shame.

အရှင်, *n.* an owner, proprietor, lord, master, သခင်; see ရှင်.

အရှင်ဘုရား, *a term applied to reverend characters.*

အရှင်ဘော, *a term applied to deity and the gods.*

အရှိန်, *n.* insufferable or excessive heat.

အရှုတ်အထမ်း, *n.* a confused collection, a jumble.

အယက်, *n.* see အချက်.

အလက်, *n.* an arm, fore-leg, *see* လက်; a limb or arm of a tree, smaller than အကိုင်း, and အခက်; a subordinate district, ကျေးလက်.

အလကား, *adj.* in vain, useless, to no purpose, အချည်းနှီး.

အလတ်, *n.* vacancy, emptiness, disengagedness.

အလတ်ရွယ်, *n.* middle age.

အလမ္ဘယ်, *n.* one skilled in catching and taming snakes; အလမ္ဘယ်သမား, do.

အလယ်, *n.* a middle, midst, centre.

အလယ်နန်း, *n.* the middle palace; the queen of the middle palace, who is the third in rank, အလယ်နန်းမိဘုရား.

အလံ, *n.* a flag, ensign, standard.

အလား, *adj.* not castrated, (applied to horses and some other animals.)

အလီ, *n.* a time, turn, အကြိမ်၊ အဝန်; *used also to form a multiplier, as* ငါးသုံးလီ, three times five.

အလီလီ, *adj.* repeatedly; အလီလီအသာသာ, do. အလီလီအဝဝ, do.

အလုံး, *pron. adj.* all, the whole.

အလုံးရုံ, do.

အလုံးအရင်း, *n.* a multitude, body of men, an army, attendants, suite, (sometimes separated, and combined with nouns, thus ဆင်လုံးမြင်းရင်း, a multitude of elephants and horses.)

အလဲလေ့, or အလဲလဲ, an interjection, expressive of pain.

အလေ့, *n.* see အလေ့လေ့.

အလေ့အကြက်, *n.* custom, habit, အာစိဏ္ဏ.

အလောက်, *adj.* about, nearly, enough, sufficient.

အလောက်အမျှ, *adv.* about as much as.

အလောင်း, (1) *n.* a dead body, a corpse, အကောင်၊ သေကောင်; အလောင်းကောင်, do. (2) *n.* a thing unfinished, imperfect, but advancing towards a finished, perfect state, as မင်းကြီးအလောင်း, or မင်းလောင်း, the rudiments of a king, one who is to be a king.

အလို, *n.* a desire, wish.

အလိုက်, *adv.* of one's own accord.

အလို့ငှါ, *v. affix,* for the sake of, or in order to.

အလိုကျူ, *n.* a species of reed.

အလိုလေ့, *an interjection, expressive of distress or astonishment.*

အလိုလို, *adv.* uselessly; doubtingly.

အလ္လာပသလ္လာပ, (*Pali,*) *n.* sociable, kind, friendly conversation; အလ္လာပသလ္လာပပြု, *v.* to converse together affectionately as intimate friends.

အလျင်, *ad.* first, beforehand, before.

အလျင်, used adverbially, as အလျင်သွား, go quick.

အလျောက်, according to, as အလိုအလျောက်, or အလိုကျအလျောက်, according to his will.

အလျှင်, see အရင်.

အလျှင်း, *adv.* wholly, entirely; as အလျှင်းမရှိ, there is none at all; လားလားမရှိ. အလျှင်းကုန်ပြီ, it is wholly spent, ထက်ထက်ကုန်ပြီ.

အလျှာ or အလျာ, *n.* a part, portion, share, what is for, အဖို့.

**အလှည့်**, *n.* a turn, a change.

အလှည့်သင့်, *v.* to come to one's turn.

အလွန်, used adverbially, as အလွန်ကြီးသည်, it is very great ; အလွန်, do. very.

အဝ, (1) *n.* an entrance, mouth, opening (as of a river, door, hole, &c. ; (2) Ava, the capital of Burmah, situated a little below Ahmerapoora, အင်းဝ၊ အင်းဝ၊ ရတနာပူရ. (3) a kind or sort, (used as a numeral auxiliary,) အထည်၊ အမျိုး.

အဝ, *n.* see အထည်.

အဝဝ, *adv.* variously, of various sorts ; hence တဝတည်း, *adv.* unitedly, at once.

အဝဇာတ, *(Pali,) adj.* inferior, (applied to a son who is not equal to his parents.)

အဝန်, *n.* a business, allotment of business, an office.

အဝါ, (1) see ဝါ, a season ; (2) *n.* appearance, colour, brightness, အဆင်း၊ အရောင်.

အဝီစိ, *n.* one of the states of punishment, (see ငရဲ.)

အဝိညာဏက, *n.* inanimate matter.

အဝိဇ္ဇော, *n.* see ဩဇာ.

အဝိုင်း, *n.* a circumference, circle.

အဂွန်း, *n.* a chief of executioners, an overseer of labourers.

အဂွင်း, *n.* surface, (applied to seas, rivers, mountains, lands, fields, gardens, &c.) အပြင်.

အသက်, *n.* health, life ; အသက်တန်း, *n.* length of life.

အသက်ကြီး, *n.* an old man, elder, အသက်ကြီးရွယ်ရင့်.

အသက်မွေး, *v.* to support life, get a living.

အသင်း, *n.* see အရှိ, also under သင်း, a collection, society.

အသင်္ချေ, (from အ, *priv.* and သင်္ချာ, number, *Pali* ;) *adj.* innumerable ; အသင်္ချေယျ, do.

အသင်းအပင်း, *adv.* socially, collectively.

အသစ်, *n.* a measure of length, one finger-breadth.

အသည် (1) *n.* a person of the common sort, who is under no special engagements to government, but is liable to be called to occasional service ; (2) *n.* an owner, proprietor, (combined with nouns,) thus, မုန့်သည်, a baker; ကြက်သည်, a fowlman, &c.

အသည်း, (1) *n.* a nail (of the fingers or toes;) (2) *n.* the liver, see သည်း; အသည်းနှလုံး, do.

အသညသတ်, a state of existence in which a man becomes as a corpse, that is, has a body without a mind, and without life.

အသန်း, *n.* the number of a million.

အသပြာ, *n.* money, whether gold, silver, or lead.

အသရေ, *n.* character, deserved reputation, ကြက်သရေ.

အသံ, *n.* sound.

အသံဗလံ, *n.* a thundering sound (as of a multitude.)

အသံသော, (from အသော;) *n.* a soft, gentle sound, သံပြောင်း၊ သံညှင်း.

အသံဩ, *v.* to be hoarse, have a dead, dull, flat voice; အသံဝင်, *v.* to fail in utterance, through exhaustion; အသံသော, *v.* do.

အသံပြိုင်ဆို, *v.* to sing together.

အသံညို, *v.* do.

အသာဝဏီ, *n.* a certain star; see နက္ခတ်.

အသား, *n.* flesh, substance (of any thing.)

အသိအကျွမ်း, *n.* an acquaintance.

အသိန်း, *n.* the number of a hundred thousand.

အသီး, *n.* fruit.

အသီးအသီး, *adv.* distinctly, variously.

အသီးအနှံ, *n.* an ear or head of grain.

အသုဘ, see ကမ္မဋ္ဌာန်း.

အသုံးအဆောင်, *n.* articles of use; riches, opulence, (ဝတ္ထု.)

အသူ, (*a contraction of* အဘယ်သူ,) who?

အသုတရာ, (*Pali,*) *adv.* very, exceedingly, (commonly applied to words of depth.)

အသူရကယ်, *n.* an Athoorakay, a kind of being inferior to man, and inhabiting one of the four states of suffering.

အသူရာ, (from အ, *priv.* and သူရာ, a happy Nat, *Pali,*) *n.* a fallen Nat, many of whom were formerly driven from the summit of Myenmo mount, to the region situate between the three stone pillars which support the mount.

အသူရိန်, *n.* Athooring, the Nat who is supposed to occasion eclipses, called also ရာဟု, and ပေ့တ်.

အသေ, (from အသေသံ, *Pali,*) *adv.* wholly, without leaving any, အကြွင်းမဲ့.

အသေက္ခ, *a term applied to the eighth, or highest kind of Areeyah ;* သေက္ခ.

အသေး, *n.* colour, appearance, အရည်.

အသဲကြိုး, *n.* the upper straps of a Burman sandal.

အသော, *n.* a certain star, (see တာရာ.)

အသောင်း, *n.* the number of ten thousand.

အသို့, (*a contraction of* အဘယ်သို့,) of what sort.

အသိုက်, *n.* a bird's nest.

အသိုက်အဝန်း, *n.* do. *figurat.* any abode, place of rest.

အသိုက်အမြုံ, (from မြုံ,) *n.* do.

အဿာဇာနည်, *n.* a kind of fabulous horse.

အဿတရ, *n.* another kind of do.

အသွင်, *n.* appearance, အဆင်း၊ အရည်.

အသွယ်, *n.* a branch, (see သွယ်.)

အသွား, *n.* the edge of a knife, or other instrument, opposed to အနှောင့်, which see; (2) *n.* appearance, အဆင်း.

အသွေး, (1) *n.* blood, see သွေး ; အသွေးအသား, *n.* offspring ; (2) *n.* appearance, အဆင်း၊ အရည်.

အဟန်, *n.* appearance, circumstance, affair, fact, အဟန်အမြစ်၊ အကြောင်း၊ အချင်းအရာ ; feigned appearance, pretence, show, အဟန်အပန် ၊ အရောင်.

အဟန်ပြု, *v.* to make a show, or appearance.

အဟိရိက, (from အ, *priv.* and ဟိရိ, modesty, *Pali,*) *n.* shamelessness, want of modesty, မရှက်ချင်း.

အံ, (1) *v.* to read, commonly applied to scholars reading ; အံရွတ်, *v.* do. (2) *n.* a drawer ; (3) *n.* a double tooth, grinder, အံသွား.

အံသွားတခဲ, *adv.* gnashingly, as with the teeth.

အံ့, *v.* to wonder.

အံ့ဩ, or အံ့သြ, *v.* to wonder, be astonished. အံ့ဖွဲ, to wonder. အံ့ရဲ, do.

အံ့သောငှါ, *v. affix*, as ပြုအံ့သောငှါ, for the purpose of doing, or in order to do.

အံ့, *v. affix*, sign of ind. mood, fut. tense. } as ပြုအံ့မည်, he will do.
အံ့မည် do. do.

အံ့ဖွယ်, or အံ့ဩဖွယ်, *adj.* wonderful.

အံ့ဖွယ်သရဲ, *adj.* very wonderful, such as was never seen before.

အံ့ဖြတ်, *n.* the light accent (့) originally a small အ, placed under a letter, and called ဖြတ်, because it interrupts the natural sound.

အာ, (1) *n.* (an abbreviation of အာသဝက္ခယဉာဏ,) a kind of wisdom which destroys the four enslaving principles; အာသဝေါလေးပါး.

အာ, (2) *n.* the inside of the mouth. အာသော်, *n.* do.

အာကျိန်း, *v.* to be rough, abusive in speech, ကျိန်းကြိတ်.

အာသော်ကျိန်း, *v.* do.

အာခေါင်း, *n.* the roof of the mouth, the whole palate.

အာဓောက်, *n.* the inner, or lower part, or bottom of the mouth.

အာရင်း, do. အာတုတ် do.

အာပေါင်, (from အပေါင်, a thigh,) *n.* the back part of the jaws.

အာစောင်, (from အစောင်, a side,) *n.* do. the sides of the mouth.

အာဖြိုရို, see ဘယ်ဖြိုရို.

အာဝုံး, *n.* the inside of the cheeks.

အာလုပ်ဆေး, *n.* a gargle.

အာလုပ်ကျင်း, *v.* to rinse the mouth.

အာ, (3) *v.* to crack open, gape, widen; to caw or croak, as a crow or raven.

အာကာ, *adj.* brave, clever, remarkable, more than common, (generally prefixed, but sometimes affixed to nouns.)

အာကာသ, *(Pali,)* *n.* space, vacuity, the expanse of heaven, ကောင်းကင်.

အာဂန္တုက, *(Pali,)* *n.* a stranger, traveller, ဧည့်သည်.

အာဂုဏ်, *commonly written* အာဂုံ, (perhaps from အာ, and ဂုဏ်,) *n.* ability to repeat without a book.

အာဂုဏ်အာဂါ, *n.* do.

အာဂုဏ်ဆောင်ရွက်, *v.* to have by heart.

အာစာရ, *(Pali,)* *n.* action, deed, အကျင့်.

အာစိဏ္ဏ, *(Pali,)* *n.* custom, habit, အလေ့အကျင့်.

အာစိဏ္ဏပြု, *v.* to form a habit, become accustomed to.

အစိဏ္ဏကံ, *n.* an action performed through long habit.

အာဇာနည်, *adj.* (from အာဇာနေယျ, *Pali,*) possessed of certain supernatural properties, (applied to men and horses.)

အာဘိန္နဆေး, *n.* a kind of medicine.

အာဏာ, *(Pali,)* *n.* power, authority, governmental dominion, အာနုဘော်.

အာဏာစက်, *n.* do.

အာဏာခွဲ, or အာဏာထား, *v.* to exercise authority; အာဏာချင်း, *v.* do.

အာဏာခေတ်, *n.* see ခေတ်.

အာဏာသား, *n.* a jailor, an executioner; an executioner, condemned to the situation on account of his own crimes, ထောင်သား၊ လက်မရွံ့.

အာဒရ, *(Pali,)* *n.* respect, ရိုသေချင်း.

အာထဗ္ဗန်, *n.* fourth book of the Vedas, which is now lost.

အာနိသင်, (from အာနိသံသော, *Pali,*) *n.* profit, advantage, အကျိုး.

အာနုဘော်, *n.* authority, energy, power, အာဏာ.

အာပတ်, *n.* fault, crime, sin, (applied to priests of Boodh,) အပြစ်.

အာပေါ, *(Pali,)* *n.* water, ရေ.

အာမ, *(Pali,)* *n.* a yes, an assent, acquiescence, agreement.

အာမခံ, (1) *v.* to agree, assent to, acquiescence in, be security for, ဝန်ခံ ခံဝံ; (2) *n.* a security, ထိုင်းခံ ခံဝံ.

အာမိသ, (1) *(Pali,)* *n.* food, အာဟာရ၊ အစာ; (2) property, ပစ္စည်း ဥစ္စာ; (3) permission, အခွင့်.

အာမေဍိတ်, (from အာမေဍိတ, *Pali,*) *n.* a sound uttered twice, thrice, or oftener, through a sudden emotion.

အာယတန, *(Pali,)* *n.* (1) a place, abode, တည်ရာ; (2) a cause, reason, အကြောင်း. Agreeably to the first signification, it denotes an abode of the mind, (စိတ္တာစိတ်တည်ရာ,) and is applied to the six senses (အဇ္ဈတ္တိကာယတန,) viz. စက္ခာယတန, the faculty of seeing; သောတာယတန, the faculty of hearing; ဃာနာယတန, the faculty of smelling; ဇိဝှါယတန, the faculty of tasting; ကာယာယတန, the faculty of touching; မနာယတန, the faculty of thinking. Agreeably to the second signification, it denotes an object with which the mind is conversant, ဝိညာဏ်ကြိုက်မွေ့လျော်ရာ, or ကျက်စားရာ, and is applied to objects of the six senses (ဗာဟိရာယတန,) viz. ရူပါယတန, appearance ; သဒ္ဒါယတန, sound ; ဂန္ဓာယတန, odour ; ရသာယတန, flavour ; ဖောဋ္ဌဗ္ဗါယတန, tangibility ; ဓမ္မာယတန, immaterial objects. See အာရုံ.

အာယုကပ်, (from အာယု, life, and ကပ္ပ, a period, *Pali,)* *n.* a period of time, during which the life of man gradually advances from the length of ten years to an indefinite extent, (အသင်္ချေ,) and returns again to the length of ten years; sixty-four of which make one intermediate period, (အန္တရကပ်.)

အာယုဝဍ္ဎနဆေး, *n.* a kind of medicine which prolongs life.

အာရုဏ်, *n.* dawn of light ; colour of light red ; glimpse, approach (of any thing,) အရုဏ်.

အာရုဏ်တက်, *v.* to dawn.

အာရုံ, (from အာရမ္မဏ, *Pali,)* *n.* an object of sense or thought, material or immaterial, (ဗာဟိရာယတန;) အာရုံပြု, *v.* to observe, form an idea of.

အာရုံရှု, *n.* see အာရုံ.

အာရုံယူ, *n.* do.

အာရှောက်ပတ်, *adv.* a term applied to the wrapping about of the clothes, or the entwining of the arms.

အာလယ, *(Pali,)* *n.* desire, အလို၊ အာသာ.

အာလိန်, *n.* an encircling gradation or story, in any pyramidical structure, အဆင့်; in pagodas, ပစ္စယံ.

အာဝဇ္ဇန်း, *(Pali,)* *n.* consideration, ဆင်ခြင်ခြင်း.

အာဝါသ, *(Pali,)* *n.* a resting place, place of shelter, abode ; *v.* to dwell.

အာသန, *n.* a place.

အာသန္န, *(Pali.)* *n.* near, nearness.

အာသန္နကံ, (from အာသန္န, near, and ကမ္မ, a deed, *Pali,*) *n.* a deed performed in the near approach of death.

အာသဝ, *n.* passion, desire.

အာသဝေါ, *n.* a band, or the act of binding.

အာသဝေါဂေါစ္ဆက, (from အာသဝေါ, a binding, *Pali,)* *n.* four restraints or bands, viz. ကာမာသဝေါ၊ ဘဝါသဝေါ၊ ဒိဋ္ဌာသဝေါ၊ အဝိဇ္ဇာသဝေါ; *see* ဩဃ.

အာသာ, *n.* desire ; see အာလယ.

အာသာဝတီ, *n.* the passion-flower vine.

အာသိသ, (*Pali,*) *n.* a longing for, တောင့်တခြင်း.

အာဟာရ, (*Pali,*) *n.* whatever affords strength ; food, nourishment, အစာ.

အား, (1) *v.* to be vacant, free, disengaged, at leisure, လစ် ; (2) *n.* strength, means, as အားဖြင့်, by means of, in regard to.

အားအန်, *n.* strength, force, valour, အန်အား။ အစွမ်း.

အားအန်သင့်, see အန်အားသင့်.

အားအန်ဖြည့်, *v.* to take refreshment, recover strength.

အားကျ, *v.* to vie with, emulate.

အားကြီးအန်တောင်, *adv.* determinately.

အားကြီးအန်ရ, *adv.* do.

အားခွန်, *n.* strength, force, ခွန်အား။ ဗလ.

အားထုတ်, *v.* to put forth strength, make exertion, be diligent.

အားနာ, *v.* to be prevented, restrained through motives of respect.

အားပေး, *v.* to give, or express satisfaction, approve, aid, countenance.

အားဖြင့်, *affix,* by means of ; in regard to.

အားပြု, *v.* to derive strength from, depend on, adhere to.

အားရ, *v.* to take satisfaction, be gratified.

အားပါးရ, *v.* do.

အားလျော့, *v.* to give out, fail, be exhausted.

အားလုံး, all, the whole, အလုံး.

အားလုံးစုံ, do. အလုံးစုံ.

အား, (3) *n. affix,* by means of, (see အားဖြင့်.)

အား, (4) (*n. aff. dative case,*) to, by, for.

အားသွန်, *v.* see အားထုတ်.

အိ, *v.* to be flabby, limber, flexible, inclined, soft, tender, delicate, နွဲ့။ ပျော့။ ပျောင်း.

အိအဲ, do.

အိထိမ်း, *v.* to be inclined, vary ; အိယိမ်း, do.

အိတ်, (1) *v.* to settle, dry up, (as paint, or any liquid substance.) အိတ်သေ, *v.* do. (2) *n.* a bag.

အိန့်, *v.* to be savoury, delicious, ဆိမ့်ထမ့်.

အိပ်, *v.* to sleep, lie down to sleep ; *see* စက်, and ကျိန်း.

အိပ်ပျော်, *v.* to be sound asleep, enjoy sleep ; အိပ်မွေ့, *v.* do. အိပ်မျည်း, *v.* do.

အိပ်ကြူ, *v.* to sleep late in the morning.

အိပ်မက်, *n.* a dream, see အိမ်မက်.

အိပ်ရာ, *n.* a bed, a place to sleep on, ဂွေ့ရာ.

အိပ်ရာခင်း, *n.* a sheet, any cloth spread on a bed.

အိပ်ပန်, (from အပန်, a turn ;) *n.* one who sleeps by turns, a centinel.

အိမ်, *n.* a house, dwelling place.

အိမ်ဦး, *n.* the front part, or entrance of a house, a porch.

အိမ်ခေါင်း, *n.* the ridge of the roof.

အိမ်ထောင်, *v.* to marry, to have sexual intercourse, to commence a family ; *n.* a family.

အိမ်ရာထောင်, *v.* do. *n.* a family.

အိမ်ထောင်ကျ, *v.* do. *n.* a family.

အိမ်ထောင်ချင်း, *n.* living in a married state.

အိမ်ထောင်ဘက်, *n.* a correlate in marriage, a spouse.

အိမ်နိမ့်, *n.* the state of being heir-apparent to the throne ; the heir-apparent himself, who lives in a palace inferior to that of the king, အိမ်ရှေ့မင်း.

အိမ်နီးချင်း, *n.* a neighbour.

အိမ်ခေါက်ကျွန်, *n.* the child of a slave.

အိမ်မ, *n.* a chief or principal house among several.

အိမ်မြှောင်, *n.* a lizard.

အိမ်ရှေ့, (*pron.* ရေ့,) *n.* heir-apparent to the throne.

အိမ်ရှေ့မင်း, do.

အိမ်ရှေ့မင်းသမီး, *n.* the wife of an heir-apparent.

အိမ်မက်, *n.* a dream, အိပ်မက်.

အိမ်း, (from ဧဝံ, *Pali,*) *int.* yes, အေး ဟုတ်ကဲ့, (*pron.* အည်း) ; hence တအိမ်းအိမ်းနေ, *v.* to remain saying yes, without doing.

အိမ့်, (1) *v.* to feign unwillingness, through pride or affection ; (2) *v.* to roll over and over, လိမ့်.

အိမ့်ညှင်, see ညှင်.

အိဒ်ပွဲ, many, much ; စကားအိဒ်ပွဲ, to be loquacious, talkative.

အီ, *v.* to be healthy, well, hearty, stout, ကျန်း မာ.

အီးသာ, *v.* do. to be lively, in good spirits.

အီးကတိုက်, see အီးတိုက်.

အီးပေါက်, *v.* to perform a certain pneumatic operation, လေထုတ်.

အီးတိုက်, *v.* to irritate, provoke, by backbiting, or misrepresentation.

အုတ်, *an astrological term.*

အုတ်, *n.* a brick, ; အုတ်ချပ်, *n.* do. အုတ်လွှာ, *n.* do.

အုတ်ခဲ, *n.* a bit of brick.

အုတ်ကြွပ်, *n.* a tile.

အုတ်ဖို, *n.* a brick-kiln.

အုတ်ကျက်, *v.* to be an overwhelming, tumultuous noise; clamorous, noisy, အုံးအောင် ၊ အုံးသဲ ၊ ရွံ့ရင် ၊ စီကျက် ၊ စီညံ ; (commonly reduplicated, and used adverbially, thus အုတ်အုတ် ကျက်ကျက်.)

အုတ်အော, *v.* do. အုတ်သဲ, *v.* do.

အုတ်နှဲ, *n.* a kind of tree.

အုတ်မွှန်း, *n.* a kind of sweet potatoe vine.

အုန်း, (1) *n.* the cocoa-tree; အုန်းဖွဲ, *n.* a kind of tree.

အုန်းသီး, *n.* a cocoa-nut ; အုန်းခွံ, *n.* a cocoa-nut shell.

အုန်းဆံ, (1) (from အဆံ,) *n.* the cocoa-nut meat ; (2) (from ဆံ, hair,) *n.* the bark of the nut, after being pounded.

အုန်းရည်, *n.* the cocoa-nut milk.

အုန်းဆီ, *n.* oil extracted from the cocoa-nut.

အုန်းမှုတ်, *n.* a dipper made of a cocoa-nut shell.

အုန်းသီးဆံချည်တွေး, *n.* the stringy substance into which the milk is converted.

အုန်းကျွန်း, *n.* the Nicobar islands.

အုန်းနှောက်, (a *corruption* of ဦးနှောက်,) *n.* the brain.

အုံး, (2) *v.* to be many, numerous, (commonly implying noise,) များ.

အုံးအောင်း *v.* to be noisy, tumultuous, clamorous, (commonly reduplicated, and used adverbially, as အုံးအုံးအောင်းအောင်း.)

အုံးအောင်းခပ်, *v.* do.

အုန်းအောင်းခပ်ပြု, *v.* to make a tumult, or uproar.

အုန်းအောင်းဆန်, *v.* do.

အုန်းအောင်းဆန်ပြု, *v.* do.

အုန်းသဲ, *v.* do.

အုပ်, (1) *n.* a box that has a conical cover.

အုပ်ဆောင်, *n.* a high conical cover, made of slight materials for occasional use.

အုပ်, (2) *v.* to superintend, preside over, ကြပ်.

အုပ်, (3) *v.* to cover, ဖုံး ; to correspond ; overwhelm, ဖိလွှမ်း ; to rule, preside over, ချုပ်၊ စိုး ; hence အအုပ်, a cover, *figurat.* a parcel, bale ; a ruler, president.

အုပ်ခြော, see ဥခြော.

အုပ်ခက်, see ဦးခက်.

အုပ်ဆက်, see ဦးဆက်, a joint of the neck.

အုပ်ထုတ်, see ဦးထုတ်.

အုပ်မှင်, see ဥမှင်.

အုပ်ရှစ်, *n.* a kind of tree.

အုပ်ကျောင်း, see ဦးကျောင်း.

အုံ, *v.* (1) to plaister, cover over, besmear, မံ ; *figurat.* to anticipate, prevent, do beforehand ; (2) *v.* to assemble, crowd together, surround, စု၊ ရုံး၊ ဝိုင်း. Hence အအုံ, a collection, assemblage ; a place where many things are collected ; implements, utensils, (collectively considered,) အဆောက်အအုံး အသုံးအဆောင် ; without the prefix အ, the body or bulging part of a pot or vessel, where the contents are collected, အိုင် ; a hut, temporary house or shed, တဲအုံ.

အုံး, *n.* a pillow ; *v.* to pillow the head, recline, repose, ခေါင်းအုံး.

အုံစည်, *v.* to plaister, &c. see အုန်, to plaister.

အုံတုံ, *n.* a kind of tree.

အုံး, *v.* to roast by covering up in the fire, the article being secured from contact with the coals, by some envelopement ; *see* ဖုတ်.

အုံးအောင်, *v.* to be tumultuous, noisy, &c. see အုတ်ကျွက်.

အုံးသဲ, *v.* do.

အုံးလှဲ, *n.* the mumps, quinsy.

အုံ, *v.* to overspread, as the clouds, မိုးအုံ.

အူ, (1) *v.* to make the noise indicated by the word; to howl as a dog or jackal; (2) to be stale, tainted, begin to putrefy —less than ပုပ်; (3) *n.* the intestines.

အူဝက်, *v.* to be rough, savage.

အူကြောင်း, *n.* the hollow which perforates certain plants; the tube of a quill.

အော, (1) *v.* see ဩ; (2) *int.* yes, အိမ်း၊ ဟုတ်ကဲ့.

အောအော, *an interjection of forbidding; also of calling.*

အဲ, (1) *v.* to be assembled, crowded together, remain in a body close and thick, စု၊ ပေါင်း၊ ရုံး; (2) a sort of verse. အဲအံ, *n.* do. (3) *int.* very well, that is right, ဟုတ်ကဲ့. အဲအဲ, do.

အဲမောင်း, *n.* a kind of spear with a long handle.

အော့, *v.* to vomit, အန်.

အောက်, *v.* to allure, decoy; draw out, detect, ဖော်.

အောက်မ, *n.* a female elephant, employed to decoy wild ones.

အောက်, *v.* to be musty, mouldy.

အောက်, *n.* a lower, or under part (of a thing;) also a term of *comparison,* as အိမ်အောက်ငယ်၏, it is smaller than the house; in which sense it supplies the place of *than.*

အောက်မှာ, under, as အိမ်အောက်မှာ, under the house.

အောက်ဗိုက်ကျိုက်, *v.* to gird up, (as the loins with a waist-cloth.)

အောက်ဗိုလုံးလုံးကျိုက်, do. ခါးတောင်းကျိုက်.

အောက်တော့ဖြူ, do. (obsolete.)

အောက်ချင်း, *n.* a kind of bird, the rhinoceros bird.

အောက်ဆဲ, *n.* a kind of vine, creeper, နွယ်ကြိမ်.

အောင်, (1) *v.* to be full, complete, not deficient in natural parts (applied to seeds, and figuratively to animals;) (2) *v.* to overcome, conquer, နိုင်; (3) *n.* a fee to the judge on gaining a cause; sometimes အင်အောင်, as အင်ကောက်အင်အောင်.

အောင်, (4) *v. affix,* so that, so as to, that, as ပြုအောင်, that he may do, or be doing.

အောင်မြင်, see အောင်, to be full, &c.

အောင်လံ, *n.* banner, flag of victory.

အောင်သူ, *n.* a victor, conqueror.

အောင်မြေ, (from မြေ,) *n.* whatever is the centre, or seat, of victory, whether a city or a monarch.

အောင်, (5) *v.* to act the part of a go-between, prepare the way, make up matters, settle difficulties, bring parties together, စေ့ဆို. အောင်ဆို, do. အောင်သွယ်, do.

အောင်သည်, *n.* a go-between, mediator.

အောင်း, (1) *v.* to be concealed, secret, hid, ကွယ်၊ ပုန်း. အောင်းဝော် အောင်းတက်, *n.* one born of the same mother; (2) *n.* the Thibet cow, bos grunniens; the tail or hair of do.

အောင်းလှံ, *n.* a spear, adorned with said tail or hair, used as a standard.

အောင်းမေ့, *v.* see အောင်းမဲ့.

အောင်းမဲ့, *v.* to recollect, call to mind, သတိရ; to meditate upon (as an absent or lost friend,) လွမ်း.

အောင့်, *v.* to retain, hold in (as the breath,) be constricted (as the bowels, or urine,) to restrain one's self, keep in, be reserved, reluctant to express one's feelings, ချုပ်တည်း.

အောင့်ကျိတ်, do. အောင့်တည်း, do. အောင့်အည်း, do. အောင့်အီး, do. အောင့်ကျင်, do.

အော်, (1) *v.* to call out, halloo, shout, to make the grunting noise of an elephant, ဟစ်၊ ကြွေး။ ကြော်; (2) *int.* O, very well! O, that's it! အော်အော်, do.

အော်ဆဲ, *v.* to rouse, summon, call to action, ဆော်မြင့်၊ နှိုးဆော်.

အော်ဂလီ, *n.* a tickling or rising in the stomach, a disposition to vomit.

အော်ဂလီဆန်, *v.* to be subject to do. အော်ဂလီတက်, do. အော်ဂလီဆ, do.

အို, (1) *v.* to be old, aged, အသက်ကြီး။ ရင့်; to look old, homely, အဆင်ဆန်; အိုမင်း, *v.* do.

အို, (2) *a vocative interjection.*

အိုဘဲ့, *an interjection denoting satisfaction and fondness.*

အိုး, *n.* a pot.

အိုးကင်း, *n.* a caldron, large iron pot or kettle; a part of a broken pot.

အိုးချမ်း, *n.* a bit of a pot, စောင်ချမ်း.

အိုးစည်, *n.* a kettle drum.

အိုးစရည်း, *n.* a large earthen pot, an unglazed jar.
အိုးထိန်း, or အိုးထိန်းသည်, *n.* a potter.
အိုးပွဲ—စကားအိုးပွဲ, *v.* to be talkative, loquacious.
အိုးဖုတ်, *n.* a little pot.
အိုးဖို, *n.* a pot-kiln.
အိုးဖိုသူ, *n.* a potter, အိုးထိန်း.
အိုးငုတ်, *n.* a short necked goglet, or earthen bottle, ငုတ်အိုး.
အိုးသူကြီး, (commonly pronounced အိုးစကြီး,) *n.* a cook.
အိုက်, *v.* to feel warm, a little different from ပူ, and နွေး.
အိုင်, *v.* to be collected, gathered together, (commonly applied to water;) *n.* a collection of water, a natural lake—larger than အင်း.
အိုင်း, *v.* to disappear by turns, seem to be gone.
အိုင်းနာ, *n.* a sore that sometimes appears to be cured, but breaks out anew.
အိုင့်, (1) *n.* a frightful wood; (2) *n.* the bulge of any thing, ဖု.

## အာ.

The second vowel of the Burman Alphabet, has no form of its own; but when initial, is represented by its symbol (ာ) combined with the vowel အ. It is, therefore, to be sought under the compounds of အ.

## ဣ

The third vowel in the Burman alphabet.
ဣ, *v.* to be flexible, tender, soft, delicate; see နု.
ဣဏ, *(Pali,)* *v.* to be connected with an object.
ဣဋ္ဌံ, *(Pali,)* *n.* desire.
ဣဋ္ဌာရုံ, (from ဣဋ္ဌံ, desire, *Pali,* and အာရုံ, an object,) *n.* a desirable object.
ဣတ္ထိလိင်, (from ဣတ္ထိ, woman, and လိင်, &c. *Pali,)* *adj.* feminine (gender.)
ဣတ္ထိ, *(Pali,)* *n.* a woman.
ဣတ္ထိဆိင်, *n.* female genitals.
ဣတ္ထိဘော, *n.* do.
ဣန္ဒ, *(Pali,)* *n.* a chief.

ဣန္ဒနီလာ, *n.* a kind of precious stone.

ဣန္ဒြေ, (from ဣန္ဒြိယံ, *Pali,*) *n.* faculties of sensation and feeling, of which there are twenty-two, including the six senses, (see အာယတန); sense, good sense, freedom from passion, composedness.

ဣန္ဒြေဆောင်, *v.* to behave well, act with propriety.

ဣန္ဒြေရ, *v.* do. ဣန္ဒြေရှိ, *v.* do.

ဣရိယာပုဒ်လေးပါး, *n.* the four positions of the body, viz. သွားခြင်း, walking; ရပ်ခြင်း, standing; ထိုင်ခြင်း, sitting; လျောင်းခြင်း, lying.

ဣလာရမ္မသိ, *n.* a kind of vine, or creeper.

ဣသိ, (*Pali,*) *n.* a holy man, an ascetic, ရသေ့.

## ဤ.

The fourth vowel in the Burman alphabet.

ဤ, (1) *pron. adj.* this, ဟယ်.

ဤသို့, *pron. adj.* such, of this sort (relating to the preceding or subsequent.)

ဤက and ဤမှ and ဤကြောင့်, hence, for this reason.

ဤမှာ, ဤမှလော, hence, concerning this.

ဤသို့က, ဤသို့မှ, from this.

ဤသို့ကြောင့်, or ဤသို့သောကြောင့်, because of this, therefore.

ဤသို့သောကြောင့်ဖြစ်သည်ဟူသော, in regard to its being thus.

ဤမည်, *pron. adj.* such, *indefinite* (used in repeating a story second hand, as, he proceeded to relate, that, in *such* a place, of *such* a man, the purchase was made.)

ဤ, (2) see အီး, to be healthy.

ဤသာ, *v.* to be well, healthy, stout.

ဤရုဗ္ဗ, *n.* one of the books of the Vedas.

## ဥ.

The fifth vowel in the Burman alphabet.

ဥ, *v.* to lay an egg. Hence အဥ, an egg; a root that protuberates like an egg.

ဥဩ, *n.* the cuckoo.

ဥကင်, *n.* the arch over a throne of state.

ဥက္ကာ, *(Pali,)* *n.* a meteor, ignis-fatuus, မီးခွ.

ဥက္ခောင်း, *n.* the head ; (*a corruption of* ဦးခေါင်း, used by the best writers.)

ဥက္ခောင်းထွင်း, *n.* a cap.

ဥကျည်, *n.* an animal of the cat kind, ကြောင်ဥကျည်.

ဥကြိုး or ဥချိုး, or ဥခြိုး *n.* a dove, ချိုး.

ဥဏ္ဏှာ, *n.* see ဦးချွဲရေး.

ဥစ္စာ, *n.* a thing, property, goods, ဝတ္ထု.

ဥစ္စာရပ်, do. ဥစ္စာရတနာ, *n.* do.

ဥဏှိ, see ဥဿုံ.

ဥဏ္ဏလုံ, *n.* the single hair which grows on a Boodh's forehead, and when stretched, is two cubits long.

ဥတု, (1) *n.* a season, one of the three seasons into which the year is divided, viz. မိုးကာလ၊ ဆောင်းကာလ၊ and နွေကာလ ; (2) see ရတု, the menses, catamenia, courses.

ဥတ္တရ, *n.* one quarter of the world, the north quarter.

ဥတ္တရကုရု, *n.* the North Island, (see ကျွန်း.)

ဥဒါန်း, (from ဥဒါန, joy, *Pali,*) *n.* a joyful utterance, speaking with joy, exultation (commonly applied to deity or inspired persons ;) accounts handed down from antiquity, traditional records relating to religion, ဥဒါန်းစကား.

ဥဒါန်းကြူး, ဥဒါန်းရင့်ကြူး, ဥဒါန်းဆို, ဥဒါန်းရွ, ဥဒါန်းမြွက်, *v.* to utter do.

ဥဒါဟရုဏ်, (from ဥဒါဟရဏ, *Pali,*) *n.* enlarged explanation or illustration, အကျယ်အားဖြင့်ဆောင်ချင်း.

ဥဒေါင်း, *n.* a peacock, ဒေါင်း.

ဥဒေါင်းမြီးစည်, *n.* the fan-tail of a peacock.

ဥဒေါင်းမြီးမျက်, *n.* the eye of a peacock's tail.

ဥဒ္ဒိ, *n.* *(Pali,)* an evil quality, or vice, see ကိလေသာ.

ဥပက္ခာ, *n.* see ပါရမီ.

ဥပက, (*Pali,*) *n.* a kind of evil spirit.

ဥပစာ, (1) *n.* a figure of speech, ထင်စားသောစကား ; (2) *n.* the suburbs of a town, or vicinity of a house.

ဥပဇ္ဈာယ်, *n.* a superior teacher, guide, monitor. Also written ဥပဇ္ဇာယ်.

ဥပဒေ or ဥပဒေသ, *n.* a precept, rule, နည်း.

ဥပဒ္ဒဝော or ဥပဒ္ဒဝေါ, *n.* an evil, calamity, အန္တရာယ် ၊ ဥပါဒ် ၊ ဘေး.

ဥပပဇ္ဇ, (*Pali,*) *v.* to be.

ဥပ္ပဇ္ဇ, (*Pali,*) *v.* to be, or proceed.

ဥပပါတ်, *adj.* produced without apparent cause; *when applied to men,* supernaturally produced; see ကရုဏ်.

ဥပမာ, *n.* a comparison, similitude, တော်ပုံ.

ဥပမေယျ, *n.* the subject of comparison.

ဥပသမ္ပဒါန်, *n.* the state attained by a priest of Boodh.

ဥပသာရ, *n.* an inseparable prefix.

ဥပါဒ်, *n.* an evil, calamity.

ဥပါဒ်, (from ဥပါဒါန်, *Pali,*) *v.* to adhere, cleave to.

ဥပါဒ်ရန်လောင်း, *n.* an evil, a calamity, ဘေး ၊ အန္တရာယ်.

ဥပါဒ်, (from ဥပါဒ်ဒါ, *Pali,*) *n.* being, ဖြစ်ခြင်း.

ဥပါဒက္ခဏ, (*Pali,*) *n.* the commencement of thought, စိတ်ဖြစ်ခြင်း; see ဌိတိက္ခဏ, and ဘင်္ဂက္ခဏ.

ဥပါဒါန်, (from ဥပါဒ်, *Pali,*) *n.* adherence, cleaving to, စွဲလမ်းခြင်း, (commonly applied to a permanent evil passion.) Four kinds are enumerated, viz. ကာမုပါဒါန် ၊ ဒိဋ္ဌုပါဒါန် ၊ သီလဗ္ဗတုပါဒါန် and အတ္တဝါဒုပါဒါန်.

ဥပါယ်, *n.* a means, expedient, device.

ဥပါယ်တမျဉ်, *n.* do.

ဥပါသကာ, (*Pali,*) (1) *n.* a layman, one who is not a priest, but who does the duties due to a priest, ဒါယကာ; *fem.* ဥပါသိကာ. (2) *n.* a kind of vine, or creeper.

ဥပုတ်, *n.* a kind of water-fowl.

ဥပုသ်, (from ဥပေါသထ, *Pali,*) *n.* performance of the duties of religion, သီတင်း.

ဥပုသ်နေ့, *n.* a duty-day, of which there are four in a month, viz. the eighth of the waxing of the moon, the full, the eighth of the wane, and the change, သီတင်းနေ့.

ဥပုသ်နေ့စောင့်, *v.* to keep or observe the duty-day.

ဥပုသ်သုံး, *v.* do.

ဥပေက္ခာ, (*Pali,*) *n.* a neutral state of mind, moderation, freedom from passion, လျစ်လျူခြင်း.

ဥပေါသထ, (*Pali,*) a kind of fabulous elephant.

ဥဒိန်ငှက်, *n.* a heron, paddy-bird, ဗိန်ငှက်.

ဥထတောဗျည်း, *n.* a kind of hermaphrodite, one who has the parts of man and woman by turns.

ဥက္ကာ, *n.* a kind of meteor.

ဥမင်, *(pron.* ဆုမ်မင်, or ဆုံမင်,) *n.* a cave, လိုဏ်.

ဥယောဇဉ်, (from ဥယျောဇ, *Pali,*) *n.* instigation, တိုက်တွန်းချင်း.

ဥယျဉ်, or ဥယဉ်, (from ဥယျာဉ, *Pali,*) *n.* an enclosure of fruit-trees or flower-plants, a garden.

ဥယျာဉ, *n.* a garden, or enclosure of fruit-trees.

ဥဿဒငရဲ, *n.* small hells, or places of punishment, by which the larger hells are encompassed.

ဥသဘ, (1) *n.* a chief; a bull, the chief of a herd; a cock; the chief disciple of Gaudama.

ဥသဘ, (2) *n.* an ookthabah, a measure of distance, equal to twenty tahs, (တာ).

ဥသဘရာဇာ, *n.* a kind of precious stone, a topaz.

ဥဿုံ, *adj.* all, the whole, without any remainder, အလုံးစုံ၊ မကျန်၊ မကျန်.

## ဦ.

The sixth vowel in the Burman alphabet.

ဦတည်ဘွား, *n.* an emperor of China.

ဦဒဂို, *adv.* without break, (applied to a train of people in motion.)

ဦရရ, *adv. an intensive.*

ဦး, (1) *v.* to polish, make bright, as gold, &c.

ဦး, (2) *v.* to begin, make a beginning, commencement, •; (seldom used as a simple verb.)

ဦး, (3) *num. affix,* (see Gram.)

ဦး, (4) *v. affix, imp. or prec.* (see Gram. *imp. mod.*)

ဦး, (5) *(pron.* အုံး,) *v. affix,* more, again, as ပေးဦးမည်, he will give more, or again.

ဦးဦး, *adv.* at first. ဦးဦးဖြားဖြား, do.

ဦးဖြာ, do. ရှေးဦးဖြာ. Hence အဦ, a beginning, အစ.

ဦး, (6) (from အဦး, a head,) *n.* the principal or most prominent part (of a thing,) ခေါင်း.

ဦးကင်း, *n.* the two protuberances on an elephant's head.
ဦးဆိုင်း, *n.* a chief.
ဦးခတ်, *n.* a kind of cap for a horse.
ဦးခေါင်း, (commonly written ဦးကျောင်း,) *n.* the head.
ဦးခေါင်းခွံ, *n.* the skull.
ဦးချိုက်, *v.* to bow the head to the feet of a person addressed; to intreat, petition.
ဦးချွားရေး, (1) *n.* the dividing line in the cranium or skull; (2) *n.* marks on the forehead indicating one's future destiny.
ဦးချို, *n.* a horn.
ဦးစား, *v.* to comply with, follow, be led by.
ဦးစောက်, or ဦးဆောက်, *adv.* stoopingly, with the head downwards.
ဦးစောက်ပန်း, *n.* artificial flowers, which are suspended under the stern of a boat.
ဦးစွန်း, *n.* the tuft of hair or feathers left on the head, a crest; *figurat.* the principal place in a kingdom, a capital.
ဦးစွန်, *adv.* straight forward.
ဦးဆက်, *n.* the back part of the neck, a joint of the neck.
ဦးဆံ, *n.* the hair of the head.
ဦးဆောက်, *n.* a kind of tree; (2) *adv.* see ဦးစောက်.
ဦးညွှတ်, *v.* to bow down, stoop; ဦးနှိမ့်, do. ဦးချ, do.
ဦးတင်, *v.* to place on the head, to assent to, acquiesce in (*respectfully.*)
ဦးတုန်း, *n.* the solid piece of wood which forms the prow of a boat.
ဦးတိုက်, *v.* to put to the head, or forehead, (as in making a religious offering.)
ဦးထုပ်, *n.* a cap, ဦးကျောင်းလွှမ်း.
ဦးနှောက်, *n.* the brain.
ဦးပြည်း, *n.* a shaven, or bald head, ခေါင်းတုံး.
ဦးပျား, *n.* the prow of a boat.
ဦးရစ်, or ဦးရန်း, *n.* a turban, ခေါင်းပေါင်း.
ဦးရည်း, *n.* an intermittent head-ache.
ဦးရီး, *n.* an uncle, a mother's brother, ဝရီး.
ဦးရှတိုင်, *n.* the principal post, or pillar of a house.

ဦးရွက်, *v.* to make the Burman obeisance, ရှိခိုး.

ဦးသစ်, *v.* to be fresh or newly polished.

ဦးသျှောင်, (*pronounced* ဦးယောင်,) *n.* the knot of hair worn by Burman men.

ဦးသျှောင်ကျင်, *n.* a certain head-dress, or ornament, ထံကျင်.

## ဧ.

The seventh vowel in the Burman alphabet.

ဧ, *v.* (1) to be cool, cold, ချမ်း။ ဖြ ; (2) to be comfortable, happy, ချမ်းသာ.

ဧက, (*Pali,*) *adj.* one.

ဧကာဒက်, *see* ဧထာဒက်.

ဧကန္တ, (*Pali,*) *adv.* certainly, verily.

ဧကဂ္ဂတာ, (see ဈာန်,) permanency, immutability.

ဧကဓိ, *adj.* of one thickness, single.

ဧကနံ, *adv.* of one width, (applied to cloth.)

ဧကမုခ်, (from မုခ, a mouth, *Pali,*) *adj.* one-mouthed, (applied to a supposed kind of cocoa-nut.)

ဧကမူလိ, *n.* a kind of vine.

ဧကရာဇ်, (from ရာဇာ, a king, *Pali,*) *n.* a sovereign of one of the four grand islands, (see ပဒေသရာဇ် and စကြာမင်း;) *according to modern use,* an independent sovereign.

ဧကဝုစ်, (from ဝစန, a word, *Pali,*) *n.* the singular number.

ဧကဝုစ်သိသ်, (from သေသော, to remain, *Pali,*) *adj.* one remaining, one only, တခုသာကျွင်း.

ဧကန်, (from ဧကန္တ, *Pali,*) *adv.* certainly, verily, အကယ်။ အမှန်.

ဧကံ, *adv. see* ဧကန်.

ဧကာဒသမ, (from ဧက, one, and ဒသ, ten, *Pali,*) *adj.* eleventh.

ဧချင်း, (from ဧ, to be cool, pleasant, and အချင်း, verse,) *n.* a kind of verse.

ဧချင်းကြူး, *v.* to repeat musically, sing.

ဧည်, (abbreviated becomes ဤ,) is used at the close of sentences, and is equivalent to ရှိသည်.

ဧည့်ခံ, (commonly pronounced ဧ့ခံ,) *v.* to give audience, receive (as a visitor.) Compare ညီလာခံ.

ဧည့်သည်, (commonly *pron.* ဧသည်,) *n.* a traveller, stranger, casual visitor, အာဂန္တုက.

ဧည့်သည်ဝတ်, *n.* the reception or entertainment of a stranger, the duties of hospitality.

ဧကိ, *n.* a kind of animal.

ဧတဒဂ်, (by corruption ဧကဒဂ်,) *n.* one who has the preference of many.

ဧတဒဂ်ရ, *v.* to attain such preference.

ဧယင်, *n.* a swinging cradle, ပခက်.

ဧရာဝတီ, *n.* the Arahwatee (Irawuddy) river.

ဧရ, *(Pali,) adj.* great, large, ကြီး; (2) *n.* the keel of a vessel.

ဧရာဝဏ်, *n.* the three-headed elephant of the Nat country.

ဧကန်, *adj.* certainly, truly.

## အဲ.

The eighth vowel in the Burman alphabet, has no form of its own; but when initial, is represented by its symbol ( ဲ ), combined with the vowel အ. It is, therefore, to be sought under the compounds of အ.

## ဩ.

The ninth vowel in the Burman alphabet.

ဩ, *an interjection, denoting various emotions.*

ဩလဲလဲ, do.

ဩကာသ, *(Pali,) n.* asking leave, အခွင့်တောင်းခြင်း.

ဩဃ, *(Pali,)* a stream or current.

ဩဃလေးပါး, (from ဩဃ, a stream, *Pali,) n.* four streams or currents which bear away creatures, viz. ကာမောဃ၊ ဘဝေါဃ၊ ဒိဋ္ဌောဃ၊ အဝိဇ္ဇောဃ; see အာသဝေါ.

ဩဇာ, (1) *(Pali,) n.* a relish, savourishness, အရသာ၊ အဖြိုက်; the food of the Nats, သုဒ္ဓဘောဇ်; *figuratively*, weight, consequence, worth, (applied to persons, and to words;) (2) the custard-apple tree.

ဩဋ္ဌဇ, (from ဩဋ္ဌ, the lips, *Pali,) adj.* labial, produced from the lips, (applied to consonants of ပ class.)

ဩဋ္ဌ, *(Pali,) n.* the lips.

ဩဋ္ဌ, *n.* a camel, ကုလားအုတ်.

ဩတ္တပ္ပ, *(Pali,)* *n.* fear of sinning, tenderness of conscience, ထန့်ချင်း caution, watchfulness, စောင့်စည်းခြင်း.

ဩလဲ, *n.* a kind of vine.

ဩဝါဒ, *(Pali,)* *n.* instruction, ဆုံးမခြင်း.

## ဪ.

The tenth vowel in the Burman alphabet, is not initial, unless used for ဩော, which see.

## က.

The first consonant in the Burman alphabet, and the first in the class of gutturals.

က, (1) *v.* to dance, moving the hands, arms, and body to the sound of music, as well as the feet. (2) *v.* to harness, bind on (as a saddle.) (3) *n.* a saddle.

ကချေသည်, *n.* a dancer.

ကကောက်, *n.* the inside of the joint of the knee.

ကတောင်း, *n.* the flaps of a saddle.

က, (4) *v. affix.* as သွားက, when he had gone, or having gone.

က်, is frequently expressed by the character (ံ) written over the preceding letter, as ရောံ, for ရောက်.

က, (5) *(n. affix, abl. case,)* from, out of. က is sometimes *nominative* also, and sometimes *vocative.*

ကဒ်, *n.* a kind of large wicker basket, see ပုဒ်.

ကက္ကဋ, see ကရကဋ်.

ကက္ကဋာ, *n.* a certain star ; (see တာရာ.)

ကက္ကူ, *n.* a kind of tree.

ကက္ကူကမည်, *n.* a kind of sea-shell.

ကက္ကောဒ်ထက်, *adv.* disputatively, quarrelsomely, ကွတ်ကောဒ်တက်.

ကင်, *v.* to roast.

ကင်ပလင်း, *n.* a kind of tree.

ကင်ပိန်, *n.* a kind of vine.

ကင်ပွန်း, *n.* a kind of vine.

ကင်း, (1) *v.* to be free of, separate from, liberated, exempted, ကွာ ရှင်း ၊ လတ် ၊ လွတ်.

ကင်း, (2) *v.* to form (as fruit in its earliest state,) ကင်းစ. Hence အကင်း, *n.* fruit in its first state, after the blossom.

ကင်းစ, *v.* to form as fruit, &c. ကင်းပွား, *v.* to produce fruit.

ကင်း, (3) *n.* a centipede, scorpion, or any similar creature.

ကင်းခြေများ, *n.* a centipede.

ကင်းဥဋ္ဌန်, *n.* a scorpion.

ကင်းမထက်မည်း, *n.* the large, black, earth-scorpion.

ကင်းမြီးကောက်, *n.* a small kind of scorpion.

ကင်းသံ, *n.* another kind of scorpion.

ကင်း, (4) *n.* a watch-house, sentinel's post.

ကင်းစမ်း, or ကင်းထိုး, *v.* to spy, reconnoitre, take a survey of the outposts.

ကင်းစောင့်, *n.* a sentinel.

ကင့်ပုံး, *n.* a kind of vine. ကင့်ပုံးလတ်ချော, *n.* a species of do.

ကစဖ်, *v.* tease, vex, play with, ကျီစယ်၊ ကျီစား၊ ပျက်ပြည်၊ ပျက်ရယ်.

ကစည်, *v.* to be ashamed, ရှက်.

ကစည်ကလျား, *adv.* in a broken, scattered manner, helter-skelter, ဖရိုဖရဲ.

ကစား, *v.* to play, amuse one's self, enjoy pleasure, မြူးထူး.

ကစေ, *v. affix*, though, notwithstanding, as သွားကစေ, though he go, or went.

ကစိမ်းကဝါး, *adv.* in a raw, inexperienced manner.

ကစီ, *n.* congee, rice-water ; ကစီရည်, *n.* do.

ကစီကရင်, *adv.* all in tumultuous confusion, စနောင်စနင်၊ ဖရိုဖရင်း.

ကဇဲ, (*Pegu,*) see လင့်ရှိ.

ကတော့, *n.* a kind of tree, ကဒ်တော့.

ကစော်, *n.* a preparation of rice, which gives it an intoxicating quality.

ကစွန်း, *n.* a kind of sweet potatoe plant.

ကဆုန်, *n.* the second month in the year.

ကဆွဲကန့်ပြု, *v.* to keep putting off, to delay, hold off, feign both willingness and unwillingness, အညှင်း၊ အနှဲ့ပြု၊ ခင်လေးနွဲ့ပြု.

ကညာ, (1) *v.* to ask help, petition, တောင်းပန် ; (2) to have pity on, relieve, သနားကယ်မ.

ကညင်, *n.* the wood-oil tree.

ကညစ်, *n.* an iron style.

ကညာ, (*Pali,*) *n.* a maiden, above seven years old, and unmarried.

ကညွတ်, *n.* a kind of plant.

ကဍွက်, *n.* a kind of plant.

ကဏ္ဌာ, *n.* (*Pali,*) the throat.

ကဏ္ဌဇ, (from ကဏ္ဌာ, the throat, *Pali,*) *adj.* guttural, produced from the throat, (applied to consonants of the က class.)

ကဏ္ဍမှူ, *n.* a disease in the ears of cows.

ကတ်, (1) *v.* to be hard, difficult, ခက်၊ ခဲ.

ကတ်သတ်, *v.* do. *also,* to be reluctant, backward.

ကတ်တွက်, do. do.

ကပ်, (2) *v.* to reach, attain, arrive at.

ကပ်လှူ, *v.* to offer or give (respectfully,) to give by way of handing.

ကတ်ကုတ်, *v.* to endeavour to overcome a difficulty, use great exertion, to be indefatigable, ကုတ်၊ ပန်းကုတ်၊ အားထုတ်၊ ကြိုးစား.

ကတ်တတ်, *adv.* contrarily.

ကတ်ကျည်း, *n.* scissors.

ကတ္တရာစေး, *n.* tar.

ကတ္တူလှေ, *n.* a kind of boat.

ကတ်ပ, *n.* a kind of tree.

ကတ်ပယ်, *n.* scales for weighing silver, ချိန်ခွင်.

ကတ်ပိုဆ်, *n.* a kind of tree.

ကတက်, (1) *n.* a kind of tree; (2) see ကတောက်.

ကတည်းက, *adv.* while or when, (referring to the past or present.

ကတည်းက, *v. affix,* from the first, as, သွားကတည်းက, from the first of his going.)

ကတတ်, *n.* a kind of vine.

ကတတ်ငန်း, *n.* a kind of tree.

ကသီ, *n.* a vessel shaped like a wine-glass.

ကတီပါ, *n.* velvet.

ကတုတ်, *n.* a temporary parapet, or mound of earth, thrown up for pefence.

ကတုန်, (1) *n.* a vessel shaped like a tumbler; (2) ***see*** **ကတွန်း.**

**ကတုံကနစ်,** *n.* a kind of vine.

ကတုံးပေါက်မ, *n.* a kind of vine.

ကတဲ, *n.* a kind of ruby, ပတဲ.

ကတော့, (1) *v.* see ကန်တော့.

ကတော့, (2) *n.* a basket made of paper, or a leaf wound into itself; e. g. ဖက်ကတော့, one made of leaf; စက္ကူကတော့, one of paper.

ကတောက်, *v.* to make the noise which the word indicates, (as fowls.)

ကတောက်ကတက်, *v.* do. *adv.* confusedly, foolishly.

ကတော်, (1) *see* ကတောက်; (2) *n.* a title formerly granted to females in high office; now used as an affix, to denote the feminine of characters above the common people; as မင်းကတော်, a governess; ဆရာကတော်, a female teacher, or the wife of a teacher.

ကတိုး, *n.* the musk-deer; musk.

ကတို, *n.* a ferryman, see ကူတို.

ကတိုက်, *v.* to provoke, irritate, ဆီးတိုက်၊ ဆီးကတိုက်၊ ဂုံးတိုက်.

ကတိုက်ကတွန်း, do. (commonly used adverbially.)

ကတွတ်မုန့်, or ကတွန်မုန့်, *n.* a kind of bread.

ကတွန်းကတိုက်, or ကတုန်းကတိုက်, *see* ကတိုက်ကတွန်း.

ကထိန်, (from ကဌိန, *Pali,*) *a term applied to certain ceremonies and offerings.*

ကတိကဝတ်, *n.* an engagement, promise.

ကန်, (1) *n.* an artificial pond, a tank, ရေကန်.

ကန်ပေါင်ဦး, *n.* a mound of earth, a bank.

ကန်စင်း, or ကန်စင်းရိုး, *n.* do. a ridge of earth in rice fields.

ကန်, (2) *v.* to kick, ကြောက်; to push off, (as a boat,) ကြောက်; to act ungratefully.

ကန်, (3) (from ကညာ, a maiden, *Pali,*) *n.* Virgo, the sixth sign of the zodiac.

ကန်, (4) a stick, cudgel, တုတ်.

ကန်တော့, (*pron.* ကတော့,) *v.* to ask pardon, make submission.

ကန်ထိတ်, *n.* a kind of tree.

ကန်း, (1) *v.* to be blind, မျက်စိကန်း; figuratively applied to the ear also; (2) *v.* to be naturally dry, not abounding in water, *different from* ခန်း, to be dried up; (3) *n.* dry land, ကုန်းကျဉ်း.

ကန့်, (1) *n.* sulphur, brimstone; (2) *v.* to cut across, obstruct, impede, hinder, prevent, တား၊ ဆည်, or ဆီး၊ ဆို့၊ တား၊ မြစ်တန့်.

ကန့်ကွက်, *v.* do.

ကန့်ကူ, (*pron.* ကင်္ကူ,) *n.* a kind of soft stone.

ကန့်ကူဆံ, *n.* a pencil made of soft stone.

ကန့်ကူထန့်, *n.* the handle of such a pencil.

ကန့်ချွပ်, *n.* a kind of tree.

ကန့်ဆိတ်, *n.* a kind of tree.

ကန့်လန့်, *adv.* right across, athwart; see ဖီလာ. Hence **အကန့်**, ***n.*** **a** line drawn across other lines; a spoke of a wheel.

ကန့်လန့်ပြု, *v.* to act contrary, be perverse.

ကန့်လန့်ကျင်, (*pron.* ကလန့်ကျင်,) *n.* a bolt, cross bar, ကျည်း; တံခါးကျင်, (*by abbreviation* ကန့်လန့်, *pron.* ကလန့်.)

ကန့်သတ်, *v.* to cut off, prevent.

ကနုက်, (1) *n.* the royal umbrella over the throne of state; (2) *v.* to erect or set up the royal umbrella.

ကနုက်ကကန်း, *n.* do. (more commonly used than ကနုက်.)

ကနို, *n.* a kind of tree.

ကနိုး, *n.* a kind of tree.

ကနဖော့, *n.* a kind of grass.

ကန္တာရ, *n.* (*Pali,*) any thing very difficult; awful, frightful, huge; (commonly applied to a difficult road, desert, &c.)

ကနား, *n.* a covering, large shed, booth for any purpose.

ကနားမြင်း, or ကနးမြင်း, *n.* a spacious roof, extending far beyond the enclosed part of the building.

ကနားဦး, *n.* a beginning, the first, အဦး၊ အစ.

ကနုကမာ, *n.* an oyster.

ကပ်, (1) *n.* a period or revolution of time, an era; see မဟာကပ်.

ကပ်သုံးပါး, *n.* three evil periods, viz. ဒုဗ္ဘိက္ခန္တရကပ်၊ ရောဂန္တရကပ်၊ and သတ္ထန္တရကပ်.

ကပ်, (2) *n.* a texture made of bamboos, split and interwoven, used to form the side of a house or room, or for other purposes.

ကပ်, (3) *v.* to join, unite, put together, ဆက်၊ ပူး၊ ရှဉ်း; (4) *v.* to adhere to, take refuge in, မှီခို; (5) *v.* to offer respectfully, ဆက်လှူ.

ကပ်ကုတ်, *see* ကုတ်ကပ်.

ကပ်ဖော, *n.* a kind of tree, ကဖော.

ကပ္ပိန္ဒု, *n.* a certain spot on a priest's garment.

ကပ္ပည်း, or ကပ္ပဲ, *n.* see ကမ္ပည်း.

ကပ္ပါ, *n.* to be near, close, to approach.

ကပ္ပိ, *(Pali,) v.* to do any service, to wait upon, minister to, (used only by priests of Boodh, in speaking to their followers,) ဆက်သည်ကိုပြု.

ကပ္ပိလ, *n.* a kind of tree.

ကဗျာ, *n.* poetry, လင်္ကာ.

ကပြောင်းကပြန်, (from ပြောင်းပြန်,) *adv.* upside down, topsy-turvy; falsely, fraudulently.

ကဖောက်ကဖက်, (from ဖောက်ဖက်, but with a change of meaning,) *adv.* remissly, heedlessly, wanting in due attention and respect; confusedly, without order, ကရောက်ကရက်၊ ဇနောင်ဇနင်၊ ဗိုးရိုးဗက်ဖက်၊ ရောက်ရက်.

ကမုဒ္ဒြာ, *n.* a kind of water-lily.

ကမ္ပည်း, (*pron.* ကပ္ပည်း, or ကပ္ပဲ,) *n.* an inscription, superscription; an account, memorandum, မှတ်စာ၊ စာရင်း.

ကမ္ဗတ်, *n.* the narrow board which, in finishing a building, is applied to cover the unsightly ends and deficiencies of the boards; the outer facing which encircles the border of a priest's garment, ဆနားပတ်.

ကမ္ဗတ်သိုင်း, *n.* the string which secures a priest's garment on the breast.

ကမ္ဗောဇ, *n.* Cambodia.

ကမ္ဗလာ, (1) *n.* cloth made of hair or wool, ထက္ကလာ; (2) a kind of Chinese carpeting; (3) *n.* a kind of tree, Sonneratia apetala, (Symmes;) the orange, လိမ္မော်.

ကမ္ဗလူ, *v.* a kind of plant.

ကမ္ဗလွေ, *n.* a wrapper or case for Burman books, made of sticks and cloth.

ကမ္ဘာ, *n.* the period of time in which an entire revolution of nature takes place; *see* လောကဓာတ်, the whole universe; the world of man, this world, လောက.

ကမ္မ, (*Pali,*) *n.* a deed, action, conduct.

ကမ္မဇ, (from ကမ္မ, a deed, and ဇာတိ, to be, or produce, *Pali,*) *adj.* caused by the influence of past deeds.

ကမ္မဋ္ဌာန်း, *n.* short sentences for repetition, of which there are forty, viz. အသုဘဆယ်ပါး၊ ကသိုဏ်းဆယ်ပါး၊ အနုဿတိဆယ်ပါး၊ အပ္ပမညာတရားလေးပါး၊ သညာတပါး၊ ဝဝတ္ထာန်တပါး၊ အရူပဈာန်လေးပါး.

ကမ္မဝါ, *n.* a writing which contains directions for initiating into the priesthood.

ကမျဉ်, (1) *n.* a kind of vine; (2) *n.* a small red ant, ကမျဉ်နီ.

ကမြင်း, *v.* to be immodest, shameless, act without regard to modesty or decency, ကလက်၊ နော၊ အရှက်မရှိ.

ကမြစ်, *v.* to instruct, discipline, correct, ဆုံးမ၊ ပဲ့ပြင်၊ သွန်သင်.

ကမ်း, *n.* (1) a raised boundary, limit; a bank, shore.

ကမ်းပါး, *n.* do. ကမ်းသင်း, *n.* do.

ကမ်းပြတ်, or ကမ်းပါးပြတ်, *n.* a broken bank, declivity, precipice, ချောက်.

ကမ်း, (2) *v.* to give, grant, bestow, ပေး.

ကယ်, *v.* (1) to help effectually, (*more than* ကူ, or ထောက်) to deliver from some evil, to save, ကယ်.

ကယ်တင်, do. ကယ်မ, do. ကယ်ယူ, do.

ကယ်ဆောင်, see ကယ်, to help, &c.

ကယ်, (2) *v.* to be full, puffed up, swollen, (applied to the bowels,) ဖယ်.

ကရ, (*Pali,*) *v.* to do.

ကရကဋ်, (from ကက္ကဋ, a crab, *Pali,*) *n.* Cancer, the fourth sign of the zodiac.

ကရကတ်, *n.* a kind of bird.

ကရင်, *adj.* pertaining to the Kaying people, who inhabit the interior of the Burman dominions.

ကရဇ, (from ကရ, to do, and ဇာ, to be or produce, *Pali,*) *adj.* produced by a generative process, as the bodies of animals on earth, not as celestial beings; *see* ဥပပါတ်.

ကရက်, *n.* muslin, fine cloth, *finer than* ခါသာ.

ကရည့်ကသီ, or ကရဲကသီ, *adv.* here and there, scattered about.

ကရိန့်, *n.* a kind of handle, or fastening of a door.

ကရမကထန်, *adv.* see ရမထန်.

ကရမက်, *n.* the bastard-sandal tree.

ကရဝိက်, *n.* a kind of fabulous bird.

ကရဝေး, *n.* the bdellium tree.

ကရား, *n.* a pitcher, or pot with a spout.

ကရုဏာ, *(Pali,)* *n.* compassion, sympathy, tenderness.

ကရုန်းကရင်း, *adv.* disorderly, confusedly; *comp.* ရုန်းရင်း.

ကရဲကစဲ, *adv.* in a broken, scattered manner, helter-skelter, ဖရိုဖရဲ.

ကရောက်ကရက်, (from ရောက်ရက်,) *adv.* heedlessly, remissly, disrespectfully, ကပေါက်ကပက် ၊ ပိုးရိုးပက်စက်.

ကရောက်ကမည်, *adv.* do.

ကရော်ကရက်, or ကရော့်ကမည့် *adv.* do.

ကလွတ်, *n.* a stand for jars, &c. composed of rattan or rope.

ကလက်, *v.* to be immodest, shameless, act without regard to modesty and decency, ကမြင်း ၊ နော့.

ကလန်, *n.* a nobleman, (obsolete.)

ကလန်သံပျင်, *n.* do.

ကလပ်, *n.* a low stand, with a concave surface, commonly used in making offerings of flowers.

ကလယ်, *adj.* pertaining to the Hindoos.

ကလလ, *n.* the fœtus in the first stage of existence, ရေကြည်း; *see* အဗ္ဗုဒ်, and ဘားထင်.

ကလာပ်, (from ကလာပေါ်, *Pali,*) *n.* a collection, union of several.

ကလာပေါ်, *(Pali,)* *n.* see ကလာပ်.

ကလိ, *v.* to disturb, be troublesome, vex, plague, ကလိ ၊ နှောင့်ယှက်.

ကလိန်, *n.* a kind of vine.

ကလိန်းကလက်, *adv.* lightly, foolishly, rudely, disrespectfully.

ကလိမ်ကလည်, (from လိမ်လည်,) *see* တလိမ်တလည်.

ကလိမ်ကမာ, *n.* falsehood, deceit, fraud.

ကလိန်ကကျစ်, *n.* falsehood, deceit, fraud.

ကလီကမာ, *n.* do.

ကလူ, *v.* to play with, divert, amuse, ပြု; *when combined with words of evil import*, to oppress, injure, abuse, as နှိပ်စက် ကလူ, or ကလူနှိပ်စက်, &c.

ကလူစား, *v.* do.

ကလူကလဲ, *adv.* playfully.

ကလေးကလား, *adv.* childishly, in an unmanly manner.

ကလေဝရ, (*Pali*, a rotten carcase,) *adj.* totally useless, idle, of no account, good for nothing.

ကလွဲ, see ကလိ.

ကလော, *n.* a kind of tree.

ကလော်, *v.* to lift up, raise out of a place, disturb, ကော် ; *figuratively*, to return evil for good, ကော်.

ကလျိုင်, *v.* to take out of the middle of a thing, dip deep, go below the surface.

ကလျှာ, see ကညာ.

ကဝံ, *n.* a kind of image.

ကဝါသည်, *n.* a washerman ; see ခဝါသည်.

ကသစ်, *n.* a kind of tree in the Tahwadeingtha Nat country.

ကသည်း, *adj.* pertaining to the Cassays.

ကသည်းမှုန့်, *v.* a kind of prepared flower or powder, used to rub on the skin.

ကဿပ, *n.* the third Boodh ; (see ဗုဒ္ဓ.)

ကသိဏံ, (*Pali*,) *n.* a collection, a whole.

ကသီကမီ, *adv.* suddenly.

ကသီလာ, *n.* a kind of coat worn in ancient times ; (obsolete.)

ကသိုဏ်း, (from ကသိဏံ, *Pali*,) *n.* a collection, a whole.

ကသိုဏ်းဆဲပါး, see ကမ္မဋ္ဌာန်း.

ကံ, (from ကမ္မ, *Pali*,) *n.* (1) a deed, action, အကြောင်း၊ အမှု; (2) the secret influence of an action on one's future destiny.

ကံ့ကော, (*pron.* ဂံ့ဂော,) *n.* a kind of tree.

ကံ့ကော်, (*pron.* ဂံ့ဂေါ်,) *n.* a kind of tree.

ကံကြေး, *n.* wages, allowance, support of any kind, whether goods or people, granted on account of service.

ကံပြင်း, *n.* a kind of tree.

ကံပြန်, *v.* to die.

ကံမြန်, *v.* to instruct, ဆုံးမ.

ကာ, *v.* (1) a shield of a certain kind, ဒိုင်းကာ; (2) *v.* to make a partition, to separate, interpose, debar, obstruct, ကန့် ၊ ဆီး ၊ တား ၊ ပြန် ၊ ဟန့်.

ကာကာ, *n.* a certain star, (see ကာဠာ.)

ကဖီ, *n.* coffee.

ကာမ, *(Pali,) n.* desire, passion, အလို ၊ လောဘ; of which there are two kinds, viz. ဝတ္ထုကာမ, and ကိလေသာကာမ.

ကာမဂုဏ်, (from ဂုဏ, a quality, *Pali,*) *n.* the passions, distinguished into five kinds, according to the five external senses.

ကာမရေ, *n.* semen, သုက်.

ကာမရာဂ, see ကာမ.

ကာမုပါဒါန်, *n.* an evil affection, or passion.

ကာမောဃ, *n.* see ဩဃ.

ကာမျှ, *adv.* merely, if merely, but merely.

ကာယ, *(Pali,) n.* a collection.

ကာယ, *(Pali,) n.* the body, ကိုယ်.

ကယန်, (from ကာယ, a collection, and အန္တ, an end, *Pali,*) *n.* a completion, finishing off.

ကာရ, *(Pali,) n.* a letter.

ကာရဏ, *(Pali,) n.* a reason, အကြောင်း.

ကာရန်, (from ကာရ, a letter, and အန္တ, an end, *Pali,*) *n.* the final letter in a syllable or word, whether a consonant, or the symbol of a vowel.

ကာလ, *(Pali,) n.* time, အခါ.

ကာလကဏ္ဍု, *n.* a kind of grass.

ကာလသုတ်, *n.* one of the states of punishment; see ငရဲ.

ကာဠာဝက, *n.* the poorest kind of elephants.

ကာဆီ, *n.* sprouts of the bang tree, after the top is broken off.

ကား, (1) *v.* to stretch out, expand, widen, spread, ပြန့် ၊ ကျယ်; to exchange, trade, barter, ဖောက်ကား; to boast, brag, ဝါကြွား.

ကားယား, *adj.* or *adv.* sprawling, spread out; obstinate, contrary.

ကား, (2) *v. affix*, as, while ; သွားကား, while he goes.

ကား, (3) *adv.* is sometimes used emphatically after other noun affixes, as အရိုက်ကိုကားခံနိုင်ပါမည်လော, can you *indeed* bear the beating? It is also used adversatively, and repeated to mark a contrast, as မြေအပြင်၌ကားခလုပ်ဆူးငြောင့်ကိုမြင်သာ၏ ။ ရေထဲ၌ကားခလုပ်ဆူးငြောင့်ကိုမမြင်နိုင်, on land it is easy to see thorns and stumps, but in the water, thorns and stumps we cannot see.

ကား, (4) *n. affix*, as to, concerning, in regard to.

ကိစ္စ, (*Pali,*) *n.* business, any work to be done, အမှု.

ကိတ်, (1) *see under* နက္ခတ် ; (2) a term in grammar.

ကိန္နရာ, *mas.* and ကိန္နရီ, *fem.* (*Pali,*) *n.* a kind of fabulous animal, a compound of man and bird.

ကိန်း, see ကျိန်း, to sleep.

ကိရိယာ, (*Pali,*) *n.* a deed, action, အကျင့် ; *in grammar*, a verb.

ကိရိကိရိ, *adv.* chirpingly.

ကိလေသာ, (*Pali,*) *n.* (1) a desire of the sexes, lust, ကိလေသာကာမ ; (2) an evil quality or vice, of which there are ten kinds, viz. လောဘ ။ ဒေါသ ။ မောဟ ။ မာန် ။ ဒိဋ္ဌိ ။ ဝိစိကိစ္ဆာ ။ ထိန ။ ဥဒ္ဓစ္စ ။ အဟိရိက ။ အနောတ္တပ္ပ.

ကိလေသာကာမ, *n.* a desire of the sexes ; see ကာမ.

ကိတ္တိ, see ကျော်စောကိတ္တိ.

ကု, *v.* to give medicine, assist in recovery from sickness, ဆေးကု.

ကုစား, *v.* do. ကုသဝ်, do. ကုမ, do. ကုသ, do.

ကုက္ကား, *n.* a certain appendage of a flag.

ကုက္ကို, *n.* a kind of tree.

ကုဏ္ဍိ, *n.* the fœtus.

ကုဋီ, (*Pali,*) *n.* (1) a building ; a small building appended to a larger.

ကုဋေ, (*Pali,*) *n.* the number of ten millions.

ကုဋ္ဌနာ, *n.* the leprosy, နူနာ.

ကုတ်, (1) *n.* a lever.

ကုတ်ကော်, see ကော်, to raise with a lever.

ကုတ်ကော်တက်, *adv.* disobediently, wilfully, contentiously, အငြင်းသန်.

ကုတ်, *v.* (2) to copulate, as a fowl, or any male bird; (3) to subtract, deduct, (in arithmetic,) နုတ်; (4) to make exertion, be diligent, အားထုတ်၊ ကြိုးစား၊ လုံ့လပြု.

ကုတ်ကတ်, *v.* to endeavour to overcome a difficulty, ကတ်ကုတ်.

ကုတ်, (5) *v.* to scratch with the nails, ခြစ်.

ကုတ်ချီ, or ကုတ်ယို, see ကုထိတမင်.

ကုတ်တိန်ကာ, *n.* a difficulty of breathing.

ကုတ်ပဲ, *n.* a kind of tree.

ကူတို, *n.* a ferryman, ကတို.

ကူတိုသည်, *n.* do.

ကူတိုလှေ, *n.* a ferry-boat.

ကူတိုစီး, *n.* one who is ferried across a stream.

ကုန်, (1) *v. affix,* sign of the plural number.

ကုန်, (2) *n.* a certain ornament for the head.

ကုန်, (3) *n.* merchandize, wares, goods for sale. ကုန်စယ်, or ကုန်စည်, or ကုန်စလယ်, do.

ကုန်သင်း, *n.* a partner in trade.

ကုန်သည်, *n.* a merchant, trader.

ကုန်သွယ်, *v.* to traffic, trade.

ကုန်, (4) *v.* to come to an end, be exhausted, wholly gone, ဆုံး၊ စင်၊ ကုံး.

ကုန်ကျ, *v.* to be spent. Hence အကုန်, *adj.* all, the whole; *adv.* wholly, entirely, အကုန်အစင်.

ကုန်း, (1) *v.* to be convex, rounded, be bent, hump-backed; (2) *n.* rising ground (frequently written ကုံး,) ကုန်း၊ ကြည်း; (3) the back of an animal, (seldom used alone,) ကျော ထိကုန်း.

ကုန်းကြည်း, *n.* dry land; see ကုန်း.

ကုန်း, *v.* (4) to stoop, bow down, (see ငုံ့.)

ကုန်းကြောင်း, *adv.* by land, တောင်ပြ.

ကုန်းနှီး, (from နှီး, to be spread out for support,) *n.* the pad of a saddle, a Burman saddle.

ကုန်းပတ်, (from ပတ်, to encircle,) *n.* the railing of a boat's deck or back.

ကုန်းဖင်, (ထမီ,) *n.* a kind of petticoat.

ကုပ်, (1) *v.* to make marks, write, ချက် ၊ ခြစ်; (2) *v.* to be curved, drawn together; to bend down the head, stoop, ကိုင်း ၊ ညွတ်; (3) to act in a humble, stooping manner.

ကုပ်ဆက်, (*pron.* ဂုတ်ဆက်,) *n.* the back part of the neck, ဦးဆောက် ၊ လည်ကုပ်.

ကုမ္ဘဏ်, *n.* one kind of the Nats, who guard Myenmo Mount.

ကုလလေးတာ, *n.* a certain measure of distance, five hundred of which make one kautha, (ကောသ.)

ကုလား, *n.* a native of any country west of Burmah.

ကုလားအုပ်, (from ဩဋ္ဌ, *Pali,*) *n.* a camel.

ကုလားကာ, *n.* a curtain or screen, made of foreign materials.

ကုလားကျင်, *n.* a lock, bolt, used by foreigners.

ကုလားပေါ်, *n.* wheat.

ကုလားထိုင်, *n.* a chair.

ကုလားမျက်စိ, *n.* a kind of vine.

ကုလီကစား, *n.* a kind of play, ဖလီကစား.

ကုလော, *n.* a kind of tree.

ကုသလ, see ကုသိုလ်.

ကုသိုလ်, (from ကုသလ, *Pali,*) *n.* merit, the reward of merit, ကောင်းမှု ၊ ကောင်းသောအကျိုး.

ကုသီထမင်း, *n.* rice given away at funerals, ကုတ်သိ.

ကုံ, (1) (from ကုမ္ဘော, a water-pot, *Pali,*) *n.* Aquarius, the eleventh sign of the zodiac; (2) see ကုန်, to be ended.

ကုံထံ, *v.* to have a sufficiency, an abundance, be rich, ပြည့် ၊ စုံ ၊ ကြွယ်ဝ ၊ ရတတ် ၊ ဝပြော.

ကုံလုံ, *v.* do. ကုံလောက်, do. ကုံဝ, do.

ကုံကုမ်, *n.* a kind of tree.

ကုံထည်, *n.* see ကုန်သည်.

ကုံး, *v.* to string, file on a string, သီ; (figuratively applied to writing, ကုံးစီ.)

ကုံ့ကုံ့, see ပုံ့ပုံ့.

ကူ, (1) *v.* to help, assist, ညီ ၊ ထောက် ၊ ပင့် ။ ပန့် ။ မ. (2) *n.* a kind of disease. (3) (from ဂုဟာ, *Pali,*) *n.* a cave.

ကူပေါင်း, *v.* to associate for mutual aid.

ကူလော, (*Pali,*) *n.* a kind.

ကုလ္လိ, *n.* a kind of boat.

ကူး, *v.* (1) to cross over, pass from one place or thing to another, သန်း၊ ဝင်; (2) to transfer, exchange, ထဲ၊ ကူးသန်း; (3) to transcribe, copy, ကူးရေး.

ကူးခပ်, *v.* see ကူး.

ကူးသန်း, *v.* to transfer, exchange, ကူး.

ကူးရေး, *v.* to transcribe.

ကူးမြောက်, *v.* to cross over, get over a difficulty, accomplish one's purpose.

ကေကေကာကာ, *adv.* deceitfully.

ကေတု, *n.* a certain star, (see တာရာ.)

ကဲ, *v.* (1) to exceed, surpass, လျွန်၊ လွန်၊ သာ; (2) to be chief, superior, ဦး၊ မြတ်. Hence အကဲ, *n.* a chief.

ကဲစိုး, *v.* to rule, govern, ချုပ်.

ကဲလား, *n.* a door which swings from the top.

ကဲ့, (1) *a euphonic affix.*

ကဲ့, (2) *v.* to hide, conceal, be secret, ထောင့်၊ ပုန်း၊ ဖွက်. (3) *v.* to do by degrees, (seldom used as a verb,) hence အကဲ့, and တကဲ့တကဲ့, *adv.* by degrees, bit by bit, တထောက်တထောက်.

ကဲ့ရဲ့, *v.* to dispraise, censure, speak evil of, revile, ရှုတ်ချ၊ ဆဲရေး.

ကဲ့သို့, *pron. adj.* such as; *also a noun affix,* (see Gram.)

ကော, *v.* to swell up, as a bank or shoal, by which the water becomes shallow; *figurat.* to be proud.

ကော, or ကောလေ, } sometimes supersede an *ind. v. affix;* otherwise *expletive.*

ကောက်, (1) *n.* the rice-plant, rice; *comp.* စပါး.

ကောက်ကြီး, *n.* rice that is long in growth.

ကောက်ယင်, (from လျင်,) *n.* rice that comes to maturity quickly.

ကောက်ရိုး, *n.* straw, rice-stalk.

ကောက်ညှင်း, *n.* a kind of rice, very gelatinous when cooked.

ကောက်, (2) *v.* to be crooked.

ကောက်ကျစ်, *v.* to be crooked and twisted, to be deceitful, perverse, လိမ်လည်.

ကောက်လိမ်, *v.* do.

ကောက်, (3) *v.* to pick up, to pick out, take from several

ကောက်တကျစ်, *adv.* crookedly, deceitfully.

ကောက်ကျိုးကောက်ကျစ်, *adv.* do.

ကေက်ကော့, *n.* a kind of tree.

ကောက်စား, *v.* to pick up, or out, take from several.

ကောက်တင်း, *n.* a rule, decision, precedent, produced as authority. Hence အကောက်, *n.* duties, custom.

ကောက်ဝန်, *n.* a head-collector of duties, collector of port-duties.

ကောက္ကုဋ, *(Pali,)* *n.* a fowl, ကြက်.

ကောင်, *num. affix,* (see Gram.)

ကောင်း, (1) (with မ prefixed to the root,) *v. affix,* as မသွားကောင်း, do not go, or it is not right to go. ကောင်း, is used with လျှင်, and other verbal affixes, in the following manner, viz. with the root repeated, as သွားကောင်းလျှင်သွားမည်, when it is proper, (I) will go, or (I) shall probably go.

ကောင်းသည်, *v. affix,* as ပြုကောင်းသည်, he may be doing, or probably is doing.

ကောင်း, (2) *v.* to be good, (by abbreviation ငေး.)

ကောင်းကြီးပေး, *v.* to praise, bless, (commonly applied to the praise or benediction bestowed by deity or celestial beings)—*more than* ချီးမွမ်း.

ကောင်းချီးပေး, *v.* do.

ကောင်းစား, *v.* to be prosperous, rise to wealth and honour, ကြွယ်ဝ.

ကောင်းမှု, *n.* merit, the reward of merit, ကုသိုလ် ၊ ကောင်းသောအကျိုး. Hence, by perversion of speech, အကောင်းအကန်း and မကောင်းမကန်း, *adj.* or *adv.* poor, worthless, of no use.

ကောင်းကင်, *n.* space, vacuity, the expanse of heaven, heaven, အာကာသ.

ကောင်းမွန်စွာ, *adv.* goodly, excellently, ကောင်းစွာ.

ကောပ္ပ, *(Pali,)* *n.* an epoch, သက္ကရာဇ်.

ကောလာဟလ, *(Pali,)* *n.* a tumultuous noise, ဆူညံဆူညံကျွက်ကျွက်သောအသံ.

ကောသ, *pron.* ဂေါသ, *(Pali,)* *n.* a kautha, a measure of distance equal to twenty ookthabahs, (ဥသဘ.)

ကော့, *v.* turn up at the edges, be concave, warp.

ကော့ရရော့, *adv.* turning up at the sides or edges.

ကော်, (1) *n.* paste, any viscous substance, glue ; (2) *v.* to raise out of a place, as with a lever ; (3) *v.* to be ungrateful, ထကော်.

ကော်ဆဲ, *v.* to reproach, revile---*more severe than* ဆဲရေး.

ကော်ဇော, *n.* a carpet.

ကော်ရော်, *v.* to respect, reverence, esteem, ရှိသေ ။ မြတ်နိုး.

ကို, (1) *n. affix,* obj. case.

ကို, (2) (from အစ်ကို, an elder brother,) a title prefixed to proper names of men, indicative of friendship, and due consideration, (commonly applied to persons older than the speaker.)

ကိုရှင်, *n.* (1) a probationer for the priesthood ; (2) a term of compellation, addressed to men, indicative of friendship and due consideration, *(commonly pron.* ကိုယင်.*)*

ကိုက်, (1) *v.* to bite, ခဲ ; to be painful, gnaw as pain, ခဲ ။ နာကျင် ; (2) to take hold (as colours on cloth, or ink on paper ;) (3) *n.* large shears used to cut metal ; (4) *n.* a kind of plane or scraper, used by blacksmiths.

ကိုင်, *v.* to hold, lay hold.

ကိုင်လုပ်, *v.* to work, လုပ်ကိုင်. Hence အကိုင်, *n.* a handle ; and အကိုင်အလုပ်, *n.* a work.

ကိုင်း, (1) *v.* to be inclined from a straight line ; to bend off, hang over. Hence အကိုင်း, *n.* the branch of a tree, အခက် ; (2) *n.* a kind of grass ; (3) *n.* a garden of culinary plants, vegetables, &c. surrounded by water, and overflowed in the rainy season, ကျွန်း.

ကိုယ်, (1) *n.* matter, material substance ; an animal body ; a person.

ကိုယ်စ, *adv.* each, each one. ကိုယ်စီ, do. ကိုယ်စီကိုယ်ဝ, do.

ကိုယ်စား, *n.* a substitute, one that acts instead of another, an agent.

ကိုယ်ပြ, *v.* to appear, show a body, (applied to beings naturally invisible.)

ကိုယ်ရံ, *n.* an attendant, body-guard.

ကိုယ်လုပ်, *n.* a female attendant, concubine.

ကိုယ်ဝတ်, *n.* the upper or principal garment of a priest of Boodh ; *comp.* သင်္ကန်း.

ကိုယ်ဝန်, (from ဝန်, a burden;) *n.* the fœtus in the womb, ဥပသန္ဓေ.

ကိုယ်ဝန်ဆောင်, or ကိုယ်ဝန်ရှိ, *v.* to be pregnant, နှတ်ပိုက်ကြီး ။ နှတ်ဝိုက်ရှိ ။ ပဋိသန္ဓေစွဲ ။ ပဋိသန္ဓေယူ.

ကိုယ်, (2) *pers. n.* one's self, i. e. myself, yourself, or himself, မိမိ.

ကိုယ်ကြွပ်, do. ကိုယ်တိုင်, do. ကိုယ်ရှင်, do. ကိုယ်ရှင်ကိုယ်, do.

ကိုယ်တော်, *pers. pron.* thou, (*mas.* or *fem.* used in addressing a superior.)

ကိုယ်စလယ်, do.

ကိယ်ရင်း, *adv.* consciously.

ကိုယ်ထူး, *adv.* alone, by one's self, venturesomely, extraordinarily.

ကိုယ်လုပ်တော်, *n.* a female attendant, or concubine of a king, မောင်းမ.

ကိုယ်ရုံကြီး, *n.* a kind of tree.

ကိုး, (1) *adj.* nine, marked by the figure ၉ ; (2) *v.* to rely on, or trust in, receive as a teacher, guide, or object of worship, to worship—*rather more than* ဆည်းကပ်, or မှီ.

ကိုးကွယ်, *v.* to worship.

ကိုးစား, *v.* to rely or trust in.

ကိုးရိုးကားယား, *adv.* improperly, wrongly.

ကိုးလိုးကန့်လန့်, *adv.* confusedly, intermixedly.

ကို့, *v.* to bend down the head, stoop ; (*com.* ကုပ် and ညွတ်.)

ကျ, *v.* (1) to fall, become low, hang down. (2) to be wanting, omitted in writing ; *act.* ချ.

ကျန်, *v.* do. do.

ကျမ, *n.* an abbreviation of ကျွန်မ.

ကျ, (3) *v.* to be settled, adjusted, put in proper place, situated ; *act.* ချ.

ကျန်, *v.* do.

ကျက်, (1) *v.* to be cooked, dressed, နပ် ; *act.* ချက်.

ကျက်, (2) to be healed (as a sore.)

ကျက်, (3) to be accustomed, acquainted, familiarised, လေ့ကျက်.

ကျက်စား, *v.* to feed in a wonted place, (as creatures in a pasture or at a trough ;) to attend to habitually, be acquainted with, accustomed to, versed in, လေ့ ၊ လေ့ကျက် ၊ လေ့လာ ၊ လေ့ကျွမ်း ၊ ကျင်လည်.

ကျက်, (4) *v.* to continue without cessation or intermission, (applied to words or sound, noise, &c. but seldom used as a simple verb.)

ကျက်ကျက်, *adv.* continually, incessantly ; *comp.* ဆူတ်ဆူတ်ကျက်ကျက် ၊ စီကျက်.

ကျယ်, (5) *v.* to stretch out, expand ; see ကား.

ကျခတ်ဝါး, *n.* the thorny bamboo.

ကျင်, (1) *n.* excrement.

ကျင်ကြီး, *n.* fœces, ordure, ချေး ၊ မစင် ၊ ဝမ်း.

ကျင်ငယ်, *n.* urine, အပေါ့ ၊ ရေယောင် ၊ သေး.

ကျင်ငယ်အိမ်, *n.* the bladder.

ကျင်ငယ်ချောင်း, *n.* the urethra, ထီး.

ကျင်, (2) *v.* to do, work, to work ore, as ရွှေကျင်သည်, to do gold, i. e. to separate gold dust from earth, (seldom used as a principal verb, but frequently as an affix.) Hence, အကျင်, *n.* a pin, bolt, bar, whatever does up, or secures a thing, combined with other words, as ဆံကျင်, a pin, or ornament, used to do up the hair ; *comp.* တံခါးကျင် ၊ ကုန်လှန်ကျင် ၊ တိတ်ကျင်.

ကျင်ခွက်, *n.* (see မိုက်,) a crucible, &c.

ကျင်, (3) *v.* to understand, be acquainted with, &c. (seldom used alone,) ကျင်လည် ၊ ကျွမ်း.

ကျင်လည်, *v.* to be acquainted, familiar with, versed or skilled in, pass through, experience ; လေ့လာ ၊ လေ့ကျက် ၊ လေ့ကျင် ၊ ကျွမ်းဝင် ၊ ကျွမ်းကျင် ; ကျင်လည်ကျင်, do.

ကျင်ကျွမ်း, *v.* do. *see* ကျွမ်း.

ကျင်း, (1) *n.* a hollow place, valley, trench, dock, concavity in the ground, or in any thing, ချိုင် ; ကျင်ချိုက်, *n.* do.

ကျင်း, (2) *v.* to put in order, set out to advantage, arrange, array, spread out, ခင်း.

ကျင်းပ, *v.* do. ကျင်းပြင်, *v.* do. ကျင်းဆင်, *v.* do.

ကျင့်, *v.* to do, perform, practise, ပြု ၊ ရှု. Hence, အကျင့်, *n.* a deed, အမှုအကျင့်.

ကျင့်နာ, *v.* to be merciful, kind, &c. (*see* သနာ.)

ကျင့်ပါ, *v.* to be natural to, အကျင့်အလေ့ပါ ၊ ဝါသနာပါ.

ကျင့်ထင့်, *v.* to be constricted, as the bowels; stiff, as the back, &c. (commonly used adverbially.)

ကျစ်, *v.* (1) to twist, လိမ်; to braid, ဝက်စုကျစ်; (2) *v.* to scratch into the ground, as an animal; (3) *v.* to be small, slender, dwarfish, ငယ် ၊ သေးကွေး ၊ လို.

ကျစ်လစ်, *v.* to be nice, exact, accurate, သေချာ ၊ သေခွေ ၊ သေသပ်.

ကျည်. (1) *n.* any tube closed at one end.

ကျည်တောက်, *n.* do. ကျည်တွန်, do.

ကျည်စေ့, *n.* a bullet, or shot.

ကျည်, (2) *v.* to be loud, or long continued, as sound, ကျယ် (commonly reduplicated, and used adverbially.)

ကျည်လောင်, *v.* do. စီလောင်.

ကျဉ်, *n.* (1) a large kind of ant; (2) *v.* to be benumbed, ထုံ.

ကျဉ်နာ, *v.* to be benumbed. Hence, အကျဉ်အခဲ, *n.* an induration, hardness, အကျိတ်အခဲ.

ကျည်ပွေ့, *n.* a pestle.

ကျည်း, (1) *n.* a kind of tree; (2) *n.* an arm, လက်ကျည်း; (3) a bolt, cross-bar, ကန့်လန့်ကျင် ၊ တံခါးကျင်; (4) *v.* to be thin, rare, (as liquid,) opposed to ပြစ်, thick, dense; (5) *adj.* pertaining to the Kyee people.

ကျည်းကျည်း, or တကျည်းကျည်း, *adv.* moderately and protractedly, (applied to words of pain.)

ကျည်းကွေး, *n.* some parts of the carved work on the roof of a Kyoung.

ကျည်းသား, *n.* small sticks used in certain plays.

ကျဉ်း, *v.* to be narrow, close, strait, confined, crowded; *act.* ချဉ်း.

ကျဉ်းမြောင်း, *v.* do. Hence, အကျဉ်း, *n.* an abridgment, compilation.

ကျတ်, *n.* a sandy, barren spot of earth.

ကျတ်တီး, *n.* do.

ကျတ်တီးပြင်, *n.* a barren plain.

ကျတ်တီးခေါင်, *n.* do.

ကျတ္တိကာ, *n.* a certain star, (see နက္ခတ်.)

ကျန်, *v.* (1) to remain, be left, ကြွင်း ; (2) *n.* a residue, balance.

ကျန်း, *v.* (1) to be well, healthy, hardy, stout, ချမ်းသာ ၊ မာ.

ကျန်းခန့်, *v.* do.

ကျန်းထော, *v.* do.

ကျန်း, *v.* (2) to be rough, savage.

ကျန်းကြွတ်, *v.* to be rough, abusive in speech.

ကျပ်, (1) *n.* a kind of box or basket ; (2) *n.* a gridiron, or any thing of the kind.

ကျပ်စင်, *n.* do. (most commonly used.)

ကျပ်ခိုး, *n.* the soot which collects on a gridiron, and hence any kind of soot, မှင် ; lamp-black.

ကျတင်, or ကျပ်တိုက်, *v.* to broil, cook by broiling.

ကျပ်, (3) *n.* a swelling, or indolent tumor, ကျပ်နာ ; (4) *n.* a kind of evil spirit ; (5) *v.* to clean out, or work upon, as the ear, or any aperture, by introducing a stick, implying some working or twisting of the thing inserted ; (6) *v.* to be intermediate ; *comp.* တိုင်ကျပ် ၊ ရက်ကျပ်.

ကျွှာ, see ကြွှာ.

ကျမ်း, *n.* (1) a floor.

ကျမ်းပိုး, *n.* a bug (so called, because dwelling in the crevices of floors.)

ကျမ်း, *n.* (2) a religious writing or book, ကျမ်းစာ.

ကျမ်းဂံ, *n.* do.

ကျမ်းကိုင်, or ကျမ်းဆို, *v.* to take an oath by, or upon, a religious book.

ကျမ်းတိုက်, *v.* to administer such an oath.

ကျမ်းစာရေး, *n.* a scribe or writer of religious books.

ကျမ်း, (3) *v.* to level, make even, ညှိ ; (4) *n.* a leveller, used in husbandry, ကျမ်းတုံး.

ကျယ်, *v.* (1) to be wide, broad, extensive ; *act.* ချဲ့.

ကျယ်ပြော, *v.* do. ကျယ်ဝင်, *v.* do. ကျယ်ဝန်း, *v.* do. ကျယ်ပိုင်, *v.* do.

ကျယ်, *v.* (2) to be loud, or long continued, as sound.

ကျံ့, *v.* (1) to besmear, rub over, anoint, လိမ်းလူး ; (2) to be affable, sweet in conversation.

ကျာ, *n.* see ဒိုင်, a piece on a gaming-board.

ကျာကျာ, *adv.* loudly, ကျိုးကျဉ်း ၊ ကြိကြိ.

ကျာဖွယ်, see ကြာဖွယ်.

ကျား, *v.* (1) to be spotted or striped, not uniform in colour, of diverse colours.

ကျားတားတား, *v.* to be a little spotted, &c.

ကျား, (2) *n.* a tiger ; (3) *n.* a piece on a gaming-board, ဒိုင်.

ကျားကွက်, *n.* a compartment on a gaming-board.

ကျားသစ်, *n.* a leopard, or hyena, သစ်ဆင်.

ကျား, (4) *n.* a prop, stay, used to support a roof, or the inclined side of a building.

ကျီ, (1) *n.* a granary ; ကျီမ, *n.* a large granary.

ကျီ, (2) *v.* to be slimy, viscous, glutinous, ချွဲ.

ကျီကျီကျွတ်ကျွတ်, *adv.* shrilly.

ကျစ်, (1) *v.* to be hard, indurated ; hard, difficult of performance or management, ခဲယဉ်း.

ကျစ်ခဲ, *v.* do. ကျစ်ခက်, *v.* do.

ကျစ်လစ်, *v.* to be properly done, exact, accurate, သေချာ.

ကျစ်လစ်သေ, *adv.* in a finished, complete, unalterable manner. Hence, အကျစ်, *n.* an induration ; a difficulty, အကျဉ်အခဲ ; အကျစ်အခဲ, do.

ကျစ်, (2) *n.* the Aurora-Borealis, or some similar appearance.

ကျစ်, (3) *n.* a kind of grass ; ကျစ်ပုတီး, *n.* a kind of tree.

ကျစ်စပါး, *n.* a kind of grain, နတ်ကောက်စပါး.

ကျစ်ကျစ်, *adv.* creakingly.

ကျစ်ဓား, *n.* a cris, dirk.

ကျိန်, *v* to swear, take an oath, imprecate evil on one's self or others, either conditionally or otherwise, curse, (one kind of ဓိဋ္ဌာန် ;) သစ္စာဆို ၊ ပန်နက် ၊ သစ္စာပန်နတ်, &c.

ကျိန်ဆို, *v.* do. ကျိန်တွယ်, *v.* do.

ကျိန်ဆဲ, *v.* to curse in anger, imprecate evil on another. Hence အကျိန်ရဲ, *v.* to dare to take an oath.

ကျိန်း, (1) *v.* to sleep, take repose, (respectful, commonly applied to clerical characters,) *see* ဆိပ်, and စက် ; to remain in a state of insensibility or stupefaction.

ကျိန်းဝပ်, *v.* to sleep, take repose; remain, dwell.

ကျိန်းစောင်း, *v.* to rest, as the fœtus in the womb.

ကျိန်း, (2) *v.* to smart, as the eyes, စပ်; (3) to be set on edge, as the teeth; (4) *n.* an astrological term, ခန်း.

ကျိပ်, *n.* a ten, (substituted for တဆယ်, in numbering rational beings, as တကျိပ်, one ten, or ten; နှစ်ကျိပ်, two tens, or twenty.)

ကျိမ်း, see ကျိန်း.

ကျီ, (1) *n.* a granary; ကျီမ, *n.* a large ditto.

ကျီကျ, *n.* do. also a treasury, storehouse.

ကျီ, (2) *v.* to separate metals from earth and sand by shaking in a vessel, ရွှေကျင် ၊ ငွေကျင်; (obsolete.)

ကျီစယ်, *v.* to tease, vex, play with, ကစား ၊ ပျက်ပြက် ၊ ပြက်ရယ်.

ကျီစား, *v.* do.

ကျီပေါ်ခွက်, *n.* see မိုက်, a crucible, &c.

ကျီး, *n.* a crow; ကျီးကန်း, *n.* do.

ကျီးအ, *n.* a raven.

ကျီးအာ, *n.* a kind of plant.

ကျီးခြေ, *n.* a staple, commonly of iron; *also* a kind of tree.

ကျီးတာရာ, *n.* a certain star, (see တာရာ.)

ကျီးသေ, *n.* a kind of tree.

ကျု, *v.* to be dirty, muddy, slimy, နောက် ၊ ညစ်.

ကျုပ်, *n.* a kind of reed.

ကျုံ, *v.* to be lean, thin, poor, to pine away, ချုံး ၊ ပိန် ၊ လှီ; ကျုံလှီ, do.

ကျုံစား *v.* do. *also* to wear away, as the ground by a stream of water.

ကျုံး, (1) *v.* to gather up, take up or away; (2) *see* ကျွင်း.

ကျုံး, *n.* (3) a moat, trench around a fortification.

ကျုံး, (4) *n.* a trap to take elephants, ဆင်ကျုံး.

ကျုံးကျုံး, *adv.* rumblingly.

ကျုံ့, *v.* to be drawn together, contracted, shrunk; (*act.* ချုံ့ ၊ ယို့ ၊ တွန့် ၊ ကျုံ့.

ကျူ, *n.* the reed plant.

ကျူကရိုင်, *n.* a coarse kind of mat, made of reeds.

ကျူငြောင်, *n.* a slender reed, one blasted in its growth.

ကျူး, (1) *v.* to go beyond, exceed, surpass, transgress, လွန် ၊ သာ.

ကျူး, (2) *v.* to produce melodious sound; to deliver, utter, express, (commonly applied to the speaking of a king or deity,) ကြွက်ရင် ၊ ဥဒါန်းကျူး.

ကျူးဇေ, *v.* do. ကျူးရင့်, *v.* do.

ကျူး, (3) *v.* to make exertion, အားထုတ်.

ကျေ, *v.* to be pulverized, reduced to powder, to be destroyed as a city or people, ကျေပွ ၊ ပြတ် ၊ ရှုန်; to be digested as food; to be versed, skilled in, accomplished, ပြီး ၊ ကျွမ်း ၊ ကျင်လည် ၊ လေ့လာ.

ကျေကွဲ, *v.* to be grieved, broken-hearted, ကွဲကျေ.

ကျေသို့, *adv.* down, as မြစ်ကျေသို့, down the river.

ကျေပွ, *v.* see ကျေ.

ကျေး, *n.* (1) a province, district.

ကျေးလက်, *n.* circumjacent parts, suburbs, environs belonging to any town or village.

ကျေးမက်, *n.* do.

ကျေးရွာ, *n.* do.

ကျေးစား, *n.* a ruler or governor of a province.

ကျေး, *n.* (2) a parrot, ကြက်တူရွေး.

ကျေးသား, *n.* do. *also*, a stick used in certain plays.

ကျေးကျွတ်, *n.* one species of parrot; ကျေးကြက်တော, *n.* another species; ကေးတမာ, *n.* another do.; ကျေးဖောင်ခါး, *n.* another do.

ကျေးငှက်, *n.* birds in general, as ရေကျေးရေငှက်, water-birds.

ကျေးမြီး, *n.* a kind of tree.

ကျေးစည်တိုင်, (*prop.* စေတိုင်,) *n.* a certain post in palaces, Kyoungs, &c.

ကျေးဇူး, *n.* advantage, profit, အကျိုး; favour conferred, obligation.

ကျေးဇူးမဲ့, *v.* to be ungrateful.

ကျေးဇူးခံ, *n.* one who receives a favour.

ကျေးဇူးရှင်, *n.* one who confers a favour, a benefactor.

ကျဲ, *v.* to be wide apart, *opposed to* စိပ်.

ကျဲကျဲ, *adv.* intensely, (applied to the heat of the sun.)

ကျောက်, (1) *v.* to kick, shove, push off, ကန် ၊ တွန်း; (2) *n.* the small-pox, ကျောက်နာ; (3) *n.* the back (of an animal,) ကျော.

ကျောက်ကုန်း, *v.* do. (most commonly used.)

ကျောက်ကပ်, (from ကပ်, to adhere to,) *n.* a kidney.

ကျောက်, *n.* (4) a stone, rock; ကျောက်ဆော်, to hew stone, ဆော်.

ကျောက်ခဲ, *n.* a stone, or rock.

ကျောက်ချဉ်, *n.* alum.

ကျောက်စေ့, or ကျောက်စရစ်, *n.* a small stone, pebble, gravel.

ကျောက်စိမ်း *n.* an emerald.

ကျောက်ဆူး *n.* an anchor, whether of stone or any other substance.

ကျောက်ထရံ, *n.* a steep rock, or precipice.

ကျောက်နီ, *n.* a ruby.

ကျောက်ပျဉ်, *n.* a flat level stone or rock.

ကျောက်ပြား, *n.* do.

ကျောက်ပြာ, *n.* do.

ကျောက်ဖြူ, *n.* an alabaster.

ကျောက်ပွင့်, *n.* sea-weed.

ကျောက်မီးသွေး, *n.* sea-coal.

ကျောက်သင်ပုန်း, *n.* a slate.

ကျောက်ဖရုံ, *n.* the long white pompion vine, ဖရုံမွှေ.

ကျောင်း, (1) *v.* to tend, feed, take care of, (as creatures,) ကျွေး၊ ထိန်း. Hence, အကျောင်း, *n.* a keeper, herdsman, &c.

ကျောင်းစား, *v.* do.

ကျောင်း, (2) *n.* a monastery, a building inhabited by priests of Boodh.

ကျောင်းကုန်း, (1) do. (2) *n.* rising ground; see ကုန်း.

ကျော့, (1) *v.* to catch in a noose or slip-knot; ကျော့ဖမ်း, do.

ကျော့ကွင်း, or ကျော့ညှတ်ကွင်း, *n.* a noose of any description.

ကျော့, (2) *v.* to be tamed, civilized, polished, decent in manners; to behave with propriety, be executed with taste, ယဉ်ကျေး၊ ပွယ်ယာ.

ကျော်, (1) *v.* to be the subject of public notice, be talked about, acquire notoriety, fame, သတင်းမြန့်; (2) (in composition,) *v.* to shout, call out.

ကျော်စော, *v.* do. *n.* fame, ကျော်စောကိတ္တိ.

ကျော်ဟုန်း, *v.* do.

ကျော်ဩ, *v.* do. *also* to shout, halloo, make a noise.

ကျော်ကြား, *v.* to be a subject of public notice; *n.* fame.

ကျော်, (3) *v.* to step over, pass over, surpass, transgress, exceed, လွှား ၊ သာ.

ကျော်, (4) *v.* to fry, ကျော်လှော်.

ကျော်ကသည်း, *adj.* Tonquinese.

ကျိုက်, (1) *v.* to gulp down, swallow at once, မြို. Hence, အကျိုက်, *n.* a swallow.

ကျိုက်, (2) *v.* to gird up, as the loins, with a waist-cloth, အောက်ဗိုက်ကျိုက် ၊ ခါးတောင်းကျိုက်.

ကျိုကျို, *adv.* loudly, noisily.

ကျွတ်ကျိုက်, *adv.* bubblingly, hissingly; tumultuously, in an uproar.

ကျိုင်း, (1) *v.* to be plump, full, large, flourishing, ထွား ၊ ဖွံ့.

ကျိုင်းတွင်း, *(pron.* ချိုင်းတွင်း,) *n.* the arm-pit, လက်ကတီး ၊ လက်ကတီ. Hence, အကျိုင်း, *n.* a branch of a tree, smaller than အခက်, and larger than အလက်.

ကျိုင်း, (2) *n.* a kind of official umbrella, carried before the owner.

ကျိုင်းကောင်, *n.* a kind of serpent.

ကျိုး, (1) *v.* to respect, reverence, be respectful, submissive, (seldom used singly,) ရိုကျိုး ၊ ရိုသေ ၊ ကျိုးဝင်.

ကျိုးနွံ, *v.* do.

ကျိုး, (2) *v.* to be broken cross-wise, *comp.* ကွဲ; (*act.* ချိုး;) see also ကြိုး, and its compounds.

ကျိုးကျည်း, *adv.* loudly, noisily.

ကျိုးကျိုး, *adv.* do. ကျွယ်ကျွယ် ၊ ကျာကျာ ၊ ကြဲကြဲ.

ကျိုးကျိုးတုတ်, *adv.* do.

ကျိုးပဲ့, *v.* see ပဲ့.

ကျိုးဖဲ့, see ဖဲ့.

ကျိုးကျွန်, see အကျွန်, under ကျွန်.

ကျုံ့, *v.* to bow down, stoop; be humbled, submissive, crouching, ကုပ် ၊ ငုံ့ ၊ လျှိုး ၊ နှိမ့်ချ.

ကျုံ့ငုံ့, *v.* do. do.

ကြ, *v. affix, sign of the plural number;* ကြကုန်, do. as ပြုကြခြင်း, their doing; ပြုကြသည်, they did.

ကြတ်, (1) *v.* to stretch out, extend.

ကြက်ကြက်, *adv.* intensely, (applied to words of heat,) ကြပ်ကြပ်.

ကြက်, (2) *n.* a fowl.

ကြက်ဦးတွန်, *n.* the time of cock-crowing in the morning.

ကြက်ခြေခတ်, *n.* the mark of a cross, or any mark resembling a fowl's foot.

ကြက်, (3) *n.* a kind of tree.

ကြက်ဆင်, *n.* a turkey.

ကြက်ဆူ, *n.* the castor oil tree, Palma Christi.

ကြက်ညှာနာ, *n.* a kind of disease.

ကြက်တက်, *n.* a kind of vine; *adv.* distinctly, (applied to words of seeing and hearing.)

ကြက်တောင်စည်း, *n.* the hair tied stiff, like a bunch of feathers.

ကြက်လျှာတံခွန်, *n.* a paper flag, in shape of a fowl's tongue.

ကြက်သည်, *n.* a fowl-merchant.

ကြက်ထက်ရည်, *n.* serum.

ကြက်တူရွေး, or ကြက်တူရွေး, *n.* a parrot, ကျေးသား.

ကြက်ပေါင်, *n.* a kind of vine.

ကြက်မဆုပ်, *n.* a kind of tree.

ကြက်မောက်, *n.* a kind of tree.

ကြက်ညိုး, *n.* a kind of vine.

ကြက်ရိုး, *n.* a kind of tree.

ကြက်ရိုးထိုးစာ, *n.* a kind of magical writing.

ကြက်သရေ, *n.* character, reputation, credit, အသရေ.

ကြက်သဟင်း, *n.* a kind of tree.

ကြက်သီး, *n.* (a contraction of ကြက်လည်သီး,) a fowl's neck.

ကြက်သီးထ, *v.* to be a subject of horripilation, to have the fine hairs of the skin erected through sudden cold, or a strong emotion of the mind, similar in appearance to the erection of feathers on a fowl's neck, when opposed to an antagonist, အမွေးထ ၊ အမွေးညှင်းထ.

ကြက်သီးမွေးညှင်းထ, *v.* do.

ကြက်သွန်, *n.* the onion plant or root.

ကြက်သွေး, (1) *n.* deep red, crimson colour, (the colour of fowls' blood.)

ကြက်ဟင်းခါး, *n.* a kind of vine.

ကြင်, *v.* (1) to feel pain, နာ၊ နာကျင်; (2) to be distressed in mind, be moved with compassion, သနား; (3) to love, esteem, have affection for, ခင်၊ နှစ်.

ကြင်နာ, *v.* do. do. do.

ကြင်စွယ်, *n.* the lower extremity of the mustaches.

ကြင့်, *v.* to do, to perform.

ကြငှန်းတိုင်, *n.* a certain post in a palace.

ကြို, *n.* a kind of tree.

ကြည်, *v.* to be familiar with, &c. see ကျင်လည်.

ကြည်, *v.* to be clear, pure, bright, (as water or colour;) to be sincere, cordial, well-disposed towards.

ကြည်လင်, *v.* do. do.

ကြည်ညို, *v.* to be sincere, kind, benevolent, cordial, &c. သဒ္ဓါ.

ကြည်နူး, *v.* do. ကြည်ဖြူ, *v.* do. ကြည်ဖြ, *v.* do.

ကြည်း, (1) *v.* to press, crush, grind down, ကြိတ်; (2) to make a grinding sound or roar, as an elephant, or the earth when convulsed; (3) *n.* dry land, ကုန်၊ ကုန်း.

ကြဉ်း, (1) *v.* to reject, refuse, avoid, shun, ပယ်၊ စဲ၊ နှိမ်၊ ငြင်း၊ နွှာ၊ ရှောင်; (2) *v.* to bear, sustain, take upon, undertake, (seldom used singly;) (3) see ကုန်း.

ကြဉ်းဆောင်, *v.* do. ဆောင်ကြဉ်း.

ကြည့်, *v.* to look, behold, look at, ရှု.

ကြတ်, *v.* to darken, grow dark, as the heavenly luminaries, to be eclipsed, (frequently pronounced ကြစ်.)

ကြတ်ကြတ်, *adv.* middling, (affixed to words of colour.)

ကြတ်စည်း, *v.* to bind, tie tight.

ကြန်, (from ကြန္တ, *Pali,*) *n.* a sign, mark, criterion, အမှတ်၊ လက္ခဏာ.

ကြန့်, *v.* to delay, be procrastinated, ကြာ.

ကြပ်, (1) *v.* to preside over, superintend, အုပ်. Hence, အကြပ်, *n.* a subordinate officer, a chief of ten.

ကြပ်, (2) to afford assistance, protection, မစ၊ ထိန်း.

ကြပ်မ, *v.* do. do.

ကြပ်, (3) *v.* to be close, tight, secure, တစ်၊ ကြူ၊ ခိုင်၊ တင်း; (4) to make tight, bind, tie hard, secure, ကြပ်စည်း; (5) to be strict, severe, ကြပ်တည်း.

ကြပ်သတ်, *v.* do. do.

ကြပ်ကြပ်, (1) *adv.* intensely, (applied to heat;) (2) firmly, strictly, tightly.

ကြပ်ထုပ်, *n.* a bag or ball for fomentation.

ကြပ်ထုပ်ထိုး, *v.* to use do.

ကြံတေ့, *(a corruption of* ပြကတေ့,*)* *n.* nature, ပကတိ.

ကြမ္မာ, (from ကမ္မ, *Pali,*) *n.* evil destiny, unpropitious influence of former deeds.

ကြမ်း, *v.* to be rough, coarse, uneven; to be unpolished, rude, harsh, severe, abusive; to be frightful, terrific.

ကြမ်းကြုတ်, *v.* do.

ကြမ်းတန်း, or ကြမ်းတမ်း, *v.* do.

ကြယ်, (1) *n.* a star; *(comp.* တာရာ and နက္ခတ်.*)*

ကြယ်ထယ်ထယ်, *adv.* provokingly, quarrelsomely.

ကြယ်, (2) *v.* to be broad, wide, extensive.

ကြယ်ပြော, *v.* do. ကြယ်ဝင်း, *v.* do. ကြယ်ဝန်း, *v.* do. ကြယ်ဝိုင်း, *v.* do.

ကြံ, (1) *v.* to spread over, besmear, anoint, လိမ်း, မံ.

ကြံ, (2) *v.* to think, consider, meditate upon, design, intend, aim at, ထ ၊ တွေး ၊ ဆင်ခြင် ၊ ရွယ်.

ကြံစည်, *(pron.* ကြံဇည်,) *v.* do. do.

ကြံ, (3) *n.* the sugar-cane.

ကြံကြံ, *adv.* noisily, ကျိုးကျိုး.

ကြံ့ပေါ, *n.* a kind of tree.

ကြံတင်း, *n.* a kind of vine.

ကြံ့, (1) *v.* to be firm, resolute, persevering, ခိုင် ၊ နိုင်; (2) *n.* a rhinoceros.

ကြာ, (1) *v.* to be distant in time, whether past or future, မြင့် ၊ ရှည်.

ကြာအောင်, *v.* do.

ကြာကြာ, *adv.* continually, permanently.

ကြာ, (2) *n.* a water-lily, plant, or flower, or any similarly shaped flower.

ကြာဖြူ, ကြာနီ, ကြာညို, ကြာပုဏ္ဍရိတ်, and ကြာသံဆိပ်, five principal varieties of the water-lily.

ကြာပဒုမ္မာ, or ကြာဂဝုတ်, or ကြာသိမ်, *n.* one kind of water-lily.

ကြာခေါင်းလောင်း, ကြာနှင်း, ကြာသိမ်, *n.* other varieties of the lily.

ကြာစွယ်, *n.* the obliquely projecting roots of the ပဒုမာ lily.

ကြာနှုတောင်း, *n.* the honey-combed pericarp of a lily.

ကြာသွတ်အိုး, *n.* a kind of jug or pot, with an open mouth, in which offerings of lilies, &c. are made, ကျောင်းရေအိုး; also some part of the spire of a pagoda.

ကြာခံ and ကြာလျှံ, *n.* other parts of the spire of a pagoda.

ကြာသပတေး, *n.* the planet Jupiter ; the fifth day of the week, Thursday.

ကြား, (1) *v.* to hear, receive information, နားဖြင့်ကြား ; (2) to inform, give information, မှာ.

ကြားငြင်း, *v.* to dislike to hear.

ကြား, (3) *v.* to be apart, separate, ကွာ ; (*act.* ချား.) Hence အကြား, *n.* a crack, opening, an interstice, intermediate space, a lane, pathway, ဝင်ကြား.

ကြိတ်, (1) *v.* to press, crush down, bruise, ကြိတ်ဖိ ; to squeeze, rub, grind as in a mill or mortar, နယ် ။ ပွတ်; to grind, as with the double teeth, ကြိတ်ဝါး ; to mix together, နယ် ။ ရော.

ကြိတ်ဆုံ, *n.* a mill, used to husk grain.

ကြိတ်, (2) *n.* large shears, used to cut metal with, ကတ်.

ကြိတ်မှန်, *n.* a kind of plant.

ကြိမ်, (1) *v.* to meet with, find, ကြုံ ။ ကြိုက် ။ ဆုံ ။ ဦး ။ တွေ့ ; (2) *n.* the ratan vine.

ကြိမ်လုံး, *n.* a ratan branch or twig ; any rod, limber stick.

ကြိမ်ဆိုခြင်း, *n.* the act of swearing, or making oath.

ကြိမ်ဖန်, (from အကြိမ်အဖန်,) *adv.* repeatedly, frequently.

ကြိမ်း, (1) *v.* to be terrified, daunted by threats, ကြောက် ။ လန့် ; (*act.* ခြိမ်း.) (2) *v.* to boast, make a display of authority, threaten, daunt, ကြုံး.

ကြိမ်းပ, *v.* to boast, threaten, &c.

ကြိမ်းမောင်း, *v.* do. ကြိမ်းဝါး, *v.* do.

ကြိယာ, see ကိရိယာ.

ကြီး, *v.* to be great.

ကြီးပြင်း, *v.* do.

ကြွတ်, (1) *v.* to rub off, as the skin—less than ပွန်း ; (2) *v.* to be dark, gloomy, black, မည်း ; (3) *n.* a kind of tree ; (4) *n.* a round box with an oval cover.

ကြွတ်ကြွတ်, *adv. prefix to words of sound.*

ကြုံ, *v.* to meet with, find, ကြိမ် ။ ကြုံ ။ ဆုံ ။ ညား ။ တွေ့.

ကြုံး, *v.* to boast, make a display ; show authority, daunt, threaten ; (*comp.* ကြိမ်း, and ခြိမ်း.)

ကြုံးပ, *v.* do. do. ကြုံးဝါး, *v.* do.

ကြူ, *v.* to emit a pleasant odour, မွှေး.

ကြူး, *v.* to be exceeded, passed by ; see လွန်.

ကြေး, (1) *v.* to be dirty, filthy, (commonly used in composition with ညစ်, as ညစ်ကြေးသည်.) Hence အကြေး, *n.* dirt, filth, အညစ် ; *also* အကြေးအညစ်, and အညစ်အကြေး, and အကြေးအချေး, do.

ကြေး, (2) *n.* lead, metal, money ; property, (frequently *pron.* ကျည်း.)

ကြေးစား, *n.* a common harlot, မိန္မရှင်.

ကြေးဖြူ, *n.* pewter, tin.

ကြေးဝါ, *n.* brass.

ကြေးနီ, *n.* copper.

ကြေးပုပ်, *n.* lead, ခဲ.

ကြေးနွတ်, *n.* a small brass drum or gong, several of which are fixed in a circle, and played on by a person standing in the middle.

ကြေးနင်း, *n.* do. *comp.* ပတ်.

ကြေးဝိုင်း, or ကြေးဆိုင်း, *n.* the whole instrument, a collection of small brass gongs, fixed in a circle, &c. *comp.* ပတ်ဝိုင်း.

ကြေးမုံ, *n.* a mirror of polished metal, a mirror of any kind.

ကြေးမြင်, *n.* do.

ကြေးငွေ, *n.* money, ငွေကြေး.

ကြေးကျွန်, *n.* a slave, subject.

ကြေးထိုက်, *v.* to be valuable.

ကြေးနဲ, *v.* to be poor, indigent, ဆင်းရဲ.

ကြေးရတတ်, *v.* to be rich.

ကြဲ, *v.* to scatter, throw about, ဖြန့် ။ ဖြူး ; to sow, as seed, မျိုးကြဲ ; to give away, စွန့်ကြဲ.

ကြော, (1) *v.* to make by tying, binding, twisting, &c. ကျစ်; to be tight, hard, မာ ၊ တင်း.

ကြောရှင်ရှာ, *adv.* evenly, neatly.

ကြော, (2) *v.* to repeat an action, do again, ထပ်.

ကြော, (3) *n.* the back, ကျောက်ကုန်း.

ကြောကုန်း, *n.* do.

ကြောက်, (1) *v.* to kick, ကန်; (see ကျောက်.)

ကြောက်, (2) *v.* to fear, be afraid, ရွံ့ ၊ ထိတ်လန့်; (*act.* ချောက်.)

ကြောက်ညှင်, *v.* do. ကြောက်ညှင်ပါ, *v.* do. ကြောက်မက်, *v.* do.

ကြောက်ဖွယ်, (1) *adj.* fearful, frightful; (2) *adv.* wonderful, extraordinary.

ကြောက်လန့်, *v.* to be timorous, fearful, apprehensive of some danger, timid.

ကြောင်, (1) to be dark in some parts, and red or yellow in others.

ကြောင်, (2) *n.* a cat.

ကြောင်ဥကျည်, *n.* a kind of cat.

ကြောင်ကြောင်, or ထကြောင်ကြောင်, *adv.* steadfastly, intently.

ကြောင်ကတိုး, *n.* the musk-cat, ဥကျည်.

ကြောင်လိမ်, *n.* a pyramid with a winding staircase in the centre.

ကြောင်ဒို, *n.* a kind of basket.

ကြောင်ပန်း, *n.* a kind of tree.

ကြောင်မြီးကူ, *n.* a kind of tree.

ကြောင်လျှာ, *n.* a kind of tree.

ကြောင်း, (1) *v.* to make, or draw a line, သား; to draw out. Hence အကြောင်း, *n.* a line, any thing drawn out in a line, a furrow, rivulet, road, &c.

ကြောင်းဝင်, *v.* do.

ကြောင်းထ, *n.* business, affair, &c. အကြောင်း ၊ ကြောင်းရာ ၊ အချင်းအရာ.

ကြောင်းရာ, *n.* do.

ကြောင်း, (2) *num. affix*, (see Gram.)

ကြောင်း, (3) *n.* a reason, cause, reason why, as ပြုရမည့်ကြောင်းကိုမသိ, why I should do it, I know not.

ကြောင့်, (by contraction ငေ့,) *noun affix*, because of, on account of.

•ကြောင့်ကြ, *v.* to be concerned, anxious, troubled about, စိုးရိမ်.

•ကြောကျဉ်း, *adv.* inadequately, insufficiently, without what is requisite.

•ကြောကြမ်း, *v.* to be rough, rude.

ကြို, (1) *v.* to boil to a pulp; to melt, as ore or metal; (2) *v.* to go to meet, advance towards, ခရီးဦးကြိုဆို; to anticipate, whether in act or thought.

ကြိုဆို, *v.* to go to meet, advance towards, anticipate. ကြိုဦ, do. ကြိုသီး, do. သီးကြို, do. Hence အကြိုနေ့, or အကြိုရက်, *n.* the day before worship-day, အဖိတ်နေ့.

ကြိုက်, (1) *v.* to meet with, find, ကြုံ၊ ကြို၊ ဆုံ၊ ညား၊ တွေ့; (2) *v.* to like, love, as an object of enjoyment, not implying a regard for, ဝင်၊ မင်; *(comp.* ချစ်.*)*

ကြိုင်, *v.* to emit a pleasant odour, ကြူ၊ မွှေး၊ သင်း.

ကြိုင်ပျံ့, *v.* do. ကြိုင်မွှန်း, do. ကြိုင်ရှား, do.

ကြိုး, (1) *v.* to endeavour, make exertion, be diligent, laborious, အားထုတ်၊ လုံ့လပြု.

ကြိုးစား, *v.* do. ကြိုးထုတ်, do.

ကြိုးပမ်း, *v.* do.

ကြိုးကုတ်, *v.* do.

ကြိုး, (2) *n.* thread doubled and twisted, a string, cord, rope; *(comp.* ချည်.*)*

ကြိုးတွန်, *n.* do.

ကြိုးကြာ, *n.* a kind of bird.

ကြိုးကြ, *adj.* diversely, unlike, some of one kind, and some of another.

ကြိုးကြိုးကြကြ, *adj.* hastily.

ကြိုးဆွဲ, *n.* a kind of game of chance.

ကြို့, (1) *n.* a hickup.

ကြို့ထိုး, *v.* to hickup.

ကြို့, (2) *n.* a kind of tree.

ကွ, (1) *v.* to be with, (used only in composition with လူ;) see လူကွ. Hence အကွ, and တကွ, *adj.* or *adv.* together with; အတူ, အတူအကွ, အတူတကွ, ကွအတူ, do.

ကွသိုးထုတ်, *v.* to geld, castrate.

ကွ, (2) *v.* to be low in stature, stinted, dwarfish, ပုနိမ့်၊ ပု.

ကွက်, (1) *v.* to make a circle, inclose in a circle, or other compartments, mark out, limit, fix bounds, ကန့်ကွက်. Hence အကွက်, *n.* a spot, place; (2) *v.* to be spotted, ပြောက်၊ ဖွံ့.

ကွင်း, (1) *num. affix*, (see Gram.)

ကွင်း, (2) *v.* to encircle, pass round, perform circuitously, ဝိုက်၊ ဝိုင်း၊ ကွေ့.

ကွင်းလှ, *v.* do. Hence အကွင်း, *n.* a circle, ring, &c.

ကွင်း, (3) *v.* to be separate, apart, detached, free from, distant, ကွာ၊ ကွေ၊ ဝေး.

ကွင်း, (4) *n.* a heath, covered with water in the rainy season.

ကွင်းပြင်, *n.* do.

ကွန်, *n.* a casting net.

ကွန်ရက်, or ကွန်ချက်, *n.* net-work.

ကွန်း, *n.* (1) a place of royal refreshment, a temporary palace, ကွန်းတော်၊ ထဲန်း; (2) a kind of building erected to a Nat, နတ်စင်.

ကွန်းတိုင်, or ကွန်းစင်တိုင်, *n.* a kind of post in kyoungs, halls of justice, and palaces.

ကွန်းစာ, *n.* a koonzah, a measure of capacity equal to a salay, (စလယ်,) about one pint.

ကွန့်, *v.* (1) to enjoy one's self, be cheerful, happy, ပျော်၊ ရွှင်.

ကွန့်, *v.* (2) to be contracted, shrunk, &c. see ကျုံ့.

ကွပ်, *v.* (1) to bind, as the rim of a wheel, or a basket, in order to secure the parts; to make fast, firm, secure, by tying, binding, &c. ခြော; (2) to chastise, discipline, punish, ဆုံး; (3) to geld, castrate, သင်း၊ ထုံး၊ အသိုးထုတ်၊ ခွေး ထိုး; (4) to execute, put to death, သတ်.

ကွပ်သင်း, *v.* to geld, castrate.

ကွပ်မျက်, *v.* to put to death.

ကွပ်ညှပ်, *v.* do. *also*, to discipline.

ကွမ်း, *n.* the beetel leaf, or vine.

ကွမ်းရွက်, *n.* the beetel leaf.

ကွမ်းပန်း, *n.* do.

ကွမ်းသီး, *n.* the beetel-nut tree, or fruit.

ကွမ်းညှပ်, *n.* an instrument to cut beetel-nut.

ကွမ်းဖတ်, *n.* chewed beetel.

ကွမ်းသွေး, *n.* beetel-spittle.

ကွမ်းဖိုး, *n.* a justice fee, present to buy beetel with, တရားကွမ်းဖိုး.

ကွမ်းထင်း, *n.* a kind of tree.

ကွယ်, (1) *v.* to hide, conceal, ပုန်း ၊ ဝှက် ၊ ဖုံး ၊ ကွယ်; (2) to disappear, conceal one's self, or be concealed, ပုန်း; (3) *pers. n.* you, (*mas.* and *fem.* used by men to equals or inferiors.)

ကွယ်တို့, *pers. n. plur.* ye, or you; (by corruption, ကွယ်ဒို့, and again, ညဒို့.)

ကွယ်, (4) *v.* see ရှိခိုးကွယ်, to worship, &c.

ကွယ်ရှိခိုး, *v.* do.

ကွာ, *v.* to become separate, implying a previous union; to go apart; *act.* ခွာ.

ကွေ, *v.* to be separated, apart, distant, free from, ကွာ ၊ ဝေး.

ကွေး, *v.* to be curved, drawn together at the ends.

ကွေ့, *v.* to move round, be circuitous, curved, serpentine, ကွေး ၊ ဝိုက် ၊ ဝိုင်း. Hence အကွေ့, *n.* a curve, bend, corner, bay, lane, road, အထောင့် ၊ အကွေ့.

ကွဲ, *v.* (1) to be divided in the midst, be broken, or severed lengthways, be split; *comp.* ပြိုး; (*act.* ခွဲ.)

ကွဲပြဲ, *v.* do.

ကွဲ, (2) *v.* to be various, diverse, ပြား ၊ ထွေ.

ကွဲထွေး, *v.* do.

ကွဲကြေ, *v.* to be divided, &c. see ကွဲ.

ကျွ, *v.* to arise, to proceed, (whether going or coming.)

ကျွက်ကျွက်, *adv. an intensive*, bubblingly, as water.

ကျွက်ဆ, or ကျွက်ထ, or ကျွက်ချွက်, do.

ကျွင်း, (1) *v.* to be a part, not the whole; (2) *n.* a residue, remnant, ကျန်.

ကျွတ်, (1) *v.* to be released, freed from, cleared, emancipated, လွတ်; to be entire, complete without remainder or exception, (used adverbially, or with a continuative affix, as သပင် ထိုကျွတ်သီးသည်, or သပင်ထိုကျွတ်ဆောင်သီးသည်, the whole tree bears.)

ကျွတ်, (2) *n.* a land-leech.

ကျွတ်, (3) *n.* a descendant of the fifth generation from one's self.

ကျွတ်, (4) *v.* to revolt, be stubborn, perverse, obstinate, ရိုင်းပျ.

ကျွန်, (1) *v.* to be feigned, have a false appearance. Hence အကျွန်, *n.* a feint, feigned appearance, (commonly constructed with simple participles, as သေကျွန်ပြုသည်, he feigns himself to be dead.)

ကျွန်, (2) *n.* a subject or slave, one under authority; (3) a slave proper, one who has no property, and is not redeemable or transferable, but at the pleasure of his master, ပေါင်သေ; (4) one who is bound to service by a specified debt, the payment of which is the only requisite to his liberation, ပေါင်ရှင်; (5) a hired servant, ပေါင်သွင်း ၊ အခစား.

ကျွန်တော်, (1) *n.* a king's subject; (2) *pers. n.* I, *mas.* (used in addressing a superior.) *Fem.* ကျွန်တော်မ.

ကျွန်မ, (1) *n.* a female slave or servant; (2) *pers. n.* I, *fem.* (used in addressing a superior,) ကျွန်တော်မ; (by abbreviation, ကျွမ.)

ကျွန်ရွာ, *n.* a slave-village, or village subject to a (စားကျေး) governor.

ကျွန်သီးတော်, *n.* (from သီး, to be distinct,) *n.* a slave of a pagoda, ဘုရားကျွန်.

ကျွန်နုပ်, *pers. n.* I, *mas.* and *fem.* (used in addressing an equal, *commonly pron.* ကျွနုပ်, or ကျုပ်.)

ကျွန်း, (1) *n.* an island. (N. B. There are four grand islands, encompassing Myenmo mount; on the north ဥတ္တရကုရု ကျွန်း; on the east ပုဗ္ဗဝိဒေဟကျွန်း; on the south ဇမ္ဗူဒီပါကျွန်း; and on the west အပရဂေါယာန်ကျွန်း, each of which is surrounded by five hundred small islands.)

ကျွန်း, (2) *n.* a garden, see ကိုင်း.

ကျွန်း, (3) *n.* the teak tree.

ကျွန်းရို, ကျွန်းမ, ကျွန်းကောင်းနွယ်, varieties of the teak tree.

ကျွမ်း, (1) *v.* to be burnt up, consumed by fire; (2) *v.* to be acquainted, familiar with, versed in, skilled, ကျင်လည် ၊ လေ့လာ; (3) *v.* to be old.

ကျွမ်းကျင်, *v.* to be acquainted with, skilled in, &c.

ကျွမ်းဝင်, *v.* do. Hence အကျွမ်း, *n.* an acquaintance; အသိအကျွမ်း, *n.* a state of acquaintance, and အကျွမ်းဝင်, *v.* to be acquainted with.

ကျွယ်, *adj.* plentiful, rich, abundant.

ကျွယ်ဝ, *adj.* do.

ကျွယ်ကျွယ်, *adv.* noisily, loudly.

ကျွံ, (1) *v.* to sink into, or through, (but not applied to water,) နစ် ၊ ဝင် ; (2) *n.* to go beyond bounds, transgress, ကျူး ၊ လွန်.

ကျွေး, (1) *v.* to call out, cry out, halloo, shout, (used only in composition,) အော် ၊ ဟစ်.

ကျွေးကျော်, *v.* do.

ကျွေးငြါ, *v.* do.

ကျွေး, (2) *v.* to feed, nourish, cherish, မွေး ; (3) *n.* a debt, မြီ ; (4) *n.* a kind of tree.

ကျွဲ, *n.* a buffalo.

ကျွဲကော, *n.* the pumplenoos, a species of lemon.

ကျွဲနရက်, *n.* a kind of bird.

ကျွဲသွားဒေါင်း, *n.* a kind of tree.

ကြွ, (1) *v.* to arise, ထ ; to proceed, whether going or coming, (respectful.)

ကြွ, *v.* to raise, (in a heap,) swell, or plump up, ရုံး ၊ ပုံ ၊ ရှိ.

ကြွက်, *n.* a rat, or mouse.

ကြွက်သယ်တောင်း, *n.* a mouse ; ကြွက်စုတ်, *n.* do.

ကြွက်ကတိုး, ကြွက်နက်, ကြွက်ဝမ်းဖြူ, varieties of the rat.

ကြွက်ရှောက်, *n.* certain cross-timbers in a house or boat, (so called, because a rat can pass and repass thereon.)

ကြွင်း, *v.* to remain, be left, ကျန်. Hence အကြွင်း, *n.* a remainder, အကျန်.

ကြွပ်, *v.* (1) to be brittle, short, crusty ; (2) *v.* to be irritable, snappish, ဆတ်.

ကြွပ်ကြွပ်, *adv.* suddenly, violently.

ကြွယ်, *v.* (1) to be abundant, plentiful ; to possess much, be opulent, wealthy, ဝ ၊ ပေါ ၊ များ ၊ ကုံထံ ၊ ပြော.

ကြွယ်ဝ, *v.* do.

ကြွယ်, (2) *see* ကြွင်, and under.

ကြွယ်ဖဲလူး, *n.* a kind of cotton.

ကြွား, *v.* to be vain, boastful, ostentatious, ဝါ ။ ကောင်လွှား ။ ပလွှား.

ကြွေ, (1) *v.* to fall off, as leaves from a tree ; *act.* ချွေ ; (2) *n.* a kind of shell-fish, the shell itself, a cowry.

ကြွေကစား, *v.* to play with cowries, to play at back-gammon, or any game of chance.

ကြွေပုကံ, *n.* a glazed dish.

## ခ.

The second consonant in the Burman alphabet, and the second in the class of gutturals.

ခ, *v.* to pay respect, wait upon, pay court to, be obsequious, submissive, endeavour to conciliate.

ခစား, *v.* do. ခချောင်း, *v.* do.

ခယ, *v.* do. ခညွတ်, *v.* do.

ခရိုး, *v.* do. ခဝပ်, *v.* do.

ခဆောင်း, *n.* a kind of tree.

ခက်, (1) *v.* to be hard, difficult, ကတ် ။ ကျွတ် ။ ခဲ ; to be harsh, austere, severe, ခက်ထန် ။ ကြမ်းထန်.

ခက်ထန်, *v.* to be harsh, austere.

ခက်ထရော်, *adv.* harshly, &c.

ခက်, (2) *v.* to tie, bind, in a transverse, oblique manner, as rattan round a jar.

ခက်ရင်း, *n.* a fork of any kind or size, (*pron.* ခရင်း.)

ခက်ရင်းခွ, *n.* do.

ခါ, (from ခါး, to be bitter,) *adj.* or *adv.* slightly bitter, bitterish.

ခင်, (1) *v.* to like, love, esteem, treat with fondness, ကြိုက် ။ နှစ် ။ မင်.

ခင်မင်, *v.* do. (most common.)

ခင်မွတ်, *v.* do.

ခင်, (2) (with မ prefixed to the root,) *v. affix*, before, as မစားခင် သွားသည်, he goes before he eats, or has eaten. ခင် sometimes takes the noun affixes after it, as မစားခင်၌, before eating. The sense is the same.

ခင်, (3) *v. affix of tense,* prior past, or prior future, according to the connection, as သွားခင်ပြီ, he had gone, and သွားခင်မည်, he will go, (that is, before some other thing happens, which is alluded to.)

ခင်ကြီး, (from သခင်, and ကြီး,) *n.* an initiated priest of Boodh, ဦး ကြီး ၊ ပဉ္စင်း ၊ ရဟန်း.

ခင်ထရင်, *n.* a kind of roof or covering, concave at the edges, used chiefly in boats of state.

ခင်ပုပ်, (1) *n.* a kind of owl, ဇီးကွက် ; (2) *n.* a kind of creeping plant.

ခင်ပွန်း, (1) *n.* a correlative in marriage, whether husband or wife, a spouse, ဇနီးမောင်ဘက် ; (2) a friend, မိတ်ခင်ပွန်း.

ခင်ဗျား, (from သခင်, and ဘုရား,) *n.* sir, or madam, *a term of compellation,* (used by men to persons rather superior, whether male or female.)

ခင်း, (1) *v.* to spread out, lay out in order, arrange, array, ဖြန့် ၊ ကျင်းပြင်.

ခင်းပ, *v.* do.

ခင်းထလျက်, *v.* do.

ခင်းနှီး, *n.* any thing spread out to lay something upon. Hence အခင်း, *n.* any thing spread out, laid out in order, a garden, a bed, &c.

ခင်း, (2) *num. auxiliary,* applied to things spread out.

ခဏ, *(Pali,) n.* (1) a certain measure of time ; (2) an instant, moment ; (3) *adv.* for a moment.

ခဏမတ္တ, *n.* an instant, moment. ခဏတဖြုတ်, do.

ခဏ်း, (from ခဏ္ဍ, to divide, *Pali,*) *n.* a section, division, distinct part, အပိုင်းအချား.

ခတ်, (1) *v.* to strike against, knock, hit, to knock on, fasten on ; to stamp, impress. *Hence,* (2) to decide the quality of uncoined money.

ခတ်တက်, *n.* an oar.

ခတ်, (3) *v.* to put into, as an article into a larger mass, to improve or complete it.

ခတောက်, *n.* a kind of tree.

ခတင်, *n.* a cot or couch, bedstead of the common kind, ပလ္လင်.

ခတတ်, *n.* a kind of tree.

ခဂ္ဂါ, *n.* a kind of land-lily.

ခထောက်, *n.* a kind of plant.

ခထောက်ကြီး, *n.* a large species of do. Pontederia dilatata, (Symms.)

ခနဲ့, *v.* to ridicule, make a laughing-stock, ပြက်ရယ်.

ခဏ္ဍီ, *n.* see ပါရမီ.

ခနောက်, see ခုံထောက်.

ခနောင်း, *n.* a whirlpool, ဝဲ.

ခနော်ခနဲ, (1) *adv.* shakingly, totteringly, as an old building; (2) *v.* to ridicule, make a laughing-stock.

ခနွဲ, *n.* a swinging dipper, used to raise water with.

ခန္ဓာ, *(Pali, a collection, အပေါင်းအစု,)* *n.* a living animal body, which, according to the learned, is composed of five parts, viz. ရူပက္ခန္ဓာ, materiality; ဝေဒနာက္ခန္ဓာ, sensation; သညာက္ခန္ဓာ, perception; သင်္ခါရက္ခန္ဓာ, will; ဝိညာဏက္ခန္ဓာ, intellect.

ခန်း, (1) *v.* to be dried up, exhausted, come to an end, be quite gone, ခြောက် ၊ ကုန် ၊ ဆုံး; (2) *an astrological term*, ကျိန်း.

ခန့်, (1) *v.* to estimate, compute quantity or extent mentally, not precisely by measure; to guess at, judge of, ချင့် ၊ ဆ ၊ ရှိန်း.

ခန့်တွက်, *v.* to estimate, enumerate, reckon, ရေတွက်.

ခန့်တွေး, *v.* to consider upon, တွေးတော. Hence အခန့်, *n.* an estimate, measurement, extent, limit, အတိုင်းအရှည် ၊ အခန့်အထား ၊ အခန့်အရှည်.

ခန့်, (2) *n.* a business, affair, အခင်း.

ခန့်တော်, or ခန့်သင့်, *v.* to suit, be suitable, convenient.

ခန့်, (3) *v.* to be about so much, (affixed to words of time or quantity, as တနှစ်ခန့်, about one year,) အလောက်; အခန့်အမျှ, do.

ခန့်, (4) *v.* to fear, respect, reverence, ရိုသေ ၊ လေးမြတ်.

ခန့်ညား, *v.* do.

ခန့်ထေး, *v.* do.

ခန့်, (5) *v.* to appoint to a work or office, commission, ခိုင်း.

ခန့်ထား, *v.* do.

ခန့်မံ, *v.* to order, direct, appoint, commission, ခိုင်း ၊ မိန့်.

ခန့်, (6) *v.* to be hard, firm, strong; see ခံ့.

ခပင်း, *adj.* all, အပေါင်း.

ခပဲ, *adj.* do.

ခပေါင်, *n.* a kind of tree.

ခပ်, (1) *v.* to dip up, take out of, draw, (as water from a well.)

ခပ်ကော်, *v.* do.

ခပ်, (2) *v.* to go through, to pass from one thing to another, ထုတ်ချင်းခပ် ၊ ကူးခပ်.

ခပ်, (3) *adv.* rather, (prefixed to reduplicated verbal roots, as ခပ်ဆိုးဆိုး, rather bad; in certain connections, used with a single root.)

ခပ်ချောက်ချောက်, *adv.* partly wet, and partly dry.

ခပ်နွယ်, *n.* a kind of vine.

ခပ်ဖြာ, *n.* brass, ကြေးဝါ ၊ တေ.

ခပ်မဆိတ်, *adv.* silently; on bad terms, quarrelsomely.

ခပ်သိမ်း, *adj.* all, the whole, အလုံးစုံ ၊ အားလုံး.

ခပ်စုံ, *adj.* do. ခပ်စုံလုံး, do.

ခပ်သိမ်းစုံ, *adj.* do.

ခမက်, *n.* a son's wife's father, or a daughter's husband's father.

ခမည်း, *n.* a father, အဖ.

ခမည်းလုလင်, *n.* husband and wife, (poetic.)

ခမီး, *n.* a son's wife's mother, or a daughter's husband's mother.

ခမုတ်, *v.* to build, construct, make; (obsolete.)

ခမဲ, *n.* a present made to a sick person, with the idea that it will facilitate his recovery.

ခမောက်, *n.* a large hat.

ခမျှာ, *adv.* pitifully, distressingly, သူခမျှာ.

ခယ်မ, *n.* a wife's younger sister; a younger brother's wife.

ခရမ်း, *n.* the egg-fruit tree.

ခရရှပ်, *n.* a kind of disease, the pulmonary consumption.

ခရုံ, see ထရုံ, or နံရုံ.

ခရာ, (1) *n.* a kind of wind-instrument, a trumpet; (2) *n.* a kind of plant; (3) *adv.* entirely, wholly.

ခရီး, *n.* a way, whether by land or water, လမ်း.

ခရီးဦးကြိုဆို, *v.* to go forth to meet.

ခရီးသည်, *n.* a traveller.

ခရု, *n.* a univalvular shell-fish; (*comp.* ယောက်သွား.)

ခရုသင်း, (1) *n.* one species of do. a conch; (2) *n.* a kind of scrofulous disease, a species of leprosy; (3) *n.* a kind of tree.

ခရုဝုတ်, *n.* a curlew.

ခရူ, *n.* a kind of plant.

ခရိုင်, (1) *n.* a central point or part, on which several other parts depend, အချုပ်; (2) *n.* the ring which holds the spokes of an umbrella, and moves on the handle; (3) *n.* a priest's water dipper, ရေစစ်, *commonly called* ခွက်ခရိုင်; (4) *n.* the single jurisdiction of a government extended over several parts, *and hence* all the parts collectively under one jurisdiction; a province, state, kingdom.

ခလာသီ, *(Hind.)* *n.* a lascar.

ခလုတ်, *n.* a stump, any thing projecting.

ခလဲ, (from အခါ and လဲ,) *n.* a turn, change, အကြိမ်.

ခလောက်, *n.* a wooden bell, such as is hung on the necks of cattle.

ခဝါရုံ, *n.* a washerman's shed.

ခဝါသည်, *n.* a washerman; in poetry, ကဝါသည်.

ခဝဲ, *n.* a kind of vine.

ခံ, (1) *v.* to receive, take, ခံယူ ၊ ခံယိမ်း; (2) *v.* to bear, sustain, enjoy, endure, as pleasure, pain, labour, service, civil or military; (3) *v.* to keep, hold, as a feast; (4) *n.* a kind of tree.

ခံစား, *v.* to bear, sustain, enjoy, &c.

ခံနိုင်, *v.* to be capable of enduring, be able.

ခံဝန်, *(an inversion of* ဝန်ခံ,) (1) *v.* to enter into an engagement, be security for, အာမခံ; (2) *n.* a security, bail, အာမခံ ၊ တိုင်ခံ.

ခံထိ, *v.* to enter into an engagement, to be security for, to pawn, pledge.

ခံတွင်း, *n.* the mouth, နှုတ် ၊ ပါးစပ်.

ခံ, (1) *v.* to be durable, firm, strong, well in health; persevering, ခိုင် ၊ မာ.

ခံ, (2) *v.* to fear, reverence, ကြောက်.

ခါ, (1) *v.* to shake, shake off or out; to evade, refuse.

ခါထွက်, *v.* do.

ခါ, (2) *n.* a partridge.

ခါခါ, *adv.* repeatedly, အခါခါ.

ခါလဲ, *adv.* do.

ခါချဉ်, *n.* a kind of ant.

ခါသာ, *n.* a kind of cloth, thinner than ပိတ်.

ခါး, (1) *v.* to be bitter; (2) *n.* the loins, waist, small of the back.

ခါးစောင်း, *n.* the loins, waist.

ခါးကြိုး, *n.* a waistband, girdle. ခါးရှန်းကြိုး, *n.* do.

ခါးစည်း, *n.* do. any thing bound round the waist.

ခါးကုန်းမြူး, *v.* to gallop.

ခါးတင်, *n.* the hip.

ခါးပတ်, *n.* a band, girdle, or any thing like a girdle, encompassing the waist or middle of a person or thing.

ခါးပန်း, *n.* do.

ခါးပုံ, *n.* a part of the waist-cloth done up in a bunch before.

ခါးပိုက်, *n.* a fold in the waist-cloth used as a pocket.

ခါးတောင်းကျိုက်, *v.* to gird up the loins in Burman fashion, ဆောင်ဖို့ကျိုက်.

ခု, (1) *num. affix,* applied to any thing which does not admit of a particular description, as သော့နှစ်ခု, two keys; (see Gram.)

ခု, (2) *v.* to support, prop, wedge up.

ခု, (3) *v.* to eke out, supply deficiencies.

ခု, (4) *v.* to bear anger without expressing it.

ခုခံ, *v.* to support, prop, wedge up; to eke out, supply deficiencies; to suppress anger without expressing it. Hence အခု, *n.* a wedge, quoin, prop; a cushion, အခုအမှီ; whatever affords support, whether a thing or person; suppressed anger or malice, အခုအခံ ၊ အခံအခု.

ခု, (5) *adv.* now, *an abbreviation of* ယခု, *which see.*

ခုတ်, (1) *v.* to chop, hew ; (2) *v.* to beat out, as a gold or silver-smith.

ခုဒ္ဒက, *n.* one division of the Boodhist scriptures.

ခုနေ့, *adv.* to-day, ယခုနေ့.

ခုန်, *v.* to leap, jump ; to roll, as waves ; to shake the feet and hands, as an angry child, ခြေ ခြေခုန်.

ခုန်ပေါက်, *v.* see ခုန်, to leap, &c.

ခုန်ချီခုန်ကျ, *adv.* up and down, helter-skelter.

ခုန်ချင်း, or ခုန်ညင်း, *n.* (1) a kind of plant ; (2) the seed of do. used by children in play ; (3) the knee-pan, ဒူးခွက်.

ခုပ်, *v.* to leap upon and catch, as a cat or a tyger ; to catch, detect.

ခုပ်လှည်း, *v.* to chop or hew down.

ခုမ်းသွားကြိ, *n.* a kind of oyster.

ခုံ, (1) *n.* a frame or case of any description ; (2) *n.* a justice of peace, ခုံမင်း.

ခုံမင်, *v.* to desire, long for, be pleased with, be happy in, အလိုရှိ၊ နှစ်သက်. Hence ခုံတမင်, and ခုံမိခုံမင်, *adv.* eagerly.

ခုံလောက်, *(pron.* ခနောက်,*) n.* the three stones which support a pot in cooking.

ခုံမိန်း, *n.* a kind of precious stone, of a green colour.

ခုံး, *v.* to be convex, rounded, ကုန်း၊ မောက်.

ခူ, (1) *n.* a certain machine, used to raise water with.

ခူ, (2) *n.* a hairy caterpillar, ဖိုးတောင်တဲ.

ခူယား, *n.* do.

ခူသီ, *n.* a kind of tree.

ခူနာ, *n.* a kind of ulcer, on the ends of the fingers or toes.

ခူး, *v.* to take up or out, as victuals from a pot or kettle ; to pluck, gather, as leaves or fruit, ဆွတ်.

ခေတ္တ, *(Pali,) n.* a field.

ခေတ်, (from ခေတ္တ, a field, *Pali,*) *n.* a state, world ; field of labour ; a certain number of Sekyah systems or worlds, in which sense there are said to be three kinds of ခေတ် ; viz. ဇာတိခေတ်, consisting of a hundred thousand millions of worlds, which are destroyed and reproduced simultaneously; အာဏာခေတ်, consisting of a billion of worlds, through which the authority of a Boodh extends; ဝိသယ ခေတ်, consisting of the whole infinity of worlds, which can only be an object of thought.

ခေတ္တခေတ, see ခေတ.

ခဲ, (1) *v.* to be hard, indurated, မာ ၊ ကျုတ်. To be hard, difficult, ခက် ၊ ကတ်.

ခဲဆတ်, *v.* to be hard to deal with, crabbed, irritable.

ခဲယဉ်း, *v.* to be hard to manage or deal with, to be close, covetous. Hence အခဲ, *n.* an induration, hardness, solid substance, solidity, materiality; အခဲအကျုတ်, do. အခဲအကျည်; *see under* ကျည်.

ခဲ, (2) *v.* to bite, ကိုက်; to bite hard, hold fast, gnaw, grind with the teeth, ကြိတ်.

ခဲ, (3) *v.* to be painful, gnaw as pain, နာကျင်.

ခဲဖွယ်, or စားဖွယ်, *n.* eatables.

ခဲအောင်, *adv.* remarkably, extraordinarily.

ခဲရော့, *adv.* do.

ခဲရဉ်း, *v.* to be hard, indurated, &c. see ကျုတ်.

ခဲ, (4) *n.* an obsolete verb.

ခဲ, (5) *n.* lead.

ခဲတံ, *n.* a lead pencil.

ခဲပုပ်, *n.* lead.

ခဲမ, or ခဲမပုပ်, *n.* do.

ခဲ, (6) *n.* a stone, ကျောက်ခဲ.

ခဲအို, *n.* an elder sister's husband, or an husband's elder brother.

ခဲထံ, *n.* a certain preparation of rice.

ခဲ့, (1) *v.* to bring, (used only in composition, as ယူခဲ့သည် ၊ ဆောင်ခဲ့သည် ၊ ခေါ်ခဲ့သည်, &c.)

ခဲ့, (2) *euphonic affix.*

ခဲ့, (3) *v. affix,* (just past,) as ပြုခဲ့သည်, he has just done.

ခဲ့, (4) *v. affix, imp.* or *prec.* (see Gram.)

ခဲ့ပြီး, *v. affix,* past tense, as ပြုခဲ့ပြီး, having, or had done

ခေါ်, (1) *v.* to stick up or out, project, rise up into a hump or knot, ကုန်း၊ မောက်.

ခေါ်, (2) *n.* a small basket, in which offerings are presented to an evil spirit.

ခေါ်စာ, *n.* an offering presented to an evil spirit.

ခေါ်ပတောင်း, *n.* a basket with a cup-like bottom, i. e. a double one, capable of being set on either end.

ခေါ်ပၢ်လၢ်, *n.* a single do.

ခေါက်, (1) *v.* to knock, rap, thump.

ခေါက်ခေါက်, *adv.* rappingly.

ခေါက်ခေါက်ခၢ်ခၢ်, *adv.* noisily, like a rapping or scratching.

ခေါက်ခေါက်ဓၢ်တၢ်, *adv.* do. do. *also,* strictly, severely, without respect to, unfeelingly.

ခေါက်ခေါက်တျၢ်တျၢ်, *adv.* rappingly; noisily, like a rapping or scratching; severely, unfeelingly.

ခေါက်ရၢ, *n.* a kind of bird.

ခေါက်, (2) *v.* to double, fold, turn back; to repeat, do over again, ထုံမြန်. Hence အခေါက်, *n.* (1) a fold, or double; (2) the bark of a tree, (because folded around;) (3) a time, turn, as တခေါက်, once, နံခေါက်, twice, အကြိမ်၊ အလီ; (see အပန်.)

ခေါက်ခေါက်, *adv.* repeatedly, အပန်ပန်.

ခေါက်နၢ်, *v.* to be decided, unwavering, မြဲသား.

ခေါင်, (1) *v.* to be high, မြင့်; (2) to be distant, remote, far, extensive, ဝေး; (3) to be long delayed, မြင့်ကြာ. Hence အခေါင်, *n.* a summit, top, highest part, အထွဋ်၊ အဖျား. (4) *v.* to be slanting, inclined, (seldom used,) ကိုင်း၊ စောင်း.

ခေါင်ကုပ်, *n.* the ridge of a roof, the upper part, or saddle of a roof.

ခေါင်ဖုံး, *n.* do.

ခေါင်ထိုင်, *n.* a post which supports the ridge of a roof.

ခေါင်လှျောက်, *n.* the ridge-beam of a roof, which receives the ends of the rafters.

ခေါင်လှျောက်နှောင်, *n.* do.

ခေါင်ရှန်း, *n.* a kind of plant.

ခေါင်း, (1) *v.* to be chief, permanent, ကဲ ၊ မိုးဆုတ် ၊ ချုပ်. Hence အခေါင်း, *n.* a master, chief, head, အကြီး ၊ အကဲ; *also* a tuberous root, အဥ. Without the prefix အ, it signifies the head, the principal part of a thing, ဦး.

ခေါင်းအုံး, *v.* to pillow the head, recline, repose; *n.* a pillow; see အုံး.

ခေါင်းခု, (from ခု, to support,) *n.* any thing placed between the head and a burden carried upon the head.

ခေါင်းမိုင်, *v.* to be head-strong, obstinate.

ခေါင်းတုံး, *n.* a shaven or bald head; (*comp.* ဦးပြည်း.)

ခေါင်းပေါင်း, *n.* a turban, or any thing wrapped round the head, ဦးရစ်.

ခေါင်းဖြူ, *n.* a grey head, *figuratively* an old man.

ခေါင်းမာ, see ခေါင်းမိုင်.

ခေါင်းရင်း, *n.* the place for the head; (*comp.* ခြေရင်း.)

ခေါင်း, (2) *v.* to be hollow; to make hollow, scoop out, excavate, ထိုက်.

ခေါင်းယက်, *v.* do. Hence အခေါင်း, *n.* an excavation, cavity, hollow place, the hollow of any thing, as of a tree, vessel, &c.

ခေါင်းပါး, *v.* to be few, scarce, နည်း ၊ ရှားပါး.

ခေါင်းလောင်း, *n.* a large bell, or one without a tongue; (*comp.* ထည်းလည်း.)

ခေါပုည်, *n.* a certain preparation of rice.

ခေါ်, (1) *v.* to call, summon, invite; to call by name.

ခေါ်ဝေါ်, *v.* do. ခေါ်ငင်, do.

ခေါ်, (2) *v.* to consider, weigh consequences, တွေး ၊ ဆင်ချင် ၊ စဥ်းစား ၊ ဆင်ခေါ်.

ခေါ်ထောက်, *v.* do.

ခို, (1) *v.* to hide, keep out of the way, avoid what is unpleasant.

ခိုမှီ, *v.* to take refuge in, adhere to, ကပ် ၊ မှီခို ၊ ဆွဲ.

ခိုဝင်, *v.* do.

ခို, (2) *n.* a kind of dove, (larger than ချိုး.)

ခိုကျော, *n.* one species of do. ခိုဖြ, *n.* another species of do.

ခိုစင်, *n.* a dove-cote; a case for any purpose.

ခိုနန်း, *n.* certain projections in a graduated roof.

ခိုမြီး, (from အမြီး, a tail,) *n.* a low house, or shed, attached to a larger.

ခိုက်, *v.* to hit, come in contact, strike against, to interfere with, trespass on, transgress against, တိုက် ။ ထိ ။ ထိပါးထိခိုက်. Hence အခိုက်, *n.* the time being; အခိုက်အတန့်, do.

ခိုက်မိ, *v.* to come in contact, strike against, interfere with, trespass on, transgress against.

ခိုက်ရန်, *n.* a quarrel.

ခိုက်ခိုက်, *an intensive,* (used with words of shaking, trembling, &c.) ချုချဲ.

ခိုင်, *v.* to be firm, strong, durable, hard; to be obstinate, obdurate, မာ ။ ခံ့. Hence အခိုင်, *n.* a stock or branch (of fruit.)

ခိုင်ကျည်, *v.* do. ခိုင်ကျန့်, *v.* do.

ခိုင်မည်း, *v.* to be obstinate.

ခိုင်း, (1) *v.* to set about any business, give orders, ခန့် ။ စေ.

ခိုင်း, (2) *v.* to compare, နှိုင်း ။ နှိုင်း ။ ပြိုင်.

ခိုင်း, (3) *v.* to put the helm to star-board; (*comp.* မတ်.)

ခိုင်းတွက်, *v.* to be particular, scrupulous, exact in making another do his part.

ခိုင်းနှိုင်း, *v.* to respect, reverence, ရိုသေ.

ခိုး, *v.* to steal. Hence သူခိုး, *n.* a thief.

ခိုးကြောင်, *v.* do.

ချ, (1) *v.* to throw down; to put down; (*neuter* ကျ.)

ချ, (2) *v.* to teach, give instruction.

ချ, (3) *v.* to settle, adjust, bring to a conclusion, put in proper place, allot, dispense; (*neuter* ကျ.)

ချ, (4) *n.* a white ant, or any ant of the genus, whether black or white.

ချအုံ, *n.* a white ants' nest.

ချပုန်း, *n.* do. တောင်ပို့.

ချက်, (1) *num. affix*, as ထီးနှစ်ချက်, two umbrellas; (see Gram.)

ချက်, (2) *v.* to cook, dress; (*neuter* ကျက်.)

ချက်, (3) *v.* to scratch, ကုတ် ။ ခြစ်.

ချက်, (4) *v.* to make marks, write, ကုပ် ၊ ခြစ်.

ချက်, (5) (from အချက်, a middle,) *n.* the navel.

ချက်မ, *n.* the navel.

ချက်ကြိုး, *n.* the penis, navel-string.

ချက်ချင်း, (from အချက်, a mark, &c.) *adv.* immediately, in the very moment.

ချက်ခြုတ်, *adv.* do.

ချင်, (1) *euphonic affix*, used in negative sentences only, (with မ repeated,) as မတိုင်မချင်ထွင်မသွားနှင့်, go not without asking leave.

ချင်, (2) *v.* to desire, (not used as a principal verb, but as an optative affix.) Hence ချင်ချင်း, *n.* desire.

ချင်, (3) *v.* to measure with a measure of capacity, ချင့်.

ချင်တွက်, *v.* do.

ချင်, (4) *n.* a musquito.

ချင်ပုန်း, *n.* do.

ချင်ခြောက်, *n.* a brush to keep away musquitoes, &c.

ချင်ထောင်, *n.* musquito curtains.

ချင်ဆီ, *n.* the marrow of bones.

ချင်ပိတ်, (from အချင်, a rafter,) *n.* a board facing the eaves of a house.

ချင်ရဲ, *v.* to be satisfied, satiated, ရောင့်ရဲ.

ချင်ရဲပြေ, *v.* do.

ချင်ရွေး, *n.* a small seed, Abrus Precatorius, ထင်ရွေး ; see ရွေး.

ချင်သေ့, *n.* a lion.

ချင်း, (1) *n.* Kyen, one district of the Burman empire ; *adj.* pertaining to the Kyen people, who mark the faces of their women with black spots.

ချင်း, (2) *adv.* mutually, one with another ; see အချင်းချင်း.

ချင်း, (3) *v. affix*, indeed ! or alas ! (see တကား.)

ချင်း, (4) *participial affix*, denotes abstract action, or being, as စားချင်း, eating ; ကောင်းချင်း, being good. It changes the verb to a noun, which admits all the noun affixes.

ချင်း, (5) *v.* to bore, pierce, penetrate, go through, ထွင်း ၊ ဖောက်.

ချင်း, (6) *n.* a basket.

N

ချင်းတောင်း, *n.* a basket.

ချင်းကြား, *n.* a cup-like basket.

ချင်း, (7) *v.* to engage, fight, as fowls, and some other animals ; come in contact, be in conjunction, as the heavenly bodies, ခွင်.

ချင်း, (8) *n.* the ginger-plant or root.

ချင်းစိမ်း, *n.* do.

ချင်းခြောက်, *n.* dried ginger.

ချင်း, (9) *(pron.* ဂျင်း, from အချင်း, a companion, &c.) *pers. n.* you, *mas.* or *fem.* (used in courts of justice.)

ချင်း, (10) *adv.* only, no more, as လူတယောက်ချင်း, one man only ; နေ့ချင်း, a day only ; ညဉ့်တွင်းချင်း, in a night only.

ချင်းချင်း, *an intensive,* used with words of redness, ရှိတ်ရှိတ်.

ချင်းချင်းတွေးတွေး, *an intensive,* do.

ချင့်, (1) *v.* to compute, calculate in the mind, form a judgment of, consider, ခန့်၊ ထင်ချင်.

ချင့်, (2) *v.* see ချင်, to measure.

ချင့်တောက်, *v.* to consider, have regard to, feel for, pity, စာ.

ချစ်, (1) *v.* to love, have affection for, regard, esteem, ခင်၊ မင်၊ ကြင်နာ၊ နှစ်သက်၊ မြတ်နိုး၊ ထေးမြတ် ; *(comp.* ကြိုက်.)

ချစ်ကြည်, *v.* do.

ချစ်, (2) *v.* to scratch, as with the paws, ကုတ်၊ ချုတ်.

ချစ်, (3) *v.* to be burnt, as food in cooking, တူး.

ချစ်ချစ်လောင်လောင်, *adv.* disagreeably, noisily.

ချည်, (1) *v.* to tie, bind, fasten by tying, နှောင်၊ ဖွဲ့၊ စည်း၊ တုပ်.

ချည်, (2) *v.* to give, as a name, or title, စည်း၊ တပ်.

ချည်, (3) *n.* thread simply spun.

ချည်ခင်, *n.* do.

ချည်ကျစ်, *n.* thread doubled and twisted.

ချည်ချောင်း, *n.* (1) a single thread ; (2) *n.* a jew's-harp.

ချည်မြှင်, *n.* do.

ချည်ဝင်, *n.* a spindle of thread.

ချည်တော့, *n.* the quill on which thread is wound from the spindle.

ချည်ခင်, (from အခင်,) *n.* a skein or hank of thread.

ချည်ထွေး, *n.* a ball of thread.

ချည်လုံး, *n.* a ball of thread.

ချည်ချည်ပျပျ, *adv.* altogether.

ချည်တစေ, *adv.* merely, only, nothing but.

ချဉ်, (1) *v.* to be sour, acid.

ချဉ်, (2) *v.* to taste unpleasant, as the mouth.

ချဉ်ထူး, *v.* to be very sour; see ထူး.

ချည်ဆား, *v.* to seek food, (applied to priests and distinguished characters.)

ချည်ဆားမြိုး, *v.* do.

ချဉ်ပေါင်, *n.* a kind of culinary plant.

ချဉ်ဖြစ, *n.* a kind of tree.

ချဉ်ရှပ်, *n.* a kind of tree.

ချည်း, (1) *adv.* only, nothing but, applied to nouns, and verbs, as လူတို့ချည်း, men only; သွားသည်ချည်း, he only goes, i. e. does nothing but go, သက်သက်.

ချည်း, (2) *n.* fœces, ordure, မစင် ၊ ကျင်ကြီး ၊ ဝမ်း.

ချဉ်း, (1) *v.* to approach, draw near, ကပ်.

ချဉ်း, (2) *v.* to make narrow, bring into a narrow compass, contract, draw together, ချုံ့; (*neut.* ကျဉ်း.)

ချည့်, *v.* to be infirm, weak, debilitated, နဲ့.

ချဉ့်ချဉ့်, *adj.* sourish.

ချန်, *v.* to leave, let remain, set aside, ချွင်း; (*neuter,* ကျန်.)

ချပ် or ချတ်, *numeral affix;* (see Gram.)

ချပ်, (1) *v.* to insert, put in, introduce, place between, သွင်း.—Hence အချပ်, *n.* the scales of fish or other animals, အကြေး.

ချပ်, (2) *v.* to flatten, to be flat, ပြား.

ချပ်, (3) *n.* a coat of mail, သံချပ်.

ချပ်ကာ, *n.* one kind of do.

ချပ်, (4) *n.* a kind of beetel-box, used by the royal family.

ချမ်း, (1) *v.* to be cool, cold.

ချမ်း, (2) to be relieved or free from pain, difficulty, &c. to be comfortable, happy, ဌ ၊ ဖြ ၊ မြေ့.

ချမ်းငြိမ်း, *n.* relief, ease, rest, happiness.

ချမ်းသာ, *v.* to be relieved, be comfortable, happy, သက်သာ.

ချမ်း, '(3) *v.* to divide into equal parts, ဝက်.

ချယ်, *v.* to variegate, diversify, စီချယ်.

ချယ်လယ်, or ချယ်လှယ်, *v.* do.

ချရား, *n.* a kind of tree.

ချရားသီး, *n.* a certain part of the spire of a pagoda, below the umbrella.

ချံ, *v.* to surround, encircle, enclose; see ခြံ, or ခြံရံ.

ချံရံ, *v.* do. see ခြံ.

ချာ, (1) *v.* to be a point of union to several parts.

ချာချုပ်, *v.* do. Hence အချာ, *n.* what unites several things, a person or thing to which several others are subordinate, အချုပ်အချာ ။ ခချိုင် ။ အချာအချုပ် ။ အချုပ်အချာ.

ချာ, (2) *v.* to take every other one, take one and leave one.

ချာချာ, *adv.* an *intensive,* (used with words of turning round.)

ချား, (1) *v.* to put a space between, divide, separate, make distinct, ရိုင်းချွင်း ။ သားခွား; to be different, diverse, unlike, dissimilar, ထူး ။ ခြား ။ သီး; *(neuter,* ကြား.)

ချားနား, *v.* do. do. Hence အချား, *n.* see အကြား; *hence also* အချား, *pron. adj.* other, တချား ။ တပါး.

ချား, (2) *n.* a machine to wind thread from, ရဟတ်ချား.

ချိ, (1) *v.* to disperse, scatter, ကြဲ ။ ဖြန့်.

ချိ, (2) *v.* to endure, hold out, be capable of enduring, ခံ ။ ထိ ခံနိုင်.

ချိတ်, (1) *v.* to hook, catch hold with a hook; (2) to use artful and indirect language, or management, စောင်း ။ ရိပ်.

ချိတ်ချိတ်, *adv. an intensive,* (used with words of redness,) ချင်းချင်း.

ချိတ်သတ်, *n.* a kind of tree.

ချိပ်, *n.* lac.

ချိန်, *v.* to weigh.

ချိန်တွယ်, *v.* do.

ချိန်ဝန်, *v.* do.

ချိန်စက်, *v.* to make equal in weight, စက်.

ချိန်ခွင်, *n.* a pair of scales or balances, ကတ်ပယ်.

ချိန်ခွင်ခွက်, *n.* the cups or scales of a balance.

ချိန်ခွင်ပေါင်, (from ပေါင်, a thigh,) *n.* the yard or cross-beam of a balance.

ချိန်ခွင်ပေါင်း, (from ပေါင်း, a kind of cap,) *n.* the handle of a balance.

ချိန်ခွင်လျှာ, *n.* the tongue of the beam.

ချိန်တာရာ, *n.* one of the constellations, see တာရာ.

ချိန်း, *v.* to appoint, fix, set, (as a time.)

ချိန်းချက်, *v.* do.

ချိန့်, *v.* to be many, numerous, များ; great, vast, ကြီး; (not used in the assertive form.)

ချိမ်း, (1) *v.* to threaten, daunt, terrify by threats, ခြိမ်းခြောက် • မောင်းမဲ; *(neuter,* ခြိမ်း.*)*

ချိမ်းခြောက်, *v.* to threaten, terrify.

ချိမ်းမဲ, *v.* do.

ချိမ်းမောင်း, *v.* do.

ချိမ်းဝါး, *v.* to threaten in a boasting manner.

ချိမ်းပ, *v.* do.

ချိမ်း, (2) see ချုန်း, to thunder.

ချိမ့်, *euphonic affix,* compounded of ချေ, and အံ့.

ချိမ့်ချိမ့် or တချိမ့်ချိမ့်, *adv.* noisily, rumblingly.

ချိမ့်ခနဲ, *adv.* do.

ချီ, (1) *v.* to lift, raise, take up, ကြွ.

ချီ, (2) *v.* to march, as troops, တက်.

ချီ, (3) *v*, to begin, make a beginning, (applied to writing.)

ချီဆောင်, *v.* undertake, conduct, as business, ဆောင်ရွက်.

ချီပင့်, *v.* to invite.

ချီထိန်း, *v.* to nurse, take care of, wait on.

ချီယ, *v.* do.

ချီး, *v.* to exalt, promote, မြှောက် • မြှင့်.

ချီးမွမ်း, *v.* to praise, applaud.

ချုန်း, *v.* to roar, as thunder; be loud, thundering, ချိမ်း.

ချုန်းခနဲ, *adv.* thunderingly.

ချုပ်, *v.* to sew, sew up, secure by sewing; to confine, bind, secure, shut up, cut off, terminate; (applied variously, as, to the constriction of the bowels, imprisonment, binding by written engagement, shutting in, as evening, မိုးချုပ်; termination of life, &c.) to have in subjection, rule, govern, have dominion over, အုပ် ၊ အစိုးရ ၊ ချုပ်ချာ.

ချုပ်ချစ်, *v.* to have but little, be in a strait for want of, be forced to pick a little here and there, as occasion offers.

ချုပ်ချယ်, *v.* to be hard to deal with, difficult, disobliging, irritating, ကပ်သပ်.

ချုပ်ချာ, *v.* see ချုပ်.

ချုပ်ချုပ်, *adv.* (1) violently ; (2) moderately, partially.

ချုပ်စာ, *n.* a written engagement, စာချုပ် ၊ သဏ္ဍာရာဂုံ.

ချုပ်တည်း, *v.* to restrain, hinder, prevent.

ချုပ်ရိုး, *n.* a seam.

ချုပ်သမား, *n.* a tailor, အချုပ်သမား ၊ အပ်ချုပ်သမား.

ချုံး, (1) *v.* to contract, draw into a narrow compass, close or shut up, ရှုံ့ ၊ ကျဉ်း.

ချုံးယုံ, *v.* do.

ချုံး, (2) *v.* to pine away, grow thin, lean, poor, ကျုံ့ ၊ ပိန် ၊ ကြုံ.

ချုံ့, *v.* to contract, draw together, ချုံးကျဉ်း ; *neuter*, ရှုံ့.

ချူ, (1) *v.* to pull out or down, with a hook or other instrument.

ချူ, (2) *n.* jingles, small round bells.

ချူကိုး, *n.* a collar of such bells.

ချူချာ, (1) *v.* to be close, niggardly, စဉ်းနဲ.

ချူချာ, (2) *v.* to be full of sores, diseases, &c. အနာထူများ.

ချူး, *n.* a kind of tree.

ချေ, (1) *euphonic affix.*

ချေ, (2) *v. affix, imp.* or *prec.* (see Gram.)

ချေ, (3) *v.* to pulverize, rub to powder ; to rub out, erase, expunge.

ချေတင်, see ချေ, to pulverize, &c.

ချေ, (4) *v.* to reply to, refute ; do a thing in return, တုံ့ ၊ တုဉ် ; (*neuter*, ကျေ.)

ချေ, (5) *n.* the porcine deer, (*pron.* ဂျီ.)

ချေပ, *v.* to reply to, refute.

ချေ, (6) *v.* to be conciliatory, pleasing, persuasive in speech, စကားချောမော ၊ စကားပြေပြစ်.

ချေလက်, and ချေလည်, *v.* do. The first is sometimes divided, and compounded with a reduplicated root, as ပြောချေပြောလက်.

ချေ့ချွင်း, or ချွ, (from ချွင်း, to throw down ;) (1) *v.* to refute ; (2) *v.* to sneeze, (frequently pronounced ချိ.)

ချေဆတ်, *v.* to sneeze.

ချေး, (1) *v.* to be soft, gentle, as sound, ညင်း.

ချေး, (2) *v.* to borrow, to lend ; to hire, to let ; the article to be returned, or its value; (commonly applied to the loan of money ;) *comp.* ငှါး.

ချေးငှင်, *v.* do.

ချေးနှီး, *v.* do.

ချေးရန်, *v.* do.

ချေး, (3) *n.* the excrement of animals, ordure, (*pron.* ချီး ;) ကျင်ကြီး မစင် ၊ ဝမ်း.

ချေး, (4) *n.* the rust of metals.

ချေးတက်, *v.* to be rusty.

ချေးယို, *v.* to evacuate the intestines, (vulgarly, ဝမ်းသွား.)

ချေးသီး, *n.* a kind of tree or fruit.

ချဲ့, (1) *v.* to widen, make wide or broad, spread open ; (*neuter*, ကျယ်.)

ချဲ့, (2) *v.* to be weak, debilitated ; *see* ချည့်.

ချဲချဲ့, *adv.* tremblingly, ခိုက်ခိုက်.

ချော, (1) *v.* to be fine, nice, smooth, handsome, ခြော ၊ မွေ့ ၊ မွတ် ၊ လှ ၊ ပြေပြစ်.

ချောမော, *v.* do. စကားချောမော, to be conciliatory, pleasant, agreeable in speech.

ချောပတ်, *v.* to be fine, smooth, nice, agreeable.

ချောချော, *adv.* nicely, finely, handsomely, agreeably.

ချော, (2) *v.* to be slippery, slimy, ကျိ.

ချော, (3) *v.* to slide, slip off, (applied to things inanimate, လျှော.)

ချော, (4) *v.* to excite a quarrel, instigate, provoke, ကုန်းချော ၊ ရန်တွေ့.

ချောစား, *v.* do.

ချောတိုက်, *v.* do.

ချောပြစ်, *v.* do.

ချောက်, (1) *v.* to be dry, dried up.

ခြောက်ထပ်, *v.* to be dry, dried up.

ခြောက်သွေ့, *v.* to become dry.

ခြောက်ခန်း, *v.* to be dried up.

ခြောက်ကပ်, *v.* do.

ခြောက်, (2) *v.* to frighten, make afraid, လှန့် *(neut.* ကြောက်.*)*

ခြောက်ခြိမ်း, *v.* to threaten, terrify.

ခြောက်, (3) *n.* a declivity, broken bank, precipice, cascade, cataract, ကမ်းပါးပြတ်.

ခြောက်, (4) *adj.* six, (marked by the figure ၆.)

ခြောက်ချက်, or တခြောက်ချက်, *adv.* quarrelsomely.

ခြောက်ချား, *v.* to shake, agitate, လှုပ်; to affect by any violent emotion, as fear, astonishment, &c.

ခြောင်, (1) *v.* to be loose, slack, not tight, မကြပ်မတင်း.

ခြောင်, (2) *v.* to be lean, thin, poor, ကျုံ့၊ ပိန်.

ခြောင်, (3) *v.* to be desolate, unfrequented; to live retired, in concealment.

ခြောင်ရှိ, *v.* do.

ခြောင်, (4) *n.* a slender basket or bamboo, used to pack tea-leaves, လက်ဖက်ခြောင်.

ခြောင်, (5) *n.* a kind of long basket, used like a wallet.

ခြောင်, (6) *n.* a pot, with a perforated bottom, used to cook by steam.

ခြောင်း, (1) *num. affix,* as အပ်နှစ်ခြောင်း, two needles, (see Gram.)

ခြောင်း, (2) *v.* to peep, look slily, pry into, ထချောင်းကြည့်.

ခြောင်းမြောင်း, *v.* do.

ခြောင်းနှောင်း, *v.* do.

ခြောင်း, (3) *n.* a cough, a hem.

ခြောင်းခြောက်, *n.* the dry cough, a disease.

ခြောင်းဆိုး, *v.* to cough, have a cold; to hem.

ခြောင်းမြို, *v.* to cough, hem.

ခြောင်းညှို့, *v.* to hem.

ခြောင်းဟန့်, *v.* do.

ခြောင်းဟက်, *v.* to hawk, raise phlegm.

ခြောင်းတဟဲဟဲ, *adv.* coughingly, gurglingly, as running water.

ခြောင်း, (4) *n.* a large brook, canal, rivulet, *larger than* မြောင်း.

ချောင်း, (5) *n.* the neck, or throat, လဲဥုဒ်.

ချောင်း, (6) *v.* see the fourth definition of ချောင်.

ချောင်းသာ, *n.* a large brook, canal, rivulet.

ချောင်းချောင်း, *adv.* ascendingly, as smoke, vapour, &c. (*fig.* applied to strong passions.) တချောင်းချောင်း, *adv.* do.

ချော့, *v.* to wheedle, coax, pacify, ဖျော့ ။ ဖြေ.

ချော့မော့, *v.* do.

ချော့မော့ပြော, *v.* to speak gently, kindly.

ချော်, (1) *v.* to slip, slide, as with the feet; (2) to err, backslide, လွဲ; (3) to play a trick with, deceive, ပျက် ။ ပျက်ရယ်; (4) to be obstinate, stiff-necked, resolute (in evil), ခက် ။ ခြောင် ။ မိတ်မာ; (5) *n.* the dross of metal.

ချို, (1) *v.* to be sweet, fresh, pleasant.

ချိုင, *v.* do. ချိုမြ, do. ချိုမြိန်, do. ချိုမြက်, do. ချိုမြေ့, do.

ချို, (2) *n.* a horn, (*pron.* ချို.)

ချိုက်, *v.* to be concave, deep, hollow.

ချိုင်, *v.* to chop, hew, ခုတ်.

ချိုင်း, (1) *v.* to be sloping, low, sunken, နိမ့် ။ ရှိုင်း ။ ငုံး; (2) *n.* a low sunken spot of ground, a valley.

ချိုင့်, (1) *v.* to be hollow, concave, deep, ခွက် ။ ခြိုက် ။ ရှိုက် ။ ယောက် ။ ဟိုက်; (2) *n.* a concavity, hollow, ကျင်းခြိုက်; (3) *n.* a cage for birds, a case for other uses.

ချိုး, (1) *v.* to be lean, thin, poor, &c. see ကျိုး.

ချိုး, (2) *v.* to break cross-wise, as any thing that is longer than it is broad; (*comp.* ခွဲ; *neuter,* ကျိုး.)

ချိုးဖဲ့, *v.* do. to break off.

ချိုး, (3) *v.* to wash, bathe, rub, as the body, with water.

ချိုးခြံ, *v.* to deny one's self, practise self-denial, perform austerities.

ချိုးခြံကျင့်, *v.* do.

ချို့, *v.* to be deficient, wanting, incomplete, defective, ယုတ် ။ တဲ့ ။ မပြည့်စုံ.

ချို့တဲ့, *v.* do.

ချိုချို, (from ချို, to be sweet,) *adj.* or *adv.* slightly sweet, sweetish.

ခြခြ, *adv. an intensive.*

ခြင်း, *part. affix*, see ချင်း.

ခြစ်, *v.* to make marks, write, ကုပ် ၊ ချက် ၊ ရေး; (*comp.* ချစ်.)

ခြည်, (1) *v. imp. affix*, as ပြုခြည်, do thou, or, do thou do.

ခြည်, (2) *n.* a ray of light, ရောင်ခြည်.

ခြမ်း, *v.* see under ဝယ်, to purchase.

ခြံ, (1) *v.* to fence in, surround, (not used singly.)

ခြံ, (2) *n.* a fence, an inclosure of any kind.

ခြံရံ, *v.* to fence, surround with a fence; to encompass, or inclose in any manner.

ခြံဝန်း, ခြံပတ်, ခြံကာ, &c. *v.* do. Hence အခြံအရံ, (1) *n.* a fence, ခြံ; (2) *n.* guards, attendants, people in waiting, အခြွေအရံ ၊ အခြံအနား.

ခြုံ, (1) *v.* to cover, overspread, as with clothes, ရုံ ၊ လွှမ်း.

ခြုံလုံ, *v.* to be tight, as a vessel, secure, safe, လုံ.

ခြုံ, (2) *n.* a bower, collection, or clump of trees, woods, ရုံ.

ခြုံပုတ်, *n.* a collection of shrubs, low bushes.

ခြူး, *n.* artificial ornaments, painted, embroidered, or sculptured.

ခြူးပန်း, *n.* artificial flowers.

ခြူးဆုံ, *n.* artificial bunches, clusters, &c.

ခြေ, *n.* a foot or leg, (sometimes *pron.* ချီ;) *comp.* အခြေ.

ခြေထောက်, *v.* do.

ခြေကျည်း, *n.* the leg from the knee to the ankles, ခြေသလုံး.

ခြေချင်း, (1) *n.* ornamental ankle-rings; (2) fetters.

ခြေချင်းဝတ်, *n.* the space between the calf and ankles.

ခြေတကောက်, *n.* the inside of the joint of the knee.

ခြေချောင်း, *n.* a toe, ခြေသန်.

ခြေစွပ်, *n.* a stocking, or boot.

ခြေဆင်း, *v.* to stretch out (the leg).

ခြေဆန့်, *v.* do.

ခြေသန်, *n.* a toe, ခြေချောင်း.

ခြေညှိုး, *n.* the toe next the great toe.

ခြေနင်း, *n.* a sandal.

ခြေတော်ရာ, *n.* an impress of a Boodh's foot, (see under ဝတ်.)

ခြေနင်း, *n.* a shoe.

ခြေနင်းခုံ, *n.* foot-stool.

ခြေဖမိုး, *n.* the upper part of the foot.

ခြေဖဝါး, *n.* the sole of the foot.

ခြေမ, *n.* the great toe.

ခြေမျက်စိ, *n.* the ankles, or ankle bone, ဖမျက်.

ခြေရင်း, *n.* the place for the feet, (to the feet;) *comp.* ခေါင်းရင်း.

ခြေလယ်, *n.* the middle toe.

ခြေသည်, *n.* a foot soldier, ခြေသည်သူရဲ.

ခြေသန်း, *n.* the little toe.

ခြေသလုံး, *n.* the leg from the knee to the ankles, ခြေကျည်း.

ခြေသူကြွယ်, *n.* the toe next to the little toe.

ခြိုက်, (1) *v.* to be hollow, concave, deep, ရှိုင်း ၊ နက်ရှိုက် ၊ တောက် ၊ ဟိုက်.

ခြိုက်, (2) *n.* a concavity, hollow, ကျင်း ၊ ရှိုင်း.

ခွ, *v.* to branch off in two parts, be forked; to be of two minds, halt between two opinions, ခွတွ ၊ တွတ်တီ. Hence အခွ, *n.* the crotch of a tree, the place of branching off in a river, a fork, &c.

ခွက်, (1) *v.* to be concave, deep, hollow, as a cup, ရှိုင်း ၊ ခြိုက်.

ခွက်, (2) *n.* a cup, bowl, or any thing of a similar shape.

ခွက်ယောက်, *n.* a cup, bowl, &c. Hence အခွက်အကျင်း, *n.* capacity (of a vessel).

ခွက်ခွင်း, *n.* a pair of brass plates, played together, လင်ကွင်း.

ခွင်, *v.* to be bent inwards, concave—*opposed to* ကုန်း, to be convex; (applied also to bandy legs and arms, which in the English idiom are said to bend *outwards.*)

ခွင်း, (1) *v.* to pierce, thrust through, slash, hew, destroy, erase, ချင်း ၊ ထိုး ၊ ခုတ် ၊ ဖျက် ၊ ချေ.

ခွင်း, (2) *n.* a kind of adze, ပဆိန်း.

ခွန်း, *num. affix,* as စကားနှစ်ခွန်း, two words; (see Gram.)

ခွန်အား, *n.* strength, force, power, အားခွန် ၊ ခွန်ပကား ၊ ဗလ.

ခွပ်, *v.* to engage, fight, as fowls and some other animals; to come in contact, be in conjunction, as the heavenly bodies, ချင်း.

ခုနစ်, *adj.* seven, (marked by the figure ၇.)

ခွာ, (1) *v.* to separate, divide, sever, cleave off, put at a distance; (*neut.* ကွာ.)

ခွာ, (2) *n.* a hoof.

ခွာညို, *n.* a kind of vine.

ခွေ, (1) *v.* to curve, curl, coil, wind into a ring.

ခွေလိပ်, *v.* do.

ခွေဝတ်, *n.* a hoop, အကွင်း.

ခွေ, (2) *v.* to gather (fuel), ထင်းခွေ.

ခွေး, (1) *n.* a ring of any description, အခွေး.

ခွေး, (2) *n.* a dog; (*in chess,*) check-mate.

ခွေးအ, *n.* a kind of wild dog, said to stammer in barking.

ခွေးဆို, *n.* the posteriors; ထင် ၊ ဝဋ္ဋဆို.

ခွေးကထက်, *n.* a low verandah, or porch.

ခွေးတောက်, *n.* a kind of vine.

ခွေးတပ္ပျက်, *n.* a kind of tree.

ခွေးလှေး, (1) (see under ခြေး,) *n.* a flea.

ခွေးလှေး, (2) *n.* a kind of vine.

ခွေ့, (1) *n.* a kind of red mineral, (*pron.* ဂွေ့,) ဓမ္ပ.

ခွေ့, (2) *v.* see ဂွေ့, to push.

ခွေ့နွမ်း, *v.* to be weak, exhausted, worn out; *see* နွမ်းခွေ့.

ခွဲ, (1) *v.* to split, divide lengthwise, (*comp.* ချိုး;) to divide into two parts; (*neut.* ကွဲ.)

ခွဲ, (2) *v.* to levy, or assess, as money, arms, &c.

ခွဲခန့်, *v.* to distribute, allot; to direct, order, စီရင်.

ခွဲခြမ်း, *v.* to divide into equal parts, separate.

ခွဲခြား, *v.* to divide into parts, make various, or many.

ခွဲဖြာ, *v.* do.

ခွဲဝေ, *v.* to divide, distribute.

ခွဲ, (3) *n.* a kway, a measure of capacity, half a ten, (တင်း.)

ခွဲ, (4) *n.* a flat basket, or wicker ladle, used to gather grass seeds with.

ချွင်း, *v.* to leave, let remain, set aside, ချန်; (*neuter,* ကြွင်း.)

ချွတ်, (1) *v.* to take out, or off, release, free, deliver, emancipate, annihilate, လွှတ်.

ချွတ်, (2) *v.* to be destroyed, lost, perished, ယွင်း ၊ ပျက်.

ချွတ်, (3) *v.* to be gone aside, be mistaken, to transgress, err, မှား ၊ လွဲ.

ချွတ်ခနဲ, *adv.* crackingly.

ချွတ်ချွတ်, *adv.* do. *also* quickly, violently, ချွံချွံ.

ချွန်, (1) *v.* to point, make pointed, sharpen; to be sharp, keen (in science or learning), ထက်; (2) *v.* to be smooth, nice.

ချွန်နေရာ, *n.* see နေညှိ.

ချွန်း, (1) *v.* to be tapering, ရှူ.

ချွန်း, (2) *n.* an iron hook used by elephant drivers.

ချွန်းတောင်း, *n.* do.

ချွံချွံ, *adv.* quickly, violently, ချွပ်ချွပ်.

ချွံချွံရက်ရက်, *adv.* do.

ချွံချွံနောင်နောင်, *adv.* jinglingly.

ချွေ, (1) *v.* to cause to fall, as leaves, fruit, &c. (*neuter*, ကြွေ.)

ချွေ, (2) *v.* to be sparing, do by degrees, bit by bit.

ချွေတာ, *v.* do. do.

ချွေး, *n.* sweat, any vapour collected in a fluid.

ချွေးထွက်, *v.* to perspire.

ချွေးယိုး, *v.* to perspire profusely.

ချွေးမ, *n.* a daughter-in-law, a son's wife.

ချွဲ, *v.* to be slimy, ropy, viscous, glutinous, ကျိ. Hence အချွဲ, *n.* any slimy substance, mucus.

ချွဲပျစ်, *v.* do.

ချွဲကန်း, *n.* phlegm, သလိပ်.

ချွဲပင်, *adv.* protractingly, procrastinatingly, ကဆွဲကနံ့.

ခြွေရံ, *v.* to surround, attend. Hence အခြွေအရံ, *n.* attendants, suite, people in waiting, အခြံအရံ.

ခြွေရွေ, *see* ခြွေရံ. Hence အခြွေအရွေ, see အခြွေအရံ.

ဂ.

The third consonant in the Burman alphabet, and the third in the class of gutturals.

ဂလိဂလိ, *adv. indicative of the sound expressed by pronouncing the word.*

ဂင်္ဂါ, *n.* the Ganges, ဂင်္ဂါမြစ်.

ဂဏ, *(Pali,)* *n.* a collection, assemblage; see ဂိုဏ်း.

ဂဏန်း, (from ဂဏနာ, *Pali,*) *n.* a numerical figure.

ဂဏန်းခြေ, *n.* do.

ဂဏန်းသင်ချာ, *v.* to count, enumerate.

ဂဏာ, *n.* rice boiled in milk, နို့ဂဏာ.

ဂဏာထွင်း, *n.* do.

ဂဏ္ဌိ, *(Pali,)* *n.* a noose, knot, difficulty, crabbed question.

ဂတိ, (1) *n.* see under ဂတိ.

ဂတိ, (2) *(Pali,)* *n.* a transition to another state of existence, လားချင်း.

ဂတိ, (3) *n.* behaviour, carriage, အကျင့်.

ဂထိ, *(a corruption of* ကထိ, *Pali, commonly written by further corruption* ဂတိ,) *n.* word, language, speech, စကား.

ဂတိဝတ်, *n.* an engagement, ကတိကဝတ်.

ဂတိစောင့်, *v.* to keep one's word, သစ္စာစောင့်.

ဂတိဆို, or ဂတိပြု, or ဂတိမူ, *v.* to promise, give one's word, make an engagement.

ဂတိတည်, *v.* to be faithful, true to one's word.

ဂတိမှန်, *v.* do.

ဂဏန်း, *n.* a crab. ဂဏန်းလုံး, a species of do.

ဂနိုင်, *n.* a grove, wood, wilderness, တောကြိုင် ၊ ရုံ.

ဂန္ဓ, *(Pali,)* *n.* smell, scent, အနံ့.

ဂန္ဓပ္ပ, *(Pali,)* *n.* a Gandappa, a kind of inferior Nat, many of whom inhabit, and guard the base of Myenmo mount, in concert with Rekkaiks, (ရက္ခိုက်,) Kōngbans, (ကုမ္ဘဏ်,) Ga-lōngs, (ဂဠုန်,) and Nagahs, (နဂါး.)

ဂန္ဓမာလာ, *n.* a kind of flower-tree.

ဂဗ္ဘ, *(Pali,)* *n.* the belly.

ဂဗ္ဘသေယက, see under ပဋိသန္ဓေ, or ဇလာဗုဇ.

ဂမန်း, *part. affix,* denotes likeness, similarity, resemblance, as သွားဂမန်း, what is like going; (also see ဘွယ်.)

ဂမိကဝတ်, (from ဂမိက, a guest, *Pali,*) *n.* the duties of hospitality, ဧည့်သည်ဝတ်.

ဂမုန်း, *n.* a kind of plant.

ဂရင်ဂျီ, *n.* a kind of disease.

ဂရု, *(Pali,) adj.* weighty, important; *adv.* respectfully, attentively.

ဂရုတ, *adv.* heavily, weightily, &c. see ဂရု.

ဂလန်, *n.* see တန်လန်ကျင်, a bolt, bar.

ဂဟေ, *n.* solder, metallic cement.

ဂဠုန်, *n.* a galōng, a kind of fabulous bird of immense size, with human face, and bird's beak.

ဂါဂရာ, *n. (Bengalee,)* a foreign female's petticoat or gown.

ဂါထာ, *n.* a stanza of Pali verse, consisting of four lines, (ပုဒ်,) each commonly containing eight syllables.

ဂါမ, *(Pali,) n.* a village, ရွာ.

ဂါဝုတ်, *n.* a Gahwōke, a measure of distance equal to four Kauthas, (ကောသ.)

ဂါး, *int.* ho! what are you about! (obsolete.)

ဂိမှာန္တဥတု, *(Pali,) n.* the warm season, နွေကာလ.

ဂုတ်, *n.* a cave, a niche.

ဂုဏ, or
ဂုဏံ, } *(Pali,) n.* a quality.

ဂုဏ်, (from ဂုဏံ, *Pali,)* (1) *n.* a good quality, attribute; *comp.* လက္ခဏ်, and ဩဇ; (2) the good resulting to others from a good quality, ကျေးဇူး; (3) the reputation of a good quality, ကျော်စော ၊ ဘုန်း.

ဂုဏ်အသရေ, *n.* reputation, resulting from good qualities.

ဂုဏ်လုပ်, *v.* to affect a good quality, be vain.

ဂုံ, *n.* a kind of creeper.

ဂုံရွှေ, and ဂုံခါး, *n.* varieties of do.

ဂုံမင်, *n.* a kind of tree.

ဂုံး, *n.* mischief.

ဂုံးချော, *v.* to excite a quarrel between other persons by backbiting, or misrepresentation.

ဂုံးတိုက်, *v.* do. ဂုံးချောတိုက်, do.

ဂုံးဖြစ်, *v.* do. ဂုံးချောဖြစ်, do.

ဂုံးစား, *v.* do. ဂုံးချောစား, do.

ဂုံးမ, *n.* a mischief-making woman.

ဂုံးသည်, *n.* a mischief-maker, fomenter of quarrels.

ဂူ, *n.* a cave; an induration in the bowels or breast.

ဂဲ, (from ခဲ, to be hard,) *n.* any thing hard.

ဂေါစရက်, *(Pali,) n.* a frequented place, ကျက်စားသောအရပ်.

ဂေါတမ, *n.* Gaudama, the fourth Boodh in the present system.

ဂေါဏာဂုံ, *n.* the second Boodh, (see ဗုဒ္ဓ.)

ဂေါရုစနာ, *n.* a kind of precious stone, found in the stomach of animals, (less valuable than အဂြေတာ.)

ဂေါ်မေဒ်, *n.* a kind of precious stone.

ဂေါ်မိတ်, *n.* do.

ဂေါ်မုတ်, *n.* do.

ဂေါ်ထရင်, *n.* a kind of parasite, taking root in the bark of trees.

ဂိုဏ်, (from ဂဏ, *Pali,) n.* a collection, assemblage, အစု၊ အပေါင်း.

ဂိုဏ်အုပ်, *n.* a bishop, one who has jurisdiction over other priests.

ဂျင်, *n.* a top, kind of play-thing.

ဂျင်ပု, *n.* a ball fixed on a pole or staff, for ornament.

ဂျပ်, *n.* a kind of serpent.

ဂျီ, *see* ချေ, the porcine deer.

ဂျုံ, (*Bengulee,*) *n.* wheat, ကုလားစပါး.

ဂျေး, *n. a corruption of* အကြေး, dirt, (sometimes *pron.* ချီး.)

ဂျိုင်း, *n.* a locust.

ဂျိုး, *n.* a kind of dove, smaller than ခို, (sometimes written ဥချိုး, or ဥချိုး, or ဥဂျိုး.)

ဂျိုးကတ, *n.* a small species of dove.

ဂျိုးကျာ, *n.* a crane, kind of bird.

ဂျိုးလင်ပြာ, *n.* a large species of dove.

ဂျိုးသိမ်း, *n.* a kind of hawk.

ဂြိုဟ်, (from ဂြဟ, *Pali,) n.* a planet.—N. B. Eight are enumerated, viz. တနင်္ဂနွေ, or နေ, the sun; တနင်္လာ, or လ, the moon; အင်္ဂါ, Mars; ဗုဒ္ဓဟူး, Mercury; ကြာသပတေး, Jupiter; သောကြာ, Venus; စနေ, Saturn; and ရာဟု.

ဂွမ်း, *n.* undressed cotton.

ဂွမ်းဖတ်, *v.* to dress cotton with a bow-string.

ဂွေးစေ့, see ဝှေးစေ့, *n.* the testicles.

ဂျွမ်း, (1) *n.* a kind of water insect, ပေါင်းလဒ်း.

ဂျွမ်းထိုး, *v.* to pitch heels over head.

ဂျွမ်းသမား, or ဂျွမ်းထိုးသမား, *n.* a tumbler, rope-dancer, &c.

ဂျွမ်း, (2) *n.* the wheel, or pendulum of a loom, ရက်ကန်းဂျွမ်း.

ဂျွံ, *adv.* altogether, without distinction, wholesale.

ဂျွံဆန်, *n.* rice which has been husked, but not completely cleaned.

## ဃ.

The fourth consonant in the Burman alphabet, and the fourth in the class of gutturals.

ဃရာဝါသ, (from ဃရ, a house, and အာဝါသ, to dwell, *Pali,*) *n.* living in the married state, having a family, အိမ်ထောင်ရှင်း.

## င.

The fifth consonant in the Burman alphabet, and the fifth in the class of gutturals.

င, (1) *v.* to be distributed; *act.* ငှ.

င, (2) *a title prefixed to proper names of men, indicative of superiority in the speaker.*

ငတ်, *v.* to desire, long for, ငံ ။ ကိုးရှင် ။ တောင့်တ.

ငကြင်းကျေး, *n.* a kind of plant.

ငချိပ်, *n.* black kind of rice, one kind of ကောက်ညှင်း.

ငင်, *v.* to pull, draw, ဆွဲ; to draw out, spin, ငင့်. Hence, by corruption, အငင်း, and ငင်းငင်း, *adv.* dealing in ready money, making immediate payment, opposed to အကြွေးစောင်း, on credit, *see* လက်ငင်း.

ငင်း, (1) *v.* to desire, long for, ငတ် ။ ငံ, (seldom used as a simple verb.)

ငင်း, (2) a contraction of ကောင်း.

ငင်းငင်းငံငံ, *adv.* see ငံငံ.

ငင့်, *v.* to pull, draw, to draw out, spin; see ငင်.

ငရိုင်ရင်, *n.* a kind of tree.

ငဆ, *int.* sirrah! you blockhead! (*obsolete.*)

ငထိုး, *int.* do. ငချွန်, do. ငပေါ, do.

ငတ်, *v.* to be hungry, or thirsty, be in want of food, စာ ။ မွတ် ။ ဆိပ်.

ငန်, *v.* to be salt.

ငန်း, (1) *n.* a goose.

ငန်း, (2) *n.* a kind of serpent, မြွေငန်း.

ငန်း, (3) *n.* a kind of violent fever, ငန်းဖျား.

ငန်း, (4) *n.* lust, desire.

ငန်းပြား, *n.* a broad spade, တူရွင်းပြား.

ငန်ငန်, (from ငန်, to be salt,) *adj.* saltish.

ငသီ, *n.* a kind of sea-weed.

ငပုတ်, *n.* the Nat who is said to occasion eclipses; see အသုရိန်.

ငြုတ်, *n.* a kind of cucumber.

ငမြိရင်, *n.* a kind of tree.

ငင်ငင်, *adv.* with longing desire, longing for, ငင်းငင်းငန်းငန်း.

ငင်လွှားလွှား, *adv.* unsatisfied, disappointed in expectation.

ငပုန်းဆေး, *n.* a kind of tree.

ငန်း, *v.* to desire, long for, ငတ်. Hence အငန်းအကျူး, *see* အကျူးအငန်း.

ငန်းငေါက်, *v.* to be loud, violent, &c. *see* ငေါက်ငန်း.

ငမျှောက်တောင်, *n.* a kind of insect.

ငယ်, *v.* to be small.

ငယ်သား, *n.* a servant, subject.

ငရနင်း, *n.* a kind of tree.

ငရုံပတူ, *n.* a kind of tree.

ငရုတ်, *n.* the red pepper plant.

ငရုတ်မိုးမျှော်, *n.* a species of do.

ငရုတ်ကောင်း, *n.* black pepper.

ငရဲ, (1) *n.* a state of punishment; (2) hell, the infernal regions, ငရဲပြည်.—N. B. There are eight central hells, ranged one above the other, viz. သိဉ္ဇီး ၊ ကာလသုတ် ၊ သင်္ဃာတ ၊ ရောရုဝ ၊ မဟာရောရုဝ ၊ တပန ၊ မဟာတပန, and အဝီစိ; each of which is encompassed with sixteen inferior hells; eight are called ဥဿဒရက်; the four next, တင်ဘုတ်; the four next, လောကန္တရိ.

ငရဲအပြစ်, *n.* a damning sin, one that deserves hell.

ငရဲသား, *n.* an inhabitant of hell.

ငလျင်, *n.* Ngalyen, a fabulous being, supposed to occasion earthquakes.

ငလျင်လှုပ်, (from ငလျင်, and လှုပ်, to shake,) *n.* an earthquake.

ငဟစ်, *n.* the large brown heron.

ငံ, *v.* to be enough, sufficient, လောက်, လောဒ.

ငံ့, *v.* to delay, tarry, wait, wait for, စောင့် ၊ ဆိုင်းငံ့ ၊ ထင့်.

ငါ, *pers. n.* I, *mas.* or *fem.* (used in speaking to one's self, of one's self, and in addressing inferiors.)

ငါး, (1) *adj.* five (marked by the figure ၅, 5.)

ငါး, (2) *n.* a fish.

ငါးကြေး, *n.* the scales of fish.

ငါးချပ်, *n.* do.

ငါးဆူး, *n.* the fin of a fish.

ငါးဆူးတောင်, *n.* the back fin.

ငါးဆောင်, *n.* a kind of fish trap.

ငါးတောင်, *n.* a fin.

ငါးပါးဟက်, *n.* the gills.

ငါးပိ, *n.* a kind of cured fish.

ငါးဖားလောင်း, *n.* a tadpole.

ငါးမျှား, *n.* a fish hook.

ငါးမျှားတံ, *n.* a fishing rod.

ငါးမျှားသုတ်, *n.* do.

N. B. Varieties of fish are as follows.

ငါးဗုပ်ဖား.
ငါးဗုံထိုး.
ငါးကကတစ်.
ငါးကာကူရံ.
ငါးကာထပေါင်း.
ငါးကာတလူး.
ငါးကြေး, a fish resembling what is called the *pout* in America.
ငါးကျဲ.
ငါးကျောင်း.
ငါးကြင်း.
ငါးခုနီ.
ငါးခုံမ.

ငါးခူ.
ငါးချင်.
ငါးငိုက်.
ငါးစင်း, the mullet.
ငါးစင်းစပ်.
ငါးစင်းပျား.
ငါးစင်းခြင်း.
ငါးစည်ပူ.
ဝါးဆကာ.
ငါးတန်.
ငါးတောက်မ.
ငါးထန်းရွက်, the sole.
ငါးတွေ.
ငါးနူလန်း.

ငါးနောက်တွား.
ငါးနက်ပြာ.
ငါးဗတ်, the boile.
ငါးပါမောင်.
ငါးပါလဘဲ.
ငါးပုဋ္ဌ.
ငါးပုတတ်.
ငါးပူထင်း.
ငါးပဲပြူ.
ငါးပြင်းသက်.
ငါးပြေ.
ငါးပြေမ.
ငါးပြေထရက်.
ငါးဗန်းမ.
ငါးဖယ်.
ငါးဖယ်ဖောင်.
ငါးဗောင်နီး.
ငါးမြင်စဝ်.
ငါးမန်း, the shark.
ငါးမြဝိုး.
ငါးမြစ်ချင်း.
ငါးမြွေ.
ငါးရင်ပေါင်ဓား.
ငါးရံ့.
ငါးရှောင်.
ငါးရွှေ.
ငါးရှင့်.
ငါးရှဉ့်, the eel.
ငါးလပိ.
ငါးလူး.
ငါးသဲ.
ငါးဝတ်.
ငါးသားလိမ်.
ငါးသဲတိုး.
ငါးသို.
ငါးသိုင်း.
ငါးဟောက်.

ငု, *n.* a kind of tree, the Cassia Lignum.

ငုတ်, *v.* to dive, go beneath; to be swallowed up, be lost, disappear, မြုပ် ၊ ပျောက် ၊ ကွယ်. Hence အငုတ်, *n.* the remains of a thing, as သစ်ငုတ်, the stump of a tree; ဘုရားငုတ်, the ruins of a pagoda; အမွေအငုတ်, an inheritance.

ငုတ်ငုတ်, *adv.* continuingly, permanently, ကြာကြာ.

ငုတ်တုပ်, (1) *n.* a kind of plant.

ငုတ်တုပ်, (2) *adv.* just, merely, (prefixed to words of sitting and remaining.)

ငုပ်, *v.* see ငုတ်.

ငုံ, *v.* to inclose, cover, shut up, as in the mouth, or a flower bud; to include, comprise. Hence အငုံ, *n.* a flower bud.

ငုံး, *n.* a quail.

ငုံ့, *v.* (1) to stoop, bow down, ကုန်း ၊ ကုပ် ၊ ငိုက် ၊ ညွတ်.

ငုံ့, *v.* (2) to enter, penetrate, go in, ဝင် ၊ တိုး.

ငူ, *v.* to project, stick up, or out, protuberate, ငေါ. Hence အငူ, *n.* a promontory, cape, headland, အငူအငေါ.

ငူ, (2) *n.* a kind of bird.

ငေး, *v.* to be so intent on one object as to be insensible to another.

ငဲ့, (1) *v.* to lean, be inclined, tipped up, as a vessel to draw off liquor, စောင်း၊ တိမ်း၊ ယိမ်း.

ငဲ့, (2) *v.* to be inclined towards, (in mind,) be partial, have regard to; (*act.* ငြဲ့.)

ငဲ့ကွက်, *v.* to be partial, have regard to.

ငေါ, *v.* to project, stick up or out, ငူ၊ ပေါ်.

ငေါက်, (1) stick up, ငေါ၊ ငေါ့.

ငေါက်, (2) *v.* to use loud, violent language, in order to daunt and terrify, ငေါ်.

ငေါက်ငမ်း, *v.* to be loud, violent, &c.

ငေါက်ဆတ်, *v.* do.

ငေါင်း, *n.* an animal said to have but one leg.

ငေါ့, *v.* to stick up.

ငေါ်, *v.* to use loud, violent language, in order to daunt or terrify, ငေါက်.

ငို, *v.* to weep, cry.

ငိုကြွေး *v.* to weep, cry, မျက်ထမ်း.

ငိုယို, *v.* do.

ငိုချင်း, *n.* a funeral song.

ငိုက်, *v.* to nod through drowsiness, to hang down the head.

ငိုက်မျဉ်း, *v.* do.

ငိုက်စိုက်, *adv.* hanging down the head.

ငြင်း, *v.* to contradict; to refuse to do.

ငြင်းခုံ, *v.* do.

ငြင်းဆန်, *v.* do.

ငြမ်း, *n.* scaffolding; scaffolding made of bamboos, for the purpose of ascending pagodas, &c.

ငြား, (1) *v.* to meet with, find, ကြုံ၊ တွေ့.

ငြား, (2) *euph. affix.*

ငြိမ်, *v.* to be still, unmoved, composed, quiet, တည်ငြိမ်.

ငြိမ်ဆိမ်, *v.* to be still, unmoved, quiet, composed.

ငြိမ်ဝပ်, *v.* do.

ငြိမ်သက်, *v.* do.

ငြိမ်း, *v.* to be free from troubles, comfortable, happy, ချမ်း၊ သက်သာ.

ငြိမ့်. *v.* to be soft, gentle, pleasant, သာယာ.

ငြိမ့်ညောင်း, *v.* do.

ငြူ, *v.* to be envious, malevolent, act an envious part, မနာလို.

ငြောင့်, *n.* a sharp stump, a thorn.

ငွါး. *v.* to be large, great, high.

ငွါးငွါးဝါ, *v.* do.

ငွါးငွါးထက်, *v.* do.

ငွေ, *n.* silver.

ငွေကြေး, *n.* money.

ငွေခွဲ. *v.* to levy, as taxes.

ငွေမွှေ, *n.* silver alloyed from ten to ninety per cent. the surface of which has the appearance of needles or hair.

ငွေတောင်, *n.* do.

ငွေတိုးပွား, *v.* to be lucrative, profitable, to increase in riches.

ငွေတော်, *n.* arbitrary taxes ; see ဆနွှံ.

ငွေရင်း, *n.* stock, capital.

ငွေသက်ငင်း, *n.* ready money.

ငွေ့, *v.* to be gentle, moderate. Hence အငွေ့, *n.* vapour, exhalation, steam, smoke, အခိုး; a glimpse, shadow, slight touch, connection, &c. အရိပ်.

ငှ, *v.* to distribute, ဝေ ; (*neut. c.*)

ငှက်, *n.* a bird.

ငှက်ကာ, *n.* a kind of bird.

ငှက်ကူ, *n.* a kind of bird.

ငှက်ပါး, *n.* a blue jay.

ငှင်မြည်, *n.* a kind of bird.

ငှက်ဆင်, *n.* a turkey, ကြက်ဆင်.

ငှက်ဆိုး, *n.* a screech owl.

ငှက်တော်, *n.* a kind of bird.

ငှက်ဖြင်, *n.* a kind of bird.

ငှက်သိန်လူ, *n.* a kind of water fowl.

ငှက်ငုစား, *n.* a kind of tree.

ငှက်ငုရှိ, *n.* a kind of fungus or mushroom.

ငှက်ပျော, *n.* the plantain; of which there are many varieties, viz.

ငှက်ပျောချက်ကြီး, a kind having the extreme part of the top end large.

ငှက်ပျောငပွဲ, a large kind.

ငှက်ပျောငရမန်, a kind having an uneven, i. e. ridged surface.

ငှက်ပျောဆင်ဖံ, a large long kind, with a smooth surface.

ငှက်ပျောဆင်ဖွယ်, a long kind, smaller than ငှက်ပျောဆင်ဖံ.

ငှက်ပျောဆင်ပေါင်, a large kind of a dark colour.

ငှက်ပျောနံ့သာပူ, the plump, yellow, sweet kind.

ငှက်ပျောနီ, a small reddish kind.

ငှက်ပျောမင်း, a large, plump, sweet kind, (*literally*, the king of plantains.)

ငှက်ပျောမယ်တော်လက်ညှိုး, a long, slender, smooth kind.

ငှက်ပျောဖီးကြမ်း, the most common kind.

ငှက်ပျောရှိုင်.

ငှက်ပျောသီးမွှေး, the long, green, fragrant kind.

ငှက်ပျောသူငယ်စား.

ငှက်ပျောဟင်းသပတားနီ, the vermilion-coloured kind.

ငှက်ဖျား, *n.* a fever occasioned by change of place or climate, &c.

ငှက်မနား, (from ငှက်, a bird, and နား, to perch,) *n.* the name of a steeple or spire, (so called, because a bird cannot perch on it.)

ငှက်မနားခင်စား, (from ငှက်, a bird, မနားခင်, before perching, and စား, to eat,) *n.* a kind of plant.

ငှါ, (1) *n.* thing, property, ဟာ၊ ဥစ္စာ၊ ဝတ္ထု၊ အရာ.

ငှါ, (2) *affix*, for, in order to.

ငှါး, *v.* to borrow, to lend, to hire, to let, (when the article is to be returned;) *comp.* ချေး.

ငှါးရမ်း, *v.* do.

ငှဲ့, *v.* to incline, tip up, as a vessel, in order to draw off liquor, စောင်း; *neut.* ငဲ့.

ငှေါက်, *v.* to smell rank, as fish, flesh, and the like, ညှီ ၊ စော်နံ, (not used singly.)

ငှေါက်ညှီ, *v.* do. ညှီငှေါက်.

## စ.

The sixth consonant in the Burman alphabet, and the first in the class of palatals.

စ, (1) *euphonic affix.*

စ, (2) *v.* to begin, make a beginning, commencement, be first, ဦး. Hence အစ, *n.* a beginning, commencement, အဦး ၊ အစအန, *n.* do. စ, and စသည်, frequently signify, &c. and so forth. သည် is sometimes used for စသည်, after က or မှ ; in the first of the two clauses, when corresponding with တိုင်, တိုင်အောင်, &c. ; in the latter clause, as တောမှသည်မြို့တိုင်အောင်, for တောမှစသည်, &c. from the woods to the city.

စန, *v.* to commence, begin, be first.

စတင်, *v.* to be the first, begin, အစတင်.

စသတ်, *v.* to make an end of, finish, အစသတ် ၊ အဆုံးသတ်.

စပြတ်, *v.* to be spent, finished, gone, အစပြတ် ၊ ကုန်.

စွာ, *adv.* at first, formerly, အစွာ.

စဦးစွာ, *adv.* do. အစဦးစွာ.

စ, (3) *n.* a part, a bit, piece, အစ ; အစအန, *n.* do.

စစ, *adv.* sundrily, အစစ ; အစစအနန, *adv.* do.

စအို, (corrupted from ဝစ္စဒွါရ,) *n.* the anus, ဖင်.

စက်, (1) *v.* to sleep, take repose, (respectful, commonly applied to royal persons ;) *comp.* အိပ် and ကျိန်း.

စက်ငြိမ်, *v.* do.

စက်ဖြန်, *v.* do.

စက်ပျော်, *v.* do.

စက်တော်ခေါ်, *v.* to sleep, take repose, equivalent to စက်တော်မူ.

စက်ဆုပ်, *v.* to be disgusting, abominable, nauseating, as carrion, or stench, ရွံရှာ ; to be disgusted with, be afraid of.

စက်, (2) *v.* to make equal in weight, ချိန်စက်.

စက်, (3) *v.* to scratch off, by a sudden jerk of the finger-nail, made by compression against the thumb.

စက်, (4) *v.* to spread, be extended, go beyond, pass over, ကျူး၊ လွန်၊ ကူး.

စက်, (5) *v.* to make a dot, or spot, to stain; to drop, fall in drops, ပေါက်၊ စွန်း. Hence အစက်, *n.* a dot, spot, အကွက်၊ အစွန်း၊ အပေါက်; a drop, အပေါက်.

စက်လက်, *adv.* droppingly, as water, &c.

စက်, (6) (from စက္က, *Pali*, which is from စကြ, *Sungskrit*,) *n.* a wheel, any thing circular and turning on an axis, ဘီး; as the wheel of a carriage, လှည်းဘီး; the wheel of a pulley, စက်နား; the wheel of a mill, or any machine, ယန္တရားစက်; a spinning wheel, or any thing of the kind, ရစ်၊ ရဟတ်၊ ချား.

စက်, (7) *n.* a wheel-rocket, စက်မီး.

စက်, (8) *n.* the zodiac, ရာသီစက်.

စက်, (9) *n.* a circular missile weapon, ပသီစက်; a thunderbolt, (supposed to whirl round,) မိုးယံကြိုးစက်; any celestial or supernatural weapon, စက်ဝရိန်၊ နတ်စက်; *particularly* the fabulous Sekyah weapon, စက်ရတနာ; any weapon, လက်နက်.

စက်, (10) *n.* power, energy, force, တန်ခိုး၊ အစွန်း၊ အား; authority, empire, အာဏာ၊ အစိုးရချင်း.

စက်, (11) *n.* any thing indicating power or right, &c. a mark, sign, indication, accomplishment (of a place or person,) စက်လက္ခဏာ; *particularly*, the characteristic marks of a Boodh's foot, or the impress of do. ခြေတော်ရာ; the foot (of a king,) ခြေဖဝါးတော်; *comp.* ဖြန့်.

စက်, (12) *n.* a circle, which though not actually circumvolving, has a centre or axis, on which it was originally turned, စက်ဝန်း.

စက်, (13) *n.* certain charms made circular, and buried in the flesh, လူ့ဒွိမြှုပ်သောစက်.

စက်, (14) *n.* a circle or mark, set up as the object of a marksman's aim, ပြစ်သောစက်.

စက်, (15) *n.* a Sekyah system or world; *see* စကြဝဠာ.

စက္ကတုန်, *n.* the name of a tree.

စက္ကဝက်, *n.* a kind of bird, the ruddy goose, (Colebrooke.)

စက္ကူ, or စက်ကူ, *n.* paper.

စက္ခု, *n.* the eye, or sense of seeing, မျက်စိ.

စက်နှား, *n.* the wheel of a pulley.

စက်ဒီး, *n.* a wheel-rocket.

စက်လက္ခဏာ, *n.* see 11th definition of စက်.

စက်ဝန်း. *n.* see 12th definition of စက်.

စက်ဝရဇိန်, *n.* any celestial, or supernatural weapon.

စကား,.*n.* a word; words, language; a speech, saying.

စကားစမည်, *n.* do. do.

စကားအစ်, စကားထစ်, စကားပြစ်, စကားတော့, စကားထောက်, စကားခေါ်, and စကားဝယ်, *v.* to be indirect in speech, in order to make some discovery, or gain some end; to draw out, try, catch in conversation, ensnare, ချိတ် ၊ စောင်း ၊ ရိပ် ၊ ရိပ်ဖမ်းသိမ်ဖမ်းပြု.

စကားဆိမ့်ဖွဲ့, စကားဆိုးဖွဲ့, စကားဖောင်ဖွဲ့, *v.* to use many words, be loquacious, talkative, စကားများ.

စကားတုံ့, *n.* a reply, answer, အဖြေ.

စကားပြန်, (1) *v.* to translate, interpret; (2) *n.* a translator, interpreter.

စကားပုံ, *n.* a comparison, similitude.

စကားတော့, *v.* to resent an injury, demand satisfaction; (see တော့.)

စကားဖွက်, *n.* a riddle.

စကားလိမ်, *n.* a rebus, made by a transposition of letters.

စကော်စကား, *adv.* incomplete, wanting, unfinished, unattained.

စကြ, (*Sungskrit,*) *see* စက်, from the sixth definition throughout.

စကြလှံ, *n.* a kind of fabulous flying spear.

စကြမင်း, *n.* a sovereign of the four great islands which surround the Myenmo mount.

စကြဝတေ, *n.* do.

စကြဝဠာ (from ဝဠာ, a division, bounded part, ***Pali,***) *n.* a Sekyah world or system, comprizing a central Myenmo mount, the surrounding seas and islands, the celestial regions, including the circumvolving luminaries, and the infernal regions.—N. B. The universe is composed of an infinity of Sekyah worlds; (*comp.* ဝေဿ.)

စကြဝဠာတိုက်, *n.* do.

စကြဝဠာတောင်, *n.* the encircling mount, which bounds a Sekyah system.

စကြာ, *n.* a four-sided roof.

စင်, (1) *v.* to be cleared away, finished, ended, gone, ကုန်.

စင်ကြယ်, *v.* to be cleared away, finished, gone, ended; to be clean, pure, innocent.

စင်, (2) *v.* to be cleared from dirt, alloy, &c. be clean, pure, innocent, ကင်း ၊ ကွာ ၊ လွတ် ၊ ရှင်း ၊ ထန်.

စင်ပြု, *v.* to be clean, pure.

စင်, (3) *n.* a frame, case, ခုံ; a stage, as ပြစင် ၊ လင့်စင်.

စင်, (4) *adv.* even, (slightly emphatic,) ပင်.

စင်္ကြံ, (from စင်္ကမ, *Pali,*) *n.* a walk, place for walking, (*pron.* စင်ဂြံ.)

စင်္ကြံသွား, *v.* to walk to and fro.

စင်စစ်, *adv.* verily, truly, certainly, really, အကယ် ၊ အတည် ၊ အမှန် ၊ မချွတ်.

စင်တိုင်, *n.* see ကွန်းတိုင်.

စင်ပြွန်း, *n.* a kind of tree.

စင်း, (1) *v.* to be extended in a straight line, တန်း ၊ ဖြောင့်. Hence အစင်း, *n.* an extended line, a stripe, အတန်း.

စင်း, (2) *v.* to be uniform in conduct, consistent.

စင်း, (3) *num. affix,* as သင်္ဘောနှစ်စင်း, two ships, (see Gram.)

စင့်, *int. affix,* as သွားစင့်, does he go ?

စစ်, (1) *v.* to filter, strain, separate one part from another; to examine, investigate, scrutinize, စီစစ် ၊ မေးမြန်း; to be unadulterated, genuine, true, pure, စင် ၊ မှန်.

စစ်ကြော, *v.* do.

စစ်ဆေး, *v.* do.

စစ်တွက်, *v.* do.

စစ်, (2) *n.* war, a battle; an army.

စစ်မက်, *n.* do.

စစ်အင်္ဂါလေးပါး, *n.* an army composed of *four parts*, viz. ဆင်စီးသူရဲ, elephanteers; မြင်းစီးသူရဲ, horsemen, or cavalry; ခြေသည်သူရဲ, footmen, or infantry; ရထားစီးသူရဲ, charioteers.

စစ်ကဲ, *n.* a lieutenant-general.

စစ်ခင်း, *see* စစ်ဆင်.

စစ်ခံ, *v.* to receive battle.

စစ်ချီ, *v.* to march to battle.

စစ်စည်, *v.* to be particular in regard to expenses, be economical, ချွေတာ.

စစ်စလီ, *n.* a kind of water-fowl.

စစ်ဆင်, *v.* to set in array, prepare for engagement.

စစ်ဆီးစစ်ဆင်, *v.* do.

စစ္ဆေ, *n.* an apparition, spectre, ghost, ထဆေ.

စစ်တံဆာ, *n.* military dress, accoutrements; weapons, instruments of war, &c.

စစ်တုန်, *n.* a kind of tree.

စစ်တုရင်, *n.* chess.

စစ်တုရင်တက်, *n.* a check, (in chess.)

စစ်ထိုး, *v.* to fight, engage in battle.

စစ်တိုက်, *v.* do.

စစ်ဘုရင်, *n.* a generalissimo, ဗိုလ်မှူး, ဗိုလ်ချုပ်.

စစ်မြေပြင်, *n.* a field of battle.

စစ်ဝတ်စစ်စား, *n.* military baggage (in general.)

စစ်ဝတ်မျည်း, *n.* a short military coat.

စစ်သည်, *n.* a soldier.

စစ်သူခက်, *n.* do.

စစ်သူရဲ, *n.* do.

စစ်သိန်, *n.* a kind of tree.

စဆာ, *n.* curree, sauce, any thing eaten with rice to give it a relish; see စဲ.

စဆံ, *n.* a small wooden porch, in front of a pagoda, commonly containing an image, ဘုရားဦးစရပ်.

စည်, (1) *adv.* while, while yet.

စည်, (2) *v.* to be many, numerous, plentiful, ပေါ၊ ဖြိုးပွားများ.

စည်ကား, *v.* do.

စည်ထွန်, *v.* do.

စည်ပင်, *v.* do. (most common.)

စည်, (3) *n.* a cask; a drum, any musical instrument, တူရိယာ.

စည်ထုပ်, *n.* a kind of drum.

စည်သုံးပါး, *n.* song, dance, and instrumental music, ကချေ.

စည်ဝိုတ်, a kind of drum.

စည်သမား, *n.* a drummer.

စည်တီး, *n.* do.

စည်လက်ခတ်, *n.* a drumstick.

စည်လည်, *v.* to act the part of a bell-man or crier.

စည်တောင်း, *n.* the air-bladder of fish.

စဉ်, (1) *v.* to place in a continuous row, စီ. Hence အစဉ်, *n.* a succession, continuity ; order, method ; *adv.* continually, always. အစဉ်မပြတ်, *v.* to be perpetual, everlasting ; *adv.* for ever. အစဉ်တစိုက်, (from စိုက်,) *adv.* in continued succession, right on ; one after another.

စဉ်ကာစဉ်လာ, *adv.* in regular rows.

စဉ်, (2) *v.* to rebound, fly off or away, လွင့်.

စဉ်, (3) *v.* to be separated, put away, ကွာ.

စဉ်, (4) *v.* to be lost, gone, ပိတ်စဉ်.

စည်း, (1) *v.* to bind, tie together, ချည် ၊ နှောင် ၊ ဖွဲ့ ၊ တုပ်.

စည်း, (2) *v.* to collect, assemble, စု ၊ ရုံး.

စည်းကြပ်, *v.* to bind tight, ကြပ်စည်း.

စည်းစား, *v.* to consider, weigh a matter, ဆင်ခြင်.

စည်းဝေး, *v.* to collect, assemble.

စည်း, (3) *n.* a temporary hedge or fence, စောင်ရန်း.

စည်းကျုန်း, *n.* the ring which secures the shaft of a cart to the yoke, လှည်းဦးနွင်.

စည်းခို, *n.* one kind of pagoda ; (*comp.* စေတီ.)

စည်းစိမ်, *n.* wealth, prosperity, sovereignty ; a sovereign.

စည်းနေရာ, *n.* a certain seat of honour ; see စနည်.

စည်းနဲ, *v.* to be close, niggardly.

စဉ်း, (1) *v.* to chop, mince.

စဉ်းတောက်, *v.* do.

စဉ်းကော, *v.* to mince, for the purpose of eating.

စဉ်း, (2) *v.* to be slender, (applied to the waist, arms, &c.)

စဉ်း, (3) *n.* a steel-yard.

စဉ်းမှိန်, *n.* do.

စဉ်း, (4) *n.* the point or head of an arrow.

စဉ်းထွား, *n.* the point or head of an arrow.

စဉ်းငယ်, *adv.* little, အနဉ်းငယ်.

စဉ်းစား, *v.* to consider, ထင်ချင်.

စဉ်းလဲ, *v.* to use artifice, (in a bad sense ;) to deceive, လှည့်စား.

စဉ့်စဉ့်, (from စေ့,) *adv.* minutely, particularly.

စဉ့်, (1) *n.* the substance used in glazing ware, prepared from the dross of silver.

စဉ့်အိုး, *n.* a glazed pot or jar.

စဉ့်, (2) *n.* a circular built granary.

စတုဂါး, *n.* a kind of plant.

စတုတ္ထ, (from စတု, *four, Pali,*) *adj.* fourth.

စတုမဓူ, *n.* a compound of parched rice, honey, sugar, and treacle.

စတုမဟာရာဇ်, *n.* the first stage of the world of Nats, situated round the waist of the Myenmo mount.

စတုရန်း, *adj.* four-cornered.

စတွေး, (a corruption of တံတွေး,) *n.* spittle.

စနဉ်, *n.* a post of honour, or place of sitting in the royal presence, of which there are five degrees, viz. တော်ဝနေရာ ၊ ထူးနေရာ ၊ စဉ်းနေရာ ၊ အတွင်းသဝါး ၊ ပြင်ဘဝါး. Besides these are two others, viz. နေရာလွတ် and နေရာချွန်.

စနဉ်း, *n.* an ominous saying.

စနဉ်းဆဉ်, *n.* an explainer of ominous sayings.

စန္ဒ, (*Pali,*) *n.* the moon, လ.

စန္ဒကုမ္ဘာ, *n.* one division of the Boodhist scriptures.

စန္ဒကူး, *n.* the sanders tree, of which there are various sorts, viz. the red, the white, the yellow, the black, &c.

စန္ဒရကန်, (from စန္ဒ, the moon, *Pali,*) *n.* a glass, supposed to produce water from the rays of the moon ; (*comp.* သူရိယာကန်.)

စန္ဒာ, *n.* a certain instrument, carried in the processions at the funerals of the great.

စန္ဒူ, *n.* some kind of entrance or aperture in the palace.

စနေ, *n.* the planet Saturn ; the seventh day of the week, Saturday.

စနောင်စနင်, *adv.* all in tumultuous confusion, ကစီကရင်း ၊ ဗရွီးဗရင်း.

စန္ဒ, *n.* the moon.

စန္ဒကံ, *n.* a glass which produces water from the rays of the moon.

စန်း, (from စန္ဒ, *Pali,*) *n.* the moon, လ.

စန့်, *v.* to be straight, ဖြောင့်၊ စင်း.

စပ်, (1) *v.* to be hot, pungent, i. e. to have the quality which excites a hot or pungent sensation in the mouth or eyes, &c. ပူ ; to feel a hot or pungent sensation, to smart, ကျိန်း၊ ပူ.

စပ်, (2) *n.* a large wooden cage, used as a place of temporary confinement.

စပ်, (3) *v.* to join, unite, connect, ကပ်၊ တွဲ၊ ပူး၊ ရှက်၊ ရှုပ်၊ ဟပ်. Hence အစပ်, *n.* a joint, seam.

စပ်ကြား, *n.* an opening, intermediate space, a lane, pathway ; it is likewise applied to different zones or climates.

စပ်ဈား, *v.* to intercede, intercept.

စပ်စပ်, *adv.* (from စပ်, to join, unite,) smackingly.

စပ်စား, (1) *v.* to join, unite, connect.

စပ်စား, (2) *v.* to make enquiries, စပ်ထပ်၊ မေးမြန်း.

စပ်ဆို, *v.* to versify, string together.

စပ်တင်, *adj.* with raised sides, (applied to boats, carts, &c. as စပ်တင်လှေ၊ လှည်းစပ်တင်.)

စပ်နှံ့, *v.* to pervade, go through all the parts, diffuse throughout ; (*by corruption,* စိမ့်.)

စပ်ဖျဉ်းဖျဉ်း, *adv.* with a smile of contempt.

စပ်လျဉ်း, *v.* to be connected with, familiar.

စပ်သမား, *n.* a coffin-maker.

စပ်ဟပ်, (1) *v.* to join, unite, connect.

စပ်ဟပ်, (2) *v.* to make enquiries, မေးမြန်း.

စပါ, *n.* a kind of odoriferous substance mentioned in ancient writings.

စပါး, or ဓည, *n.* (1) any plant of the grass genus, in which sense there are said to be one hundred and two species.

စပါး, (2) *n.* any plant which bears esculent seeds, whether grain or pulse ; in which sense there are said to be seven kinds, viz. ထထေးစပါး၊ ကောက်စပါး၊ မုယောစပါး၊ လူး၊ ထတ်၊ ပြောင်း, and ပဲ.

စပါး, (3) *n.* the rice plant or grain, ကောက်.

စပါးကျီ, *n.* a granary.

စပါးကြီးမြွေ, *n.* a kind of snake.

စပါးခွံ, *n.* a husk or hull.

စပါးနှံ, *n.* an ear or spike of grain.

စပါးဖုံ, *n.* leaves which cover the ear.

စပါးဖျင်း, *n.* unsubstantial grain, an ear without grain or fruit.

စပါးလင်, *n.* lemon-grass.

စပျစ်, *n.* the grape vine.

စပျစ်နွယ်, *n.* do.

စပျစ်ရည်, *n.* wine.

စပွယ်, or စတွယ်, *part. affix*, see တွယ်.

စမ်း, (1) *v. affix imp.* or *prec.* (see Gram. *imp. mood.*)

စမ်း, (2) *v.* to feel, as with the hand; to use means to know or discover, to try, make trial of, စုံစမ်း; see Gram.

စမ်းသပ်, *v.* to feel, to stroke.

စမ်း, (3) *n.* a spring of water.

စမ်းရေ, *n.* spring-water.

စမာ, *n.* a water course.

စမုတ်, *n.* the covering or roof over a long passage or entrance way.

စမုတ်စပါး, *n.* henbane.

စမုန်, *n.* a plant, of which there are several kinds.

စမုန်နီ, *n.* cresses.

စမုန်ပြ, *n.* dill, a kind of plant.

စမဲ, *n.* sauce of any kind, or any thing eaten with rice to give a relish, ဟင်းလျာ.

စမဲစထာ, *n.* do.

စမ္ပ, *n.* Tsampa, a country, situate between Cambodia and Cochin China.

စမ္ပယ်, *v.* to enjoy, take delight in, be happy; *see* under စံ.

စမ္ပါယ်, *n.* a kind of flower-plant.

စမြင်းခေါ်သ, *n.* indurated fæces.

စဖြိတ်, *n.* a kind of plant.

စဖြိန်စထုပ်, *n.* a bag in which boiled rice is put.

စဖြောင်, *n.* a petty constable, peace-officer.

စဗွတ်, *n.* a kind of plant.

စရ, *(Pali,)* *v.* to do, perform.

စရည်, *n.* a kind of tree.

စရန်, *n.* a pledge, earnest, any thing given in advance.

စရနပ်, *v.* to mix together, assimilate by commixing.

စရပ်, *(pron.* ဇရပ်,) *n.* a building erected for public accommodation.

စရာ, (1) *part. affix,* denotes what is for any particular purpose, as စားစရာ, what is for eating, that is, victuals; ပြောဝံ့စရာ, what may be ventured to be spoken.

စရာ, (2) *n.* a short trumpet, နှဲတို.

စရိတ်, (1) *(pron.* ဇရိတ်, from စား, to eat, and ရိက္ခာ, provision,) *n.* provisions, necessaries of life, expenses of living, any expense.

စရိတ်စက, *n.* do.

စရိတ်, (2) *n.* shot.

စရိယ, *(Pali,)* *n.* a deed, အကျင့်.

စရုံဆိမ်, (from စား, ရုံ, and ဆိမ်,) *n.* a low room attached to the principal building, used to eat in, ထင်းကုပ်.

စရု, *n.* a kind of vine.

စရိုက်, *n.* custom, habit, way; see စာရိတ်.

စရုတ်, *n.* a tsaroot, measure of capacity, equal to two pyees, (ပြည်.)

စရွေ, *n.* a mortise.

စရွေပေါက်, *n.* do.

စလယ်, *n.* a tsalay, a measure of capacity equal to one-fourth part of a pyee, (ပြည်) ကိုန်းစား.

စသိ, or စသိသိ, *part. affix,* see ဘွယ်.

စလုပ်, *(pron.* ဇလုပ်,) (1) *n.* a cavity or basin, made by a fall of water.

စလုပ်, (2) *n.* a small vessel, junk.

စလုပ်, (3) *n.* the crop, or craw of a bird.

R

စလုံ, *n.* a bowl, with a foot.

စလုံး, (*a substitute for* အလုံး,) *adj.* all, the whole.

စလောင်း, *n.* the cover or lid of a vessel, အဖုံး၊ အဖိတ်.

စနှိ, *n.* a gouge.

စလွယ်, *n.* a thread of distinction, worn over the left shoulder and under the right arm; as the Brahminical thread, or the insignia of nobility used in Burmah.

စံ, (1) *v.* to enjoy, take delight in; to enjoy one's self, be happy, ပျော်မွေ့.

စံစား, *v.* do.

စံပယ်, or စွယ်, *v.* do.

စံပယ်တင်, *v.* to wear the upper garment over the left shoulder and under the right arm, လက်ဝဲတော့ထိုး.

စံ, (2) *n.* a sample, specimen, တန်း; a pattern, representation, ပုံ၊ သက်သေ.

စံ, (3) *n.* a custom, way, ထုံး၊ နည်း; a rule, precept, နည်း၊ ဥပဒေသ.

စံ, (4) *n.* standard gold.

စံခိုင်, *n.* a judge, or appraiser of gold.

စံကား, (*pron.* စကား,) *n.* the champa tree, bearing a yellow flower.

စံကော, (*pron.* စကော,) (1) *n.* a shallow, flat bottomed basket, used to separate grain of different qualities by shaking and tossing; *comp.* ပျာ.

စံကော, (2) *n.* a kind of tree.

စံပါ, *n.* the wood of the champa tree.

စံတို, *n.* see အတံ.

စမုန်နက်, *n.* the black cummin plant.

စံ, *int. affix,* as, သွားစံ, does he go?

စိမ့်, (*a corruption of* စိမ့်,) *v.* to pervade; see စိမ့်.

စာ, (1) *n.* a writing.

စာအုပ်, *n.* a book bound on the back.

စာကုံး, *v.* to write, compose.

စာကြည့်, *v.* to peruse, read to one's self.

စာချီ, (*pron.* စချီ,) *n.* a secretary.

စာချုပ်, *n.* an engagement, an obligatory writing, ချုပ်စာ.

စာချွန်, *n.* a governmental order, written on a pointed leaf.

စာစီ, *v.* to write, compose.

စာစွဲ, *v.* to lodge a complaint in writing.

စာထား, *v.* do.

စာဆိုတော်, *n.* a king's reader, rehearser.

စာညှင်, *n.* writing in letters, distinguished from ဂဏန်း, figures.

စာတုမဟာရာဇ်, *n.* one state of Nats, နတ်ဘုံ.

စာထင်ခုံ, *n.* a study-table.

စာပြင်, *n.* an open, or light, verandah; place to read in.

စာရင်း, *n.* a record, account.

စာရေး, *n.* a writer, scribe.

စာရေးတံပြု, *v.* to cast lots, မဲချ.

စာရေးတံဆွဲ, *v.* do.

စာလုံး, *n.* a letter of the alphabet, အက္ခရာ.

စာ, (2) *n.* a sparrow, of which there are various kinds.

စာခထော, *n.* a small kind of sparrow.

စာပေါင်းသောင်း, *n.* one that makes a hanging nest.

စာဝတီး, *n.* do.

စာသင်ကန်း, *n.* a yellow sparrow.

စာ, (3) *v.* to consider, have regard to, feel for, pity, ထောက်၊ ချင့်၊ ထောက် ၊ ညှာတာ ၊ သနား.

စာနာ, *v.* do. *(most common.)*

စာဂ, *(Pali,)* *n.* charity, almsgiving, စွန့်ကြဲချင်း.

စာစာ, or တစာစာ, *adv.* without intermission, မပြတ်, (applied to words of sound.)

စာတ်, *n.* the influence of certain days, &c. on one's future destiny, စုတ်.

စာမရီ, *n.* a kind of beast.

စာရိတ်, (from စရိတ္တ, *Pali,)* *n.* custom, habit, way, အလေ့အကျက်, (commonly written, စရိုက်.)

စာယို, *n.* see စအို.

စာရိတ္တ, *(Pali,)* *n.* a deed.

စား, (1) *v.* to eat.

စား, (2) *v.* to divide (in arithmetic,) ascertain how many times one number is contained in another, ကုတ်.

စားကျက်, *n.* a wonted feeding place, as a pasture, trough, &c.

စားကျေး, *n.* a ruler of a province.

စားကြူးသောသူ, *n.* a glutton.

စားကြွင်း, *n.* leavings after eating, orts, စားနှုပ်စားပေါက်.

စားကြွင်းစား, *n.* one that lives on orts, or fragments.

စားခန်း, (*pron.* စခန်း,) *n.* a stage, resting place, place of refreshment, cantonments, စားခန်းစားနား.

စားခန်းထောက်, *n.* do.

စားခန်းထောက်ချ, *v.* to encamp.

စားခန်းချ, *v.* do.

စားတော်ကဲ, *n.* a king's cook.

စားတော်ခေါ်, *v.* to eat, applied to great personages, equivalent to စားတော်မူ.

စားနပ်, *n.* food, eatables.

စားနှုပ်စားပွဲ, *n.* fragments, bits of food, orts, leavings of the table, စားကြွင်း.

စားနှုပ်စားပေါက်, *n.* do.

စားပန်း, *n.* a piece of mat-work, used for a plate.

စားရိုးနင့်, *v.* to be satiated, sick with repletion.

စားပွဲ, (*pron.* စပွဲ,) *n.* a table, eating board.

စပွဲထင်, or စားပွဲထင်ခုံ, *n.* do.

စားဖို, (*pron.* စဖို,) *n.* a hearth, fire-place, cooking-place; *comp.* ဖို.

စားဖိုဆောင်, a cook-house.

စားဖိုသည်, *n.* a cook, စိုးသူကြီး.

စားဖွယ်, *n.* eatables, ခဲဖွယ်.

စားမြိန်စာ, *n.* relishing food; any food.

စားမြုံ့, *n.* the cud, (from မြုံ့, *v.* to chew.)

စားမြုံ့ပွတ်, *v.* to chew the cud.

စားမြုံ့ပြန်, or စားမြုံ့တေ့, *v.* do.

စားဝင်, *n.* the throat, or gullet.

စိစစ်, *v.* to be discriminating, particular, exact; to scrutinize, မေးမြန်း ၊ စစ်ကြော.

စိစိ, *adv.* strictly, tightly, firmly, ကြပ်ကြပ်.

**စိတ်**, (1) *v.* to divide lengthwise or crosswise, separate, sever, ပိုင်း ၊ ခွဲချိုး ; to divide into four parts. Hence အစိတ်, *n.* a division, part, a quarter.

**စိတ်**, (2) *n.* a tsike, a measure of capacity, equal to a quarter of a ten, (တင်း,) or two tsaroots, (စလွတ်.)

**စိတ်**, (3) (from စိတ္တ, *Pali,*) *n.* mind, နှလုံး ; soul, ဝိညာဉ် ; spirit, နံ.

**စိတ်နှလုံး**, *n.* mind.

**စိတ်ခံ**, *v.* to endure anger or malice without expressing it, to bear malice, ငုံ.

**စိတ်**, *v.* (4) *affix*, expressing willingness.

**စိတ်ချဉ်**, *n.* a kind of tree.

**စိတ်စိတ်**, *adv.* gently, moderately.

**စိတ်စွဲ**, *n.* to attract the mind, to have the mind set on any object.

**စိတ်ငဲ့ကွက်**, *v.* to be biassed in mind, be partial to.

**စိတ်ဆိုး**, *v.* to be angry, အမျက်ထွက်.

**စိတ်ထန်း**, *v.* to have the mind set on an object, စိတ်စွဲ.

**စိတ်တို**, *v.* to be easily offended, irritable.

**စိတ်ထား**, *v.* to be obstinate, determined (in a good or bad sense.)

**စိတ်တားခံ**, see စိတ်ခံ.

**စိတ်မာ**, *v.* to be obstinate, stiff-necked, untractable.

**စိတ်ရှည်**, *v.* to be longsuffering, forbearing, slow to anger.

**စိတ်ရှုပ်**, *v.* to be confused, troubled, perplexed in mind.

**စိတ္တက္ခဏ**, (from စိတ္တ, mind, and ခဏ, a moment, time being, *Pali,*) *n.* a certain state of mind or thought, either commencing, continuing, or terminating ; *see* ဥပါဒက္ခဏ ၊ ဌိတိက္ခဏ ၊ ဘင်္ဂက္ခဏ.

**စိတ္တဇ**, (from စိတ္တ, mind, and ဇ, to be or produce, *Pali,*) *adj.* caused by mind.

**စိတ္တုပ္ပါဒ်**, (from စိတ္တ, mind, and ဥပ္ပဇ္ဇိ, to be, *Pali,*) *n.* the exercise of mind, thought.

**စိန်**, (1) *n.* a diamond.

**စိန်**, (2) *n.* a blunderbuss, swivel.

**စိန်ပြောင်း**, *n.* do. (most common.)

**စိန္နပဋ်**, *n.* Madras.

**စိန်တင်ပေါ်**, *n.* a kind of plant.

စိန်ခေါင်, *n.* an ornament, or badge of rank, worn around the forehead. *Also,* a certain ornament or decoration in architecture.

စိန်ပန်း, *n.* a kind of vine.

စိန်ပွင့်, ငိန်ဖြန်, ဧနှုး, *n.* certain parts of the ornamental work of a spire or steeple.

စိပ်, (1) *v.* to be close together, crowded—opposed to ကျဲ.

စိပ်, (2) *v.* to count beads, while performing religious duties, ပုတီးစိပ်; to repeat a number of formula, in order to preserve it in memory, မန္တန်စိပ်; *comp.* ငုပ်.

စိပ်, (3) *v.* to be accurate, exact, nice.

စိပ်ပုတီး, *n.* a rosary, string of beads used to keep count while performing religious duties.

စိပ်စိပ်, *adv.* intently, စိမ်းစိမ်း.

စိမ်, *v.* to steep, soak in liquor; to imbue.

စိမ်စိမ်ဖြေဖြေ, *adv.* moderately, slowly, စိမ့်စိမ့်လေးလေး.

စိမ်း, (1) *v.* to be green, of a green colour; to be green, unripe, immature, မမှည့် ၊ မရင့်.

စိမ်း, (2) *v.* to be raw, not cooked, မကျက် ၊ မနပ်. Hence အစိမ်းစား, *adj.* not requiring to be cooked in order to be eaten; အစိမ်းစားထောပတ်, *n.* butter.

စိမ်း, (3) *v.* to be fresh, handsome, လတ် ၊ လန်း.

စိမ်း, (4) *v.* to be unacquainted, not familiar, not versed; to be a "fresh," or "raw hand," မကျက် ၊ မကျွမ်း ၊ မလေ့မလာ.

စိမ်းကား, *v.* to be destitute of natural affection.

စိမ်းစိမ်း, *adv.* intently, steadily, perseveringly.

စိမ်းညို, *v.* to be of a green colour.

စိမ်းပတ်, *v.* do.

စိမ်းမြ, *v.* do.

စိမ်းလဲ့, *v.* to be of a bright green.

စိမ့်, (1) (compounded of စေ, and အံ,) *causal affix,* as သွားစိမ့်, will cause to go.

စိမ့်သော်ငှါ, *v. affix,* in order to cause, as သွားစိမ့်သော်ငှါ, in order to cause to go.

စိမ့်, (2) *v.* to ooze out, leak; to ooze into, penetrate, ယို.

စိမ့်, (3) *n.* a marsh, swamp, fen.

စိမ့်ဆိ, *v.* to ooze, &c.

စိမ့်ရေ, *n.* spring-water.

စိမ့်စိမ့်, *adv.* moderately, slowly.

စိမ့်စိမ့်လေးလေး, *adv.* do. စိမ့်စိမ့်ဖြေဖြေ, do.

စီ, (1) *v.* to place in order, in a continuous row, စဉ်; to arrange, put in order, ကျင်းဆင်; to direct, order, ခွဲခန့်.

စီချယ်, *v.* to variegate, diversify, ချယ်.

စီထား, *v.* to place in a continuous row; to arrange, put in order.

စီရင်, *v.* to direct, order, ခွဲခန့်; to do, perform, make, လုပ် ၊ ဖန်ဆင်း; to decide, pass sentence, ဆုံးဖြတ်.

စီမံ, *v.* do.

စီလျော်, *v.* to be regular, even, ညီညွတ်; to be proper, suitable, harmonious, agreeable, ဖွယ်ရာ ၊ လျောက်ပတ် ၊ ပြေပြစ်.

စီရရီ, *adv.* in due order, orderly, harmoniously, handsomely; numerously.

စီ, (2) *adv.* each, a piece, as တယောက်စီ, each one; ကိုယ်စီ, each person; တခုစီ, each thing, one a piece.

စီကျက်, *v.* to be noisy—less than ဆူကျက်.

စီညံ, *v.* do.

စီလောင်, *v.* do.

စီး, (1) *v.* to be mounted on, (any vehicle, animate or inanimate,) to ride on; to possess, as a spirit.

စီးနင်း, *v.* do.

စီး, (2) *num. affix*, as မြင်းနှစ်စီး, two horses; (see Gram.)

စီး, (3) *v.* to flow, run in a stream.

စီးမျော, *v.* to float down or along.

စီးဆင်း, *v.* to flow, run as water.

စီး, (4) *v.* to increase, augment, (*neut.*) တိုး ၊ ပွါး.

စီးပွါး, (1) *v.* to increase, augment.

စီးပွါး, (2) *n.* increase, profit, advantage, အကျိုး ၊ အမြတ်.

စီးဖြန်း, *v.* to repeat mentally or vocally, သရဇ္ဈာယ်.

စု, *v.* to collect, assemble, စည်း ၊ ရုံး.

စုဆောင်း, *v.* to collect together, (applied to things,) ဆောင်းစု.

စုညီရာ, *n.* a place of arbitration, where the parties are confronted, စုံရာ.

စုရုံး, *v.* to gather together; to collect.

စုဝေး, *v.* to call together, assemble, as people, စည်းဝေး. Hence အစု, *n.* a collection, or whole, အပေါင်း; (frequently drops the အ.) Hence, *also*, အစုခွဲကျွန်, *n.* a slave that is redeemable, (ရွေးနိုင်,) but has no other rights.

စုတ်, (1) *v.* to be torn, rent; to be disordered, confused, tangled, frizzled, shaggy, (*act.* ဆုတ်.)

စုတ်ဖွား, *v.* to be disordered, &c. as the hair of a shaggy dog.

စုတ်, (2) *v.* to suck with the mouth; to draw, as a pump; to suck in, absorb.

စုတ်, (3) *n.* a hair-pencil, a painting brush, a Chinese pen, a reed, a grass-pen, a sharp tatooing-iron.

စုတ်, (4) *n.* the influence of certain days, &c. on one's destiny, ဇာတ်, (an astrological term.)

စုတေ, (from စုတိ, *Pali,*) *v.* to remove, depart, die, ရွေ့ ၊ သေ.

စုတ်ခနဲ, *adv.* suddenly, instantaneously, ပြတ်ခနဲ ၊ ယုတ်ခနဲ.

စုတ်ချည်း, *adv.* do.

စုတ်စုတ်, *adv.* do. *also*, an intensive to words of sourness.

စုတ်စုတ်ငေါ့ငေါ့, *adv.* protrusively, (applied to the lips,) poutingly.

စုန်, *v.* to go down (a river;) to go before (the wind)—opposed to ဆန်.

စုပ်, *v.* to charm, infuse virtue into by repeating a muntra, မန်း ၊ မန္တန်စုပ်.

စုင်နှ, *v.* to be disrespectful, မရိုမသေပြု.

စုလစ်, *n.* small ornamental spires, summits, elevations, &c. on the roof or steeple of royal or sacred buildings, including ဒုရင် ၊ မှန်ကင်း. &c. ပွန်းဆွန်း ၊ ပွန်းပေါင်း.

စုလျား, *n.* a garment, worn by men over the shoulders, an upper garment; *comp.* တပက်.

စုံ, (1) *v.* to be double, form a pair, be even; to be complete, ပေး ၊ ပြည့်. Hence အစုံ, *n.* an even number, a pair, a collection, a whole, အစု ၊ အပေါင်း. Hence, also, အလုံးစုံ, and ပစ်သိမ်းစုံ, which see.

စုံ, *v.* to be complete.
စုံစီ, *v.* do.
စုံလင်, *v.* do.
စုံညီ, *v.* to be even, complete, &c. see စုံ.
စုံရာ, *n.* a place of arbitration, where the parties are confronted, စုညီရာ.
စုံဖက်, *n.* a partner, အပေါင်းဖက်.
စုံ, (2) *n.* a grove, wood, wilderness, ဝိုင် ၊ မြိုင် ၊ ရုံ.
စုံစမ်း, *v.* to try, make trial of, scrutinize, စမ်း ၊ စူးစမ်း.
စုံမက်, or စုမက်, (1) *v.* to like, ကြိုက်; to love, esteem, ချစ်; to be pleased with, နှစ်သက်; (2) *v.* to grudge, be unwilling to part with, နှမြော; (3) *v.* to feel for, pity, ကြင်နာ ၊ သနား.
စုံမြိုင်, *n.* a grove, wood, wilderness.
စုန်း, *n.* a conjurer.
စုန်းမ, *n.* a witch.
စုံစုံ, *adv.* completely, fully, အကုန်.
စုံ, *v.* to raise up (in a heap,) plump up, swell up, ကြွ ၊ ပုံ ၊ .ဖို.
စူ, (1) *v.* to be tapering, projecting in a point, ချွန်း.
စူ, (2) *v.* to set up on end, ထောင်, (provincial.)
စုဖာ, *v.* to patch, mend, repair by patching.
စူလာနှဟာ, *n.* a kind of plant.
စူလာ့ဗိတ်, *n.* a kind of plant.
စူဠာ, *n.* a constellation ; (see တာရာ.)
စူး, *v.* to prick, pierce ; *n.* a piercer, awl, punch.
စူးစမ်း. *v.* to try, make trial of ; see စုံစမ်း.
စူးစူး, (1) *adv.* straight forward, direct, တည့်တည့် ၊ တူရူ ၊ ရှေ့ရှူ.
စူးစူး, (2) *int.* away ! right on ! (used in setting on dogs.)
စူးတိုက်, *v.* to set on (as dogs ;) to provoke a quarrel, ရန်တိုက်.
စူးဝင်, *v.* to pierce, penetrate.
စေ, (1) *v.* to send, send away, လွှတ်.
စေ, (2) *v.* to commission, order, command, ခန့် ၊ ခိုင်း.
စေဆော်, *v.* to excite to action, stimulate, quicken.
စေစား, *v.* to commission, order, direct, command.
စေပါ, *v.* do.
စေပါခံ, *v.* to serve, obey. Hence အစေခံ, and အစေအပါ, *n.* a servant.

စေ, (3) *v. affix,* causative, as ပြုစေသည်, to cause to do.

စေအောင်, *v. affix,* in order to cause, as ပြုစေအောင်, in order to cause to do, or that (he) might cause to do.

စေကောင်းပြီ, *v. affix,* as ပြုစေကောင်းပြီ, may have caused to do, or probably has caused to do.

စေခလို, *v. affix; prec. mood,* as သွားစေခလို, may he go, let him go.

စေတနာ, *(Pali,)* (1) *n.* a union or accordance of mind with an object, inclination, motive, စေဆော်ချင်း.

စေတနာ, *n.* (2) good-will, kindness, benevolence, ကြည်ညိုချင်း.

စေတသိတ်, (from စေတ, mind, and ဿုတ, to be connected, ***Pali,)*** ***n.*** exercise of mind, thought, feeling.

စေတီ, *(Pali,)* *n.* a monument erected to a Boodh, a Sub-boodh, or a Rahandah, ပုထိုး ၊ ဘုရား.—**N. B. Those erected to Gaudama, the last Boodh, are the only extant.**

စေတိုင်, *n.* see ကျေးစည်တိုင်.

စေသတည်း, or စေသော, *v. affix,* sign of the precative mood, as သွားစေသော, may he go? or, let him go.

စေပြီးလျှင်, *v. affix,* having caused, as ပြုစေပြီးလျှင်, having caused to do.

စေး, (*commonly pron.* စည်း,) (1) *v.* to stick, adhere, ကပ်. Hence အစေး, *n.* gum, any glutinous matter.

စေး, (2) *v.* to grudge, be loth to part with, be close, niggardly, ချူချာ ၊ နှမြော ၊ ဝန်တို.

စေးနဲ, *v.* to grudge, &c.

စေးခြုံ, *v.* to cover, overspread, as with clothes; see ခြုံ.

စေးနဲ, *n.* a kind of tree.

စေးပျစ်, *v.* to be close, thick (as a wood,) ထူထပ်.

စေးမဒန်း, *n.* a kind of tree.

စေ့, (1) *v.* to join by a perfect union of parts, စေ့စပ်.

စေ့, (2) *v.* to unite, reconcile, bring together, အောင်သို.

စေ့, (3) *v.* to be nice, accurate, finished, သေချာ.

စေ့, (4) *v.* to be complete, ကုံ ၊ ကုံလင် ၊ ပြည့်စုံ.

စေ့, (5) *v.* to be diffused throughout, နှံ့ ၊ နှံ့စပ်.

စေ့ကြပ်, *v.* to be close, thick, crowded.

စေ့င, *v.* to be complete.

စေ့ငု, *v.* do.

စေ့စပ်, (1) *v.* to reconcile, bring together, unite in mind.

စေ့စပ်, (2) *v.* to be nice, finished, accurate, complete, particular, exact, scrupulous.

စေ့စပ်, (3) *v.* to be close, thick, crowded.

စေ့စပ်, (4) *v.* to solder, join by metallic cement ; to be joined by a perfect union of parts.

စေ့စပ်, (5) *v.* to be diffused throughout, or through all the parts.

စေ့ဆော်, (1) *v.* to solder, join by metallic cement, ဆော်.

စေ့ဆော်, (2) *v.* to reconcile, bring together, unite in mind, စေ့စပ်.

စေ့ဆို, *v.* do.

စေ့ပွတ်, *v.* to be nice, particular, exact, scrupulous.

စေ့ငှ, *adj.* various.

စေ့ပြ့, *v.* to be nice, accurate, finished, complete.

စဲ, *v.* to cease, stop, break off.

စဲနုံး, *n.* a sand-bank ; see သဲနုံး.

စဲ, *n.* a circular granary, ကျီ.

စော, (1) *v.* to be early. Hence အစော, *adv.* early, and အစောကြီး, very early.

စောစော, *adv.* very early.

စောစောကြီး, *adv.* do.

စော, (2) *n.* a title prefixed to proper names, *indicative of respect ;* but in conversation, is commonly ironical.

စောက်, (1) *v.* to be steep, whether deep, (နက်,) or high, (မြင့်.) Hence အစောက်, (sometimes စောက်,) *n.* steepness, depth, height.

စောက်, (2) *n.* female genitals, (vulgar,) ရှုဗွိဆိုင် ၊ ရှုဗွိဆော.

စောက်ပတ်, or စောက်ပုတ်, *n.* do.

စောက်စေ့, *n.* the nymphæ clitoris.

စောက်ဖို, *n.* an enlargement of do.

စောက်ထင်း, *n.* a term of abuse.

စောက်, (3) *v. affix,* sign of the *poten. mood,* as သွားစောက်, he can go.

စောက်ထိုး, *adv.* with the head down, upside down, topsy-turvy, ဦးစောက် ၊ လင်းပြန်.

စောက်ထိုးကျ, *v.* to fall headlong.

စောကြော, *v.* to enquire, investigate ; to criminate, find fault with ; see စောဒနာ.

စောင်, (1) *v.* to lay by for future or occasional use, သိမ်း.

စောင်, (2) *v.* to be waiting to engage in fight, to be on the point of engaging, (as two cocks.)

စောင်, (3) *n.* a sheet, a large loose covering of cotton or silk wove in a separate piece.

စောင်ချမ်း, *n.* a bit of a pot, အိုးချမ်း.

စောင်ရန်း, *n.* a temporary hedge or fence, စည်း.

စောင်ရှား, (*pron.* စောင်ရား,) *n.* the cringe tree.

စောင်း, (1) *v.* to incline, set obliquely, lay on one side, look obliquely, ငဲ့.

စောင်း, (2) *v.* to use artful or indirect language or management, in order to injure another ; *comp.* ရိပ်, and ချိတ်.

စောင်းမြောင်း, *v.* do. (*most common.*)

စောင်းပင်း, *v.* do.

စောင်း, (3) *n.* a lute or harp.

စောင်းကောက်, *n.* a curved do.

စောင်းတန်း, *n.* steps, stairs, လှေကား, (commonly appropriated to the high steps of pagodas.)

စောင်းဖိ, (from အစောင်း, a side, and ဖိ, to press,) *adv.* lying on one side.

စောင်းမာန်, *n.* pride ; *see* မာန်.

စောင့်, (1) *v.* to delay, tarry, wait for, ငံ့ ၊ ဆိုင်း ၊ ဖင့် ၊ လင့်.

စောင့်, (2) *v.* to watch, keep watch, as a sentinel ; to watch over, take care of, protect, ထိန်း.

စောင့်ကြပ်, *v.* to superintend.

စောင့်စည်း, *v.* to beware, shun, ကြဉ်ရှောင်.

စောင့်မ, *v.* to take care of, attend upon, ထိန်း ; to aid, assist, မစ.

စောင့်ရှောက်, *v.* to watch over, protect.

စောဒနာ, (1) *v.* to enquire, question, examine, investigate, မေးမြန်း ၊ ဆေးမေး.

စောဒနာ, (2) *v.* to find fault with, criminate, အပြစ်ထင်.

စော်, *v.* to smell offensively, နံ.

စော်ကား, *v.* to behave without regard to the feelings of others, be rude, insolent, ရိုင်းကား.

စော်ကဲ, *n.* a hereditary chief or prince, subject to a more powerful sovereign, (appropriated to the chiefs of several tribes in the Burman empire.)

စော်ဘွား, *n.* do. (appropriated to the Siamese princes, who do homage to the Burman monarch.)

စို, *v.* to be wet, moist, စွတ် ၊ ရွှမ်း; to be fresh, green, flourishing, စိမ်း ၊ ရွှန်း ၊ လန်း; to be abundant, ဖြိုး ၊ ပြည့်ဖြိုး; to be beautiful, လှ.

စိုဟန်း, *v.* do. do.

စိုက်, (1) *v.* to be erect, မတ်; to be direct, straight forward in looks or motion (*comp.* ငုံ့ ၊ တူရူ ၊ ငေးရူ;) or to look straight forward, in the direction of the face, though downwards; to erect, set upright, as a post, ထူ ၊ ထောင်; to set, plant, as trees or plants, ပျိုး; to sow, as seeds, ကြဲ.

စိုက်ပျိုးလုပ်, *n.* husbandry.

စိုက်, (2) *v.* to act instead of, to substitute, employ instead of, အစားစိုက်.

စိုက်, (3) *v.* to advance, pay in advance, နှိုက်ထုတ်.

စိုက်ကြဲ, *v.* to scatter, or sow, as grain.

စိုက်ချည်း, *adv.* directly, immediately, ဖြိုက်ချည်း.

စိုက်ထုတ်, *v.* to advance, pay in advance.

စိုင်, (1) *v.* to adhere together, be compact, consolidate, တွေ. Hence အစိုင်, *n.* a lump, any adhesive mass.

စိုင်, (2) *n.* a kind of wild cow.

စိုင်ကျော့, *adj.* of a bay colour (applied to horses.)

စိုင်း, *v.* to drive fast (in riding.)

စိုင်းနှင်, *v.* do.

စိုင်းပြင်း, *v.* to deliberate (what to do,) make a calculation; ချိန်ဆယ်.

စိုး, (1) *v.* to preside over, rule, have dominion, အုပ်ချုပ် ၊ စိုင်; to be chief, superior, ကဲ ၊ ဦး ၊ မြတ်.

စိုးမြန်း, *v.* do. do. Hence အစိုးရ, *v.* to be master of, have authority over, govern, rule.

စိုး, (2) *v.* to be concerned, anxious, troubled about, fear, ကြောင့်ကြ.

စိုး, (3) *v.* to enjoy, possess.

စိုးနှောင့်, *v.* to be concerned, anxious, troubled about, fear.

စိုးရိမ်, *v.* do. (most common.)

စိုးစဉ်း, *adv.* a little, အနည်းငယ် ၊ စဉ်းငယ် ၊ တစိုးတစိ.

စိုးလို့, *affix*, lest, for fear that, စိုးသောကြောင့်.

စို့, (1) *v.* to suck, as an infant, စုပ်.

စို့, (2) *v.* to go a little beyond the mark, ပျို.

စို့, (3) a rainbow, so called when it appears in the west, (*comp.* သက်တံ;) a broken part of a rainbow.

စို့, (4) *n.* a sharp peg, a punch, a short chisel used in cutting money, (from တံစို့.)

စို့, (4) } 
စို့အံ့, } *v. affix*, 1*st pers. plur. imp.* as သွားစို့, let us go.

စွ, *v. affix*, indeed, (generally connected to the root by a euphonic affix,) as ကြီးလေစွ, it is great indeed.

စွက်, *v.* to add, superadd, ဆောင်း.

စွက်စွက်, or စွက်ခနဲ, or စွက်ချည်း, *adv. indicative of the sound made by a sudden dash in water.*

စွင့်, *v.* to be erect, to stick up, ထောင်; to be high, မြင့်.

စွင့်ယှန်း, *v.* do.

စွတ်, *v.* to be wet, moist, စို.

စွတ်ယှန်း, *v.* do.

စွတ်စွတ်, *adv. intensive to words of colour.*

စွတ်ပလွတ်, *n.* a kind of tree.

စွန်, (1) *v.* see စွန်း, to be the end of, &c.

စွန်, (2) *v.* to have a painful sore on the eyelid, မျက်စိစွန်.

စွန်, (3) *n.* a kite, (bird of prey;) a kite, (of paper.)

စွန်ထောင်ဆွဲ, *v.* to pull up, (as the corner or side of a garment.)

စွန်ပလွံ, *n.* the date tree.

စွန်လက်သဲ, *n.* a kind of vine.

စွန်း, (1) *v.* to stain, be stained, spotted.

စွန်း, (2) *v.* to desire, lust after, covet, ထပ် ၊ မက်.

စွန်းမက်, *v.* do.

စွန်း, (3) *v.* to be in advance, foremost, ဦး; to be the end or extreme part of a thing, စွန်. Hence အစွန်း, *n.* an end, extremity, edge, side, border, အစွန် ၊ အဖျား ၊ အနား ၊ အပြိတ်.

စွန့်, *v.* to part with, give up, give away, refuse, reject.

စွန့်ကြဲ, *v.* to give away, be charitable, scatter abroad.

စွန့်ခွာ, *v.* to sever, exclude, cast off, as any thing useless or injurious.

စွန့်စား, *v.* to be adventurous, ready to give up all.

စွန့်ပေး, *v.* to give away, give up, part with.

စွန့်ပစ်, *v.* to throw away, abandon, reject.

စွန့်လွှန်း, *v.* to be adventurous, ready to give up all.

စွန့်လွှန်းထမောဖြ, *v.* do.

စွန့်လွှတ်, *v.* to release, cast off, reject, or give up.

စွပ်, (1) *v.* to put in or on, as clothes, or as the foot into a shoe, တပ်.

စွပ်, (2) *v.* to accuse, charge with a crime, impeach, ဦး.

စွပ်စွဲ, or စွပ်ဆွဲ, *v.* to accuse, &c.

စွပ်ကြောင်း, *n.* the track of any thing drawn along on the ground.

စွပ်ဖား, *n.* the runners of a sledge, or like vehicle.

စွမ်း, *v.* to be strong, powerful, able, အားရှိ. Hence အစွမ်း, *n.* strength, အား.

စွမ်းနိုင်, *v.* do.

စွမ်းအား, *n.* strength, power, အန်အား ၊ စွန်အား ၊ ဗလ.

စွမ်းပကာ, *n.* do. စွမ်း.

စွမ့်, *v.* to leave, give up, relinquish, စွန့်.

စွယ်စုံ, *n.* a double tusked elephant; an able person.

စွယ်တော်, *n.* a kind of tree.

စွယ်ရန်း, *n.* the projecting arms of a chariot seat.

စွံ, *v.* to get rid of in selling, ရောင်းချစွံ.

စွာ, (1) *euph. affix.*

စွာ, (2) *adv. affix,* as ကောင်းစွာ, well, excellently.

စွေ, (1) *v.* to squint with one eye, မျက်စိစွေ.

စွေ, (2) *v.* to rain incessantly, မိုးထစ်စွေ.

စွေးစွေး, *adv. modifying words of colour.*

စွေ့, *v.* to pucker, or contract, (as the lips.)

ဒြိ, *v.* to cleave or cling to, hang on, adhere, ကပ်၊ တွယ်.

ဒြိလမ်း, *v.* do. commonly denoting adherence to sentiment, opinion, &c.

ဒြိမှတ်, *v.* do.

ဒြိယူ, *v.* do.

ဆ.

The seventh consonant in the Burman alphabet, and the second in the class of palatals.

ဆ, *v.* to consider, deliberate on, implying doubt and uncertainty, တွေး၊ ရှိန်း.

ဆက်, (1) *v.* to connect, join, unite, by the ends or in a continuation, (not literally as ရှည်, &c.) to offer respectfully, present, as to a governor or king; (*comp.* ကပ်.) Hence အဆက်, *n.* a junction, or union, a joint. *Also* အဆက်ဆက်, *adv.* connectively, successively; future time, used in opposition to မျက်မှောက်, present time. အဆက်ဆက်ဌပဒေသ, *n.* traditionary precepts.

ဆက်ကပ်, *v.* to offer respectfully, present, as to a great personage.

ဆက်သ, *v.* do.

ဆက်ဆုတ်, *v.* to dislike, abhor, be disgusted.

ဆက်ဍ, *v.* to offer respectfully.

ဆက်, (2) (*pronounced* ဇက်,) *n.* the bits of a bridle.

ဆက်ဒြိ, *v.* to put in the bits of a bridle.

ဆက်သိုး, or ဆက်းသိုးကြိုး, *n.* the reins of a bridle.

ဆက်သိုးကြိုး, *n.* do.

ဆက်, (3) *n.* a descendant of the seventh generation from one's self.

ဆက်, (4) *n.* a kind of goat.

ဆကာ, *n.* a sieve.

ဆကာနှင့်ချ, *v.* to sift.

ဆက်ကလိ, *n.* the armpit, လိုင်းတွင်း၊ လက်ကတီး.

ဆတ်ဆက်, *adv.* certainly, truly, အကယ်၊ အတပ်အမှန်၊ ဧကန်၊ စင်စစ်၊ ဆတ် ဆတ်ပိ၊ သေ၊ မချွတ်.

ဆက်ဆံ, *v.* to be congenial, of like properties, assimilated, have connection with ; to be, or have, in common.

ဆက်ကြိုင်, *n.* the back part of the neck, လည်ကုပ်.

ဆင်, (1) *v.* to put in order, make ready, adorn, ပြင်.

ဆင်ရင်, *v.* do. Hence အဆင်တော်, or အဆင်သင့်, *v.* to be convenient, အခန့်သင့်.

ဆင်, (2) *n.* an elephant.

ဆင်ဦးစီး, *n.* an elephant driver.

ဆင်က, *n.* a howdah.

ဆင်ကပ်, *n.* a landing place, stage ; an uncovered verandah.

ဆင်ကဲ, *n.* a chief of elephanteers.

ဆင်ကျုံး, *n.* an elephant trap.

ဆင်ခြေလျှောမြေ, *n.* a side-hill, declivity.

ဆင်စီးသူရဲ, *n.* an elephanteer, or soldier who fights on an elephant; *comp.* စစ်အင်္ဂါလေးပါး.

ဆင်ဖေါက်, *n.* a male elephant.

ဆင်ပြောင်, *n.* a male elephant in full prime.

ဆင်ခြင်, *v.* to consider, တွေးတော.

ဆင်ခြင်ခြင်း, *n.* consideration, meditation.

ဆင်ခြေ, *n.* a register of evidence in law.

ဆင်တာရာ, *n.* one of the constellations ; see တာရာ.

ဆင်ယင်, *n.* see တန်ဆာ.

ဆင်ငို, ဆင်နား, ဆင်နီ, ဆင်နှာမောင်း, ဆင်ပုသဲ, ဆင်သမနွယ်, (from ဆင်, an elephant, &c.) *n.* various kinds of grass and plants.

ဆင်း, (1) *v.* to descend, (opposed to တက်, to ascend ;) to succeed as a generation.

ဆင်းသက်, *v.* do. do.

ဆင်း, (2) *v.* to stretch out (the leg or arm,) ခြေဆန့်.

ဆင်း, (3) *v.* to cleanse, make fine, by sifting, shaking, &c.

ဆင်းတု, (from ရုပ်ဆင်း and အတု,) *n.* an image, idol.

ဆင်းရဲ, (1) *v.* to be poor, destitute ; to be unhappy, afflicted, miserable.

ဆင်းရဲ, (2) *n.* unhappiness, misery, ဒုက္ခ.

ဆင့်, (1) *v.* to place one upon another, ထပ် ; to accumulate, ဆည်းကျုံး ; to repeat or enforce (an order.)

ဆင့်ဆို, *v.* to repeat or enforce (an order.)

ဆင့်, (2) *n.* the transverse supporters of a floor, which rest upon the longitudinal timbers, and pass through the posts or pillars, (ရက်မ.)

ဆင့်လောင်း, *v.* to add, accumulate, or put one thing upon another.

ဆစ်, (1) *v.* to have a joint, or to be jointed at certain distances, as the limbs of the body, and of certain trees; to be knotty, knobby; to be hard, difficult, dangerous, ခဲ. Hence အဆစ်, *n.* a joint, &c.

ဆစ်ပူး, *v.* do. do.

ဆစ်, (2) *v.* to cheapen, offer at a lower price. Hence အဆစ်, *n.* any thing thrown into the bargain.

ဆစ်ဆွတ်, *v.* do.

ဆစ်, (3) *v.* to hew, carve in stone, &c. ထုတ်.

ဆည်, *v.* to cut across, obstruct, shut up, ကန်၊ ပိတ်.

ဆည်း, (1) *v.* to prevent; *see* ဆီး.

ဆည်း, (2) *v.* to collect, accumulate, treasure up, စု၊ ပေါင်း.

ဆည်းပူး, or ဆည်းဘူး, *v.* do. (most common.)

ဆည်း, (3) *n.* a soft, gentle sound.

ဆည်းကပ်, *v.* to adhere to, be under the care or guidance of, မှီ.

ဆည်းကျူ, *v.* to be soft, gentle, pleasant (in sound,) ညင်း.

ဆည်းဆာ, *n.* dusk, twilight.

ဆည်းညံ, *v.* *see* ဆည်းကျူ.

ဆည်းလည်း, (*commonly pron.* ဆွဲလဲ, or ဆွဲဆွဲ,) *n.* a small bell with a tongue; (*comp.* ခေါင်းလောင်း.)

ဆဋ္ဌမ, (from ဆ, six, *Pali.*) *adj.* sixth.

ဆတ်, (1) *v.* to be brittle, short, crusty; to be irritable, snappish, ကြွပ်.

ဆတ်, (2) *v.* to hew (stone,) carve (in stone,) ဆစ်၊ ကျောက်ထုတ်.

ဆတ်, (3) *v.* to separate (inferior rice from good,) by shaking in a flat basket, (ဗ်ကော,) ဆန်ပြွန်းဆတ်.

ဆတ်, (4) *n.* a kind of grain; see ပေါ.

ဆတ်, (5) *n.* a kind of wild cow.

ဆတ်, (6) *n.* a descendant of the sixth generation from one's self.

ဆတ်ချည်း, (1) (from ဆတ်, to be brittle, &c.) *adv.* suddenly.

ထတ်ချောင်း, (2) *v.* to sneeze; *see* ချေဆတ်.

ထတ်ဆတ်, *adv.* certainly, truly; *see* ထင်ဆတ်.

ထတ်ဆတ်မြားမြား, *adv. intensive.*

ထတ္တာသည်, *n.* a barber.

ထတ်သွား, *n.* a kind of tree.

ထတ်သွားဖူး, (1) *n.* do.

ထတ်သွားဖူး, (2) *n.* the bulging part of a spire or steeple, just above the umbrella.

ထဒ္ဒါန်ဆင်, *n.* a kind of fabulous elephant.

ထဒ္ဒါန်ဆင်မင်းသခင်, *a title of the emperor of Burmah.*

ထန်, *v.* to go up (a river,) to go against (the wind,) ဆန်; (opposed to စုန်.)

ထန္ဒ, *(Pali,) n.* desire, ဆန္ဒ.

ထန္ဒဂတိ, *n.* do.

ထန်း, (1) *v.* to differ, vary, exceed others, be more than common, extraordinary, ထူး ၊ ပြား.

ထန်းကြွယ်, *v.* do. ထူးထန်း.

ထန်းပြား, *v.* do. *also,* to use artifice, be false.

ထန်း, (2) *n.* a certain astrological book.

ထန်း, (3) *v. affix,* just, only, nothing more, as ကြီးထန်းကြီးသည်, he is only large, that is, possessed of no other qualities.

ထန့်, (1) *v.* to stretch out straight; *neut.* ဆန့်.

ထန့်တန်း, *v.* do.

ထန့်, (2) *v.* to be opposite, adverse, uncongenial, quarrelsome, ရန်တွေ့.

ထန့်ကျင်, *v.* do. (most common.)

ထန့်ကန်, *v.* do.

ထန့်ကျင်ဘက်, *n.* an opposite.

ထပ်, (1) *v.* to repay.

ထပ်, (2) *n.* the smallest kind of land-leach.

ထပ်ကျိုးရစ်, *n.* a kind of vine, or creeper.

ထပ်ဆပ်ချည်, *n.* a kind of plant.

ထပ်ပြာ, *n.* salt-earth, used in washing; soap of any kind.

ထမ်း, *v.* to scatter over, pour or put upon (as curry-gravy on rice.)

ဆယ်, *v.* to take up or out, deliver, extricate, arrest in progress (as a floating boat,) ကယ် ၊ ယူ.

ဆယ်တင်, *v.* do.

ဆရာ, *n.* a teacher, master of any art or science.

ဆလင်ကျွန်း, *n.* Junkseylon Island.

ဆံ, (1) *n.* the hair of the head, ဦးဆံ.

ဆံပင်, *v.* do.

ဆံစု, *n.* a collection of hair, a false club.

ဆံထုံး, *n.* the knot of hair worn on a woman's head.

ဆံကျင်, *n.* a certain ornament worn to keep the hair in order.

ဆံချပ်, *n.* another do. ဆံထိုး, *n.* do.

ဆံချင်တာရာ, *n.* a certain constellation; see တာရာ.

ဆံကျစ်, *n.* braided hair.

ဆံလျဉ်, *n.* short hair on the forehead.

ဆံ, (2) (from ဆန်,) *n.* husked rice.

ဆံမွဲ, *n.* small broken rice, the poorest sort.

ဆံနုပ်, *n.* do. ဆံဖွန်း, do.

ဆံဖွန်းဆော်, *v.* to clean rice, &c. see ဆော.

ဆံပွား, *n.* the next poorer sort; see ဆံမွဲ.

ဆံလတ်, *n.* the middling sort.

ဆံလုံးတီး, *n.* rice, partially husked, as it comes from the mill. N. B. After it is completely husked by pounding, but not separated into different sorts, it is called ဂုံ့ဆံ; see ဂုံ့.

ဆံရင်း, *n.* the best sort of rice.

ဆံပုပ်, *see* ဟင်္သာ, or ပဲခူး, Pegu.

ဆံသည်, *n.* a dealer in rice.

ဆံတေး, *n.* a kind of tree.

ဆံ့, *v.* to be capable of (receiving, containing, sustaining, &c.) ဝင်နိုင် ၊ နိုင်.

ဆာ, (1) *v.* to be hungry or thirsty, to hunger or thirst for, ငတ် ၊ မွတ် ၊ သိပ်.

ဆာမွတ်, *v.* do. ကြိုက်လှည်း ၊ ပူဆာ.

ဆာလောင်, *v.* do.

ဆာ, (2) *v.* to feel uneasy, uncomfortable, be in slight pain.

ဆာနွမ်း, *v.* to be weak, exhausted, worn out; *comp.* နွမ်း.

ဆာပါ, *n.* a bandanna handkerchief.

ဆား, *n.* salt.

ဆားပျား, *n.* do. (used in certain connections, as ဆားပျားငါးပိ, salt and preserved fish.)

ဆားစိမ်, (from စိမ်,) *adj.* salted, impregnated with salt.

ဆိတ်, (1) *v.* to be still, silent, quiet, solitary, တိတ်.

ဆိတ်ကွယ်, *v.* do.

ဆိတ်ညိမ်, *v.* do.

ဆိတ်, (2) *v.* to pinch, nip, to peck (as a fowl.) Hence အဆိတ်, or တဆိတ်, *n.* a pinch, i. e. a little quantity, တဆိတ်ခလေး. *Also* ဆိတ်စာ ။ ဆိတ်စိ ။ ဆိတ်ခလေး ။ ဆိတ်စိခလေး.

ဆိတ်, (3) *n.* a goat.

ဆိတ်ကုလား, *n.* a sheep, သိုး.

ဆိတ်မြွှာ, *n.* the common goat.

ဆိတ်သိုး, *n.* a sheep.

ဆိတ်ချဉ်း, *n.* a kind of tree, ပလိ.

ဆိတ်နံ, *n.* a kind of tree.

ဆိတ်ဖူး, *n.* a kind of plant.

ဆိတ်ပွား, (a corruption of ဇီဝေါ, life, *Pali,*) *interj.* May you live long ! (said to children, when they sneeze.)

ဆိတ်ဘီလူး, *n.* a kind of tree.

ဆိပ်, *n.* a shore, landing place.

ဆိမ့်, *v.* to be pleasant to the taste, savoury, delicious, ဆိမ့်နှ.

ဆီ, (1) *n.* presence, nearness, အထံ.

ဆီမှာ, *affix,* in presence of, as မင်းဆီမှာ, in presence of the governor.

ဆီ, (2) *n.* oil, fat, grease, အဆီ.

ဆီကြည်, *n.* oil.

ဆီဥ, *n.* fat.

ဆီခဲ, *n.* do.

ဆီမီး, *n.* a lamp-fire or light.

ဆီမီးစာ, *n.* a wick.

ဆီမီးခွက်, *n.* the cup of a lamp.

ဆီစောင်, *n.* the medicinal oil tree, a kind of plant, ရှားစောင်.

ဆီမီးဖက်, *n.* a kind of serpent.

ဆီမီးတောက်, *n.* a kind of plant.

ဆီလျော်, *v.* to accord, agree, suit, လျော်.

ဆီး, (1) *v.* to prevent, obstruct, interrupt, impede, stop, ဆို့ ။ ကာ ။ ဆည်း ။ တား ။ မြစ် ။ ပိတ်.

ဆီး, (2) *v.* to clothe, cover, bind, (as the waist.)

ဆီးကြို, *v.* to go forth, to meet, to anticipate, ကြိုဆို.

ဆီးငေါ်, *v.* to consider, deliberate upon, weigh consequences.

ဆီးဆ, *v.* to consider, deliberate upon, implying doubt and uncertainty.

ဆီးဆို့, see ဆီး, to prevent, &c.

ဆီးထောက်, *v.* to consider, deliberate, to have reference or regard to.

ဆီး, (3) *n.* the urethra, ကျင်ငယ်ချောင်း.

ဆီးအောင့်, *v.* to have a stoppage of urine; *see* အောင့်.

ဆီး, (4) *n.* dew, mist, fog, frost, snow, နှင်း.

ဆီးနှင်း, *n.* do.

ဆီးခဲ, *n.* ice, frost.

ဆီးနှင်းခဲ, *n.* do.

ဆီးသွား, *v.* to evacuate urine.

ဆီးတောက်, *n.* a kind of bird.

ဆု, *n.* a reward conferred by a superior; a favour conferred by deity, or a celestial being, whether a reward or a gift.

ဆုလာဘ်, *n.* do.

ဆုတောင်း, *v.* to ask a reward or favour; to pray.

ဆုယူ, *v.* do. to wish well, desire good for others. (N. B. Not applied to asking a favour for one's self.)

ဆုတ်, (1) *v.* to draw back, retreat, recede, move out of the way, ယုတ်.

ဆုတ်, (2) *v.* to become less, inferior, be diminished, ယုတ် ။ လျော့.

ဆုတ်, (3) *v.* to tear, rend, sever, *(neut.* ပြုတ်.*)*

ဆုတ်ကပ်, *n.* a kind of game.

ဆုတ်သွား, *v.* to retreat, go back, move out of the way.

ဆုံးဆ, *v.* to consider, ဆင်ချင်.

ဆုပ်, *v.* to lay hold of (with the hand,) to clinch, or double up, as the fist.

ဆုပ်နယ်, *v.* to squeeze, press.

ဆုမ, (1) *v.* to instruct, discipline, correct, whether by reproof or punishment, သွန်သင် ၊ ပဲ့ပြင် ၊ ကွပ်.

ဆုမ, (2) *v.* to geld, castrate, ကွပ် ၊ သင်း.

ဆုမခက်, *v.* to be obstinate, not to receive instruction or reproof.

ဆုံ, (1) *v.* to meet, come together, ကြုံ ၊ ကြုံ ၊ ကြိုက် ၊ ပြား ၊ တွေ့.

ဆုံ, (2) *n.* a mortar.

ဆုံကျဉ်, *n.* the concavity of do. see ကျဉ်; any tube closed at one end.

ဆုံး, (1) *v.* to come to an end, be finished, terminated, destroyed, ကုန် ၊ ခန်း ၊ ပျောက်, *(opposed to* စ.) Hence အဆုံး, *n.* an end, termination, အဆုံးစွန်; *adj.* last, final.

ဆုံးပါး, *v.* do.

ဆုံး, (2) *affix*, sign of the superlative degree.

ဆုံး, (3) *v.* to be unable, unequal to, &c. see ရှုံး.

ဆုံးစွန်, *v.* to be last, final.

ဆုံးဖြတ်, *v.* to bring to a conclusion, finish, decide, settle.

ဆုံး, (4) *n.* some kind of red mineral, as cinnabar.

ဆူ, (1) *v.* to bubble, boil, ပွက် ၊ ဝေ; to be agitated, restless, disturbed, distressed.

ဆူပွက်, *v.* to bubble, boil, to be agitated, restless, disturbed, distressed.

ဆူလောင်, *v.* to be distressed, &c. ပူပန် ၊ ပွက်ကျဉ်း.

ဆူ, (2) *v.* to be fat, corpulent, ဝ; to be plentiful, abundant, ဝ.

ဆူ, (3) *num. affix*, as ဘုရားနှစ်ဆူ, two gods, (see Gram.)

ဆူလှယ်, *adv.* by turns, alternately.

ဆူး, (1) *v.* to be very sour, sharp, piercing, *(comp.* ချဉ်;) to smart, as the eyes, ကျိန်း.

ဆူး, (2) *n.* a thorn, any thing pointed.

ဆူးပန်း, *n.* the safflower plant.

ဆူးကျင်, ဆူးခေါက်နက်, ဆူးတံခါး; ဆူးပတောင်း; ဆူးပလွှ, ဆူးပုပ်, ဆူးဖြူ, ဆူးချစ်, ဆူးလေ, ဆူးသိုးခွ, various thorn plants, trees, and creepers.

ဆေး, (1) *v.* to clean, clean by washing; polish (as a blade.)

ဆေးကြော, *v.* do.

ဆေးသန့်, *v.* to engrave, transcribe fairly.
ဆေး, (2) *v.* to investigate, စစ်.
ဆေးကြော, *v.* do.
ဆေးမေး, *v.* do. မေးမြန်း.
ဆေး, (3) *n.* a drug (of any kind,) medicine, paint, tobacco.
ဆေးကု, *v.* to give medicine.
ဆေးကျဉ်း, *n.* a kind of tobacco, on which mould appears.
ဆေးချယ်, *v.* to paint, ဆေးရေး.
ဆေးတံ, *n.* a pipe.
ဆေးတောင့်, *n.* a bolus.
ဆေးဒန်း, *n.* some kind of yellow mineral, yellow orpiment.
ဆေးပြား, *n.* a trochisch lozenge.
ဆေးမှုန့်, *n.* medicinal powder.
ဆေးရေး, *v.* to paint.
ဆေးတိုက်, *v.* do.
ဆေးလိပ်, *n.* a cigar.
ဆေးထိုက်, *v.* medicine takes effect.
ဆေးဝါ, *n.* medicine.
ဆေးသင့်, *v.* medicine suits or takes effect.
ဆေးခါးကြီး, ဆေးတလုံး, ဆေးပုန်းတုပ်, ဆေးပုလဲ, ဆေးပဲစိတ်, ဆေးပွတ်ကိုး, ဆေးဝင်ခြင်း, ဆေးဝါကြီး, various medicinal plants, trees, &c.
ဆေးလေး, *v.* to be slow, dilatory, to delay, procrastinate, နှေး၊ နှဲ.
ဆဲ, (1) *v.* to revile, abuse in words.
ဆဲရေး, *v.* do. ရေးရွတ်.
ဆဲဆို, *v.* do.
ဆဲ, (2) *v. affix*, sign of the ind. mood, pres. tense.
ဆဲသည်, *v. affix*, do.
ဆော, *v.* to be quick, မြန်၊ လျင်; seldom used singly.
ဆောက်, (1) *v.* to build, erect, တည်, (sometimes written ဆောင်.)
ဆောက်တည်, *v.* to perform habitually, maintain, observe, promote any design, (applied to religious duties.)
ဆောက်, (2) *n.* a chisel.
ဆောက်, (3) *n.* a kind of tree.
ဆောက်ဝန်း, *n.* a circular edged chisel.
ဆောက်ပုတ်, *n.* a mallet, short club.

ဆောက်တိုင်, *n.* a pole erected in the manner of a flag-staff, တိုင် ၊ တိုင်ရိုက်.

ဆောက်ဒိုက်, *n.* a mallet.

ဆောက်ခတ်, *n.* do.

ဆောင်, (1) *num. affix*, as စာနှစ်ဆောင်, two books, (see Gram.)

ဆောင်ကြဉ်း, *v.* to bear, sustain, &c. see ဆောင်.

ဆောင်, (2) *v.* to bear, carry, ရွ; to sustain, carry on, accomplish, ရွက်; to use, employ, သုံး; to do, perform, ကျင့် ၊ ပြု ၊ မူ. *It frequently derives a specific meaning from the connection.*

ဆောင်ရှောင်, *v.* do. do. Hence အဆောင်အရှောင်, *see* အခမ်းအနား.

ဆောင်နှင်း, *v.* to give in marriage, ထိမ်းမြား ၊ ပေးစား.

ဆောင်ပနိုး, *n.* a short deck on the prow of a boat, or something similar in the forepart of a cart.

ဆောင်ရွ, *v.* to bear, carry.

ဆောင်ရွက်, *v.* to bear, carry, sustain, carry on, accomplish, &c.

ဆောင်း, (1) *v.* to cover with an umbrella, a hat, or high raised cover, &c.

ဆောင်း, (2) *v.* to pay something extra, in consideration of the inferior quality of money, မီးဆောင်း.

ဆောင်း, (3) *n.* a high conical open work cover, with an aperture at the top, used to catch fish, and for various other purposes.

ဆောင်းစု, *v.* to bring or collect together, (applied to things;) see စုဆောင်း.

ဆောင်းကာလ, *n.* the cold season; *comp.* ဥတု.

ဆောင်းကျွတ်, *n.* the end of the cold season.

ဆောင်းပါး, *n.* an epistle in verse.

ဆောင်းမေးခါး, *n.* a kind of drug.

ဆောင့်, *v.* to thrust, push, butt, stamp, &c. by a sudden violent jerk, ထိုး.

ဆောင့်မိ, *v.* to hit, ထိ.

ဆောင့်အောင့်, *v.* to shew temper, obstinacy, resistance of authority.

ဆောင့်ကြောင့်, *adv.* in a squatting posture.

ဆော့, *v.* to be restless, meddling, troublesome, rude.

U

ဆော့ကြွတ်, *v.* to be restless, rude.

ဆော်, (1) *v.* to rouse, excite to action, urge on, stimulate, quicken, နှိုး ၊ လှုံ့.

ဆော်ဩော်, *v.* do. ဩော်ဆန်း.

ဆော်ပံ, *v.* do.

ဆော်ကြော်, *v.* do.

ဆော်, (2) *v.* to solder, join by metallic cement, စေ့ဆော်.

ဆို, *v.* to speak, say, tell, ပြော.

ဆိုလို, *v.* to mean, signify, import.

ဆိုမည်, *v.* to complain, murmur, မည်ညည်း.

ဆိုက်, *v.* to arrive, ရောက်; to reach, hit, မှန် ၊ ထိ; to bring, or come alongside, as a boat, a cart, &c.

ဆိုင်, (1) *v.* to have a right to, have concern in, or with, ပိုင်.

ဆိုင်, (2) *v.* to be engaged together, whether in union of action or in rivalry, ပြိုင်; to meet, ပြိုင် ၊ အချင်းချင်းတွေ့.

ဆိုင်, (3) *n.* a shop, stall.

ဆိုင်း, (1) *v.* to delay, tarry, wait, wait for, ငံ့ ၊ စောင့် ၊ ဝင့် ၊ လင့်.

ဆိုင်းဆိုင်း, *adv.* spreadingly, overshadowingly, extendingly, (as vines and the like.)

ဆိုင်း, (2) *v.* to sling up, suspend, တွဲ. Hence အဆိုင်း, *n.* a cluster, bunch (of flowers, fruit, &c.)

ဆိုင်း, (3) *n.* a sling to carry things in, suspended at the ends of a porter's yoke.

ဆိုင်း, (4) *n.* see ပတ်ဆိုင်း.

ဆိုင်း, (5) *v.* to be fresh, luxuriant, full of leaves, or, *figuratively*, of other good things, ပြိုင်း ၊ ပြိုင် ၊ ရှိန်း.

ဆိုး, (1) *n.* to be bad, not good, မကောင်း; poor, mean, vile, hurtful, injurious; evil, wicked.

ဆိုး, (2) *v.* to dye, colour, ထဲ.

ဆိုးကြံ, *v.* to design, think, or meditate evil.

ဆိုးရွာ, *v.* to be bad, poor, mean, vile.

ဆို့, *v.* to stop up, obstruct; *comp.* ထို့, &c. Hence အဆို့, *n.* a stopper.

ဆို့ပိတ်, *v.* to stop up, &c.; *figuratively*, to be covetous; see ဝမ်းဆို့.

ဆို့ဆို့, *v.* to be sick, inclined to vomit, အော့အန်.

ဆွ, *v.* to scratch up, dig lightly, agitate, irritate.

ဆွတ်, (1) *v.* to pluck, gather, ခူး.

ဆွတ်, (2) *v.* to sprinkle, scatter, (as water,) ဖျန်း.

ဆွတ်ဖြူး, *v.* to scatter, (as powder,) ဖြူး.

ဆွတ်, (3) *v.* to be very white, *(used also as an intensive with other words of colour.*

ဆွတ်လွတ်, or ဆွတ်ဆွတ်လွတ်လွတ်, *adv.* indicative of emotion or feeling, &c.

ဆွံ့, *v.* to be scarce, deficient, wanting, နည်း၊ ရှား၊ ပါး.

ဆွမ်း, *n.* cooked rice, *(clerical,)* ထမင်း.

ဆွမ်းခံဝင်, *v.* to receive rice, as a priest.

ဆွမ်းစည်, *v.* to set rice in order before a priest.

ဆွမ်းဘုန်း, *n.* cooked rice.

ဆွမ်းဘုဉ်းပေး, (from ဆွမ်း, cooked rice, and ဘုဉ်းပေး, to eat, *clerical,*) *v.* to eat cooked rice.

ဆွယ်, *v.* to attach to, connect with, lean on, ကပ်၊ တွယ်၊ မြှောင်.

ဆွံ့, *v.* to be deficient in some faculty, as in strength, &c. to be imperfect.

ဆွေဉာတကာ, *n.* a friend, မိတ်ဆွေ.

ဆွေရင်းမျိုးချာ, (from အဆွေ, &c.) *n.* an own relation, အဆွေအမျိုးစစ်.

ဆွေပါ, *n.* an acquaintance, friend, အဆွေ.

ဆွေး, *v.* to be decayed, rotten, ယို၊ ယိ.

ဆွေးနွေး, *v.* to enquire into, investigate, discuss, မေးမြန်း၊ ဆေးမေး၊ နှိုးနှော.

ဆွေးနွှေး, *v.* do.

ဆွေးမြန်း, *v.* do.

ဆွေးမြေ့, *v.* to be decayed, rotten, ယို၊ ယိ.

ဆွေ့ဆွေ့ခုန်, *v.* to shake the hands or feet, as a child, through anger or fear.

ဆွဲ, (1) *v.* to pull, draw; to hang up, suspend, တွဲ.

ဆွဲငင်, *v.* to pull, draw.

ဆွဲ, (2) *n.* large scales, or balances, ရာဇူ.

ဆွဲလဲ, *n.* a small bell with a clapper; see ဆည်းလည်း.

ဆွဲလွဲ, *n.* do.

## ဇ.

The eight consonant in the Burman alphabet, and the third in the class of palatals.

ဇ, (1) *(Pali,)* *v.* to be, or produce.

ဇ, (2) *(contraction of* ဇာတက,) *n.* one portion of the Boodhist scriptures.

ဇက်ရက်, *n.* the mina, a kind of bird, ဇရက်.

ဇင်ကလယ်, *n.* small dishes which children play with, ဇိုးပွတ်.

ဇင်ရော်, *n.* a kind of white bird.

ဇက်, *n.* the neck, လည်ပင်း.

ဇာတက, *n.* one portion of the Boodhist scriptures.

ဇနပဒ, *(Pali,)* *n.* see ဇနပုဒ်.

ဇနပုဒ်, (from ဇနပဒ, *Pali,*) *n.* a small village.

ဇနိကာ, *(Pali,)* *n.* a mother.

ဇနီး, (from ဇနိကာ, *Pali,*) *n.* a daughter.

ဇနီးမိလ်ရှင်, *n.* husband and wife collectively, လင်မယား ၊ သမီးမိလ်ရှင်.

ဇနီးခင်ပွန်း, *n.* do. သမီးခင်ပွန်း.

ဇနီးမောင်နှံ, *n.* do. သမီးမောင်နှံ.

ဇမ္ဗူဒိပ်, (from ဇမ္ဗူ, the eugenia tree, and ဒီပ, an island,) *n.* the great south island on which we live, one of the four grand islands which surround the Myenmo mount; *comp.* ကျွန်း.

ဇမ္ဗူဒီပ, *n.* see ဇမ္ဗူဒိပ်.

ဇမ္ဗူဇရီ, *n.* a kind of tree.

ဇမ္ဗူရာဇ်, *n.* the most precious kind of gold, being that produced from the gold eugenia tree.

ဇမ္ဗူသပြေ, *n.* the gold eugenia tree, said to grow on the northern extremity of Zamboodebah Island.

ဇရက်, *n.* the mina, a kind of bird.

ဇရစ်, *n.* a kind of plant, ဇရာဓိ.

ဇရပ်, *n.* see စရပ်.

ဇရာ, *(Pali,)* *n.* old age, အိုခြင်း.

ဇရာဓိ, *n.* a kind of plant, ဇရစ်.

ဇရဲ, *n.* a kind of tree.

ဇခြေ, *(frequently pron.* စချွေ,) *n.* a kind of bird.

ဇထပ်, *n.* a kind of tree.

ဇလာကပင်, *n.* a kind of boat.

ဇလာဗုဇာ, (*Pali,*) *n,* a womb; the transit of mind from one body to another ; see ပဋိသန္ဓေ.

ဇလား, *n.* a four cornered vessel of different sizes, used as a measure.

ဇလုံ, *n.* a deep iron pot, a caldron.

ဇထဲ, *n.* a kind of tree.

ဇဝက်, *n.* doubt, uncertainty, indecision, နှောင့်နှေးချင်း.

ဇဝက်သာ, *n.* sal-ammoniac.

ဇဝါ, *n.* painting, picture-work in colours or gold.

ဇာ, (from ဇာတိ, to be or produce, *Pali,*) *adj.* caused, or produced, used as a formative increment, with words of Pali origin, as ကမ္မဇာ, caused by the influence of past deeds. N. B. ဇာ becomes ဇ in composition, as ကမ္မဇရုပ်, a body caused by the influence of past deeds.

ဇာဂဏာ, *n.* compasses.

ဇာတ်, (from ဇာတိ, to be, or produce, *Pali,*) (1) *n.* existence, ဖြစ်ချင်း.

ဇာတ်, (2) *n.* mode of existence, nature, ပကတိ၊ သဘော.

ဇာတ်, (3) *n.* a race, kind, cast, အမျိုး.

ဇာတ်, (4) *n.* the organs of generation.

ဇာတ်, (5) *n.* an account of one's own existence, or life, given by one's self ; commonly applied to different existences of Boodhs, and particularly to the different existences, or lives of Gaudama, the last Boodh, 550 of which are counted in the extant Boodhist scriptures : 10 of these, distinguished from the rest in regard to interest and celebrity, are as follows : viz.

| | | | |
|---|---|---|---|
| တေမိ, *marked* | တေ. | စန္ဒကုမာ, *marked* | စ. |
| နေမိ, .... | နေ. | ဝေသန္တရာ, .... | ဝေ. |
| ဇနက, .... | ဇ. | သုဝဏ္ဏသျှံ, .... | သု. |
| မဟော်, .... | မ. | ဘူရိဒတ်, .... | ဘူ. |
| နာရဒ, .... | နာ. | ဝိဒူရ, .... | ဝိ. |

ဇာတာ, *n.* time and circumstances of one's birth, or a record of the time and circumstances of one's birth, used for astrological purposes.

ဇာတာပေတာ, *n.* do.

ဇာတိ, (1) *(Pali,)* *v.* to be, exist, produce.

ဇာတိ, (2) *adj.* clear, pure, genuine, အတိ၊ အစစ်.

ဇာတိခေတ်, *n.* a certain division of Sekyah systems, consisting of a hundred thousand millions of worlds, which are destroyed and reproduced simultaneously ; see ခေတ်.

ဇာတိဿရ, (from ဇာတိ, to be, and သရ, to bring to mind, *Pali,)* *n.* knowledge of one's own existence in a past state.

ဇာဒိဖိုလ်, *n.* a nutmeg.

ဇာဒိဖိုလ်ပွင့်, *n.* mace.

ဇာလိမာလာ, *n.* a kind of tree.

ဇီကွက်, *n.* a screech owl, ခင်ပုပ်.

ဇီဇီ, *adv.* indicating certain noises.

ဇိန, *(Pali,)* a Zeena or Boodh, မာရ်ငါးပါးကိုအောင်သောသူ ; a person who has overcome the five evils, or tyrants, viz. ခန္ဓာမာရ်, animal constitution ; အဘိသင်္ခါရမာရ်, subjection to the operations of the four causes ; ကိလေသာမာရ်, the passions ; မစ္စု မာရ်, death ; and ဒေဝပုတ္တမာရ်, the most powerful evil Nat.

ဇီယာ, *n.* the cummin plant.

ဇီဝက, *n.* Zewakah, a noted physician ; *figuratively*, any skilful physician.

ဇီဝစိုး, *n.* a kind of bird, a pheasant.

ဇီဝေါ, *(Pali,)* *n.* life.

ဇိဝှါ, *(Pali,)* *n.* the tongue, လျှာ.

ဇိဝှါဝိညာဏ်, *n.* the sense of taste.

ဇီး, *n.* the fœtus, (commonly applied to animals.)

ဇို, *n.* nine-pins, or any thing of the kind ; *also*, pieces used in certain other plays.

ဇော, (from ဇောတိ, *Pali,)* *n.* a sudden active emotion, or exercise of mind.

ဇောဖြန့်, *v.* to be thrilled with a sudden violent emotion.

ဇောက်ရှင်သောင်း, *n.* a kind of tree.

ချောက်ချင်း, (1) *n.* a fragment, or broken bit of a pot.
ချောက်ချင်း, (2) *n.* a kind of tree.
ချောင်ပတွေး, *n.* a kind of tree.
ချောင်း, *n.* a stable, မြင်းချောင်း ၊ မြင်းတင်းကုပ်.
ချောင်းဂေါ်, *n.* a certain disease of horses.
ချောတ, *n.* a kind of precious stone.
ချောတချုပ်, *n.* do.
ချောဂ်ဂီ, *n.* a Jogi, a performer of certain religious austerities.
ချောဂ်ဂီဆုပ်ထုပ်, *n.* a kind of mushroom, or fungus.
ချွတ်တချွတ်, *adv.* rudely, disrespectfully, improperly, badly, ဆဲနိ.
ဇွန်း, *n.* a spoon.

## ဈ.

The ninth consonant in the Burman alphabet, and the fourth in the class of palatals.

ဈာ, *n.* lace, open work in cloth, paper, or boards.
ဈာန်, (from ဈာန, *Pali,*) *n.* a certain attainment, or state of mind, which enables the possessor to traverse different worlds. It is divided into five constituent parts, viz. ဝိတက္က, thought, design; ဝိစာရ, consideration, reflection; ပီတိ, pleasure, joy; သုခ, bliss, happiness; ဧကဂ္ဂတာ, permanency, immutability.
ဈာန်သမာပတ်, *n.* do.
ဈာန်အဘိညာဉ်, *n.* do.
ဈိုး, *n.* a kind of tree, of which there are various species.
ဈေး, *n.* a market, bazar.
ဈေးကြို, *n.* a kind of fair, or resting place, where country people stop and dispose of their goods to the market people.
ဈေးချွပ်စု, *n.* small silver change, used in the market.
ဈေးချွပ်စုသည်, *n.* a market man, or woman.

## ည.

The tenth consonant in the Burman alphabet, and the fifth in the class of palatals.

ည, (*a contraction of* ညဉ့်,) *n.* night.
ညက်, *v.* to be made fine, as powder, မှုန့်.

ညင်ပါး, *v.* to be frightened, lose courage, run away, ကြောက်ညင်.

ညင်ပါးကြောက်ညင်, *v.* do.

ညင်း, (1) *v.* to be gentle, soft, quiet, pleasant, ငြိမ်း၊ သာ.

ညင်း, (2) *v.* to contradict, dispute, deny; see ငြင်း.

ညင်းဆို, *v.* do.

ညင်းဆန်, *v.* do.

ညစ်, *v.* to be dirty, မစင်; to be sorrowful, distressed; နှစ်ထိုမသာ၊ ညှိုးနွမ်း; to be vile, wicked, ဆိုး. Hence အညစ်, dirt, filth, အညစ်အကြေး၊ အကြေးအညစ်.

ညစ်ထျု, *v.* to be muddy, filthy, dirty, slimy, နောက်.

ညစ်ကြေး, *v.* to be rusty, dirty, filthy.

ညစ်ညမ်း, *v.* to be dirty.

ညစ်ညှိုး, *v.* to be gloomy, sorrowful, distressed.

ညစ်ထာ, *v.* to be filthy, dirty, mean.

ညစ်ထည်း, *v.* do.

ညှည်တည်း, *v.* to be afraid, &c. see ညင်ပါး.

ညည်း, (1) *v.* to sigh, groan, be distressed in mind.

ညည်းညံ, *v.* do.

ညည်းညူ, *v.* do.

ညည်းတွား, *v.* do.

ညည်းပူန်, *v.* do.

ညည်း, (2) *n.* a friend, used as a term of address, by a woman to other women, or to her husband; or by a man to his wife, or other women; to his equals, or inferiors, ဆွ.

ညဉ့်, *n.* night.

ညဉ့်ဦး, *n.* evening.

ညဉ့်စား, *n.* evening food, supper.

ညဉ့်နေ, *n.* afternoon, latter part of the day.

ညတ်, *n.* a certain portion of the writing used at the initiation of priests, ကမ္မဝါ.

ညတ်ညတ်, *adv.* indicative of the noise made by a frog, or chicken, when frightened.

ညပ်, *v.* to be pinched, squeezed between two substances; *act.* ညှပ်.

ညမ, *n.* a younger sister, ညီမ.

ညံ, (1) *v.* to be protracted (as sound), be noisy, ဝီညံ ၊ ညီညံ.

ညံ, (2) *n.* a kind of animal.

ညံ, (3) *n.* a kind of tree.

ညံသော, *v.* to be protracted (as sound), be noisy.

ညံ့, (1) *v.* to be fine, soft, delicate, နု ၊ နူး ၊ ပျော့ ၊ သိမ်.

ညံ့သက်, *v.* do.

ညံ့, (2) *v.* to be poor, mean, inferior, deficient, ယုတ် ; to grow less, decrease, be diminished, လျော့.

ညာ, (1) *v.* to lay eggs, ဥ.

ညာ, (2) *v.* to come to one's help, (not used alone, but combined with other words, as ကူညာ ၊ ညီညာ, &c.)

ညာ, (3) *n.* the right side,—*opposed to* ဘယ်.

ညာကမိုး, *n.* a jar appropriated to drinking-water.

ညာဏ်, (from ညာဏ, *Pali,*) *n.* intellect, sense, wisdom.

ညာတကာ, (*Pali,*) *n.* relations, အဆွေအမျိုး.

ညာသို့, *affix,* up, as မြစ်ညာသို့, up the river; ပြည်ညာသို့, up the country.

ညား, (1) *v.* to meet with, find, get, တွေ့ ၊ ကြုံ ၊ ကြို.

ညား, (2) *euphonic affix.*

ညိ, *v.* to hitch upon, hang or suspend upon; to be caught, as by a nail, thorn, fire, disease, &c.

ညိစွန်, *v.* do.

ညိတ်, *v.* to nod, as the head.

ညိတ်ညိတ်, *adv.* an intensive to words of sound.

ညိမ်, *v.* to be still, unmoved, composed, quiet, ငြိမ်.

ညိင်း, *v.* see သတ်.

ညီ, (1) *v.* to be even, like, as much as, မျှ ; *act.* ညှိ.

ညီညာ, *v.* do.

ညီညွတ်, *v.* do. Hence တညီတညွတ်, of one accord, alike.

ညီလာ, *n.* audience, a levee.

ညီလာခံ, *v.* to give audience, hold a levee, *(royal ;) comp.* ဧည့်ခံ.

ညီ, (2) *v.* to help, aid, assist, ကူ ၊ မ.

ညီညာ, *v.* do.

ညီ, (3) *n.* a younger brother of a brother.

ညီအစ်ကို, *n.* a brother.

ညီမ, *n.* a younger sister.

ညိုး, (1) *v.* to be dissatisfied, uneasy, discontented.

ညိုးငွေ့, *v.* do.

ညီး, (2) *v.* to be glittering, flaming, တောက်.

ဉေယျဓံတရားငါးပါး, (from ဉေယျ, knowledge, and ဓမ္မ, law, *Pali,*) *n.* five principles, or laws, viz. သင်္ခါရ, the principle of mutability; ဝိကာရ, the principle of existence, or mode of existence; လက္ခဏာ, the principle of discriminating marks, signs, &c. နိဗ္ဗာန်, the principle of absorption, or annihilation; and ပညတ်, *which see.*

ညှဲ, *n.* a friend, &c. *see* ညှဉ်း.

ညှဲမင်းငယ်, *n.* a doll, puppet, ရုပ်မင်း.

ညောင်, *n.* the banyan tree, *Ficus Indica.*

ညောင်ဗောဓိ, *n.* the sacred banyan, *Ficus Religiosa,* under which Gaudama was perfected, ပညောင်.

ညောင်ဗုဒ္ဓဟော, *n.* do.

ညောင်ကုတ်ပဲ, ညောင်ကျုတ်, ညောင်ကျွတ်, ညောင်ချည်, ညောင်မြေတောက်, ညောင်ပိန်းခဲ, and ညောင်သမြေ, varieties of the banyan.

ညောင်စောင်း, *n.* a kind of bedstead.

ညောင်ရေ, (from ညောင်, the banyan, and ရေ, water,) *n.* holy, or sanctified water, poured around the banyan.

ညောင်ရေအိုး, *n.* the pot in which holy water is kept, or offered, ကြာသွတ်အိုး.

ညောင်း, *v.* to be wearied through inaction; to pay attention to by the eye or ear, *(polite and respectful,)* မျက်စိညောင်း။ နား ညောင်း.

ညောင့်, *n.* a sharp stick; a thorn, ငြောင့်.

ညို, (1) *v.* to be dark in colour, approaching to black; of a deep blue, or green, မှိုင်း; opposed to ဖြူ.

ညို, (2) *v.* to be sorrowful, grieved, gloomy.

ညို, (3) *v.* to be faded, shrivelled, withered, contracted.

ညိုကျည်း, *n.* the shin bone, ခြင်းခေါင်း, *(comp.* ကျည်း, an arm, &c.)

ညှိုးငြင်, or ညှိုးညင်, *v.* to be poor, distressed, miserable, ဆင်းရဲ.

ညံစီ, *v.* to be noisy, ဆူ.

ညိုပြောင်, *v.* to be of a beautiful dark colour.

ညိုး, *v.* to feel ill-will towards, wish to injure, indulge malice, feel revengeful, မုန်းထား၊ ရန်ငြိုးဖွဲ့.

ညွတ်, (1) *v.* to stoop, bow down the head, hang down, ငုံ့၊ ကုန်း၊ ကိုင်း.

ညွတ်, (2) *v.* to assent to, be inclined in mind. Hence တညွတ်, *adv.* of one mind, with one accord.

ညွတ်နူး, *v.* to be pleased or gratified with, ကြည်နူး၊ နှစ်သက်.

ညွတ်ကျုတ်, *v.* to stoop, bow down, be low.

ညွတ်ဍုံ, *v.* to bow down together, as a multitude.

ညွန်, *n.* mud, mire, ရွှံ့.

ညွန်ချောင့်, *n.* a muddy ditch, a miry place.

ညွန့်, *v.* to taper, run out into a point, ချွန်း၊ ပြူးသွယ်. Hence အညွန့်, *n.* a sprout, a young twig, a branch ; *adj.* fine, nice, of the best quality, (applied to silks, &c.)

ညှက်, *v.* to be slender, poor, weak.

ညှင်း, (1) *v.* to cut into long slices.

ညှင်း, (2) *n.* a cutaneous disease, white spots on the skin.

ညှင်း, (3) *n.* a kind of trumpet, a French-horn.

ညှင်း, (4) *v.* to be soft, gentle, as sound.

ညှစ်, *v.* to squeeze, or press, in order to extract liquor or milk ; to milk.

ညှဉ်း, *v.* to hurt, injure, treat unjustly or severely, နှိပ်စက်.

ညှဉ်းဆဲ, *v.* do.

ညှဉ်းပန်း, *v.* do.

ညှဉ်းဆိုး, *v.* to be distressed, miserable.

ညှပ်, (1) *v.* to pinch, squeeze, compress between two substances ; *neut.* ညပ်.

ညှပ်, (2) *n.* nippers, pincers, tongs, snuffers, shears, scissors, &c.

ညှပ်ရိုး, *n.* the collar bone ; lower jaw bone.

ညှာ, *v.* to have regard to, pity, help, စာနာ၊ ထောက်.

ညှာတာ, *v.* do.

ညှာတွယ်, *v.* do.

ညှိ, (1) *v.* to kindle, to catch fire, တွန်း ; *neut.* ညီ ; to take along with one, ဆွေး.

ညှိ, (2) *v.* to make even, alike ; *neut.* ညီ.

ညှိညွှတ်, *v.* do.

ညှိ, (3) *v.* to compare, နှိုင်း ၊ ယှဉ်.

ညှီ, *v.* to be rank in regard to smell, to smell offensively, ညှော် ၊ ဟောက်.

ညှော်, *v.* to smell as burnt flesh.

ညှော်သင်, *v.* do.

ညှိုး, *v.* to be dull, faded, withered, နွမ်း ၊ သွမ်း ; to be of a sad countenance, နွမ်း ၊ သမ်း ; to be sorrowful, distressed in mind, ညစ် ၊ ညှဉ်း ၊ နှိုး ၊ နွမ်း ၊ ပျပ်.

ညှိုးငယ်, *v.* do.

ညှိုးဖြ, *v.* do.

ညှိုးမြည်း, *v.* do.

ညှို့, (1) *v.* to charm, lure, decoy, ဖမ်းစား.

ညှို့, (2) *v.* to blow the nose.

ညှို့, (3) *n.* a bow-string, the string of a musical instrument.

ညွတ်, (1) *v.* to bend down, ကုန်းဆေ ၊ ကိုင်းဆေ.

ညွတ်, (2) *v.* to incline the mind, persuade, ဖျားယောင်း.

ညွတ်, (3) *n.* a noose, a collection of nooses, ကျော့ကွင်း.

ညွှန်, *v.* to show, point out, ပြ.

ညွှန်း, *v.* do.

## ဋ

The first consonant in the class of linguals, which is called the ဋ class.

ဋီကာ, *n.* a commentary on the original Pali text, (supplementary to the inspired commentary of the Yahandahs, which is called အဋ္ဌကထာ.)

ဋီကာဆရာ, *n.* a commentator on do.

## ဌ

The second consonant in the class of linguals.

ဌာန, *(Pali,)* *n.* a place, အရပ် ; a receptacle.

ဌာပနာ, *(Pali,)* *v.* to enshrine.

ဌီ, (from ဌိတိ, *Pali,*) *n.* continuance, တည်ခြင်း.

ဌိတိက္ခဏ, *n.* the continuance of thought ; see စိတ္တက္ခဏ.

## ဍ.

The third consonant in the class of linguals.

## ဎ.

The fourth consonant in the class of linguals.

## ဏ.

The fifth consonant in the class of linguals.

## တ.

The first consonant in the class of dentals, which is called the တ class.

တ, (1) *v.* to regret, တသ.

တ, (2) *num. adj.* one, *(a contraction of* တစ် *; also a contraction of* တခြား, other.)

တ, (3) *n.* a formative prefix, used especially in forming adverbs; (see Gram.)

တရုင်တဈာ, *adv.* numerously, confusedly.

တက်, (1) *v.* to go up, ascend; opposed to ဆင်း, to descend.

တက်, (2) *v.* to advance, increase.

တက်, (3) *n.* a paddle.

တဏ္ဍုတွန်း, *n.* a gross heretic, one whose sentiments are fundamentally erroneous; *comp.* တိတ္ထိ.

တက်ခတ်, *v.* to pull an oar, to row.

တုတ်တတ်, *adv.* an intensive, ကျွတ်ကျွတ်.

တက်တူ, *n.* a kind of large brown lizard.

တက်နာ, *n.* a convulsion fit.

တက်မ, *n.* a rudder or helm.

တက်မကိုင်, *n.* a helmsman, ပဲ့နင်း.

တက်မရိုင်း, *v.* to put the helm to starboard.

တက်မယက်, *v.* to put the helm to larboard.

တကယ်, *adv.* right, certain, true, အကယ်.

တက်လှော်, *v.* to paddle.

တက်ဝန်း, *v.* to assemble round, encircle, &c. ဝိုင်း.

တက်ဝယ်, *adv.* in a cross-legged manner.

တကာ, (1) (from ဒါယကာ, *Pali,*) *n.* one who contributes to the support of religious characters, a layman, ဥပါသကာ.

တကာမ, *n.* a female do.

တကာ, (2) *adj.* all, the whole.

တကား, *adv. affix*, indeed! alas!

တကဲ့တကဲ့, *adv.* by degrees; see ကဲ့.

တကျည်ပကတ်, *n.* a kind of tree.

တကျဉ်း, *n.* a principal nerve or tendon in the bowels.

တကျဉ်းကျဉ်း, *adv.* moderately and protractedly, applied to pain.

တကွ, *adv. affix,* together, together with, as ဆရာတကွ, with the teacher.

တကွနက်, (from တစ်, one, အကွ, together, and အနက်, a collection,) *adv.* at once, all together, တပြိုင်နက်.

တခါ, *adv.* once.

တခါတည်း, *adv.* one time only, at once.

တခု, (from တစ်, one, and အခု, a numeral auxiliary,) some one; one out of several.

တခုတခု, *adv.* one after another, whether every one, or several.

တခုတလေ, or တလေတခု, *adj.* few, now and then one, or here and there one. N. B. Other numeral auxiliaries are used in a similar manner, as တခါတလေ, or တလေတခါ, sometimes, now and then; တယောက်တလေ, &c. a few persons, now and then a person.

တခုလပ်, *n.* a woman who has lost her husband by death, or divorce.

တခဲ, (from တစ်, one, and ခဲ, to be hard,) *n.* a hard substance; a number of materials blended into one mass.

တခဲနက်, (1) (from အနက်, a collection,) *n.* do. do.

တခဲနက်, (2) *adj.* commingled, blended, assimilated, (frequently applied to sound, and colours.)

တခဲနက်, (3) *adv.* altogether, တကွနက်; တပြိုင်နက်.

တခေါက်, *adv.* once; နှစ်ခေါက်, twice, &c. (see ခေါက်.)

တခြမ်း, *n.* a half.

တခြား, see အခြား, under ခြား, other.

တချိုင့်ချိုင့်, *adv.* noisily.

တချောင်းချောင်း, *adv.* see ချောင်းချောင်း.

တချို့, see အချို့, some.

တင်, (1) *v.* to put, or place upon ; တင်စည်, *v.* do.

တင်, (2) *v.* to stretch, as a bow, i. e. to place the string upon the catch.

တင်, (3) *v.* to be alive, not dead, ရှင်.

တင်လျှင်, *v.* to be beforehand, as တင်လျှင်ချ၍ပြောသည်, to speak beforehand.

တင်, (4) *n.* the posteriors, ခွေး ၊ ဆုံ ၊ ပဦဆုံ.

တင်သား, or တင်ဆီး, *n.* do. (most common.)

တင်ပါး, *n.* the sides of do.

တင်္ကား, *n.* coin, money.

တင်ကူး, *v.* to cross a river obliquely, setting above the place aimed at in order to counteract the force of the current ; to take a similar course to gain any point.

တင်ကျည်, *n.* the cross-piece, or yoke, for the back of an animal.

တင်ကျီ, *n.* a kind of bird.

တင်စား, (1) *v.* to use a figure of speech ; (2) to mislead by using language which is susceptible of more than one meaning ; (3) to cheat.

တင်ဆတ်, *n.* a kind of bird.

ထင်တင်, *adv.* clearly, conspicuously.

တင်ပြင်, *adv.* in a cross-legged manner, တက်ဝယ်.

တင်ပြင်ခွေ, *adv.* do.

တင်မိ, *v.* to be beforehand, to get the advantage.

တင်ရှိန်း, *n.* a saddle-cloth.

ထင်လဲ, *n.* molasses, boiled juice of the palm or cane.

တင်း, (1) *v.* to be firm, hard, ခိုင်း ၊ မာ.

တင်း, (2) *v.* to be tight, not slack, မလျော့.

တင်း, (3) *n.* a measure of capacity ; see အတင်း.

တင်းကုပ်, *n.* a shed, low house, place of business, distinguished from a dwelling house.

တင်းကုပ်ရုံ, *n.* do.

ထင်းကျမ်း, (*pron.* ခင်းကျမ်း,) *adv.* very, very much, complete, &c.

တင်းတင်း, *adv.* see တျင်းတျင်း, an intensive.

တင်းတိမ်, (1) *v.* to be satisfied, have enough, (negative တင်းမတိမ်.)

တင်းတိမ်, (2) *n.* a screen.

တင်းလင်း, *adj.* or *adv.* unfinished, လက်စမပြီး.

တင်းဝါး, *n.* a kind of bamboo.

တင့်, *v.* to appear well, be comely, handsome. Hence အတင့်, *adv.* appearing well, but not in reality.

တင့်အပ်, *v.* do.

တင့်တယ်, or တင့်တည်, *v.* do. (most common.)

တစ်, (1) *adj.* one, (marked ၁.)

တစ်, (2) *v.* to be tight, not slack, ကြပ်.

တစ်, (3) *v.* to cut in pieces. Hence အတစ်, *n.* a piece, bit.

တစည်း, *n.* a kind of adze, ဋင်း.

တစပြင်, *n.* a place of performing funeral rites.

တရစာ, *adv.* without intermission.

တစိ, *n.* or *adv.* a little bit, အနည်ငယ် ၊ နည်းငယ် ၊ နိုးနည်း ၊ ဆိတ်စိ ၊ တစိုးတစိ.

တစုံတခု, *adj.* some one, one only. N. B. Other numerals are construed in a similar manner ; တစုံတယောက်, some one person.

တဝ, *adv.* merely, only, သက်သက်.

တစောင်တိုက်, *v.* to instigate a quarrel by underhand management, ဋုတိုက်.

တစောင်းချောင်း, *v.* to peep, look slily, pry into.

တစိုးတစိ, see တစိ, or နိုးနည်း.

တဆ္ဆနှိဖြိ, *n.* a small particle of dust.

တစ္ဆေ, or တဆေ, *n.* a ghost, (see စစ္ဆေ.)

တဆုပ်တဆုန်း, *adj.* one, a single one.

တဆာ, *n.* see တန်ဆာ.

တဆိတ်, *n.* a pinch, that is, a small quantity.

တဆိတ်ကလေး, *adv.* very little.

တဆေး, *n.* leaven or yeast.

တရှင်, *n.* a file.

တကျောင်တပ်, *n.* the flank of an army.

တည်, *v.* (1) to build up, erect, set up, establish, ထောက်, ထောင်.

တည်တား, *v.* do. *also*, to establish, make firm, settle, compose, agree to, make binding.

တည်ကြည်, *v.* to build up, erect, set up, establish, &c.

တည်ကြား, *v.* do.

တည်တံ့, *v.* do.

တည်ကျွေး, *v.* to feast to satiety, ရစ်ဝ.

တည်, (2) *n.* a basket, measuring one တင်း.

တည်, (3) *n.* the fig tree, တည်ပင်.

တည်, (4) *n.* an elephant with one tusk only.

တည်ရာ, *n.* a building, an abode.

တညင်း, *n.* a kind of tree.

တည်း, (1) *affix,* used in asking questions, to designate the point on which the question turns, and is nearly equivalent to *or*, and *either*.

တည်း, (2) *adv.* only, as တခုတည်း, one thing only.

တည်း, (3) *v.* to remain for a little while, to secure for a little while, တဲ.

တည်း, (4) *v.* to be, used at the close of a simple sentence, as အမည်းကားမောင်လောက်တည်း, his name is Moung Louk.

တည်းစပ်, (from တည်း, and စပ်,) *n.* an instrument used by tailors to stitch work together.

တည့်, (1) *v.* to be strait forward, direct from one point to another, မစောင်း၊ မတိမ်း.

တည့်, (2) *(pron.* ဒဲ့,) *affix,* shows that the words to which it is affixed are a quotation, or repeated from the mouth of another.

တည့်တည့်, *adv.* straitly, directly, strait forward, ဖြူးဖြူး.

တညီး, *adv.* evenly, alike, like as.

တဏှာ, *n.* passion, လောဘ၊ ဆန္ဒ.

တတ်, (1) *v.* to know, know how, be accustomed to, skilled in, understand, လည်.

တတ်နိုင်း, *adv.* according to one's skill, by one's own ability.

တတ်, (2) *v. affix,* equivalent to ရှိသည်. It is used at the close of a parenthesis, or paragraph.

တတ်စွမ်, *v.* to be able, possess ability.

တတ်လွယ်, *v.* to be intelligible, easy to be understood.

တတိယ, (from တိ, or တြိ, three, *Pali,*) *adj.* third.

တတောက်တတောက်, *adv.* by degrees ; see ကဲ့.

တခဏ, *adv.* a little while, a moment, ခဏ.

တဒတ္ထသမ္ပဒါန်, *(in Grammar,) n.* the dative case, when it terminates in ၌, *(Carey.)*

တဒါရုံ, *n,* idea, memory, မှတ်မြဲသောအမှုကိုအမှတ်ပြုခြင်း.

တန်, (1) *v.* to accord with, be enough, suitable, worthy of, တော် ၊ ထိုက် ၊ လောက် ၊ ရာ ၊ လျော် ၊ သင့်.

တန်, (2) *v.* to be mean, worthless, unbecoming, unsuitable, out of character, wrong, vile, ညိုးညစ် ၊ ညံ့ ၊ တေ ၊ ဖျင် ၊ ယုတ်.

တန်, (3) *n.* filth, dirt, *(obsolete.)*

တန်, (4) *n.* an evil, calamity, ဘေး ၊ အန္တရယ်.

တန်, (5) *num. affix,* as အကျိုးနှစ်တန်, two rewards.

တန်ကျွန်, *n.* a kind of vine.

တန်ခိုး, *(frequently pron.* တခိုး,) *n.* power.

တနင်္ဂနွေ, *n.* the sun in character of a planet ; *comp.* ဂြိုဟ် ; the first day of the week, Sunday.

တနင်္လာ, *n.* the moon in character of a planet ; *comp.* ဂြိုဟ် ; the second day of the week, Monday.

တနင်္သာရီ, *n.* Tenasserim, the southernmost town in the Burman dominions.

တန်စက်, *n.* the eaves of a roof, အမိုးစွန်.

တန်စယ်, *(pron.* တစယ်,) *n.* a field on the margin of a river, cultivated in the dry season, and overflowed in the rains, မှုရင်.

တန်ဇိတွင်း, *n.* a reservoir, a receptacle of filth, *(pron.* တဇိတွင်း.)

တန်စွက်, *(pron.* တစွက်,) *n.* a kind of boat.

တန်စွက်ပန်း, *n.* a kind of tree.

တန်ဆာ, *(frequently pron.* တဆာ,) *n.* an ornament or article of embellishment ; an implement or article of use ; an appendage of any kind.

တန်ဆေး, *(pron.* တဆေး,) *n.* yeast, or any fomenting substance.

တန်ဆောင်, *(pron.* တဆောင်,) *n.* a portable pyramidical structure offered in worship.

တန်ဆောင်တိုင်, *n.* do.

တန်ဆောင်မုန်း, *(pron.* တဆောင်မုန်း,) *n.* the eighth month in the year.

တန်ဆောင်း, (*pron.* တဇောင်း,) *n.* a four-cornered edifice, with a roof which commonly consists of two or three gradations, erected at the corners of fortresses, for the purposes of defence; or elsewhere, for religious purposes; (*comp.* ပြာသာဒ်.)

တနည်းကား, *adv.* moreover, furthermore.

တဏှ, *n.* a robber, a ravisher, &c.

တံတား, (*pron.* တဒါး,) *n.* a bridge, causeway, wharf; *figuratively*, a messenger.

တန်တူ, (*pron.* ဒန်တူ,) *adj.* or *adv.* alike, equal.

တံတိုင်း, (*pron.* တဒိုင်း,) *n.* a brick, or stone wall.

တံပြက်, (*pron.* တပြက်,) *n.* a kind of creeper.

တံမြက်, (*pron.* တမြက်,) *n.* a broom.

တံမြက်စည်း, *n.* do. (*by corruption*, တမြက်စည်း.)

တံမြက်ချေး, *n.* sweepings.

တနွယ်, *n.* a large spot of deep mud.

တံသား, *n.* a carpenter's rule, a ruled line.

တန်း, (1) *n.* an extended line, စင်း. Hence အတန်း, *n.* an extended line, အစင်း; a row, အစဉ်; length, duration, as အသက်တန်း, length of life.

တန်း, (2) *n.* a place of detention, or moderate confinement, for debt, or slight offences.

တန်းသား, *n.* a keeper of do.

တန့်, (1) *v.* to stop, put a stop to, တန့်ဆီး; (2) *v.* to stop, remain. Hence အတန့်, *n.* a mark drawn across, a limit, stop. အတန့်တန့်, *adv.* one after another, successively.

တပ်, (1) *v.* to fix in or on, tie, နှပ်.

တပ်, (2) *v.* to dye, colour, ဆိုး.

တပ်, (3) *v.* to desire, covet, lust after, နှမ်း ၊ မက်.

တပ်, (4) *v.* to be certain, (*not used alone.*) Hence အတပ်, *adv.* certainly.

တပ်အပ်, *adv.* certainly, အကယ် ၊ အမှန်.

တပ်တပ်, *adv.* do.

တပ်, (5) *n.* a fortification of wood; *comp.* မြို့.

တပ်, (6) *n.* a regiment of soldiers, or a squadron of military boats.

တပ်ဦး, *n.* advanced troops.

တပ်စီးပြ, *n.* a parade of troops.

တပ်တာ, *n.* a fortification, a regiment of soldiers, a squadron of military boats.

တပ်တောင်, *n.* do.

တပ်ဖျား, *n.* advanced troops.

တပ်မ, *n.* a chief fortification, the main body of an army, or of military boats.

တပ်မှူး, *n.* a military officer, a captain, or colonel.

တပ်သင်္ဘော, *n.* a war-ship, " a man of war."

တပတ်, *n.* a garment worn by women over the shoulders, a shawl.

တပဆေး, *n.* a kind of tree.

တပည့်, *n.* a disciple; see တပြည့်.

တပါး, *pron. adj.* other, another, အခြား၊ တခြား၊ အထူး၊ တထူး.

တပ္ပုရိသ, *(a grammatical term,) n.* the fourth class of compound sentences, made by compounding a noun in any case with a verb, *(Carey.)*

တပေါင်း, *n.* the twelfth month in the year.

တပိုတပါး, *adv.* more or less.

တပိုးခင်, *n.* the mouth-piece of a musical instrument.

တပို့တွဲ, *n.* the eleventh month in the year.

တမြက်စည်း, *(a corruption of* တံမြက်စည်း,) *n.* a broom.

တပြင်တကွဲ, *adv.* diversely, in different directions.

တပြင်တပါး, (from အပြင်, an outside, and တပါး, other,) *adv.* or *adj.* elsewhere; pertaining elsewhere, or to some other place.

တပြည့်, *n.* a disciple, a scholar.

တပြည့်တော်, (1) *n.* a disciple of an eminent teacher; (2) *pers. n.* I, *mas.* (used in addressing a priest, or religious teacher.)

တပြည့်တော်မ, *fem. of* တပြည့်တော်.

တပြောင်းပြန်ပြန်, *adv.* backward and forward, interchangeably.

တပြိုင်နက်, (from တစ်, one, ပြိုင်, to be or do together, and အနက်, a collection,) *adv.* at once, all together, တကွနက်.

တဖန်, *adv.* again, once more.

တဖန်ဖန်, *adv.* again, repeatedly.

တဖံ, *adv.* again, once, once more.

တဖံတုံ့, *adv.* again, once more.

တဖျတ်ဖျတ်, *adv.* see ဖျတ်ဖျတ်.

တဖြုတ်, *adv.* an instant, instantly, ခဏတဖြုတ် ၊ ဖြုတ်ခနဲ.

တဘန်, *adv.* see တဖံ.

တဘောင်, *n.* a proverb, common saying, a song.

တမ်း, *v.* to be dissatisfied with, feel uneasy on account of, to regret the want of, တ၊ လွမ်း.

တမ်းဆို, *v.* do.

တင်းဆွတ်, *v.* do.

တမ်းညွတ်, *v.* do.

တမ, *n.* the past; the future, လွန်ချင်း.

တမင်, *adv.* therefore; see သို့တမင်.

တမန်, *n.* a messenger.

တမန်း, *n.* mud in rice fields, သမန်း.

တမဟုတ်, *n.* an instant, moment; *see* မဟုတ်.

တဗ္ဗ, *n.* the poorest kind of gold, being that in common use, ရွှေ.

တမာ, *n.* a kind of tree.

တမုတ်ကြိုး, *n.* ornamental cords or ropes, trappings.

တမုံ့, used after an assertive affix, is merely expletive, as သွားသည်တမုံ့, he goes.

တမူ, *affix*, see တမုံ့.

တမူကား, *v. affix*, implies supposition, as, သွားတမူကား; if he go, or if he had gone. It is also an affix of tense, as သွားတမူကား, when he went, or had gone; having gone.

တမျည်း, see တမြည်း.

တမြန်နေ့, *n.* the day before yesterday.

တမြည်း, *n.* the art of telling where lost goods can be found, နိမိတ်.

တမြင်း, *n.* a rule, or measuring rod, မြင်း.

တမြိတ်, *n.* a kind of plant.

တမှိန်းတွေတွေ, *adj.* lost, or confused, in thought.

တမျှ, *adv.* as, like as, &c. see ဆမျှ.

တမှုတ်, *n.* a kind of royal umbrella.

တယ်, (1) *v.* to be very, (good or bad;) as, တယ်ချောကောင်းသည်, or တယ်ကောင်းသည်, it is very good. In conversation it has various other applications.

တယ်, (2) *interj.* extraordinary ! သယ်.

တယု, *v.* to regret, ယုတ ၊ တ ၊ တမ်း.

တရက်, *n.* Tartary, the name of a country.

တရင်, *an astrological term.*

တရပတ်, *n.* a kind of fan.

တရပတ်သမား, *n.* a ship-caulker, တေးတတ်သောသူ.

တရံ, (1) *n.* a fence, enclosure.

တရံ, (2) *n.* a time, turn, as တရံသောခါ, at one time, at the same time.

တရား, (1) *n.* the universal, and immutable laws of the moral world, collectively considered, or any particular moral principle or law; whatever accords with the laws of the moral world, or with the established system of just retribution; justice, right.

တရား, (2) *v.* to accord with any law or moral principle, to be just, right. Hence မတရား, unjust, illegal, sinful.

တရားတသောင်း, *n.* see တရား.

တရားကွမ်းဘိုး, *n.* see ကွမ်းဘိုး.

တရားခံ, *n.* a defendant in a suit at law.

တရားထင်ကုပ်, *n.* an inferior tribunal.

တရားတွေ့, *v.* to engage in a lawsuit.

တရားလမ်း, (from တရား, a moral principle, and လမ်း, a road,) *n.* the path of duty, a moral course, morality.

တရားလို, *n.* a plaintiff.

တရားသူကြီး, *n.* an administrator of justice, a magistrate, judge.

တရုပ်, *n.* China.

တရေးရေး, *adv.* steadily, uniformly, consistently.

တယော, *n.* a violin.

တယောထိုးတံ, *n.* a fiddlestick.

တရှော်, *n.* a kind of tree.

တရွင်း, *n.* a spade.

တရှောင်ရှောင်, *adv.* moderately and of long standing, as a chronic disease.

တလင်း, *n.* a clean level spot of ground.

တလင်းပြင်, *n.* do.

တလား, *n.* a coffin, or any receptacle wherein a corpse is placed to receive funeral rites.

တလားဖုတ်, *n.* a low cook-house; a name given particularly to the place near Kyoungs, where those who are candidates for the priesthood cook their rice.

တလိမ်လည်, (from လိမ်, and လည်,) *adv.* hypocritically, dissemblingly.

တလုပ်ဆိမ်, *n.* a compartment in a sacerdotal garment.

တလိုမွေးမွေး, *adv.* concernedly.

တလုံလဲလဲ, *adv.* repeatedly, တလဲလဲ.

တဆေတခု, see တခုတဆေ.

တလိုင်း, *adj.* pertaining to the Peguese. တလိုင်းပြည်, *n.* Pegu.

တလိုင်းနို့, *n.* a kind of tree.

တလျှောက်လုံး, *adv.* all along.

တဝန်းတလျှာ, *n.* a division, part, portion.

တဝတည်း, *adv.* unitedly, (in regard to time,) all at once.

တဝေ့လည်လည်, *adv.* round and round, like a whirlpool.

တသ, *v.* to regret, တ ၊ တမ်း ၊ တယူ.

တံကူး, (*pron.* တဂူး,) *n.* the first month in the year.

တံကဲ, (*pron.* တဂဲ,) *n.* a support for the back, any thing to lean against.

တံကဲလူ, *n.* a substantial man, one who affords support to others.

တံကျင်, (*frequently pron.* တဂျင်,) *n.* a spit, or any thing of the kind, တံရှု.

တံကွမ်, *n.* see တံခွန်.

တံခါး, (*pron.* တဂါး,) *n.* a door or gate.

တံခါးကျင်, *n.* a bolt, bar, ကန့်လန့်ကျင် ၊ ကျည်း.

တံခါးခုံ, *n.* a threshold.

တံခါးပေါင်, *n:* the back part of the leaf of a door, terminating in a point above and below, upon which the door turns, supplying the place of proper hinges; *comp.* ဆပေါင်.

တံခါးမုတ်, *n.* an arch or frame over a door or gate.

တံခါးရွက်, *n.* the leaf or fold of a door.

တံခါးချူ, *n.* a long pole used to gather fruit with.

တံခွန်, (*pron.* တဂွန်,) (1) *n.* a kind of flag, made of cloth or paper, and offered in worship.

တံခွန်, (2) *n.* the tail of a comet, or of a meteor.

တံခွန်ကုက်ကား, *n.* a flag suspended from a bending staff.

တံငါတာရာ, *n.* one of the constellations; see တာရာ.

တံငါး, (*pron.* တငါး,) *n.* a fisherman.

တံစဉ်း, (*pron.* တရှဉ်း,) *n.* a file.

တံစည်, (*pron.* တရှည်,) *n.* a sickle.

တံစည်း, (*pron.* ရှည်း,) *n.* an adze.

တံစူးဝါး, (*pron.* တရှူးဝါး,) *n.* a poker used at funerals.

တံစိုး, (*pron.* တဆိုး,) *n.* a present made in order to gain some end, a bribe; တံစိုးကိုစားသည်, he lives by bribery.

တံစိုးထိုး, *v.* to bribe.

တံစို့, (*pron.* တဆို့,) *n.* a spit, or any thing of the kind.

တံဆိပ်, (*frequently pron.* တဆိပ်,) *n.* a mark or impression made by stamping, a stamp.

တံဆိပ်ခတ်, *v.* to make an impression with a stamp, to stamp, seal.

တံဆုံး, *n.* a stamp.

တံတင်း, *n.* a kind of box or basket, (*obsolete.*)

တံတောင်, (*pron.* တဒေါင်,) *n.* the elbow, the arm from the elbow to the fingers' ends.

တံတောင်ဆစ်, *n.* the elbow, the joint of the elbow.

တံတောင်ပွတ်, *n.* the elbow.

တံထဘ, *n.* a kind of cloth.

တံတွေး, (*pron.* တထွေး,) *n.* spittle; *by corruption,* ဓတွေး.

တံဒုတ်, (*pron.* တဒုတ်,) *n.* a corruption of တံသုတ်, which see.

တံပူ, (*pron.* တဘူ,) *n.* a tooth-brush; a tongue-scraper, နံနက်စား.

တံပူစာ, *v.* to use a tooth-brush, or tongue-scraper.

တံပိုး, (1) *n.* a horn, or trumpet, a kind of wind-instrument.

တံပိုး, (2) *n.* a wave, လှိုင်း.

တံမြာ, (*pron.* တမြာ,) *n.* a rod, stick, a bunch of rods.

တံဘောင်, (*frequently written and pron.* တဘောင်,) a proverb, a common saying or song.

တံမြော, *n.* a short kind of wind-instrument.

တံရှည်, *n.* a long kind of wind-instrument.

တံရှူးဝါး, *n.* a poker used in burning a corpse at funerals.

တံလျှပ်, *n.* the dazzle of the sun's beams, reflected from a sandy plain, occasioning an appearance like water.

တံသျှပ်, *n.* do.

တံစို့, (*pron.* ဒံစို့,) *n.* a spy, သူလျှို.

တံသင်း, *n.* a peg or stick, driven into the ground to fasten any thing by, or upon.

တံသုတ်, (*pron.* ဒံသုတ်,) *n.* a leveller, whether small, such as is used to level grain in a measure, or large and heavy, such as is used to level ground.

တံသုတ်ကျင်း, *n.* do.

တာ, (1) *v.* to measure with a tah, (တာ.) Hence အတာ, *n.* a measure of length equal to 7 cubits; measure in general, distance; allotment, portion of business, အငန်း ၊ အဝန်.

တာ, (2) *n.* a box, သေတ္တာ, (*obsolete.*)

တာကျ, *v.* to come to one's turn.

တာတတ်, *v.* do.

တာသင့်, *v.* do.

တာတွယ်, *v.* to be attached to, တွယ်တာ ၊ ငြာတာ ၊ စွဲ.

တာပန, *n.* one of the states of punishment; see ငရဲ.

တာရာ, (*Pali,*) *n.* a star or constellation, ကြယ်. N. B. Nine principal ones are enumerated, corresponding to the 27 Nekkats (နက္ခတ်), viz. ကာကာ, a crow, ကြိုးတာရာ; ဟံသာ, a kind of bird, ဟင်းသာတာရာ; ကဏ္ကဋ, a species of crab-fish, ပုစွန်တာရာ; တူလာ, scales, ချိန်တာရာ; စူဠာ, a crest; an ornament used to fasten up the hair, ဆံကျင်တာရာ; ကေဝဋ္ဋ, a fisherman, တံငါတာရာ; ဟတ္ထိ, an elephant, ဆင်တာရာ; အဿ, a horse, မြင်းတာရာ; ဗကော, a heron, a paddy bird, ဗျိုင်းတာရာ.

တာလီ, *n.* a certain golden ornament, formerly worn around the neck, ဓါလီ.

တာလုဇာ, (from တာလု, the palate, *Pali,*) *adj.* palatal, produced from the palate, applied to consonants of the စ class.

တာဝတိံသာ, *n.* the second stage of the world of Nats, situate on the summit of the Myenmo mount; *compare* နတ်ပြည်.

တား, *v.* to impede, obstruct, prevent, ဆီး ၊ ဖြီး.

တားတား, *adv.* middling, (affixed to words of quality.)

တိ, (1) *v.* to pare off (an end,) in order to make even, to cut off (a little bit.)

တိ, (2) *(Pali,) adj.* one.

တိတ္ထိ, *n.* one whose sentiments are partially erroneous ; *comp.* တဏ္ဍတွန်း.

တိတ္ထိယပက္ကန္တက, *n.* a proselyte to erroneous sentiments.

တိတ်, (1) *v.* to be still, silent, quiet, ဆိတ်.

တိတ်, (2) *n.* an omen, နိမိတ်.

တိတ်တိတ်, *adv.* silently, quietly, privately.

တိတ်ထုံး, *n.* a writing explanatory of omens.

တိတ်ငေါ့, *v.* to have regard to, consider, ငဲ့.

တိထိ, *(pron.* ဒိဒိ, *Pali,) n.* a lunar day, the 30th part of a lunation.

တိန်ညင်း, *n.* a kind of bird.

တိန်နဂါးငွေ့, *n.* the galaxy, milky-way.

တိန်းညက်, *n.* the logwood tree.

တိန်းညင်, *n.* a tame animal used to decoy wild ones.

တိမ်, (1) *v.* to be shallow, of little depth, မနက်.

တိမ်, (2) *n.* a cloud.

တိမ်လွှာ, *n.* do.

တိမ်ငါးကြင်းကြေး, *n.* clouds which lie in the manner of the scales on a fish.

တိမ်ထိုက်, *n.* a thick heavy cloud.

တိမ်ထပ်, *n.* clouds which lie behind one another.

တိမ်ပုပ်, *n.* a dark gloomy cloud.

တိမ်မြုပ်, *v.* to disappear, be lost, obliterated, buried in oblivion.

တိမ်ဆင့်, *n.* clouds which lie behind one another.

တိမ်း, (1) *v.* to incline, put on one side, set obliquely, ငဲ့ ၊ စောင်း ၊ ယိမ်း.

တိမ်း, (2) *v.* to go aside or out of the way, be indirect, စောင်း ၊ လွဲ.

တိမ်းတိ, *adv.* lying on one side, စောင်းတိ.

တိမ်းတိတိမ်းပါး, *adv.* do.

တိရစ္ဆာန်, (from တိရစ္ဆာန, *Pali,) n.* a brute animal, any animal between man and insects, whether bird, beast, or fish.

တိ, (1) *v.* to clear up, as wild ground, ထွင်.

တိ, (2) *n.* a descendant of the fourth generation.

တိ, (3) *n.* an earth-worm.

တိတီတွတ်, *n.* a kind of bird.

တီတွတ်, *v.* to warble, chirp, chatter, talk much, make a continued noise, as in chanting, lamenting, scolding, &c. ယောက်တီမည်တွန်.

တီတော့, *v.* to gurgle ; *see also* တီတွတ်.

တီး, (1) *v.* to strike in order to produce sound, as on a drum or any musical instrument ; to beat, as the breast.

တီးမှုတ်, *v.* to produce any musical sound, by beating and blowing.

တီး, (2) *v.* to shake by sudden jerks, as rice in a basket, for the purpose of cleaning it, &c. ဇကောငံ့တီး.

တီးတုတ်, (*pron.* ဒီးဒုတ်,) *n.* a large horned owl.

တီးတိုး, *adv.* softly, gently.

တီးတောက်, *v.* to complain, murmur, find fault with, မည်တွန်၊ စောင်ကပ်တီး.

တု, *v.* to emulate, rival, pretend to an equality, ပြိုင် ; to imitate in appearance or manners.

တုပ, *v.* do. do.

တုတ်, (1) *v.* to break without severing the parts.

တုတ်, (2) *v.* to drink a large quantity, drink to excess.

တုတ်, (3) *n.* ascarides.

တုတ်, (4) *v.* to tie, bind, ချည်၊ တုပ်.

တုတ်တုတ်, (from တုတ်,) *adv. of various applications.*

တုန်, *v.* to shake, tremble, လှုပ်.

တုန်ခိုက်, *v.* do.

တုန်တုန်, *adv.* an intensive.

တုန်ယား, *n.* the fever and ague.

တုန်ရင်, *v.* to shake, tremble.

တုန်း, *n.* time being ; see အတုန်း.

တုန်းတုန်းတင်းတင်း, *adv.* loudly.

တုပ်, (1) *v.* to sting ; to pierce with a jerk ; to strike backward or forward with a short quick jerk.

တုပ်, (2) *v.* to kneel, bend (the knees,) ပုဆစ်တုပ်, ပုဆစ်ချ.

တုပ်ကွ, *v.* do. *Also,* to pay respect, homage, ရှိခိုး.

တုပ်, (3) *v.* to be full, plump, bulky, large in compass, compared with the height or length.

တုပ်, (4) *v.* to tie together as a bundle, ချည်, စည်း.

တုပ်, (5) *n.* a plank, piece of timber placed as a support or guard.

တုရင်တိုင်, *n.* a certain post planted near a door or gate.

တုသိတာ, *n.* see နတ်ပြည်.

တို့, (1) *affix,* applied to nouns, is expletive.

တို့, (2) *euph. affix.*

တို့, (3) *int. affix;* (colloquial.)

တို့, (4) *n.* a sect of Boodhist priests, distinguished by their manner of wearing the upper sacerdotal garment, ဒုကုဋ်.

တို့ဖြန်, *v.* to double, fold, repeat, do over again.

တို့မင်, *n.* a kind of wind instrument, or drum.

တို့ဝပ်, *v.* to respect, reverence; see ရိုသေ.

တိုး, (1) *n.* a tube filled with powder, and made to run on wheels, when fired, ဒုံး.

တိုး, (2) *v.* to be blunt, pointless; not sharp. Hence အတိုး, *n.* a log, block, stump.

တိုးစပ်, *n.* the adjutant bird.

တိုးတိုး, *adv.* continually.

တိုးလိုး, *adv.* lying all along.

တုံ့, (1) *v.* to reply, refute, do a thing in return, ခေါက် ၊ ပြန် Hence အတုံ့, *n.* any thing given, or done in return.

တုံ့, (2) *v.* to stoop through fear or respect, ကျုံ့ ၊ ဝပ်; (not used singly.)

တုံ့ဝပ်, *v.* do. (most common,) ဝပ်တုံ့.

တုံ့ယပ်တုံ့ပယ်, *adv.* backward and forward; alternately.

တူ, (1) *v.* to be erect, set upright, ထောင်.

တူ, (2) *v.* to be the same, like, similar, ညီ ၊ မျှ. Hence အတူ, *n.* likeness, sameness, (frequently written အတု;) *adv.* together with.

တူကွ, *v.* to be in company with, together with, ကွတူ. Hence အတူအကွ, *adv.* together with, အကွအတူ.

တူ, (3) *n.* the son of a man's sister, နှမ၏သား; the son of a woman's brother, မောင်၏သား.

တူ, (4) *n.* a hammer.

တူ, (5) (from တုလာ, scales, *Pali,)* *n.* Libra, the seventh sign of the zodiac.

တူထပ်မျှား, *v.* to be crowded, huddled together.

တူရိယာ, *n.* a musical instrument of any kind.

တူရူ, *adv.* strait forward, direct, ရှုံးရူတည့်တည့်၊ ဖြောင့်.

တူလာ, (from တုလာ, scales, *Pali.)* (1) *n.* see တာရာ; (2) *n.* a certain class of diseases, supposed to have their seat in the waist, or centre of the body.

တူလာသရော, *n.* certain diseases; see တူလာ.

တူး, (1) *v.* to dig.

တူးဆွ, *v.* to root up (the ground,) as a hog.

တူး, (2) *v.* to be burnt, as food in cooking, ချွန်.

တူးတည်, *v.* to make firm, establish; see တည်ကြည်.

တူးလေး, *n.* a cross-bow.

တေ, (1) *v.* to beat, pound, in order to make pliable, consistent, &c. ထု.

တေ, (2) *v.* to be exhausted, spent, ကုန်.

တေ, (3) *v.* to be mean, worthless, vile, ယုတ်၊ ညံ့၊ ထန်.

တေ, (4) *v.* to do repeatedly.

တေ, (5) *n.* brass, ကြေးဝါ၊ ဝင်ဂြာ.

တေဇော, *(Pali,)* (1) *n.* fire, မီး.

တေဇော, (2) *n.* power, glory, တန်ခိုးတော်.

တေမိ, *n.* one division of the Boodhist scriptures, (marked တေ.)

တေလောနှမင်, *n.* publican, tax-gatherer.

တေး, *n.* a kind of short song.

တေးချင်း, *n.* do. (most common.)

တေးကျာ, *n.* do.

တေးတွံ, *n.* do.

တေးခံ, *n.* a chorus or response.

တေးကိုယ်, *n.* the body of a song.

တေ့, *v.* to bring near, place in contact, join, to lay together, compare, collate.

တေ့တေ့တဒ်တင်, *adv.* face to face.

တဲ, (1) *v.* to remain a little while, တည်း.

တဲ, (2) *n.* a temporary abode, a place of rest, a tent, &c.

တဲဆို, *n.* do.

တဲစခန်း, *n.* a resting place, place of refreshment, camp, an encampment.

တဲနန်း, *n.* a temporary palace, place of royal refreshment.

တဲရှင်, *n.* a moveable tent, a vehicle.

တဲတဲ, *adv.* a little, အနည်းငယ်.

တဲ့, *v.* to be straight forward, direct, တည့်.

တော, (1) *v.* to resent an insinuation, demand satisfaction, စကား တော့; see တော့.

တော, (2) *n.* a wood, forest, wilderness.

တောအုပ်, (from အုပ်, to overspread,) *n.* a thick forest.

တောအုံ, (from အုံ, to be crowded together,) *n.* a thicket, a thick forest.

တောကစား, *v.* to go into the woods for pleasure.

တောခွေး, *n.* a wolf; a jackal.

တောဖြိုးသစ်ပင်, *n.* a tree which fructifies without affording blossoms.

တောနက်, *n.* an extensive or deep forest.

တော, (3) *adj.* wild, untame, as တောစား, wild food; တောသား, wild beasts; တောငှက်, birds of the forest.

တောက်, (1) *v.* to strike away with the thumb and finger, or with a stick; *see also under* ခေါက်.

တောက်, (2) *v.* to poison, inebriate, make dizzy, sicken, dispose to vomit.

တောက်အန်, *v.* do.

တောက်, (3) *v.* to shine, be bright, ထွန်း၊ ထိန်၊ ပြောင်.

တောက်ပ, *v.* do.

တောက်, (4) *n.* a stick used to hamper a creature, or to keep him at a distance.

တောက်ဆတ်, *adv.* irritably, provokingly.

တောက်တော, *n.* a kind of plant.

တောက်တီး, *v.* to complain, murmur, find fault with, မြည်တွန်.

တောက်တီးတောက်တက်, *adv.* erroneously, blunderingly.

တောက်တဲ့, *n.* the great lizard, peculiar to India beyond the Ganges.

တောက်တဲ့ပြူးကျူ, *n.* a small species of do.

တောက်တဲ့လက်ဝါး, *n.* a kind of plant.

တောင်, (1) *v.* to desire, lust after.

တောင်, (2) *v.* to measure with a cubit. Hence အတောင်, *n.* a cubit, a measure of length equal to two spans, (အထွာ.) In composition the အ is dropped, as တတောင်, one cubit; နှစ်တောင်, two cubits, &c.

တောင်, (3) *n.* a hill, a mountain.

တောင်ပို့, *n.* a hillock raised by white ants, ချပို့.

တောင်ဖြေ, *adv.* by land, ကုန်းကြောင်း.

တောင်, (4) *n.* the south.

တောင်ညာ, *n.* the queen of the south palace, the first in rank.

တောင်ညာနန်းမ, *n.* do.

တောင်နန်း, *n.* the south palace; the queen of the south palace, the first in rank.

တောင်ဂမုန်း, *n.* a kind of medicinal vine.

တောင်ရှလပ်, *n.* a kind of flower.

တောင်တဲ, *n.* a hairy caterpillar.

တောင်ပံ, *n.* the end of a bird's wing.

တောင်ပိစူး, *n.* a kind of bird.

တောင်ဖြောင့်, *adv.* steadily, intently.

တောင်ဝှေး, *n.* a corruption of တောင်ဝေး.

တောင်ဝေး, *n.* a long staff.

တောင်သူ, (1) *n.* a certain race of people who are addicted to husbandry; (2) *n.* a husbandman.

တောင်း, (1) *v. affix*, indeed. It is generally connected to the root by a euphonic affix, as ကြီးပေတောင်း, it is great indeed.

တောင်း, (2) *v.* to ask, ask for, to require, demand.

တောင်းပြီး, or တောင်းဆို, *v.* do.

တောင်းပန်, *v.* to ask pardon, (less than ကန်တော့;) to ask in a respectful manner, implying a wish to be pardoned for asking; to ask permission, ခွင့်ကြာ.

တောင်းရမ်း, *v.* to ask, ask for; to require, demand.

တောင်း, (2) *v.* to be short, as a garment, တို.

တောင်း, (3) *n.* a basket, (of various sizes.)

တောင့်, (1) *v.* to hide, conceal, be secret, ဝှက်.

တောင့်, (2) *v.* to be stiff, firm, နိုး । တင်း । မာ.

တောင့်, (3) *n.* a quiver, မြားကျည်တောက်.

တောင့်တ, *v.* to long for, express a longing desire after.

တော့, (1) *v. affix*, implying slight necessity, as သွားတော့မည်, must go; သွားတော့, go.

တော့, (2) *v.* toss and catch, to catch in conversation, ကောက်တော့ । ကောက်ထိန်; see under ကော.

တော်, (1) *v.* to be suitable, fit, sufficient, တန် । ကိုက် । ထိုက်.

တော်ကြား, *v.* do.

တော်, (2) *v.* to be connected, related, ဆိုင်.

တော်, (3) *v.* to guess, presume, (not used singly.)

တော်ဆ, *v.* do. ရမ်းဆ.

တော်, (4) *adj.* excellent, (applied to things sacred, royal, divine, &c.)

တော်, (5) *a term of compellation*, used by women to either sex, not disrespectful, but rather impolite.

တော်နေရာ, *n.* a certain honourable seat; see ဓနည်.

တော်မူ, *v. honorific affix*, is always used when speaking of any thing done by a great personage, as ရှင်တော်မူသည်, he *(that is, some great personage)* does. The negative is made by prefixing မ to မူ, as ရှင်တော်မမူ, he does not.

တော်ချော်, *adv.* contrarily, perversely.

တော်လည်း, *v.* to be loud, thundering, ပုံထင်းဝင်.

တော်လှန်, *v.* to be liberated, obtain freedom, as from slavery.

တော်လော်, *v.* to misunderstand, to take one word for another.

တော်သလင်း, *n.* the sixth month in the year.

တို, *v.* to be short, မရှည်.

တိုတောင်း, *v.* do.

တိုက်, (1) *v.* to hit, come in contact, strike against, engage in combat, ခိုက်; to bring into contact, provoke, to quarrel or fight; to put together, compare, နှိုင်းယှဉ်; to rub

တိုက်ခိုက်, *v.* to fight.

တိုက်, (2) *v.* to transport by carriage.

တိုက်, (3) *v.* to give to drink.

တိုက်, (4) *n.* a tight secure place, a repository, whether a room, house, city, kingdom, or Sekyah world.

တိုက်ကျု, *n.* do.

တိုက်တာ, *n.* do.

တိုက်တွန်း, *v.* to investigate, excite, to do any thing.

တိုက်တွန်းလှည့်စား, *v.* to tempt to evil.

တိုက်မောင်း, *n.* a small gong.

တိုက်ရိုက်, *adv.* strait forward, direct, တည့်တည့်.

တိုင်, (1) *v.* to take to witness; to ask leave, အခွင့်တောင်း။ ပန်ကြား.

တိုင်ကြား, *v.* do. do.

တိုင်ခံ, *n.* a security, bail; *v.* to be security, အာမခံ။ ဝန်ခံ.

တိုင်တည်, *v.* to take to witness.

တိုင်တန်း, *v.* to take to witness; to ask leave.

တိုင်တော, *v.* to take to witness.

တိုင်, (2) *v.* to arrive at, reach, obtain, ရောက်.

တိုင်အောင်, *affix,* until, as far as, unto, as သွားသည်တိုင်အောင်, until he goes; အိမ်တိုင်အောင်, as far as the house; ကာလတိုင်အောင်, until the time.

တိုင်တိုင်, *affix,* through, throughout, during, as ပြည်တိုင်တိုင်, through the country; ကာလတိုင်တိုင်, during, or throughout time. In the use of this affix, တို့, or သို့, is understood after the noun.

တိုင်ထက်အဆွန်, *adv.* even to the extremity.

တိုင်, (3) *n.* a post.

တိုင်, (4) *n.* a measure of distance, equal to about two miles; see အတိုင်.

တိုင်ပင်, *v.* to consult, deliberate together.

တိုင်း, (1) *v.* to compare together, to measure or estimate one thing by another, နှိုး။ နှိုင်.

တိုင်းရှည်, *v.* do. Hence အတိုင်းအရှည်, or အတိုင်းအရှည်, *n.* a measurement, estimate.

တိုင်းထွာ, *v.* to be suitable, fit, to be a proper estimate, or measurement.

တိုင်းတာထက်အလွန်ကြီး, *v.* to be beyond measure.

တိုင်း, (2) *n.* a country, or a kingdom, (more extensive than မြို့.)

တိုင်းကား, *n.* do.

တိုင်းကျပ်, *n.* the intermediate space, or boundary between two countries.

တိုင်းခြား, *n.* do.

တိုင်းစွန်း, *n.* the outskirts or borders of a country.

တိုင်းစွန်းမြို့ပြား, *n.* do.

တိုင်းနိုင်ငံ, *n.* a kingdom.

တိုင်း, (3) *adj.* every. It is placed after its substantive, as လူတိုင်း, every man; နေ့တိုင်း, every day.

တိုး, (1) *v.* to advance, increase, add to, be enlarged, ပွါး. Hence အတိုး, increase, interest.

တိုး, (2) *v.* to push, butt, shove against, ဝှေ့; to press into (presence of,) to make submission to, pay homage, wait upon.

တိုးကပ်, *v.* do.

တိုးဝင်, *v.* do.

တိုး, (3) *n.* a kind of animal.

တိုးတိုး, *adv.* softly, not loud.

တို့, (1) *n. affix,* expresses plurality, as လူ, man; လူတို့, men.

တို့, (2) *pers. n.* an abbreviation of ငါတို့, we.

တို့, (3) *v.* to touch lightly.

တျက်တျက်, *(pron.* တက်တက်,) *adv. an intensive.*

တျင်းတျင်း, *(pron.* တင်းတင်း,) *adv.* do.

တျာတျာ, *adv. an intensive to certain words.*

တြိ, *(Pali,) adj.* one.

တြိကဋုက်, *n.* a mixture of ငရုတ်, and ပိတ်ချင်း, (different kinds of pepper,) with ချင်း, (ginger.)

တွ, (1) *v.* to sling up, suspend, ဆိုင်း.

တွ, (2) *v.* to move slow through weakness or fatigue, to be dull, stupid, ထိုင်း၊ ထိုင်းမှိုင်း.

တွက်, (1) *v.* to strike backwards.

တွက်, (2) *v.* to count, enumerate, compute, ရေတွက်. **Hence** အတွက်, a reckoning, account; a matter, concern.

တွက်ကြိန်း, *v.* do.

တွက်ချက်, *v.* do.

တွင်, (1) *v.* to distinguish by name, သမုတ်.

တွင်, (2) *v.* to dispatch, perform expeditiously; to be capable of dispatching, adequate, clever, skilful.

တွင်ကြယ်, *v.* do.

တွင်, (3) *n.* a cupping-glass.

တွင်ခွက်, *n.* do.

တွင်, (4) *affix*, (generally locative,) in, among, as အိမ်တွင်, in the house; သွားသည်တွင်, in going, or while going. တွင် is sometimes possessive.

တွင်မှာ, *affix*, in, within, among.

တွင်ဝန်, *n.* a private minister of state.

တွင်း, *n.* a hole, a pit, as ရေတွင်း, a well; ခံတွင်း, the mouth.

တွတ်တွတ်, *adv.* musically, pleasantly.

တွန်, (1) *v.* to crow, as a cock; to low, bellow, as a cow.

တွန်, (2) *v.* to be poor or thin (on the sides or ribs,) နံတွန်.

တွန်း, *v.* to shove, kick, push, thrust at, to rub off.

တွန်းပယ်, *v.* do.

တွန်းငုံ, *n.* a large wooden hoe, or scraper.

တွန့်, (1) *v.* to move as clouds, waves, smoke, &c. လိမ့်.

တွန့်, (2) *v.* to be wrinkled, shrivelled, drawn up, ရှုံ့; to draw back, as a snake through fear, ကုပ်.

တွန့်ဆုတ်, or တွန်ဆုတ်, *v.* to flinch from a purpose, be wavering, distrustful, နတွန့်; to be close, niggard, ဆို့ပိတ်.

တွန့်တာ, *n.* a retraction of the genitals.

တွပ်, *v.* to cut or polish, as precious stones; to enchase.

တွပ်တွပ်, *adv. an intensive.*

တွယ်, *v.* to join or stick together, make adhesive; to stick, adhere, ကပ်.

တွယ်တာ, *v.* to adhere, be attached to, တာတွယ် ။ ကြွတာ ။ နှံ.

တွံတေး, *v.* to produce a pleasant melodious sound; see ရင့်ကျူး.

တွား, *v.* to creep, or crawl.

တွားတွားပျက်, *v.* to be destroyed, as a city or people.

တွေ, (1) *v.* to be confused in thought, absent, stupified, astonished, *(seldom used singly,)* မိန်း၊ ငိုင်.

တွေဝေ, *v.* do. (most common,) မိန်းမော.

တွေငေါ့, *v.* do.

တွေ, (2) *v.* to stiffen, make firm, တောင့်စေ၊ မာစေ ; to be stiff, fat, ဝ.

တွေ, (3) *v.* to consolidate, unite, make adhere together, စိုင်.

တွေစု, *v.* to be assembled, crowded together, remain in a close body, စု.

တွေပေါက်တိုင်, *n.* a roll of adhesive, combustible materials, saturated with oil, used for a candle.

တွေး, *v.* to consider, deliberate upon, (implying doubt or uncertainty,) ဆ၊ ရှင်း.

တွေးတော, *v.* do.

တွေးခေါ်, *v.* do. ခေါ်တွေး.

တွေးတွေး, *adv.* an intensive to words of redness, ချင်းချင်းမြိုက်မြိုက်.

တွေ့, *v.* to find, meet with, ဆုံ ; to come in contact, to feel ; တရားတွေ့ဆို, to sue at law ; တရားတွေ့ဘက်, the parties opposed in law.

တွဲ, (1) *v.* to put together, unite, ပူး၊ ချုပ်၊ ဖက်၊ ပေါင်းရက်.

တွဲ, (2) *v.* to hang up, suspend, ဆွဲ.

တွဲလောင်း, တွဲလဲ, တွဲရွဲ, *v.* do. (commonly used adverbially.)

တွဲရရွဲ, *adv.* an intensive to words of hanging, suspending, and other words of similar signification.

ဍွဲ, (1) *v.* to suspend, တွဲ.

ဍွဲ, (2) *v.* to hang back, pretend to be reluctant, နွဲ့.

## ထ.

The second consonant in the class of dentals.

ထ, *v.* to arise, get up, ဖြ ; to grow up.

ထ, (2) *euph. affix.*

ထမြောက်, *v.* to arise, as from sickness, or trouble, to recover ; be relieved.

ထမြောက်လုံ့လ, *n.* diligence.

ထနောင်, *n.* a kind of tree.

ထက်, (1) *v.* to be sharp, keen, ချွ ၊ ချွန် ၊ မတုံး.

ထက်, (2) *affix*, than, *a term of comparison.*

ထက်ကြပ်, *adv.* close to, together with, အတူ.

ထက်ခြမ်း, *n.* a half, တခြမ်း.

ထက်ခြမ်းခွဲ, *v.* to divide into halves.

ထက်စည်, *n.* a kind of drum, ပတ်သာ.

ထက်မှာ, *affix*, above, as အိမ်ထက်မှာ, above the house.

ထက်ဆုံး, (from အထက်ဆုံး,) *affix*, through or to the end of, as အသက်ထက်ဆုံး, through or to the end of life.

ထက်ရပ်, *n.* a kind of boat.

ထက်ဝက်, *n.* a half, တဝက်.

ထက်ဝက်ခွဲ, *v.* to divide into halves.

ထက်ဝန်း, (1) *v.* to surround, encircle, ဝန်း.

ထက်ဝန်း, (2) *n.* a circuit; environs.

ထက်ဝန်းကျင်, (1) *v.* to surround, encircle, ပတ်လည် ၊ ပတ်ဝန်းကျင်.

ထက်ဝန်းကျင်, (2) *n.* a circle; environs.

ထက်ဝယ်, *adv.* in a cross-legged position, တင်ပြင်.

ထက်ဝယ်ဖွဲ့, or ထက်ဝယ်ဖွဲ့နေ, or ထက်ဝယ်ဖွေယ်, *v.* to sit in a cross-legged position, တင်ပြင်နေ.

ထက်မကိုင်, *n.* a helmsman; see ပဲ့နင်း.

ထင်, *v.* to be visible, appear, be conspicuous, ပေါ်; to appear to the mind: *hence*, to think, suppose, &c. မှတ်.

ထင်ထင်, *adv.* conspicuously.

ထင်ရှား, *v.* to be visible, appear, be conspicuous.

ထင်း, *n.* fuel, fire-wood.

ထင်းခွေ, *v.* to gather fuel.

ထင်းရှူး, *n.* the pine, or fir-tree.

ထင်းရှူးရည်, *n.* turpentine.

ထစ်, *v.* to break the uniformity of an even line by gaps and protuberances; to interrupt a continuous sound by stops and breaks, as in stuttering, (စကားထစ်,) or in a succession of thunderclaps, (မိုးထစ်,) &c. to catch in conversation, or go round about in order to gain a point, or make some discovery. See under စကား.

ထည်, (1) *v.* to be decent, respectable in appearance; to be showy, vain, assuming, ဝါ ၊ ကြွား.

ထည်, (2) *v.* to exchange, barter, ထည်း, (infrequent.)

ထည်, (3) *num. affix,* as အင်္ကျီနှစ်ထည်, two coats, (see Gram.)

ထည်း, *v.* to be filthy, dirty, mean, ညစ်.

ထည်းညစ်, *v.* do. ညစ်ထည်း.

ထည့်, (1) *v.* to put, or place in, သွင်း.

ထည့်, (2) *affix,* quick, instantly.

ထတ်, (1) see ထပ်.

ထတ်, (2) *affix,* equivalent to ရှိသည်, (used at the close of a paragraph, or parenthesis;) see ထည်း.

ထန်, *v.* to be redundant, excessive, violent, ပြင်း ၊ ထည်း.

ထနောင်း, *n.* a kind of tree.

ထန်း, *n.* a palm tree.

ထန်းကျင့်, *n.* a kind of tree.

ထန်းနို့, *n.* the branch of the male palm tree, whence the liquor distils.

ထန်းဘထပ်, *n.* the bark which clusters round the trunk at certain intervals.

ထန်းကျော်, *n.* do.

ထန်းရည်, *n.* the liquor of the palm tree.

ထန်းလျက်, or ထန်းညက်, *n.* the coarse sugary substance into which the molasses made of the liquor or juice (ထနိသဲ) is ultimately converted.

ထန်းသီးမြင်, *n.* ploughed land, which has the appearance of the palm fruit.

ထန်းတူ, *adj.* alike, equal, on a par.

ထန်းပေါက်, *n.* a young palm tree.

ထပ်, (1) *v.* to place one upon another, add to, ဆင့်; also used as a numeral with the verb စား; as, တထပ်စားသည်, to eat once, &c.

ထပ်, (2) *v.* to exchange, barter, ထည်.

ထပ်, (3) *v.* to repeat an action, do again, ကြော.

ထပ်မံ, *v.* do.

ထပ်တူ, *adj.* alike, equal, on a par, ထန်းတူ.

ထပ်တူရှိ, *v.* to be alike, equal, &c.

ထပ်တူပြု, *v.* to make equal, or to treat as if equal.

ထပ်မျှ, *adj.* alike, equal, on a par, ထပ်တူ.

ထဘီ, *n.* a Burman petticoat, ထမိန်, ထမီ.

ထမင်း, *n.* boiled rice.

ထမင်းဖတ်, *n.* rice when cleared from water.

ထမင်းချိုး, *n.* burnt rice at the bottom of the pot.

ထမင်းချက်, *v.* do.

ထမင်းနှပ်, *n.* rice boiled to a pulp, ယာဂု.

ထမင်းဆုတ်ကြီး, *n.* a kind of tree.

ထမိန်, see ထဘီ.

ထမီ, see ထဘီ.

ထမ်း, *v.* to bear, or carry on the shoulder; to do work, or service of any kind, ဆောင်; to carry on the head.

ထမ်းစင်, *n.* a kind of litter, uncovered vehicle.

ထမ်းရွက်, *v.* to do work, or service, ဆောင်ရွက်.

ထမ်းပိုး, (1) *n.* a yoke for the neck of a draught animal; (2) a porter's yoke; (3) interest, when equal to the principal.

ထမ်းပိုးကျည်း, *n.* the arms of a yoke, by which it is secured to the neck of the creature.

ထမ်းသမား, *n.* a porter, carrier of burdens.

ထယ်, *n.* a ploughshare, a plough; *comp.* ထွန်.

ထယ်, *v.* to plough; (scarcely used by a Burman.)

ထယ်ဒိုးကင်း, *n.* a cast-iron pot; see ဒိုးကင်း.

ထရံ, *n.* the side of a house, or high fence made of woven bamboos, (ထပ်.)

ထံ, *affix*, presence, nearness; see အထံ.

ထံထံ, *adv.* partly wet and partly dry, ခပ်ခြောက်ခြောက်.

ထံမှာ, *affix*, in presence of, as မင်းထံမှာ, in presence of the governor.

ထံပါး, *n.* presence, in presence of; see အထံ.

ထံရင်း, *n.* presence, in presence of; see အထံ.

ထာဝရ, *(Pali,)* (1) *n.* uniformity, constancy, အမြဲတည်ခြင်း; (2) *adv.* unchangeably, constantly.

ထား, *v.* to put, place, ထို့ ; to set aside, postpone, except, not to mention.

ထား, (2) *n.* see ဓား, a knife.

ထိ, (1) *v.* to touch, come in contact, hit, တွေ့ ၊ ခိုက်.

ထိ, (2) *v.* to trespass against, molest, assault, ခိုက် ၊ တိုက်.

ထိခိုက်, *v.* see both definitions of ထိ.

ထိပါး, *v.* do.

ထိကထောက်, *n.* an instrument used by thieves to retain fire, and give light when needed.

ထိကပေါက်, *n.* a buckle.

ထိကပေါက်ကြိုး, *n.* a girth.

ထိကရုံး, *n.* the sensitive plant.

ထိတ်, (1) to startle, be frightened, လန့်.

ထိတ်ကြား, *v.* do. ထိတ်ပျာ, *v.* do. ထိတ်ချိ်, *v.* do.

ထိတ်, (2) *n.* stocks for confinement.

ထိတ်ကြင်, ထိတ်ကျင်, or ထိတ်ကျဉ်း, *n.* the cross bar of do.

ထိတ်ထိတ်, *adv.* fearfully, timorously.

ထိန်, (1) *v.* to be bright, shining, brilliant, တောက် ၊ ထွန်း ၊ ပြောင်.

ထိန်, (2) *(Pali,)* *n.* want of reverence or respect; impudence, စိတ်ကြီးမခန့်ချင်း.

ထိန်း, *v.* to take care of, attend on, protect, စောင့်. Hence အထိန်း, *n.* a nurse, guardian, &c.

ထိန်းချုပ်, *v.* to nurse, take care of, wait upon.

ထိန်းထိန်း, *adv.* loud, thunderingly.

ထိန်းယ, *v.* to take care of, attend on, protect.

ထိန်းသိမ်း, *v.* to take under protection, preserve, lay up securely, take care of.

ထိန့်, used subjunctively or adverbially, as an intensive to verbs, particularly verbs of noise, tumult, &c.

ထိန့်လန့်, do. ထိန့်လန့်ချင်း, do.

ထိပ်, *n.* end, extremity, point, အဖျား ; head, summit, အထွဋ် ၊ ခေါင်.

ထိပ်တင်, *n.* a title politely given to females of the blood royal.

ထိမ်, (1) *v.* to keep back, conceal, secrete, ဝှက် ၊ ထိမ်း.

ထိမ်ကြံ, *v.* do.

ထိမ်တန်, *v.* do.

ထိမ်ခြွတ်, *v.* to conceal, &c. see ထိမ်.

ထိမ်, (2) *n.* a kind of tree.

ထိမ်း, *v.* to feed, take care of, &c. see ထိန်း.

ထိမ်းမြား, *v.* to marry, unite in marriage, perform some marriage ceremony, ပေါင်းဖော်.

ထိမ်းမှတ်, *v.* to give a name, သမုတ်; to give an order, enact a law, ပညတ်.

ထိမ်းသည်, *n.* a potter; see အိုးထိမ်း.

ထိ, *v.* to fear, reverence, stand in awe of, ခန့် ၊ လေး.

ထိမတင်, *adv.* fearlessly, without due regard, မလေး.

ထိတမာ, *n.* things, (indefinite.)

ထီး, (1) *n. affix*, mas. gen. as ခွေး, a dog; ခွေးထီး, a male dog.

ထီး, (2) *v.* to be single, alone, solitary, deserted. Hence အထီး, *adj.* alone, as အထီးကြင်, or အထီးကျံ, a solitary devotee, one who lives and practises by himself.

ထီး, (3) *n.* an umbrella.

ထီးတွိုင်, or ထီးတွိုင်ကာ, *n.* a kind of large bird.

ထု, (1) *v.* to pound, hammer, beat, ခတ် ၊ နှက်.

ထု, (2) *v.* to carve, engrave, ထုလုပ်.

ထုတ်, *v.* to take out, produce, bring to light, ပေါ်; to put out, expel, နှင်ထုတ်; to extract, as from a book, ထုတ်ယူ.

ထုတ်ချင်း, *adv.* straight through.

ထုတ်ချောက်, *adv.* do.

ထုတ်ချင်းခပ်, *v.* to go through; see ခပ်.

ထုတ်ထုတ်, *adv.* prefixed to words of shaking.

ထုတ်သန်း, *v.* to be straight, make straight, straight through, &c. see ထုတ်ချင်း, and သန်း.

ထုပ်, (1) *v.* to wrap up, as in a bundle. Hence အထုပ်, *n.* a bundle.

ထုပ်ဒိုက်, *v.* do.

ထုပ်ပိုး, *v.* do.

ထုပ်, (2) *n.* the upper transverse beams of a house; *com.* ချောက်.

ထုပ်စီး, *n.* do.

ထုပ်တုလင်, *n.* do.

ထုပ်, (3) *v.* to extract, pull or take out; see ထုတ်.

ထုပ်ဆီး, *v.* to engage in a certain play (of boys.)

ထုရွင်ပြား, *n.* a wide spade.

ထုံ, (1) *v.* to perfume, make odorous by infusing and mixing, or by spreading over, anointing, pouring, &c. Hence အထုံ, *n.* any fragrant preparation.

ထုံဖြ, *v.* do.

ထုံ, (2) *v.* to be benumbed, ကျဉ်; to be stupid, dull, အ.

ထုံထိုင်, *v.* to be stupid, dull.

ထုံး, (1) *v.* to tie in a knot, ဖွဲ့.

ထုံး, (2) *v.* to sever, divide, ပိုင်း.

ထုံးဖြတ်, *v.* to decide, settle, စီရင် ၊ ဆုံးဖြတ်.

ထုံးဖွဲ့, or ထုံးရွက်, *v.* to direct, order, ခွဲခန့် ၊ စီရင်.

ထုံး, (3) *n.* a custom, way, manner, စံ ၊ နည်း ၊ အထုံး.

ထုံးစံ, *n.* do. (most common.)

ထုံး, (4) *n.* chunam, lime.

ထုံး, (5) *n.* a pond, lake by the side of a river, formed by the overflowing of the stream, ထုံးအိုင်.

ထုံးဖွဲ, *n.* custom, manner, &c.

ထူ, (1) *v.* to set up, erect, ထောင်; to set up for one's self, ထူထောင်.

ထူ, (2) *v.* to be thick, not thin, မပါး ၊ မကျဲ; to be thick, close, crowded, စိပ် ၊ မကျဲ ၊ မပါး; to be numerous, ပေါ ၊ များ.

ထူထပ်, *v.* do. ထူထဲ, *v.* do.

ထူး, *v.* to differ from others, whether for the better or worse; to be singular, uncommon, ထူးချား ၊ ထူးခြား; *comp.* ဆန်း. Hence အထူး and တထူး, *pron. adj.* other; *hence also*, အထူးသဖြင့်, an abbreviation of အထူးဖြစ်သဖြင့်, (used as an intensive to other verbs.)

ထူးလည်, *v.* to differ from others, &c. see ထူး.

ထူးဆန်း, *v.* to differ, &c. see ထူး.

ထူး, (2) *v.* to reply to a call.

ထူး, (3) *n.* a pit, hole, (either perpendicular or horizontal.)

ထူး, (4) *n.* a cord used fetter-like to confine the feet of animals.

ထူးနေရာ, *n.* see စနည်.

ထေယျသံဝါသက, (from ထေယျ, to steal, and သံဝါသ, to associate, ***Pali,***) *n.* one who assumes the appearance of a priest, and thereby obtains the fellowship of the priests.

ထေရ်, (from ထေရော, *Pali,*) *n.* a priest of Boodh, ရဟန်း.

ထေရီ, *n.* a priestess of Boodh, ရဟန်းမ ၊ မထေရ်မ.

ထေး, *v.* to calk.

ထေးကျစ်, *v.* do.

ထဲ, *affix,* in, within, inside.

ထဲမှာ, *affix,* within, as အိမ်ထဲမှာ, within the house.

ထဲ့, see ထည့်, *v.* to put or place in, &c.

ထောက်, (1) *v.* to prop up, ခု; to support, maintain, afford assistance, ကူ ၊ ချီး ၊ ပင့် ၊ ပံ့ ၊ မ.

ထောက်, (2) *n.* a stay, a prop.

ထောက်တို, *n.* do. (so called, because shorter than the other parts.)

ထောက်ခွ, *n.* a supporting crotch.

ထောက်, (3) *v.* to consider, deliberate, ချင့် ၊ စာ ၊ ထေ ၊ ထွေး; to have regard for, စာ ၊ ညှာ; to have reference to, refer to.

ထောက်ရှု, *v.* do. ထောက်ထွေး, *v.* do.

ထောက်ထား, *v.* to have regard for, whether from pity or respect.

ထောက်တန်, *v.* to be proper for consideration, worthy of attention.

ထောက်ကြံ့, *n.* a kind of tree.

ထောက်ရှား, *n.* a kind of tree.

ထောင်, (1) *v.* to entrap, catch.

ထောင်, (2) *v.* to erect, set up, ထူ.

ထောင်ထား, *v.* to be proud, ostentatious, haughty, unyielding, obstinate, မာန်ထောင်.

ထောင်လွှား, *v.* to be proud, &c. မာန်ထောင်လွှား.

ထောင်, (3) *n.* a prison, jail, လှောင်အိမ် ၊ လျှောင်အိမ်.

ထောင်သား, *n.* a jailer, executioner, အာဏာသား.

ထောင်မှူး, *n.* a sheriff.

ထောင်း, *v.* to pound with a pestle (or any thing of the kind.)

ထောင်းထောင်း, *adv.* fine as powder; rising, ascending, as smoke, dust, &c. (figuratively applied to passion.)

ထောင့်, (1) *v.* to hide, conceal, ကွယ် ၊ ထိမ် ၊ ဖွက် ၊ [illegible] ၊ ဝှက်.

ထောင့်, (2) *v.* to bend, curve, make a corner, ကွေ့. Hence အထောင့်, *n.* a corner, an angle, a bend, အကွေ့ ၊ အကွေး.

ထောဘနာ, *n.* see ထောမနာ.

ထောမနာ, *(Pali,)* *v.* to praise, laud, ချီးမွမ်း.

ထောလပတ်, *n.* a kind of plant.

ထော့နဲ့, *adv.* limpingly.

ထော်, *v.* to stick up, or out, one-sidedly, or obliquely, ငေါ.

ထော်ထော်, *v.* do. *Also,* to act contrary, be perverse, ကန့်လန့်ဖြ.

ထော်မော်, *v.* do.

ထော်ရငေါ်, *adv.* contrarily, perversely.

ထို, *pron. adj.* that. ထို is sometimes doubled to form a kind of plural, as ထိုထို, those.

ထိုက, ထိုမှ, from that; ထိုကြောင့်, because of that.

ထိုမှာ, ထိုမှာကား, among them, in that.

ထိုသို့, *pron. adj.* such, of that sort.

ထိုသို့က, ထိုသို့မှ, from such, from that manner.

ထိုသို့ကြောင့်, or ထိုသို့သောကြောင့်, because of such, because it is thus.

ထိုက်, *v.* to be worth, worthy of, adequate, sufficient, fit, suitable, ထန် ၊ တော် ၊ လျော် ၊ သင့်.

ထိုက်တွန်း, *v.* to instigate.

ထိုင်, *v.* to sit.

ထိုင်း, *v.* to be stupid, dull, slow, inert, တွ ၊ ထုံ ၊ နှေး.

ထိုင်းတွ, *v.* do. (most common.)

ထိုင်းမှိုင်း, *v.* do.

ထိုး, (1) *v.* to thrust at, in, or through, ဆောင့်.

ထိုး, (2) *v.* to make figures, marks, &c. on any substance, to engrave, write, cut in stone, ရေး ၊ ထုပ် ၊ ချက် ၊ ဖြစ်.

ထိုးကျင့်, *v.* to thrust, penetrate, as pain in the body.

ထိုးထွင်း, *v.* to pierce, penetrate.

ထိုးတံ, *n.* a fiddlestick; a spit; a rammer, or any thing of the kind.

ထိုးမုန့်, *n.* a kind of bread.

ထွက်, *v.* to go, or come out. Hence အထွက်နေ့, *n.* the day after a worship day.

ထွက်ကုန်, *v.* to export, as articles of trade. Hence အထွက်ဥစ္စာ, *n.* exports.

ထွက်ဝန်, *v.* do.

ထွက်စည်, *v.* to export, &c. see ထွက်ကုန်.

ထွက်နုပ်, *v.* to present, offer, *(obsolete;)* *n.* a present.

ထွင်, *v.* to clear, make clear, purify, &c. ရှင်း ၊ သုတ်သင် ၊ ပြင် ၊ တီ.

ထွင်း, *v.* to make a hole into by excavating part of the substance, as by a chisel or gouge. Hence အထွင်း, a mortise.

ထွတ်, *v.* to be tender, delicate, နု.

ထွတ်နာ, *n.* a kind of leprosy.

ထွတ်ဖြင်း, *n.* an indolent humour, ဖြင်းလု.

ထွန်, (1) *n.* a kind of harrow used for a plough, ထယ်.

ထွန်, (2) *v.* to harrow.

ထွန်သွား, *n.* the tooth of a harrow.

ထွန်ကိုင်း, *n.* the curved handle of a harrow.

ထွန်သန်, *n.* the shaft of do.

ထွန်တုံး, *n.* the block in which the teeth are fixed.

ထွန်တုံးထောင်, *v.* to set up the ploughing business, to plough.

ထွန်း, *v.* to kindle, ညှိ ; to shine, တောက် ၊ ထိန် ၊ ပြောင် ; to appear, be distinguished, conspicuous, ပေါ် ၊ ထင်ရှား.

ထွန်းပ, *v.* to shine, ထွန်းလင်း.

ထွန့်, *v.* to twitch gently.

ထွာ, (1) *v.* to shave, or slice off, ထွှာ.

ထွာ, (2) *v.* to measure with a span. Hence အထွာ, *n.* a span, a measure of length equal to twelve finger breadths, a half cubit.

ထွား, (1) *v.* to be plump, full, large, flourishing.

ထွားကျိုင်း, *v.* to be plump, &c.

ထွားဖွံ့, *v.* do.

ထွား, (2) *v.* to be made fine, pulverized, ကျေ ၊ ညက် ၊ မှုန့်.

ထွေ, *v.* to be various, များပြား ၊ ထူး ; to be numerous, များ.

ထွေလည်, *v.* do. do.

ထွေထွေ, *adv.* variously.

ထွေး, (1) *v.* to mix together, to jumble, confuse, ရော ၊ နှော ၊ ရှုပ်.

ထွေး, (2) *v.* to wind into a ball, လုံး.

ထွေး, (3) *v.* to be the youngest, နှောင်း.

ထွေး, (4) *v.* to spit out.

ထွေးအင်, or ထွေးခံ, *n.* a spitting pot, ဖြတ်ရို.

## ဒ.

The third consonant in the class of dentals.

ဒက်, *n.* a kind of ornament, *(obsolete.)*

ဒကူ, *n.* the ribs of a vessel.

ဒင်္ဂါး, *n.* money, coin; see တင်္ကား.

ဒင်္ဂါးပုံ, *n.* mint, for coining.

ဒင်လေးချိ, *adv.* dilatorily, procrastinatingly, လဆွဲကန့်.

ဒဏ္ဍာရီ, *n.* a fable, fiction.

ဒနိ, *n.* a species of palm tree.

ဒနုံး, *n.* a kind of tree.

ဒန္တဇာ, (from ဒန္တ, a tooth, *Pali,*) *adv.* dental, produced from the teeth, (applied to consonants of the တ class.)

ဒန္တလွန်, *n.* see ဒန့်သလွန်.

ဒန်း, (1) *n.* a swing.

ဒန်း, (2) *n.* a kind of tree.

ဒန့်ကွဲ, *n.* the cassia-fœtida plant, *(Carey.)*

ဒန့်ဒသက်, *n.* the myrtle tree.

ဒန့်သခွား, *n.* a kind of vine.

ဒန့်သလွန်, *n.* the Indian horseradish plant.

ဒရင်ကောက်, *n.* a kind of plant, fern.

ဒရယ်, *n.* a small kind of deer.

ဒရွတ်, *adv.* dragging along on the ground, ရှည့်ဆီ.

ဒရွတ်ဆီ, *adv.* do. see ဆီ.

ဒလေ့, *n.* manner, custom, way; see အလေ့.

ဒလယ်, *n.* a kind of roof or covering over a boat or vehicle, belonging to a person of rank; comp. ပေါင်း.

ဒသ, *(Pali,) adj.* ten, တဆယ်.

ဒသမ, (from ဒသ, ten, *Pali,*) *adj.* tenth.

ဒဟတ်, *n.* a kind of tree.

ဒဟတ်သကြီ, *n.* a kind of tree.

ဒဟတ်သကြိုင်း, *n.* a kind of tree.

ဒိတ်, *n.* metal.

ဒိဏ်, *(Pali,* from ဒဏ္ဍာ,) *n.* chastisement, punishment.

ဒိန်, *(Pali,* ဒဏ္ဍာ,) *n.* an evil, a calamity, ဘေး ၊ အန္တရယ်.

ဒါန, *(Pali,)* (1) *n.* a gift, အလှူ.

ဒါနဝတ္ထု, *n.* do.

ဒါန, (2) *n.* a giving, လှူခြင်း.

ဒါယဇ္ဇ, *(Pali,)* *n.* an heir, အမွေခံ.

ဒါယကာ, *(Pali,)* *n.* one who contributes to the support of religion and religious characters, a layman, ထကာ၊ ဥပါသကာ.

ဒါလီ, *n.* certain golden ornaments, formerly worn around the neck, ထာလီ.

ဒါးဝယ်မှိုင်း, *n.* a kind of tree.

ဒိ, *(an abbreviation of* ဒိဗ္ဗစက္ခုဉာဏ်, *Pali,)* *n.* celestial wisdom, the wisdom of Nats; *comp.* ပု, and အာ.

ဒိဃ, *n.* one division of the Boodhist scriptures.

ဒိဗ္ဗံပေါက်, *n.* divination.

ဒိဗ္ဗစက္ခု, see ဒိ, &c.

ဒိဋ္ဌိ, *(Pali,)* (1) *n.* opinion, doctrine, အယူ; (2) *n.* false opinions, heresy, မှားသောအယူ၊ မိစ္ဆာဒိဋ္ဌိ.

ဒိဋ္ဌုပါဒါန်, *n.* an evil passion or affection.

ဒိဋ္ဌုံ, *n.* a writing explanatory of omens, တိတ်ထို.

ဒိဃောဃ, *n.* a stream, current; see ဩဃ.

ဒိန်, *n.* curd, cheese.

ဒိန်ခဲ, *n.* do.

ဒိန်ညှဉ်း, *n.* a kind of bird, a cormorant, ဒိန်ညင်း.

ဒီ, *n.* the tide.

ဒီတက်, *n.* flood tide.

ဒီကျ, *n.* ebb tide.

ဒီဃ, *v.* to be drawn out, lengthened, be long, အရှည်; in reading, to draw out the sound of a letter or syllable with a singing tone.

ဒီပ, *(Pali,)* *n.* an island.

ဒီပရာဇ်, (from ဒီပ, an island, and ရာဇ, a king, *Pali,)* *n.* the sovereign of an island.

ဒု, *n.* depth, thickness; see အထု.

ဒုကုဋ်, *n.* the outside garment of a priest of Boodh, worn over the shoulders; *comp.* ထဘိန်း.

ဒုက္ကဋ်, (from ဒုက္ကဋ, *Pali,)* *n.* a crime, guilt, (clerical.)

ဒုက္ခ, *(Pali,)* *n.* unhappiness, misery, pain, ဆင်းရဲချင်း, (opposed to သုခ, bliss.)

ဒုက္ခိတ, (from ဒုက္ခ,) *n.* one who is unhappy.

ဒုစ္စရိုက်, (from ဒု, bad, and စာရိတ္တ, a deed, *Pali,)* *n.* a bad deed, မကောင်းသောအကျင့်, (opposed to သုစရိုက်, a good deed.)

ဒုတ်, *n.* a stick, a staff.

ဒုတ်ရှည်, *n.* a long stick, a pole.

ဒုတ္တာ, *n.* blue vitriol.

ဒုတိယ, (from ဒွိ, two, *Pali,)* *adj.* second.

ဒုဗ္ဘိက္ခန္တရကပ်, *n.* an evil period ; see ကပ်သုံးပါး.

ဒုရင်, (1) *n.* small pointed projections upon the roof or steeple of distinguished buildings.

ဒုရင်, (2) *n.* a kind of coat.

ဒုဿီလ, see ပုထုဇန်.

ဒုံး, (1) *n.* a tube filled with gunpowder, and made to run on wheels when fired ; see တုံး.

ဒုံး, (2) *n.* a kind of boat.

ဒူး, *n.* the knee, ပုဆစ်.

ဒူးဆစ်, *n.* the joint of the knee.

ဒူးခွက်, *n.* the knee-pan, ဒုနီချင်း.

ဒူးထောင်, *v.* to bend the knee.

ဒူးနေရာ, *n.* see စနည်.

ဒူးလေး, *n.* a cross-bow.

ဒူးပေါင်ကား, *v.* to sit in a squatting posture.

ဒူးရင်း, *n.* a species of the jack tree, the doorean tree.

ဒေဝ, *(Pali,)* *n.* a Devah, or Nat ; see နတ်.

ဒေဝန်း, or ဒေဝန်းတိုက်, *n.* a royal custom-house, or depository, တိုက်တော်.

ဒေဝပုတ္တ, *n.* the most powerful evil Nat.

ဒေဝိန္ဒ, (from ဒေဝ, a Devah, and ဣန္ဒ, a chief, *Pali,)* *n.* a sovereign of the Devahs, နတ်မင်း ၊ သကြားမင်း.

ဒေသ, *(Pali,)* *n.* a place, country, အရပ်.

ဒေသစာရီ, (1) *(Pali,)* *v.* to go, သွားချင်း.

ဒေသစာရီ, (2) *adv.* itinerantly, from place to place.

ဒေသနာ, *(Pali,)* *n.* a declaration, ဟောချင်း.

ဒေသနာကြား, *v.* to confess, acknowledge, (clerical.)

ဒေသနာ, *n.* a declaration, ဟောချင်း.

ဒေါက်ခွါ, *n.* a kind of cap sometimes worn by priests of Boodh.

ဒေါက်ရှပ်, *n.* a kind of tree.

ဒေါင်း, *n.* a peacock.

ဒေါင်းဖြံ, *n.* a kind of fence allowed to people of rank.

ဒေါင်းပေါင်, *n.* a round box with a conical cover, raised on several legs.

ဒေါင်းနိ, *n.* an ornament or guard worn about the ears, နားတောင်း.

ဒေါင်းလန်း, *n.* a round tray or salver, raised on several legs, and used to eat upon.

ဒေါင့်ဆပ်ပြာ, *n.* a kind of tree.

ဒေါင့်သထိတ်, *n.* a kind of plant.

ဒေါန, *n.* a kind of tree.

ဒေါသ, *(Pali,)* (1) *n.* blame-worthiness, guilt, အပြစ်.

ဒေါသ, (2) *n.* anger, အမျက်.

ဒိုင်, *n.* a judge or arbiter of games.

ဒိုင်း, *n.* a kind of shield, လွှား.

ဒိုင်းဝန်, *n.* a certain minister of state.

ဒြပ်, (from ဒဗ္ဗ, *Pali,)* *n.* a substance; opposed to ဂုဏ်, a quality.

ဒွတ္တိံသာ, *n.* the body; see ကာယ.

ဒွန်, (from ဒွန္ဒ, *Pali,)* *n.* duality, အစုံ.

ဒွန္ဒ, *(in grammar,)* *n.* the first class of compound sentences; *(Carey.)*

ဒွန်းစဏ္ဍာ, *n.* a person of no character, as a beggar, တောင်းစား; or one employed in disposing of dead bodies, သုဘရာဇာ.

ဒွါဒသမ, (from ဒွိ, two, and ဒသ, ten,) *adj.* twelfth.

ဒွါရ, *(Pali,)* *n.* a hole, politely substituted for အပေါက်၊ ပေါက်, &c.

ဒွိဂု, *n.* the fifth class of compound sentences, made by compounding a numeral with its auxiliary; *(Carey.)*

ဒွေး, *n.* a small seed used in weight, ရွေး.

## ဓ.

The fourth consonant in the class of dentals.

ဓနွက်, *n.* a kind of tree.

ဓနု, (*Pali*, a bow,) *n.* Sagittarius, the ninth sign of the zodiac.

ဓမ္မ, (*Pali,*) see တရား.

ဓမ္မက္ခန္ဓာ, (from ခန္ဓာ, a collection, *Pali,*) *n.* a section of the Boodhist scriptures, of which there are eighty four thousand.

ဓမ္မခိုင်, *n.* see ခိုင်.

ဓမ္မတာ, (from မတ္တာ, a measure,) uniformity, custom, nature.

ဓမ္မဝတ်, *n.* religious duties, righteousness.

ဓမ္မသတ်, (from သတ်, to decide,) *n.* a law; (commonly such as is defined in ancient law books.)

ဓမ္မာသန, (from ဓမ္မတရား, and အာသန, a place, *Pali,*) *n.* a place from which a preacher addresses his audience; a pulpit.

ဓလေ့, *n.* custom, way, manner; see အလေ့.

ဓံ, an abbreviation of ဓမ္မ, (sometimes used in composition.)

ဓာတ်, (from ဓာတု, *Pali,*) (1) *n.* an element, constituent part of any thing, material or immaterial; the root of verbs in *Pali.* N. B. Four principal elements are reckoned, viz. ပထဝီဓာတ်, earth; အာပေါဓာတ်, water; တေဇောဓာတ်, fire; ဝါယောဓာတ်, air; to which some add, အာကာသဓာတ်, space. *comp.* မဟာဘုတ်.

ဓာတ်တော်, *n.* relics of Boodh, သရီရဓာတ်.

ဓာတ်, (2) *n.* temper, disposition.

ဓာတ်, (3) *n.* a mineral.

ဓာတ်နှာ, *n.* a consumption.

ဓား, *n.* a knife, sword.

ဓားဦး, *n.* the point of do.

ဓားမ, *n.* a large knife, a cleaver.

ဓားလွယ်, *n.* a sword, suspended knife.

ဓားပြ, *n.* a knife shewer, that is, a robber.

ဓားမြ, *n.* do.

ဓားမြတိုက်, *v.* to rob, plunder.

ဓားမောက်, *n.* a knife with a protuberant back.

ဓားမြှောင်, *n.* a short dagger.

ဓားနိုင်, *v.* to have the power of life and death.

ဓားဝယ်, *n.* Tavoy.

ဓိဋ္ဌာန်, (from အဓိဋ္ဌာနံ, to establish, ဆောက်တည်, *Pali,)* *v.* to make a future good or evil depend on a certain specific condition by an appeal to fate or Deity; or to make the appeal, though the virtue of the appellant may not be sufficient to ensure the thing demanded; to take an oath, to vow, promise; *comp.* ကျိန်, and သစ္စာပြု.

ဓိဓိ, *adv.* an intensive.

ဓုတင်, *n.* a certain kind of austerity, of which there are thirteen.

ဓုပ်ရုံ, *adv.* with the head covered, as in a cloak or hood.

ဓူမိကာ, *n.* the bulging part of a graduated steeple, (ပြာသဒ်,) beneath the umbrella; *compare* ဟင်းရုံပူး.

ဓူဝံ, *n.* the north-star.

ဓေဓေ, or တဓေဓေ, *adv.* repeatedly, constantly.

ဓေ့ဓေ့, or တဓေ့ဓေ့, *adv.* by little and little.

ဓောင်ချွေးသွား, *n.* royal guards, *(obsolete.)*

## န.

The fifth consonant in the class of dentals.

နက်, (1) *v.* to be deep, not shallow, မတိမ်.

နက်နဲ, *v.* to be deep, profound, difficult of attainment, ခက် ။ ခဲ.

နက်, (2) *v.* to be dark, of a black colour, မည်း.

နကျယ်, (from နကျည်,) *n.* a wasp.

နက္ခတ်, (from နက္ခတ္တံ, *Pali,)* *n.* a nekkhat, a particular star or constellation, of which there are twenty-seven, viz. အဿဝဏီ ။ ဘရဏီ ။ ကြတ္တိကာ ။ ရောဟဏီ ။ မိဂသီ ။ အဒြ ။ ပုဏ္ဏဖုသျှ ။ ဖုသျှ ။ အသလိဿ ။ မာဃ ။ ပြုဗ္ဗာဘရဂုဏီ ။ ဥတ္တရာဘရဂုဏီ ။ ဟဿ ။ စိတ္တရ ။ သွာတိ ။ ဝိသာခါ ။ အနုရာဓ ။ ဇေဋ္ဌ ။ မူလ ။ ပြုဗ္ဗာသဠ ။ ဥတ္တရာသဠ ။ သရဝဏ် ။ ဓနသိဋ္ဌ ။ သတ္တဘိသျှ ။ ပြုဗ္ဗာပုရိုက် ။ ဥတ္တရာပုရိုက်, and ရေဝတီ; to which was formerly added ဘိဇ်, which is now lost.

နက်ဖြန်, *adv.* to-morrow, နံဖြန်.

နက်သတ်, *n.* anciently used for နက္ခတ်.

နဂံ, *(a corruption of* နှင်တံ,) *n.* a driving-stick, a whip.

နဂါး, (1) *n.* a Nagah, a kind of sea dragon.

နဂါးငွေ့, *n.* the galaxy, milky-way.

နဂါးပတ်, *n.* a fabulous kind of noose.

နဂါး, (2) *n.* twisted timber, သစ်နဂါး.

နဂါးသွဲ့, *n.* a kind of precious stone.

နဂိုရ်, *n.* constitution, nature, real character, origin, stock, မူလ; *in astrology*, permanent residence, opposed to ယာယီ.

နင်, (1) *v.* to choke, stop in the throat, ဆို့.

နင်, (2) *pers. pro. mas. or fem.* you, (used to inferiors.)

နင်း, *v.* to tread upon.

နင်းချွဲနင်းကျွံ, *adv.* walking in the mud, slipping, sinking, &c.

နင့်, *v.* to cram, stuff; သိပ်, to be tight, constricted, ကြပ် ၊ သိပ်.

နစ်, (1) *v.* to sink into, be immersed, မြုပ်; *act.* နှစ်.

နစ်, (2) *v.* to be thick, sticky, ပျစ်.

နစ်မွန်း, *v.* to sink into, be immersed.

နစ်, (3) *v.* to return, ပြန်.

နစ်နစ်, *adv.* an intensive to words of whiteness.

နည်း, (1) *v.* to be few, not many, မများ ၊ ပါး.

နည်း, (2) (from နယ, *Pali,*) *n.* a rule, precept, ဥပဒေ; a kind, sort, way, manner, custom, အတန်း ၊ စံ ၊ ထုံး.

နည်းနာ, *n.* do.

နည်းတူ, *adv.* in the same manner. Hence တနည်းကား, moreover, furthermore.

နည်း, (3) *int. affix,* as ဘယ်ကိုသွားသနည်း, whither does he go? see Gram.

နည်းနည်းညက်ညက်, *adv.* an intensive to words of destroying.

နတ်, *n.* a Nat, Devah, (ဒေဝ,) a supposed being superior to man, but inferior to Bramha, (ဗြဟ္မာ;) some of whom are said to inhabit the inferior celestial regions, and others to have dominion over different portions of the earth and sky.

နတ်ပြည်, *n.* the Nat country, the inferior celestial regions, of which there are said to be six stages, or stories, viz. စတုမဟာရာဇ် ၊ တာဝတိံသာ ၊ ယာမာ ၊ တုသိတာ ၊ နိမ္မာနရတိ, and ပရနိမ္မိတဝသဝတ္တီ.

နတ်ဘုံ, *n.* Nat country; *see the preceding word.*

နတ်ဆိုး, *n.* a demon, evil spirit.

နတ်ဝင်, *n.* a magician, conjurer, &c.

နတ်ရကာ, *n.* an offering to a Nat.

နတ်ကောက်စပါး, *n.* a kind of grain.

နတ်ကောင်, *n.* a kind of wild rice plant.

နတ်စင်, *n.* a kind of building erected to a Nat.

နတ်စက်, *n.* any celestial, or supernatural weapon; see စက်.

နတ်တော်, *n.* the ninth month in the year.

နတ်ရှုး, *n.* a sovereign or ruler of Nats.

နန်း, (1) *n.* a royal palace, abode of a king, နန်းတော်.

နန်းမတော်, *n.* the chief queen, တောင်နန်း.

နန်းလောင်း, or နန်းလျာ, *n.* the heir apparent of the crown, အိမ်ရှေ့မင်း.

နန်း, (2) *n.* an iron plate, perforated with small holes.

နန်းချည်, *n.* wire.

နန်းကြိန်, *n.* Nankin.

နန်းလုံးကျိုင်, *n.* a kind of tree.

နန့်, *v.* to shake, လှုပ်.

နန့်သာ, *n.* an odoriferous substance; see နံ့သာ.

နပ်, *v.* to be done sufficiently, i. e. carried through a process, and brought to the desired state, as, food cooked, fruit ripened, business accomplished, acquaintance formed, &c. &c. Hence ဆနပ်, *a numeral auxiliary* applied to meals.

နပန်းဖွန်း, (from နဘပန်း,) *n.* the end of an axletree.

နပန်းဖွန်းတိုင်, *n.* the linchpin.

နပန်းလုံး, *v.* to wrestle, လုံးထွေး.

နပန်းထွေး, *v.* do.

နပုံလိင်, (from နပုံ, and လိင်,) *n.* the neuter gender.

နပုံ, (from နပုံသက, *Pali,)* *n.* one that is neither male nor female.

နဖား, *n.* the eye of a needle or other instrument, any hole through the end of a thing, နဖားပေါက်.

နဖူး, *n.* the forehead.

နဖူးစာ, *n.* marks on the forehead indicative of one's destiny, ဦးချွန်ရေး; fate, destiny, fortune, ကံ.

နဗူး, *n.* a kind of vine.

နမသလေး, see သလေး.

နမော်နမဲ့, *adv.* heedlessly.

နမ်း, *v.* to smell, receive scent.

နယ်, (1) *v.* to squeeze, press.

နယ်, (2) *v.* to stir up with, mix together, ရော ၊ နှော.

နယ်, (3) *n.* all the component parts of a territory or judicatory, whether principal or subordinate, collectively taken, ပယ်.

နယ်နိမိတ်, *n.* do. see နိမိတ်.

နယ်စပ်, *n.* the boundary between two countries, အပိုင်းအခြား.

နယ်, (4) *n.* the curved stick that stretches the cloth on a loom.

နယ်ကိုင်း, *n.* do.

နယ်ဆူး, *n.* the iron points of do.

နယုန်, *n.* the third month in the year.

နရည်, *n.* a long trumpet, နှဲရှည်.

နရတင်း, *n.* an ornament or guard worn about the ears, being an appendage to a crown, ထရတု.

နရပစေတ, *(Pali,) n.* mortar, or plaster, အင်္ဂတေ ၊ ထရွတ်.

နရပတိ, *n.* a kind of plant.

နဝင်း, *an astrological term.*

နဝမ, (from နဝ, nine, *Pali,*) *adj.* ninth.

နဝရတ်, (from နဝ, nine, and ရတန, a gem, *Pali,*) *n.* nine kinds of precious stones, ရတနာကိုးပါး.

နသံ, *n.* a kind of worm, ပိုးနသံ.

နံ, (1) *v.* to smell offensively, စော်.

နံ, (2) *n.* the day of the week on which one is born, a birth day.

နံနက်, *adv.* to-morrow, နက်ဖြန်.

နံသား, *n.* the child of such or such a day.

နံ, (3) (from နာမ, *Pali,*) *n.* mind, spirit, (opposed to ရုပ်,) including စိတ်, and စေတသိက်.

နံ, (4) (from အနံ,) *n.* the side of a body, animate or inanimate.

နံပါး, *n.* do. နံရပ်, do. နံဘေး, do. နံတောင်း, do.

နံရံ, *n.* the raised side of an inanimate thing, as the side of a house, well, &c.

နံစ, *n.* the part of a man's side that is tattooed.

နံရိုး. *n.* a rib.

နံကာ, *n.* the fifth month in the year, ဝါခေါင်, *(obsolete.)*

နံနက်, *n.* morning, (by corruption, မနက်.)

နံနက်စား, *n.* a tooth-brush, တံပူ.

နံတွန်, *v.* to be poor on the side or ribs.

နံနံ, *n.* the fennel plant.

နံနံရွက်, *n.* the leaves of fennel.

နံနွင်း, *n.* the turmeric plant, or root, သနွင်း.

နံရံ, *n.* see တံရံ.

နံ့သာ, *n.* an odoriferous substance. N. B. In ancient writings, five kinds are mentioned, viz. နံ့သာနီ ၊ နံ့သာဖြူ ၊ အကျော် ၊ စံပါ, and ကရမက်.

နံ့သာပျောင်း, *n.* a fragrant ointment.

နံ့သာမှုန့်, *n.* fragrant powder.

နံ့သာရည်, *n.* fragrant essence.

နာ, (1) *v.* to listen, hearken, attend to.

နာခံ, *v.* do.

နာ, (2) *v.* to be sick, feel in pain ; to be hurt in feelings, distressed in mind ; to suffer loss. Hence အနာ, *n.* a pain, disease, ရောဂါ ; *sometimes written* အမာ.

နာကျင်, *v.* do. *(expletive.)*

နာကြင်, (from ကြင်,) *v.* do.

နာကြည်း, *v.* do.

နာရွတ်, (from ရွတ်, to be old,) *n.* a scar, အမာရွတ်.

နာဋ, *(Pali,)* *n.* union of song, dance, and instrumental music, စည်သုံးပါး.

နာနတ်, (1) *n.* the pine-apple plant.

နာနတ်, (2) *(pron.* နာနာ, various, *Pali,)* *n.* a dissimilarity, variety.

နာမ်, (from နာမ, *Pali,)* *n.* a noun.

နာမ, (from နာမံ, *Pali,)* *n.* a name, အမည်.

နာမည်, *n.* do.

နာမံ, *(Pali,)* *n.* a noun, a name.

နာဍုး *n.* one division of the Boodhist scriptures, (marked နာ.)

နာဠိ, (*Pali,*) *n.* a Naree; a measure of time, equal to twenty-four minutes, or the sixtieth part of a natural day; a watch, time-piece.

နာဠိခွက်, *n.* a watch.

နား, (1) *v.* to cease from motion or action, through desire of rest; to light, perch, as a bird.

နား, (2) *n.* the ear, နားရွက်; (*pron.* နာ, when combined with nouns.)

နားဆုံ, *n.* the bulge of the ear.

နားကပ်, *n.* a certain ornament worn in the ear.

နားကျ, *v.* to accord with, acquiesce.

နားငြောင်း, *v.* to pay attention to by the ear; see ငြောင်း, to be weary through inaction.

နားတောင်း, *n.* a hollow cylinder, worn in the perforated hole of the ear.

နားတင်, *n.* the part behind the ear.

နားထောင်, (from ထောင်, to erect,) *v.* to listen, hearken, &c. နား.

နားပင်း, (from ပင်း, to stop up,) *v.* to be deaf.

နားထိုင်း, *v.* do.

နားပန်, *n.* (from ပန်, to adorn,) an amulet, or preservative from evil, worn in the ears.

နားပန်း, *n.* the temple, side of the head, near the ear.

နားပန်းဆံ, *n.* hair about the temples or ears.

နားပူနားကျပ်, *adv.* teasingly, importunately.

နားဖြင့်ကြား, *v.* to hear, receive instruction.

နားဖာ, *n.* ear-wax.

နားဖာကော်, *n.* an ear-pick.

နားမှာ, *affix,* as အိမ်နားမှာ, by the house.

နားယောင်, *v.* to hear indistinctly.

နားရွတင်း, *n.* an ornament or guard worn about the ears.

နားရွက်, *n.* the ear, *literally* the leaf of the ear.

နားလည်, *v.* to understand; see လည်.

နားလို, *v.* to love to hear, to be pleased with, approve, နှစ်သက်.

နားဝင်, *v.* to enter the ear, gain access to the mind, be persuaded.

နားသယ်, *n.* the part under and behind the ear.

နားသံ, *n.* an ear-ring.

နားသံသီး, *n.* an ear-drop.

နားသွင်း, *v.* to attend to, persuade.

နားသွယ်ပန်း, *n.* a certain ornament for the ear.

နိကယော, *n.* a collection.

နိကယ်ငါးပါး, (from နိကယော, a collection, *Pali,*) *n.* five parts into which the Boodhist scriptures are divided, according to a certain distribution, ဒီဃ ၊ မဇ္ဈိမ ၊ သံယုတ္တ ၊ အင်္ဂုတ္တရ, and ခုဒ္ဒက.

နိက္ခမ, *(Pali,)* *n.* a departure into a wilderness, တောသို့ထွက်ချင်း.

နိဂုံး, *n.* a conclusion, (in writing,) အဆုံးချုပ်ချင်း.

နိဂုံ, (from နိဂမော, *Pali,*) *n.* a small town, a village, a little trading place.

နိဂ္ဂဟိတ်, *n.* the character (ံ), သေးသေးတင်. It is placed over a letter, and has the sound of final မ.

နိဂ္ဂဟိတ, *see* နိဂ္ဂဟိတ်.

နိစ္စ, *adj.* permanent, unchanging.

နိဒါန်း, *n.* an introduction, exordium.

နိဒ္ဓါရဏအဓိကရဏ, *(in Grammar,)* *n.* the locative case, when terminating in တွင် ; *(Carey.)*

နိမ်, *v.* to be low, put down, depressed, *(of various applications ;)* act. နှိမ်.

နိပါတ်, (1) *n.* in *Pali*, an indeclinable particle, whether a part of speech or an expletive.

နိပါတ်, (2) *n.* a species of writing.

နိဗ္ဗာန်; (from နိဗ္ဗာနံ, *Pali,*) *n.* an emancipation from all evil, annihilation, အကျွတ်တရား.

နိမ္မာနရတိ, *n.* see နတ်ပြည်.

နိမ့်, *v.* to be low, လျော့ ၊ ဝဲ ; to be short in stature ; act. နှိမ့်.

နိမိတ်, (1) *n.* the suburbs of a city, the immediate dependencies of a government.

နိမိတ်, (2) *n.* the genitals, whether male or female, အင်္ဂါဇာတ် ၊ သော ၊ ထိင်.

နိမိတ်, (3) *n.* a sign of any thing to come, an omen, တိတ်.

နိမိတ်တမျှဉ်, or နိမိတ်တမျှည့်, *n.* a sign, an omen; see နိမိတ်.

နိမိတ်အဓိကရဏ, *(in Grammar,)* *n.* the locative case terminating in ကြောင့်; (*Carey.*)

နိမိတ်ဖတ်, *v.* to explain or interpret an omen, to divine.

နိယံ, *n.* a certain writing.

နိရုဇ္ဈ, *adv.* stationarily, as a planet or star.

နိရုတ္တိပဋိသမ္ဘိဒါ, *n.* a kind of intuitive knowledge, a knowledge of different religions, &c.

နိသီဒုန်, or နိသီဒိုင်, *n.* a quilt or cushion, for a priest to sit upon.

နိဿရည်း, (from နိဿယ, *Pali,*) *n.* a support, guide; something to lean upon or adhere to, as a teacher, or an interpretation.

နိဿျ, *n.* a translation; *see also the preceding word.*

နီ, *v.* to be red, be of a reddish colour.

နီကျန်, *v.* do.

နီချင်, *v.* do.

နီတွေး, *v.* to be of a bright red.

နီမြန်း, *v.* do.

နိဓိ, (*Pali*, a gold pot,) *n.* a book of directions (whether relating to domestic, civil, or religious concerns).

နီပါးဆေး, *n.* a kind of tree.

နီလာ, *n.* a sapphire, or amethyst.

နီး, *v.* to be near, not far distant, မဝေး.

နီးမှာ, *affix*, near to, as အိမ်နီးမှာ, near the house.

နု, *v.* to be fine, tender, delicate, ညံ့ ၊ ထွတ် ၊ နွေ့ ၊ သိမ်.

နုနယ်, *v.* do. Hence အနုကြမ်း, *adv.* at first gently, then forcibly, as a sly robber. အနုဓိ, or အနုတက်, *v.* to act at first in a gentle, then in a forcible manner.

နုတ်, *v.* to pull out; see နှုတ်.

နုန်း, *v.* to be weak, exhausted, worn out, နွေ့ ၊ နွမ်း.

နုန်းနွေ့, *v.* do.

နုန်းနယ်, *v.* do.

နုပ်, *v.* to be small, fine, ငယ် ၊ ပွ ၊ လျော့ ၊ သိမ် ၊ သေး.

နုပ်သိမ်, *v.* do.

နုပ်စု, *n.* small silver change, used in the market; see ငွေနုပ်စု.

နုမော, (*an abbreviation of* အနုမောဒ,) *v.* to rejoice.

နုံး, *n.* fine mud, နုသောညွန်.

နုံးနစ်, *n.* do.

နုံ့, *v.* to be loose, unstable, နဲ့ ၊ မခိုင် ; to be weak, debilitated, infirm, ချည့် ၊ နဲ့ ; to move by starts and twitches ; *act.* နှုံ့.

နူ, *v.* to be leprous, have the leprosy.

နူဝဲ, *v.* do.

နူနာ, *n.* leprosy, ကုဋ္ဌနာ.

နူး, *v.* to be soft, mellow, gentle, easy, ညံ့ ၊ ပျော့ပျောင်း ၊ သိမ် ; to be well disposed towards, affectionate, pleased with, ညွတ် ၊ ကြည်ညို ၊ နှစ်သက် ; *act.* နှူး.

နေ, (1) *v.* to remain, continue. Hence အနေကျ, *n.* continuance, uniformity, (commonly used to form verbal nouns, as သွားနေကျသည်, he constantly goes.)

နေ, (2) *n.* the sun.

နေဝန်းပေါ်, *n.* the rising sun.

နေဆိမ်ခွဲ, *n.* the halo of the sun.

နေကြာ, *n.* the sun-flower.

နေခြည်, *n.* a ray of light.

နေစာလှုံ, *v.* to bask in the sun.

နေတိုင်း, (from နေ, the sun, and တိုင်း, to compare,) *n.* a quadrant.

နေထွက်, *n.* sunrise, sunshine.

နေပြောက်, *n.* a spot of light made by the sun's shining through an aperture.

နေဝင်, *n.* sunset.

နေကြာမျက်, *n.* a kind of grass, မြေကြာမျက်.

နေမိ, *n.* one division of the Boodhist scriptures, (marked နေ.)

နေ့, *n.* a day, from sunrise to sunset, opposed to ညဉ့်, *(comp.* ရက်*)*

နဲ, (1) *v.* to be few ; see နည်း.

နဲ, (2) *v.* to be soft, pulpy, ပျော့.

နဲ, (3) *n.* a fawn, (in chess.)

နဲ့, *v.* to be loose, infirm, နုံ့ ; to be weak, debilitated, ချည့် ; *act.* နှဲ့.

နောက်, (1) *v.* to be dirty, foul, muddy, (applied to liquids ;) not transparent, မကြည်လင် ; *act.* နှောက်.

နောက်, (2) *v.* to be behind in place; to be subsequent, or posterior in time, နောင်, (seldom used assertively.) Hence အနောက်, *n.* the west; အနောက်တောင်, *n.* south-west; အနောက်မြောက်, the north-west.

နောက်, (3) *n.* a hinder part; posterior time; *comp.* အရှေ့.

နောက်, (4) *affix*, behind, after, afterwards, as သွားသည်နောက်, after he goes, had gone, or has gone.

နောက်မှာ, *affix*, behind, as အိမ်နောက်မှာ, behind the house.

နောက်ချေးပိုး, *n.* a kind of beetle.

နောက်ပိတကိုင်း, *adv.* with the back towards a person.

နောက်ဒယ်, *n.* the back part of the head.

နောင်, (1) *v.* to be later, subsequent, posterior in time.

နောင်, (2) *n.* posterior time; *act.* နှောင်း.

နောင်, (3) *n.* a man's elder brother, အစ်ကို; (anciently used as a term of compellation by men in addressing women.)

နောင်တ, (from နောင် and တ,) *n.* regret, repentance.

နောင်တရ, *v.* to regret, be sorry for, be penitent.

နောင်နှင်, *adv.* backward and forward, alternately.

နော့, *v.* to be immodest, indecent, ကမြင်း၊ ကလက်.

နော်, *affix*, used in soliciting acquiescence, as သွားတော့မည်နော်, I will go, shall I?

နိုင်, (1) *v. affix*, sign of the potential mood, as သွားနိုင်, he can go, &c.

နိုင်, (2) *v.* to be master of, have authority over, ပိုင်၊ အစိုးရ; to prevail, conquer, overcome, အောင်.

နိုင်ချင်း, *adj.* mutually or equally prevalent.

နိုင်ငံ, *n.* a country under one jurisdiction or government, တိုင်း နိုင်ငံ; *figuratively*, will, pleasure.

နိုင်ထက်, *v.* to use violence. Hence အနိုင်အထက်, *adv.* by force, forcibly.

နိုး, *v.* to awake; *act.* နှိုး.

နိုးကြား, *v.* to be diligent.

နိုးချွတ်, *v.* do.

နို့, (1) *n.* milk; a breast, one of the two breasts, သားမြတ်.

နို့အုံ, *n.* a breast.

နို့ခဲ, နို့ရိုင်, နို့တင်, or နို့စဲ်, *n.* curdled milk, curd.

နို့ဃနာ, *n.* rice boiled in milk.

နို့စို့, *n.* a suckling.

နို့ညှစ်, *v.* to milk.

နို့ကိုင်, *n.* a teat.

နို့ထိန်း, *n.* a wet-nurse.

နို့ရည်, *n.* milk, နို့.

နို့သီး, *n.* a nipple, pap.

နို့, (2) thus, (*a corruption of* သို့.)

နို့သော်လည်း, but, nevertheless; see သို့သော်လည်း.

နို့မို့, therefore, if so; see သို့မို့.

နွမ်း, *v.* to be dull, faded, withered; to be exhausted, worn out; to be dejected, sorrowful, distressed, ညှိုး ၊ သမ်း ၊ ညှစ် ၊ နွမ်းညည်း ; (*act.* နွမ်း.)

နွမ်းနယ်, *v.* do.

နွယ်, *v.* to meet, to stretch along in the manner of a vine. Hence အနွယ်, *n.* a vine or creeper (of any kind.)

နွယ်ချို, *n.* liquorice.

နွယ်တာ, *n.* the twelfth month in the year, တပေါင်း, (*obsolete.*)

နွဲ့, *v.* to hang down, become low, (applied to inanimate things,) ကျောက်ကိုင်ကျ ၊ ကိုင်း ၊ ညွတ် ; to be submissive, respectful, crouching, (applied to intelligent beings,) ကျိုး ၊ ကျိုး ၊ နိမ့်ချ ၊ ပျပ် ၊ ဝပ် ; (*act.* နှိမ့်.)

နွား, *n.* bull, cow, ox.

နွားမ, *n.* a cow; နွားမကြူး, *n.* a fine large cow.

နွားထီး, *n.* a bull.

နွားတိုး, *n.* do.

နွားသိုး, *n.* do.

နွားပြိုး, *n.* an ox.

နွားဖိုက်, *n.* do.

နွားနောက်, *n.* an animal between a cow and buffalo.

နွားငြောင်, *n.* a kind of plant.

နွားပြိုးစွဲ, *n.* a species of bird, the fork-tailed shrike.

နွားမြေရင်း, *n.* a kind of grass.

နွားလျှာကြီး, *n.* a kind of vine.

နွားသေးသောက်, *n.* a kind of bird.

နွေး, *v.* to be warm—*less than* ပူ.

နွေးကာလ, *n.* the hot season ; *comp.* ဥတု.

နှဲပေါက်ငှက်, *n.* a kind of bi;d.

နွဲ့, (1) *v.* to be limber, pliable, flexible, ဆိ၊ ပျော့ပျောင်း.

နွဲ့, (2) to tease, be contrary, တွဲ့.

နွဲ့နှောင်း, *v.* to be limber, &c.

နှက်, *v.* to beat, (*commonly* to beat in, or down,) ရိုက်၊ ပုတ်.

နှင်, *v.* to drive along, drive away, မောင်း.

နှင်ထုပ်, *v.* do.

နှင်ထုတ်, *v.* to drive out, expel.

နှင်တံ, *n.* a stick to drive with, a whip, ကြိမ်လုံး.

နှင်နှင်, (1) *adj.* common, middling, not distinguished, သာမည.

နှင်နှင်, (2) *adv.* only, merely, nothing but, ချည်းတသေ၊ သက်သက်.

နှင်း, (1) *v.* to give, deliver over, transfer the owning of, for a time, or for ever, ပေး၊ အပ်နှင်း.

နှင်း, (2) *n.* dew, mist, fog, frost, snow, ဆီး.

နှင်းခဲ, *n.* snow.

နှင်း, (3) *n.* the common white lily.

နှင်းဆီ, *n.* the oil of roses, the rose tree.

နှင်းဆီပင်, *n.* a rose bush.

နှင်းဆီပွင့်, *n.* a rose.

နှင်းရည်, *n.* rose water.

နှင့်, (1) *n. affix*, on account of; by means of, by.

နှင့်, (2) *n. affix*, with ; together with.

နှင့်အညီ, *adv.* even as, as far as, in as much as, like as, according to, agreeable to, as သွားသည်နှင့်အညီ, according to the going.

နှင့်ပြီး, *v. affix*, sign of the pluper. tense, as သွားနှင့်ပြီး, he had gone.

နှင့်မည်, *v. affix*, sign of 2nd fut. tense, as သွားနှင့်မည်, he will have gone.

နှင့်, (3) (with မ prefixed to the root,) *v. affix*, prohibitory, as မသွားနှင့်, go not.

နှင့်အတူ, *affix*, together with, as ဆရာနှင့်အတူ, together with the teacher.

နှင့်တကွ, *affix*, together with, &c.

နှင့်အတိုင်း, see နှင့်အညီ.

နှင့်အမျှ, *affix*, as much as, as ဆရာနှင့်အမျှတတ်သည်, to know as much as the teacher.

နှင့်အတူ, *affix*, with, together with, as ဆရာနှင့်အတူ, with the teacher.

နှစ်, (1) *v.* to immerse, make to sink, မြုပ်; *neut.* နစ်.

နှစ်, (2) *n.* the heart; see နှစ်လုံး.

နှစ်သက်, *v.* to be pleased with, have pleasant feelings towards; *either*, to love, esteem, approve, (ကြည်ညို ၊ ချစ် ၊ စုံမက် ၊ နားလည် ;) *or*, to be gratified with, rejoice in, အားရ ၊ ဝမ်းမြောက်.

နှစ်ခြိုက်, *v.* do. do.

နှစ်မြို့, *v.* do. do.

နှစ်လို, *v.* do. do.

နှစ်သိမ့်, *v.* do. *also*, to be composed, quiet, easy in mind.

နှစ်မြော, (*pron.* နှမြော,) (1) *v.* to grudge, be unwilling to part with, စုံမက်.

နှစ်မြော, (2) *v.* to feel for, regard, commiserate, ကြင်နာ.

နှစ်, (3) *n.* a year.

နှစ်ချော်ပွဲ, *n.* an anniversary festival.

နှစ်လည်, *v.* to turn a year, be above a year old, အခါလည်.

နှစ်, (4) *adj.* two, (marked by the figure ၂.)

နှစ်မ, (*pron.* နှမ,) *n.* a man's sister.

နှစ်လုံး, (*pron.* and frequently written, နှလုံး, from အနှစ်, the substantial part of a thing, and အလုံး, round,) *n.* the heart, the mind, စိတ်.

နှစ်လုံးထား, *v.* to consider, reflect, မှတ်.

နှစ်ပွား, *v.* to love, feel delight in, နှစ်သက်.

နှစ်မူ, *v.* to meditate on, lay up in the mind, နှစ်လုံးသွင်း.

နှစ်လုံးပိုက်, *v.* do.

နှီး, *v.* to be silly, foolish, သွပ်.

နှပ်, (1) *v.* to mature, bring to a proper state; act. of နပ်, which see.

နှပ်, (2) *n.* the mucus of the nose.

နှပ်ချိ, *n.* a kind of tree.

နှပ်း (1) *v.* to be speckled, spotted, ပြောက်.

နှင်း, (2) *n.* a kind of tree.

နှင်းဆီ, *n.* an oil expressed from the seed of do.

နှင်းဖတ်, *n.* the refuse after the oil is expressed; see နှင်းဆီ.

နှယ်, (*see* နည်း,) *n.* a kind, sort, manner, (commonly used with pronominal adjectives,) as ဘယ်နှယ်, how? သည့်နှယ်, thus.)

နှံ, (1) *v.* to commit, deliver up, give in charge, အပ်.

နှံ, (2) *n.* a grasshopper, နှံကောင်.

နှံ. (3) *n.* an ear, or spike of grain.

နှံကြပ်, *n.* a kind of creeper.

နှံစုတ်, (from အနှံ and စုတ်,) *n.* a kind of bird, ဗိုလ်ထို့.

နှံမြည်စုတ်, *n.* a kind of bird.

နှံဘဲ, (*pron.* နှဘဲ,) *n.* a kind of tree.

နှံ့, *v.* to pervade, go over all the parts, diffuse throughout, ပျံ့.

နှံ့ပြား, *v.* do. (most common.)

နှံ့စပ်, *v.* do.

နှာ, *n.* the nose.

နှာခေါင်, (from အခေါင်, a summit, ridge,) *n.* do.

နှာခေါင်း, (1) (from အခေါင်း, a hollow,) *n.* a nostril.

နှာ:ခေါင်း, (2) *n.* any medicinal odoriferous preparation.

နှာစ, *n.* the ridge of the nose.

နှာ:စေး, *v.* to have the nose stopped up, as by a cold.

နှာနှတ်, *n.* any medicinal, odoriferous preparation.

နှာမောင်း, (from မောင်း, an arm,) *n.* an elephant's proboscis, or tusk, လမောင်း.

နှာရောင်, *n.* the ridge of the nose; the ridge of a roof, ခေါင်ချုပ်.

နှာရှုပ်, *v.* to string the nose (of a creature;) to make a serpent harmless, by a charm, နှာရှုပ်ထည့်.

နှာဝ, *v.* to be heavy in the head, as with a cold.

နှာသီး, *n.* the end of the nose.

နှိပ်, *v.* to press down, crush, squeeze, oppress.

နှိပ်နယ်, *v.* do.

နှိပ်စက်, *v.* to crush, put down, oppress, vanquish, put or keep in subjection, ညှဉ်းဆဲ; *act. of* နိပ်.

နှိပ်စက်ကလူ, *v.* to play with, divert; to tease, vex; see ကလူ.

နှိမ့်, *v.* to put down, make low; *neut.* နိမ့်.

နှိမ့်ချ, *v.* do. *also,* to be humble, to bow down, be submissive.

နှီး, (1) *v.* to spread out for the purpose of receiving and supporting, (uniting the ideas of ခင်း, and ခံ;) to place, put, in order to receive an accumulation, as a capital or stock in trade, ရင်း. Hence အနှီး, *n.* a sheet spread, child's cloth. အနှီးအခင်း ။ အနှီးအချ, a capital or stock in trade, အရင်း.

နှီး, (2) *n.* split bamboo, used in weaving mats.

နှီးခေါက်, *n.* the outer rind, or bark of a bamboo, peeled off for making mats.

နှီးနှော, *v.* to discuss in conversation, ဆွေးနွေး ။ ဖော်ပြီး.

နှုတ်, (1) *v.* to pull out, extract, subtract; refute.

နှုတ်, (2) *n.* the mouth, ခံတွင်း ။ ပစပ်.

နှုတ်ကပတ်, (from ပါတ, to arrive, *Pali,*) *n.* a divine speech or utterance, မုခွတ်.

နှုတ်ကျက်, *adv.* by heart, by rote.

နှုတ်ကြမ်း or နှုတ်ကြမ်းကြုတ်, *v.* to be abusive, or harsh in speech.

နှုတ်ခမ်း, *n.* a lip. N. B. အထက်နှုတ်ခမ်း, the upper lip; အောက်နှုတ်ခမ်း, the lower lip.

နှုတ်ခမ်းဖြဲ, *v.* to grin, to express anger or contempt by drawing out the lips.

နှုတ်ငုံ့တ်, *n.* an amulet or charm kept in the mouth.

နှုတ်ဆက်, *v.* to make mutual enquiries of civility, to converse together, salute.

နှုတ်တိုက်, *v.* to teach by mouth, dictate.

နှုတ်လှန်ထိုး, *v.* to contradict, (as an inferior a superior.)

နှုတ်သီး, *n.* a lip; a bird's bill, နှုတ်ခမ်း.

နှုတ်သီးကောင်း, *v.* to be a scold.

နှုတ်ပွက်, *v.* to speak, (honorific.)

နှုတ်ရိုက်, *n.* pregnancy, ပဋိသန္ဓေ.

နှုတ်ရိုက်ကြီး, or နှုတ်ရိုက်ရှိ, *v.* to be pregnant, ကိုယ်ဝန်ဆောင် ။ ပဋိသန္ဓေစွဲ.

နှိုင်း *v.* to compare, ရိုင်း ။ တိုင်း ။ နှိုင်း ။ ပြိုင်.

နှိုင်းထမ်း, *v.* do.

နှိုင်းရှိုင်, *v.* do.

နှိုး, *v.* to loosen, weaken, enfeeble, နှဲ့; to make start, to excite, stimulate; *neut.* နိုး.

နှုပ်, *n.* the mouth, နှုတ်.

နှူး, *v.* to make soft, mellow ; *act. of* နူး, *which see.*

နှေး, *v.* to be slow, not quick, မလျင် ၊ မမြန်.

နှဲ, *n.* a kind of trumpet.

နှဲတို, *n.* a short do.

နှဲရှည်, *n.* a long do.

နှဲ့ဝဲ, *n.* a kind of tree.

နှဲ့, *v.* to loosen, weaken, enfeeble, နှဲ့ ; *neut.* နဲ့.

နှော, (1) *v.* to mix together, mingle, ရော.

နှော, (2) *n.* a kind of tree.

နှောမွေ, *v.* see နှောက်.

နှောက်, *v.* to stir up, make muddy (as water ;) agitate, throw about, put into confusion, mix together, molest, distress, နှော ၊ မွှေ ; *neut.* နောက်.

နှောင်, *v.* to tie up, bind, make fast, ချည် ၊ ဖွဲ့.

နှောင်သွင်း, *v.* do.

နှောင်အိမ်, *n.* a prison, ထောင် ၊ လှောင်အိမ်.

နှောင်း, *v.* to place after, in time, cause to be posterior, or later, to be youngest ; *neut.* နောင်း.

နှောင့်, *v.* to molest, trouble, worry, vex, pull to pieces, destroy, မှောင့် ၊ ရှောင့် ၊ ဖျက်ဆီး.

နှောင့်ရှက်, *v.* do.

နှောင့်နှေး, *v.* to be in suspense, doubt, anxiety, not to know what to think or do.

နှိုက်, (1) *v.* to penetrate, drive into, with the hand or an instrument.

နှိုက်နှဲ, *v.* do. (commonly applied to literary or scientific researches,) ထိုးထွင်း.

နှိုက်, (2) (by abbreviation ၌) *n. affix*, in, among.

နိုင်, (1) *v. affix*, sign of the potential mood, as သွားနိုင်, he can go.

နိုင်, (2) *v.* to overcome, conquer ; see အောင်.

နိုင်ရှည်, *v.* to quarrel, or fight.

နှိုင်း, *v.* to compare, နိုင်း ၊ တိုင်း ၊ နှိုး ၊ ပြိုင်.

နှိုင်းရှည်, *v.* do.

နှိုး, *v.* to wake, waken, နိုးစေ; to rouse, to excite, urge to action, ဆော် ၊ ညှို့.

နှိုးဆော်, *v.* do. do.

နွှင်, *v.* to peel off, skin, နွှာ ၊ သင်.

နွှမ်း *v.* to make dull, faded, &c. *act. of* နွမ်း, *which see.*

နွှယ်, *v.* to connect together in succession, စဉ် ၊ ဆက် ၊ နွယ်; *neut.* နွယ်. Hence အနွှယ်, *n.* a lineal succession, descent, race, အစဉ်အဆက် ၊ အမျိုး.

နှိမ့်, *v.* to bend down, make low, နှိမ်နှိမ့်; *neut.* နိမ့်.

နွှာ, *v.* to peel off, skin, နွှင် ၊ သင်.

နွှေး, *v.* to slice, cut in thin pieces, ထွာ ၊ မွှင်းကြိုး ၊ လွှာ.

နွှဲ့, (1) *v.* to procrastinate, delay, ငင့် ၊ လေးလေး.

နွှဲ့, (2) *v.* to loll, lean against, ထိမ်း ၊ ယိမ်း.

## ပ

The first consonant in the class of labials, which is called the ပ class.

ပ, (1) *v.* to shine, (used only in composition with words of similar import;) see တောက် ၊ ထွန်း, &c.

ပ, (2) *v.* to offer to a demon, or evil spirit, ပူဇော်.

ပသ, *v.* do. (most common.)

ပ, (3) *v.* to put aside, or out, ရွှေ့; to neglect, disuse, မသုံး. Hence အပ, *n.* an outside, an outer part, အပြင်.

ပမှာ, *affix,* without, or out of, as အိမ်ပမှာ, without the house.

ပ, (4) an ancient abbreviation of အတယ် or ဘယ်, as ပသို့, for အဘယ်သို့.

ပအုံးရည်, *n.* vinegar, ပုံးရည်.

ပက်, (1) *v.* to throw or toss up, with a scooping motion, as water with the hand, or a dipper; to squirt, as with a syringe; to throw up, as a hog; to beat in, as rain.

ပက်, (2) *v.* to be shallow, as a dish, မစောက်.

ပကတိ, *(Pali,) n.* nature, သဘော.

ပဂိုး, *n.* Pegu, ပဲခူး.

ပက္ခဆွမ်း, *n.* rice given on the first day of the waxing or waning of the moon, လဆန်းပက္ခ ၊ လဆုတ်ပက္ခ.

ပက်စက်, *v.* to be careless, heedless, ill-mannered.

ပက်လက်, *adj.* or *adv.* lying on the back, supine.

ပကူး, *n.* do.

ပက်ကျိ, *n.* a snail.

ပခက်, *n.* a swinging cradle ; see ပုခက်.

ပခုံး, *n.* the shoulder.

ပချုပ်, *n.* a small basket with a cover.

ပဂံ, *n.* a plate, dish ; see ပုဂံ.

ပင်, (1) *v.* to be fatigued, tired, (in body or mind,) ပန်း ၊ မော (used only in composition with words of a similar import.)

ပင်ပန်း, *v.* do. (most common.)

ပင်ရှား, *v.* do.

ပင်, (2) *num. affix*, as ပင်နှစ်ပင်, two trees ; (see Gram.)

ပင်, (3) *adv. affix*, even, (slightly emphatic,) placed either before or after other affixes.

ပင်စိမ်း, *n.* a mint plant.

ပင်တိုင်, *adv.* firmly, perseveringly.

ပင်လယ်, *n.* a sea, an ocean, သမုဒ္ဒရာ.

ပင်လယကသစ်, *n.* a kind of celestial tree.

ပင်း, (1) *v.* to help, aid, assist, ကူ ၊ ညီ ၊ ထောက် ၊ ပံ့ ၊ မ.

ပင်း, (2) *v.* to impede, obstruct, (as a stream,) ကန့်, &c.

ပင်းကုံ, see ပုကုံ, *(obsolete.)*

ပင်းတကား, *n.* a kind of yoke put on men as a mark of disgrace.

ပင့်, (1) *v.* to raise, lift up, ချီး ၊ မြှောက် ; to exalt, promote, ချီး ၊ မြှင့် ; to draw in the breath, inspire.

ပင့်, (2) *v.* to invite, (more respectful than ဖိတ်.)

ပင့်ဆောင်, *v.* do.

ပင့်ဖိတ်, see ဖိတ်.

ပင့်ကူ, *n.* a spider.

ပင့်ကူမွှေး, or ပင့်ကူမြှေး, or ပင့်ကူအိမ်, *n.* a spider's web.

ပင့်ခေါ်, *v.* to invite, call by way of invitation.

ပစပ်, *n.* the mouth, ခံတွင်း ၊ နှုတ်.

ပစ္စ, (*Pali*,) *n.* the past.

ပစ္စင်, (1) (from ပြစ်, to shoot, and စင်, a frame,) *n.* a scaffold or terrace within a fortification, whence missive weapons are discharged, ပြစ်စင်.

ပစ္စင်, (2) *n.* a kind of litter, (*obsolete,*) ထမ်းစင်.

ပစ္စည်း, (from ပစ္စယော, *Pali,*) *n.* a cause, အကြောင်း ; a thing, property, goods, ဥစ္စာ ၊ ပဿု ; *in Pali,* a formative particle.

ပစ္စည်း, (3) *n.* a kind of tree.

ပစ္စယာ, *n.* a lower story of a pagoda, ပစ္စယာဆင့် ၊ အာလိန်.

ပစ္စယုပ္ပန်, (from ပစ္စယော, a cause, and ဥပ္ပန်, to proceed, *Pali,*) *n.* a consequence, result, အကျိုး.

ပစ္ဆိမဘဝ, *n.* the state before the present, အရင်းကဘဝ.

ပစ္စု, *n.* a canopy, ဗိတာန်.

ပစ္စုပ္ပန်, (from ပစ္စ, the past, and ဥပ္ပန်, to be, proceed, *Pali,*) *n.* the present, ယခု.

ပစ္စေကဗုဒ္ဓါ, (from ပစ္စေက, distinct, and ဗုဒ္ဓါ, a Boodh, *Pali,*) *n.* a semi-Boodh.

ပစ်ယံ, *n.* a cause, &c. see ပစ္စည်း.

ပဆုပ်မနှိ, *n.* a kind of hornet.

ပဍာ, *adv.* why ? wherefore ?

ပဍာကြောင့်, do.

ပဉ္စ, (*Pali,*) *adj.* five.

ပဉ္စကာနိ, *n.* a kind of tree.

ပဉ္စင်း, (1) (from ပဉ္စ, five, and အင်္ဂါ, a part, *Pali,*) *adj.* consisting of five parts.

ပဉ္စင်း, (2) *n.* a priest of Boodh, proficient in the five requisite qualifications, ထေရ် ၊ ရဟန်း.

ပဉ္စင်း, (3) see ပစ္စင်.

ပဉ္စပဉ္စ, *n.* a kind of creeper.

ပဉ္စမ, (from ပဉ္စ, five, *Pali,*) *adj.* fifth.

ပဉ္စသီလ, (*by abbreviation,* ပဉ္စသီ, from ပဉ္စ, five, and သီလ, a religious performance, a duty, *Pali,*) *n.* the five grand duties ; see သီလငါးပါး.

ပညတ်, (from ပညတ္တိ, *Pali,*) (1) *n.* a name ; *v.* to give a name, နာမ.

ပညတ်, (2) *v.* to command, ထိန်းမှတ် ; *n.* a command.

ပညတ္တိ, (*Pali,*) *n.* a command, precept.

ပညာ, (*Pali,*) *n.* wisdom.

ပညာရှိ, *n.* a wise man, လူမိန်.

ပညောင်, or ပဉ္စညောင်, *n.* the sacred banyan, ညောင်ဗုဒ္ဓယော.

ပဋိဃာတ်, (from ပဋိဃာတ္တ, *Pali,*) *n.* malice, ရန်ငြိုးဖွဲ့ခြင်း.

ပဋိညဉ်, (from ပဋိညာဏ်, *Pali,*) *n.* acquiescence, promise, ဝန်ခံခြင်း.

ပဋိပတ်, (from ပဋိပတ္တိ, *Pali,*) *n.* a duty, သီလ.

ပဋိပါဠိ, (*Pali,*) *n.* drift, course, order, အစဉ်.

ပဋိဘာန်, (from ပဋိဘာန, *Pali,*) *n.* knowledge, wisdom, ပညာ.

ပဋိဘာဏ, see ပဋိဘာန်.

ပဋိရူပ, (*Pali,*) *n.* comeliness, agreeableness, တင့်တယ်လျောက်ပတ်ခြင်း.

ပဋိသန္ထာရ, (*Pali,*) *n.* a connection or interchange of conversation, စကားစပ်ခြင်း၊ နှုတ်ဆက်ခြင်း.

ပဋိသန္ဓေ, (from ပဋိ, again, and သန္ဓိ, to connect, *Pali,*) *n.* the connection between a former and subsequent state of existence ; i. e. the transition of mind from one body into another, of which there are four, viz. အဏ္ဍဇာ၊ ဇလာဗုဇာ၊ သံသေဒဇာ, and ဥပပါတ် ; conception, pregnancy.

ပဋိသန္ဓေစွဲ, ပဋိသန္ဓေယူ, ပဋိသန္ဓေနေ, &c. *v.* to conceive, be pregnant, နှုတ်နှုတ်ကြီး၊ ကိုယ်ဝန်ဆောင်.

ပဋိသမ္ဘိဒါ, *(Pali,)* *n.* certain intuitive knowledge.

ပဋိသိဓ်, (from ပဋိသေဓ, *Pali,*) *n.* an interruption, prevention, prohibition, မြစ်တားခြင်း.

ပတ္ထနာ, *(Pali,)* *v.* to pray, ask a favour of a divine or celestial being ; *(one kind of* ဆုတောင်း.)

ပတ္ထနာ, (2) *n.* a prayer.

ပဌမ, *(Pali,)* *adj.* first.

ပဘဝ, (*Pali,*) *n.* an origin, root, stock, နဂိုရ်၊ မူလ၊ အရင်း.

ပဏ္ဍုက်, (from ပဏ္ဍကော, *Pali,*) *n.* a man subject to certain debilities, ပန်းပုတ်.

ပဏ္ဏာ, (*Pali,*) *n.* a gift, present, လက်ဆောင်.

ပဏ္ဏာကာရ, *n.* do.

ပတ်, (1) *v.* to crack, open, gape, ဟက်.

ပတ်, (2) *v.* to wind round, encircle, encompass, go round, ရစ်၊ လည်၊ ဝန်း၊ ဝိုင်း၊ ထက်ဝန်း. Hence အပတ်, *n.* a circuit ; sometimes written အပဒ်.

ပတ်လည်, ပတ်ဝန်း, ပတ်ဝန်းချင်း, *v.* do. *n.* the environs, or circuit of a thing, ဝန်းကျင်၊ ထက်ဝန်းကျင်.

ပတ်လည်, *affix,* around, as အိမ်ပတ်လည်, round the house.

ပတ်လုံး, (1) *affix*, during, or throughout, as ကာလပတ်လုံး, during, or throughout time.

ပတ်လုံး, (2) *n.* a whole circuit, or duration, (commonly applied to words of time,) ပန်လုံး.

ပတ်ကုံး, *n.* do.

ပတ်ဝိုင်း, *v.* to wind round, &c. see ပတ်.

ပတ်, (3) *n.* a small cylindrical drum.

ပတ်တုံ, *n.* do.

ပတ်ဆိုင်း, or ပတ်ဝိုင်း, *n.* a circular frame, in which several *pats* are fixed, and played on by a person standing in the middle; *comp.* ကြေးဆိုင်း.

ပတ်သာ, *n.* a small *pat* (ပတ်,) used singly, တုံသာ.

ပတ်မ, *n.* a large do.

ပတ်ကုတ်, see ပန်းကုတ်.

ပတ္တမြား, *n.* a ruby, or carbuncle, ကျောက်နီ.

ပတ္တမြားနီ, *n.* do.

ပတ္တမြားပြောက်, *n.* a spotted ruby.

ပတ္တရသချို, *n.* a kind of plant which takes root on the leaves of certain trees.

ပတ္တလား, *n.* a kind of stringed musical instrument.

ပတ္တာ, *n.* a brass or iron hinge, မျှောက်လက်.

ပတ္တုနီ, *n.* a kind of cloth.

ပတ္တုပြယ်, *n.* do.

ပတ္တူ, *n.* a kind of coarse woollen cloth.

ပတူ, (1) *n.* a hornet, a kind of wasp.

ပတူ, (2) *n.* a sucker, made of reed, quill, &c.

ပတ်ိ, *n.* a kind of precious stone, ထတ်ိ.

ပတ်ကော, *n.* a species of ginger-plant.

ပထကာ, see ပဂကာ.

ပထဝီ, (*Pali,*) *n.* the earth, မြေကြီး.

ပဒပုရဏ်, (from ပဒ, a poetic line, and ပူရဏ, completion, *Pali,*) *n.* the completion of a line in poetry, its being complete or full.

ပဒါး, (see ပြဒါး,) *n.* quicksilver.

ပဒုမ္မာ, (*Pali,*) *n.* a kind of water-lily; *comp.* ကြာ.

ပဒေသရာဇ်, (from ဒေသ, a country, and ရာဇာ, a king, *Pali*,) *n.* the sovereign of a division of one of the four grand islands, တဝန်းတလျှားအစိုးရသောမင်း ; *comp.* ဓိကရာဇ်, and စကြာမင်း.

ပဒေသာ, *n.* (1) a kind of tree, supposed to grow on the great north island, and to produce every thing that contributes to the happiness of life.

ပဒေသာ, (2) *n.* an artificial tree laden with religious offerings.

ပန္တက်, *n.* a short stake driven into the ground to mark out a limit.

ပန္တက်ဘဲ, *n.* do.

ပန္တက်တိုင်, *n.* do.

ပန်, (1) *v.* to make, to adorn, decorate, by sticking on flowers, decorations, &c. to receive an order with submission and respect.

ပန်ဆင်, *v.* do.

ပန်, (2) *v.* to ask leave, beg, petition, အခွင့်တောင်း ၊ တိုင်.

ပန်ကြား, *v.* do.

ပန်တွာ, *v.* do.

ပန်နတ်, *v.* do. *also* to imprecate evil on one's self, take an oath, ကျိန်ဆို ၊ သစ္စာပြု.

ပန်လုံး, see ပတ်လုံး.

ပန်း, (1) *v.* to be tired, fatigued, harassed in body or mind, ပင်ပန်း ၊ မော ; to pant, breathe with difficulty, as when labouring under the asthma. Hence အပန်း, *n.* a fatiguing business, a difficulty. အပန်းကြီး, *v.* to be of great consequence, requiring great exertion. Hence also တပန်းတကြီး, *adv.* earnestly, indefatigably, with great exertion, အပတ်တကုတ် ; အပန်းကြီးစွာ, *adv.* do.

ပန်းစတ်, see ပဍ္ဍုတ်.

ပန်းကုတ်, (*commonly* ပတ်ကုတ်,) *v.* make fatiguing exertion, (generally used adverbially.)

ပန်း, (2) *n.* a flower, blossom, အပွင့် ၊ ပန်းပွင့် ; (*sometimes used expletively in composition, as* ကွမ်းပန်း ၊ ထွမ်းပန်း, &c.) A general term, including several varieties of flower trees and plants.

ပန်းကလပ်, see ကလပ်.

ပန်းကုံး, *n.* a garland, wreath, chaplet of flowers.

ပန်းဆိုင်း, *n.* do.

ပန်းတောင်း, or ပန်းပုံတောင်း, *n.* a flower basket, with a foot or stand.

ပန်းရုက်, *n.* the essence or juice of flowers.

ပန်းမွှန်, *n.* flowers, (in general.)

ပန်းသည်, *n.* a florist.

ပန်းချီ, (*sometimes pron.* ပချီ,) *n.* a painter.

ပန်းစုတ်, see ပန္နလုတ်.

ပန်းဆိုးသွား, *n.* a dyer of cloth, &c.

ပန်းတဉ်း, (*pron.* ပခဉ်း,) *n.* a brazier.

ပန်းထိမ်, (*sometimes pron.* ပဒိမ်,) *n.* a gold or silver-smith, a jeweller.

ပန်းတုံး, *n.* a pole crowned with a bunch of grass or leaves, and set up; a government notice, or interdict.

ပန်းထိုင်း, (*pron.* ပဒိုင်း,) *n.* a kind of tree.

ပန်းတွဲ, *n.* ornaments suspended from the stern of a boat.

ပန်းထည်, *n.* a kind of red cloth.

ပန်းထိုးသွား, *n.* an embroiderer.

ပန်းပု, (*sometimes pron.* ပဗု,) *n.* a carver in wood.

ပန်းပဲ, (*sometimes pron.* ပဘဲ,) *n.* a blacksmith.

ပန်းပွတ်, *n.* a turner.

ပန်းမှိုက်ကျုံး, *n.* a pagoda slave, one who gathers up flowers, and the refuse of offerings, ကျွန်သိမ်တော် • ဘုရားကျွန်.

ပန်းမှိုက်ဖွန်, or ပန်းဖွန်, *n.* do.

ပန်းယွန်း, *n.* one that works in lacquer.

ပန်းရန်, (*pron. and commonly written* ပုရန်,) *n.* a mason.

ပန်းသွန်း, *n.* a founder.

ပမာ, an abbreviation of ဥပမာ.

ပမာဏ, (*Pali,*) *n.* a measurement, size, standard, အတိုင်းအရှည်.

ပမာဏပြု, *v.* to regard, have respect to, esteem, value.

ပဗ္ဗ, *n.* a kind of tree.

ပယ်, (1) *v.* to put aside or away, to reject, ဖဲရှား.

ပယ်, (2) *n.* a piece of ground 560 cubits square.

ပယ်စားမြေ, *n.* taxable ground.

ပတိ, (3) see နတိ.

ပယောဂ, (*Pali,*) *n.* an instigator, principal agent.

ပရင်း, *n.* a kind of precious stone,—yellowish, opaque.

ပရဆေးသည်, *n.* a druggist.

ပရစ်, *n.* a cricket.

ပရဆေး, *n.* medicine.

ပရဂ္ဂ, *n.* one of the six glories of Boodh, *see under* ဘုန်းတော် ခြောက်ပါး.

ပရိနိဗ္ဗာနတော်ကြီး, *n.* see နတ်ဖြစ်.

ပရက်, (*Pali,*) *n.* completion, fulness.

ပရန်, (*a contraction of* ပန်းရန်,) *n.* a mason.

ပရမတ္တ, (*Pali,*) *adj.* excellent.

ပရပေါ်, *n.* a kind of plant.

ပရိုက်, *n.* a kind of heretic.

ပရမတ်တရားလေးပါး, (from ပရမတ္တ, excellent, *Pali,*) *n.* four principles, viz. စိတ်, mind; စေတသိတ်, the operations of mind; ရုပ်, body, or matter; and နိဗ္ဗာန်, absorption or annihilation.

ပရမာဏုမြူ, *n.* the finest conceivable particle,—invisible to sight.

ပရမ်းပတာ, (*from* ရမ်းတော,) *adv.* thrown about, scattered, dispersed, ပြန့်ပရဲ.

ပရဝုန်, (from ပရဝေန်, to appropriate, *Pali,*) *n.* a fence, enclosure, appropriated place, အရံအတား.

ပရဝိုင်း, *n.* a fence around a kyoung or monastery.

ပရိက်, (1) *n.* furniture, appendages.

ပရိက်, (2) *n.* certain religious exercises.

ပရိက္ခရာ, (*Pali,*) *n.* a utensil, article of use, အသုံးအဆောင် ၊ ဝန်တာ.

ပရိတ်, (from ပရိတ္တ, *Pali,*) *n.* a kind of invocation or prayer, used as a preventative of evil.

ပရိတ်ရွတ်, *v.* to repeat do.

ပရိတ်ချည်, *n.* thread used as a charm.

ပရိတ်ရေ, *n.* charmed or holy water.

ပရိနိဗ္ဗာန်, *n.* absorption, or annihilation; see နိဗ္ဗာန်.

ပရိယတ်, (from ပရိယတ္တိ, *Pali,*) *n.* learning; study, application to books, သင်ရင်း.

ပရိယာယ်, (from ပရိယာယော, *Pali,)* (1) *n.* a means, expedient, artifice, device, ဥပါယ် ၊ မာယာ ၊ ဝေဝုစ်.

ပရိယာယ်, (2) *n.* a synonymous word, one by which the same thing is expressed.

ပရိသတ်, *(from* ပရိသာ, *Pali,)* *n.* an attendant on instruction, an auditor.

ပရုတ်, *n.* camphor.

ပရွမ်းပရင်း, *adv.* (from ရွမ်းရင်း,) confusedly, riotously.

ပရောဟိတ်, (from ပရောဟိတ, *Pali,)* *n.* a Brahmin of a certain order.

ပရောဟိတ်ပုဏ္ဏာ, *n.* one who prognosticates, a prophet or fortune-teller.

ပချောက်ပချက်, *adv.* (from ချောက်ချက်,) confusedly, &c.

ပရွက်, *n.* an ant.

ပရွက်ဆိတ်, *n.* do.

ပလင်း, *n.* a bottle.

ပလာ, *(pron.* ဗလာ ; *from* ပလာဘော, *Pali,)* *adj.* or *adv.* open, naked, bare, vacant, empty.

ပလိမ်းပကျံ့, (from လိမ်း and ကျံ့,) *adv.* flatteringly, deceitfully.

ပလီ, (1) *v.* to be cunning, crafty, artful, ထန်းပြား.

ပလီ, (2) *n.* a ball thrown, and caught by a bat, as a cricket ball ; or by a cord attached to it, as a discus, ဝက်.

ပလီလုံး, *n.* do.

ပလီတံ, *n.* a bat, in the game of cricket.

ပလုတ်တုတ်, *n.* a kind of drum.

ပလုံး, *n.* a kind of basket.

ပလုံးပထွေး, (from လုံး and ထွေး,) *adv.* confusedly.

ပလုံတောင်သံ, *n.* a kind of plant.

ပလူ, *v.* to be obsequious, to fawn.

ပလျှက်, *v.* do.

ပလဲပတင်, *adv.* backward and forward, interchangingly, တပြောင်းပြန်ပြန်.

ပလောင်းပလဲ, (from လောင်း and လဲ,) *adv.* falsely, deceitfully, putting one thing for another.

ပထောင်းပလုပ်, *adv.* do.

ပလ္လင်, *(pron.* ပလင် ; *from* ပလ္လင်္ကော, *Pali,)* *n.* a raised seat, a throne.

ပဍ္ဍား, *v.* to be vain, boastful, ostentatious, ဝါ ၊ ကြွား.

ပဝါ, *n.* a handkerchief, a towel.

ပါဌ, *n.* an opinion, a sentiment; see ပါဋ.

ပဝါရဏာ, *(Pali,) n.* a certain religious ceremony, an act of fellowship, performed by priests in full assembly, wherein a mutual invitation to tell each other's faults is given and accepted.

ပသာဒရုပ်, (from ပသာဒ, visible, sensible, and ရုပ, matter, *Pali,*) *n.* matter which perceives, i. e. the organs of sense; *comp.* ဝိသယရုပ်.

ပသိမ်, *n.* Bassein.

ပသီ, *n.* a Musulman, Moorman.

ပသျှူး, *adj.* pertaining to Malay.

ပဟိုရ်, *n.* a period of time, division of day and night.

ပဟိုရ်စည်, *n.* a royal drum, beat at certain houses to tell the time of day or night.

ပဟိုရ်စင်, *n.* the frame of do.

ပံသုကူ, (from ပံသု, dirt, and ကူလော, a kind, *Pali,*) *n.* food or clothing thrown away in the dirt for any person to take.

ပံ့, *v.* to help, aid, assist, ကူ ၊ ညို ၊ ထောက် ၊ ပင့် ၊ မ.

ပါ, (1) *v.* to have, to take or bring with.

ပါ, (2) *affix,* sign of the imperative or precative mood. When applied to nouns, it is expletive; *also,* when used after an indicative affix.

ပါစေ, *prec. affix,* as ဖြစ်ပါစေ, may it be.

ပါလေစေ, *prec. affix,* as သွားပါလေစေ, let him go.

ပါ့, (3) *euphonic affix,* (polite, respectful.)

ပါတ, (*Pali,*) *v.* to arrive, ရောက်; to come.

ပါဋိဟာ, *(Pali,) n.* a divine communication.

ပါဠိ, *n.* an original text or reading.

ပါဒ်, (from ပါဒ, *Pali,*) *n.* a measure of time, equal to one fourth part of a naree, (နာရီ.)

ပါဒရုပ်, (from ပါဒ, the foot, *Pali,*) *n.* the cause of a certain class of diseases, so called because supposed to ascend from the feet.

ပါဒချက်တက်, *v.* to ascend, &c. see the preceding word.

ပါရမီ, *(Pali,) n.* an accomplishment, or virtue (ပြည့်စုံချင်း,) of which there are ten kinds, viz. ဒါန ၊ သီလ ၊ နိက္ခမ ၊ ခန္တီ ၊ မေတ္တာ ၊ ပညာ ၊ ဝိရိယ ၊ သစ္စာ ၊ အဓိဋ္ဌာန ၊ ဥပေက္ခာ.

ပါရသီ, *n.* a Parsee.

ပါရာဇိက, *(Pali,) n.* a crime which deserves the lowest hell.

ပါသိနတ်စာ, *n.* an offering made to a Deva, or Nat.

ပါဠိ, *n.* an original word or language opposed to the vernacular; the Pali language, a dialect of the Sungskrit, in which the Boodhist scriptures are written, မာဂဓပါဠိ.

ပါဠိနက်, *n.* a translation, an interpretation, နိဿယ.

ပါဠိနံ, *n.* do.

ပါဠိပါဌ်, *n.* see ပါဌ်.

ပါး, (1) *num. affix,* as ဆရာနှစ်ပါး, two teachers ; *(see Gram.)*

ပါး, (2) *v.* to send (a thing.)

ပါးလိုက်, *v.* do. *(most common,)* ပေးလိုက်.

ပါး, (3) *v.* to be thin, not thick, လျော ၊ လျော့ ၊ လွှာ ၊ မထူ ; to be wide apart, set thinly, not close, ကျဲ ၊ မစိပ် ၊ မထူ ; to be few, not many, နည်း ၊ မများမထူ ; to be scarce, ရှား.

ပါး, (4) *v.* to recede, depart, be gone, spent, finished, လွင့်.

ပါးရော, *v.* do.

ပါး, (5) *n.* a cheek, side of the face.

ပါးစောင်, *n.* do.

ပါးရိုး, *n.* the lower jaw.

ပါးချိတ်, *n.* the end of the lower jaw.

ပါးမွေး, *n.* the hair of the cheek, the whiskers.

ပါးဟက်, *(pron.* ဘဟက်,) *n.* the gills of a fish.

ပါးပျဉ်း, *n.* the cheeks hanging down ; the head of a cobra di capello.

ပါးကာ, *n.* a guard for the cheeks.

ပါးလျှာ, or ပါးလျက်, (from လျှာ, and လျက်,) *v.* to lick the face, as a dog ; to fawn, be obsequious.

ပါးလျှာနားလျှာ, *adv.* fawningly, obsequiously, &c. see ပါးလျှာ.

ပါးလျက်နားလျက်, *adv.* do.

ပိ, *v.* to press, flatten, crush, be flat, ချပ် ၊ ပျား.

ပိစပ်, *adj.* or *adv.* flat, pinched up, contracted.

ပိဋကတ်သုံးပုံ, (from ပိဋကာ, a basket, *Pali,*) *n.* the three grand divisions of the Boodhist scriptures, viz. ဝိနည်း, သုတ္တန်, and အဘိဓမ္မာ.

ပိဏ္ဍပတ်, *n.* a daily offering of rice to the priests.

ပိတင်, *n.* a window; see လေသာ.

ပိတ်, (1) *v.* to shut, shut up, to close, stop up, ပင်း ၊ ဆို့; to pre-engage.

ပိတ်, (2) *n.* cotton cloth.

ပိတ်ထုပ်, *n.* a bale of do.

ပိတ်, (3) *n.* the dysentery, or flux.

ပိတ်ကိုက်နာ, *n.* do.

ပိတ်နီ, ပိတ်ဖြူ ၊ ပိတ်ကြောင်, *n.* varieties of do.

ပိတ်ကျည်, *n.* a kind of wind instrument.

ပိတ်ချင်း, *n.* a species of the pepper plant.

ပိတ်ထကျည်း, *n.* a kind of tree.

ပိတ်တော့, an interjection, expressive of joy that a thing is destroyed, (in low use.)

ပိတ်တော့ပြီး, *n.* do.

ပိတ်ပေါင်း, *n.* a close thick wood.

ပိတ်မှာန်, see ပိမှာန်.

ပိတ်သင်းကတ်, *n.* a kind of tree.

ပိတ်သည်းပိတ်နည်း, *adv.* grudgingly.

ပိတာ, (*Pali,*) *n.* a father, အဘ.

ပိတာန်, (*sometimes* ပြတာန်; *from* ပိတာနံ, *Pali,*) *n.* a canopy, any thing stretched over the head, မျက်နှာကြက်.

ပီတိ, (*Pali,*) joy, pleasure, နှစ်သက်ချင်း ၊ ဝမ်းမြောက်ချင်း.

ပိတုဿ, *n.* see ပိတာ.

ပိတုန်း, *n.* a large blue insect.

ပိတောက်, *n.* a kind of tree.

ပိဒုက္ခ, (from ပိတာ, and ဒုက္ခ,) *n.* an evil incurred by ill-treating a father.

ပိန်, *v.* to be lean, poor, thin, to pine away, ကြုံ ၊ လှီ ၊ ဖဝ.

ပိန်ညင်, *n.* a kind of water-fowl, ငှက်ဘဲ.

ပိန်း, (1) *v.* to be close together, without an opening; to be crowded, numerous, &c. see ထူ.

ပိန်း, (2) *n.* a plant of the mint kind, of which there are several varieties.

ပိန်းဖော, *n.* a canoe made of a single piece of timber.

ပိန္နဲ, *n.* the jack tree; the fruit of do.

ပိန့်, *v.* to swell slightly, rise up, as the skin, from the effects of a blow, or bite. Hence အပိန့်, *n.* a rising of skin, a blister, pustule, &c.

ပိမ့်, *v. affix,* fut. tense, as ပြုပိမ့်မည်, he will do, or will be doing.

ပိမ့်, (from ပဲ, and လေ,) *euph. affix.*

ပိဿာ, *n.* a pikthah, or viss; a weight equal to one hundred kyats, or tickals, (အကျပ်.)

ပိသုကာ, *(Pali,)* *n.* a master workman, chief artist, director, superintendent.

ပီတာသ, an intensive to negative assertions; see ပေတာသ.

ပီတား, *n.* a kind of shell fish.

ပီတု, *n.* a kind of bird, ငှက်.

ပီးပီး, *adv.* an intensive.

ပု, (1) *n.* to be short, dwarfish, stunted, ကွ.

ပု, (2) *(an abbreviation of* ပုဗ္ဗေနိဝါသဉာဏ, *Pali,)* *n.* wisdom which can discern the past; *comp.* ဒိ, and စ.

ပုကန်, (1) *(pron.* ပကန်,*)* *n.* a glazed earthen dish, bowl, &c.

ပုကန်ပြား, *n.* a glazed dish, plate, saucer, &c.

ပုကန်လုံး, *n.* a glazed cup, bowl, &c.

ပုကန်, (2) *n.* a kind of tree.

ပုခက်, *(pron.* ပခက်,*)* *n.* a swinging cradle, ဇလင်.

ပုဂ္ဂိုလ်, (from ပုဂ္ဂလ, *Pali,)* (1) *n.* being, or state of being in general, သတ္တဝါ.

ပုဂ္ဂိုလ်, (2) *n.* a priest of Boodh, who has the controul of a kyoung or monastery, an abbot; an unmarried man who devotes himself to the instruction of others.

ပုစဉ်း, *(pron.* ပစဉ်း,*)* *n.* a kind of locust.

ပုစဉ်းထိုး, *n.* a kind of bird.

ပုစ္ဆာ, *(Pali,)* *n.* a question, အမေး.

ပုဇွန်, *(pron.* ပဇွန်,) *n.* a species of crab fish ; *comp.* ဂဏန်.

ပုဇွန်တာရ, *n.* a certain star or constellation ; see တာရ.

ပုဇွန်တုပ်, *n.* a prawn, a lobster.

ပုဇွန်ဆိတ်, *n.* a shrimp.

ပုဇွန်လုံး, *n.* a species of crab fish.

ပုဇွန်စာ, *n.* a kind of plant.

ပုဇွန်တပက်, *n.* a kind of vine, or creeper.

ပုဆစ်, *n.* a knee, ဒူး.

ပုဆစ်တုပ်, *v.* to kneel.

ပုဆိန်, *n.* an axe.

ပုဆိုး, *(pron.* ပဆိုး,) (1) *n.* cloth in general.

ပုဆိုး, (2) *n.* a waist-cloth, the garment worn by Burman men around the waist.

ပုဆိုးကျုန်း, *n.* a part of a waist-cloth, an old piece of cloth, a rag.

ပုညာ, (*Pali,*) see ကုသိုလ်, and ကောင်းမှု.

ပုဏ္ဏား, *(Pali,)* *n.* a Brahman.

ပုဏ္ဏဖုသျှ, *n.* a certain star or constellation ; (see နက္ခတ်.)

ပုဏ္ဏေး, *n.* a Brahmanee.

ပုတ်, *v.* (1) to strike, beat, ရိုက် ၊ နှက်.

ပုတ်, (2) *n.* a large square wicker basket ; see ထက်.

ပုတ်ခတ်, *v.* to fight, &c. see under သတ်.

ပုဒ်, (3) *n.* punctuation, a period.

ပုဒ်ချ, *v.* to punctuate, make a mark in punctuation.

ပုဒ်မ, *n.* a full point, or period.

ပုတတ်, *n.* *(pron.* ပုဒတ်,) a kind of cameleon.

ပုတတ်စာ, *n.* a kind of plant.

ပုတ်ပြတ်, *adv.* all together, by the lump, wholesale.

ပုတ်သင်, *n.* a kind of cameleon.

ပုတီး, *(pron.* ပဒီး,) (1) *n.* a bead, or string of beads.

ပုတီးစိပ်, *v.* to count beads, while performing religious duties, &c.

ပုတီး, (2) *n.* a kind of plant, ဗုဒ္ဓသရကာ.

ပုတီးပြိ, *n.* a kind of tree.

ပုထုဇဉ်, (from ပုထုဇ္ဇနော, *Pali,*) *n.* one that has not attained the state of an Areeya, (အရိယာ.)

ပုထုဇန်, or ပုထုဇ္ဇန်, *n.* a priest of Boodh, or one who performs the duties of a priest.

ပုထိုး, (*pron.* ပထိုး,) *n.* a pagoda; see စေတီ.

ပုဒ်, (from ပါဒ, *Pali,*) (1) *n.* a line of Pali verse, commonly consisting of eight syllables, the fourth part of a stanza, (ဂါထာ); (2) *n.* a line of Burman verse consisting of four syllables, or more.

ပုန်ကန်, *v.* to rebel.

ပုန်စား, *v.* do.

ပုဏ္ဍရိက်, *n.* a kind of water-lily; see ကြာ.

ပုန်ကျော, *n.* see ရက်မ.

ပုန်း, *v.* to conceal one's self, keep out of the way, hide, ကွယ် ၊ တိမ်း ၊ ရှောင် ၊ လွှဲ.

ပုန်းညက်, *n.* a kind of tree.

ပုန်းတမ်းကစား, *v.* to play at hide and seek.

ပုန်းတလုတ်ကစား, *v.* to play, as at blind man's buff.

ပုန်းမဲစာ, *n.* a kind of tree.

ပုန်းရည်စာ, *n.* a kind of tree.

ပုပ်, (1) *v.* to be putrid, rotten.

ပုပ်စပ်, *v.* do.

ပုပ်, (2) *v.* to be dark, gloomy in countenance, ညို ၊ မည်း.

ပုပ်, (3) *v.* to be left, as shreds of cloth.

ပုဗ္ဗ, (*Pali,*) what is future, ရှေး ၊ နောင်.

ပုဗ္ဗနိမိတ်, *n.* a mark, sign, &c. see နိမိတ်.

ပုဗ္ဗေနိဝါသာနုဿတိ, (*Pali,*) *n.* prescience.

ပုဗ္ဗေနိဝါသဉာဏ်, (*Pali,*) *v.* to know the past, and future; ရှေးအဖြစ် နောက်အဖြစ်ကိုမြင်သည်.

ပုရပိုက်, (*pron.* ပရပိုက်,) *n.* a plate, thin substance, whether of paper, cloth, or metal, folded backward and forward, used to write upon.

ပုလ္လိင်, (from ပုရိသော, *n.* a male, ဆိုဒ်, &c. *Pali,*) *n.* the male genitals; masculine gender.

ပုလဲ, *n.* a pearl.

ပုသိမ်, (*pron.* ပသိမ်,) *n.* Bassein.

ပုံ, (1) *v.* to heap up, collect in a heap, accumulate. Hence အပုံ, *n.* a heap, a great quantity.

ပုံ, (2) *n.* a pattern, ပုံစံ; a rule, နည်း ၊ ဥပဒေ; a figure, similitude, comparison, ဥပမာ.

ပုံပြင်, *n.* do.

ပုံစီ, *v.* to compose, as a printer, to set up types, &c.

ပုံထား, *v.* to heap, pile up.

ပုံတောင်, *n.* the nave of a wheel.

ပုံဘော, (from ပုရိသော, a male, and ဘော, *Pali,*) *n.* the male genitals.

ပုံသေ, *adv.* certainly, truly, အမှန် ၊ ဆတ်ဆတ်, &c.

ပုံး, *n.* a kind of clothes-basket; see also ရေပုံး.

ပုံးရည်, *n.* vinegar; see ပဆုံးရည်.

ပုံ့, *v.* to plump up, swell up in a heap.

ပုံ့ပုံ့ကြွ, *v.* do. (most common.)

ပူ, (1) *v.* to bore with a gimblet.

ပူ, (2) *v.* to be hot, pungent; to be troubled in body or mind, distressed, harassed.

ပူစပ်ပူလောင်, *v.* to be inflamed, be troubled, distressed, harassed.

ပူပန်, *v.* to be distressed, troubled, &c.

ပူပင်, *v.* do.

ပူဆွေး, *v.* do.

ပူဆာ, *v.* do.

ပူ, (3) *n.* a round basket with a cover.

ပူတာ, *n.* do.

ပူဇော်, (from ပူဇာ, *Pali,*) *v.* to make an offering to a being, in token of homage or worship.

ပူဇော်သကာ, *n.* an offering.

ပူး, *v.* to join, unite, put together, ကပ် ၊ စပ် ၊ တွဲ ၊ ရှက် ၊ ယှဉ် ၊ တပ်.

ပေ, (1) *v.* to have the edge or point worn off, so as to be dull, blunt, &c.

ပေ, (2) *n.* an anvil.

ပေ, (3) *n.* the palmyra tree or leaf.

ပေ, (4) *euphonic affix,* as ပြုပေသည်, he does or is doing; (see Gram.)

ပေ, (5) *v. affix,* imp. or prec. (see Gram. imp. mood.) When applied to nouns, it is expletive.

ပေတာယ, *adv.* an intensive to negative assertions.

ပေး, *v.* to give, ကမ်း.

ပေးစား, *v.* to give in marriage, ဆောင်နှင်း ; *comp.* ထိမ်းမြား.

ပေးလိုက်, *v.* to send (a thing,) ပါးလိုက်.

ပေးဝေ, *v.* to divide, distribute ; see ဝေပေး.

ပဲ, (1) *n.* a *bai,* a weight equal to six or eight seeds of Abrus precatorius, ရွှင်ရွေး.

ပဲ, (2) *n.* a leguminous plant, one that bears seeds in a pod ; pulse, of which there are many varieties.

ပဲတောင့်, *n.* the pod.

ပဲဆံ, or ပစေ့, *n.* the seed ; peas, beans, &c.

ပဲသီး, *n.* the pod and contents.

ပဲခူး, *n.* Pegu, ပဂိုး.

ပဲခွပ်, *n.* a short handled adze.

ပဲ့, (1) *v.* to be broken off, as a small piece from a larger, ကျိုးပဲ့ ; *act.* ဖဲ့.

ပဲ့, (2) *n.* the stern of a boat or vessel.

ပဲ့စင်, *n.* the place of a helmsman.

ပဲ့တိုး, *n.* the piece of timber which forms the stern of a Burman boat.

ပဲ့တက်, *n.* the helm, or rudder, တက်မ.

ပဲ့နင်း, *n.* a helmsman, တက်မကိုင်၊ ပဲ့သွား.

ပဲ့တင်, *n.* (1) an echo ; (2) *n.* any loud thundering noise.

ပဲ့တင်ခတ်, *v.* to be a loud thundering noise, ဟောင်လည်း.

ပဲ့တင်ထပ်, *v.* to echo.

ပဲ့ပြင်, *v.* to instruct, guide, discipline, correct, ဆုံးမ၊ သင်.

ပေါ, *v.* (1) to be plentiful, not scarce, ထူ၊ မရှား.

ပေါရွန်, *v.* do.

ပေါရွယ်, *v.* do.

ပေါ့, (2) *affix,* when applied to nouns, is expletive ; *also* when used after ind. affix.

ဖေါ, (3) *v.* see ဖယ်.

ပေါ်လော, *adv.* or *adj.* buoyant, or floating on the water.

ပေါ်လော, *adv.* backward and forward, in a disorderly manner.

ပေါက်, (1) *v.* to be pierced, penetrated, have a hole made into or through, to have a dot made on, စက်; to sprout, (as vegetation;) to come out, appear, (as a hole;) ထွက် ၊ ပေါ်; to arrive, ရောက်; (*act.* ဖောက်.) Hence အပေါက်, *n.* a hole; a dot, အစက် ၊ ဗိန္ဒု; a drop, အစက်.

ပေါက်ဖြာ, *v.* do.

ပေါက်ဖွား, *v.* to be born, brought forth; see ဖွား.

ပေါက်, (2) *v.* to paw with the fore feet, (as a horse.)

ပေါက်, (3) *n.* a kind of tree.

ပေါက်ခြိုက်, (*pron.* ပေါင်ခြိုက်,) *n.* a kind of cap worn as a mark of distinction; *comp.* ပေါင်.

ပေါက်ဆိန်, *n.* an axe; see ပုဆိန်.

ပေါက်တူး, *n.* a hoe.

ပေါက်ပန်းဖြူ, *n.* a kind of tree.

ပေါက်ပေါက်, *n.* parched rice.

ပေါက်ပန်းပွင့်, *n.* do.

ပေါက်ဖတ်, *n.* a kind of fly.

ပေါက်ဖော်, *n.* a person born of the same mother; a near relative, အဆွေအမျိုး.

ပေါင်, (1) *v.* to superadd, attach to for the purpose of strengthening or improving.

ပေါင်, (2) *v.* to pawn, mortgage.

ပေါင်နှံ, *v.* do.

ပေါင်သေ, *n.* a slave who is at the entire disposal of his master.

ပေါင်ရှင်, *n.* a slave who is transferable at his own pleasure.

ပေါင်ဘွင်, *n.* a hired servant, အခစား; *comp.* ကျွန်.

ပေါင်, (3) *n.* the thigh; *comp.* အပေါင်.

ပေါင်ချုန်, *n.* the groin, inside of the thigh.

ပေါင်ဆစ်, *n.* the hip joint.

ပေါင်ဒိုး, *n.* a swelling of the groin.

ပေါင်ထောင်, *v.* to squat, sit in a squatting posture.

ပေါင်ထောင်ထောက်ထား, *v.* to sit in a squatting posture, with the hands resting on the knees.

ပေါင်ရိုး, *n.* the hip bone.

ပေါင်, (4) (*pron.* ဗောင်,) *n.* a kind of cap, insignia of rank.

ပေါင်ထရပု, *n.* do.

ပေါင်ကျွပ် ; ပေါင်ထုတ် ; ပေါင်ပျင်, varieties of do.

ပေါင်, (5) *n.* a kind of mat.

ပေါင်း, (1) *v.* to collect and unite in one—more than ပု and ရုံး.

ပေါင်း, (2) *n.* a sum total. Hence အပေါင်း, *n.* or *adj.* many, the many, all.

ပေါင်းဖက်, *v.* to associate.

ပေါင်းဖော်, *v.* do.

ပေါင်း, (3) *v.* to bake, to distil.

ပေါင်းအချောင်, *n.* a pot with a perforated bottom, used to cook by steam.

ပေါင်း, (4) *n.* an arched covering or roof over a carriage, boat, or palanquin, ပေါင်းမိုး ; the vehicle itself.

ပေါင်းကုပ် ; ပေါင်းရှုပ် ; ပေါင်းသင်, *n.* varieties of do.

ပေါင်းကူး, (from ကူး, to cross over,) *n.* an arch, arched passage, မုဒ်.

ပေါင်းကွပ်, *n.* certain transverse timbers which support a floor.

ပေါင်းဘီ, *n.* pantaloons, small clothes.

ပေါ့, *v.* to be light, not heavy, မလေး ; to be quick, လျင် ; to be light, worthless, ထိန် ။ ဆုံ ။ ယုတ် ; to be slightly deranged, ပျံ့လွင့်,

ပေါ့ပါး, *v.* do.

ပေါ့တာ, *v.* to be light, worthless, ချွတ်ပေါ်.

ပျောက်, *v.* to be lost, gone, missing, be forgotten.

ပေါ်, (1) *v.* to appear, come to light ; *act.* ဖော်.

ပေါ်ထွေး, *v.* to be improperly done ; see ချွတ်ပေါ်.

ပေါ်ချွတ်, *v.* do.

ပေါ်မှာ, *affix*, above, as အိမ်ပေါ်မှာ, above the house.

ပေါ်, (2) *v.* see ပြန်, to return, &c.

ဖို, (1) *v.* to heap up above the level or surface, to make more than full, to cause to exceed in any respect, ထို. Hence အဖိုနေ့, *n.* the day after a worship day, when kept as a work of supererogation.

ဖို, (2) *n.* a long oval wicker basket, used in transporting goods.

ပို, (3) *n.* see ပြိုက်, a piece on a gaming-board, ကျား.

ပိုက်, (1) *v.* to hold in the arms, to hug, both the arms being under the object; *comp.* ဖက်.

ပိုက်ထွေး, *v.* to take care of, lay up, သိမ်းဆည်း.

ပိုက်, (2) *v.* to make stops in writing, to mark off sentences or lines. Hence အပိုက်, *n.* a portion inclosed in marks or stops.

ပိုက်, (3) *n.* a sweep net.

ပိုက်ကွန်, *n.* a net.

ပိုက်ဆံ, *n.* the hemp plant.

ပိုင်, (1) *v.* to own, possess, have a right to, have authority over, အစိုးရ.

ပိုင်ဆိုက်, *v.* do.

ပိုင်သ, *v.* do.

ပိုင်နက်, (from အနက်, a collection) *n.* property, what belongs to one.

ပိုင်, (2) *v.* to be soft, pulpy, but of such consistence as to bear handling; *compare* နှဲ.

ပိုင်း, (1) *v.* to sever, divide, ထုံး.

ပိုင်းခြား, *v.* to make a separation between, to draw a dividing line, distinguish, make distinct, ခြား ၊ သားနား.

ပိုင်း, (2) *n.* a part, as ဆယ်ပိုင်းတပိုင်း, one tenth part, or one part of ten.

ပိုး, (1) *v.* to fix or fasten one on another, suspend—more than ဆင် and ထင်.

ပိုး, (2) *n.* an insect, or worm; any small animal without distinguishable sounds; the silk-worm, silk.

ပိုးဖြူ, *n.* the white ant.

ပိုးကာ, (from ကာ, to interpose,) *n.* sheathing boards, so called because they defend from worms; thin narrow boards.

ပိုးစာ, *n.* the silk-worm's food; the mulberry tree.

ပိုးစုန်းကြူ, *n.* a fire-fly, a glow-worm.

ပိုးစုန်းကြူး, *n.* do.

ပိုးဖြင်ဖြိုး, *n.* do.

ပိုးခဲကောင်, *n.* a large green fly, or bug.

ပိုးတောင့်တဲ, *n.* a hairy caterpillar.

ပိုးနှသံ, *n.* a kind of worm.

ပိုးပရှန်, *n.* a kind of fly.

ပိုးဟပ်, *n.* a kind of bug; a cock-roach.

ပိုးစုန်းကြူး, *n.* a fire-fly.

ပိုးရိုး, *adv.* see ပိုးရိုးပက်စက်.

ပိုးရည်ဖြူ, *n.* a fire-fly.

ပိုးရိုးပက်စက်, *adv.* remissly, heedlessly, wanting in due respect and attention, ကဗောက်ကဗက် ၊ ရှောက်ရိရှောက်ရက်; *comp.* ပက်စက်.

ပို့, (1) *v.* to carry or bring, to conduct, ဆောင်.

ပို့, (2) *v.* to teach, instruct, သင်.

ပို့, (3) *v.* to offer, as a good wish or blessing.

ပို့သ, *v.* to carry, &c. see ပို့.

ပို့, (4) to be thrown into, or upon; *act.* ပို့.

ပျ, *n.* a kind of ant, from whose nests lac is procured.

ပျက်, *v.* to be destroyed; *act.* ဖျက်.

ပျက်စီး, *v.* do.

ပျက်ပျား, *v.* to be destroyed.

ပျက်, (2) *v.* to trick, play a trick with, deceive, ချေ့ ၊ သဝေ့.

ပျက်ချော်, *v.* do. (most common.)

ပျက်ပြယ်, *v.* do.

ပျက်ပြည်, *v.* do.

ပျက်ရယ်, *v.* do. *also* to jest, joke.

ပျက်, (3) *v.* to add, put into, as a little into a large mass, ခပ် ၊ ဖွက် ၊ လောင်း.

ပျက်, (4) *v.* to spread out in the sun for a little while.

ပျက္ခဒိန်, *n.* some astrological scheme, which forms the basis of subsequent calculations.

ပျက်သီ, *adv.* a little, အနည်းငယ်; see ပျက်.

ပျင်း, *v.* to be lazy, ရိ.

ပျစ်, *v.* to be thick, dense, not rare, မကျည်.

ပျဉ်, (1) *v.* to make flat, level.

ပျဉ်, (2) *n.* a board, plank, ပျဉ်ပြား.

ပျဉ်း, (1) *v.* to be tough, to bear bending without breaking, မဆတ်; to be stupid, dull, insensible of discipline, ထုံ.

ပျဉ်း, (2) *v.* to be loose, pulpy, hanging down, as the skin of the cheek, the breasts, &c. တွဲလွဲ.

ပျဉ်း, (3) *n.* a kind of tree ; of which there are several varieties.

ပျပ်, *v.* to be low, နိမ့်, ဝပ် ; to be in a low posture, to stoop, squat, &c. commonly implying respect, ဝပ်.

ပျပ်ဝပ်, *v.* do.

ပျပ်ခွေ, *v.* do.

ပျပ်ကလပ်, see ကလပ်, to be immodest, &c.

ပျပ်ပျပ်, *adv.* droppingly, drop by drop.

ပျပုံချည်ချည်, *adv.* all together, wholly.

ပျမ်း, *v.* to distribute equally throughout, မျှ.

ပျယိုးယား, *adv.* all together.

ပျံ, *v.* to fly.

ပျံ့, (1) *v.* to be scattered, spread, diffused, ပြန့်, (act ပျံ့ ;) to be diffused as pleasant odour ; fragrant, odorous, ထုံ ၊ ကြူ ၊ ကြိုင် ၊ မွှေးသင်း.

ပျံ့, (2) *v.* to be pleasant, agreeable, သာယာ ; to be pleased, joyful, ရွှင်.

ပျံ့ပျူး, *v.* to be pleasant, or pleased.

ပျံ့ရှား, *v.* to be fragrant, pleasant, &c. see ပျံ့.

ပျံ့လွင့်, *v.* to be scattered, dissipated.

ပျာ, (1) *v.* to toss up as rice, when cleaning it by fanning, (စကော.)

ပျာ, (2) *v.* to be distressed in mind, agitated, distracted, စိတ်ပျာ.

ပျား, (1) *v.* to be flat, level, ညပ်.

ပျား, (2) *n.* a honey-bee.

ပျားအုံ, *n.* a collection of bees, a bee-hive.

ပျားအုန်း, *n.* a swarm of bees.

ပျားတူ, (*pron.* ပတူ,) *n.* a hornet.

ပျားရည်, *n.* honey.

ပျားလပို, *n.* a honey-comb.

ပျားသငယ်, *n.* young bees.

ပျားသထက်, *n.* cells for young bees.

ပျူငှာ, *n.* courteous behaviour, kind attention, politeness, ဧည့်ဝတ်.

ပျူတာ, *n.* courteous behaviour, &c. see ပျူငှါ.

ပျူပျူတာတာ; *adv.* courteously, engagingly, politely.

ပျောက်, *v.* to be lost, to disappear, be gone; *act.* ဖျောက်.

ပျောက်လွင့်, *v.* do.

ပျောက်ရှ, *v.* do. (applied to goods only.)

ပျောင်း, *v.* to be limber, pliant, flexible, ဆိ ၊ နွဲ့ ၊ မတောင့်; *act.* ဖျောင်း.

ပျော့, *v.* to be soft, tender, yielding, not hard, မမာ.

ပျော့ပျ, *v.* do.

ပျော်, *v.* to enjoy one's self, be pleased, satisfied, happy, မွေ့လျော်; *act.* ဖျော်.

ပျော်ပါး, *v.* do. ပျော်မြိုက်, do. ပျော်ပွယ်, do. ပျော်ကြွား, do. ပျော်မွေ့, do. ပျော်ဒွိန်း, do. ပျော်ရွှင်, do.

ပျို, *v.* to be young, fresh, in prime, not old. Hence အပျို, *n.* a young unmarried woman, အိမ်မထောင်သောမိန်း; (*comp.* လူပျို.) အပျိုကြီး, or အပျိုဟိုင်း, *n.* an old maid.

ပျိုရွ, *v.* to be young, &c. see ပျို.

ပျိုဖြန်း, *n.* a female just arriving at pubescence.

ပျိုမျစ်, *v.* to be young, &c. see ပျို.

ပျိုရွယ်, *v.* do.

ပျိုး, (1) *v.* to sow, as seed, ကြဲ ၊ စိုက်.

ပျိုး, (2) *v.* to set, plant, စိုက်.

ပျိုး, (3) *n.* a plant.

ပျို့, *v.* to be sick at the stomach, disposed to vomit, ရင်ပူ; to be sick with passion, as love, hatred, &c.

ပျို့အန်, *v.* do. do.

ပျို့ဆိန့်, *v.* to be sick at the stomach, ဆို့ပျို့.

ပြ, (1) *v.* to show, point out, direct, ညွှန်.

ပြ, (2) *n.* a raised frame or scaffold, for various purposes, with or without a roof—if on a fortress, for the purpose of defence, ပင်.

ပြဆိုး, *n.* do.

ပြစင်, *n.* do.

ပြထင့်, *n.* do.

ပြကတေ့, *(from the Sungscrit,)* (1) *n.* nature, ပကတိ ၊ သဘော.

ပြကတေ့, (2) *v.* to be natural.

ပြက်ပြက်, *adv.* clearly, conspicuously, ထင်ထင်.

ပြက်ရယ်, *v.* to ridicule, ခနဲ့.

ပြင်, (1) *v.* to put in order, prepare, repair, adorn.

ပြင်ဆင်, *v.* do.

ပြင်လျာ, *v.* do.

ပြင်လွင့်, *v.* to be gone aside, out of the way, &c.

ပြင်, (2) see အပြင်, outside.

ပြင်, (3) *affix*, besides, as သည်ပြင်, besides this; ထိုပြင်, besides that.

ပြင်မှာ, *affix*, without, outside, as အိမ်ပြင်မှာ, without the house.

ပြင်ဘဝါး, *n.* see ဖနည့်.

ပြင်ဝန်, *n.* a public minister of state; *comp.* အတွင်းဝန်.

ပြင်း, *v.* to be violent, သည်း.

ပြင်းပြ, *v.* do.

ပြင်းထန်, *v.* do.

ပြစ်, (1) *v.* to throw away, reject, စွန့်.

ပြစ်, (2) *v.* to throw at, shoot.

ပြစ်မှတ်, *n.* a mark set up to aim at.

ပြစ်, (3) *v. is sometimes used for* ပစ်, *which see.*

ပြစ်လိုက်, *v.* to throw away, reject; to throw at, shoot.

ပြစ်မှား, *v.* to sin against, transgress.

ပြည်, (1) *v.* to be loosened, untied; *act.* ဖြည်.

ပြည်, (2) *v.* to jest with, &c. see ပြယ်.

ပြည်, (3) *n.* a country; division of do. a district, city.

ပြည်ထောင်, *n.* do.

ပြည်တံခါ, *n.* the opening of a country; a pan; a custom-house.

ပြည်တန်ဆာ, *n.* a courtezan, distinguished harlot, မိဗ္ဗြ.

ပြည်တံခွန်, *n.* the clergy, literati.

ပြည်စား, *n.* governors of provinces.

ပြည်မျက်စိ, *n.* do.

ပြည်လက်ရုံး, *n.* the great officers of state.

ပြည်ထဲရေး, *n.* the internal affairs of a country.

ပြည်, (4) *n.* a pyee, a measure equal to five စလယ်, or one sixtieth part of an တင်း.

ပြည်, (5) *n.* pus.

ပြည်ပန်း, *n.* a kind of tree; ပြည်ပန်းညို.

ပြည်း, (1) *v.* to be numerous, plentiful, ထူ၊ များ၊ ပေါ; (used in composition with other words of like import.)

ပြည်း, (2) *v.* to be finished, spent, gone, exhausted, ကုန်၊ စင်၊ ခန်း၊ ဆုံး၊ ပြိုန်း.

ပြည်းတော, *n.* a kind of boat.

ပြည့်, *v.* to be full; (*act.* ဖြည့်.)

ပြည့်ကျပ်, *v.* to be full, crowded, full as any vessel.

ပြည့်မွမ်း, *v.* do.

ပြည့်စုံ, *v.* to be complete, perfect; accomplished, fulfilled, စုံညီ၊ စုံလင်.

ပြည့်စင်, (*pron.* ပြည့်ရှင်,) *n.* a kind of tree.

ပြဋ္ဌာန်း, (from ပဋ္ဌာန, *Pali,*) (1) *v.* to decide, ဆုံးဖြတ်.

ပြဋ္ဌာန်း, (2) *n.* a characteristic, essential difference.

ပြတ်, *v.* to be cut in two, to be cut off, ended; to be broken off, to stop as a stream; to be decided, distinct, clear, ပြတ်သား; *act.* ဖြတ်.

ပြတ်လပ်, *v.* to be cut in two, to be cut off, ended; to break.

ပြတ်သတ်, *v.* to be cut in two, to be cut off, ended; to break, or be broken; to be decided, distinct, clear.

ပြတ်သား, *v.* to be decided; distinct, clear; see ပြတ်.

ပြတင်း, *n.* a window, လေသွင်းတံခါး.

ပြတင်းပေါက်, *n.* do.

ပြတာန်, *n.* a canopy; see ဗိတာန်.

ပြဒါး, (*pron. and commonly written* ပဒါး,) *n.* quicksilver.

ပြဋ္ဌိ, *n.* a spitting box or pot, ထွေးအင်၊ ထွေးခံ.

ပြန်, (1) *v. affix,* again, as သွားပြန်သည်, he goes, or is going again.

ပြန်, (2) *v.* to return, to repeat, do again or in return, တုံ့၊ ပေါက်; to die, (colloquial.)

ပြန်ကြား, *v.* to relate, repeat (an account.)

ပြန်ဆို, ပြန်ပြော, &c. *v.* to answer.

ပြန်လွှား, *n.* a kind of bird.

ပြန့်, (1) *v.* to be spread out, extended; *act.* ဖြန့်.

ပြန့်, (2) *v.* to be enlarged, multiplied.

ပြန့်ပြော, *v.* to be spread out, &c. *see both definitions of* ပြန့်.

ဖြန့်ပွား, ဖြန့်များ, ဖြန့်ကျယ်, &c. *v.* see both definitions of ဖြန့်.

ဖြယ်, (1) *v.* to come to an end, to put out of the way, be extirpated, ကုန်။ ပျောက်။ ပျက်.

ဖြယ်, (2) (*originally* ဖြယ်,) *v.* to show and laugh, to jest with, put to the blush, as young persons of different sexes, to make indelicate allusions, ကိလေသာနှင့်စပ်ရှက်ဖွယ်စကား ; *one kind of* ပျက်ချော်, or ပျက်ရယ်.

ဖြယုတ်, (from ပယောဂ, *Pali,*) *n.* an illustration, proof.

ဖြဲ့, *v.* to misguide, deceive.

ဖြသန်, *n.* a kind of wasp.

ဖြသဒ်, (from ပါသာဒ, *Pali,*) *n.* a four-cornered graduated steeple, attached to palaces, royal boats, kyoungs, &c.

ဖြသဒ်ဦးဖြည်း, (*commonly written* ဖြသဒ်ဥဖြည်း,) *n.* do. shaven headed, not rising to a point.

ဖြဿနာ, *n.* a subject for discussion.

ပြာ, (1) *v.* to be blue.

ပြာ, (2) *v.* to be dim, as the eyes from dazzle, weakness, age, &c. မှုံ ; *comp.* ဝါး.

ပြာ, (3) *n.* ashes.

ပြာသိုလ်, *n.* the tenth month in the year.

ပြား, (1) *v.* to be divided into several parts, (*act.* ဖြား ;) to be spread abroad, diffused, ပျံ့ ; to become many, be numerous, multiplied, များ. Hence အပြား, *n.* breadth, width, &c. အကျယ် ။ အနံ ။ ပျက် ; *hence also* အပြားအားဖြင့်, (used adverbially,) numerously, very ; *hence also* အပြားပြား, *adv.* variously.

ပြားစား, *v.* to be divided, &c. see ပြား.

ပြား, (2) *num. affix*, as ပြည်နှစ်ပြား, two countries ; (see Gram.)

ပြိတ်, *v.* to wink or make signs with the eyes.

ဖြိုး, *v.* to be idle, vain, unsubstantial, ပျင်း ; (applied to persons and language.)

ဗြိစ္ဆာ, (*Pali, a scorpion,*) *n.* Scorpio, the eighth sign of the Zodiac.

ပြိတ္တာ, or ပြိတ်, (from ပေတော, *Pali,*) *n* a Pyittah, a kind of being inferior to man, inhabiting one of the four states of suffering ; *see* အပါယ်. There are several varieties ;

*see* ဧင္ဂ and ပုတ်. It includes the lower orders of the brute creation, as insects, worms, serpents, fish, &c. *see* တိရိစ္ဆာန်.

ပြိဿ, *(Pali, a bull,)* Taurus, the 2d sign of the Zodiac.

ပြိ, *v.* to be accurate, exact.

ပြိပြင်, *v.* do.

ပြိသ, *v.* do.

ပြီး, (1) *v.* to be finished, accomplished, done, ပြည့်စုံ.

ပြီးစီး, *v.* do. Hence အပြီးနေ့, *n.* a worship day, *comp.* အကြိုနေ့ ၊ အဝိ ထင်နေ့ ၊ အထွက်နေ့, and အပိုနေ့.

ပြီး, (2) *v. affix*, sign of ind. mood, past tense.

ပြီးလျှင်, *v. affix*, sign of the past tense, or sub. mood, as ပြုပြီးလျှင်, if he complete or finish, or when he has completed or finished.

ပြီးလျက်, *v. affix*, subj. mood, past tense, as ပြုပြီးလျက်, had he done, or finished doing. Also when he had done, or finished doing.

ပြု, *v.* to do, perform, ကျင့်ဆောင် ၊ မှု ; to make one's self be, become, or act like ; see မှု.

ပြုစု, *v.* to take care of, administer to.

ပြုပြင်, *v.* to repair, put in order ; see ပြင်.

ပြုတ်, (1) *v.* to boil ; ချက်ပြုတ်, to cook by boiling.

ပြုတ်ဆေး, (1) *n.* a decoction.

ပြုတ်, (2) *v.* to be unloosed, put out of place, dislocated, deranged, ပြည် ၊ ကျွတ် ; *act.* ဖြုတ်.

ပြုတ်ပြုတ်, *adv.* expressive of the sound which is produced by pronouncing the word itself.

ပြုတ်ရှပ်, see ရှပ်.

ပြုဗ္ဗဝိဒေဟာ, *n.* the East Island ; see ကျွန်း.

ပြုန်း, *v.* to be worn away, be exhausted, become extinct, ခန်း ၊ တုံး ၊ ပြည်း ; *act.* ဖြုန်း.

ပြုန်းတီး, *v.* do.

ပြုန်းပြည်း, *v.* do.

ပြုံ, *v.* to remain unaltered or unaffected in passing through an operation.

ပြုံး, *v.* to smile.

ပြုံးပြုံး, *adv.* expressive of the sound which is produced by pronouncing the word itself.

ပြုံ့ပြုံ့, *adv.* smilingly.

ပြူ, *v.* to project a little, appear beyond, ထိုး၊ ပေါ်.

ပြူတိုး, *adv.* projectingly.

ပြေ, (1) *v.* to be done away, settled, appeased; *act.* ဖြေ.

ပြေ, (2) *v.* to be made agreeable, be pleasant, comfortable.

ပြေချော, *v.* to be agreeable, pleasant, comely, handsome, ချောမော.

ပြေပြစ်, *v.* do.

ပြေလည်, *v.* do.

ပြေစာ, *n.* a certificate of settlement, discharge, acquittal, &c.

ပြေ, (3) *v.* to be dark in colour, of a deep blue, ညို.

ပြေး, *v.* to run, flee.

ပြေးလွန်, *v.* to run by, outrun.

ပြဲ, (1) *v.* to gape, expand, lie open, be bell-mouthed, ဟန်း; *act.* ဖြဲ.

ပြဲ, (2) *v.* to be exhausted, &c. see ပြည်း.

ပြော, (1) *v.* to speak, say, tell, ဆို.

ပြောပ, *v.* do.

ပြော, (2) *v.* to be wide, extensive, ကျယ်; to be many, numerous, plentiful, ထူ၊ များ; (seldom used alone.)

ပြောက်, (1) *v.* to be spotted, variegated, whether by colours, or carved work. Hence အပြောက်, *n.* pointed, carved, or embroidered work. အပြောက်အပြန်း, *n.* do.

ပြောက်, (2) to be obliterated, &c. (generally written ပျောက်, *which see.*)

ပြောင်, (1) *v.* to be bright, shining, brilliant, တောက်၊ ထိန်၊ ထွန်း.

ပြောင်, (2) *v.* to be hard, not soft, မာ; to be hardened, obstinate, untractable, ခေါင်း၊ စိတ်မာ.

ပြောင်တောင်, *adv.* steadily, intensely, တောင်ပြောင်.

ပြောင်, (3) *n.* a kind of wild cow.

ပြောင်ပြ, *n.* a royal military howdah.

ပြောင်း, (1) *v.* to be tender, soft, &c. (generally written ပျောင်း;) see ပြော.

ပြောင်း, (2) *v.* to put one thing in place of another, လဲ; to remove, change place, နေရာပြောင်း.

ပြောင်းပြန်, *v.* to put upside down, or one end for the other.

ပြောင်း, (3) *n.* a tube.

ပြောင်း, (4) *n.* a kind of grain.

ပြောင်းဖူး, *n.* Indian corn.

ပြော့, *v.* to be tender, soft, delicate, limber, flexible, နူး.

ပြေန်, *v.* to sleep quietly, be in a sound sleep, ငွေ၊ အိပ်ပြေန်.

ပြို, *v.* to break down, tumble to pieces, come to ruin; *act.* ဖြို.

ပြိုပျက်, *v.* do.

ပြိုလဲ, *v.* do.

ပြိုက်ပြိုက်, *adv.* droppingly, (as tears.)

ပြိုင်, *v.* to put together, side by side, ယှဉ်; to compare, နှိုင်း၊ ထိုင်း၊ နှိုင်း; to engage together, whether in union or rivalry, ဆိုင်း; to meet together, အချင်းချင်းတွေ့.

ပြိုင်း, *v.* to be full, abundant, well furnished, whether in size or numbers.

ပြိုးပြက်, *v.* to glitter, မှိုးရှက်; (commonly reduplicated, and used adverbially.)

ပြို, *n.* sacred verse, in lines of four syllables.

ပြိုဝတ်စာ, *n.* do.

ပွ, (1) *v.* to be brittle, easily crumbled.

ပွ, (2) *v.* to rise up soft, be pulpy.

ပွက်, (1) *v.* to bubble, as boiling liquid, ဆူ; or as water when agitated by fish, or otherwise, ပွက်ထ၊ ဝေ. Hence အပွက်, *n.* a bubble, froth, scum, အမြှုပ်.

ပွက်, (2) (from အပွက်,) *n.* mud, mire, ညွှံပွက်.

ပွက်, (3) *v.* to speak, (honorific;) နှုတ်ပွက်.

ပွင့်, *v.* to expand, open, be opened, to blossom; *act.* ဖွင့်. Hence အပွင့်, *n.* a blossom.

ပွင့်ချပ်, *n.* the petals of a blossom.

ပွင့်ထင်း, *v.* to be brought to light, be manifest.

ဖွင့်ထွက်, *v.* to expand, &c. see ပွင့်.

ပွတ်, (1) *v.* to rub, တိုက်; to wash as clothes.

ပွတ်, (2) *n.* a turner's lathe.

ပွတ်ခံ, *v.* to use a turning lathe.

ပွတ်ခုံသမား, *n.* a turner.

ပွတ်ခုံပွတ်ကျဉ်း, *n.* a turner's lathe.

ပွတ်တိုင်, *n.* a post, balustrade, or any thing of the kind which is prepared by a turning lathe.

ပွန်း, *v.* to rub off, wear away by friction.

ပွင့်, *v.* to be open, not stopped up, မဆို့ ၊ မပိတ်.

ပွား, *v.* to increase in number or size, များ ၊ တိုး.

ပွေး, (1) *n.* a mole, (an animal.)

ပွေး, (2) *n.* a ring-worm.

ပွေးကိုင်း, *n.* senna.

ပွေးသစင်ငွေ, *n.* a ring-worm.

ပွေ့, *v.* to support on the arms.

ပွဲ, *n.* a feast or festival (of any kind;) an assemblage, concourse; the place of assembling or holding a festival, သဘင်; a place of eating, a table, eating board, as စားပွဲ ၊ ထမင်းပွဲ &c.

ပွဲခ, *n.* a banker's commission.

ပွဲစား, *n.* a dealer in uncoined money, an appraiser of do. a banker, sirkar.

ပွဲတော်ကဲ, *n.* a king's cook, စားတော်ကဲ.

ပွဲတော်ဖို, *n.* a king's cook-house.

ပွဲတော်သား, *n.* people employed in do.

ပွဲလမ်း, *n.* a festival, entertainment.

ပွဲသဘင်, *n.* a feast, festival; an assembly, or concourse of people; the place of holding a festival.

ပွဲရက်, *n.* the gum of a certain tree, ဆင်တွဲ.

ဖြက်, (1) *v.* to bubble, boil, &c. see ပွက်.

ဖြွက်, (2) *v.* to utter, speak, *(honorific,* မြွက်*).*

ဖြိုက်, (1) *v.* to grow in clusters. Hence အဖြိုက်, *n.* a cluster, bunch.

ဖြွတ်, (2) *n.* a squirt, syringe, any instrument which throws out water with force; *(frequently pron.* ပွတ်.)

ဖြွတ်တံ, *n.* a pump.

ဖြွတ်ဖြွတ်, *adv.* in a squirting manner, like water squirted from a syringe; *applied to speech,* rapidly, fluently.

ပြွန်, (1) *v.* to be versed, skilled in, accomplished, ကျွေ ။ ကျင် ။ ထည် ။ ကျွင်း.

ပြွန်တီ, *v.* do. (most common.)

ပြွန်, (2) *n.* any conductor of water or other liquids, an aqueduct, pipe, tap, spout, &c.

ပြွန်တံ, *n.* a pump.

ပြွမ်း, *v.* to mix together, commingle, ရော ။ နှော.

ပြံ, *v.* to be in advance, go beyond, exceed.

ပြွေ, *n.* a kind of musical instrument, a flute.

## ဖ

The second consonant in the class of labials.

ဖ, (1) *n. affix*, mas. gen. as ကြက်, a fowl; ကြက်ဖ, a cock.

ဖ, (2) *n.* an abbreviation of အဖ, a father.

ဖဖေ, *n.* a father.

ဖခင်, *n.* do.

ဖကြီး, *n.* a father's elder brother; a mother's elder sister's husband; comp. ဦးရီး, or ဝရီး.

ဖထွေး, *n.* a father's younger brother; a mother's younger sister's husband; a step-father.

ဖက်, (1) *num. affix*, as လက်နှစ်ဖက်, two hands; (see Gram.)

ဖက်, (2) *v.* to embrace, hug in the arms, to form corresponding parts in union, to unite, associate, ပေါ် ။ ပေါင်းပေါ် ။ ပေါင်း ဖက်. Hence အဖက်, *n.* a corresponding part in a union; a companion, associate, အပေါ်.

ဖက်ယမ်း, *v.* to embrace, hug.

ဖက်, (3) *n.* a leaf, အရွက်.

ဖက်ကတော့, see ကတော့.

ဖက်ခန်, *n.* a kind of fine silk.

ဖက်ဦးရေလောင်း, *adv.* conjointly, in regard to profits and expenses; in fellowship.

ဖက်ဗွန်, *n.* a kind of water-dipper, without a handle.

ဖက်ဆွတ်, *n.* a kind of tree.

ဖက်ညွန်, *n.* a kind of cloth.

ဖက်ချာ, *n.* a kind of tree.

ဖက်သက်တရေဒ်, *n.* a kind of tree.

ဖက်သကပ်, *n.* a kind of disease.

ဖက်သချွာ, *n.* a kind of disease.

ဖက်သနီး, *n.* a kind of tree.

ဖခက်, *n.* a swinging cradle, ပေထင်.

ဖင်, *n.* the anus, စအို.

ဖင်ဝ, *n.* do.

ဖင်စု, *n.* dung.

ဖင်ပုပ်, *n.* ordure.

ဖင့်, *v.* to procrastinate, prolong time, put off, delay, နှေး၊ လေးလေး.

ဖင့်စား, *v.* do.

ဖင့်နှိုးဖင့်နှေး, *adv.* slowly, procrastinatingly.

ဖခေါင်, *n.* the side of the hand or foot.

ဖတ်, (1) *v.* to read audibly, ဖတ်ရွတ်.

ဖတ်, (2) *v.* to interpret, explain (a dream or omen,) &c.

ဖတ်, (3) *v.* to dress (cotton) with a bow-string, ဂွမ်းဖတ်.

ဖတ်, (4) *v.* to be beautiful (used with words, expressive of appearance or colour; also, in a reduplicated form, as an intensive of various applications.)

ဖတ်, (5) *n.* sediment, &c. see အဖတ်.

ဖတ်လျင်, *n.* a bed-stead, ခတင်.

ဖန်, (1) *v.* to give a form or appearance, to form, create, make, စီရင်၊ လုပ်; to assume an appearance, အသွင်ဆောင်.

ဖန်ဆင်း, *v.* do.

ဖန်ခင်, *v.* to do, perform, make, direct the making of a thing.

ဖန်, (2) *v.* to clean cotton, by pulling and picking, previously to dressing it, ဝါဖန်.

ဖန်, (3) *v.* to be astringent (in taste.)

ဖန်ရည်, *n.* astringent liquor, (commonly applied to decoctions of barks, roots, &c.)

ဖန်, (4) *n.* glass.

ဖန်ကတီ, *n.* a wine glass.

ဖန်ကတုန်, *n.* a glass tumbler.

ဖန်ကပ်, *n.* a kind of glass ornament.

ဖန်ခွက်, *n.* a glass cup or vessel.

ဖနောင့်, *n.* the heel.

ဖနောင့်ဖကျဉ်း, *n.* do.

ဖန်ခါး, *n.* a kind of tree.

ဖန်ဝေ, *v.* see ဝေဖန်, to distribute, &c.

ဖန်း, *v.* to catch, lay hold of, apprehend.

ဖန်းယူ, *v.* do.

ဖန်းဆီး, *v.* to apprehend, catch, prevent.

ဖန်းတား, *v.* do.

ဖန်, *v.* to dry up, be dry.

ဖပ်ဖပ်, *adv.* an intensive to words of moistness, liquidity, &c.

ဖမိုး, *n.* the back of the hand, or upper part of the foot.

ဖမျက်, *n.* the ancles, ခြေမျက်စိ.

ဖမ်း, *v.* to catch, မိ ၊ ရ; to try to catch.

ဖမ်းစား, *v.* to seize, possess (as a spirit,) to bewitch, charm, စွဲ.

ဖမ်းဆီး, *v.* to apprehend.

ဖယ်, *v.* to go aside, shun, reject, avoid, ဆိမ်း ၊ ရှားရှောင် ၊ လွှဲ ၊ ကြဉ်.

ဖယာ, *n.* a certain quantity of tea leaf ; (obsolete.)

ဖယ်ရမ်း, *adv.* in a straddling manner, throwing out the legs.

ဖယ်လယ်, *adv.* out of the way, indirectly, obliquely.

ဖရင်ဂျီ, *n.* a Portuguese, or descendant of do.

ဖရုံ, *n.* a pumpkin, of which there are many varieties.

ဖရုံနွဲ, *n.* a long white species of pumpkin, ကျောက်ဖရုံ.

ဖရုံဆုံ, *n.* the posteriors, ခွေးဆုံ ၊ တင်.

ဖရဲ, *n.* the melon, of which there are many varieties.

ဖယောင်း, *n.* wax.

ဖယောင်းတိုင်, *n.* a candle.

ဖယောင်းခုံ, *n.* a candlestick.

ဖယောင်းဆီ, *n.* ointment, salve.

ဖယောင်းပန်း, *n.* a kind of tree.

ဖရိုးဖရဲ, *adv.* in a broken, scattered, disordered manner, ပရမ်းပတာ.

ဖလဋ္ဌာန်, (from ဖလ, profit, and ဌာန, a receptacle, *Pali,*) *n.* one who has attained either of the four grand rewards or blessings ; *comp.* ဖိုလ်.

ဖလှယ်, *v.* to exchange, လဲ.

ဖလံ, *n.* the Bauhinia dyphylla ; (Symes.)

ဖလံတောင်ပေါ, *n.* a kind of tree.

ဖလံပြူ, *n.* a kind of insect.

ဖလား, *n.* a kind of cup, or bowl.

ဖလုကပ္ပလီ, *n.* Andaman.

ဖလီစက်, *n.* a circular missile weapon.

ဖဝါး, *n.* the palm of the hand, or sole of the foot.

ဖဝါးခြေထပ်, *adv.* following, treading in another's footsteps.

ဖဿ, *(Puli,) n.* perception, အာရုံကိုတွေ့ခြင်း.

ဖာ, (1) *v.* to mend, repair.

ဖာ, (2) *n.* a four-cornered basket, with a cover.

ဖာလာ, *n.* the tree which produces cardamoms.

ဖာလာနုဒိ, *n.* a kind of tree.

ဖာလာနုဒိတ်, *n.* a kind of tree.

ဖား, (1) *v.* to hang loosely about, be flowing, full, luxuriant, ပေ.

ဖားရား, *adv.* hanging loosely about.

ဖားလား, *adv.* do.

ဖား, (2) *n.* a frog, (many varieties.)

ဖားပြုပ်, *n.* a toad.

ဖိ, *v.* to keep down, press, crush; to squeeze together.

ဖိတ်, (1) *v.* to invite, (more respectful than ခေါ်;) to offer to give, invite to take; *comp.* ပင့်.

ဖိတ်မန်, *v.* do.

ဖိတ်ကြား, *v.* do. Hence အဖိတ်နေ့, *n.* the day before a worship day, အကြိုနေ့.

ဖိတ်, (2) *v.* to spill over; to wash.

ဖိတ်စည်, *v.* to spill over, wash away, be lost, gone.

ဖိတုံး, (from ဖိ and တုံး,) *n.* logs of wood used to keep down a corpse when burning in a funeral.

ဖိန်းဘာ, *n.* the fourth day from the present.

ဖိန်းနွဲ, *n.* the third day from the present.

ဖိန်းပက်လက်, *n.* the fifth day from the present.

ဖိမ်နေ့, *n.* the third day after the present.

ဖီ, *v.* to prevent, hinder, press, ဆီး၊ တား.

ဖီထွား, *v.* do. (most common.)

ဗိဆန်, *v.* to contradict, oppose, ငြင်း.

ဗိလာ, *adv.* obliquely, across ; (comp. ကန့်လန့်.)

ဗီး, *n.* a comb. *v.* to comb.

ဗိလုံး, *n.* a kind of bird.

ဘု, *v.* to be a knot, or bulb, to be knobby, knotty, &c.

ဘုတ်, (1) *v.* to roast, or burn, by putting in the fire without covering.

ဘုတ်ကြည်း, *v.* to burn in a funeral.

ဘုတ်, (2) *n.* an evil spirit, ghost, ဘုတ်ကောင်,—one kind of ပြိတ္တာ.

ဘုတ်, (3) *n.* dust, dirt.

ဘုတ်လူငုတ်, *n.* a kind of bird.

ဘုတ်, (4) *n.* a kind of insect.

ဘုတ်, (5) *adj.* diminutive; see ဆင်ဘုတ် ၊ ဆိုးဘုတ်, and ခြုံဘုတ်.

ဘုတ်ဘုတ်, *adv.* expressive of the sound which it imitates.

ဘုန်းကြီး, *n.* a priest of Boodh.

ဘုန်းတောလုတ်, *n.* a kind of play.

ဘုန်းပေး, *v.* to eat; (clerical.)

ဘုန်းလွှမ်း, *v.* to cover up, to hide.

ဘုံ, (1) *v.* to be fine, dusty, powdery, မှုန့်; to be acquainted with, familiar; (comp. ဖျေ, dust,) အရှုန် ၊ ရှိ.

ဘုံဘုံထ, *v.* to rise in dust.

ဘုံ, (2) *n.* a bed, stuffed quilt, မွေ့ရာ.

ဘုံး, *v.* to cover, cover up, အုပ်; to hide, ထိမ် ၊ ဝှက် ၊ လျှို့ ၊ ဖွတ်.

ဘူး, (1) *v.* to bud, swell into little protuberances, as trees, skin, &c. Hence အဘူး, *n.* a bud, pimple, small boil.

ဘူး, (2) *v.* to meet, see, behold, မြင် ၊ တွေ့ ၊ ကြုံ; *(respectful.)*

ဘူးရုရှုး, *adv.* in pimples.

ဘေး, (1) *v.* to seal over.

ဘေး, (2) *v.* to be gentle, easy.

ဘဲ, (1) *v.* to cast away, reject, ပယ် ၊ ငြင်း ၊ နှင်; to go aside or out of the way, to go out, ရှောင် ၊ ရှား.

ဘဲရှား, *v.* do.

ဘဲ, (2) *n.* fine silk.

ဘဲ, (3) *n.* a card, (in gaming.)

ဘဲစား, *v.* to play at cards.

ဖဲကစား, *v.* to play cards.

ဖဲ့, *v.* to break off, as a small piece from a large one, ချိုးဖဲ့ ; *neut.* ပဲ့.

ဖော, *v.* to be a little swelled, ဖန်း.

ဖောက်, (1) to make a hole into or through ; (*neut.* ပေါက်.)

ဖောက်ထွင်း, *v.* to penetrate, make a hole through.

ဖောက်, (2) *v.* to change, be changed, changeable, ပြောင်းပြန် ; to be wrong, uncertain, false, မှား၊ ယွင်း.

ဖောက်ပြန်, *v.* do. (most common.)

ဖောက်လွှဲ, *v.* do.

ဖောက်လွန်, *v.* do.

ဖောက်ပြား, *v.* do.

ဖောက်, (3) *v.* to exchange goods, to trade, implying frequency or continuance, ကုန်သွယ်၊ ရောင်းဝယ်.

ဖောက်ကား, *v.* do. (most common.)

ဖောင်, *n.* a raft or float ; an accommodation boat.

ဖောင်ပျံ, *n.* a flying roofed do.

ဖောင်ဖွဲ့, *v.* to unite, connect, tie, or fasten as a raft. It is also applied to speech, as စကားဖောင်ဖွဲ့, to use many words, be loquacious, talkative.

ဖောင်ဖောင်, *adv.* expressive of the sound which it imitates.

ဖောင်ဖွဲ့, *v.* to unite, fasten, or tie, as a raft.

ဖောင်း, (1) *v.* to be much swelled, puffed up.

ဖောင်း, (2) *n.* a cornice, or facing.

ဖောင်း, (3) *n.* a kind of grass.

ဖောင်းဝတ်, *adj.* grey, (applied to horses.)

ဖောဋ္ဌဗ္ဗ, (*Pali,*) *n.* tangibility, အတွေ့.

ဖောဋ္ဌဗ္ဗာရုံ, (see အာရုံ,) *n.* tangibility, an object of feeling.

ဖော့, (1) *v.* to float by an effort.

ဖော့, (2) *n.* a kind of tree.

ဖော့ဂိုး, *n.* a kind of turban.

ဖော်, (1) *v.* to produce, bring to light, ထုတ် ; neut. ပေါ်.

ဖော်ပြ, *v.* to show, make known, confess.

ဖော်, (2) *v.* to associate, keep company, ပေါင်း၊ ဖက်၊ ရော၊ တွဲ. Hence အဖော်, *n.* a companion, associate, အဖက်၊ အပေါင်းအဖော်.

ဖို, (1) *v.* to be barren, without offspring or fruit, မြုံ.

ဖို, (2) *n.* a Burman bellows.

ဖိုကျင်, *n.* do.

ဖို, (3) *n.* a fire-place, မီးဖို ; *comp.* ရုက်ဖို ၊ and ဖေါ့ဖို.

ဖိုလ်, (from ဖလ, *Pali,*) *n.* gain, profit, fruit, attainment, reward, အကျိုး.

ဖိုလ်လေးတန်, *n.* the four grand attainments, viz. သောတာပတ္တိဖိုလ် ၊ သကဒါဂါမိဖိုလ် ၊ အနာဂါမိဖိုလ်, and အရဟတ္တဖိုလ် ; *comp.* အရိယာ.

ဖိုလ်, (2) *n. affix,* mas. gen. as ငန်းဖိုလ်, a gander.

ဖိုသူတော်, see under သိတင်းသုံး.

ဖိုး, (from အဖိုး, a grandfather,) *n.* a title prefixed to the names of aged men, ဦး.

ဖိုးကြီး, *n.* a grandfather ; an aged man.

ဖိုးဖေ, *n.* do.

ဖို့, (1) *v.* to throw in or upon, ထပ် ၊ လောင်း ; neut. ဖို့.

ဖို့, (2) *v.* to pant, breathe quick, ဟိုက်.

ဖို့, (3) *part. affix,* sometimes used for ရာ, which see.

ဖို့, (4) (from ငှါ, or အလို့,) for, on account of, as အိမ်ဖို့, for the house ; စားဖို့, for eating, &c.

ဖျ, *v.* to be fine, gentle, as sound.

ဖျဖျ, *adv.* quickly, လျင်လျင်.

ဖျက်, *v.* to destroy ; neut. ပျက်.

ဖျက်ဆီး, *v.* do.

ဖျက်ဖျက်, *adv.* moderately.

ဖျင်, *n.* cotton cloth made by Burmans.

ဖျင်လက်, *n.* a kind of gown.

ဖျင်း, (1) *v.* to be many, numerous, များ ၊ ထူ ၊ ပေါ ၊ ပြည့်.

ဖျင်း, (2) *v.* to be empty, void, worthless, unsubstantial, အနှစ်မဲ့.

ဖျဉ်နာ, *n.* the dropsy.

ဖျဉ်းဂစ်ဂစ်, or ဂစ်ဖျဉ်းဖျဉ်း, *adv.* with a smile of disregard or contempt.

ဖျဉ်း, (1) *n.* an open-mouthed pot, ဖျဉ်းအိုး.

ဖျဉ်း, (2) *n.* a kind of dropsy.

ဖျတ်ဖျတ်, or တဖျတ်ဖျတ်, *adv.* with repeated slaps, repeatedly ; *also* of various other applications.

ဖျန်း, *v.* to scatter, or sprinkle, as water.

ဖျင့်, *v.* to cast (a shadow,) အရိပ်ဖျင့်.

ဖျံ, *n.* a kind of wild animal.

ဖျုံ့ဖျုံ့, *adv.* intensive.

ဖျုံ့, *v. act. of* ပျုံ့, which see.

ဖျာ, (1) *v.* to separate, divide, ခွဲ.

ဖျာ, (2) *n.* a mat.

ဖျား, *v.* to be in a fever.

ဖျားယောင်း, *v.* to persuade, use persuasive arts, be persuasive; to deceive, seduce, ဖြူထိ ၊ ချောင်ပုံ့.

ဖျိ, see ဖိ, *v.* to press.

ဖျီး, see ဖီး, *v.* to comb.

ဖျုတ်, *n.* a kind of insect.

ဖျောက်, (1) *v.* to lose, obliterate, destroy; neut. ပျောက်.

ဖျောက်ဖျဉ်း, *v.* do.

ဖျောက်, (2) *v.* to scratch, as a consequence of itching.

ဖျောင်း, *v.* to make limber, yielding; neut. ပျောင်း.

ဖျောင်းဖျ, *v.* to persuade, be persuasive, ဖျားယောင်း.

ဖျော့, *v.* to be faded, be of a yellowish colour, look sickly.

ဖျော့တော့, *v.* do.

ဖျော်, (1) *v.* to please, satisfy, &c. *(act. of* ပျော်, which see,) ချော့ ၊ ဖြေ.

ဖျော်ဆိတ်, *v.* do. see ပျော်.

ဖျော်, (2) *v.* to dilute, make thin. Hence အဖျော်, *n.* sweet liquor.

ဖျော်ဖျော်, *adv.* intensive.

ဖြိုး, *v.* to swell up, be plump, full, heaping, convex, ဖွံ့ ၊ မောက်.

ဖြင့်, *n. affix*, inst. case, by means of; by.

ဖြစ်, (1) *v.* to be, ရှိ; to become, to come into existence, to be practicable; (frequently used as a qualifying verbal affix, and sometimes written ဖြစ်.) Hence အဖြစ်အပျက် ၊ အဖြစ်အဆင်, &c. events, adventures, affairs.

ဖြစ်ရာ, (compounded of အဖြစ်, and အရာ,) *n.* matters, events, &c. *see the respective roots.*

ဖြစ်ပွား, *v.* to become numerous, to increase, &c. see ပွား.

ဖြစ်ကောင်း, *v.* to be practicable, probable.

ဖြစ်နိုင်, *v.* to be able to be or become, to be practicable.

ဖြဲ, (2) *v.* to rub, pull, or twist to pieces.

ဖြည်, *v.* to untie, loosen, unrol, unfold; neut. ပြည်.

ဖြည်း, (1) *v.* be slow, moderate, gentle, easy, pleasant, နှေး၊ သာယာ.

ဖြည်းညှင်း, *v.* do.

ဖြည်းဖြ, *v.* do.

ဖြည်း, (2) *v.* to shave (the head.)

ဖြည့်, *v.* to fill, make full, complete, ဖြည့်ဆ; to replenish, recruit, ဖြည့်တင်း.

ဖြည်ံ, *v.* to restrain, moderate, appease.

ဖြုံသား, *v.* do.

ဖြတ်, (1) *v.* to cut in two, to decide; neut. ပြတ်.

ဖြတ်, (2) *v.* to bring a person, for the sake of gain, into trouble.

ဖြန်ဖြန်, *adv.* qualifying words of sound.

ဖြန့်, (1) *v.* to spread out, extend, expand, ကား; neut. ပြန့်.

ဖြန့်, (2) *v.* to step, extend the foot, walk; (highly honorific,) ရွှေစထ်တော်ဖြန့်၊ ခြေတော်ဖြန့်.

ဖြား, *v.* to divide into several parts, make many, numerous; act. of ပြား, which see.

ဖြီး, *v.* to finish, complete a thing.

ဖြုတ်, *v.* to unloose, dislocate, derange; neut. ပြုတ်.

ဖြုတ်ခနဲ, *adv.* instantly, suddenly, ရုတ်ခနဲ၊ ယုတ်ခနဲ.

ဖြုတ်ချည်း, *adv.* do.

ဖြုတ်ဖြုတ်, *adv.* do. also expressive of the sound produced by pronouncing the word itself.

ဖြုန်း, *v.* to wear away, exhaust; (neut. ပြုန်း, which see.)

ဖြုန်းဖြုန်း, *adv.* expressive of the sound produced by pronouncing the word itself.

ဖြူ, (1) *v.* to be white; to be pleasant or pleased—opposed to ညို.

ဖြူဖွ, *v.* do.

ဖြူဆွတ်, *v.* do.

ဖြူစင်, *v.* to be white, clean, pure, စင်ဖြူ၊ စင်ကြယ်၊ သန့်ရှင်း.

ဖြူဖွား, *v.* do.

ဖြူ, (2) *n.* a porcupine.

ဖြူဆူး, *n.* a porcupine's quill.

ဖြူဆံ, *n.* a kind of grass.

ဖြူး, (1) *v.* to sprinkle, scatter, as powder; ဆွတ်ဖြူး.

ဖြူး, (2) *v.* to be drawn out slender, be taper, (applied to height, or length;) သွယ်.

ဖြူး, (3) *v.* to hiss as a serpent; ကျူ.

ဖြေ, (1) *v.* to coax, pacify; do away, settle; see ချော့.

ဖြေ, (2) *v. act.* of ပြေ, which see; *also*, to answer (a question;) opposed to မေး, to enquire.

ဖြေဆည်, *v.* to refute.

ဖြေး, see ဖြည်း, to be slow, gentle, &c.

ဖြဲ, *v.* to open, pull open, make gape; neut. ပြဲ.

ဖြေန်, *v.* to sleep, take rest.

ဖြောင့်, *v.* to make strait, be strait.

ဖြောင့်သား, *v.* do.

ဖြောင့်ဖြောင့်, *adv.* straitly, strait forward.

ဖြောင့်ဖြောင့်သန့်သန့်, *adv.* do. do.

ဖြောင့်မတ်, *v.* to be strait up, erect, upright, just; (applied to matter or mind.)

ဖြို, *v.* to break down, destroy; neut. ပြို.

ဖွက်, *v.* to hide, conceal, secrete; see ဖွတ်.

ဖွက်ထား, *v.* do.

ဖွင့်, *v.* to open, လှစ်; neut. ပွင့်.

ဖွတ်, (1) *v.* to hide, conceal, secrete, ကွယ် ၊ ထိမ် ၊ ထောင့် ၊ ဖုံး ၊ ဝှက် ၊ သိုမှီး.

ဖွတ်, (2) *n.* a guana, (species of lizard.)

ဖွပ်, *v.* to cleanse, make clean, white, စင်ဆေး ၊ ရှင်း ၊ သန့်; (commonly applied to pounding rice or clothes by beating.)

ဖွယ်, (1) *v.* to be suitable, fit, proper, comely.

ဖွယ်ရာ, *v.* do. (most common,) လျောက်ပတ်.

ဖွယ်, (2) *v.* to be inadhesive, မစေး.

ဖွယ်, (3) *n.* Siamese silver money.

ဖွယ်, (4) *part. affix*, see ဘွယ်.

ဖွယ်လိဂမန်း, do. see တွယ်.

ဖွံ့, *v.* to be full, plump, large, flourishing, ကြိုင်း ၊ ထွား.

ဖွာ, *v.* to branch out into several parts, be divided into many, ပြား.

ဖွား, *v.* to bear, bring forth, as animals, မွေး.

ဖွားဖက် or ဖွားဘက်, *n.* one born at the same time with another.

ဖွားမြင်, *v.* to be born, or to bear, bring forth.

ဖွားဖေ, *n.* a grandmother, အဘွား.

ဖွားဘက်, *n.* a kind of tree ; see also ဖွားဖက်.

ဖွေ, *v.* to seek, look after, search for, ရှာ.

ဖွေး, *v.* to be white, ဖြူ.

ဖွဲ, (1) *v.* to be small, fine, သေး.

ဖွဲ, (2) *n.* the husks or chaff of grain.

ဖွဲကြမ်း, *n.* the coarser part of the husks which is rubbed off in the mill.

ဖွဲရင့်, *n.* do.

ဖွဲနု, *n.* the finer part of grain which is separated by pounding, shaking, &c.

ဖွဲသင့်, *n.* do.

ဖွဲ့, *v.* to bind together, ချည် ၊ နှောင် ; to unite, connect, ပေါင်း ၊ ရှက် ၊ ပူး ; to string together, ဆက် ၊ စီ.

ဖွဲ့ဆို, *v.* to connect in verse or song.

ဖွဲ့ဖက်, or ဖွဲ့ဘက်, *n.* a companion, an associate.

## ဗ.

The third consonant in the class of labials.

ဗဇော, *n.* a certain star or constellation ; see တာရာ.

ဗဒ္ဒကပ်, (from ဗဒ္ဒ, good, and ကပ္ပ, a period, *Pali,*) *n.* a grand revolution or period of time, which is distinguished by five Boodhs in succession ; comp. ဗုဒ္ဓ.

ဗဒ္ဒကပ်ကမ္ဘာ, *n.* do.

ဗန္ဓ, (*Pali,*) *n.* a connection, junction, အနှောင်အဖွဲ့.

ဗရပြစ်, *adv.* numerously, innumerably.

ဗရုန်းဗရင်း, *adv.* all in tumultuous confusion.

ဗလ, *(Pali,)* *n.* ability.

ဗဠဝါမုခ, *(Pali,)* *n.* a violent whirlpool, gulf, အာကြီးသောဝဲ.

ဗလိကစား, *n.* a kind of play.

ဗလုံ, *n.* the bubble of boiling liquid.

ဗလော့ဗလာ, *adv.* from လော့လာ, which see.

ဗလောင်ဆန်, *v.* to be noisy, confused, tumultuous, (not used assertively.)

ဗဟိဒ္ဓ, (from ဗဟိ, without, *Páli,) n.* what is foreign or irrelative.

ဗဟု, *(Pali,) adj.* many, အများ.

ဗဟုဗ္ဗီဟိ, *(in grammar,) n.* the second class of compound sentences, *(Carey.)*

ဗာလဗျင်ကွေ, *n.* a kind of military accoutrement worn around the shoulders.

ဗာဟိရာယတန, *n.* an object of sense or thought, whether material or immaterial, အာရုံ.

ဗိတ်, *n.* Mergui, the name of a place.

ဗိန္ဒု, *(Pali,) n.* a dot, အပေါက်.

ဗိမာန်, *(pron. and frequently written* ဗိတ်မာန်, *from* ဝိမာန, *Pali,)* *n.* a house, mansion, habitation.

ဗီဇကံ, (from. ဗီဇ, a seed, *Pali,) adj.* produced from seed sown; comp. ဘုရကံ.

ဘီး, *n.* a comb. *v.* to comb, brush.

ဘီးဝက်မှင်, *n.* a brush made of bristles.

ဘီးတောင်ရှည်, *n.* a kind of bird.

ဗုတ်, (1) *n.* a species of pheasant.

ဗုတ်, (2) *n.* balls used in certain plays.

ဗုဒ္ဓ, *(Pali,) n.* a Boodh; a being in the form of a man, who, in point of wisdom and virtue, is unrivalled throughout the Sekyah system, and is the supreme object of worship, both during his existence and after his annihilation, until the appearance of another Boodh, သဗ္ဗာလေးပါးကိုသိတော်သည်. N.B. In the present grand period of မဟာကပ်, four Boodhs have already appeared, viz. ကကုသန် ၊ ကောဏာဂုံ ၊ ကဿပ, and ဂေါတမ; the fifth, အရိမေတ္တေယျ, is yet to come; comp. ဗုဒ္ဓကပ်.

ဗုဒ္ဓသရက, *n.* a kind of plant, ပုတီး.

ဗုဒ္ဓဘော, or ဗုဒ္ဓပေါ်, *n.* a species of the banyan; see under ညောင်.

ဗုဒ္ဓဟူး, *n.* the planet Mercury; the fourth day of the week, Wednesday.

ဗုံလုံ, *n.* a kind of vine.

ဗေဒင်, (from ဗေဒေါ, *Pali,)* *n.* the Vedas in three books, viz. သာမ, ယဇု, and ဣရုဗ္ဗ; the fourth, အာထဗ္ဗန်, being lost;) the mathematics, *particularly* astrology.

ဗဲဗို့, *adv.* obstinately, unyieldingly, ဇွတ်တရွတ်.

ဗဲ့ဗျား, *n.* a kind of tree.

ဗောက်, *n.* a kind of tree.

ဗောက်ချေး, *n.* a kind of tree.

ဗောက်ဗက်, *v.* to be troublesome, disorderly, rude, ရောက်ရက်.

ဗောက်သောက်, *n.* a kind of tree.

ဗောင်းလှန်, *v.* be more than full, heaped, running over.

ဗောရကိုင်း, *n.* a kind of tree.

ဗောဓိပင်, *n.* the species of tree under which a Boodh is perfected; in the case of Gaudama, the Ficus religiosa, ညောင်ဗုဒ္ဓေါ ၊ ပညောင်.

ဗောဓိသတ်, (from ဗောဓိသတ္တော, *Pali,)* see ဘုရားလောင်း.

ဗိုင်း, *n.* cotton made up in rolls for spinning.

ဗိုင်းတော, *n.* a harlot, မိန္မရှင်.

ဗိုလ်, (1) (from ဗလ, *Pali,*) *n.* strength, အစွမ်းအား; force, military force, soldiers, troops, စစ်သူရဲ; a colonel, chief of a regiment, တပ်ဦး.

ဗိုလ်ကြီး, or ဗိုလ်ချုပ်, or ဗိုလ်မှူး, *n.* a chief general, commander in chief, စစ်ဘုရင်.

ဗိုလ်ခြေ, or ဗိုလ်ပါ, *n.* forces, troops.

ဗိုလ်, (2) *n.* a piece on a gaming board, ကျာ.

ဗိုလ်, (3) *n.* a bo, a weight equal to five kyats, (အကျပ်.)

ဗျက်, *n.* breadth, width, အနံ.

ဗျဂ္ဃာစာရဂြိ, or ဗျဂ္ဃာစရိယဂြိ, (from ဗျဂ္ဃာ, a tiger, and စရိယာ, a deed, practice, *Pali,*) *v.* to retrograde, as the heavenly bodies; comp. သီဟစာရဂြိ.

ဗျည်း, (from ဗျဉ္ဇန်, *Pali,)* *n.* a consonant.

ဗျာဒိတ်, (from ဝါဒိတာ, *Pali,)* *n.* a divine communication of any kind, frequently a prophetical intimation; (by courtesy applied to kings.)

ဗျာဒိတ်ထား, *v.* to utter a divine communication.

ဗျာဒိတ်ပြ, *v.* to make a display of any divine attribute.

ဗျာဓိ, (*Pali,*) *n.* sickness, နာခြင်း ၊ ဖျားခြင်း.

ဗျာပါ, (from ဗျာပါဒ, *Pali,*) *n.* anxiety, distress of mind, စိုးရိမ်ခြင်း.

ဗျုန်းငွေ, *n.* a kind of plant.

ဗျူဟာ, *n.* a book on military tactics.

ဗျော, *n.* a kind of drum.

ဗျောတီးသမား, *n.* a drummer.

ဗျောလက်ခတ်, *n.* a drumstick.

ဗျိုင်း, see ဥဗျိုင်း, a heron, paddy bird.

ဗျိုင်းတာရာ, *n.* a certain star, or constellation; (see တာရာ.)

ဗြဟ္မစရိယတရားလေးပါး, (from ဗြဟ္မ, excellent, and စရ, to perform, *Pali,*) *n.* four excellent principles, viz. မေတ္တာ ၊ ကရုဏာ ၊ မုဒိတာ, and ဥပေက္ခာ; see အပ္ပမညာ.

ဗြဟ္မဝိဟာရ, *n.* do.

ဗြဟ္မာ, (*Pali,*) *n.* a Bramha, a being superior to men and Nats (နတ်,) inhabiting the higher celestial regions.

ဗြဟ္မပြည်, *n.* see ဗြဟ္မာ့ဘုံ.

ဗြဟ္မာ့ဘုံ, *n.* an abode of Bramhas, the superior celestial regions, of which there are twenty stages or stories, (comp. နတ်ပြည်,) sixteen material (ရူပဘုံ,) and four immaterial or invisible (အရူပဘုံ,) which are named as follows: ဗြဟ္မပါရိသဇ္ဇာ ၊ ဗြဟ္မပုရောဟိတာ ၊ မဟာဗြဟ္မာ ၊ ပရိတ္တာဘာ ၊ အပ္ပမာဏာဘာ ၊ အာဘဿရာ ၊ ပရိတ္တသုဘာ ၊ အပ္ပမာဏသုဘာ ၊ သုဘကိဏှ ၊ ဝေဟပ္ဖိုလ် ၊ အသညသတ် ၊ အဝိဟာ ၊ အတပ္ပါ ၊ သုဒဿာ ၊ သုဒဿီ ၊ အကနိဋ္ဌာ ၊ အာကာသာနဉ္စာယတန ၊ ဝိညာဏဉ္စာယတန ၊ အာကိဉ္စညာယတန, and နေဝသညာနာသညာယတန.

ဗြဲ, *n.* a Pegu title.

ဗျွတ်, *n.* a kind of bird.

ဗျွတ်ဆိုး, see ဆိုးဗျွတ်.

## ဘ.

The fourth consonant in the class of labials.

ဘက်, (1) *n.* a corresponding part or side; see အဖက် under ဖက်.

ဘက်, (2) *adv.* even, (slightly emphatic, used in conversation.)

ဘင်, (1) *n.* ordure, မစင်.

ဘင်ဘုတ်, *n.* a class of inferior hells.

ဘင်, (2) (from ဘင်္ဂ, *Pali,*) *n.* destruction, ပျက်ခြင်း.

ဘင်္ဂ, (1) *n.* a kind of tree.

ဘင်္ဂ, (2) *n.* a kind of plant, which takes root on certain trees.

ဘင်္ဂဉာဏ, (see ဘင်, destruction, and ဝိဇ္ဇဉာဏ, a mental exercise,) *n.* a termination of thought, စိတ်ကြံပျက်ခြင်း.

ဘင်း, *n.* the bang plant, gaṅja.

ဘဏ္ဍာ, *(Pali,) n.* a treasure.

ဘဏ္ဎာ, *n.* do.

ဘဏ္ဍာန်, *n.* materiality, visibility, appearance.

ဘဏ္ဍာစိုး, *n.* a steward, a keeper of treasures.

ဘတ်, (from ဘတ္တံ, *Pali,*) *n.* cooked rice ; ထမင်း၊ ထွမ်း.

ဘနန်း, *adv.* as if, as, (affixed to verbal roots ;) မတတ်.

ဘန်း, (1) *n.* a shallow flat-bottomed basket; (comp. ဗန်ကော.)

ဘန်း, (2) *n.* a sample, specimen, ဝံ.

ဘယ်, (1) *n.* the left side, လက်ဝဲ—opposed to ညာ.

ဘယ်ပြောင်းညာပြန်, *v.* to turn from side to side.

ဘယ်, (2) (an abbreviation of အဘယ်,) what? ဘယ်နှယ်, do.

ဘယ်စာ, do. (provincial.)

ဘယ်ပြုလို့, *adv.* why?

ဘယ်ကို, which? where?

ဘယ်သို့, where? how?

ဘယ်က, whence?

ဘယ်ကြောင့်, why? wherefore?

ဘယ်မှ, whence?

ဘယ်မှာ, where? wherein?

ဘယ်ကြောင့်နည်းဟူမူကား, wherefore.

ဘယ်သို့က, what? how? why?

ဘယ်သို့မှ, where?

ဘယ်သို့ကြောင့်, wherefore?

ဘယ်သို့မှာ, where? wherein?

ဘယ်သို့ကြောင့်နည်းဟူမူကား<br>ဘယ်သို့သောကြောင့်နည်းဟူမူကား, } wherefore, because.

ဘယ, *(Pali,) n.* fear, ကြောက်ခြင်း.

ဘယက်, *n.* ornaments for the neck, (as beads.)

ဘရွပ်တိုက်, *v.* to scuff, shuffle, as the feet.

ဘဝ, *(Pali,)* (1) *n.* a state of existence, a world ; ကာမဘဝ, the world of passions, including the four states of punishment; ကာမလောကဘုံ, the state of man and the six inferior heavens; ရူပလောက, the world of visible objects, including the sixteen material superior heavens; and အရူပလောက, the world of invisibles, including the four immaterial superior heavens.

ဘဝ, (2) *n.* a time of existence, time of life; comp. ဘုံ and လောက.

ဘဝရှင်, *n.* a king, monarch, မင်းတရား၊ ရှင်ဘုရင်.

ဘဝဂ်, (from ဘဝဂ္ဂ, *Pali,*) *n.* the summit of a Sekyah world or system of the universe.

ဘဝင်, (from ဘဝ, and အင်္ဂ,) *n.* the stamina or substance of the mind; or the mind considered abstractly from its exercises.

ဘဝင်မချား, *adv.* instantly.

ဘဝေါဃ, *n.* see ဩဃ.

ဘာ, *a contraction of* ဘယ်ဟာ, what thing? what? ဘယ်ငှါ.

ဘာဖြလို့, *adv.* why? for what reason? wherefore?

ဘာဝနာ, *(Pali,) adv.* many times, repeatedly.

ဘာသာ, *(Pali,) n.* a language, စကား; mode of practice, custom, way, ဓ၊ ထုံး၊ နည်း.

ဘာသာလေ, *adv.* of one's own will and way, အလိုလို.

ဘိ, *euph. affix,* (mostly used before သိက်, abbreviated to ဘ.)

ဘိက္ခု, (*Pali,*) *n.* a priest of Boodh, ရဟန်း.

ဘိက္ခုနီ, *n.* a female do. ရဟန်းမ.

ဘိချိုင့်, *n.* a basket or vessel flattened at the ends.

ဘိင်္ဂရာဇ်, *n.* a kind of bird.

ဘိတ်ဘိတ်ကျိုး, *adv.* in total ignorance.

ဘိနပ်, *n.* a sandal; the base of a pagoda; an elephant's foot.

ဘိနပ်ထိုးသမား, *n.* a sandal maker.

ဘိန်း, (1) *n.* opium. (2) see ဘီး, a wheel.

ဘိန်းနွဲ့, *n.* a kind of tree.

ဘိသိက်သွန်, *v.* to perform a certain ceremony in coronation.

ဘီလူး, *n.* a Beeloo, a kind of monster which eats human flesh, and possesses certain super-human powers.

ဘီလူးတံတွေး, *n.* the frothy excrescence on plants.

ဘီလူးတောင်ဝေး, *n.* a kind of tree.

ဘီထူးဝါ, *n.* a kind of tree.

ဘီး, *n.* a wheel; see စက်.

ဘု, *v. affix*, past tense, as ပြုဘုသည်, he has been doing.

ဘုပြီး, *v. affix*, do. as ပြုဘုပြီး, he had done.

ဘုတ်, (from ဘူတ, visible, *Pali*,) *n.* matter; comp. မဟာဘုတ်.

ဘုန်လွှန်, see ဖုန်လွှန်.

ဘုန်း, *n.* glory, power, ဘုန်းဒါန်း ၊ ဘုန်းကြက်သရေ.

ဘုန်းအသရေ, *n.* perfection, glory, power.

ဘုန်းတော်ခြောက်ပါး, *n.* six glories of Boodh, viz. ဣဿရိယ ၊ ဓမ္မ ၊ ယသ ၊ သိရိ ၊ ကာမ, and ပယတ္တ.

ဘုန်းစား, *n.* a mendicant.

ဘုန်းကြီး, (pron. ဖုန်းကျီး,) *n.* a priest of Boodh; ရဟန်း; a minister of religion, ဓမ္မဆရာ.

ဘုန်းလဒ်သဒ်ပကာ, *n.* profit, any thing gained or obtained; see လဒ်.

ဘုဘမသိ, *v.* to know nothing at all (alluding to the story of Miss Boo and her father.)

ဗုံး, *n.* a bomb.

ဘုမ္မစိုးနတ်, (from ဘုမ္မ, or ဘုမိ, the earth, *Pali*; စိုး, to rule, and နတ်, a Nat,) *n.* a Nat which has dominion over some part of the earth.

ဘုမ္မတီး, *n.* a kind of bird.

ဘုမ္မရာဇာ, *n.* a kind of plant.

ဘုမ္မသိန်, *n.* the camphor tree.

ဘုမ္မိနက်သန်, *n.* a good place or spot of ground.

ဘုမ္မိရတ်, (see အဂ္ဂိရတ်,) *n.* the business or science of searching the ground for hid treasures.

ဘုရင်, *n.* a chief, sovereign; comp. စဝ်ဘုရင်, and ရှင်ဘုရင်.

ဘုရား, (1) (pron. ဖယား,) *n.* a god, object of worship, a lord, master, အရှင်၊ သခင်; (2) *n.* a pagoda, စေတီ.

ဘုရားဦးစွယ်, *n.* see ဆွဲ.

ဘုရားသခင်, *n.* the supreme object of worship, a Boodh, ဖြစ်ဗွားဘုရား.

ဘုရားရှင်, *n.* do. also an idol.

ဘုရားလောင်း, (see အလောင်း,) *n.* one who is destined to be a Boodh.

ဘုရားကျွန်, *n.* a slave to a pagoda, one who has the care of a pagoda, and lives on the offerings, ကျွန်သီးတော်.

ဘူရိဒါတ်, *n.* one division of the Boodhist scriptures, marked ဘူ.

ဘုံ, *n.* a mansion, abode, ဗိမာန် ; a state of existence, of which there are thirty one, viz. အပါယ်လေးဘုံ, the four states of punishment ; ကာမဘုံခုနှစ်ပါး, the seven states of passion or pleasure, i. e. the state of man, and the six inferior heavens, (which eleven states are collectively called ကာမဘဝ;) ရူပဘုံဆယ်ခြောက်ပါး, the sixteen visible states (ရူပဘဝ ;) and အရူပ ဘုံလေးပါး, the four invisible states, အရူပဘဝ.

ဘုံ, (2) *n.* a superadded gradation of a graduated roof, ပြာသာဒ်.

ဘုံ, (3) *n.* a kind of drum ; see ပတ်ဘုံ.

ဘုံလှိုချအုံး, *n.* a large pillow used to support the body.

ဘုံသာ, *n.* a kind of drum ; (see ပတ်ဘုံ.)

ဘူတ, (*Pali,*) *n.* that which is visible, ဘူတ်.

ဘူရက်, (from ဘူရ, a sprout or twig, *Pali,*) *adj.* produced from a root or stump, set out or planted, (not from seed sown ;) comp. ဗီရက်.

ဘူး, (1) *n.* the gourd plant, of which there are many varieties ; a gourd.

ဘူး, (2) *n.* a bottle or phial, ပုလင်း.

ဘူးဆို့, *n.* the stopper of a bottle or phial, a cork.

ဘူးတား, *n.* a certain appendage to a spindle.

ဘူး, (3) *v. affix*, sign of past tense, as သွားဘူးသည်, he went.

ဘူး, (4) (*with* မ *prefixed to the root,*) makes the negative of verbs, as မသွားဘူး, he goes not.

ဘူးတောင်း, *n.* a broken gourd, or a piece of a gourd.

ဘေး, (1) (from ဘယ, fear, *Pali,*) *n.* evil, calamity, အန္တရာယ်.

ဘေးဒါဏ်, *n.* do.

ဘေးဘျမ်း, *n.* a great calamity.

ဘေး, (2) a great-grandfather ; see အဘေး.

ဘေးမ, see အဘေးမ, a great-grandmother.

ဘဲ, (with မ prefixed to the root,) *v. affix*, without, as မစားဘဲ သွားသည်, he went without eating. It sometimes takes the noun affix နှင့် after it, as မစားဘဲနှင့်, without eating ; but it does not change the sense.

ဘဲတောင်, *n.* the side of an animal differing in colour from the rest of the body.

ဘဲရုံ, *n.* the gilt fringe or border of a garment.

ဘော, (1) (*Pali*, from ဘဂ,) *n.* the genitals, male or female, အင်္ဂါဇာတ် ၊ နိမိတ် ၊ လိင်.

ဘော, (2) *v.* to be protracted, as sound, be noisy, ဆူဘော.

ဘောက်ခနဲ, *adv.* suddenly, ယုတ်ခနဲ.

ဘောင်, *n.* company, congregation, society.

ဘောဇဉ်, (from ဘောဇန, *Pali,*) *n.* food, eatables, ခဲဖွယ် ၊ စားဘွယ်.

ဘော်, *n.* pure silver.

ဘိုး, (from အဘိုး,) *n.* a grandfather.

ဘိုးစဉ်ဘောင်ဆက်, *adj.* inherited from one's ancestors.

ဘို့, (from အဘို့ or အဘို့) *affix*, for, as အိမ်ဘို့, for the house.

ဘျား, (from ဘုရား,) *n.* a familiar term of compellation used by men.

ဘွယ်, *part. affix*, denotes what is fit for, worthy of, or adapted to, any particular purpose, as စားဘွယ်, what is fit to eat; အံ့ဘွယ်, what is wonderful; ချစ်ဘွယ်, what is lovely, &c. see Gram.

ဘော့, *n.* a natural mark on animals.

ဘွဲ့, *n.* an honorary title; the badge of do.

## မ.

The fifth consonant in the class of labials.

မ, (1) *n. affix*, fem. gen. as ရဟန်း, a priest; ရဟန်းမ, a priestess.

မ, (2) *v.* to support, bear up, assist, help, relieve, ကူ ၊ ချီ ၊ ထောက် ၊ ပင့် ၊ ပံ့.

မ, (3) (from အမ, an elder sister,) *n.* a title prefixed to names of women, indicative of equality.

မ, (4) (from အမ, a female, or mother,) *adj.* chief among many; main, principal, as လမ်း, a road; လမ်းမ, the main, or mother road.

မ, (5) *adv.* not, (prefixed to verbs.)

မကူ, *n.* a kind of tree.

မဆေ, *n.* a mother, အမယ် ၊ အမိ ၊ အမေ ၊ မိခင်.

မက်, (1) *v.* to desire, covet, နှိုး ၊ ထင်.

မက်မော, *v.* do.

မက်, (2) *v.* to dream, အိပ်မက်.

မက်, (3) *v.* to put helm to larboard; *comp.* ရိုင်း.

မက်, (4) *v.* to be caught, as by a thorn or nail, &c. as by fire, by disease, &c. see ညှိ.

မက, *v.* to be uneven, more than; to exceed, လွန်; (used only in the negative form, and most commonly adverbially, without an affix, as တကျပ်ထက်မက, or briefly, တကျပ်မက, more than a tical.)

မကန်, *n.* (from မကာရ, *Pali,*) a certain sea-animal.

မကာရ, *(Pali,) n.* Capricorn; the tenth sign of the zodiac.

မကောင်းမှု, *n.* demerit, the punishment of demerit, အကုသိုလ် ၊ မကောင်းသော အကျိုး.

မကိုဋ်, *n.* a crest, ornament of the head.

မကိုဋ်ရောင်ချွန်, *n.* do.

မကျိုးမကျဉ်, *adv.* disrespectfully.

မချွတ်, *adv.* truly, verily, ဧကန်အမှန် ၊ မလွဲ.

မဂ်, (from မဂ္ဂေါ, *Pali,*) *n.* a passage, way; a course of duty.

မဂ်လေးတန်, *n.* the four grand ways, viz. သောတာပတ္တိမဂ် ၊ သကဒါဂါမိမဂ် ၊ အနာဂါမိမဂ်, and အရဟတ္တမဂ်; *comp.* အရိယာ.

မဂဓ, *n.* South Behar, Magada; the language of do. ပါဠိ.

မဂ္ဂင်ရှစ်ပါး, (from မဂ္ဂေါ, a way, and အင်္ဂါ, a part, division,) *n.* the eight (good) ways; viz. သမ္မာဒိဋ္ဌိ, right opinion; သမ္မာသင်္ကပ္ပ, right intention; သမ္မာဝါစာ, right words; သမ္မာကမ္မန္တ, right actions; သမ္မာအာဇီဝ, right way of supporting life; သမ္မာဝါယာမ, rightly directed intelligence; သမ္မာသတိ, good heed, caution; and သမ္မာသမာဓိ, composure, serenity.

မဂ္ဂဉာဏ်, (from မဂ္ဂေါ, and ဉာဏ, *Pali,*) a person who is perfect in one or more of the four grand courses of duty; comp. မဂ်လေးတန်.

မင်, *v.* to love or like, ခင်; (either ကြိုက်, or ချစ်.)

မင်္ဂလာ, (from မင်္ဂလံ, *Pali,*) *n.* whatever is propitious; whatever gives happiness, or removes evil; a blessing, a religious rite or ceremony, a sacrament.

မင်း, (1) *n.* a ruler, governor.

မင်းကြီး, *n.* a king, monarch, a great minister of state, ပြင်စန်၊ ဝန်ကြီး.

မင်းတရား, *n.* a monarch, ရှင်ဘုရင်၊ ဘဝရှင်.

မင်းလုလင်, (*pron.* မင်းသလင်, or မင်ဒုလင်,) *n.* people who execute the orders of a governor.

မင်း, (2) *pers. pro.* you, *mas.* used in addressing one somewhat inferior.

မင်းမ, do.

မင်းမယ်, or မမယ်, do. (obsolete.)

မင်းကွတ်, *n.* a mangoosteen.

မင်းတုပ်, *n.* a bolt.

မင်းလွင်, *n.* dust raised by a gentle wind—of a particular appearance, exhibited in the hot season.

မစ, *v.* to aid, assist; see စောင့်မ.

မစင်, *n.* ordure, ကျင်ကြီး၊ ဘင်.

မစင်တီးပြင်, *n.* do.

မစင်တချစ်, *adv.* disrespectfully.

မစ္စု, *(Pali,)* death, သေခြင်း.

မစ္ဆရိယ, *(Pali,) n.* covetousness, ဝန်တိုခြင်း.

မဆိတ်, *adv.* immediately, without delay, as သွားမဆိတ်သေမည်, on going, without delay, he will die.

မဈ, (from မ negative, and ဈ, an obsolete verb,) *impersonal,* if not yet being, i. e. before, prévious to, (used adverbially.)

မဈက, or မဈမှီ, or မဈမှီက, do.

မဇ္ဈိမ, *n.* one division of the Boodhist scriptures.

မဇ္ဈိမဒေသ, (from မဇ္ဈိမ, middle, and ဒေသ, place, *Pali,) n.* the middle part of the world, including 16 great countries, the scene of the sacred histories of Boodh.

မညီငွေ့, *v.* see ရှုဆိတ်.

မည်, (1) *v.* to complain, find fault with, scold, တောက်တီး.

မည်ထမ်း, *v.* do. *also,* to lament, bewail, express grief.

မည်တွန်, *v.* do. do.

မည်, (2) *v.* to sound, produce sound, အသံပြု.

မည်, (3) *v.* to be named, have a name, be called. Hence အမည်, *n.* a name, နာမ.

မည်, (4) *pron. adj.* what? (interrogative;) whatever.

မည်သည်, *pron. adj.* whatever.

မည်ရွာ, and မည်ဝါ, do. (variously reduplicated and construed.)

မည်, (5) *v. affix*, sign of the ind. mood, fut. tense.

မည်သို့, *pron. adj.* of what sort? *(interrogative,)* အဘယ်သို့.

မဉ္ဇူ, *n.* a kind of tree.

မည်သဒိ, *n.* red velvet.

မဉ္ဇူးပန်း, *n.* a kind of tree.

မည်း, *v.* to be of a dark black colour, နက်.

မဏ္ဍပ်, (from မဏ္ဍပံ, *Pali,)* *n.* a large shed or booth, a building erected for a temporary occasion.

မဏ္ဍိုင်, (from မဏ္ဍလံ, a circle, *Pali,* and တိုင်, a post,) *n.* the tree under which a Boodh is perfected, ဗောဓိပင်.

မတ်, (1) *v.* to be erect, perpendicularly straight.

မတ်တတ်, မတ်ထန်, or မတ်လတ်, *adv.* in an upright posture.

မတ်မတ်, *adv.* do.

မတ်, (2) *n.* a husband's younger brother; a woman's younger sister's husband; (*comp.* ခဲအို.)

မတ်, (3) *n.* a mat, a weight which is equal to four great pays (ပဲ,) or five small ones.

မတ်, (4) see အမတ်, a person of rank.

မတတ်, *part. affix,* as, like as, as if; see တနန်း, and ဂမန်.

မတရားသောအမှု, *n.* sin, transgression.

မထီမဲ့မြင်, *adv.* disrespectfully, irreverently.

မထေမဲ့မြင်, *(from* ထီ, to reverence,) *adv.* disrespectfully, irreverently, saucily, မရှိမသေ.

မထေရ်, (see ထေရ်,) *n.* an elderly priest of Boodh, ရဟန်းကြီး.

မထေရ်မ, *n.* a female do.

မထောင်းတာ, *v.* to be pretty well, in regard to health, or other circumstances; (used in the negative only.)

မန, *(Pali,)* *n.* mind, စိတ်.

မနက်, *a corruption of* နံနက်, the morning.

မနသိကာရ, *(Pali,)* *n.* meditation, နှလုံးသွင်းချင်း.

မနာလို, *v.* to be envious, malevolent, ငြူ.

မနီးမကမ်း, *adv.* not near nor distant.

မနုသီဟ, *(Pali,)* *n.* a fabulous monster, viz. man and lion compounded.

မနေ့, *(an abbreviation of* ယမန်နေ့,) *n.* yesterday.

မနောထင်ပန်း, *n.* a kind of salver.

မနိုင်မကန်, *adv.* submissively.

မန်ကျည်း, *(pron.* မကျည်း) *n.* the tamarind tree.

မန္တတ်မင်း, *n.* a sovereign of the four great islands, စကြာမင်း.

မန္တန်, *n.* a charm or spell.

မန္တရား, *n.* do.

မန္တန်စိပ်, *v.* to repeat a charm, in order to retain it in memory.

မန္တန်မှုတ်, *v.* to charm, &c. see မှုတ်.

မန်း, (1) *v.* to charm, infuse virtue into, by repeating a mantra, မှုတ်.

မန်း, (2) *n.* a kind of swelling or sore; (3) *n.* a charm.

မန်းရည်, *n.* the thin water of a blister or other sore, သားနာ့ရည်.

မမ, *n.* a mistress, madam.

မယ်, (from အမယ်, a mother,) *n.* a title prefixed to the names of women, indicative of sincerity, or expressive of respect.

မယ်န, *n.* a nail (of iron), သံချွန်.

မယ်မင်း, *n.* a term of compellation, addressed to women, indicative of disrespect or anger.

မယ်ရှင်, *n.* a madam, respectful matron.

မယ်သီလရှင်, *n.* *(the ultimate pron.* ယင်,) *n.* a vestal, unmarried deaconness, or priestess.

မယား, (1) *n.* a wife.

မယား, (2) *n.* a kind of tree.

မရဏ, *(Pali,)* *n.* death.

မရဏာသန်, (from အာသန္န, near, *Pali,)* *n.* the near approach of death.

မရန်း, *n.* Mayan tree.

မရီး, *n.* a wife's elder sister; a man's elder brother's wife; *comp.* ခယ်မ.

မရေမရာ, *adv.* idly, to no purpose.

မဒီး, see မုဒီး, a kind of tree.

မရှင်, *n.* mistress, madam.

မလန်းပေါက်ခတ်, *v.* to slap one's own arms.

မလိန်, *n.* a kind of tree.

မဆေးပွား, *n.* paper ornaments, streamers, &c. attached to flags.

မလွယ်, *n.* a small entrance, or side door, used occasionally, when the larger door is closed.

မဆိုင်, *n.* a certain preparation of curdled milk.

မဇ္ဈ, *n.* a kind of tree.

မသာ, (from မ negative, and သာ, to be pleasant,) *n.* a funeral.

မသာခင်း, *n.* do. *also*, preparations, or appendages of a funeral.

မသာချ, *v.* to convey the corpse to the place of interment, or burning.

မသူတော်, (see သူတော်,) *n.* a bad man.

မဟာဂုဏ်, (from မဟာဂုဏော်, *Pali,*) *n.* excellent mental attainments, ဖြစ်သောအပြစ်သို့ရောက်ချင်း.

မဟင်လွတာ, *n.* a certain ornament worn over the shoulders.

မဟာ, *(Pali,) adj.* great, အကြီး ; excellent, အမြတ်.

မဟာကပ်, (from မဟာ, great, and ကပ္ပ, a period, *Pali,*) *n.* a period in which an entire revolution of nature is performed, subdivided into four grand periods, each of which is again subdivided into sixty-four intermediate periods, and each of these is again subdivided into sixty-four life periods, as they may be called.

မဟာဒကာ, *n.* a kind of tree.

မဟာဒုတ်, *n.* a royal barber.

မဟာဘုတ်လေးပါး, *n.* the four material elements, earth, water, fire, and air ; see ဘုတ်, and ဓာတ်.

မဟာဝံ့, *n.* a brick wall round a pagoda, တန်တိုင်း.

မဟာကျေကား, *n.* a kind of creeper.

မဟာရောရုဝ, *n.* one of the states of punishment ; see ငရဲ.

မဟာတာပန, *n.* another of do. see ငရဲ.

မဟော, *n.* one division of the Burman scriptures.

မဟုတ်, (from မဟုတ္တာ, *Pali,*) *n.* an instant (commonly used with တ, as တမဟုတ်.)

မဟူရာ, *n.* a cornelian.

မံ, *v.* to anoint, spread over, besmear; *comp.* မွမ်.

မံ့, *v. affix*, sign of the 2d pers. imp. mood; (obsolete.)

မာ, *v.* to be hard, ကြော ။ ထင် ။ တောင့်; to be healthy, well, ဤ ။ ကျန်း.

မာမြင်း, *v.* do.

မာမြန်း, *v.* do.

မာကြီး, *n.* tar and oakum, used to caulk vessels.

မာခါကတ်ကညွန်း, *n.* a kind of medicine.

မာချော်, *n.* a kind of drug.

မာတာ, *(Pali,)* *n.* a mother, အမိ ။ မအေ.

မာတုဂါမ, *(Pali,)* *n.* a woman, မိန္မ.

မာတုဃ္ဃ, (from မာတာ, and ဃ္ဃ,) *n.* evil incurred by ill-treating a mother.

မာနထောင်, *v.* to be proud, obstinate, unyielding.

မာန်, (from မာန *Pali,)* *n.* pride; an evil; a tyrant, မာရ်.

မာန်မာန, *n.* do.

မာန်စောင်, *n.* do.

မာန်ထောင်လွှား, *v.* to be proud, haughty.

မာန်ရှိ, *v.* do.

မာန်မူ, *v.* to be angry, အမျက်ထွက်.

မာန်ပြု, *v.* do.

မာတုဃာ, *(Pali,)* *n.* a woman or wife; (clerical.)

မာယာ, *n.* a means, expedient, artifice, device, လှည့်ပတ်ချင်း ။ ပရိယာယ်.

မာရ်, (from မာရော်, *Pali,)* *n.* pride, &c. see မာန်.

မာရ်ငါးပါး, *n.* the five masters or tyrants, viz. ခန္ဓာမာရ်, animal constitution; အဘိသင်္ခါရမာရ်, subject to the repairs and operations of the four causes (အကြောင်းတရားလေးပါး;) ကိလေသာမာရ်, passion; မစ္စုမာရ်, death; and ဒေဝပုတ္တမာရ်, the most powerful evil Nat (မာရ်နတ်သား.)

မာရ်နတ်သား, *n.* a powerful evil Nat or spirit, who resides in the highest inferior heaven, and has dominion over all the lower parts of the universe.

မာရပင်, *n.* a recess in a room.

မာလကာ, *n.* the guava tree.

မာလကာကျုံ, *n.* the saffron plant.

မာလိန်, *(Bengalee,)* *n.* a ship's officer or pilot.

မား, *v.* to be high, မြင့် ၊ စွင့်.

မိ, (1) *v.* to obtain, ရ.

မိ, (2) *euph. affix.*

မိဂသီ, *n.* a certain star or constellation; (see နက္ခတ်.)

မိ, (3) from အမိ, *n.* a mother.

မိခင်, *n.* a mother.

မိကြီး, *n.* a mother's elder sister; a father's elder brother's wife; *comp.* အရီး.

မိထွေး, *n.* a mother's younger sister; a father's younger brother's wife; a stepmother.

မိဘ, (from အဖ, a father,) *n.* parents, father and mother.

မိ, (4) (from အမိ, a daughter,) *n.* a title prefixed to the names of girls and young women, indicative of superiority in the speaker.

မိဂဒါဝန်, (from မိဂ, deer, or any game, and ဝန်, a forest, *Pali,*) *n.* a game-forest.

မိစ္ဆာ, *(Pali,) n.* falsehood, delusion, error.

မိစ္ဆာဒိဋ္ဌိ, *n.* do. *also* a heretic; (see ဒိဋ္ဌိ.)

မိတ်, (from မေတ္တာ,) (1) *n.* affection, friendship.

မိတ်ဆွေ, *n.* a friend, အဆွေခင်ပွန်း.

မိတ်ဖက်ဖွဲ့, *v.* to be united in friendship, as a married couple.

မိတ်သဟာယ, or မိသဟာယ, (from သဟာယ, to associate,) *n.* a union of friendship; friendly intercourse.

မိတ်, (2) *n.* an efflorescence of humours on the skin, the prickly heat.

မိတ်လင်စုံ, (from မိတ်, love, and *figurat.* a wife, လင်, a husband, and စုံ, a pair,) *n.* a married couple; an original text, accompanied with a translation, (နိဿယ.)

မိတ္တေယျ, (by corruption, မိတ်,) see အရိမေတ္တေယျ.

မိဒ္ဓ, *(Pali,) n.* want of reverence, စေတသိက်ကြီးခန့်ညားခြင်း ; *comp.* ထိန်.

မိန်, (1) *v.* to long for, တောင့်တ.

မိန်မော, *v.* do.

မိန်, (2) (from မိန, a fish, *Pali,*) *n.* Pisces, the twelfth sign of the zodiac.

မိန်, (3) *n.* a screech-owl, ငှက်ဆိုး.

မိန္ညိ, *n.* a military coat with sleeves, worn over the coat of mail, (ချင်.)

မိန်း, *v.* to be confused, lost in thought, absent, stupefied, astonished.

မိန်းမော, *v.* do. (most common,) တွေဝေ.

မိန်းမှိုင်, *v.* do.

မိန်းမ, *n.* a woman.

မိန်းမသန်, *v.* do.

မိန်းမစိုး, *n.* a eunuch, one who has the charge of women.

မိန်းမရှင်, *n.* a harlot.

မိန်းမလျှာ, *n.* a hermaphrodite or eunuch ; a womanish, effeminate man.

မိဘုရား, *n.* a queen.

မိန့်, *v.* to speak, (honorific.)

မိမိ, *pers. pro.* one's self, i. e. myself, yourself, or himself, according to the connection, ကိုယ်.

မိဗ, *n.* a woman, မိန်းမ.

မိဗစိုး, *n.* one who has the care of women, a eunuch.

မိလက္ခ, *(Pali,) n.* a certain race of wild people, တောင်သူ.

မိဿာ, *n.* a kind of Chinese ware, made of brass or copper, and cemented.

မိဿ, *(Pali,* a goat,*) n.* Aries, the first sign in the zodiac.

မိဿထင်, *n.* a kind of tree.

မီး, (1) *n.* fire.

မီး, (2) *n.* that which is paid extra in consideration of the bad quality of money, discount.

မီးအိမ်, *n.* a lantern.

မီးကသပ်, *n.* a censer.

မီးကြည်, *n.* fire-works.

မီးခတ်ကျောက်, *n.* a flint to strike fire from.

မီးခုံ, *n.* a candlestick.

မီးခဲ, *n.* a live coal.

မီးခိုး, *n.* smoke.

မီးချေး, *n.* a live coal.

**မီးခွက်, *n.* a cup to burn oil in, a lamp, ဆီမီးခွက်.**

မီးစ, *n.* a stick kindled at one end, a fire-stiek.

မီးစာ, *n.* a wick.

မီးညှပ်, *n.* tongs, snuffers.

မီးထောင်း, *v.* to pay something extra in consideration of the bad quality of money.

မီးတင်းကုပ်, *v.* a fire-shed.

မီးတိုင်, *n.* a candle.

မီးတိုက်, *v.* to burn with fire, မီးရှို့.

မီးပါသေနတ်, *n.* a fire-lock.

မီးပုံစာရေး, *n.* a pile of wood, raised and kindled on certain days of worship.

မီးပေါက်, *n.* a drop of fire, a spark, မီးပွား.

မီးပေါက်လက်နက်, *n.* fire-arms.

မီးပျံ, *n.* flying fire, a rocket.

မီးပွား, *n.* a spark, မီးပေါက်.

မီးပုံး, *n.* a lantern, မီးအိမ်.

မီးဖို, *n.* a fire-place, a hearth.

မီးမယ်ဖြူ, *n.* a kind of chaffing dish, with a conical cover, ထောင်း.

မီးမွေး, *v.* to make a fire.

မီးရှူး, *n.* a torch.

မီးရှို့, *v.* to burn with fire.

မီးလင်ဖွေ, *n.* a kind of rocket which hisses in falling.

မီးလျှံ, *n.* a flame.

မီးသွေး, *n.* dry fire, i. e. a dead coal, charcoal.

မီးကျောင်း, (1) *n.* an alligator, a crocodile.

မီးကျောင်း, (2) *n.* a kind of creeper.

မီးကျောင်း, (3) *n.* a kind of stone, ကျောက်မီးကျောင်း.

မီးစောင်း, *n.* a kind of harp.

မီးဖြူ, *n.* tried silver,—best kind.

မီးရပ်, *n.* the menses, ဥတု.

မုခ, *(Pali,) n.* a mouth.

မုခွတ်, *n.* a divine speech or utterance.

မုခပါတ် (from မုခ, a mouth, and ပါထ, to come, *Pali,) n.* a divine speech or saying, နှုတ်ကပတ်.

မုခ္ချ, (from မုချ, *Pali,) n.* certainty, reality, genuine, အမှန်ဖြစ်ချင်း.

မုဆိတ်, *(pron.* မုတ်ဆိတ်,*)* *n.* the beard of the chin.

မုဆိုး, *(pron.* မုတ်ဆိုး,*)* *n.* a huntsman.

မုဆိုးဖို, *n.* a widower.

မုဆိုးမ, *n.* a widow.

စုဋ္ဌာ, *(Pali,)* *n.* a pagoda with a recess in each side.

မုဋ်, (1) *v.* to measure with the breadth of the fist, the thumb being closed down on the side of the finger. Hence တမုဋ်, *n.* a measure of length equal to five finger breadths, (တသစ်.)

မုဋ်, (2) *n.* aloes.

မုဋ်ကာပူး, *n.* do.

မုဒ်, (3) *n.* an arch, arched passage, ပေါင်းကူး.

မုဒ်ကူး, *n.* do.

မုဒ်ဝ, *n.* do.

မုတ်ဆိတ်, *n.* see မုဆိတ်.

မုဒ်ဆိတ်နား, *n.* a kind of tree.

မုတ်ဆိုး, *n.* see မုဆိုး.

မုတ္တမ, *n.* Martaban.

မုတ်နား, *n.* see မုဆိတ်.

မုဒ်ပုတီး, *n.* a kind of bead.

မုဒ်သုံဖြန်, *n.* a woman kept by a foreigner.

မုဒုရက်, *n.* the Bassia latifolia.

မုဒိတာ, *(Pali,)* *n.* joy, ဝမ်းမြောက်ချင်း.

မုဒိန်း, *n.* a kind of drum.

မုဒိမ်း, *n.* a ravisher, one who commits a rape.

မုဒ္ဓဇာ, (from မုဒ္ဓ, the head, tip, top, *Pali,*) *adj.* lingual, produced from the tip (of the tongue,) နိဂ္ဂုမုဒ္ဓဇာ, (applied to consonants of ဋ class.)

မုန်, *n.* a temporal juice, which at times exudes from the elephant's temples; see အမုန်.

မုန်း, *v.* to dislike, hate, detest, မြင်ဖြင်.

မုန်းထား, *v.* to bear malice, ငြိုး.

မုန့်, *n.* bread.

မုန့်သည်, *n.* a baker.

မုန့်ဥာက်, *n.* property.

မုန့်ညက်, flour.

မုယော, *n.* a kind of grain ; see ဂေါ်း.

မုရင်, see တန်စယ်.

မုရန်, *n.* myrrh, (as used in the translation of the **N. T.**)

မုရာ, *n.* a kind of tree.

မုဠိ, *n.* a kind of tree.

မုဠိစည်, *n.* a kind of drum.

မုလေး, *n.* the woodbine, မြတ်လေး.

မုသာ, *(Pali,)* (1) *n.* falsehood, မမှန်သောစကား.

မုသာ, (2) see ဒိုက်, a tray, &c.

မုဿ, *n.* an intumescence of the testicles.

မုသာဝါဒ, *v.* to deceive, tell a falsehood.

မုံ, *v.* to begin to form, as a bud. အမုံ, *n.* an incipient bud.

မုံးတား, *v.* to hate, bear malice.

မုံ့, *n.* bread.

မုံ့ကာ, *n.* a kind of silk.

မုံ့ညင်း, *n.* the mustard plant, mustard.

မုံ့တိုင်း, *n.* a violent wind, tempest, gale, hurricane.

မုံ့လာ, *n.* the radish plant.

မုံ့သည်, *n.* a baker.

မှု, (1) *v.* to do, perform, ကျင့်၊ ပြု၊ ဆောင်; to make one's self be, become, or act like ; as မင်းမှု, to make one's self a king ; နဂါးမှု, to act like a Nagah, ပြု၊ လုပ်. Hence အမှုအကျင့်, and အမှုအရာ, &c. a deed, action, conduct, behaviour.

မှု, (2) *n.* an original writing, from which a copy is made.

မှု, (3) *v. affix,* as သွားမှု, if he go ; when he had gone, having gone.

မှုကား, *v. affix,* do.

မှု, (4) *euph. affix.*

မှု, (5) *n. affix,* as to, concerning, in regard to.

မှုကား, *n. affix,* do.

မူလ, *(Pali,)* *n.* an origin, bottom, foundation, အရင်း၊ အမြစ်; origin of action or motion, တိတ်.

မူး, (1) *v.* to be giddy, dizzy, partly intoxicated—less than

မူး, (2) *n.* a small river, a rivulet.

မူး, (3) *n.* a weight, of which there are two kinds, the great and the small—the great being equal to two great pays, (ပဲ) or one 8th of a kyat; and the small being equal to two small pays, or one 10th of a kyat.

မူး, (4) *n.* a person of rank; see အမူး.

မူးမတ်, *n.* do. see အမူး.

မူးတော်မတ်တော်, *n.* do.

မေတ္တာ, *(Pali,) n.* benevolence, affection, love, ချစ်ခြင်း; an expression of good will or benevolence, a blessing; a prayer for the good of another.

မေတ္တာပြု, မေတ္တာပို့, or မေတ္တာသက်, *v.* to wish well to another, bless, pray for.

မေတ္တာရပ်ခံ, *v.* a petition, (clerical.)

မေခုန်, *n.* sexual intercourse, သံဝါသ.

မေထုန်, or မေခုန်, (from မေထုံ, *Pali,*) (1) *n.* sexual intercourse.

မေထုန်, (2) *n.* Gemini, the third sign of the zodiac.

မေး, (1) *v.* to enquire, ask, မြန်း.

မေးမြန်း, *v.* do.

မေးမြန်းစုံစမ်း, *v.* to make enquiries.

မေး, (2) *n.* the chin.

မေးစေ့, *n.* the extremity of the chin.

မေ့, *v.* to forget, be inadvertent, အမှတ်မရှိ.

မေ့ကျန်, *v.* do.

မေ့လျော့, *v.* do. (most common.)

မဲ, (1) *v.* to threaten, terrify, မောင်း.

မဲ, (2) *v.* see မည်း, to be dark, black, to be dark in mind, ignorant, foolish, မိုက်.

မဲမဲသဲသဲ, *adv.* darkly, very dark, &c.

မဲ, (3) *n.* a lot, စာရေးတံ.

မဲချ, *v.* to cast lots.

မဲ, (4) *n.* the indigo plant, indigo.

မဲနယ်, *n.* indigo.

မဲနွယ်, *n.* a species of indigo plant.

မဲ, (5) *n.* a weight put into one side of the balance with the article weighed, in order to have a surplus for duties.

မဲထီး, *n.* a kind of tree.

မဲပန်းညို, *n.* a kind of plant.

မဲသီးချစ်, *n.* a kind of grass.

မဲ့, (1) *v.* be drawn aside, distorted, as the face, ရွဲ့.

မဲ့, (2) *v.* to be wanting, not to be မရှိ; (commonly used without a modal affix.)

မော, *v.* to be tired, fatigued, ပင်ပန်း.

မောဒါ, (*Pali,*) *n.* joy.

မောက်, *v.* to be convex, elevated in the centre, မို့. Hence အမောက်, *n.* a hairy or fleshy protuberance, as a peacock's crest, or a cock's comb.

မောက်တို, *n.* a kind of bonnet or cap.

မောက်မာ, *v.* to be strong, firm, သန် ၊ ခိုင်း ၊ တင်းမာ.

မောက်လူ, *n.* a kind of crown with a crest.

မောင်, *n.* the brother of a woman; a title prefixed to names of men, indicative of equality.

မောင်ရှင်, *n.* a probationer for the priesthood; a term of compellation addressed to men younger than one's self, (commonly used by women;) *comp.* ကိုရှင်.

မောင်နှံ, *n.* a husband, လင်.

မောင်မင်း, *pers. pro.* you, *mas.* (used to inferiors.)

မောင်မဂေါ်, *n.* a kind of plant.

မောင်း, (1) *v.* to threaten, terrify by threats, ခြိမ်း ၊ မဲ; to drive away, နှင်.

မောင်း, (2) *v.* to be of a dark red colour.

မောင်း, (3) *n.* the arm, လက်မောင်း.

မောင်းစွပ်, *n.* a sleeve or any ornament worn on the arm.

မောင်း, (4) *n.* a gong, a plate of metal, with a convexity in the middle which is beaten to produce sound.

မောင်း, (5) *n.* a mortar in which rice is cleaned.

မောင်း, (6) *n.* a well-pole.

မောင်းမ, *n.* a female attendant or concubine of a king, ကိုယ်လုပ်တော်.

မောင်းမမိတ်သံ, *n.* do.

မောင်းမမိဿံ, *n.* do.

မောင့်မာ, *v.* see မောက်မာ, to be strong, &c.

မောဂ္ဂိဝါကျောက်, *n.* a kind of precious stone.

မောဟ, *(Pali,) n.* darkness, ignorance, folly, မိုက်မဲတွေဝေခြင်း.

မှော, *v.* to appear, come to light ; see မော်.

မော်, (1) *v.* to turn up the face, look up, မော့.

မော်, (2) *v.* to stick up or out, ငေါ ၊ ငေါက်. Hence အမော်, *n.* a steep place.

မော်, (3) *v.* to be haughty, insolent, ငေါ ၊ ငေါက်.

မော်ကား, *v.* to be haughty, insolent, rude, စော်ကား ၊ ရိုင်းကား.

မော်မိမော်မနိုး, *adv.* idly, carelessly, without an object.

မော်ယော်, *n.* a kind of silk.

မို, *v.* to be elevated, raised in the centre, convex, မောက်.

မိုက်, (1) *v.* to be dark, မှောင် ; to be ignorant, foolish, မဲ.

မိုက်, (2) *v.* to measure with the fist and thumb erected. Hence အမိုက်, *n.* a maik, a measure of length equal to eight finger breadths, (အသစ်.)

မိုက်, (3) *n.* a crucible.

မိုက်, (4) *n.* a tray used to separate grains of metal from the earth by shaking, ကျင်ခွက် ၊ ကျိုရာခွက်.

မိုဃ်း, (from မေဃော်, *Pali,*) *n.* the sky, visible heavens ; clouds, rain.

မိုဃ်းဖွဲ, *n.* a small cloud, မိုဃ်းငယ်ခဲသေး.

မိုဃ်းဆွေ, *v.* to rain incessantly ; see ဆွေ.

မိုဃ်းကာလ, *n.* the rainy season ; *comp.* ဥတု.

မိုဃ်းကောင်းကင်, *n.* the sky.

မိုဃ်းကျ, *v.* to rain.

မိုဃ်းကြိုး, *v.* to thunder in a loud crash. *n.* a thunderbolt.

မိုဃ်းစက်, or မိုဃ်းကြိုးစက်, *n.* a thunderbolt.

မိုဃ်းချိမ်း, see မိုဃ်းချုန်း.

မိုဃ်းချုန်း, *v.* to thunder in a protracted rumbling osund.

မိုဃ်းချုပ်, or မိုဃ်းချုတ်, *v.* to shut in, as evening.

မိုဃ်းထစ်, *v.* to thunder in short claps.

မိုဃ်းဝက်, *v.* to beat in or against, as rain.

မိုဃ်းပေါက်, *n.* a drop of rain.

မိုဃ်းမြည်, *v.* to rumble in the sky, to thunder.

မိုဃ်းမည်, *v.* do.

မိုးရွာ, *v.* to rain.

မိုးသက်, *v.* do.

မိုးသက်လေ, *n.* wind preceding a storm.

မိုးသီး, *n.* hail.

မိုးသောက်, *n.* the morning.

မိုးစာ, *n.* a kind of bird, ဒိန်ညင်; a waterfowl.

မိုးမွှေး, *n.* a kind of tree.

မိုးနံ့, *n.* a kind of tree.

မိုးခြံ, *n.* a field, or spot of ground for a particular purpose; see ဝတ်မိုး.

မိုင်း, *v.* to cover, ဖုံ.

မိုင်းမ, *v.* to help, ညီညာ.

မိုး, (1) *v.* to cover, overspread, လွှမ်း. Hence အမိုး, *n.* a cover, a roof. အမိုးစွန်း, *n.* the eaves of a roof.

မိုး, (2) *v.* to excel, surpass, be chief, preeminent, ကဲ ၊ မြတ် ၊ လွန်. Hence အမိုး, *n.* a chief, အကဲ.

မိုးထုပ်, *v.* to be chief; be permanent; see ခေါင်း.

မို့, *affix*, because, as သွားမို့, or သွားလျှင်မို့, or သွားသော်မို့, because of going.

မို့တုံး, *neg. affix*, as သွားသည်မို့တုံး, he goes not.

မျက်, (1) *v.* to be angry, စိတ်ဆိုး. Hence

အမျက်, *n.* anger, ဒေါသ.

အမျက်ထွက်, *v.* to be angry, မျက်.

အမျက်ဖင်, *v.* do.

အမျက်ထိ, *v.* to be angrily disposed.

အမျက်မံ, *v.* to pretend to be angry.

အမျက်ခံ, *v.* to restrain anger, ခုံ.

မျက်, (2) *v.* to stick in (the throat.)

မျက်, (3) *n.* grass.

မျက်ပုတ်, *n.* a clump of grass.

မျက်, (4) *n.* a gem, precious stone.

မျက်စုံ, မျက်မွန်, မျက်ရှင်, *n.* do.

မျက်ရွဲ, do. *also* a particular kind of precious stone, ကျောက်မျက်ရွဲ.

မျက်, (5) *n.* the eye, (seldom used but in composition,) မျက်စိ.

မျက်အိမ်, *n.* the socket of the eye.

မျက်ကွင်း, *n.* do.

မျက်ကွယ်, *adv.* out of sight.

မျက်ခမ်း, *n.* an eyelid.

မျက်ခုံး, *n.* the long arch over the eye, မျက်မှောင်.

မျက်ခုံးမွေး, *n.* the eyebrow.

မျက်ချေး, *n.* the dirt of the eye, မျက်ဝင်.

မျက်ဖြေ, *n.* the reach of the eye, eyesight.

မျက်ခွက်, *n.* the face.

မျက်စဉ်း, *n.* medicine for the eyes.

မျက်စိ, *n.* the eye.

မျက်စိစောင်း, *v.* to be cross-eyed.

မျက်စိထိုးကြည့်, *v.* to look stern, to frown.

မျက်စိညောင်း, (see ညောင်း, to be tired through inaction,) *v.* to pay attention to by the eye.

မျက်စိတိမ်, *n.* a film, or cataract upon the eye.

မျက်စောင်းရိပ်, *v.* to wink, make signs with the eyes.

မျက်စောင်းထိုး, *v.* to cast a back side-glance.

မျက်ဆန်, *n.* the pupil of the eye.

မျက်တောင်, *n.* the eye-lashers.

မျက်ထောင့်, *n.* the corner of the eye.

မျက်နက်, *n.* the iris of the eye.

မျက်နှာ, *n.* the face, countenance.

မျက်နှာကြက်, *n.* a canopy, ပိတာန်.

မျက်နှာကြီး, မျက်နှာများ, *v.* to have many friends.

မျက်နှာစာ, *n.* presence, အထံ ၊ ထံ.

မျက်နှာညို, *v.* be downcast in countenance ; blush.

မျက်နှာပန်း, *n.* a kind of tree.

မျက်နှာရ, *v.* to gain countenance, obtain favour.

မျက်နှာမူ, *v.* to have the face towards.

မျက်နှာသိ, *n.* an acquaintance.

မျက်ရည်, *n.* a tear, မျက်ချည်.

မျက်ဝန်, *n.* an expletive used with မျက်လုံး ၊ မျက်နှာ, &c.

မျက်ဖြူ, *n.* the white of the eye.

မျက်မာန်ကြုတ်, see မျက်မှောင်ကြုတ်.

မျက်မုန်း, or မျက်မုန်းထိ, see မျက်မုန်းကြိုး.

မျက်မုန်းကျိုး, *v.* to resent, feel ill will.

မျက်မှန်း, *n.* the eye's desire, what the eye is fixed upon.

မျက်မှောက်, *n.* in presence of, presence ; the present time, (sometimes used adjectively.)

မျက်မှောက်ပြု, *v.* to make an absent thing present.

မျက်မှောင်, *n.* the long arch over the eye, the eyebrow.

မျက်မှောင်ကြုတ်, *v.* to look stern, dark, angry, threatening.

မျက်မှောင်ချီ, *v.* to raise the eyebrows, look stern.

မျက်ရစ်, *n.* any thing which encircles the eye ; a precious stone, or valuable object which intoxicates the eye.

မျက်ရည်, *n.* tears.

မျက်လုံး, *n.* the eyeballs.

မျက်လေ, *v.* to be deceived by the eye.

မျက်လှည့်, *v.* to deceive the eye.

မျက်လှည့်သမား, *n.* a juggler.

မျက်လွှာ, *n.* an eyelid.

မျက်ဝပ်, *n.* the dirt of the eye, မျက်ချေး.

မျက်ပါး, *n.* a thin leaf (of gold.)

မျက်ရတနာကျောက်, *n.* see ရတနာ.

မျည်, see မည်, *v.* to complain.

မျည်တမ်း, see မျည်, *v.* to complain, be distressed.

မျဉ်း, (1) *v.* to be sleepy, or to sleep, (not used singly.)

မျဉ်း, (2) *v.* to be weak, exhausted, dejected, နွမ်းငွေ.

မျဉ်း, (3) *n.* a short military coat, စစ်ဝတ်မျဉ်း.

မျဉ်းနီ, *n.* do.

မျှဉ်း, (1) *v.* to be moderate, gentle.

မျှဉ်း, (2) *n.* a ruler, or ruling line, တမျှဉ်း.

မျဉ်းကြိုး, *n.* a ruling line.

မျှဉ်းတံ, *n.* a ruler.

မျှာ, or မျှာတိုင်, *n.* the short supporters of a roof, resting on a lower floor.

မျှား, *v.* to be many, ထူ ၊ မနည်း.

မျှားတွဲ, *adv.* in a hanging, suspensive manner.

မျော, (1) *v.* to float.

မျှော, (2) *n.* a pole, slender post.

မျောက်, (1) *n.* a monkey—many varieties.

မျောက်, (2) *n.* the potato, or yam plant.

မျောက်ဒေါင်း, or မျောက်ဥ, *n.* the potato or yam.

မျောက်ငုံ့နွယ်, *n.* a kind of creeper.

မျောက်ဒို, *n.* the Lythrum fructicosum.

မျောက်ဆိတ်, *n.* a kind of tree.

မျောက်နို, *n.* a kind of tree.

မျောက်မ, *v.* to commit adultery.

မျောက်မျဉ်း, *v.* to be half asleep and half awake.

မျောက်လက်, *n.* a brass, or iron hinge, ပတ္တာ.

မျောက်လက်ဝါး, *n.* a kind of creeper.

မျောက်လုပ်, *n.* a kind of tree.

မျောက်လျှော်ကူး, *n.* a kind of creeper.

မြို, *v.* to swallow.

မျိုးစေ့, (from အမျိုး, a race, kind,) *n.* seed, seed-grain.

မျိုးပဲ, *n.* do.

မျိုးရိက္ခာ, *n.* stated provision ; see ရိက္ခာ.

မြ, (1) *v.* to be cold, ဆ ၊ ချမ်း ၊ အေး.

မြ, (2) to be sharp, keen, ထက် ၊ မြက်.

မြ, (3) *n.* an emerald, ကျောက်စိမ်း.

မြ, (4) *n.* a kind of tree.

မြက်, (1) *v.* to be sharp, as a knife, ထက် ; to be pungent, as flavour.

မြက်, (2) see မျက်, grass, &c.

မြင်, (1) *v.* to be distant in time, whether past or future ; see မြင့်.

မြင်ကြာ, *v.* do.

မြင်, (2) *v.* to see.

မြင်ပြင်း, *v.* to hate or dislike to see, ရွံ့.

မြင်မက်, (see မက်,) *v.* to dream, be in a reverie.

မြင်း, *n.* a horse.

မြင်းထိန်းကျွန်, *n.* a horse-keeper, a groom.

မြင်းစီးသူရဲ, *n.* a trooper.

မြင်းခြိုး, *n.* a gelding.

မြင်းတာရာ, *n.* a certain star or constellation ; see တာရာ.

မြင်းထီး, (1) *n.* a stallion; see အထီး; (2) *n.* a mule.

မြင်းက, *n.* a kind of creeper.

မြင်းခေါင်း, *n.* the shin bone, ခြိကျည်း.

မြင်းခွာ, *n.* a kind of creeper.

မြင်းပု, *n.* an indolent tumour, ထွတ်မြင်း.

မြင်းမိုရ်, *n.* the Myenmo mount; the centre of the Sekyah system, (စကြ.)

မြင်းဖြူသေ, *n.* a kind of tree.

မြင်းဝါး, *n.* a species of bamboo.

မြင်းသခြိက်, *n.* the piles, a kind of disease.

မြင်းသီလာ, *n.* a kind of stone.

မြင့်, *v.* to be high, မြင့်မား; to be distant in time, ကြာ၊ ရှည်; (act. မြှင့်.)

မြစ်, (1) *v.* to impede, obstruct, prevent, ဆီး၊ တား; to warn, instruct, as a teacher of religion; to prohibit.

မြစ်, (2) *n.* a river, i. e. the channel of a river.

မြစ်မ, *n.* a main river. N. B. There are five main rivers, which run southward, on the great south island, (ဇမ္ဗူဒိပ်,) viz. ဂင်္ဂါ၊ အစိရဝတီ၊ ယမုန္နာ၊ သရဘူ, and မဟီ.

မြစ်, (3) *n.* a grand-child.

မြစ်ငွေး, *n.* a kind of bird.

မြည်, (1) see ပျည်, to produce sound.

မြည်, (2) see မည်, to be named.

မြည်း, *n.* an ass, မြ.

မြိည်း, *n.* a ruler, measuring rod.

မြည့်, *v.* to be crumbling, easily pulverized, မွ.

မြတ်, *v.* to be excellent; to exceed, be an overplus, be gain, profit. Hence အမြတ်, *n.* gain, overplus; အမြတ်အဖွား, do. အမြတ်အစွန်, do.

မြတ်နိုး, *v.* to love; to reverence, esteem.

မြတ်လေး, (1) *v.* do. see လေးမြတ်.

မြတ်လေး, (2) *n.* the woodbine, မုလေး.

မြန်, *v.* to be quick, swift, သော၊ လျင်.

မြန်ထက်, *v.* do.

မြန်မြန်, *adv.* quickly, hastily.

မြန်မာ, (commonly written မြမ္မာ, and pron. ဗမ္မာ,) *adj.* of, or pertaining to Burmah or the Burmans—under which are included seven divisions or distinct races, viz. မြမ္မာကြီး, or ရခိုင်, the Aracan; မြမ္မာပဒေါင်, the Burman proper; တလိုင်း, the Pegu; ချင်း, the Kyen; ကရင်, the Ka-yan; ယော, the Yaw; and ဓားဝယ်, the Tavoy.

မြန်း, (1) *v.* to enquire, ask, မေး.

မြန်း, (2) *v.* to have possession of, enjoy, ခံ ။ စိုး.

မြန်း, (3) *v.* to be dull, faded, withered, shrivelled, ညှိုး ။ ထေး.

မြမ္မာ, see မြန်မာ, Burman, or pertaining to Burmah.

မြား, *n.* an arrow.

မြားကျည်တောက်, *n.* a quiver, တောင့်.

မြားမွှတ်, *n.* the feather of an arrow.

မြားလျှော, *n.* do.

မြတ္တာ, *n.* see အတ္တာ.

မြိန်, *v.* to relish, be pleased with, enjoy.

မြိန်ရှက်, *v.* do.

မြီ, *n.* a debt, ကြွေး.

မြီရှင်, *n.* a creditor.

မြီစား, *n.* a debtor.

မြီချ, *v.* to put out interest.

မြီထပ်, *v.* do.

မြီယူ, *v.* to receive interest, borrow money.

မြီး, (from အမြီး,) *n.* a tail.

မြီးညှု. *n.* the root of a tail.

မြီးတိုး, *n.* do.

မြီးကျွမ်, *n.* a crupper.

မြုပ်, *v.* to be immersed, overwhelmed, swallowed up, နစ်; *act.* မြှုပ်.

မြုပ်ခြီး, *n.* the scapula, or shoulder blade.

မြုံ, (1) *v.* to be barren, (applied to animals.)

မြုံ, (2) *v.* to divide, split, ခွာ.

မြုံ, (3) *v.* to conceal one's self, hide, keep still, အောင်း ။ ကွယ် ။ ပုန်း.

မြုံ, (4) *n.* a basket or cover to keep fish in water after they are caught.

မြုံ့, *v.* to work about in the mouth, to chew (the cud)—a little different from ဝါး, to chew. Hence အမြုံ့, the cud, စားမြုံ့.

မြူ, (1) *v.* to play with, divert, amuse.

မြူ, (2) *n.* dust, a minute particle, an atom, အမှုန်.

မြူတော, *n.* a pot with a long neck and an open mouth.

မြူး, (1) *v.* to enjoy pleasure, exult in, delight, ရွှင်.

မြူး, (2) *v.* to glitter, play about, as rays of light or dust.

မြူးထူး, do. do. (most common.)

မြူးစား, do. do.

မြူးနွဲ့, do. do.

မြေ, *n.* the earth, ground.

မြေကျုံ, *n.* a mixture of earth, dung, or other substances, used as plaster or mortar.

မြေကြီး, *n.* the earth.

မြေနှစ်မြေဆီ, *n.* the fat or riches of the ground.

မြေခွေး, *n.* a jackal.

မြေစား, *v.* to moulder, turn to dust.

မြေတိုင်, *n.* a certain country officer.

မြေပဲ, *n.* a Manilla root, earth-bean.

မြေဇာမြက်, *n.* a kind of grass, နေဇာမြက်.

မြေပြန်, *n.* a kind of plant, purslain.

မြေး, *n.* a grandchild.

မြေးသားကျည်မြေးဆက်, *n.* posterity.

မြေ့, (1) *v.* to be cool, cold, အေး ၊ ချမ်းမြ.

မြေ့, (2) *v.* to be fine, nice, ချော.

မြဲ, (1) *v.* to be tight, close, secure, ကြပ် ၊ တင်း ၊ ခိုင်.

မြဲ, (2) *v.* to continue the same, permanent, unchangeable.

မြဲမြံ, *v.* do.

မြဲခိုင်, *v.* do. Hence အမြဲ, *n.* permanency; အမြဲတည်, do.

မြဲ, (3) (freq. pron. မြည်း,) *v.* to taste of, try by tasting.

မြဲစမ်း, *v.* do.

မြဲ, (4) see မြည်း, an ass.

မြောက်, (1) *ordinal auxiliary adj.* as နှစ်ရက်မြောက်, the second day; သားနှစ်ယောက်မြောက်, the second son, &c. see Gram.

မြောက်, (2) *v.* to be raised, elevated, placed on high; to be raised above (a difficulty;) to gain, accomplish; *act.* မြှောက်.

မြောက်, (3) *n.* the north.

မြောက်နန်း, *n.* the north palace; the queen of do. who is second in rank.

မြောက်စည်, *n.* a kind of drum.

မြှောက်စား, *v.* to praise, glorify, ချီးမွမ်း.

မြောင်မ, *n.* an adulteress, လင်ငယ်.

မြောင်မထား, *v.* to commit adultery, (as a woman,) လင်ငယ်ထား.

မြောင်လက်, *n.* a brass or iron hinge.

မြောက်သား, *n.* a correlate in marriage, whether husband or wife, အိမ်ထောင်ဘက် ၊ ခင်ပွန်း.

မြောင်, *v.* to be long, narrow, သွယ်; (*act.* မြှောင်.) Hence အမြောင်, a valley, a narrow road or path.

မြောင်း, *n.* an artificial water-course, a canal, channel, rivulet—smaller than ချောင်း.

မြိုက်, *v.* to be singed, scorched; *act.* မြှိုက်.

မြိုက်မြိုက်, *adv.* engagedly, intently.

မြိုင်, (1) *n.* a forest, grove, ရှို.

မြိုင်, (2) *v.* to be full, crowded.

မြိုးမြက်, *v.* to be sharp, pungent, delicious, မြိုက်.

မြို့, *n.* a fortified place, a city, chief town, &c.

မြို့ဦး, *n.* a fortification.

မြို့မ, *n.* a metropolis, chief city.

မြို့ရိုး, *n.* the wall of a fortress; *comp.* ထပ်.

မြို့ရိုးတည်, *v.* to build a fortification, to fortify.

မြို့ဝန်, *n.* the governor of a city, a viceroy.

မွ, *v.* to be crumbling, easily pulverized, ကြေ.

မွတ်, *v.* to hunger, thirst after, ငတ် ၊ ဆာ ၊ သိပ်.

မွန်, (1) *v.* to be good, excellent, ကောင်း ၊ မြတ်.

မွန်ချည်, *v.* do.

မွန်, (2) *adj.* see ထိုင်း.

မွန်း, *v.* to be overwhelmed, suffocated, astonished, stupefied; (*act.* မွှန်း.)

မွန်းတည့်, *v.* to be noon.

မွန်းတယ်, *v.* to be after noon.

မွမ်း, *v.* to be anointed, spread over, besmeared, covered; (see *act.* မှွမ်း.)

မွမ်းချွန်း, or မွမ်းဝေါင်း, see ဒုထစ်.

မွမ်းမံ, *v.* to be spread over, decorated, adorned.

မံ့, *adv.* yes, (obsolete.)

မွေး, (1) *n.* hair of the body; see အမွေး.

မွေး, (2) *n.* a sacred relic of deity; see ဓာတ်.

မွေး, (3) *v.* to feed, nourish, cherish, ကျွေး.

မွေး, (4) *v.* to bring forth, as animals; see ဖွား.

မွေးကျွေး, *v.* to feed, nourish, cherish.

မွေးစား, *v.* do.

မွေးမြူ, *v.* do.

မွေ့, (1) *v.* to sleep, sleep soundly, အိပ်.

မွေ့, (2) *v.* to enjoy one's self, be satisfied, ပျော်ပါး.

မွေ့, (3) *v.* to be fine, soft, gentle, delicate, နူး၊ ညံ့.

မွေ့ရာ, *n.* a mattress, bed, stuffed quilt.

မွေ့လျော်, *v.* to enjoy, take delight in.

မြွက်, *v.* to speak, utter.

မြွက်ဆို, *v.* do.

မြွေ, *n.* a serpent, snake.

မြွေငန်း, *n.* a species of serpent.

မြွေဆိုး, *n.* a poisonous serpent.

မြွေပါ, *n.* an animal.

မြွေမွေး, *n.* a species of serpent.

မြွေဟောက်, *n.* the cobra de capello.

မြွေးတုပ်, *n.* a certain charm, found in the bodies of animals, in the shape of a hair.

မှ, (1) *v. affix*, when, as သွားမှ, when he had gone, or having gone.

မှ, (2) *n. affix*, from, out of, besides, except.

၍, an abbreviation of မည်.

မှက်, *n.* a gnat, large fly.

မှင်, *n.* soot, blacking, ink.

မှင်အိုး, *n.* an inkstand.

မှင်ကြိုက်, *v.* to be entranced, walk in sleep.

မှင်ကြိုက်မိ, *v.* do.

မှင်ဆံ, *n.* the mane of a horse, stiff coarse hair.

မှင်တံ, (1) *n.* a pen.

မှင်တံ, (2) *n.* bristles, stiff coarse hair.

မှည့်, (1) *v.* to be ripe, mellow, ပျော့ ၊ ရင့်.

မှည့်, (2) *v.* to produce sound.

မှည့်, (3) *v.* to name, give a name. Hence အမှည့်, *n.* a name.

မှည့်, (4) *n.* a mole, natural mark upon the body.

မှည့်ရှင်, *n.* a mole, natural mark.

မှတ်, *v.* to note, mark down, remark, consider, think, be of opinion. Hence အမှတ်, a mark, sign, observation, supposition, opinion.

မှတ်ကျွ, *v.* to remark, take notice of.

မှတ်ကျောက်, *n.* a touchstone to try metals.

မှတ်ခံ, *v.* to grind, as upon a grindstone.

မှတ်ချက်, *n.* any thing written, a government order, &c.

မှတ်စာ, *n.* an index, catalogue, list.

မှတ်မှတ်ရရ, *adv.* prefixed to မှတ်, ပြော, and ထား, to denote an action to be remarked, observed, taken notice of.

မှတ်မှား, *v.* to mistake, as in taking one thing for another.

မှတ်သား, *v.* to observe, mark, think, suppose, be of opinion, ထင်; to remember, recollect, ရည်.

မှန်, (1) *n.* a looking-glass, mirror.

မှန်, (2) *v.* to be true, right, exact, proper.

မှန်, (3) *v.* to hit, as a mark.

မှန်ကင်, *n.* an extremity, point, top, summit, အဖျားထိပ်.

မှန်ကင်း, *n.* small spires upon distinguished buildings; see ငုတ်.

မှန်ကန်, *v.* to be true, right, exact, proper, မဖြောင့် ၊ မလွဲ. Hence အမှန်, *n.* truth; and အမှန်ကျ, *v.* to hit right, be adapted to a case; to be in the right.

မှန်ကူ, *n.* an inclined triangled square, an obtuse triangle.

မှန်း, *v.* to mark, remark, observe, aim at any object, မှတ်.

မှန်းထား, *v.* to mark, remark, &c.

မှာ, (1) *v.* to tell, order, commission.
မှာကြား, *v.* do.
မှာစာ, *n.* a note, letter of intelligence, memorandum.
မှာထား, *v.* do.
မှာ, (2) *affix*, (used with verbal, and other nouns,) in, while, among, in presence of; as to, concerning, in regard to.
မှား, (1) *v.* to err, be false, wrong, uncertain, လွဲ ၊ ယောင် ၊ ထွေး.
မှား, (2) *v.* to transgress, sin against; commit adultery, ဖြစ်မှား.
မှားယွင်း, *v.* to sin, transgress, commit adultery.
မှားရှက်, *v.* do.
မှိ, *v.* to nod, nap, be in a deep study, မှိုင်.
မှိတ်, *v.* to wink with the eye, ဝိတ်; see ဆန္ဒ.
မှီ, (1) *v.* to be on account of, for the sake of, touching, relative to.
မှီ, (2) (with မ prefixed to the root,) *affix*, before, as မစားမှီသွားသည်, he goes before he eats. It sometimes takes a noun affix after it, as မစားမှီမှ; but the sense appears to be the same.
မှီ, (3) *v.* to reach, come up or at, overtake, find, touch, attain to.
မှိ, (4) *v.* to be even, alike, similar, equal; be even, regular, (as a row of trees.)
မှီအုံး, *n.* a cushion, to sit or lean upon.
မှီကွာမှီကွာ, *adv.* slightly different.
မှီခို, *v.* to adhere to, be under protection, take refuge in, ခိုလှုံ.
မှီခိုရာ, *n.* an object of trust, confidence, or worship; a refuge from a storm, a shelter, resting place.
မှီဝဲ, *v.* to have sexual intercourse.
မှီဝဲး, *v.* to depend on, rely upon, ဆည်းကပ်.
မှူး, *n.* a minister of state.
မှုတ်, *v.* to blow with the mouth, to blow or play on an instrument.
မှုန်, (1) *v.* to be dim, as the eyes, from age or weakness.
မှုန်, (2) *v.* to pervade, diffuse, become many, နှံ့ ၊ စပ်.
မှုန့်, *v.* to pulverize, reduce to powder, ကြေ ၊ ညက် ၊ မှုံ့.

မှုန့်, or မှုန့်ညက်, *n.* flour.

မှုန့်မှုန့်ညက်ညက်, *adv.* an intensive to words of fineness.

မှူး, (1) *n.* a minister of state.

မှူး, (2) *v.* to rule over, govern, ကဲရိ.

မှေ့, (1) *v.* to doze, be partly asleep.

မှေ့မှိတ်, *v.* do.

မှေ့, (2) *v.* to be unsound, distempered, (applied to the eyes,) မှိုင်း.

မှေး, *v.* to be besmeared all over, soiled.

မှေးလက်, *v.* do.

မှဲ့, (1) *v.* see မှည့်.

မှဲ့, (2) *n.* a wart, mole.

မှောက်, (1) *v.* to turn over, capsize ; be convex, ကုန်း.

မှောက်, (2) *n.* a helmet, kind of hat.

မှောက်ခုံ, *adv.* turned over, pronely, face downwards.

မှောက်လူ, *n.* a sort of helmet, worn by viceroys as an honorary reward.

မှောင်, (1) *v.* to be dark, gloomy, မိုက် ၊ မှိုင်း ၊ မဲ.

မှောင်, (2) *v.* to be weak, deficient in strength, as the eyes, မှိုင်း.

မှောင့်, *v.* to vex, trouble, to be subject to trouble from anxiety or desire.

မှို, *n.* a toadstool, mould, fungus.

မှိုင်, *v.* to be stupid, lost in thought, astonished, confused. Hence တမှိုင်တွေတွေ, *adv.* in an absent manner, as when one is lost in thought ; confusedly, intently.

မှိုင်မှိုင်တွေတွေ, *adv.* confusedly, &c.

မှိုင်မှိုင်ငေငေ, *adv.* do.

မှိုင်း, (1) *v.* to be of a dark colour.

မှိုင်း, (2) *v.* to be partly blind, through disease or age, မှုန် ၊ မှေး ၊ မှောင်.

မှိုင်းမှိုင်, *adv.* spreadingly, overshadowingly, covering over, extendingly, (as a plant or creeper,) ဆိုင်းနှိုင်းဝေဝေ.

မှိုတက်, *v.* to be mouldy, become musty.

မှိ, *n.* a material used for making pillows, consisting of flowers not unlike fine silk, or cotton.

မျှ, (1) *v.* to be enough, sufficient, လောက် ၊ ငံ ၊ လောင်.

မျှ, (2) *affix,* as much as, နှ ၊ မျှလောက်.

မျှ, (3) *v.* to distribute, divide, assign a portion, ဝေ ၊ ငှ. Hence အမျှ, *n.* a portion, distribution.

မျှ, (4) *v.* to be even, alike.

မျှ, (5) *adv.* even, even all, အမျှ.

မျှင်, *v.* to strip, tear off in strips.

မျှင့်, (1) *v.* to lift up, make high, exalt, မျှောက်.

မျှင့်, (2) *v.* to become small, long, stringy, (as hair or fruit,) သေးသွယ်.

မျှား, (1) *n.* a hook of any kind; an arrow.

မျှား, (2) *v.* to hook up or on, take as a fish.

မျှား, (3) *v.* to deceive, allure, liken, consent, agree to.

မျှော, *v.* to float, cause to float.

မျှောက်, *v.* to promote, exalt, lift up, honour.

မျှော့, *n.* a leech.

မျှော်, *v.* to look up with astonishment, to look forward with hope or anxiety.

မျှော်ငံ့, *v.* do. မျှော်ထောက်, *v.* do. မျှော်ထင့်, *v.* do.

မျှော်တာင်, *v.* to consider, look into.

မြှိုင်, (1) *n.* a small fish.

မြှိုင်, (2) *v.* to be insensible, stupid.

မြှစ်, *n.* a young sprout of bamboo.

မြှတ်ရိုး, *n.* the collar bone, ညှပ်ရိုး.

မြှုတ်, (1) *v.* to swallow up, suffocate, immerse; to bury, cover up, deposit in the earth, နှစ် ၊ နှုန်း.

မြှုတ်ထား, *v.* do.

မြှုတ်ချ, *v.* do.

မြှုတ်, (2) *v.* to bubble. Hence အမြှုတ်, *n.* a bubble, ရေမြှုတ်.

မြှုပ်, *v.* to sink down, immerse, overwhelm, နှစ်; (*neut.* မြုပ်.)

မြှုံး, *n.* a kind of bamboo trap or net to catch fish.

မြှူ, *v.* to please, delight, allure.

မြှေး, *v.* to be entangled, to entangle, involve.

မြှောက်, *v.* to exalt, elevate, &c. (*neut.* မြောက်; which see.)

မြှောင်, *v.* to make lean on, connect with, attach to.

မြှောင်း, *v.* to make long or narrow; see မြောင်း.

မြှိုက်, *v.* to scorch, singe; see မြိုက်.

မှင်း, *v.* to cut in thin slices, slice, နွှေး ၊ ထွာ ၊ လှီး ၊ လွှာ.

မွတ်, *v.* to be smooth, delicate, handsome, ချော ၊ ပြေပြစ်.

မွန်း, *v.* to overwhelm, suffocate; astonish, confound, နှစ် ၊ မြုပ် ၊ မိန်းမော ၊ တွေဝေ.

မွမ်း, (1) *v.* to spread over, besmear, anoint, မံ ၊ လိမ်း ၊ လူး ၊ ကြိ; (*neut.* ပွမ်း.)

မွမ်း, (2) *v* to decorate, adorn.

မွှာ, *v.* to cut in slices, divide, split, ခွဲ ၊ ခိတ် ၊ ဆုတ်.

မွား, *v.* be small, be atom-like.

မွားကောင်, *n.* a tick.

မွှေ, *v.* to stir up, about, or into; make search, wander about, vex, plague.

မွှေနှောက်, *v.* do.

မွှေး, *v.* to smell, perfume, be fragrant, odoriferous. Hence အမွှေး, *n.* an odoriferous scent, fragrance, perfume.

မွေ့ရာ, *n.* a mattress, stuffed quilt.

မွေ့လျော်, *v.* to enjoy, take delight, be happy, [illegible].

မွှား, *n.* a tick, small insect.

## ယ.

ယက်, (1) *v.* to scratch, scrape together, rake up, ခြစ်.

ယက်, (2) *v.* to stir, agitate, paddle, churn, မွှေ ၊ လှော်.

ယက္ခ, (*Pali,*) *n.* a fabulous animal (of the ဂုမ္ဘဏ်, or ဘီလူး race.)

ယခင်, *adv.* former, formerly (referring to something previous.)

ယခု, or ယှု, *adv.* now, immediately.

ယခုနေ့, *adv.* to-day, ယနေ့ ၊ ခုနေ့.

ယင်, (1) *adv.* before, previously.

ယင်, (2) *conj.* so, that, if.

ယင်, (3) *pro.* the same, that.

ယင်, (4) *n.* a fly, or gnat.

ယင်ပျား, *n.* a small sort of bee.

ယင်ရဲ, *n.* a large fly, or gnat.

ယင်သောခါ, *adv.* then, at that time.

ယင်သို့, *adv.* as before, so, if so, (referring to the preceding sentence.)

ယင်သို့မဟုတ်, *adv.* if not so.

ယဉ်, (1) *n.* any vehicle or animal on which a person is carried, (seldom used.)

ယဉ်, (2) *v.* to be tamed, broken in (as a horse.)

ယဉ်, (3) *v.* to be polished, sociable, gentle in language or conduct, သိမ်မွေ့ ၊ နူးညံ့.

ယဉ်, (4) *v.* to be tender, delicate, sleek, handsome, ချော ၊ လှ.

ယဉ် (5) *v.* to be composed, steady.

ယဉ်, (6) *v.* to be beautiful (in a moral sense,) on account of observing the duties of religion.

ယဉ်ကျေး, (1) *v.* to be handsome, beautiful, be well informed, act becomingly.

ယဉ်ကျေး, (2) *n.* (from ယာန,) a while, a space of time.

ယဉ်ချေး, *v.* to be handsome, &c. see ယဉ်.

ယဉ်, *n.* a kind of disease, ရိန္နာ.

ယှဉ်ပေါင်း, *v.* to cohabit, have sexual intercourse.

ယစ်, (1) *v.* to be intoxicated, မူး; to be inadvertent, careless, ပေါ့လျော့.

ယစ်ဝ, *v.* to feast to satiety, တင်းတောင်း.

ယစ်, (2) *n.* (from ယဇ္ဇ, *Pali*,) a Nat, Devah; see နတ်.

ယစ်ဆရာ, *n.* a priest, one who offers sacrifice.

ယစ်တလင်း, *n.* an altar.

ယစ်ပူဇော်, *v.* to make offerings to Nats, worship them; to worship by the sacrifice of beasts.

ယဇု, *n.* one book of the Vedas.

ယပ်, or ယပ်, (1) *n.* a fan.

ယပ်, (2) *v.* to fan.

ယပ်, (3) *v.* to beckon with the hand.

ယပ်ခတ်, *v.* to fan another, တွား.

ယပ်ခံ, *v.* to be fanned.

ယပ်တောင်, *n.* the fan of a priest.

ယပ်ရိုး, *n.* the handle of a fan.

ယပ်ရွက်, *n.* the leaf of a fan.

ယပ်ခွက်ပြား, *n.* the border of the leaf of a fan.

ယသ်ရာ, *n.* glory, magnificence, ဘုန်းကြက်သရေ.

ယသ်ရာရ, *v.* to obtain glory, or magnificence.

ယန္တရာ, (*Pali,*) *n.* a charm; an astrological calculation impressed on metals, or on any substance, and deposited in the earth, over which (on account of its magical powers) it is supposed an enemy cannot pass.

ယန္တရာမြှုပ်, *v.* to deposit do.

ယန္တရာထား, *v.* do.

ယန္တရာရှင်, *n.* the act of proving a charm to be correct, either by books or the event itself.

ယန်, *v.* to be wetted, softened, moistened, နှစ် ၊ နိ.

ယန္တရား, *n.* machinery.

ယန္တရားစက်, *n.* wheel machinery.

ယန်ယန်, *adv.* soft, muddy, &c. နှစ်နှစ်.

ယန်း, *n.* gunpowder.

ယနေ့, *adv.* to-day, this day.

ယပ်, see ယတ်.

ယပ်တောင်, see ယတ်တောင်.

ယမက, (*Pali,*) *n.* a final sentence, ဆုံးဖြတ်ချင်း.

ယမကာ, (*Pali,*) *n.* a kind of sweet liquor, အဖျော်.

ယမနတ်, *n.* the Nat who presides over death, သေမင်း.

ယမန်, *adv.* before, previous, ago, (applied to days or years,) formerly, previously.

ယမနေ့, *adv.* yesterday, (vulgarly, မနေ့.)

ယများ, *n.* an offering of strips of cloth hung on a flagstaff.

ယမုနာ, *n.* one of the five grand rivers; see မြစ်.

ယမ်း, *v.* to embrace, hug in the arms, ဖက်.

ယမ်းယမ်း, *adv.* an intensive to words of affection.

ယသ, *n.* see under ဘုန်း.

ယံ, (from ယာမ, *Pali,*) *n.* ime denoting the watches of the night, as ညဦးယံ, evening; သန်းခေါင်ယံ, midnight. It also signifies the place of, or place about, and is constructed with nouns.

ယံသာ, *n.* a certain star or constellation; see တာရာ.

ယာ, *n.* an enclosure, either of trees, vegetables, or flowers, (of one year's growth,) လယ်.

ယာကွတ်, *n.* a medicinal drug.

ယာစကာ, (1) *n.* a beggar, or wandering mendicant.

ယာစကာ, (2) *n.* a priest to offer sacrifices.

ယာစကာ, (3) *n.* a harlot, ယာစကာမ.

ယာဂု, *n.* rice water, congee, rice boiled to a pulp.

ယာဂုထမင်း, *n.* do.

ယာဉ်, (from ယာန,) *n.* a palanquin with a ridged roof.

ယာဉ်ပေါင်, *n.* one with a round roof.

ယာမ, (*Pali,*) *n.* a watch of the night.

ယာမာ, *n.* see နတ်ပြည်.

ယာယီ, *n.* a calamity removed, that is, a ယဂ္ဂရာ, which is supposed to occasion evil, removed; see ယဂ္ဂရာ.

ယိ, *v.* to be rotten, decayed, ယဲ့.

ယိုင်း, *v.* to be inclined, hang over, lean on one side.

ယိမ်း, (1) *v.* to be crooked, as a road; to go in an indirect, crooked manner.

ယိမ်း, (2) *v.* to bend backward and forward, as grass moved by the wind.

ယိမ်း, (3) *v.* to lean against, ထိမ်း.

ယုတ်, (1) *v.* to be void of understanding, inferior, poor, mean, worthless; ညံ့.

ယုတ်, (2) *v.* to be profligate, vile, wicked.

ယုတ်, (3) *v.* to be diminished; to diminish, ထုတ်; to be lessened, not full, empty, လတ် ၊ လျော့ ၊ မပြည့်.

ယုတ်, (4) *n.* or *adj.* dead, a dead body.

ယုတ်, (5) *v.* to deteriorate, draw back, fall from, as from good sentiments, or excellence of character, လျော့.

ယုတ်ကျ, *v.* to fall from, as from good sentiments, or excellence of character.

ယုတ်ခနဲ, *adv.* suddenly, quickly, ချက်ချင်း ၊ ဖုတ်ခနဲ.

ယုတ်မာ, *v.* to be profligate, vile, wicked.

ယုတ်လျော့, *v.* see ယုတ်ကျ.

ယုန်, (1) *n.* a hare, rabbit, ယုံ.

ယုန်, (2) *n.* the fourth year of a cycle of 12 years, ယုန်နှစ်.

ယုန်, (3) *n.* used in astronomy to mean dark spots in the sun.

ယုံ့, *v.* to be contracted, shrunk.

ယုယ, *(Pali,)* *n.* the act of handling in a soft tender manner, or of speaking delicately.

ယုံ, (1) *n.* a hare, or rabbit.

ယုံ, (2) *v.* to believe, credit, be trusty.

ယုံကြ, *v.* do. do.

ယုံကြည်, *v.* do. do.

ယုံမှား, *v.* to err in matters of faith.

ယုံ့, *v.* to crouch up, be drawn together, as a serpent or other animal when frightened, ကျုံ့ ၊ ရှုံ့.

ယူ, *v.* to take, hold, possess, ဆောင်.

ယူဆံ, *v.* to admit, embrace, (as a doctrine,) မှတ် ၊ ယူ. Hence အယူ, *n.* a doctrine, sentiment.

ယူခဲ့, *v.* to bring.

ယူငင်, *v.* do. (less common than ယူခဲ့.)

ယူဇနာ, *n.* a measure of distance, (above 12 miles,) ချောက်တိုင်ယုံးယ တွင်းတယူဇနာ.

ယူပ, *(Pali,)* *n.* a shape, appearance, အဆင်း.

ယိ, *v.* to be rotten, decayed, ဆိ.

ယော, *n.* the name of a country in the Burman empire.

ယောက္ခမ, *n.* a mother-in-law or father-in-law.

ယောက်, (1) *num. affix*, as လူနှစ်ယောက်, two men, (see Gram.)

ယောက်, (2) *v.* to sprout, as a plant, or the horns of an animal, ပေါက် ၊ ပေါက်ယောက်.

ယောက်ျား, *n.* a man, male.

ယောက်ျားကောင်း, *n.* a champion, သူရဲကောင်း.

ယောက်ချို, *n.* a kind of ladle, used for stirring up rice or curry.

ယောက်မ, *n.* do. ဟင်းချို.

ယောက်ဖ, *n.* a brother-in-law.

ယောက်သွားခုံး, *n.* a kind of oyster, ခုံးသွားကျဲ.

ယောင်, *v.* to be in a heedless inattentive state of mind, to wander in thought, be in a reverie.

ယောင်ကန်းကန်း, *adv.* (done) confusedly, wrongly.

ယောင်မ, (1) *n.* a husband's younger sister.

ယောင်မ, (2) *n.* a ladle.

ယောင်ယန်, *v.* to be heedless, inattentive, lost in thought, (*sometimes written* ရောင်ရန်.)

ယို, (1) *v.* to penetrate, ooze, leak through, flow as tears, run out as spittle, စိမ့် ၊ ထွက်.

ယိုကျ, *v.* do.

ယိုစီး, *v.* to trickle down, as tears, or water.

ယို, (2) *v.* to be destroyed, ယွင်း ၊ ပျက်စီး ၊ ကျိုးပဲ့.

ယို, (3) *n.* a kind of bread.

ယိုင်, *v.* to be inclined, lean over.

ယိုယွင်း, *v.* to be lost, destroyed, withdrawn, ပျက်.

ယိုး, *v.* to accuse, impeach, စွပ်စွဲ ၊ အပြစ်တင်.

ယိုးစွပ်, *v.* do. (most common.)

ယိုးမယ်, *v.* to make an excuse.

ယိုးမယ်ဖွဲ့, *v.* do.

ယိုးမယ်ဖြု, *v.* do.

ယွင်း, (1) *v.* to be withdrawn, lost, destroyed, လစ်.

ယွင်း, (2) *v.* to commit adultery.

ယွင်း, (3) *v.* to start aside or out of proper place.

ယွင်းစု, *v.* to be ambiguous. double minded.

ယွင်းမှား, *v.* to err, go out of the way, transgress.

ယွင်းလွဲ, *v.* do.

ယွန်း, (1) *n.* Siamese, ရှမ်း.

ယွန်း, (2) *v.* to become inclined, incumbent, hang over, တော့င် ၊ စောင်း ၊ တိမ်း; to become old, or mature, as fruit or leaves.

ယွန်းရှိ, *v.* to become old, ripe, mature.

ယွယ်, *v.* to aim at, take aim, ရေ့ ၊ ရည်.

ယွို, *v.* to move out of place, ယွင်း ၊ ယို.

## ရ.

ရ, (1) *v.* to obtain, find, get, ရထိုက် ၊ မိ.

ရ, (2) *v. affix*, must, or can, as သွားရမည်, I must go.

ရအောင်, *v. affix*, in order to, for the purpose of.

ရကာ, *n.* a species of verse.

ရကုန်, *n.* a shrub, bush, any large spreading bush or shrub.
ရကိုင်, *n.* do.
ရကျွက်, *n.* one of the monsters which guard the Myenmo mount, of the ဘီလူး kind.
ရက်, (1) *n.* a day, နေ့.
ရက်, (2) *v.* to scratch, scrape together, ခြစ် ၊ ခြက် ၊ တူး.
ရက်, (3) *v.* to paddle.
ရက်လှူ, *v.* do. ရက်ကန်, *v.* do. ရက်သဲ, *v.* do.
ရက်, (4) *v.* to be able, နိုင်.
ရက်, (5) *v.* to weave, make a net, &c. ယှင်း ၊ လျှို.
ရက်, (6) *v.* to stir up, or about, agitate, churn, put in motion.
ရက်ကန်ဂွန်, *n.* a wheel or pendulum loom.
ရက်ကန်မြှောက်, *n.* do.
ရက်ကန်ပင်, *n.* the warp, or woof, ဖတိုင်.
ရက်ကန်း, (1) *n.* a loom ; (2) *v.* to weave.
ရက်ကန်းရင်, *n.* a loom, or *v.* to weave.
ရက်ကန်းရှည်, *v.* to place threads lengthwise in weaving.
ရက်စက်, *v.* to be cruel, unmerciful, void of affection, not care about, be unconcerned.
ရက်ထားရာ, *adv.* (prefixed to ကျန်, or ကျန်ကြမ်း,) very or exceedingly savage, rough, &c.
ရက်ဖောက်, *n.* a weaver's quill with the yarn upon it, ခွန်းသီး.
ရက်ဖောက်လုံး, *v.* to wind, or fill a quill.
ရက်ဖောက်သီး, *n.* the quill destitute of yarn, ခွန်းသီးခေါင်း.
ရက်မ, *n.* the longitudinal timbers which support a floor, ပုန်လျှာ.
ရက်ရော, or ရက်ရောကြမ်းကြုတ်, *v.* see ရက်စက်.
ရက်လည်, (from ရက်, a day, and လည်, a turn,) *n.* a turn of seven days, from one day until the return of the same day again, that is, a week.
ရက်ထိုး, *n.* a weaver's shuttle, ခွန်း.
ရခိုင်, *n.* Arracan.
ရညံ, *(Pali,)* *n.* a wilderness, forest ; see ဂိုင်.
ရင်, (1) *v.* to speak, utter ; see ဖြက်.
ရင်, (2) *n.* the breast, chest.
ရင်, (3) *n.* a fly.

ရင်ဖုတ်, *n.* the breast, chest.

ရင်ကန်ပန်, *n.* a kind of rattan, which bears a delicious fruit.

ရင်ခတ်, *n.* a species of tree.

ရင်ခွင်, *n.* the lap.

ရင်ခွင်ထိုင်, *v.* to sit in a leaning posture, that is, leaning forward.

ရင်ခြောက်, *n.* see သားမြီးယပ်.

ရင်ဆိုင်, *v.* to meet in the way, ခရီးရင်ဆိုင် ; to march, approach, come in contact, ကြုံ.

ရင်ဆိုင်တွေ့, *v.* do. ရင်ဆိုင်ကျ, *v.* do.

ရင်ဆိုင်နေ, *v.* to remain in a place of meeting.

ရင်ညွန့်, *n.* the pit of the stomach.

ရင်တား, *n.* a two leaved door or gate.

ရင်ပူ, ရင်ထာ, ရင်ဆူ, ရင်ကား, *n.* varieties of sickness at the stomach.

ရင်နှိုး, *v.* to be sick at the stomach.

ရင်ဖတ်, (1) *n.* the breast, stomach.

ရင်ဖတ်, (2) *n.* the heartburn.

ရင်စွဲ, *n.* the string tied round the breast of a priest during the time of religious ceremonies.

ရင်မဲ့ရဉ်း, *n.* a green fly, bred in filth.

ရင်ဝ, *n.* the breast, from shoulder to shoulder.

ရင်း, (1) *v.* to place or put for the sake of accumulating.

ရင်း, (2) *v.* to be near, close, to approach, နီး။ ကပ်.

ရင်း, (3) *v. affix*, as, while.

ရင်း, (4) *part.* one's own, (not used singly, but combined with other words, as ရင်းနှစ်, an own child ; ရင်းဥစ္စာ, own goods.)

ရင်းလျှောက်, *n.* a scaffold, or terrace within a fortification, whence missive weapons are discharged, (not used in conversation,) ရွေလောင်း။ ပခွင်.

ရင်းသွေး, *n.* an own child.

ရင့်, (1) *v.* to be ripe, mellow, mature, hardened, old, advanced in life.

ရင့်, (2) *v.* to be in an advanced state of pregnancy.

ရင့်, (3) *v.* to be fit, accomplished, complete, as language, စကားကောင်း.

ရင့်ကျူး, *v.* to produce a pleasant melodious sound, တွံလူး.

ရစ်, (1) *n.* a spinning wheel, or any thing of the kind.

ရစ်, (2) *v.* to twist, turn round, encircle, ထိင် ၊ ပတ်.

ရစ်, (3) *adverbial affix,* remaining behind, as ပြုရစ်သည်, remaining behind, he did it.

ရစ်, (4) *v.* to be intoxicated, မူး ၊ ဝေ.

ရစ်, (5) *v. affix, imp.* or *prec. mood,* (see Gram. *imp. mood.)*

ရုပ်မင်း, *n.* a doll or puppet, ရုပ်မင်းငယ်.

ရစ်ဝ, *v.* to feast to satiety, တည်ကျွေး.

ရည်, (1) *n.* colour, appearance, အရည် ၊ အသား.

ရည်, (2) *n.* strength, courage, valour, heroism.

ရည်, (3) *v.* to be strong, valiant, courageous.

ရည်, (4) *v.* to remember, recollect, observe, remark, meditate upon, မှတ် ၊ နှစ်လုံးသွင်း.

ရည်စူး, *v.* to contemplate, meditate upon, &c.

ရည်ထောင်, *v.* to remember, recollect particularly, take notice, aim at, mark out.

ရည်ညွှန်း, *v.* do.

ရည်ပေး, *v.* do.

ရည်မှတ်, *v.* to be of opinion, feel confident of, be positive.

ရည်း, (1) *v.* see ရည်.

ရည်း, (2) *v.* to be covetous, lustful, anxious.

ရည်းငံ, *v.* to be in love, possess regard for, ချစ်ကြည်.

ရဉ်း, *n.* a mode of conveyance, that is, of riding, whether upon the back of an animal or by other means.

ရဉ့်, *v.* to hang down, or drag along the ground, as the belly of a very fat animal.

ရဉ့်သိ, *v.* do.

ရတတ်, (1) *v.* to understand how to get; to have a sufficiency, be rich, ကြွယ် ၊ ကြွယ်ဝ.

ရတတ်, (2) *n.* a rich person, သူဌေး ၊ သူကြွယ်.

ရတန, *n.* see ရတနာ.

ရတနာ, (1) *n.* a gem, precious stone, မျက်ရတနာကျောက်, of which there are seven kinds, ခုနစ်ပါး.

ရတနာ, (2) *n.* gold, silver, property of any kind.

ရတနာ, (3) *n.* the three objects of worship, or of religious observance, viz. God, his precepts or holiness, and the assembly, that is, his attendants, ရတနာသုံးပါး.

ရတနာဃရ, (1) *n.* a certain kind of house, made of precious stones, and built by the Nats, in which Gaudama fasted seven days.

ရတနာဃရ, (2) *n.* one division of the Burman sacred writings.

ရတနာတွင်း, *n.* a mine of precious stones.

ရထား, (1) *n.* a chariot, carriage, cart.

ရထား, (2) *n.* the castle in chess.

ရထားစီးသူရဲ, *n.* a charioteer.

ရထားပေါင်းချုပ်, *n.* a covered carriage, or chariot.

ရန်, (1) *v. affix,* for the sake of, for the purpose of, ဖို့.

ရန်, (2) *v.* to quarrel, dispute (in anger,) &c.

ရန်ကူ, *v.* to help or assist another in a quarrel.

ရန်ကြမ်း, *v.* to be outrageous, furious (in a quarrel.)

ရန်ငြိုး, *v.* to quarrel, be at enmity, dispute.

ရန်ဆိုက်တွေ့, *v.* to pick a quarrel, to meet or come together, as two disputants or quarrelers.

ရန်ငူး, *n.* the king (because he reigns over, and subdues all his enemies; *used in poetry.*)

ရန်ဆ, *v.* to guess, surmise, form an estimate of any number.

ရန်ငြိုးဖွဲ့, *v.* to feel ill-will towards, to be malicious, hostile, revengeful, မုန်းထား.

ရန်တမ်း, *n.* a disease resembling the small-pox.

ရန်တစ္ဆ, *n.* do.

ရန်တုံ့, or ရန်တုန့်, *v.* to retaliate, turn in anger.

ရန်တိုက်, *v.* to excite a quarrel, provoke, ဒုံးချော.

ရန်ဖွေ, *v.* to quarrel, dispute, be at enmity.

ရန်ပြု, *v.* to act like an enemy, fight.

ရန်ဘန်, *adv.* sometimes, occasionally.

ရန်ဘန်ရန်ဘန်, *adv.* again and again, repeatedly.

ရန်ရှာ, *v.* to seek a quarrel.

ရန်သူ, *n.* an enemy, foe.

ရန်း, (1) *n.* gunpowder.

ရန်းပွက်, *n.* do.

ရန်းစိမ်း, *n.* saltpetre, nitre, ရန်း.

ရန်း, (2) *v.* to swell, be bloated, speak in a haughty manner.

ရန်းကား, *v.* do.; *also,* to be insulting, irritating, စော်ကား.

ရန်းကြီး, see ဒါးကြီး.

ရန်းဆ, *v.* see ရမ်း, to try, guess at, &c.

ရှန်းချောင်, *v.* see ရန်းကား.

ရပ်, (1) *num. auxiliary,* as စကားနှစ်ရပ်, two languages; (see Gram.)

ရပ်, (2) *v.* to stop, stand still; to place, be situated; to cease, as from speaking, တည်. Hence အရပ်, a place.

ရပ်စဲ, *v.* do.

ရပ်စောက်, *v.* to be erect, upright, perpendicularly strait, မတ်တတ်.

ရပ်ဝန်း, *n.* the border or suburbs of a town, country, &c.

ရပ်ဝန်းရွာ, *n.* a village in the borders of a large town, or country.

ရပ်တည်, *v.* see ရပ်, to stop, &c.

ရပ်တန့်, *v.* see ရပ်, to stop, &c.

ရပ်ရပ်, *adv.* (1) motionless, permanently, တည်တည်.

ရပ်ရပ်, *adv.* (2) various places.

ရဗ, *n.* a kind of flat basket.

ရဗ္ဗိ, *(transferred from the Greek, and used in the translation of the New Testament,) n.* Rabbi.

ရမက်, *v.* to covet, have a desire after or for.

ရမထီ, *n.* a kind of cloth of superior quality.

ရမ်, *v.* to set or place uprightly, as a post, &c. မတ်.

ရမ်သစ်, *n.* rough timber, for posts, &c.

ရမ္မက်, *n.* a strong passion, အလိုကြီး.

ရမ်း, *v.* to guess at, try, put to the test, examine, ဆ၊ ခန့်၊ ချင့်.

ရမ်းကား, *v.* to be haughty, proud, insolent, မော်ကား.

ရမ်းဆ, *v.* to try, &c. see ရမ်း.

ရယ်, *v.* (1) to cough, ဟ.

ရယ်, *v.* (2) to laugh.

ရယ်ခိုး, *v.* to cough secretly; to turn the face aside and laugh.

ရယ်ပြုံး, *v.* to cough, or laugh.

ရယ်မော, *v.* do.

ရယ်ရွှင်, *v.* do.

ရသ, see အရသာ.

ရသာ, *n.* flavour ; see အရသာ.

ရဿ, *(Pali,) v.* to be short, တို ၊ မရှည်.

ရသေ့, *n.* a devotee, sage, an austere man.

ရသေ့ဆံ, *n.* a small kind of rice, which possesses a fragrant smell, and is eaten by persons of high rank.

ရဟတ်, *n.* a machine to wind thread ; a wheel, any thing that moves round, စက်.

ရဟတ်ချား, *n.* do.

ရဟတ်ရိုး, *n.* an axletree, ဝင်ရိုး.

ရဟန်း, *n.* a mendicant, a priest of Boodh.

ရဟန်းဒဏ်, *n.* punishments inflicted by the priests upon their disciples.

ရဟန်းဝတ်, (1) *n.* the duties of a priest.

ရဟန်းဝတ်, (2) *n.* punishments inflicted by priests on their disciples.

ရံ, (1) *num. affix,* applied to pairs of things, as ခြေအိတ်နှစ်ရံ, two pair of stockings.

ရံ, (2) *v.* to desire, wish.

ရံ, (3) *v.* to surround, encircle, enclose, ခြံ ၊ ခြံရံ. Hence အရံ, an enclosure, fence.

ရံဖန်, *adv.* seldom, once in a long time.

ရံဂ, *n.* desire, passion, လောဘ ၊ တဏှာ ၊ ကိလေသာ.

ရံသူ, *n.* adherents, attendants, surrounding people or multitude, followers.

ရာ, (1) *part. affix,* denotes the object of an action, or the place where a thing is done, as နှစ်သက်ရာ, an object of love ; ပစ်ပြစ်ရာ, a place of throwing away.

ရာ, (2) *v.* to be suitable, fit, proper, worthy of, တော်.

ရာ, (3) *n.* ridges of earth cultivated for raising vegetables.

ရာဂ, *n.* passion.

ရာဇဒဏ်, *n.* punishment inflicted by kings, or by magistrates according to the king's order.

ရာဇဒဏ်, *n.* do.

ရာဇပလ္လင်, *n.* a throne.

ရာဇမတ်, *n.* works upon astrology, ဗေဒင်စာ.

ရာဇမတ်, *n.* a fence on each side of a road, erected on public occasions, made of bamboos horizontally crossed, peculiarly royal; any badge of royalty

ရာဇဝင်, *n* a history of kings.

ရာဇပုံ, *n.* do

ရာဇကဏ်, *n.* do.

ရာဇဝတ်, *n* the proceedings of a king, governor, or magistrate.

ရာဇဝတ်တွေ့, *v.* to be convicted, become guilty.

ရာဇဝတ်သင့်, *v* to be criminal, to deserve public punishment.

ရာဇသတ်, *n* the decrees or laws of a king.

ရာဖို, *v* to coil, wind round

ရာဇာ, *n* *(Pali)* a king, ruler.

ရာဒိ, or ရာအဒိ, see ရာ, *part affix,* which denotes the object of an action, &c.

ရာသကျည်, *n* the name of a certain tree.

ရာဿီ, *(Pali,)* (1) *n* the moon, လ.

ရာသီ, *(Pali,)* (2) *n* a month, that is, a lunar month.

ရာသီ, or ရာဿီ, *n* a sign of the zodiac, a time, season.

ရာသီစက်, *n* the zodiac.

ရာသီခွင်, *n.* the twelve signs of the zodiac, ဆဲ့နှစ်ရာသီ.

ရာသီရည်, *n* menses, monthly courses

ရာဟု, *n* (1) one of the planets, (not discoverable,) which is the habitation of the Nat who occasions eclipses.

ရာဟု, (2) *n* the name of the said Nat, (3) an eclipse.

ရား, *v* to itch, feel an itching sensation.

ရားနာ, *n* the itch.

ရိ, (1) *v* to be lazy, idle, ပျင်းရိ.

ရိ, (2) *v* to be fatigued, uneasy, harassed, either in body or mind, မော ။ ညောင်း ။ ပင်ပန်း.

ရိ, (3) *n.* a gonorrhœa, gleet, strangury.

ရိက္ခာ, *n.* provisions, any thing required in travelling.

ရိဖြဲ, *v* to have a gonorrhœa, gleet, or strangury.

ရိတ်, *v.* to reap, cut, shave.

ရိနာ, *n.* gonorrhœa, gleet, strangury.

ရိဋ္ဌမာ, *(Pali,)* *n.* a kind of fabulous flying spear, ဓါးလှံ.

ရိပ်, (1) *v.* to wink, or make signs with the eye, ပြတ် ၊ မျက်စောင်း ရိပ်.

ရိပ်, (2) *v.* to be slanting, leaning, inclining ; to speak indirectly, စောင်း.

ရိပ်ဖမ်းသံဖမ်းပြု, *v.* do.

ရိပ်ဖန်း, *v.* to be distrustful, suspicious, take according to appearance ; see သံဖန်း.

ရိပ်မိ, *v.* to guess, form an idea, to glance at, have a glimpse of.

ရိပွတ်, *v.* to be lazy, idle, &c. see ရိ.

ရီ, (1) *v.* to laugh, ရယ်.

ရီ, (2) *v.* to be dark, gloomy, မှောင်.

ရီတရိုက်, is prefixed to အချိန်, (time,) to signify the dusk of the evening.

ရီတရော, do.

ရုက္ခစိုး, *n.* that division of the Nats which presides over trees.

ရုတ်, (1) *v.* to take from, confiscate, သိမ်းယူ.

ရုတ်, (2) *v.* to gather, collect.

ရုတ်, (3) *v.* to be deficient, wanting.

ရုတ်ခနဲ, *adv.* immediately, instantly, ပြုတ်ခနဲ ၊ ဖုတ်ခနဲ.

ရုတ်ချည်း, *adv.* do. ပြုတ်ချည်း.

ရုတ်ရက်ရှိ, or ရုတ်ရုတ်ခပ်သည်း, *v.* to be in a hurry, be in a bustle.

ရုပ်, *n.* a form, image, likeness, whatever has a specific form or shape, အဆင်း.

ရုပ်တရက်, *adv.* quickly, instantly.

ရုပ်တု, *n.* an image, form, shape.

ရုပ်နာမ်, *n.* the body and mind.

ရုပ်နံ့, (1) *n.* do.

ရုပ်နံ့, (2) *v. affix,* denoting probability.

ရုပ်နံ့သေးပွဲ, *n.* a puppet-show, a comedy.

ရုပ်ရုပ်, *adv.* quickly, instantly, ဖုတ်ဖုတ် ၊ သုပ်သုပ်.

ရုံ, *n.* a large shed, temporary house, ရုံး.

ရုန်း, (1) *v.* to jerk, extricate from the hold of another, twitch away.

ရုံး, (2) *n.* a court of justice.

ရုန်း, (3) *v.* to collect together, assemble, စု.

ရုန်း, (4) *v.* to pull, draw, as oxen.

ရုန်းဒြုန်း, *adv.* collectively.

ရုပ့်ရင်း, *v.* to be stout, well, healthy; see ကျန်း.

ရုံ, (1) *(obsolete,)* is now written ရုံ, which see.

ရုံ, (2) *v.* to cover, overspread, as with clothes, ခြုံ.

ရုံ, (3) *n.* a bower, a collection or clump of trees, ခြုံ.

ရုံ, (4) *v.* see ရုန်.

ရုံ, (5) *v.* to be enough, sufficient, လောက်.

ရုံ, (6) *v. affix*, just, just enough.

ရုံ, (7) *v.* to believe, credit, be confident in.

ရုံကြည်, *v.* to believe, credit, be confident in.

ရုံကျေ, *v.* to be satisfied, settled in mind, free from anxiety.

ရုံတန်ရုံ, *adv.* sufficiently.

ရုံသာ, *adv.* but just, only just, as ရောက်ရုံသာ, but just arrived.

ရုံး, or ရုန်း, *v.* to pull, draw, as oxen, ငင်; to pull, or draw out, as out of the mud, ဆွဲ.

ရုံးတော်, *n.* a court of justice.

ရုံးပတေ, *n.* ramtoory, the name of a plant.

ရုံးရင်, *adv.* (prefixed to words of doing,) confusedly.

ရုံးရင်း, *v.* to be insolent, riotous, noisy.

ရုံးရင်းခပ်, *v.* to become suddenly confused, tumultuous, noisy.

ရုံးရင်းဆန်မြှုပ်, *v.* to become suddenly confused, confused in conversation.

ရုံးရင်းသာမြှုပ်, *v.* do.

ရုံးရင်းတက်, *v.* do.

ရုံးရင်းထက်မြှုပ်, *v.* do.

ရုံ့, *v.* to swell, or heap up, ဖုံ ၊ ကြွ ၊ ပုံ.

ရူပ, *(Pali,)* (1) *n.* materiality; (2) visibility, appearance.

ရူပကာယ, *n.* materiality.

ရူပက္ခန္ဓာ, *n.* see ခန္ဓာ.

ရူပထသယ်ခြောက်ဘုံ, *n.* the sixteen superior visible heavens, the abode of Bramhas.

ရူပဘဝ, *n.* a visible or material state.

ရူး, *v.* to be mad, insane, stupid.

ရူးကျွန်ပြု, *v.* to feign madness.

ရူးမူး, *v.* to be distracted, confused mentally.

ရေ, *n.* water.

ရေအိုး, *n.* a water-pot.

ရေကံ, *n.* a tank, pool, pond, ရေကန်.

ရေကူး, *v.* to swim upon or in water, to cross water.

ရေကျွံစား, *v.* to undermine with water.

ရေကျေး, *n.* a kind of water-fowl.

ရေကျောက်, *n.* a disease resembling the small-pox, ကျောက်ပြု.

ရေကြက်, *n.* a water-fowl ; a duck, ဝမ္ဗဲ.

ရေကြည်, *n.* the fœtus.

ရေချိုး, *v.* to bathe.

ရေငှက်, *n.* a general name for water-fowls.

ရေစက်, *n.* a drop of water.

ရေစက်ချ, *v.* to drop or pour out water, as a religious ceremony, calling heaven and earth to witness the vows which are made.

ရေစစ်, *n.* a priest's water-dipper, ဓမ္မခိုင်.

ရေစည်, *n.* a barrel.

ရေစုတ်, *n.* the stick on which is placed the rag or sponge of a syringe.

ရေဆိုင်, *n.* a pair of water-pots, as carried on the shoulder.

ရေညှိ, *n.* slime.

ရေတကောင်း, *n.* a goglet.

ရေတံခွန်, *n.* a fall of water, a cascade.

ရေတွက်, *v.* to count, enumerate, value, esteem. Hence အရေအတွက်, *n.* an enumeration, number.

ရေတွင်း, *n.* a well of water.

ရေထ, *n.* spring tides.

ရေပက်, *v.* see ရေဖြန်းကစား.

ရေပုံး, *n.* a water-bucket.

ရေပေါက်, *n.* a conductor of water, an aqueduct, spout, tap.

ရေပြွတ်, *n.* a syringe.

ရေပြွန်, *n.* see ရေပေါက်.

ရေဖရဲသီး, *n.* the water-melon.

ရေဗျဉ်းနာ, *n.* the dropsy, လေဗျဉ်းနာ.

ရေဖြန်း, *v.* sprinkle water.

ရေဖြန်းကစား, *n.* to play by spirting water, (particularly observed by the Burmans on the first day of their year,) ရေပက်.

ရေဘူး, *n.* a goglet, coojah.

ရေဘုန်း, *n.* a water-bucket.

ရေမျက်, *n.* a spring of water.

ရေမျို, *n.* the throat, gullet.

ရေမြောင်း, *n.* a canal.

ရေမြှုပ်, *n.* a bubble. Hence အမြှုပ်, *n.* do.

ရေယဉ်, *adj.* vapid.

ရေယုန်, *n.* a disease of the erysipelatous kind.

ရေဒီ, *n.* a kind of tree.

ရေရွတ်, *v.* to talk, speak, converse; to abuse, revile.

ရေလျှံ, *n.* a flood; *v.* to be a flood.

ရေဝဲ, *n.* a whirlpool, ခနောင် ၊ ဝဲ.

ရေသနုတ်, *n.* a bathing gown.

ရေသဗ္ဗယ်, *v.* to bathe.

ရေသပန်း, *n.* the name of a tree.

ရေသဗ္ဗယ်, *v.* to bathe.

ရေယောင်, *n.* a polite term for urine.

ရေး, *v.* to write.

ရေးကူး, *v.* to transcribe.

ရေးစား, *n.* an excelling, being better.

ရေးစားမယူ, *n.* one who is more prosperous, or better off than another.

ရေးထား, *v.* to write, compose, make, as a book.

ရေးမှတ်, *v.* to write, put on record.

ရေးရာ, *n.* an affair, business, circumstance, အရှ.

ရေးရေးစားစားရှိ, *v.* to be more prosperous, or better off than another.

ရဲအလံ, *n.* a flag, or standard.

ရဲတံခွန်, *n.* do.

ရဲရဲ, *adv.* an intensive to words of redness.

ရဲလှေ, *n.* a war-boat, တိုက်လှေ.

ရဲး, (1) *v.* to be fierce, bold, courageous, savage.

ရဲး, (2) *v.* to be red, light, brilliant, ထိန် ၊ ပြောင်.

ရဲးစွမ်း, *v.* to be bold, fierce, savage, courageous.

ရဲးတင်း, *n.* a battle-axe.

ရဲးတင်းပေါက်ဆိန်, *n.* do.

ရဲးမက်, *n.* an army, စစ်.

ရဲးရင်, *v.* to be bold, courageous, bold, savage.

ရဲးရဲးရှူးရှူး, *adv.* intently.

ရဲးရဲးတောက်, *v.* to glitter, or glisten, as a burnished instrument of war.

ရဲးဝံ့, *v.* to be bold, savage, courageous.

ရော, (1) *connective affix,* used for သော, before words of time.

ရော, (2) *v. affix, imp.* or *prec. mood ;* (see Gram.)

ရော, (3) *v.* to mix, mingle, နှော.

ရောဂန္ဓရက္ခစ်, *n.* see ကဝ်သုံးပါး.

ရောဂါ, *n.* disease, sickness, distress.

ရောဂါဝေဒနာ, *n.* do.

ရောရစ်, *v.* to wind, twist round, as vines, or creepers.

ရောရုဝ, *n.* one of the states of punishment ; see ငရဲ.

ရောရှက်, *v.* to mix, mingle, to sympathize with.

ရောရှက်ပေါင်းပေါ်, *v.* to have mutual feeling, to sympathize with.

ရောဟိနိ, *n.* a certain star ; see နက္ခတ်.

ရောက်, *v.* to arrive, attain, obtain, incur, ရ.

ရောက်ရက်, *adv.* confusedly, (prefixed to words of action.)

ရောက်ရက်ခပ်, *v.* to act mischievously, childishly, ဆော့ဆော့ကြွတ်.

ရောက်ရိုးရောက်ရက်, *adv.* remissly, heedlessly, wanting in due respect, ကပေါက်ကပက် ၊ ဖိုးဖိုပက်စက်.

ရောင်, (1) *v.* to be swollen, ယော.

ရောင်, (2) *v.* to shine, glitter, emit a brightness, တောက်ပ ၊ ထွန်း ၊ ထိမ် ၊ ပြောင် ၊ လျှံ.

ရောင်ချည်, *n.* a ray of light, နေခြည်.

ရောင်တော်, *n.* a resplendence or glory emitted from deity, said to be in six streams of different colours, ရောင်တော်ခြောက်သွယ်.

ရောင်ထုံး, *n.* the knot of hair worn by Burman men.

ရောင်ရမ်း, *v.* to be swollen; to be proud, confused, vacant, heedless in mind, not to have one's thoughts about one.

ရောင်ကျွန်, *n.* that part of a pagoda which is directly under the umbrella.

ရောင်း, *v.* to sell.

ရောင်းချ, *v.* to sell.

ရောင်းပစ်, *v.* to get rid of, or part with by selling.

ရောင်းဖော်ရောင်းဘက်, *n.* partners in trade, or business.

ရောင်းရင်း, *n.* do.

ရောင့်, *v.* to molest, trouble, worry, vex, မျှောင့် ၊ နှောင့် ၊ ရှက်.

ရောင့်ရဲ, *v.* to be enough, be satisfied.

ရော့, (1) *affix*, denotes a slight uncertainty. It is sometimes used like the affix အောင်, which see.

ရော့, (2) *v.* to slip or slide off, &c. see လျှော့.

ရော့, (3) *v.* to be lessened, diminished, abated, as the price of an article; see လျှော့.

ရော်, (1) *v.* to crow, or make a noise like a hen when her brood is in danger.

ရော်, (2) *v.* to become old, as the leaves of trees, ရင့် ၊ ယွန်း.

ရို, *n.* sweetmeats, ရို့.

ရိုခိုး, *v.* to reverence, respect, &c. see ရိုသေ.

ရိုခ, *v.* to attend upon, be in waiting, present one's self, pay obeisance, reverence.

ရိုယွင်း, *v.* to be partially spoiled, become ruined, destroyed.

ရိုသေ, *v.* to respect, pay regard to, behave in a becoming manner towards a superior, to reverence, worship.

ရိုသေစွာရှိခိုး, *v.* do.

ရိုး, (1) *n.* custom, habit, manner, precept, ထုံးရိုး.

ရိုး, (2) *v.* to be strait, upright, (applied to either matter or mind,) မတ် ၊ ဖြောင့် ၊ ဖြူ.

ရိုး, (3) *v.* to blame, charge with fault, စွပ်.

ရိုးစွပ်, *v.* to alledge a fault, blame.

ရိုးထုံး, *n.* a custom, manner, precept, ထုံးရိုး.

ရိုးရှက်, *v.* to glitter, glisten, (commonly reduplicated and used adverbially,) ရိုး ၊ ပြက် ၊ အရောင်ထွက်.

ရိုးရာ, *n.* a successor, the succeeding.

ရိုက်, *v.* to strike, hit, hammer, beat, ပုတ်.

ရိုင်, (1) *v.* to lean, incline, be incumbent, တိမ်း ၊ ညွတ် ၊ လှိုင်း.

ရိုင်, (2) *n.* a coarse bamboo mat, used to line carts to prevent grain, &c. from falling through.

ရိုင်း, *v.* to be uncultivated, rude, be in a wild state, unpolished, untamed, unlearned.

ရိုင်းပျ, *v.* to revolt, be stubborn, perverse, obstinate, ကျွတ်.

ရိုင်းဖျန့်, (1) to divide, separate, make distinct, ရှင်းခြား.

ရိုင်းဖျန့်, (2) to rebel, be obstinate, သောင်းကျန်း ၊ ပုန်ကန်.

ရွ, *v.* to be brittle, be easily broken, to crumble, ပွ.

ရွက်, (1) *n.* a leaf; the sails of a ship.

ရွက်, (2) *v.* to carry, bear, (as an offering, or as goods, in any manner,) ရိုး ၊ ထမ်း ၊ ဆောင်.

ရွက်, (3) *v.* to possess, have in charge; carry on, accomplish, transact business.

ရွက်, (4) *v.* to sustain, endure, as pain, or affliction, ခံ. (It is applied to things both of the present and future state.)

ရွက်ကြိုး, *n.* the ropes in the rigging of a ship.

ရွက်ခံ, *v.* to sustain, endure, as pain or affliction.

ရွက်တိုင်, *n.* the mast of a ship.

ရွက်နား, *n.* the edge, or border of a sail.

ရွက်နုသန်, *v.* to sprout, put forth leaves.

ရွက်နီ, *n.* silver, not pure, but less than 25 per cent. discount.

ရွက်ဖျား, *n.* the top of a mast.

ရွက်ထက်, *n.* the yards of a ship.

ရွက်ထုတ်လျှင်, *v.* to undertake any business.

ရွင်း, *v.* to be withdrawn, lost, destroyed; to err, be void, vacant, လွတ် ၊ ချွတ်; to be missing, absent, fall off, be wanting, လစ်.

ရွတ်, (1) *v.* to read, peruse, prŏnounce, ဖတ်.

ရွတ်, (2) *v.* to be old, mature.

ရွတ်, (3) *n.* a lever.

ရွတ်ဆင်ချင်, *v.* to read, and consider upon, to commit to memory.

ရွတ်တိုက်, *v.* to apply a lever.

ရွန်, *v.* to move as clouds, waves, smoke, တွန့် ၊ လိပ်.

ရွန်စည်, *n.* a kind of drum, စည်.

ရွပ်ရွပ်, *adv.* an intensive to words of quickness.

ရွမ်, (1) *v.* to dislike, abhor, be disgusted with, consider abominable.

ရွမ်, (2) *n.* a weaver's shuttle, လွန်း.

ရွမ်ရှာ, *v.* to dislike, abhor, be disgusted with, ဆက်ဆုတ်.

ရွမ်သီး, *n.* a weaver's quill.

ရွမ်သီးသောင်း, *n.* the quill destitute of yarn.

ရွံ့, *v.* to dread, fear, be reluctant, ကြောက်.

ရွယ်, (1) *v.* to aim, intend, design, ကြံ.

ရွယ်, (2) *v.* to dart as a spear, to threaten, ခြောက် ၊ ဆ.

ရွယ်, (3) *v.* to put water into a vessel, as a charm for the purpose of removing sickness.

ရွယ်, (4) *n.* age, time of life.

ရွယ်ချက်, *v.* to have a purpose, to intend, design.

ရွယ်လတ်, *n.* middle age.

ရွံ, *v.* to dislike, abhor, be disgusted with, ရွမ်.

ရွံရှာ, *v.* to dislike, to avoid through disgust, to abhor.

ရွာ, (1) *v.* to threaten, make the appearance of striking, ရွယ်.

ရွာ, (2) *n.* a village.

ရွာစား, *n.* a village officer.

ရွာတည်သစ်, *n.* an astrological book, by which is determined the proper time to found cities, and by which their future destinies are known.

ရွေ, (1) *v.* to associate, keep company with, ပေါ ၊ ပေါင်း ၊ ဆက်.

ရွေ, (2) *v.* to clear away, prepare; to plane, to hew and square timber; prepare bamboo for baskets, &c.

ရွေ, (3) *v.* to carry, as a wallet, under the arm.

ရွေငင်, *v.* to be clean, smooth, nice, (as any thing planed.)

ရွေပေါ်, *n.* a carpenter's plane.

ရွေဘော်, *v.* to be born at the same time, be adherents.

ရွေတောင်း, *n.* a terrace, platform within a wall or fortification, whence missive weapons are discharged, ရင်းကျောက်.

ရွေး, (1) *v.* to elect, choose, pick out, select.

ရွေး, (2) *v.* to purchase, ransom, (as a slave.)

ရွေး, (3) *n.* a small seed, used in weight.

ရွေးကောက်, *v.* to choose, pick out, select.

ရွေးချယ်, *v.* to choose, select, pick out.

ရွေးစယ်, *v.* do.

ရွေးတွင်းပိတ်, *n.* what cannot be got back, or redeemed.

ရွေးပေး, *v.* to purchase, ransom, (as a slave.)

ရွေးယူသင့်နေ, *v.* to purchase a slave woman for the purpose of cohabiting with her.

ရွေ့, (1) *v.* to change place, situation, or position; to die, ပြောင်း, (*act.* ရွှေ့.)

ရွေ့, (2) *conj.* or *adv.* and, even, also, as much as, (generally contracted to ရှ်)

ရွေ့ကျ, *v.* to fall, fall down.

ရွေ့ပြောင်း, (1) *v.* to change place.

ရွေ့ပြောင်း, (2) *v.* to die, ဆုံး ၊ သေ.

ရွှေ့လျှော, *v.* to fall, fall down.

ရွေး, (1) *n.* a small black and red seed, used as beads and weights.

ရွေး, (2) *v.* to be drawn aside, distorted.

ရွေးကြီး, *n.* a seed used in weight, one of which is equal to two ချင်ရွေး.

ရွေးတွင်း, *n.* to make beads.

ရွေးသမား, *n.* a maker of beads.

ရှ, *v.* to cut, wound, gash, lop off, ပြတ်.

ရှက်, (1) *v.* to intersect, join ends, dovetail, ဆက် ၊ ပူး ၊ ရှက်.

ရှက်, (2) *v.* to be ashamed, modest.

ရှက်, (3) *v.* to mix together, jumble, confuse, ရော ၊ ရှုပ်. Hence အရှက်, modesty, want of confidence; အရှက်ခွဲ, *v.* to put to shame, to disgrace.

ရှက်စနိုး, *v.* to be almost ashamed, appear to be ashamed.

ရှက်တင်, *v.* to mix, confuse; also to come together, cohabit after marriage, ပေါင်းဖော်. Hence အရှက်အတင်, *n.* a mixture, mingling, confusion.

ရှက်ရွံ့, *v.* to be or feel ashamed.

ရှင်, (1) *n.* a young priest, or one who has taken the yellow cloth, but has not attained the full condition of a priest, သာမဏေ.

ရှင်, (2) *n.* life.

ရှင်, (3) *v.* to be alive, have life, have health.

ရှင်, (4) *n.* lord, master, ruler; sir, *(voc.)*

ရှင်ဆချုပ်, *n.* a chief of hereticks, one notoriously mistaken in sentiment, တက္ကတွန်း.

ရှင်ခင်းရှင်းဖွာ, *n.* life.

ရှင်ခင်းရှင်ရှ, *n.* life, sustenance.

ရှင်စော, *n.* lord, master, (used in addressing deity.)

ရှင်ဘုရင်, *n.* king, monarch, &c. ဆရှင် ၊ ဘဝရှင် ၊ မင်းတရား.

ရှင်ဘုရင်ဘုရား, *n.* do.

ရှင်း, *v.* to clear away, make clear, or light, ထင်း; to disperse, remove, as rubbish, ဝင်ရှင်း; to become separate, go apart, (implying a previous union,) ကွာ; to be clean, pure, innocent, စင်ကြယ် ၊ သန့်ရှင်း.

ရှင်းကွာ, *v.* to become separate, go apart.

ရှင်းထွင်, *v.* to clear away, disperse, as rubbish.

ရှင်းရှင်း, *adv.* wholly, entirely.

ရှဉ့်, *n.* a squirrel.

ရှိန်ရှား, *n.* the name of a certain tree.

ရှည်, *v.* to be long, (applied to time or distance.)

ရှည်လျား, *v.* to be long, (applied to time or distance.)

ရှဉ်, (1) *v.* to unite, put together, (edge to edge,) bring in contact, yoke together, စပ် ၊ ရှက်.

ရှဉ်, (2) *v.* to resemble, be even, alike, equal, (applied to objects and sentiments.

ရှဉ်, (3) *v.* to be agreeable, suitable, proper, သင့် ၊ တော်.

ရှဉ်, (4) *v.* to compare, ချိန်နှိုင်း ၊ တိုင်း ၊ နှိုန်း.

ရှဉ်ပြဉ်, *n.* boards for uniting edge to edge, thin planks, used in the sides of ships.

ရှိ, *v.* to cut, destroy, hurt, ဖြတ်ဖီး.

ရှမ်း, *adj.* Siamese, pertaining to Siam, ယွန်း.

ရှထိ, *v.* to stretch in a transverse manner, (as the strings of a drum.)

ရှရာ, *n.* a wound, a gash.

ရှာ, (1) *v. affix,* indeed, alas! It conveys the idea of affection or regret in the speaker, as သွားရှာသည်, he goes, alas! သားခလေးသေရှာသည်, ah, alas! my little son is indeed dead.

ရှာ, (2) *v.* to seek or look after, make search for.

ရှာကြံ, *v.* do.

ရှာဖွေ, *v.* do.

ရှာမှီး, *v.* do.

ရှား, (1) *v.* to be scarce, high, dear in price, ဆွန့်.

ရှား, (2) *v.* to recede, drive away, လွင့်ပါး.

ရှား, (3) *v.* to be diffused, as odour, သင်း ၊ မွှေး ၊ ကြိုင် ၊ ထှိုင်.

ရှား, (4) *n.* a kind of tree.

ရှားစေး, *n.* Japan earth.

ရှားစောင်, *n.* the medicinal oil-tree, နံ့နှာင်.

ရှားစောင်ကြီး, ရှားစောင်ချုပ်, ရှားစောင်မြင်းနှား, ရှားစောင်လက်ဆက်, ရှားစောင်ပြဿဒ်, ရှားစောင်ထက်ပတ်, ရှားစောင်သိင်္ဂနိတ်, *n.* varieties of the medicinal oil-tree.

ရှားစောင်း, *n.* a general name for the varieties of the prickly pear, or euphorbium.

ရှားပါး, *v.* to be scarce, dear, high in price.

ရှိ, *v.* to be, have, become, ဖြစ်.

ရှိခိုး, *v.* to worship, pay homage, by putting the hands together, and raising them to the forehead.

ရှိတုန်းခါ, or ရှိတုန်းတွင်, *adv.* while; see ဆတုန်း.

ရှိန်, *v.* to be insufferably hot. Hence အရှိန်, *n.* insufferable or excessive heat.

ရှိန်ဖော, *v.* do.

ရှိရှား, *n.* the name of a certain tree.

ရှိရှိ, *adv.* even with, like as.

ရှိလေသမျှ, *adv.* all whatsoever, as much as there is.

ရှိသမျှ, *adv.* do.

ရှု, *v.* to look at with attention, see, behold, ကြည့်.

ရှုဆိတ်, *v.* to long to see, feel anxious to behold, not averse to, ကြည့်ချင်း ၊ မငြီးငွေ.

ရှုတ်, *v.* to be confused, jumbled together, ထွေး. Hence အရှုတ်အထင်း, *n.* a confused collection, a jumble.

ရှုတ်ချ, *v.* to reproach, defame, slander, disgrace; to lessen, in value, esteem, or height.

ရှုံး, *v.* to lose, as in a law-suit; receive or suffer loss, be defeated, overcome.

ရှုံးနိမ့်, *v.* do.

ရှိုက်, (1) *v.* to smell, kiss, ရှူ ၊ နမ်း.

ရှိုက်, (2) *v.* to swallow, inhale, as the breath, ယူ ၊ ရှူ.

ရှိုက်, (3) *v.* to be diminished, contracted, (applied to the mind,) လော့.

ရှိုက်ချ, *v.* to be diminished, contracted.

ရှုမျှော်, *v.* to look forward, behold at a distance, anticipate, expect, မျှော်လင့်.

ရှိုင်း, *v.* to be unattainable, unequal to, (as means to the end;) to lose, (as a bet,) ဆုံး ၊ ရှုံး.

ရှုံ့, *v.* to shrink up, shrivel, be contracted.

ရှုံး, *v.* see ရှိုင်း.

ရှုံ, *v.* to stick out, as the lips, to pout.

ရှုံ့, *v.* to shrink, shrivel, be contracted.

ရှူ, *v.* to draw up, or in, as the breath, to respire, inhale, kiss, smell, ရှိုက် ၊ နမ်း; to send out the breath with a hissing noise.

ရှူးပျံ, *n.* a flying squirrel.

ရှေး, *n.* before time, ancient time.

ရှေးကခန့်, or ရှေးကခန့်ထား, *v.* to predestinate.

ရှေးကပြော, *v.* to predict, foretel.

ရှေ့, *adv.* or *prep.* forward, before, near, in presence of.

ရှေ့တော်ရေး, *n.* a royal register.

ရှေ့ထိုး, *n.* the mark placed over ာ, thus ါ.

ရှေ့နေ, *n.* a pleader, a substitute, one who speaks for another.

ရှေ့နေစကား, *n.* a plea.

ရှေ့နေပြော, *v.* to plead.

ရှေ့ပေါက်, *n.* the mark း, tending to lengthen the syllable; see Grammar.

ရှေ့ရွတ်, *v.* to read onward.

ရှေ့ဘက်, *n.* the front side, the east side.

ရှေ့မျက်နှာ, *n.* towards the east, in an eastern direction.

ရှေ့, *prep.* before, as အိမ်ရှေ့, before the house.

ရှေ့ရှု, *adv.* before, (in presence,) strait before.

ရှေ့သွား, *v.* to go forward, go before (another.)

ရှဲ, *v.* to shun, avoid, to put, or go on one side, လွှဲ ၊ ဝယ် ၊ လွှဲဝယ် ၊ ရှောင် ၊ ဖဲ ၊ ရှောင်ရှား.

ရှောက်, (1) *n.* a citron.

ရှောက်, (2) *n.* an adulterer.

ရှောက်, (3) *v.* to walk or cross over, (as a road, bridge, or plank.)

ရှောက်ချို, *n.* the name of a certain tree, the sweet citron.

ရှောက်ဖောင်, *n.* an adulterer, ထင်ဖောင်.

ရှောင်, (1) *v.* to shun, avoid, go out of the way, err, လွှဲ.

ရှောင်, (2) *v.* to conceal, secrete, cover up, ပုန်း ၊ ကွယ်.

ရှောင်ကြဉ်, *v.* to shun, avoid, err, go out of the way.

ရှောင်တခင်, *adv.* immediately, quickly, ချက်ချင်း ၊ ရှောင်တခင်အပင်ပေါက်, to sprout, or spring up immediately or very soon.

ရှောင်ရှား, *v.* to shun, avoid, err, go out of the way.

ရှောင်လွှဲ, *v.* do.

ရှော့, *v.* to let go by degrees, to lessen, diminish, လျှော့.

ရှော်, (1) *v.* to wash, as clothes, (commonly written လျှော်.)

ရှော်, (2) *n.* strips of trees for the purpose of binding bundles.

ရှီးရှီး, or ရှီ့ရှီးရှိန်း, or ရှီးရှီးရှိန်းရှိန်း, *adv.* intensive to words of taste or colour.

ရှို, *v.* to hide, conceal, secrete, ဖွက် ၊ ကွယ်.

ရှိုက်, *v.* to grieve, sigh. Hence အရှိုက်, *n.* a sigh.

ရှိုင်း, *v.* to be hollow, deep, concave, နိမ့် ၊ ရှိုင်း ၊ ဟိုက် ၊ တောက်.

ရွှင်, *v.* to rejoice, exult, be delighted, ပြုံးထူး.

ရွှင်ပ, ရွှင်လျော်, ရွှင်ပြုံး, ရွှင်လန်း, *v.* do. မိန္ဒရွှင်, *n.* a distinguished harlot.

ရွှန်း, (1) *v.* to be bright, shining, ပြောင် ၊ လင်း.

ရွှန်း, (2) *v.* to be wet, moist, စို ၊ စွတ်; to shed tears, weep profusely, ဦ.

ရွှန်း, (3) *v.* to be full, luxuriant, as a tree with leaves or fruit; to be green and flourishing, ဖြိုင်း ၊ စိမ်း.

ရွှန်းယို, *v.* to be wet, moist, shed tears.

ရွှန်းရွှန်း, *adv.* denoting clearness, free from confusion.

ရွှန်းရွှန်းကြည်ကြည်, *adv.* do.

ရွှန်းရွှန်းလန်းလန်း, *adv.* do.

ရွှန့်, *n.* mud, mire, ညွန်.

ရွှန့်ရွှန့်, *adv.* soft, muddy.

ရွှဲ, *v.* to be wet, soft, soaked, စွတ်.

ရွှံ့, *v.* to be soft, muddy, ညွန်.

ရွှံ့ဗွက်, *n.* mud, mire.

ရွှေ, *n.* gold; *adj.* royal, (sometimes prefixed to proper names.)

ရွှေကပ်, *v.* to gild, overlay with gold.

ရွှေကျင်, *v.* to sift earth in search of gold.

ရွှေကျင်ဦး, *n.* gold found in the earth.

ရွှေစက်တော်, *n.* the golden or royal feet.

ရွှေထုံး, *n.* an image made of wood, and overlaid with gold; a bar, or log of gold.

ရွှေတောင်, *n.* a state of royalty.

ရွှေတောင်တက်, *v.* to ascend a throne, or attain a state of royalty.

ရွှေတောင်ရ, *v.* do.

ရွှေထီး, *n.* a gilt (or what is termed a gold) umbrella.

ရွှေနန်း, *n.* a royal palace.

ရွှေပန်း, *n.* a royal flower; (figuratively, the male or female genitals, previous to puberty.)

ရွှေပန်းထိမ်, *n.* a goldsmith.

ရွှေပလ္လင်, *n.* a royal seat, or throne.

ရွှေပြည်စိုး, *n.* a species of bird of a yellow colour.

ရွှေဖဝါးတော်, *n.* the under part of the foot of a king, or of deity.

ရွှေဘဝါးတော်ဆောက်, *n.* a royal footstool.

ရွှေဘွား, *n.* the under part of the foot of a king, or of deity.

ရွှေဘွားတော်, *n.* do.

ရွှေရွှေ, (1) *adv.* smoothly, handsomely.

ရွှေရွှေ, (2) *adv.* expressive of the sound made by pronouncing the word itself.

ရွှေလုံး, *n.* gold beads, or beads gilt with gold.

ရွှေလောင်း, *n.* a gilt or royal boat.

ရွှေလှေ, *n*. a royal or gilt boat.

ရွှေ့, *v*. to cause to change place or situation, to move, shove out of the way.

## လ.

လ, (1) *n*. the moon.

လ, (2) *n*. a month. The months have 29 and 30 days alternately, and every third year admits of an intercalary month.

လဆိန်ဝိုင်, *n*. the halo or disk of the moon.

လက်, (1) *num. affix*, as သေနတ်နှစ်လက်, two muskets; (see Gram.)

လက်, (2) *n*. a certain term used in astrology.

လက်, (3) *n*. the hand.

လက်အုပ်, *n*. the hands joined together, as in the act of worship.

လက်အုပ်ချီ, *v*. to join the hands as in the act of worship, and raise them to the forehead; to worship.

လက်ဦး, *adv*. before, previous, ရှေးဦး.

လက်ဦးတင်, *v*. to lift the hands to the forehead in act of obedience or respect.

လက်ကတီး, *n*. the armpit, ချိုင်းတွင်း ၊ လက်ကလိ.

လက်ကတော့ထိုး, *v*. to wear the upper garment over the left shoulder, and under the right arm.

လက်ကောက်, *n*. bangles, or rings for the wrist.

လက်ကောက်သက်ကြွင်, *adv*. discreetly, (used with words of time.)

လက်ကောက်ဝတ်, *n*. the wrist.

လက်ကျဉ်း, *n*. the whole arm.

လက်ကျားလမ်း, *n*. a lane, small road.

လကနင်, *n*. mortar, plaster.

လကုန်, *n*. the close of a lunar month.

လကူး, *n*. the change of the moon.

လကြတ်, *n*. a lunar eclipse.

လကျာ, *n*. the right hand side.

လကြေး, *n*. marble, or alabaster.

လင်္ကွင်း, *n*. a pair of brass plates played together.

လကွယ်, *n*. the disappearing of the moon, as at the change.

လက်ခ, *n.* wages for services or business in handicraft.

လက္ခ, *n.* do.

လက္ခဏာ, *n.* a sign, mark, token, a specific mark.

လက္ခဏာကျမ်း, *n.* works on physiognomy.

လက်ခတ်, *n.* a mallet, mall, ဆောက်ပွတ်.

လက်ခပ်, *n.* the lathe of a loom.

လက်ခံ, (1) *n.* a copy of any writing.

လက်ခံ, (2) *v.* to harbour, protect, screen from justice.

လက်ခံ, (3) *v.* to agree, consent to, acquiesce in.

လက်ခုပ်, (1) *n.* the hand joined together, as in the act of holding water. Hence တလက်ခုပ်, *n.* a handful.

လက်ခုပ်, (2) *n.* the name of a certain tree.

လက်ခုပ်, (3) *v.* to catch, or lay hold of, with a striking motion.

လက်ခုပ်ခတ်, *v.* to clap the hands by way of derision.

လက်ခုပ်တီး, *v.* do.

လက်ခုပ်လက်ဝါး, *adv.* turning over and over.

လက်ခုပ်သီး, *n.* the block of a ship.

လက်ခုံ, *n* the back of the hand.

လက်ခေါက်, *n.* the knuckles.

လက်ချည်း, *adv.* empty handed.

လက်ချား, *n.* borax.

လက်ချောင်း, *n.* the fingers, လက်ညှိုး.

လက်ခြေကျည်း, *n.* the arm and leg.

လက်ငင်း, *n.* giving payment individually, ready money.

လက်စတာင်းလင်း, *adv.* or *adj.* unfinished.

လက်စမ်း, *v.* to lift or feel of with the hand by way of trial.

လက်စမပြီး, *adj.* unfinished, incomplete.

လက်စသတ်, *v.* to finish off, give the finishing stroke.

လက်စားချေ, *v.* to retaliate, revenge, take satisfaction.

လက်စွပ်, *n.* any thing worn on the hand ; a ring.

လက်စွဲ, *v.* to take in the hand, to cleave to the hand.

လက်ဆစ်, *n.* a finger joint, wrist joint.

လက်ဆန့်, *v.* to stretch out the arm.

လက်ဆုပ်, *v.* to double up the fist.

လက်ဆောင်, *n.* a present, gift.

လက်ဆောင်ကာရ, *n.* do.

လက်ဆောင်ထိုး, *v.* to bribe.

လက်ဆောင်ပဏ္ဏာ, *n.* a gift, present.

လက်ဆွမ်း, *n.* the hands formed into a cavity for the purpose of holding water, grain, &c. လက်ဖက်.

လက်ညှိုး, *n.* the forefinger, the fingers in general.

လက်တဆုပ်, (from လက်ဆုပ်,) *n.* a handful.

လက်တော်, *n.* an artificer.

လက်ထပ်, *v.* to join together, to join in marriage.

လက်တဖက်, *n.* (from လက်ဖက်,) the arms full, or a handful.

လက်တံ, *n.* an arm ; an arm or limb of a tree.

လက်ထက်, *n.* the reign of; the days of.

လက်ထပ်, *v.* to marry, join together in marriage.

လက်ထပ်မင်္ဂလာ, *n.* marriage.

လက်ထိပ်, *n.* the tip of the finger.

လက်ထုပ်, *n.* the name of a certain tree.

လက်နက်, *n.* a weapon of any kind ; see ဝက်.

လက်နက်ကိုင်, *n.* a soldier, one who holds weapons of war.

လက်နက်စုံ, *n.* an armour complete.

လက်ပန်း, *v.* to strike the shoulders with the palms of the hands previous to fighting, as a kind of defiance, or for the same purpose that a person disposed to fight strikes his fists together.

လက်ပန်းပေါက်, *v.* to clap the hands, လက်ခုပ်.

လက်ပန်းပေါက်ခတ်, *v.* do.

လက်ပံ, *n.* the large cotton tree.

လက်ပြင်, *n.* a shoulder blade.

လက်ပြန်ချည်, *v.* to tie the hands behind, နှောင်.

လက်ပွေ *v.* see လက်ပန်း, to strike, &c.

လက်ပွေခတ်, *v.* see လက်ပန်း, to strike, &c.

လက်ဖက်, (1) *v.* to fold in the hands or arms.

လက်ဖက်, (2) see လက်ဆွမ်း.

လက်ဖက်, (3) *n.* the tea leaf.

လက်ဖက်အိုး, *n.* a tea-pot.

လက်ဖက်ချင်း, *n.* a slender basket for the purpose of packing tea leaves.

လက်ဖက်ထင်, *n.* do.

လက်ဖက်ချောင်း, *n.* a bamboo filled with tea, given as a present at funerals.

လက်ဖမိုး, *n.* the back of the hand.

လက်ဖျံ, *n.* the arm between the wrist and elbow.

လက်ဖျောက်တီး, *v.* to snap, rub, or make a noise with the thumb and finger.

လက်ဖြစ်, *v.* to rub the thumb and finger together.

လက်ဖြစ်တီး, *v.* to make a noise by rubbing the thumb and finger together.

လက်ဖွဲ့, (1) *n.* a charm bound upon the arm.

လက်ဖွဲ့, (2) *v.* to bestow a portion, heritage, or dowry.

လက်ဖွဲ့ဥစ္စာ, *n.* a heritage, portion, dowry.

လက်မ, *n.* the thumb.

လက်မတင်, *n.* about the length, breadth, or size of the thumb.

လက်မည်း (လူ,) *n.* an executioner.

လက်မောင်း, *n.* the arm above the elbow.

လက်မှတ်, *n.* a certificate, signature.

လက်ယာ, or လက်ျာ, *n.* the right hand, or side.

လက်ယာနံတောင်း, *n.* the right side.

လက်ရ, *n.* what comes to hand, a prisoner, &c.

လက်ရပ်, *v.* to beckon with the hand.

လက်ညာနံတောင်း, *n.* the right side.

လက်ညာနံပါး, *n.* do.

လက်ရုံး, *n.* the arm.

လက်ရေး, *n.* a manuscript.

လက်ရေးပုံ, *n.* the copy of a handwriting.

လက်ရှက်, *v.* to join the hands, intertwine the fingers.

လက်ရှိန်က, *v.* to dance, that is, to move the hands with the feet, after the manner of eastern dancing.

လက်လည်, or လက်လယ်, *n.* the middle finger.

လက်လီအသေးဝိတ်, *v.* to retail, deal out by little and little.

လက်ဝါး, *n.* the palm of the hand.

လက်ဝါးဆုပ်, *v.* to cover with the palms of the hand.

လက်ဝါးကပ်, *n.* a cross, or any thing to which the palms of the hands are fastened.

လက်ဝါးကပ်တိုင်, *n.* do.

လက်ဝဲ, *n.* the left hand, or side.

လက်သစ်, *n.* a finger's breadth.

လက်သည်း, *n.* the finger nails.

လက်သန်း, *n.* the little finger.

လက်သမား, or လက်သွား, *n.* a carpenter.

လက်သမိုး, *n.* the back of the hand.

လက်သာ, *n.* a barber, ဆတ္တာသည်.

လက်သီး, *n* the fist.

လက်သီးနှင့်ထိုး, *v.* to box, or strike with the fist.

လက်သီးဆုပ်, *n.* the fist.

လက်သုင်း, *n.* the arm of a chair, staircase.

လက်သုံး, *n.* do.

လက်သူကြွယ်, *n.* the finger next to the little one.

လက်သဲ, *n.* the finger nails.

လပုတ်ဖန်း, *n.* the seizure of the moon by ပုတ်, or အသူရိန်, *i. e.* an eclipse.

လင်, *n.* a husband.

လင်္ကာ, *n.* any well-written piece of composition, poetry.

လင်ခွင်း, *n.* cymbals.

လင်ငေါင်, *n.* an adulterer, သတော်ကော် ၊ ရှောက်.

လင်ငေါင်ထား, *v.* to commit adultery, (as a man.)

လင်ပန်း, *n.* a tray, or any flat vessel of metal.

လင်တိုင်, *n.* a kind of fish.

လင်မယား, *n.* husband and wife.

လင်း, *n.* light ; *v.* to be light, bright, clear, ကြည်.

လင်းအား, *adv.* dawn of day, early in the morning.

လင်းအားကြီး, *adv.* do.

လင်းခါနီး, *adv.* do.

လင်းဆွဲ, *n.* the hanging bat, or flying fox.

လင်းတ, *n.* a vulture.

လင်းထို, *n.* the membrane on leather, or skin previous to tanning.

လင်နို့, *n.* the small mouse-sized bat.

လင်းပြန်, *adv.* head downwards, upside down.

လင်းမြီး, *n.* a small black imitation bird, having a short bill, and long tail.

လင်းယဉ်, (1) *n.* a sail of a ship or boat, &c.

လင်းယဉ်, (2) *n.* the top of a ship's mast.

လင်းဒေါ်, *n.* a species of hawk larger than the kite, an eagle.

လင်းပျံ, *n.* a species of fish.

လင်းလင်းရှိ, *v.* to be enlightened, have a knowledge of a subject.

လင်းကျ, *adv.* dawn of day, early in the morning.

လင်းလေး, (1) *n.* a bow from which arrows are discharged.

လင်းလေး, (2) *n.* Sagittarius.

လင်းလွန်း, *n.* the name of a certain tree.

လင်ဝက်, *n.* the largest kind of bat.

လင့်, (1) *n.* a stage, platform.

လင့်, (2) *v.* to tarry, wait for, ငံ့ ၊ ဝင့် ၊ စောင့်; to expect, anticipate, မျှော်.

လင့်, (3) (with မ prefixed to the root,) *v. affix,* expressing prohibition, as မသွားလင့်, go not.

လင့်ကစား, *v. affix,* though, as သွားလင့်ကစား, though he go.

လင့်စင်, *n.* a stage, platform; *also* a watch-tower, watch-house.

လင့်ပြီး, *v. affix,* sign of the pluperfect tense.

လင့်မည်, *v. affix,* sign of the second future tense.

လစ်, *v.* to leave behind, forget, mistake, to be lost, missing, မေ့လျော့ ၊ လျော့ ၊ သတိလစ် ၊ သတိလစ်ဟင်း. (*act.* လှစ်.)

လစ်ဟိုရှင်း, *v.* to be vacant, empty, opened, ရှင်း.

လစ်လတ်, *v.* do. (most commonly used.)

လစ်ထျူ (ရှိသည်,) *v.* to be doubtful, dubious, uncertain, at a stand about what to do or say.

လစ်ဟင်း, (1) *v.* see လစ်လတ်.

လစ်ဟင်း, (2) *v.* to be bewildered, stupefied, drunken.

လဆန်း, *n.* the waxing of the moon.

လဆန်းပက္ခ, see ပက္ခကာလတ်.

လဆုတ်, *n.* the waning of the moon.

လဆုတ်ပက္ခ, *n.* see ပက္ခကာလတ်.

လည်, (1) *v.* to turn, walk or move round, wander about, လည်သွား၊ လှည့်ပတ်.

လည်, (2) *v.* to understand, သိ၊ တတ်၊ နားလည်.

လည်, (3) *n.* the secret parts of men.

လည်, (4) *n.* the neck, throat.

လည်ကုတ်, *n.* the bottom of the back part of the neck, ဂုတ်ဆစ်.

လည်ချောင်း, *n.* the upper part of the alimentary canal, the gullet.

လည်ချောင်းရှည်, *n.* do. ရေမြို.

လည်ခြိုင်, *n.* the bottom of the neck.

လည်ဆံ, *n.* down or hair on the neck.

လည်တိုင်, *n.* the neck, throat.

လည်ပင်, *n.* do. ချောင်း.

လည်ပင်စည်း, *n.* a neckcloth.

လည်ပြည်း, *n.* a dewlap.

လည်မြို, *n.* the throat, gullet, ရေမြို၊ စားဝင်.

လည်ဆွဲ, *n.* a necklace, of any kind.

လည်း, (1) *conj.* and, also; သော်လည်း, though, notwithstanding.

လည်း, (2) *v.* to change, exchange, လည်.

လည်း, (3) *int. affix,* (see Grammar.)

လည်း, (4) *adv. affix,* also, (applied to any part of speech.)

လည်း, (5) *v. affix, subj. mood,* if; see လျှင်.

လည်း, (6) *v. affix,* sign of the second pers. imp. mood.

လည်း, (7) *v.* to lie, lean, be recumbent, လဲ.

လည်းကောင်း, *conj.* and, also, (by contraction ၎င်း, or ၎.)

လည်းလျောင်း, *v.* to lean, be reclined, low, in a recumbent posture, တိမ်း၊ လျောင်း.

လတ်, (1) *v.* to be fresh, good, new, beautiful, စိမ်း.

လတ်, (2) *v.* to be empty, vacant, exempt, without, လစ်၊ လွတ်၊ လွတ်လပ်. Hence အလတ်, *n.* emptiness, vacancy, disengagedness. အလတ်ရွယ်, or ရွယ်လတ်, middle age.

လတ်တလော, *adv.* in an instant, in a moment, instantly.

လတ္တံ့, or လတ်တံ့, *v. affix,* sign of the indicative mood, future tense.

လက်လတ်, or လတ်လတ်လန်းလန်း, *adv.* flushingly, gaudily.

လတ်လန်း, *v.* to be fresh, new, good, beautiful.

လထီးဆောင်း, *n.* halo, or disk of the moon.

လန်, *v.* to turn over, or round, capsize, ပြောင်းပြန်.

လန်း, (1) *v.* to gape, expand, be open, &c. see ပြဲ.

လန်း, (2) *v.* to be fresh, look beautiful, be verdant, လင်းလယ် ၊ လှ ၊ စိမ်း.

လန်းပြတ်, *v.* to be fresh, look beautiful, be verdant.

လန်းလန်း, *adv.* gaudily, flushingly.

လာဘ်, (1) *euph. affix,* mostly used before လော်.

လာဘ်, (2) *n.* profit, any thing gained or obtained, a blessing, ဆုလာဘ်.

လာဘ်, (3) *an astrological term.*

လာဘ်သာဘ်, *n.* any thing gained or obtained, (as a present.)

လာဘ်သာဘ်ပဏ္ဏာ, *n.* an offering, a gift.

လာဘ်သာဘ်ပဏ္ဏာရ, *v.* to get gain, obtain profit.

လာဘ်သာဘ်ပဏ္ဏာရောက်, *v.* do.

လပု, *n.* a hermaphrodite, သယောင်.

လပို့, *n.* the hump on the shoulders of cattle.

လပြည့်, *n.* full moon.

လပြည့်ကျော်, *n.* the moon when past the full.

လမုသီး, *n.* a kind of fruit growing in salt-water ground.

လမ်း, (1) *n.* a road, way, path.

လမ်း, (2) *v.* to step, move, သွား ၊ ရွေ့.

လမ်းကြား, *n.* a lane, small road, ကွေ့.

လမ်းကြောင်း, *n.* a road, path, way.

လမ်းခရီး, *n.* do. ခြီး.

လမ်းဆုံ, *n.* the end of a way, a confluence of ways.

လမ်းပြသည့်, *n.* a guide.

လမ်းမ, *n.* a main or principal road.

လမ်းမွှာ, *n.* a small road, or pathway.

လမ်းဝ, *n.* a bye-path, lane, the opening of a road.

လမ်းဆော်, *n.* do.

လယ်, (1) *v.* to understand, လည် ၊ နားလည်.

လယ်, (2) *n.* a field, paddy field.

လယ်ကွက်, *n.* rice fields marked out into parcels, an inclosure.

လယ်ခေါင်ရုံး, *n.* a kind of flower, destitute of fragrance.

လယ်ထွန်သမား, *n.* a ploughman.

လယ်ပြင်, *n.* an extensive field, or surface.

လယ်လုပ်, *v.* to plough or cultivate a field.

လယ်သည်, *n.* a husbandman.

လယ်သား, *n.* a countryman, in distinction from a townsman.

လရောင်, *n.* moon-light.

လဝန်းပေါ်, *n.* the rising moon.

လသာ, *v.* to be moon-light, the moon is beautiful.

လဟာ, (*Pali,*) *n.* vacuity, emptiness.

လဟုတာ, (*Pali,*) *n.* quickness, lightness, လျင်၊ချင်း.

လံ, *v.* to grow long, become extended, ရှည်.

လံထား, *v.* to tie up with a long string; to be appointed to a remote situation.

လာ, (1) *v.* to come, arrive, ရောက်.

လာ, (2) *int. affix*, used in a familiar manner.

လာလေ, *v. affix*, see လေ.

လား, (1) *v.* to go, move, go from, depart, သွား.

လား, (2) *n.* a mule, မြင်းလား.

လားချင်း, *n.* a transition from one state of existence to another, ဂတိ.

လားလား, *adv.* at all, as လားလားမပြု, he does nothing at all.

လိ, *part. aff.* see ဘွယ်.

လိင်, (1) *n.* a sort, kind.

လိင်, (2) *n.* a kind of turtle.

လိင်, (3) *n.* organs of generation, whether male or female.

လိင်သကတ်, (from လိင်္ဂ, a shape, and သကတ္တ, self,) *n.* identity, or one's own shape or features, in distinction from that of others.

လိတ်ကျည်, *n.* the name of a certain tree.

လိတ်လက, *adv.* glitteringly.

လိန်, *n.* the penis, လီး၊ တော၊ နိမိတ်.

လိပ်, (1) *n.* a title, signature, address, (as of a book or letter.)

လိပ်, (2) *n.* a turtle, tortoise.

လိပ်, (3) *v.* to roll up, or fold, ခေါက်၊ ရစ်.

လိပ်ပြာ, *n.* a butterfly, ပိလန်.

လိပွယ်, *part. affix*, see တွယ်.

လိဗန်, *n.* frankincense.

လိမ်, *v.* to twist, wrench, twist round, to use deceit.

လိမ်ညို, *v.* to dissemble, deceive, (applied to trade.)

လိမ္မာ, *v.* to be wise, cunning, prudent, knowing, ထက်.

လိမ္မော်သီး, *n.* a lemon, or orange.

လိမ်ထစ်, *v.* see လိမ်.

လိမ်လည်, *v.* to dissemble, play the hypocrite, ကောက်လိမ်.

လိမ်း, *v.* to spread, spread over, anoint, besmear, လူး ၊ ကျံ ၊ မံ.

လိမ်းသပ်, *v.* do.

လိမ့်, (1) *v.* to roll over and over, ဆိမ့်.

လိမ့်, (2) *a euph. affix.*

လီစယ်, *v.* to ask, enquire, interrogate, မေးမြန်း.

လီဆယ်, *v.* to plan, scheme, design, ခင်းကြင်း ၊ ကြံစည်.

လီး, *n.* the penis.

လီးဥ, *n.* the scrotum.

လီးမွေး, *n.* the hair about the genitals.

လု, (1) *v.* to plunder, take by force, seize at random.

လု, (2) *v. affix, future tense infinitive mood*, as သွားလု, about to go. This affix retains the same meaning whatever affixes of tense may be superadded; see Gram.

လုင်, *n.* an abbreviation of လုလင်, which see.

လုဆို, *v.* to contradict, dispute, ငြင်းခုံ.

လုဘ်, *v.* to make, perform, do, ပြု ၊ ကိုင်.

လုတ်, (2) *v.* to shake, tremble, တုန်; (*act.* ရှုတ်.)

လုတ်ကတ်, *v.* to be difficult of performance, ဆောကတ်.

လုတ်ကိုင်, *v.* to do, make, perform.

လုတ်ကျ, *v.* to fall, slip off, or away.

လုတ်ကျွေး, *v.* to serve, administer to, feed. Hence အလုတ်အကျွေး, *n.* a servant, attendant.

လုတ်သတ်, *adv.* tremblingly, shiveringly.

လုနီးပြီ, *v. affix*, about to be.

လုပ်, *v.* to do, make, perform, လုတ်.

လုပ်ကိုင်, *v.* to work, do work, perform.

လုပ်ကျင်း, (1) *n.* a gargle.

လုပ်ကျင်း, (2) *v.* to gargle the mouth.

လုပ်ကြံ, *v.* to destroy, kill, put to death.

လုပ်ဆေး, *n.* a gargle.

လုပ်ဆောင်, *v.* to work, do, do work, perform.

လုပ်ကျိုင်း, *n.* a burying place, သုသာန် ၊ သင်္ချိုင်း.

လုပ်ရည်ကြံရည်, *n.* skill, faculty.

လုမ်, (1) *v.* to cover, overspread, be concealed, covered.

လုမ်, (2) *v.* to be water-proof, air-tight, perfectly secure, ခြုံ ၊ လုံခြုံ.

လုမ်လ, *n.* see လုံ့လ.

လုယက်, *v.* to plunder, take by force, seize at random.

လုရက်, *v.* do.

လုလင်, *n.* an inferior officer, a sheriff, constable.

လုံ့လ, *n.* exertion, diligence, အားထုတ်. လုံ့လပြုသဖြင့်, by using diligence, by perseverance, by or through exertion.

လုံ, (1) *v.* to be warm.

လုံ, (2) *v.* to be tight, secure, safe.

လုံခြုံ, *v.* to be tight, secure; to cover, overspread.

လုံဝတ်, *adv.* all round, the whole of, around the circumference of any thing.

လုံပနီသီး, *n.* a kind of fruit.

လုံလုံ, *adv.* tightly, safely, securely.

လုံး, (1) a contraction of အလုံး, which see.

လုံး, (2) *v.* to wind, twist round, as into a ball.

လုံး, (3) an affix to nouns and verbs, and conveys the idea of wholly, entirely, all, the whole, &c. as တလျှောက်လုံး, all along; သင်္ဘောတစင်းလုံး, the whole ship.

လုံး, (2) *num. affix*, as အိုးနှစ်လုံး; two pots, (see Gram.)

လုံးထွေး, *v.* to wrestle, နပန်းလုံး.

လုံးပတ်, (1) *n.* a circuit, circumference, ပတ်လုံး.

လုံးပတ်, (2) *v.* to collect around, assemble, စု ၊ ဝေး ၊ ပေါင်း.

လုံးရင်း, *v.* do.

လူ, *n.* a man, mankind; sometimes used in a vague sense to mean the three orders of rational beings, viz. Men, Nats, and Bramhas.

လူစု, *n.* a collection of people, a multitude.

လူစေးနှဲ, *n.* a miser.

လူထွက်, *v.* to renounce the priesthood, and become a common man again.

လူပု, *n.* a dwarf, a man short in stature.

လူပြု, *v.* to perform the duties of a man, in distinction from those of a priest; to act like a man.

လူပျို, *n.* a young man.

လူပျိုနာ, *n.* the venereal disease.

လူယောင်, *n.* the appearance of a man, လူရောင်.

လူရှုပ်, *n.* a mob, riot, confused collection of people.

လူဝံ, *n.* an ourang-outang.

လူသငယ်, *n.* a child, children.

လူသေကောင်, *n.* a dead body, a corpse, အလောင်း.

လူး, (1) *n.* one kind of paddy, barley.

လူး, (2) *v.* to turn over, remove from side to side.

လူး, (3) *v.* to anoint, rub over, besmear, ကြိန်း လိမ်း. Hence အလူးလူး, *adv.* dirtily, filthily.

လူးစပါး, *n.* one kind of paddy, barley.

လူးလာ, *v.* to go backwards and forwards.

လူးလာသွား, *v.* do. Hence တလူးလာလာ, *adv.* backwards and forwards.

လေ, (1) *n.* wind.

လေ, (2) *v. affix, imper. or prec.* (see Gram.)

လေ, (3) *euph. aff.* used with nouns and verbs; ပြုလေပြီး, or ပြုလေခဲ့ပြီး, having, or had done.

လေ, (4) *v. affix*, persistive, as ရှိသည်လေ, it certainly is.

လေခတ်, *v.* the wind blows, or strikes, လေပုတ် ၊ လေတိုက်.

လေချွန်, *v.* to whistle.

လေညှင်း, *n.* a moderate breeze, a zephyr.

လေထကျင်, *n.* the pleurisy.

လေတက်, *n.* wind rising in the stomach.

လေတံခွန်, *n.* a paper-kite.

လေတုလာ, *n.* a species of rheumatism.

လေတိုက်, *v.* the wind blows, or strikes.

လေထုတ်, *v.* see ဆီးပေါက်.

လေနာနှိပ်စက်, *n.* the colic, flatulence.

လေပြင်း, *n.* a strong wind.

လေပြည်, *n.* a cool wind.

လေပြည့်နာ, *n.* the dropsy.

လေပြေ, *n.* a gentle breeze.

လေပွေ, *n.* a whirlwind.

လေမုန်တိုင်း, *n.* a tempest, hurricane.

လေရာရာ, *adv.* wherever, wheresoever.

လေလံ, *n.* an auction.

လေသာ, *n.* a window, because it pleasantly admits the wind, ပိတင်း.

လေသာတံခါး, *n.* do. ပြတင်း.

လေသွင်းတံခါး, *n.* do.

လေး, (1) *adj.* four.

လေး, (2) *v.* to fear, reverence, be in awe of, ထိ.

လေး, (3) *n.* a bow.

လေး, (4) *v.* to be heavy, ponderous. Hence အလေး, *n.* weight.

လေးချ, *v.* to discharge an arrow.

လေးကိုင်း, *n.* the rim or wooden part of a bow.

လေးစား, *v.* to fear, reverence.

လေးညှင်း, *n.* cloves.

လေးကြိုး, *n.* a bow-string.

လေးတင်, *v.* to draw a bow.

လေးထောင့်, *n.* four cornered.

လေးဒူး, *n.* the handle of a bow.

လေးနက်, *v.* to be pleasant, satisfying, cheering, အရာသည်လေးနက်သည်.

လေးပြစ်, *v.* to discharge arrows from a bow.

လေးမျက်နှာ, *n.* four points of the compass, four sides.

လေးမြင့်, see အခါထည်, *v.* to delay, be distant in time, be a long time, အခါလေးမြင့်.

လေးမြတ်, *v.* to love, esteem, respect, မြတ်နိုး၊ နှစ်သက်.

လေးမြား, *n.* an arrow, မြား.

လေးလန်, *v.* to be slow, to delay.

လေးသမား, *n.* an archer.

လေ့, *v.* to be acquainted with, accustomed to.

လေ့ကျက်, *v.* do.

လေ့ကျင့်, *v.* do.

လေ့ကျွန်း, *v.* do.

လေ့ကျွမ်းဝင်, *v.* to enter into an acquaintance with.

လေ့လာ, *v.* to be industrious, diligent, be perfect, or versed in, (as in learning,) be instructed ; to speak, order, direct.

လေ့လာကျေပြွံ, *v.* to be versed in, perfected, accomplished.

လဲ, (1) *v.* to change, exchange one thing for another. Hence အလဲလဲ, *adv.* interchangeably, by turns.

လဲ, (2) *int. affix*, see Gram.

လဲဖို့, *n.* a kind of soft woolly substance, used as stuffing for pillows, &c. ရှို.

လဲး, *v.* to fall, slide down, ကိုင်း ၊ ကျ ၊ လျှော.

လဲ့လဲ့, *adv.* an intensive to words of colour.

လော, *v.* to repeat, do again, ထပ်.

လော, (2) *v. affix, 2d pers. imperative.*

လော, (3) *interrogative aff.* used in a formal or reserved manner.

လောက်, (1) *v.* to be enough, sufficient, တန်.

လောက်, (2) *adv.* about, nearly ; သို့မျှလောက်, about so much ; အဘယ်မျှလောက်, so much ; how much? အလောက်, enough, so much, as much as, about so, or how much.

လောက်, (3) *n.* a maggot.

လောက်စာ, *n.* balls for a bow.

လောက်ပတီ, *n.* a sling.

လောက်လက်, *adj.* unsteady, moving, in motion.

လောက်လန်း, *n.* a small insect that darts about in the water, ဂုဏ်.

လောက်လေး, *n.* a bow for discharging balls.

လောက်သွဲ, *n.* a sling.

လောက, *n.* this world, mankind, ကမ္ဘာ.

လောကထံ, or လောကဓံ, (from လောကဓမ္မ,) *n.* what befals or happens to a person in this life, enumerated as follows, လာဘော ၊ အလာဘော ၊ ယသော ၊ အယသော ၊ နိန္ဒာ ၊ ပသံသာ ၊ သုခံ ၊ ဒုက္ခ ; these collectively are called လောကဓံရှစ်ပါး.

လောကဝတ်, *n.* customs, manners, courteous behaviour, polite attentions, politeness, ယွင်္ကါ.

လောကီ, *adj.* worldly, pertaining to this world merely, opposed to လောကုတ္တရာ.

လောကီဈာန်, *n.* certain miraculous powers, possessed by deities and their immediate disciples.

လောကုတ္တရာ, *n.* whatever pertains, or has reference to a future state.

လောင်, *v.* to burn, consume, be in a flame, to singe, တောက်.

လောင်လင်, *n.* restlessness, perplexity, distress.

လောင်း, (1) *v.* to pour out, pour over, into, or upon any thing, throw or cast water ; (*act.* လျှောင်း.)

လောင်း, (2) *v.* to cast as a bet, lay a wager.

လောင်းစား, *v.* to lay a wager, cast as a bet, &c.

လောင်းတန်း, *v.* to guess, bet, lay a wager.

လောင်းတန်းဥစ္စာ, *n.* goods or money, employed in a bet or wager.

လောဗန်, *n.* frankincense.

လောဘ, *n.* passion, desire, တဏှာ.

လောလော, *adv.* quickly ; twingeingly, as pain.

လောဝါး, *n.* the pole or bamboo of a cage used to allure birds.

လောဟကုမ္ဘီ, *n.* see under ငရဲ.

လော်ယာ, *v.* to be unsteady, unstable ; also to do, or speak what a person ought not, လျှပ်ပေါ်.

လို, (1) *v.* to desire, wish, ရုံချင်း ၊ အလိုရှိ. အလိုက်, of one's own accord.

လို, (2) *v. affix*, implying similarity or likeness, as သွားသည့်လို, like going.

လိုက်, (1) *v.* to follow, accompany, ထပ် ၊ ပါ ၊ ထံ.

လိုက်, (2) *v. affix*, sign of the imperative or precative.

လိုက်, (3) (from ရုံ and လေ,) *a euphonic affix.*

လိုက်နာ, (1) *v.* to sting.

လိုက်နာ, (2) *v.* to attend to one's instructions, follow advice.

လိုဏ်, *n.* a cave ; niche, ဥမင် ၊ ဂူ.

လိုဏ်မုထိတော်, *n.* a pyramid with one, or more long caves, or excavations.

ရှိရှိ, *affix*, signifies a little like, a slight similarity, as သွားသည်ရှိရှိ, a little like going.

ရှိုး, *v.* to cause to enter, shove in and out, push in, ရှိုးသွင်း.

ရှိ့, *v. affix*, because.

ရှိ့လည်း, *v. affix*, do.

လျ, *v.* to become small, taper away, become thin, narrow, spin out, သွယ်၊ ငိုက်.

လျလျချပ်ချပ်, *adv.* an intensive to words of thinness.

လျက်, (1) *v.* to suck, lick, taste, စုပ်.

လျက်, (2) *v. affix, subj.* as, ပြုလျက်, if he have done, or was doing.

လျက်, (3) *v. affix, past tense,* as ပြုလျက်, having done, or when he had done.

လျက်, (4) *continuative, v. affix,* as ပြုလျက်, while he does, or is doing.

လျင်, (1) *v.* to be quick, swift, fast, မြန်.

လျင်, (2) *n.* a kind of sauce for rice.

လျင်, (3) *a euphonic affix.*

လျင်စွာ, *adv.* quickly, swiftly.

လျင်ထံ, or လျင်ခံ, *adv.* do.

လျင်လျင်, *adv.* do.

လျင်လျား, *v.* to be quick of understanding.

လျစ်လျူ, (1) *v.* to be exempt from passion, to be in a state of indifference with regard to objects.

လျစ်လျူ, (2) *adj.* tolerable, moderate, middling.

လျပ်, *adv.* an intensive to words of thinness, as ပါးလျပ်သည်, it is extremely thin, လွှး.

လျပ်လျပ်, (1) *adv.* glitteringly.

လျပ်လျပ်, (2) waving about, as a flag.

လျာ, (1) *an affix,* all, the whole, (as တသက်လျာ, during life,) လုံး၊ တိုင်တိုင်.

လျာ, (2) *affix,* for, for the sake of.

လျား, *v.* see လျှား.

လျှောကား, *n.* the upper transverse beams of a house.

လျောက်, (1) *n.* the longitudinal timbers of a roof.

လျောက်, (2) *v.* to be proper, fit, suitable, လျော်.

လျောက်ပတ်, *v.* do. Hence အလျောက်, *n.* according to the ability of any thing.

လျောင်း, *v.* to lie down, lean, be recumbent.

လျော့, *v.* to be loosened, enfeebled, exhausted ; to become little, recede, subside, နည်း ; to diminish in bulk, value, price, or quantity, ယုတ် ; see ရှော့. Hence အလျော့, *n.* a fine, deduction, discount.

လျော်, (1) *v.* to pay damages, make up loss, repay.

လျော်, (2) *v.* to be fit, suitable, proper, beautiful, တော် ၊ သင့်.

လွင်, (1) *v.* to be flat, level, even, ညီ.

လွင်, (2) *n.* an extensive tract of land, fit for cultivation, ကွင်း.

လွင်, (3) *v.* to be glossy, fine, shining, beautiful, any thing new.

လွင်ကျွင်း, *n.* any cleared, open, level spot, &c.

လွင်တလင်း, *n.* do.

လွင်တီးခေါင်, *n.* a soil or field, on which nothing grows.

လွင်မှို, *n.* see တဲ.

လွင့်, (1) *v.* to be blown away, sailed, departed, as by the wind.

လွင့်, (2) *v.* to go outside, or without, recede, depart, ပါး ၊ ပြင် လွင့် ; (*act.* လွှင့်.)

လွတ်, (1) *v.* to be free, exempt from, emancipated, delivered, ကျွတ် ၊ လတ် ၊ ကင်း.

လွတ်, (2) *v.* to be disengaged, unemployed. Hence အလွတ်နေ, to be disengaged.

လွတ်, (3) *v.* to be unoccupied, empty, as a room, လပ်.

လွတ်နေရာ, *n.* see စနည်း.

လွတ်လတ်, *v.* see လွတ်.

လွတ်လွတ်, *adv.* see ထွတ်လွတ်.

လွတ်လွတ်ရက်ရက်, *adv.* generously, liberally.

လွန်, (1) *v.* to be exceeded, surpassed, gone by or beyond, to excel, ကဲ ၊ သာ ၊ ကျော် ၊ ကြူး.

လွန်, (2) *n.* a rope, ကြိုး ၊ ကြိုးလွန်.

လွန်, (3) *n.* a gimblet, piercer, awl.

လန်, (4) *n.* a kind of tree.

လွန်, (5) *v.* to die, သေ ၊ သေလွန်.

လွန်ကြင်, *n.* a kind of bird.

လွန်ပြန်, *v.* to pass by, go from place to place.

လွန်ဘူ, *n.* a gimblet, or any thing of the kind.

လွန်သေ, *v.* is dead, (implying some distance of time.)

လွန်း, *n.* a weaver's shuttle.

လွန့်, *v.* to move, stir, twist about, လှုပ် ၊ လိမ်.

လွမ်း, *v.* to remember, recollect, reflect upon, regret the loss of, တမ်း ၊ အောင်းမေ့ ၊ တ ၊ တမ်းတ.

လွမ်းချင်း, *n.* a kind of song, တေးချင်း ၊ သီချင်း.

လွမ်းဆွတ်, *v.* see လွမ်း.

လွမ်းတန်း, *v.* see လွမ်း.

လွယ်, (1) *v.* to hang over, swing, be suspended, ဆွဲ ၊ ဆိုင်း ၊ ငိုး.

လွယ်, (2) *v.* to be easy of obtaining or doing, မခက်.

လွယ်, (3) *v.* to carry, as a wallet, over the shoulder and under the arm, ဆောင် ၊ ယူ.

လွယ်ကူ, *v.* to be easy of obtaining.

လွယ်ငိုး, *v.* to suspend, as a burden from the head.

လွယ်လင့်တကူ, *adv.* quickly, easily.

လှော့ လှ, *adj.* satisfactory, healthy, void of blemish.

လွဲ, (1) *v.* to err, to be incorrect, be passed by, or on one side, or over, to be inclined, move obliquely, to slip, backslide.

လွဲ, (2) *v.* to suspend, hang up, တွဲ ၊ ဆွဲ.

လွဲ, (3) *v.* to be different, diverse, ကွဲ ၊ မတူ.

လွဲ, (4) *v.* to descend, as the sun from his meridian.

လှ, (1) *v.* to be handsome, pretty, beautiful, ရွှန်.

လှ, (2) *v.* *affix*, very, as ကြီးလှသည်, it is very great.

လှ်, *n.* an abbreviation of လည်.

လှင်, *n.* a stick, cudgel; the shaft of a carriage or cart.

လှင်ကန်, *n.* do.

လှင်တန်, *n.* the largest, or lowest part of a branch; a ruler, short stick.

လှစ်, *v.* to be, or make vacant, ဟ; to open, ဖွင့်.

လှည်း, (1) *n.* a carriage, or cart.

လှည်း, (2) *v.* to put or lay down; to throw, cast, or cut down, ထိတ် ၊ ခုတ်; to strike, as colours, when an army is defeated.

လှည်း, (3) *v.* to sweep, as a floor.

လှည်း, (4) *v.* to feel uncomfortable, have a slight pain, ကိုက် ၊ ဆာ.

လှည်းအိမ်, *n.* the body of a cart.

လှည်းဦးစွပ်, *n.* a ring which secures the shaft of a cart to the yoke.

လှည်းကုန်သည်, *n.* a cart-maker.

လှည်းကြောင်း, *n.* a cart path or track.

လှည်းရုံ, *n.* a wooden shovel, with the handle in the side.

လှည်းချ, *v.* see လှည်း, to put, or lay down, &c. to strike, as colours, &c.

လှည်းစပ်ဘိုင်, *n.* the sides or railing of a cart.

လှည်းထား, *v.* to put or lay down, to throw, cut or cast down; to strike, as colours, when an army is defeated.

လှည်းပေါင်း, *n.* the covering of a cart.

လှည်းဘီး, *n.* a wheel of a cart, &c. ဘိန်း ၊ စက်.

လှည်းရှုး, *n.* the owner of a cart, a cartman, လှည်းရှင်.

လှည်းဝင်ရိုး, *n.* an axletree.

လှည်းသမား, *n.* a cart-maker.

လှည့်, (1) *v.* see ချေ, to pulverize, &c.

လှည့်, (2) *v.* to turn, turn round, over, back, or upside down, လှန် ၊ ပြန်.

လှည့်, (3) *v.* to walk, ဝတ်.

လှည့်, (4) *v.* to encircle, encompass. Hence အလှည့်, *n.* a turn; အလှည့်သင့်, to come to one's turn; အလှည့်အလှည့်, *adv.* by turns; နှစ်ရက်တလှည့်, a turn every other day.

လှည့်စား, *v.* to deceive, impose upon, lie, မုသာဝါဒ.

လှည့်ပတ်, *v.* to walk backward and forward, encircle, encompass, peregrinate, walk around, ဝန်း ၊ ရစ်.

လှည့်ဖြား, *v.* to entice, excite, flatter, or promise with an intention of deceiving, ဖြားယောင်း ၊ တိုက်တွန်း ၊ ချော့ ၊ လှည့်စား ၊ လှည့်ပတ်; to use false or flattering language.

လှည့်လှည့်, *adv.* (from လှည့်,) in an encircling, encompassing manner; round about, this way and that, upside down, &c.

လျည့်သွား, *v.* see လျည့်ပတ်.

လှန်, *v.* to turn over, as a leaf or fold, to open, ဖွင့်; to return, ပြန်.

လှန်း, *v.* to spread out, as in the sun; extend, as the hand, expand, lay out.

လှန်းလျည့်, *an imperative termination.*

လှန့်, *v.* to frighten, make afraid, ခြောက်.

လှစ်, (1) *v.* to open, or be opened, ဟ.

လှစ်, (2) *v.* to be light, vain, unsubstantial.

လှပ, *v.* to be handsome, fit, proper, nice, လှ ၊ လျောက်ပတ်.

လှမ်း, (1) *v.* to reach out, stretch out the hand towards an object for the purpose of receiving it.

လှမ်း, (2) *v.* to step forward, advance.

လှံ, *n.* a spear.

လှံရိုး, *n.* the handle of a spear.

လှံထိုး, *v.* to throw as a spear.

လှံထိုးမိ, *v.* to throw as a spear, and hit the object.

လှာ, *a euphonic affix.*

လှို့, *v.* to be small, dwarfish, ကျုံ.

လှီး, *v.* to cut up, slice, pare off, သွာ ၊ ထွာ ၊ ရှင်း.

လှီးဖြတ်, *v.* do.

လှီးယောက်, *v.* do.

လှုပ်, *v.* to shake, tremble, လှုတ်.

လှုပ်ရှား, *v.* do.

လှုံ, (1) *v.* to take refuge in, adhere to, မှီ.

လှုံ, (2) *v.* to warm as by a fire.

လှုံခင်, *n.* the uvula.

လှုံ့, *v.* to rouse, excite, move to action, နှိုးဆော်.

လှူ, *v.* to give, bestow, (clerical,) ကပ် ၊ ပေး.

လှူဒါန်း, *n.* a gift, or offering.

လှူဒါန်းသည်, *n.* one who bestows a gift, or makes an offering.

လှူတန်း, *v.* to bestow a gift, make an offering.

လှေ, *n.* a boat.

လှေဦး, *n.* the prow of a boat.

လှေစပ်, *n.* the wash-board of a boat.

လှေထက်, *n.* a boat of any description.
လှေတုံး, *n.* any large clumsy boat.
လှေပဲ့, *n.* the stern of a boat.
လှေမှူး, *n.* the commander of a boat.
လှေလောင်း, *n.* an unfinished boat, the hull of a boat.
လှေလှော်, *n.* the paddle or oar of a boat.
လှေသင်္ဘော, *n.* a ship.
လှေး, *v.* to be small, diminished, ယုတ် ၊ လျော့.
လှေကား, *n.* steps or stairs, a ladder.
လှေကားထစ်, *n.* the steps of stairs, or of a ladder.
လွှေ့, *v.* to fly, or blow away, as chaff; recede, လွင့်.
လှည်း, *n.* a carriage, or cart.
လှည်းဘီး, *n.* the wheel of a cart.
လှည်းဘိန်း, *n.* do.
လှည်းဝင်ရိုး, *n.* an axletree.
လှည်းသန်, *n.* the shaft of a cart.
လှည်းသမား, *n.* a carter.
လှဲ့, *v.* to change, turn, &c. see လှည့်.
လျှောက်, *v.* to increase, add to, ထပ် ၊ ကန်း ၊ သာ.
လှောင်, (1) *v.* to secure, shut up, imprison.
လှောင်, (2) *n.* a prison, ထောင် ၊ နှောင်အိမ်.
လှောင်, (3) *v.* to pour, pour into, or upon, to introduce, cause to enter, သွင်း ၊ ထား.
လှောင်အိမ်, *n.* a prison, place of confinement.
လှောင်ထား, *v.* to secure, put into, shut up, imprison.
လှော်, (1) *v.* to paddle, as a boat, stir up, stir about, as to parch rice, ရက် ၊ နှဲ့.
လှော်, (2) *v.* to associate, keep company with, ပေါင်း.
လှော်ကားလှေ, *n.* a boat of state, having a very high stern, the ornaments of which denote the owner's rank in office.
လှော်လှေ, *n.* a boat which is propelled with oars, a row-boat.
ရှိုက်, (1) *v.* to excavate, hollow, or scoop out, ဖေါင်း.
ရှိုက်, (2) *v.* to pant, breathe quick, ဒိုး ၊ ဖို.
ရှိုက်, (3) *v.* to feel uneasy, uncomfortable, လှည်း ၊ ဟာ.
ရှိုက်လှည်း, *v.* to feel uncomfortable, uneasy.

လှိုင်, (1) *v.* to diffuse, or spread, as perfume; to perfume; to extend, ပြန့် ၊ ပြိုင်.

လှိုင်, (2) *n.* a cave, ဥမင်.

လှိုင်ခေါင်း, *n.* do.

လှိုင်ဝ, *n.* do.

လှိုင်ဂှင်း, *n.* do.

လှိုင်း, (1) *n.* a wave, or billow, တံပိုး.

လှိုင်းတံပိုး, *n.* do.

လှိုင်း, (2) *n.* a sheaf, bundle, as of grain, &c. ကောက်လှိုင်း.

လျှ, *v.* to be thin, not thick.

လျှင်, (1) *v. affix, past tense,* as သွားလျှင်, having gone, or when he had gone.

လျှင်, (2) *v. affix, subj. mood,* as သွားလျှင်, if he go, if he have gone, &c.

လျှင်ထန်, *n.* a hand weapon, a cudgel, stick, used for the purpose of driving, နှင်တံ.

လျှင်း, *v. affix,* as, while, as သွားလျှင်း, while he goes.

လျှဉ်လူ, *adv.* a little, in a small degree.

လျှတ်ပေါ်, *v.* to do any thing improperly.

လျှန်, *v.* to ascend, glide, as a flame, to roll, as waves or smoke, to overflow.

လျှန်သွား, *v.* do.

လျှပ်, (1) *n.* lightning.

လျှပ်စစ်, *n.* do.

လျှပ်စစ်နွယ်, *n.* do.

လျှပ်ပြက်, *v.* to lighten.

လျှပ်စစ်ထပြက်, *n.* a flash of lightning.

လျှပ်, (2) *v.* to bring a person into trouble or distress for the sake of gain, ပြတ်.

လျှပ်စား, *n.* profit arising from thus bringing a person into trouble.

လျှပ်ပြတ်, *v.* to bring a person into trouble for the sake of gain.

လျှပ်, (3) *v.* to be thin, like paper, လွှာ ၊ ပါး.

လျှပ်လျှပ်, *adv.* thinly, လွှာလွှာ; *also,* instantaneously, immediately, (prefixed to words of action.)

လျှပ်, (4) *v.* to scorch, singe.

လျှပ်, (5) *v.* to be worthless, vain, unsubstantial.

လျှပ်ပေါ်, *v.* to be vain, worthless, unsubstantial, improper.

လျှံ, *v.* to ascend, glide, as fire or a flame, to flame, burn brightly, shine; to roll, as waves or smoke, တောက် ၊ လွှမ်း.

လျှာ, (1) *v.* to decide, fix or settle the mind upon an object.

လျှာ, (2) *n.* the tongue, *(pron.* ရှာ,) နှုတ်.

လျှာခင်, *n.* the uvula, ဆခင်.

လျှား, (sometimes written လျား,) *v.* to be long, in regard to time or distance, ရှည်.

လျှော, *v.* to slip, slide off, glide down, ရှော.

လျှောက်, (1) *v.* to speak, utter, (as a petition,) to deliver a speech in a regular form, to address, တင် ၊ ပြော.

လျှောက်ထား, *v.* do.

လျှောက်စာ, *n.* a written address, or petition.

လျှောက်, (2) *v.* to walk or cross over, as over a bridge, plank, &c. (sometimes written ရှောက်.)

လျှောက်, (3) *v.* to slip, or slide along.

လျှော့, *v.* to make loose, diminish, abate; to fall, subside.

လျှော်, *v.* to wash, as clothes; to rub or scour, as the head in bathing, &c. ဖွပ် ၊ ဆေး; see ရှော်.

လျှို, *v.* to pierce, thrust through, string, cause to enter, to weave, ထောက် ၊ ထိုး ၊ သီ.

လျှိုး, *v.* to penetrate, enter, go in, ငုံ ၊ ဝင်.

လျှိုး, *v.* to stoop, bow down.

လျှို့, *v.* to hide, conceal, ဝှက်.

လျှို့ဝှက်, *v.* do.

လွှ, *n.* a saw.

လွှင်, *v.* to be glossy, bright, beautiful, handsome, ပြောင် ၊ တောက် ၊ ချော.

လွှင့်, *v.* to cause to depart, leave, sail, as by the wind; to scatter, disperse to a distance, to scatter to the wind, နှင် ၊ လေ ၊ ပြေ.

လွှတ်, (1) *v.* to emancipate, make free, deliver, send, save.

လွှတ်, (2) *n.* a house of lords, or where the ministers of state assemble, ရွှေလွှတ်တော်.

လွှတ်တော်, *n.* the king's supreme court.

လွှန်, *v.* to cause to exceed, excel, surpass; to step, or cross over, pass by, go beyond bounds, transgress.

လွှန်ကဲ, *v.* do.

လွှန်း, *v.* to cover, overspread, shut up.

လွှမ်း, *v.* to cover, overspread, shut up, ပိတ် ၊ ဖုံး.

လွှမ်းမိုး, *v.* to overspread, cover, overwhelm.

လွှာ, (1) *v.* to be thin, like paper, ပါး ၊ လျှပ်.

လွှာ, (2) *v.* to shave, slice off, cut in slices, လွှာ ၊ လှီး ၊ ချွေ ၊ ခြင်း.

လွှာ, (3) *num. auxiliary*, as အရွက်နှစ်လွှာ, two leaves.

လွှာလွှာ, *adv.* thinly.

လွှား, (1) *v.* to jump up, or over, as upon a horse, ခုန် ၊ ကျော်.

လွှား, (2) *n.* a large square shield, ကာ.

လွှား, (3) *v.* to fan a person, ယပ်ခတ်.

လွှဲ, (1) *v.* to cause to pass by, or on one side, or beyond; to err, disobey, မှား ၊ လွှဲဖယ်.

လွှဲ, (2) *v.* to transfer business.

လွှဲ, (3) *v.* to discharge a debt to another, by paying his creditor.

လွှဲ, (4) *v.* to swing the arms as in walking, or as a person on a rope.

လွှဲဖယ်, *v.* see လွှဲ, to cause to pass by, &c.

## ဝ.

ဝ, (1) *n.* an entrance, opening; as တံခါးဝ, the entrance of a door; လမ်းဝ, the entrance of a road.

ဝ, (2) *v.* to be fat, corpulent, bulky, ထွား ၊ ဖြော ၊ ကြီး ၊ ပွ.

ဝ, (3) *v.* to be satisfied, have enough, sufficient, plenty, ဝန် ၊ တော ၊ ပြည့်.

ဝဖြော, *v.* to be plenty, abundant.

ဝက်, (1) *v.* to divide into equal parts; (see ချွမ်း;) တဝက်, one half, or one part.

ဝက်, (2) *n.* a hog, swine.

ဝက်အူ, *n.* a screw.

ဝက်အူကျစ်, *v.* to turn a screw.

ဝက်အူလိန်, *n.* a screw.

ဝက်ဂွမ်း, *n.* picked cotton, ဝါဂွမ်း.

ဝက်ကြွပ်, *n.* a kind of plant.

ဝက်ခြင်, *n.* a small kind of vermin, lying under the skin in different parts of the face.

ဝက်ခြုပ်, *n.* a pimple.

ဝက်ခြုတ်, *n.* small vermin squeezed from the nose.

ဝက်စွယ်နှားပင်း, *n.* a boar's tusk which is solid, used as a charm.

ဝက်နှစ်, *n.* the 12th year in a cycle of 12 years.

ဝက်ပေါင်, *n.* the leg or thigh of a swine, a ham.

ဝက်ရူး, *n.* a species of insanity ; under the influence of which a person makes a noise like a hog.

ဝက်လက်, *n.* the leg or shoulder of a swine.

ဝက်လိန်, *n.* a screw.

ဝက်ဝန်, *n.* a bear.

ဝက်ဝံ, *n.* do.

ဝက်သက်, *n.* measles.

ဝင်, (1) *n.* race, descendant; history, (applied only to persons.)

ဝင်, (2) *n.* to penetrate, enter, go in, ထိုး ၊ ငုတ်.

ဝင်္ကပါ, *n.* the mountain to which Wathandria was banished.

ဝင်ရိုး, *n.* an axletree, ရဟတ်ရိုး.

ဝင်လာ, *v.* to enter, penetrate, invade.

ဝင်သား, *n.* attendants on governors or kings, swordsmen.

ဝင်း, (1) *n.* a fence, enclosure, တံ့.

ဝင်း, (2) *v.* to shine, glitter, be brilliant, be yellow, ထိန် ၊ တောက် ၊ ပြောင် ၊ လျှံ ၊ ထွန်း. Hence တဝင်းဝင်းတထိန်ထိန်, *adv.* brilliantly, glitteringly.

ဝင်းကာ, *v.* to arrange, as a fence.

ဝင်းခင်း, *v.* to arrange, put in order, as guards, troops, &c.

ဝင်းခတ်, *v.* to fence, make a fence.

ဝင်းရံ, *v.* to set or place around, place in order, as a body guard, &c.

ဝင်းရိုး, *n.* a fence, yard ; a guard, suite.

ဝင်းသား, *n.* see ဝင်သား.

ဝင့်, *v.* to spin, draw out, extend, ဝိုက် ၊ ငင်.

ဝင့်ရိုး, *n.* see ဝင်ရိုး.

ဝစံ, (*Pali,*) *n.* a word.

ဝစီမုခံ, *n.* an exordium, introduction, စကားဦး.

ဝစနာ, *n.* a word, speech, စကား.

ဝဉ္စနာ, *v.* to deceive, လှည့်စား.

ဝုဋ္ဌိ, *v.* to rain ; *n.* rain, မိုးဆစ်ရွာခြင်း.

ဝဋ္ဋ, (1) *n.* transmigration ; passing from one state of existence to another, သံသရာစက်.

ဝဋ္ဋ, (2) *n.* situation or circumstances, in one state of existence, corresponding with the character formed in a previous state ; the influence of past good or bad deeds.

ဝဋ္ဋ, (3) *n.* a deed, action, ကံ၊ အကျင့်.

ဝဋ္ဋ, (4) *n.* a duty, or that which a man is naturally or morally bound to perform, such as a subject to his king, a slave to his master, children to parents, &c. ဝဋ္ဋတရား.

ဝဋ္ဋခံ, *v.* to receive or suffer the reward of former deeds.

ဝဋ္ဋစံစား, *v.* to enjoy the happiness which results from the performance of former good deeds.

ဝဋ္ဋဆင်းရဲ, *v.* to be poor, destitute, indigent, as a consequence of former bad deeds.

ဝဋ္ဋတရား, *n.* see ဝဋ္ဋ, a duty, &c.

ဝဋ္ဋကျက်ပြု, *v.* to be habitual in the performance of duties, သောက်တည်.

ဝဋ္ဋပြု, *v.* to perform one's duty, be obedient, pay respect to.

ဝဋ္ဋဖြစ်, *v.* to become a duty.

ဝတ်, (1) *v.* to remain, stay, (*respectful,*) ကျိန်းဝတ်၊ နေ.

ဝတ်, (2) *v.* to sleep, lie down, (*respectful,*) ကျိန်းစက်.

ဝတ်, (3) *n.* business, employment, work, provision, articles, appendages, အကျင့်.

ဝတ်, (4) *v.* to dress, put on, decorate. Hence အဝတ်, *n.* clothes, dress.

ဝတ်, (5) *v.* to tie or bind on, ဆွဲ.

ဝတ်စွန်း, *n.* the border, or end of a garment.

ဝတ်ဆင်, *v.* to tie or bind on, ဆွဲ.

ဝတ်ဆံ, (1) *n.* the stamina of a flower, ဆူးဝန်း.

ဝတ်ဆံ, (2) *n.* an ornament of flowers, or of any kind.

ဝတ, (*Pali,*) *adj.* unstable, not permanent, ဆန္ဒာ.

ဝတ္ထု, (1) *n.* a religious story or history.

ဝတ္ထု, (2) *n.* goods, things ; reason, cause ; an effect, ဥစ္စာ. This term is used by priests of Boodh, to signify gold, silver, &c. because they are obliged to look upon it as an inferior article, အသပြာ.

ဝတ္ထုကာမ, see ကာမ.

ဝတ်ပြုည်, *v.* to worship, pay respect to, ပူဇော်ရှိခိုး.

ဝတ်မိုဃ်, *n.* a spot of ground bestowed for religious purposes, မိုဃ်မြေ.

ဝတ်မြိတ်, *n.* the end or border of a garment.

ဝတ်မြေ, *n.* see ဝတ်မိုဃ်.

ဝတ်လုံ, *n.* a cloak, great coat.

ဝတ်လဲ, *n.* a garment, robe.

ဝတ်သန့်စကောင်း, *n.* good things, good food and raiment.

ဝဒညူ, (1) *n.* large offerings, အပေးအကမ်းများ.

ဝဒညူ, (2) *v.* to be accustomed to use pleasant or agreeable language, သာယာစကားဆိုတတ်သည်.

ဝန်, (1) *n.* a burden, cargo, load, goods.

ဝန်, (2) *n.* an office.

ဝန်ကိုပြု, *v.* to commission, order, direct.

ဝန်ကျုံးသူ, *n.* one who sustains an office.

ဝန်ကြီး, *n.* a prime minister, of which there are eight, viz. တွင်းဝန်, four, and ပြင်ဝန်, four ; or four internal, and four external : these ministers are frequently called မင်းကြီး.

ဝန်ခံ, *v.* to consent, agree to, comply with.

ဝန်ချ, *v.* to unlade, disburden.

ဝန်ချုပ်, *n.* an officer next in authority to the king.

ဝန်တင်, *v.* to load, place a burden upon.

ဝန်တို, *v.* to be of a little mind, unwilling to part with any thing, greedy, covetous.

ဝန္ဒာမိ, (*Pali,*) *v.* to worship, bow down.

ဝန်ရို, *n.* a pelican, ဝန်လို.

ဝန်ရို့, *n.* a gatherer of taxes, a publican, ငွေတော်ခို့ဝန်.

ဝန်လေး, *v.* to be important, weighty, burthensome.

ဝန်ထိ, *n.* a kind of bird.

ဝန်း, (1) *v.* to assemble round, go round, encircle, hem in, ဝိုင်း ၊ ရံ.

ဝန်း, (2) *n.* a circumference, the horizon, ဝန်းကြင် ၊ အဝန်း ၊ အဝိုင်း.

ဝန်းကြင်, *n.* a circuit, circumference ; a district, an adjacent country. Hence အဝန်း, a circle ; အိမ်ဝန်းကြင်, round the house ; တဝန်းတလျှာ, a division, part, portion ; (see ပတိထည်.)

ဝန်းတား, *v.* to assemble round, hem in, go round, &c.

ဝန်းဆီး, *v.* do.

ဝနံ, *(Pali,)* *n.* a forest.

ဝန္ဒနာ, *n.* worship, reverence, respect, ရှိခိုးခြင်း.

ဝန္ဒီ, *n.* a panegyrist.

ဝနိတာ, *n.* a woman ; a servant.

ဝပ်, (1) *v.* to be prostrate, be recumbent, ဝပ်ငုံ့.

ဝပ်, (2) *v.* to bow the body, in reverence, ယှပ်.

ဝပ်, (3) *v.* to become fixed, steadfast, ငြိမ် ၊ ခိုင်ခံ့ ; to become settled, quiet, သေဝပ်.

ဝပ်ငုံ့, *v.* to prostrate, be recumbent.

ဝပ်ထီးဝေါ, *adv.* disrespectfully, irreverently.

ဝပ်သွား, *v.* to creep, as on the belly ; be prostrate on the face, as before superiors, to do obeisance, be obsequious.

ဝပ်ဝင်ပျး, *v.* to enter under, stoop underneath.

ဝပြော, *v.* to be full, have sufficiency, be satisfied.

ဝမ်း, (1) *n.* the belly, abdomen.

ဝမ်း, (2) *n.* the fœces, ordure, မစင်.

ဝမ်းကျ, (1) *n.* a looseness of the bowels.

ဝမ်းကျ, (2) *v.* to have a looseness of the bowels.

ဝမ်းကြက်ကြက်, *v.* to be empty bellied, hungry.

ဝမ်းခေါင်း, *n.* the cavity of the belly.

ဝမ်းချိုင်, (1) *n.* costiveness.

ဝမ်းချိုင်, (2) *v.* to be costive.

ဝမ်းချ, *v.* to purge, produce purging.

ဝမ်းဆွဲ, *n.* a midwife.

ဝမ်းတို, *v.* to be covetous, illiberal, ထိုစိတ်.

ဝမ်းနည်း, *v.* to grieve, be dissatisfied, distressed, displeased, မ ညစ်ထမ်း.

ဝမ်းနည်း, *v.* to grieve, complain, be dissatisfied.

ဝမ်းနုတ်, *v.* to purge, produce purging.

ဝမ်းပန်းသာ, *v.* to rejoice, be delighted, ရွှင်မြူး.

ဝမ်းပိတ်, (1) *n.* costiveness.

ဝမ်းပိတ်, (2) *v.* to be costive.

ဝမ်းဘဲ, *n.* a duck.

ဝမ်းဗိုး, *n.* the fœtus, ကလလ.

ဝမ်းဖြစ်, *v.* to be inclined, disposed to, desire.

ဝမ်းမြောက်, *v.* to rejoice, be delighted, ရွှင်မြူး.

ဝမ်းရွှင်, *v.* do.

ဝမ်းသက်, *v.* to have a looseness of the bowels.

ဝမ်းသာ, *v.* to rejoice, be delighted.

ဝမ်းသွား, *v.* to evacuate the intestines naturally.

ဝယ်, (1) *v.* to purchase, ယူ၊ ဖြမ်း.

ဝယ်, (2) *n.* *affix*, in, within.

ဝရဇိန်, *n.* thunderbolt, မိုဃ်းကြိုးစက်.

ဝရီး, *n.* an uncle, mother's brother, ဦးရီး.

ဝဏ္ဏန်, *n.* see ကမ္ဗဏ္ဍာန်း.

ဝဿာ, *n.* the rainy season.

ဝသီ, *v.* to have a multitude of wives, be vulgar, obscene.

ဝသုန်, *n.* the earth.

ဝသုန္ဒရာ, *n.* the earth.

ဝသုန္ဒရေ, (1) *n.* the earth.

ဝသုန္ဒရေ, (2) *n.* the Nat who watches over the earth, မြေစောင့်နတ်.

ဝဂ္ဂါ, *(Pali,) n.* a division, bounded part.

ဝံ, *n.* applied to animals which resemble a bear.

ဝံခံ, *v.* to agree to, acquiesce in; see ဆာခံ.

ဝံပိ, *n.* a wild cat.

ဝံလက်, *n.* a kind of bird.

ဝံလို, *n.* do.

ဝံ့, *v.* to be daring, bold, to be courageous, fearless, desperate, ရဲ. It is also used as an auxiliary, as ပြုဝံ့သည်, he dares to do.

ဝံ့စား, *v.* do.

ဝံ့ရဲ, *v.* do.

ဝါ, (1) *v.* to be yellow, ဝင်း.

ဝါ, (2) *n.* cotton.

ဝါ, (3) *n.* brass.

ဝါ, (4) *n.* a time, season, as ထဝါ, a season; the season of lent, which continues three months.

ဝါ, (5) *n.* an opinion, belief, အယူ.

ဝါ, (6) *v.* to boast, brag, exult, be self-conceited, proud, foppish, ဝါကြွား ၊ ပလွှား ၊ ထောင်လွှား ; to speak bombastically, ကြွား.

ဝါကတ်, *v.* to perform the duites of lent, ဝါဆို.

ဝါကတ္တိသိ, *n.* a mattrass or pillow used by priests, made of a kind of grass.

ဝါကရာ, (from ဝါ, 2; က, 1; and ရာ, 4;) *n.* the 214 orders of beings who inhabit the several states of happiness and misery.

ဝါကား, *v.* to be of a yellow colour.

ဝါကျပ်, *n.* one of the sacred books, သုဗောဓာလင်္ကာရ.

ဝါကျွတ်, *n.* October, သတင်းကျွတ်; the end of lent.

ဝါကြိတ်, *n.* a wheel used to refine cotton.

ဝါကြွား, *v.* to boast, brag, ကား.

ဝါခင်း, *n.* a field of cotton.

ဝါခေါင်, *n.* the fifth month in the year.

ဝါခြည်, *n.* cotton thread.

ဝါဂွမ်း, *n.* picked cotton.

ဝါစာ, *(Pali,)* *n.* language, စကား.

ဝါဆို, *n.* the fourth month in the year; *v.* to observe lent.

ဝါတွင်း, *n.* one season of the year, embracing the three months of lent.

ဝါဒ, *(Puli,)* *n.* an opinion, belief, အယူ.

ဝါပင်, *n.* the cotton tree.

ဝါဖတ်ချင်း, *n.* a large basket used to bleach cotton in.

ဝါဝှန်, *v.* to clean cotton previous to dressing it.

ဝါယာမော, (*Pali,*) *n.* diligence, exertion, လုံ့လ.

ဝါယော, (*Pali,*) *n.* air, လေ.

ဝါရိတ္တသီလ, *n.* a general term which embraces all those religious duties which consist in avoiding objects unfit to be used, eaten, handled, and worn ; also those places where it is improper to go, and improper to remain.

ဝါရှောင်, *v.* to fast, avoid food.

ဝါလ, (*Pali,*) *n.* a time, season.

ဝါသနာ, (*Pali,*) *n.* a desire, inclination, အကျင့်အလေ့ ; an effect ; an inclination of the mind towards any course of conduct, a natural aptitude to any thing.

ဝါသနာပါ, *v.* to be natural to, အကျင့်ပါ.

ဝါသီး, *n.* the cotton pod or fruit before it is opened.

ဝါး, *n.* a bamboo.

ဝါး, *v.* to chew, ဖြုံ.

ဝါးကြမ်း, *n.* a bamboo floor or bridge.

ဝါးဦ, *n.* a bamboo without thorns.

ဝိဘာဝ, (*Pali,*) *n.* existence, ဖြစ်ခြင်း ; mode of appearance, form, လက္ခဏာ.

ဝီမံသာ, (*Pali,*) *n.* reflection, consideration.

ဝိစာရ, (*Pali,*) *n.* consideration, reflection ; see ဈာန်.

ဝိစ္ဆာ, (*Pali,*) *n.* a term which comprizes all the words that are repeated from compound words, meaning all, the whole.

ဝိစိကိစ္ဆာ, (*Pali,*) *n.* dissipation, warding off thought, စိတ်ပျံ့လွင့်ခြင်း.

ဝစီ, (*Pali,*) *n.* the tongue, or the organs of speech.

ဝစီဝိညတ်, *n.* transgression or sin in speech, နှုတ်ဖြင့်ကျူးလွန်ခြင်း.

ဝစီဝိညတ်ကံ, *n.* the influence of sin in speech (committed in a former state,) upon one's circumstances in the present state.

ဝိဇ္ဇာ, (*Pali,*) *n.* knowledge, light, wisdom, understanding, အလင်း၊ ပညာ.

ဝိဇ္ဇာဓိ, *n.* see ဝိဇ္ဇာဓိုရ်.

ဝိဇ္ဇာဓိုရ်, (*Pali,* from ဝိဇ္ဇဓိုရ,) *n.* one who possesses knowledge ; *also* an aërial spirit which guards the သုဒ္ဓရောင် tree, which is said to produce fruit in shape like the human species.

ဝိညာဉ်, or ဝိညာဏ်, *n.* the spirit, soul, mind, စိတ်.

ဝိညာဏက္ခန္ဓာ, *n.* see ခန္ဓာ.

ဝိတက္က, (*Pali,*) *n.* thought, intention, design, purpose, အကြံ၊ အစဉ် ; see ဈာန်.

ဝိတက်သုံးပါး, *n.* a general term which embraces three particulars, viz. ကာမဝိတက်, cherishing lascivious desires, (ကိလေသာစပ်လည် နှင့်ကြံစည်ခြင်း ;) ဗျာပါဒဝိတက်, cherishing hatred or malice towards another, (ရန်ငြိုးဖွဲ့သောသူတို့နှင့်ကြံစည်ခြင်း ;) and ဝိဟိင်္သာဝိတက်, meditating oppression or cruelty towards another, (သူတပါး တို့အားညှဉ်းဆဲခြင်းနှင့်ကြံစည်ခြင်း.)

ဝိထိသုံးပါး, (from ဝိထိ, a way, *Pali,*) *n.* the three grand courses of the planets around Myenmo mount, viz. အင်္ကြာဝိထိ, the inner course ; ဗာဟိရဝိထိ, the outside course ; and မဇ္ဈေဝိထိ, the middle course. The sun enters အင်္ကြာဝိထိ in တပေါင်းလပြည့်, and continues in that course until ဝါဆိုလပြည့် (July.) This is the hot season. It emerges from အင်္ကြာဝိထိ on ဝါဆိုလပြည့်, and enters မဇ္ဈေဝိထိ on တန်ဆောင်မုန်းလပြည့်. This is the rainy season. On တန်ဆောင်မုန်းလပြည့်, it leaves မဇ္ဈေဝိထိ, and enters ဗာဟိရဝိထိ, in which course it continues until တပေါင်းလပြည့် (March.) This is the cold season. These three courses constitute the three seasons of the year ; see ဥတု.

ဝိဍုရ, *n.* one division of the Boodhist scriptures, (marked ဝိ.)

ဝိနည်း, *(Pali,)* *n.* a division of the sacred books, which comprizes the commands of Gaudama for the observance of his priests.

ဝိနည်းစောင့်, *v.* to observe the command of the ဝိနည်း.

ဝိပဿနာ, *(Pali,)* *n.* the duties of a priest, ရဟန်းကျင့်ဝတ်.

ဝိပဿီ, *n.* one of the twenty-eight Boodhs ; see ဆိခင်ဘုရား.

ဝိပ္ပယုတ်, *n.* disconnection, disunion.

ဝိပါက်, (from ဝိပါက,) *n.* a reward, an effect.

ဝိဘက်, *n.* the influence of former bad deeds or actions ; fate, destiny, (used only in a bad sense,) မကောင်းသောကံ.

ဝိဘတ်, *n.* the termination of a noun ; (from ဝိဘတ္တိ.)

ဝိဘတ္တိအပါဒါန်, (in grammar,) the ablative, when terminating in အောက်, or ထက်.

ဝိမတိစ္ဆေဒနာပုစ္ဆာ, *n.* the act of making enquiries for the purpose of removing erroneous sentiments which may have been embraced, ယုံမှားသံသယရှိလျှင်ယင်းကိုပယ်ဖျောက်လိုသောကြောင့်မေးခြင်း.

ဝိမံသိဒ္ဓိပါဒ်, *n.* the power of using means to attain any object.

ဝိပ္ပတ္တိငါးပါး, *(Pali,)* *n.* the five great evils, viz. ဇာတိဘေး, birth; သေချင်း, death; ဗျာနာချင်း, sickness; ညှိဉ်းဆဲချင်း, oppression; ဆင်းရဲချင်း, poverty.

ဝီရိယ, *(Pali,)* *n.* exertion, endeavour, diligence, လုံ့လ.

ဝိရိယသံ, *n.* diligence, exertion.

ဝိရိယိန္ဒြေ, *n.* a disposition to exertion or diligence, လုံ့လဖြိုထောင်ခြင်း.

ဝိရိယိဒ္ဓိပါဒ်, *n.* the power of arriving at an object by means of diligent exertion.

ဝိရူပက္ခနဂါး, *n.* the king or chief over one race of Nagahs; (see နဂါး.)

ဝိဝဋ္ဋ, *n.* one period in a complete revolution of nature; see မဟာကပ်. In this period the waters which deluged the universe disappear, (see သံဝဋ္ဋ,) and, according to the eternal laws of nature, the sun, moon, and stars break forth, every thing comes into sudden existence, and Bramhas descend and people the earth, but they can return to the upper regions when they please.

ဝိဝဋ္ဋဋ္ဌာယီ, *n.* a period in a complete revolution of nature; see မဟာကပ်. At the commencement of this period the Bramhas, *(see under* ဝိဝဋ္ဋ,) commence eating a kind of earth, by which they lose the power of ascending, the period of life begins to shorten, and continues to do so until a person is old at the age of ten years, after which it begins to lengthen, and continues to do so until the system is destroyed by water; see သံဝဋ္ဋ.

ဝိဝေက, *(Pali,)* *n.* composedness, quietness: it is divided into three parts, viz. စိတ္တဝိဝေက, quietness of mind, freedom from passion; ဥပဓိဝိဝေက, exemption from instability, annihilation; and ကာယဝိဝေက, quietness of body.

ဝိဝေကငါးပါး, *n.* this term embraces five particulars; viz. တဒင်္ဂဝိဝေက, the reward of passion, (ကာမကသိုဏ်;) ဝိက္ခမ္ဘနဝိဝေက, see မဟာဂုတ်; သမုစ္ဆေဒဝိဝေက, the four ways, (see မဂ်လေးတန်;) ပဋိပဿဒ္ဓိဝိဝေက, the four rewards, (see ဖိုလ်လေးတန်;) and နိဿရဏဝိဝေက, absorption, annihilation, (နိဗ္ဗာန်.)

ဝိသုဒ္ဓိဒေဝ, *n.* see ဒေဝ.

ဝိညာဏ်, *(Pali,)* *n.* perception, sensibility, consciousness ; the state of being affected by any object : it is divided into five parts, viz. ရူပါရုံ, seeing, မြင်ချင်း။ သဒ္ဒါရုံ, hearing, ကြားချင်း။ ဂန္ဓာရုံ, smelling, နံချင်း။ ရသာရုံ, tasting, လျက်ချင်း။ ဖောဋ္ဌဗ္ဗာရုံ, feeling, တွေ့ချင်း. By another division, it is divided into seven parts ; see ပရမတ်ကျမ်း.

ဝိသယ, *n.* an object of sense.

ဝိသယရုပ်ခုနစ်ပါး, *n.* the seven objects of sense, viz. ရူပါရုံ, the idea formed of a visible object, an object seen ; သဒ္ဒါရုံ, the idea of sound, sound heard ; ဂန္ဓာရုံ, the idea of smell, odour smelt ; ဖောဋ္ဌဗ္ဗာရုံ, the idea of tangibility, an object felt ; ပထဝီဓါတ်, earth ; တေဇောဓါတ်, fire, heat ; and ဝါယောဓါတ်, air.

ဝိသာခါ, *n.* Wethakah, a female mentioned in the Burman sacred books, who was famous for her beauty, religious character, &c.

ဝိသေသန, *n.* a word or sentence expressing or denoting the quality of a noun, an adjective, (a term in grammar.)

ဝိသေသျ, *n.* a word whose quality is expressed by a ဝိသေသန, (a term in grammar.)

ဝိဟိံသာဝိတက်, *n.* see under ဝိတက်သုံးပါး.

ဝိစိကိစ္ဆာ, (*Pali,*) *n.* dissipation of mind, wandering of thought, စိတ်ပျံ့လွင့်ချင်း.

ဝုဍ္ဎိသုံးပါး, *n.* a general term which embraces three things, viz. ဇာတိဝုဍ္ဎိ, excellent pedigree, (အမျိုးမြတ်တည်း ;) ဂုဏဝုဍ္ဎိ, great by means of good qualities, (ဂုဏ်မြင့်ကြီးသည် ;) and ဝယဝုဍ္ဎိ, great by means of age, (အရွယ်မြင့်ကြီးသည်.)

ဝေ, (1) *v.* to divide, set apart.

ဝေ, (2) *v.* to bubble, boil, ဆူ.

ဝေ, (3) *v.* to be giddy, intoxicated, ရစ်.

ဝေ့, *v.* to divide, distribute, set apart.

ဝေနတေယျ, *n.* one race of Galongs, (see ဂဠုန်,) whose king or chief is said to be of immense size, each wing being above 600 miles long, (ယူဇနာငါးဆယ် ;) the distance between the wings the same ; the length of the body above

6000 miles, (ယူဇနာငါးရာ ;) the crest upon his head above 36 miles, (ယူဇနာသုံးခု ;) and his bill, above 1800 miles, (ယူဇနာတရာငါးဆယ်.)

ဝေဒနာ, *n.* pain, anguish.

ဝေဒနာက္ခန္ဓာ, *n.* the suffering pain or anguish; see ခန္ဓာ.

ဝေနေယျ, (1) *n.* a multitude, assembly, ပရိသတ်.

ဝေနေယျ, (2) *n.* a being capable of receiving instruction, an intelligent being, ဆုံးမအပ်သောဝေနေယျ.

ဝေနဲ, *v.* to be close, niggardly.

ဝေပေး, *v.* to disperse, divide among, hire, ငှ ၊ ပေးသေ.

ဝေဖန်, *v.* to distinguish, discern.

ဝေဖန်စီမံထုံးဖွဲ့, *v.* to perform, execute.

ဝေဠဉ်, *n.* a device, means, artifice, expedient.

ဝေဠုတ်, *n.* do.

ဝေလာဟက, *(Pali,) n.* a kind of fabulous horse that dwells in the regions of air.

ဝေသာလ္လရာ, *n.* one division of the Boodhist scriptures (marked ဝေ.)

ဝေသာလီ, *n.* Wathallee, the name of a country mentioned in the sacred books.

ဝေဿဘူ, *n.* one of the twenty-eight Boodhs; see ထိမ်ဝင်ဘုရား.

ဝေဠုဝန်, *n.* a bamboo jungle.

ဝေး, *v.* to be far, distant; တယ်လောက်ဝေးသလော, how far is it?

ဝေးချင်းလေးပါး, *n.* the four things which are far distant from each other, viz. from one shore of the great ocean to the other, မဟာသမုဒ္ဒရာထိပ်မှာဘက်နှင့်ဤမှာဘက်လည်းဝေး၏; from the rising to the setting of the sun, နေထွက်တောင်နှင့်နေဝင်တောင်လည်းဝေး၏; from the earth to the top of Myenmo mount, ဘဝတ်နှင့်မြေ နှင့်လည်းဝေး၏; and above these, the distance between a wicked man and one who is religious, ထိုထက်ကားသူယုတ်နှင့် သူတော်ကောင်းနှင့်လည်းဝေး၏.

ဝေးလံ, *v.* to be far distant.

ဝဲ, *n.* a whirlpool.

ဝဲး, (1) *n.* the roof of a house of distinction, the hinder part of which projects over the front.

ဝဲ, (2) *v.* to be low ; see နိမ့်.

ဝဲ, (3) *v.* to fly without moving the wings, to soar or sail, as a bird.

ဝဲချောက်, *n.* the itch.

ဝဲစွဲ, *v.* to be mangy, have the itch.

ဝဲနာ, *n.* the itch.

ဝဲယားနာ, *n.* do.

ဝေါ, *n.* a large kind of palanquin, borne by 40 or 50 men, used only by kings.

ဝိုက်, *v.* to spin, turn round, ဝဲ့.

ဝိုင်း, (1) *v.* to help, aid, assist, ဆို့ ၊ ညီ ၊ ကူ.

ဝိုင်း, (2) *v.* to go or move round the circumference of any thing, ဝန်း. Hence အဝိုင်း, a circumference or horizon.

ဝိုင်းဝိုင်းကွင်း, *v.* to encircle, make a circle or circumference.

ဝိုးဝါ (ရှိသည်,) (1) *v.* to be doubtful, uncertain, not able to assign a reason, ဝိစိကိစ္ဆာ.

ဝိုးဝါ (ရှိသည်,) (2) *n.* twilight, dusk, not light enough to distinguish objects.

ဝိုးဝင်း, *adv.* glitteringly, brilliantly, ဝင်းဝင်း.

ဝှက်, (1) *v.* to steal, ခိုး.

ဝှက်, (2) *v.* to hide, conceal, keep back ; to be obscure, ထိန် ၊ ထိန်ဝှက် ၊ လျှို့ဝှက်.

ဝှန်, *v.* to rise up, burst up as water, to explode, ထက်. It is also applied to news or fame, သတင်းဝှန်ထက်.

ဝှန်ဝါ, *n.* glory, excellence, fame, အဝှန်အဝါ.

ဝှမ်, *v.* to be declivious, deep, ရှိုင်း.

ဝှမ်း, *v.* to be level, flat. Hence အဝှမ်း, a surface, a flat, level place.

ဝှေးစေ့, *n.* the testicles.

ဝှေ့, *v.* to push, propel, drive along or against, တိုက်.

## သ.

သ, (1) *v.* to make anew, do afresh, make over again.

သ, (2) *v.* to bring with, to offer, present, ရှိဆောင်.

သ, (3) an abbreviation of the connective and verbal affixes, သော and သည်.

ဿ, an abbreviation of သဿ.

သက်, *v.* to descend; to drop or fall down, ဆင်း ။ ဆင်းသက်.

သက်ကယ်, *n.* a kind of grass used for thatch.

သက္က, *(Pali,)* (1) *n.* sugar, sweetness, သကြား.

သက္က, (2) *n.* a race of kings, သာကီဝင်.

သက္က, (3) *n.* patience, forbearance, သည်းခံခြင်း.

သက္ကဋ္ဌဒါန်, *n.* see under သဒ္ဓရိုသဒါန်.

သက္ကာယ, *(Pali,)* *n.* a disposition to covet the goods of others, covetousness.

သက္ကရ, *(Pali,)* *n.* worship, homage paid.

သက္ကရာဇ်, (from သက္ကရာဇ,) (1) *n.* an era, a date fixed upon by the king, era of a monarchy.

သက္ကရာဇ်, (from သက္ကရာဇ,) (2) *n.* a written engagement, as a slave-bond.

သက္ကလတ်, *n.* woollen cloth of any kind.

သက္ကလတ်ကျောက်နုံး, *n.* fine woollen cloth, broad cloth.

သက္ကလတ်ပက္ကူ, *n.* flannel.

သက္ကလတ်ဖုံရှိုင်း, *n.* a coarse kind of flannel.

သက္ကာရ, see ဈာန်.

သက္ကော, *(Pali,)* (1) *n.* a deity who has descended from a race of kings, သာကီဝင်မျိုးဖြစ်သောဘုရား.

သက္ကော, (2) *n.* strength, power, ခွန်အား.

သက်ဆင်း, *v.* to descend, as an office or employment, from father to son; to be hereditary.

သကတ်, *(Pali,* သကတ္တ,) substance, or that to which a quality belongs.

သက်တန့်, *n.* a rainbow, (in the east.)

သကဒါဂါမိ, *n.* the second state attained by an Areeyah, (အရိယာ.)

သကဒါဂါမိမဂ်, *n.* the duties of said state.

သကဒါဂါမိဖိုလ်, *n.* the rewards of performing the duties of said state.

သကဒါဂါမိမဂ္ဂဋ္ဌာန်, *n.* one who has performed the duties of said state.

သက်ပန်း, *n.* wormwood.

သကန်, *n.* a form, pattern, rule, ဥပဒေ.

သကလံ, *(Pali,)* (1) *n.* a quarter, fourth part, အစိတ်.

သကလံ, (2) *n.* all, the whole, အလုံးစုံ.

သကလံ, (3) *n.* a small stone, a pebble, ကျောက်စရစ်.

သကလော, *(Pali,)* (1) *n.* all, the whole, ခပ်သိမ်း.

သကလော, (2) *n.* a half, ထက်ဝက်.

သက်သက်, (1) *adv.* empty-handed.

သက်သက်, (2) wholly, entirely, only, nothing but, applied to nouns and adjectives, as မေတ္တာနှင့်သက်သက်ပြုမည်, I will do it from affection merely; အနက်သက်သက်ရှိ၏, it is entirely black.

သက်သာ, *v.* to be tranquil, enjoy quiet, to be pleasant, သာရှိ.

သက်သေ, (1) *n.* a representation, pattern, ပုံ၊ မံ.

သက်သေ, (2) *n.* a witness, testimony.

သက်သေခံ, *v.* to bear witness, give in testimony.

သကာ, *n.* the hardened sediment of molasses.

သကုဏ, *(Pali,)* *n.* a bird, ငှက်.

သကုန္တာ, *(Pali,)* *n.* a bird; a bird that can talk, စကားဆိုတတ်သောငှက်.

သကဲ့သို့, or ကဲ့သို့, *an affix,* in the same manner, like as, as if.

သကော, *(Pali,)* (1) *n.* a drinking-cup, သောက်ခွက်.

သကော, (2) *pron.* own, one's own, one's own self, မိမိ.

သကျသီဟော, *n.* deity, who is more excellent than the race of kings, သာကီဝင်မင်းတို့ထက်မြတ်သောဘုရား.

သကျမုနိ, *(Pali,)* *n.* deity, who is descended from the race of kings, သာကီဝင်မင်းမျိုးမှဖြစ်သောဘုရား.

သကျော, *(Pali,)* *n.* a race of kings, သာကီဝင်မျိုး.

သကြိဉ်, *n.* embroidered or carved work.

သကြား, *n.* sugar.

သကြား, *n.* a kind of sweetmeat.

သကြားခဲ, *n.* sugar-candy.

သကြားပွင့်, *n.* do.

သခင်, *n.* lord, master, ruler, husband, အရှင်.

သခါ, *(Pali,)* *n.* a friend, one who seeks the prosperity of his companion, စီးပွါးရှာဘက်.

သခိ, *(Pali,)* *n.* a friend, a companion, ခင်ပွန်း.

သခွတ်, *n.* a kind of tree.

သခွါးသီး, *n.* a cucumber.

သခွားခင်း, *n.* a cucumber field.

သခွားကြီး,<br>
သခွားကြောင်,<br>
သခွားချည်,<br>
သခွားငပြုတ်,<br>
သခွားဆစ်,<br>
သခွားဆပ်,<br>
သခွားနီ,<br>
သခွားပြုတ်,<br>
သခွားဖြူ, } *n.* varieties of the cucumber.

သဂ္ဂဝါသိနော, (*Pali*,) *n.* a person who resides in the Nat country, နတ်ပြည်၌နေလေ့ရှိသောသူ ; the name of a Nat, နတ်အမည်.

သဂ္ဂါ, (*Pali*,) (1) *n.* giving alms, စွန့်ကြဲခြင်း.

သဂ္ဂါ, (2) *n.* nature, disposition, သဘော.

သဂ္ဂါ, (3) *n.* the act of forming or creating, ဖန်ဆင်းခြင်း.

သဂ္ဂါ, (4) *n.* the place where happiness or enjoyment continues permanent for a great length of time ; the Nat country, စည်းစိမ်ချမ်းသာတို့ကြာမြင့်စွာတည်ရာ.

သင်, (1) *pers. pro. mas. or fem.* thou, (used in writing.)

သင်, (2) *v.* to learn, receive instruction.

သင်, (3) *v.* to make clean, press, prepare, clear away, as a forest, သုတ် ၊ ရှင်း ၊ ပျင်.

သင်, (4) *v.* to peel, skin off, ခွာ ၊ နွှာ ၊ နွှင်.

သင်အမတေ, *n.* a charm, found in certain plants.

သင်ကန်း, or သင်္ကန်း, *n.* a priest's garment, the yellow cloth. There are four articles belonging to a priest, viz. သင်္ကန်း ၊ ဆွမ်း ၊ ကျောင်း ၊ ဆေး, collectively called ပစ္စည်းလေးပါး.

သင်္ကန်းပွဲ, *n.* a feast in the month တဆောင်မုန်း.

သင်္ကန်းလွှာ, *n.* a kind of petso or cloth worn round the body.

သင်္ကဋော, (*Pali*,) *v.* to be narrow, close, strait, confined, crowded, ကျဉ်းမြောင်း.

သင်္ကပ္ပါ, (*Pali*,) *n.* thought, consideration, design, အကြံ.

သင်္ကာ, *v.* to doubt, fear, dread, ရွံ့ရှာ ; to suspect, be suspicious.

သင်္ကု , (*Pali,*) *n.* a thorn, ငြောင့် ; a peg or stick driven into the ground to fasten any thing to or upon, တံသင်း ; a weapon, လက်နက်.

သင်္ကျန်, *n.* a feast ; an assemblage or concourse of persons, ပွဲသဘင်.

သင်ကြတ်, *n.* an ornament worn by officers of state.

သင်ကြား, *v.* to learn, receive instruction.

သင်ကြိုဟ်, (1) *v.* to preach, give instruction from the sacred books.

သင်ကြိုဟ်, (2) *v.* to support, maintain, relieve, &c.

သင်ခမ်, *n.* a garden, grove, hermitage, ဆရိုက်.

သင်္ခန်း, *n.* a temporary building for priests to inhabit during the performance of those ceremonies which require their being away from their regular places of abode.

သင်္ခါရ , (*Pali,*) *n.* liability to change, instability, ပျက်တတ်ခြင်း ၊ ဖောက်ပြန်ခြင်း.

သင်္ခါရတရား, *n.* the principles or law of mutability.

သင်္ခါရက္ခန္ဓာ, *n.* will, disposition ; see ခန္ဓာ.

သင်္ခါရလောက, being produced and reproduced.

သင်္ချာ, *v.* to enumerate, count, ဂဏန်းသင်္ချာ; *n.* an inconceivably large number.

သင်္ချေ, *n.* a number beyond enumeration, but less than သင်္ချာ.

သင်ခွေချုပ်, *n.* a kind of animal.

သင်္ဂ, (*Pali,*) *n.* associating together, being in company with, ပေါင်းဖော်ခြင်း.

သင်္ဂမာ, (*Pali,*) *n.* do.

သင်္ဂမာ, *adv.* accurately, minutely.

သင်္ဂဟော, (*Pali,*) *n.* the act of lifting up, helping, giving assistance, exalting, ချီးမြှင့်ခြင်း.

သင်္ဂါမော, (*Pali,*) *n.* coming together, as antagonists, fighting; စစ်ထိုးခြင်း.

သင်္ချိုင်း, *n.* a burying place, သုတ်သာန် ၊ သုသာန်.

သင်္ဂြိုဟ်, (1) *v.* to help, aid, assist, ထောက်ပံ့ ၊ ထောက်မ.

သင်္ဂြိုဟ်, (2) *v.* to burn a dead body, or deposit it in the ground ; to perform funeral ceremonies.

သင်ဃါ, or သင်္ဃာ, *n.* a general name for all manner of religious mendicants, or devotees ; a society, assembly.

သင်္ဃါတ, *n.* one of the states of punishment ; see ငရဲ.

သင်္ဃါဒ်, *n.* an assemblage of priests, collected for the purpose of performing pontifical duties, ဝတ်ကျင်သင်္ဃါမြားမြားရဟန်းပိုးကြီး.

သင်္ဃါနော, *n.* the chief of a kyoung, (ကျောင်း.)

သင်္ဃါပုံ, *n.* a collection of priests who live in one kyoung.

သင်ဃါယနာ (တင်သည်,) *v.* to utter or repeat in concert, as an assembly of priests, (properly in the presence of deity.)

သင်တုံး, *n.* a razor, ဓါးရွဝ်.

သင်တိုင်း, *n.* a kind of jacket, made so as to cover the head.

သင်တွဲး, *n.* verdigris.

သင်ရုံးလှူရသောအကျိုးငါးပါး, the five rewards obtained by the person who makes a religious offering of a razor, viz. numerous good friends ; perfection in diligence ; patience ; wisdom ; and purity.

သင်ဝင်, *n.* the rattan of which a kind of mats is made.

သင်ပိတ်, *n.* a pot in which the priests receive the offerings made by the people to them.

သင်ပုတ်, *n.* the offerings which the priests receive in their pots.

သင်ပုံး, *n.* a term used for all the Burman characters and compounds ; a lesson, or pattern for learning.

သင်ပြင်, *v.* to reprove, chastise, correct, ဆုံးမ.

သင်ဖျာ, *n.* a kind of mat.

သင်ဖြူး, *n.* a kind of mat.

သင်္ဘော, (1) *n.* a ship.

သင်္ဘော, (2) *n.* the papaya tree.

သင်္ဘောသခွား, *n.* the papaya tree.

သင်္ဘောဩဇာ, *n.* noona, the custard apple.

သင်္ဘောကျရု, *n.* black myrobalans.

သင်္ဘောဆိပ်, *n.* a harbour for shipping.

သင်္ဘောသရက်, *n.* custard apple or nut, ထရုဝ်သရက်.

သင်္ဘောမုန်လာ, *n.* cabbage, radish, lettuce, &c.

သင်္ဘောသီးနို, *n.* a sort of sweetmeat.

သင်ဖိုး, *v.* to imitate, mock by means of gestures.

သင်ယူ, *v.* to learn, receive instruction.

သင်သရာ, *n.* the future world or state.

သင်သရာဘဝ, *n.* do.

သင်း, (1) *adj. pro. mas. fem.* or *neut.* this, that: it is generally used substantively.

သင်း, (2) *v.* to unite, associate, collect in one, ပေါင်း.

သင်း, (3) *v.* to emit a pleasant odour, မွှေး၊ ကြိုင်.

သင်း, (4) *n.* the organs of generation.

သင်း, (5) *v.* to geld, castrate, အစိုးထုတ်.

သင်းကြက်တူရွေး, *n.* a species of turtle whose head resembles a parrot's bill.

သင်းခြော, *n.* a large brown shining lizard.

သင်းကြွပ်, *n.* the earth which peels off the surface of land after an inundation.

သင်းချော, *v.* to be all of one sort or substance, all the same.

သင်းချော, *n.* see သင်းခြော.

သင်းချိုင်း, *n.* a place of interment, burying ground, သုသာန်၊ သင်္ချိုင်.

သင်းချို, *n.* do.

သင်းစင်, *n.* a castrated bull, an ox.

သင်းပင်း, *n.* an attendant, an assembly, အသင်းအပင်း.

သင်းပိုင်, *n.* the lower garment of a priest, which is secured by the ခါးပန်း, or girdle.

သင်းပေါင်း, *v.* to unite, associate, collect in one.

သင်းဖော်, *v.* do.

သင်းဖက်, *v.* do.

သင်းဖွဲ့, *v.* do. အသင်းဖွဲ့၊ စည်းကြွပ်.

သင်းမှူး, *n.* the head, or chief of an association of people.

သင်းလိပ်, *n.* an animal resembling a turtle, (native of China.)

သင့်, (1) *v.* to be suitable, fit, proper, consistent, တော်; to agree together; to be ready, finished.

သင့်, (2) *v.* to be, become, hang about or over, as fogs or frost.

သင့်, (3) *v.* to unite, cement, မှီဝဲ; to unite, marry, cohabit, as man and wife.

သင့်သင့်, *v.* see သင့်, to be suitable, &c.

သင့်နေ, *v.* to live with a woman as a mistress.

သစ်, (1) *v.* to be new, just made; to be fresh, not stale, not old, ထွင်.

သစ်, (2) *n.* timber, wood.

သစ်, (3) *n.* an astrological book.

သစ်ကုံးပိုး, *n.* cinnamon, cassia lignea.

သစ်ကျား, *n.* a leopard.

သစ်ကျုတ်, *n.* a small kind of leopard.

သစ်ကြံ့ပိုး, *n.* a cinnamon tree.

သစ်ကြား, *n.* a walnut.

သစ်ကြောင်း, *n.* a forked branch.

သစ်ကြောင်းဗြီး, *n.* the base of a forked branch.

သစ်ခက်, *n.* the branch of a tree.

သစ်ခက်တတ်, *n.* a tent, a temporary place of residence.

သစ်ခဝတ်, *n.* a fabulous tree, (in Athoora.)

သစ်ချ, *n.* a Burman nut, a Malay chesnut.

သစ်ခွ, *n.* a parasitical plant.

သစ်ခွတ်, *n.* see သစ်ခဝတ်.

သစ္စံ, *(Pali,)* *n.* see the definitions of သစ္စာ.

သစ္စာ, (1) *adj.* true, right.

သစ္စာ, (2) *n.* truth.

သစ္စာ, (3) *n.* an engagement, oath, promise.

သစ္စာစောင့်, *v.* to keep one's word, fulfil an engagement, keep an oath, perform one's vows.

သစ္စာပြု, *v.* to make an agreement, make a vow; imprecate evil on one's self, if he speak not according to truth, and to desire good, if he do speak the truth; to take an oath, to swear.

သစ္စာဆို, *v.* do.

သစ္စာတရား, *n.* true precepts, righteousness.

သစ္စာဖွဲ့, *v.* see သစ္စာပြု.

သစ္စာပန်, *(Pali,)* *n.* believing, crediting; acting according to truth, အမှန်ပြုခြင်း.

သစ္စာရေ, *n.* water drunk when the oath of allegiance to the king is taken, or when any other agreement is made.

သစေ, *(Pali,) conj.* expressing doubt, conditionality, or probability, if, အတွေနိုပါလိ.

သစ္ဆန္ဒာ, *(Pali,) v.* to act according to one's own will or disposition, အလိုအလျောက်ကျင့်ထတ်ခြင်း.

သစ်ဆင်, *n.* a leopard.

သစ်ဆိမ့်, or သစ်ဆိမ့်, *n.* a kind of tree.

သစ်တတ်, (1) *n.* a wall made of wood, as round a city or town, a wooden stockade.

သစ်တာ်, (2) *v.* to measure with the breadth of the finger. Hence လက်သစ်, *n.* a finger-breadth.

သစ်တတ်, (3) *n.* a leopard.

သစ်ထတ်တည်, *v.* to encamp, pitch a tent, &c.

သစ်တာ, *n.* a chest, box, trunk.

သစ်တော်သီး, *n.* an apple.

သစ်တောက်, *n.* a wood-pecker.

သစ်တိုင်, *n.* a post.

သစ်နဂါး, *n.* an omen, prodigy, နဂါးပတ်.

သစ်နတ်, *n.* a kind of tree from which cloth or paper is sometimes made.

သစ်ပင်, *n.* a tree, any large tree, timber.

သစ်ပင်ရေ, or ရည်, *n.* the juice of a tree.

သစ်ပုပ်, *n.* the name of a certain tree.

သစ်မင်း, *n.* the name of a certain tree.

သစ်သား, *n.* timber, wood.

သစ်သီး, *n.* fruit of any kind.

သစ်သီးဝလံ, *n.* fruit of any description.

သဂုနော, (*Pali,*) *n.* an acquaintance, friend, အဆွေ၊ ကိုယ်ထွ.

သစိဝါ, (*Pali,*) *n.* an intimate of a king or governor, a king's counsellor, မင်းတို့တိုင်ပင်အမတ်.

သနိဝေါ, (*Pali,*) *n.* a person who lives with a king or governor; a royal counsellor.

သဇ္ဇု, (*Pali,*) *n.* a moment, an instant, ခဏ.

သဇ္ဇုလသော, (*Pali,*) *n.* the gum of a tree, ပွဲချက်.

သဇ္ဈု, (*Pali,*) *n.* silver, ငွေ.

သည်, (1) *adj. pron.* this, ဤ.

သည်, (2) *n. affix*, sign of the nominative case; သည် is sometimes used for ၏သည်; see ၏.

သည်, (3) *connective affix*, (by contraction သ,) used to connect nouns with adjectives, and frequently is construed like the relative who, which, and that.

သည်, (4) *v. affix*, sign of the assertive or indicative mood, as သွားသည်, he goes, or is going.

သည်, (5) *n.* a post.

သည်, (6) *n. affix*, denoting the profession of a person, as ကြက်သည်, a fowl-seller; အမှုသည်, a claimant; မုံ့သည်, a baker, &c.

သည်က, from this, hence, from this place.

သည်ကလောက်, so much, as much as this.

သည်ကား, *affix*, as to, concerning or in regard to this.

သည်ကဲ့သို့, thus, like this.

သည်ကြောင့်, therefore, on this account.

သည်ငှါ, *adj. pron.* this (thing.)

သည်တိုင်, *n.* a post.

သည်တွင်, here, in this place; ထိုတွင်, there, in that place.

သည်ပြင်, besides this, besides; ထိုပြင်, besides that.

သည်မှုကား, relative to this, concerning this.

သည်မှ, from this, hence, from this place.

သည်မှာ, in this, in this place.

သည်လျှာ, *n.* a person beloved.

သည်သို့, *pron. adj.* such, of this sort, thus.

သည်သို့က, from this manner, from this method.

သည်သို့ကြောင့်, or သည်သို့သောကြောင့်, because it is thus, because of this manner.

သည်သို့မှ, from this manner, from this method.

သည်သို့မှာ, in this way, in this manner.

သည်း, (1) *v.* to roar, be excessive, violent, cry from anguish or pain, as an infant, or any one in distress, to make a loud piercing noise, သည်းထန် ၊ ပြင်းထန်.

သည်း, (2) *n.* sand, သဲ ၊ သလဲ.

သည်း, (3) *n.* the liver.

သည်းဦးဆက်ကပ်, *v.* to give to a superior out of fear.

သည်းခံ, *v.* to be forbearing, endure with patience, be quiet under injuries and abuse.

သည်းခံအကျိုးငါးပါး, *n.* the five rewards of patience or forbearance, viz. the universal love of mankind, ခပ်သိမ်းသောသူတို့နှစ်လိုသည် ; peace, ငြိမ်းသည် ; few faults, အပြစ်နည်းသည် ; peace of mind in death, မတွေမဝေသေသည် ; and deliverance from the four states of punishment after death, အပါယ်လေးပါးမလားရသည် ; on the other hand there are five rewards of impatience which are directly the opposite of those just named.

သည်းချေ, *n.* the gall-bladder.

သည်းခြေ, *n.* the gall.

သည်းညည်း, *v.* see သည်းခံ.

သည်းထန်, or ထန်, *v.* see သည်း, to roar, &c.

သည်းသန်, *v.* to become severe, excessive, as pain or sickness.

သဉ္ဇူဟော, *(Pali,)* *n.* a collection, a whole, အပေါင်း.

သဉ္ဇာတိဒေသ, *(Pali,)* *n.* the place where a thing is, or where an event occurs, scene of action, ဖြစ်ရာ.

သဉ္ဇာနနံ, *(Pali,)* *n.* knowledge, perception, သိခြင်း.

သညာ, (1) *n.* perception.

သညာ, (2) *v.* to know, perceive.

သညာ, (3) see တဋ္ဋဒွါန်း.

သညာက္ခန္ဓာ, *n.* perception.

သဌေး, *v.* to be rich, opulent.

သဋ္ဌံ, *(Pali,)* *n.* using artifice or deceit, စဉ်းလဲခြင်း.

သဏ္ဌာန်, *n.* likeness, shape, form, as အိုသည်သဏ္ဌာန်, to have the appearance of old age; နုသည်သဏ္ဌာန်, to have a youthful appearance.

သဏ္ဌာနံ, *(Pali,)* *n.* a mark, sign ; see also သဏ္ဌာန်.

သဏ္ဍာသော, *(Pali,)* *n.* nippers, snuffers, shears, &c. ညှပ်.

သတ်, *v.* to kill, fight, destroy, cut off, quench, or extinguish, as fire, or a candle; to decide, order, command, as a king; to strike, beat, တိုက်၊ ဖြတ်၊ ပယ်၊ ထိုး၊ ပုတ်ခတ်၊ ကွပ်၊ ကွပ်မျက်၊ ငြိမ်း. Hence အသတ်, a sentence, a mute letter.

သတင်ကျွတ်, *n.* October.

သတင်း, *n.* news, tidings, သတင်းစကား.

သတင်းပြန့်, *v.* to be notorious, talked about, acquire fame.

သတင်းကျွတ်, *n.* the seventh month in the Burman year, that is, October.

သတတ်, *v. affix*, denoting supposition.

သတ္တဌာန်, *n.* the seven postures in which Gaudama is said to have been found.

သတ္တမ, (*Pali,*) *ordinal adj.* seventh.

သဿတံ, (*Pali,*) *n.* permanency, stability, အမြဲ.

သဏ္ဌံ, (*Pali,*) *v.* to continue, be permanent, တည်နေ.

သတ္တရဘံ, *n.* the seven ranges of mountains which surround Myenmo mount, and which separate the seven rivers in regular succession.

သတ္တလောက, *n.* being, a state of being, a living being.

သတ္တဝါ, *n.* a general term for all intelligent beings.

သတ္တဟံ, *n.* the space of seven days.

သတ္တဟံစောင့်, *v.* to keep or observe a fast of seven days.

သတ္တံဒရက္ခဝ်, *n.* see ကဝ်သုံးပါး.

သတ်ပုံ, *n.* a sort of dictionary, or spelling book.

သဝ်မြှင်, *n.* the mark ်, which shows a letter to be final.

သတံ, (*Pali,*) (1) *n.* strength, ability, အား.

သတံ, (2) *n.* a subject, matter, principle, law, တရား၊ ထရား.

သဝံ, (3) see သဏ္ဌာန်.

သတ္တိ, *n.* strength, might, power.

သတိ, (*Pali,*) (1) *n.* a woman who is entirely under the control of her husband, လင်၏အလိုဖြင့်သာဖြစ်တတ်သောမိန်းမ; one who endeavours to please her husband, လင်ကိုဖြင်းစေတတ်သောမိန်းမ.

သတိ, (2) *n.* recollection, care, attention, determination.

သတိဇြေ, *n.* an attentive, thoughtful disposition, free from forgetfulness, မမေ့မလျော့တတ်ခြင်း.

သတိဆောင်, *v.* to use caution, take heed, perform with attention.

သတိနှင့်, with or by means of care, attention, &c.

သတိပြု, *v.* to use caution, take heed, &c.

သတိပဋ္ဌာန်လေးပါး, *n.* the four subjects of attention and care; ကာယနုပဿနာသတိပဋ္ဌာန်, (ကာယ, the body; နုပဿနာ, to observe, watch,) one that watches over the body; စိတ္တနုပဿနာ, one that watches over the mind; ဝေဒနာနုပဿနာ, one that attentively considers the miseries of life; and ဓမ္မာနုပဿနာ, one that attentively observes the duties of religion.

သတိဝေါဿဂ္ဂ, *(Pali,)* *n.* being destitute of knowledge or perception, သတိလွတ်ခြင်း; being forgetful, မေ့လျော့ခြင်း.

သတိရ, *v.* to recollect, call to mind.

သတိလစ်, *v.* to forget, not to remember, မေ့လျော့.

သတိလစ်ဟင်း, *v.* do.

သတိလျော့, *v.* do. မိန်းမော ၊ တွေဝေ.

သတို့သမီး, *n.* the daughter of a king or other great personage.

သတို့သား, *n.* the son of a king or other great personage.

သဒြံ, *(Pali.)* *n.* making religious offerings; giving stability, အမြဲပေးခြင်း.

သဒန်, *(Pali,)* *n.* a house, place of habitation; a sheath, အိမ်.

သဒ္ဒါ, *n.* sound, articulation; grammar; a noun.

သဒ္ဒါယတန, *n.* the sense or faculty of hearing.

သဒါဒါန, *n.* see under သဒ္ဓြိုသဒါန.

သဒ္ဒါရုံ, *n.* the idea of sound.

သဒိသမာန်, *n.* one kind of pride, viz. feeling an equality with superiors, ထိုသူကားငါနှင့်အတူတူသာတည်းဟူမာန်မူခြင်း.

သဒ္ဓါ, (1) *v.* to will, feel a pleasure in doing any thing; to do any thing from pure motives; to confer honour or favour, be gracious, ကြည် ၊ ကြည်လင် ၊ ကြည်ဖြူ.

သဒ္ဓါ, (2) *n.* a motive, an excitement to action, strong desire.

သဒ္ဓါဗလ, *n.* intensity of application.

သဒ္ဓိဆန္ဒ. *n.* a disposition to habitual kindness, or cordiality, ကြည်ညိုတတ်ချင်း.

သန်, (1) *n.* the rainy season, ဝဿ.

သန်, (2) *v.* to be strong, luxuriant, thriving, flourishing, healthy.

သန်ကြမ်း, *v.* do.

သန်စွမ်း, *v.* do.

သနင်း, *n.* a king, governor, မင်းကြီး.

သန်, (3) see သန်စတော်မူ.

သန်စတော်မူ, *v.* to void urine, or fæces, a term used by the best authors, when speaking of this act in great personages.

သဏ္ဌာန်, *n.* state, circumstances, affairs, အဖြစ် ၊ အကြောင်း.

သန္တန်, *n.* the period of a man's life, length of life.

သန္နိဋ္ဌာန်, *(Pali,) n.* a decision, a resolve, ဆုံးဖြတ်ချင်း.

သန္ဓေ, *(Pali,) n.* pregnancy, a state of pregnancy ; *v.* to connect with, unite.

သန္နိဋ္ဌာန်ချ, *v.* to come to a decision, make a resolve.

သံသေဒဇ, *n.* one of the four ways of generation, viz. as worms in filth.

သန္တာ, *n.* a coral.

သန္တု, *(Pali,)* the month of October, သီတင်းကျွတ်.

သနပ်, (1) *n.* pickles.

သနပ်, (2) *n.* the name of a plant.

သနပ်ခါး, *n.* the name of a certain tree, the bark of which is fragrant.

သနပ်ခါးမှုန့်, *n.* the bark of do. pulverized, used by women to rub upon their faces.

သန်လယ်, *n.* a field cultivated in the rainy season.

သနပ်, *n.* state, circumstances, affairs, အဖြစ် ၊ အကြောင်း.

သံ, *(Pali,) n.* sex, whether male or female.

သန်း, (1) *v.* to be strait, make strait, ဖြောင့် ; to cross or pass over from one place to another.

သန်း, (2) *n.* a gape.

သန်း, (3) *n.* a louse.

သန်းခေါင်, *n.* midnight.

သန်းဈ, *n.* a net.

သန်းမ, *n.* a large kind of louse.

သန်းသန်း, *adv.* straitly, in a strait line.

သန်းသန်းဖြောင့်ဖြောင့်, *adv.* do.

သန့်, *v.* to be clear, intelligible, plain, ရှင်း.

သန့်ပျို့, *v.* do. to be pure, free from fault.

သန့်ရှင်း, *v.* to be pure, perfectly clean, free from any fault or blemish, စင်ကြယ်.

သန့်သက်ရေ, *n.* water used by kings after an evacuation of nature ; also by priests.

သန့်သန့်, *adv.* purely, clearly, innocently.

သနား, *v.* to be merciful, gracious, kind, to show favour or kindness, ကျင့်နား.

သန္တာန်, *n.* state, circumstances, affairs, အဖြစ် ၊ အကြောင်း.

သပ်, *v.* to smooth, rub down, stroke gently, ချော ၊ ညှိ ၊ သုံးသပ်.

သပင်, *n.* a kind of mat, သပေါင်.

သဗ္ဗကာ, *(Pali,)* *n.* a favour conferred by a superior.

သဗ္ဗညု, *adj.* divine, belonging to deity.

သဗ္ဗညုတ, *adj.* omniscient.

သဗ္ဗညုတဉာဏ်, *n.* a perfect knowledge of the five general principles or laws, အလုံးစုံသောဉေယျဓမ္မတရားတို့ကိုသိသောဉာဏ် ; see ဉေယျဓမ္မတရားငါးပါး.

သပ်ဝတ်, *n.* beautiful, comely, divinely elegant, applied to deity, တင့်တယ်.

သပရ, *(Pali,)* *v.* to be near, (so as to touch.)

သပ်သပ်ရှင်းရှင်း, *adv.* perfectly clear, free from confusion.

သပ္ပါယ်, (1) *v.* to bathe, (applied to a priest.)

သပ္ပါယ်, (2) *v.* to be handsome, suitable, elegant, လှ ၊ တော်.

သဗ္ဗေ, *(Pali,)* *adj.* all, the whole, ခပ်သိမ်း.

သပ္ပိနာမ, (*Pali,*) butter, ghee, ထောပတ်. The priests are allowed to use three kinds of butter or ghee, viz. that made from the milk of cows, goats, and buffaloes.

သပိတ်, *n.* an open-mouthed pot, in which the priests receive their rice.

သပိတ်မှောက်, *n.* a certain place in a pagoda, where relics are deposited.

သပိတ်အိပ်, *n.* a kind of bag suspended from the neck, in which the သပိတ် is carried.

သပိတ်ခြေ, *n.* a stand or pedestal for a သပိတ်.

သပိတ်လှူရသည့်အကျိုးဆယ်ပါး, the ten rewards which the person obtains who makes an offering of a သပိတ် ; viz. dishes ornamented with precious stones, &c. ; the necessaries of life at all times ; deliverance from evil ; freedom from oppression ; the reverence of mankind ; easily obtaining food, clothing, a place to sleep, and a place of habitation ; happiness and enjoyment which shall not be destroyed ; a settled and contented mind ; a love for the divine law ; few sexual desires, and complete freedom from anxieties.

သပေါင်, see သပင်.

သပြာ, (a contraction of အသပြာ,) (1) *n.* money, whether gold or silver.

သပြာ, (2) *n.* a clam.

သပြေ, *n.* the Eugenia tree ; Jomboo fruit in general.

သဘက်, *n.* the day after to-morrow.

သဖန်း, *n.* Myrobalans.

သဖြင့်, *affix*, by means of, by.

သဗွယ်, *affix*, like as, ကဲ့သို့.

သဗ္ဗ, *(Pali,) adj.* all, the whole, ခပ်သိမ်း.

သဗ္ဗုဒ္ဓိသဒါန, *n.* five particulars relative to offerings ; viz. သဒ္ဓါဒါန, making an offering in expectation of the reward, (ကံကိုအကျိုးကိုယုံကြည်၍လှူခြင်း ;) သက္ကစ္စဒါန, making an offering of proper materials, and which are free from blemish, (လှူအပ်သောဝတ္ထုကိုသန့်ပြန့်စွာလှူခြင်း ;) ကာလဒါန, giving to travellers the best of flowers and fruits in a time of famine, (ဧသည်ခရီးသွားတို့အားလည်ကောင်းရှားပါးခေတ်မှတ်သောကာလ၌လည်ကောင်းပန်းဦးသစ်သီးဦးတို့ကိုလှူခြင်း ;) အနုဂ္ဂဟိတဒါန, making offerings when one is in very indigent circumstances, (မိမိစည်းစိမ်ကိုချို့တတ်မစွမ်းရက်ရက်လှူခြင်း ;) the fifth is not mentioned.

သတင်, *n.* an assembly, congregation, gathering of people ; the place of assembling.

သဘော, *n.* the mind, disposition, nature.

သဘောချု, *v.* to overcome a person's disposition or resolution, to resolve, determine.

သဘောကျွမ်း, *v.* to be acquainted with, or know a person's mind or disposition.

သဘောရောက်, *v.* to feel favourably disposed ; to fall in love with a woman ; have lustful feelings.

သဘောသက်, *v.* do.

သဘောမေတ္တာ, *v.* do.

သမ်, *v.* to be of a dull colour, dim, cast down.

ထမက်, *n.* a son-in-law.

သမ်ညှိ, *v.* to be of a dull colour, dim, cast down.

သမင်, *n.* a large kind of deer.

ထမတိ, *adv.* before, formerly, perpetually.

သမ်း, (1) *v.* to gape, yawn, ဟ.

ထမ်း, (2) *v.* to cut or strike across, ကူး ၊ ဖြတ်.

သမ်းဥခေါင်း, *n.* the head of a louse; a measure of distance, seven of which make စပါးတလုံး, or one rice-kernel.

သမန်း, *n.* mud in rice fields, ထမန်း.

သမ္ဗုဇ္ဈည်, *n.* wisdom, learning.

သမ္ဗုဒ္ဓ, see ဗုဒ်.

သမ္ပဒါန်, (in grammar,) the dative case, terminating in အား and ငှါ.

သမ္ပတ္တိစက်လေးပါး, *n.* a general term, embracing four particulars; viz. the privilege of living in an elegant and delightful place of abode; having an old stock of merit for good deeds performed in previous states of being; doing well for one's self; and the privilege of associating with upright and religious persons.

သမ္ဗန်, *n.* a boat, လှေ.

ထမ္ဗန်, (in grammar,) the possessive case, two terminations, ၏ and တွင်.

သမ္ပယုတ်, *n.* union, agreement, ရှဉ့်ချင်း.

ထမ္ဗရာသီး, *n.* a lemon or lime.

ထမ္မပ္ပဓာန်လေးပါး, *n.* a general name which embraces four things; viz. using exertion to prevent demerit, while as yet the person has done nothing blameworthy, မဖြစ်သေးသောအကုသိုလ်တရားတို့ကိုမဖြစ်အောင်လုံ့လပြုခြင်း; using exertion to prevent the increase of demerit after the person has already done that which is sinful, ဖြစ်ပြီးသောအကုသိုလ်တရားတို့ကိုမပွါးရအောင်လုံ့လပြုခြင်း; endeavouring to do that which will procure merit, while the person is yet destitute of it, မဖြစ်သောကုသိုလ်တရားတို့ကို ဖြစ်ပွါးအောင်လုံ့လပြု ခြင်း; and endeavouring, after a person has a stock of merit, to excel in meritorious actions, ဖြစ်ပြီးသောကုသိုလ်တရားတို့ကိုအတွန်ပွါးများအောင်လုံ့လပြုခြင်း.

သမ္မာ, *(Pali,) adj.* good, right, just.

သမ္မာအာဇီဝေါ, *n.* the right way of supporting life.

သမ္မာကမ္မန္တော, *n.* right actions.

သမ္မာဒိဋ္ဌိ, *n.* good stability, being established in good sentiments.

သမ္မာဋ္ဌိတိ, *n.* good continuance.

သမ္မာဓိ, *(Pali,) n.* embracing good sentiments, holding sound doctrine.

သမ္မာဒိဋ္ဌေ, *n.* a disposition to embrace good sentiments or sound doctrine, ကောင်းသောအယူဟူတတ်ခြင်း.

သမ္မာဝါစာ, *n.* proper language.

သမ္မာသင်္ကပ္ပေါ, *n.* right intention.

သမ္မာပါဒ်, *n.* a kind of trance, in which evil cannot affect the person.

သမ္မာဝါယာမော, *n.* intelligence rightly directed.

သမ္မာသတိ, *n.* proper care or attention, good heed.

သမ္မာသမာဓိ, *n.* composure, serenity.

သမ္မာသမ္ဗုဒ္ဓ, *n.* one of the four classes of Boodhs; viz. the highest class, or a divine being, သမ္ဗုဒ္ဓဘုရားသခင်သည်သမ္မာသမ္ဗုဒ္ဓမည်၏.

သမှို, *v.* to be of a dull colour, dim, depressed, cast down.

သမား, *n.* an artificer, one skilled in any business, as ဆေးသမား, a physician.

သမားဟူရာ, *n.* do.

သမားညို, *n.* an astrologer.

သမားပြို, *n.* an astrologer.

သမိတ, *(Pali,) v.* to consume with fire, ဓိးစား.

သမိတိ, *(Pali,) n.* an assemblage, collection, the place of assembling, သတင်း ၊ အပေါင်း.

သမိတော, *(Pali,) n.* peace, comfort, ease, pleasure, ငြိမ်သက်ခြင်း.

သမီး, or သ္မီး, *n.* a daughter.

သ္မီးကညာ, *n.* the daughter of a king, presented to another king.

သ္မီးကညာဆက်, *v.* to present a king's daughter to another king.

သ္မီးအိမ်ရှင်, *n.* husband and wife.

သ္မီးခင်ပွန်း, *n.* husband and wife.

သမီးမောင်နှံ *n.* do.

သမီးခြောက်သား, *n.* cousins, by affinity.

သမုဒါ, *(Pali,) n.* the present time, things present, မျက်မှောက်.

သမုဋ္ဌာဒိဝေက, *n.* see under ဝိဝေကငါးပါး.

သမုတ်, *v.* to give or bestow, as a title or name.

သမုဒ်, *n.* a command, a law, ပညတ်.

သမုဒ္ဒံ, *(Pali,) n.* a house, place of residence, အိမ်.

သမုဒ္ဒိ. *(Pali,) n.* sea-salt, သမုဒ္ဒရာဆား.

သမုဒ္ဒေါ, *(Pali,) n.* the sea or ocean, သမုဒ္ဒရာ.

သမုဒ္ဒရာ, *n.* a sea, an ocean, ပင်လယ်.

သမုဒ္ဒရာနက်ဆန်းဖွယ်ရှစ်ပါး, *n.* the eight wonders of the sea; viz. the water's continually rising into swells, and sinking into vallies, အစဉ်အတိုင်လှိုင်းထွန်းသည်; that the waters do not overspread the shores, ကမ်းကိုမလွှမ်းသည်တပါး; that it throws dead bodies upon the shore, အကောင်ပုတ်ကိုကမ်းသို့ဖြစ်တင်သည်တပါး; that the five great rivers lose their names when they reach the sea, မြစ်ကြီးငါးစင်းသမုဒ္ဒရာသို့ရောက်လျှင်အမည်ကိုစွန့်သည်တပါး; that its waters never are diminished or increased, ယုတ်ခြင်းတက်ခြင်းမရှိသည်တပါး; that the salt is so mingled with the water as to become but one, တခုတည်းသောဆားငံရေရှိသည်တပါး; that it is the repository of precious stones, &c. ရတနာတို့၏တည်ရာဖြစ်သည်တပါး; and that it is the residence of Nats, နတ်တို့၏နေရာဖြစ်သည်တပါး.

သမုဒ္ဒိသင်္ဃာ, *(Pali,) n.* a priest of Boodh.

သမုဒိယ, *(Pali,) v.* to call or distinguish by name.

သမုတိဝေါဟာရ, *n.* the giving of arbitrary names.

သမိုက်, *v.* to measure, take the measurement.

သမိုင်း, *n.* an ancient record.

သမြိတ်, *n.* a polite name for the breasts of a female.

သယ်, (1) *v.* to remove from one place to another.

သယ်, (2) *v.* to perform, transact business, ဒိ.

သယ်, (3) *v.* to carry, bear away, ဆောင်ရွက်.

သယ်, (4) *int.* indicative of surprise.

သယ်, (5) *adv.* an intensive to other words.

သယ်, (6) *affix,* denoting the profession or business of a person.

သယ်နှယ်, *adv.* how? ဘယ်နှယ်.

သယ်ပိုး, *v.* to perform, transact business.

သယောက်, *n.* an adulterer.

သယောင်, *n.* a hermaphrodite, ထပုံး.

သထိလေ, *int.* indicative of surprise.

သရ, (1) *v.* to remember, to call to mind.

သရ, (2) *n.* a vowel.

သရက်သီး, *n.* a mango; သရက်, *n.* the mango tree.

သရဏ္ဍန်, *n.* the sanders tree, of which there are many varieties.

သရဆယ်, *v.* to repeat, rehearse, စီးဖြန်း၊ ရွတ်၊ ဖတ်.

သရဇ္ဈာယ်, *v.* to repeat mentally or vocally, စီးဖြန်း; to worship.

သရဏဂုဏ်, *n.* the three objects of worship, viz. deity, law, and priests.

သရဏံ, *(Pali,) v.* to injure, cut off, destroy, သတ်၊ ညှဉ်းဆဲ.

သရဘူ, or ဘူ, *n.* one of the five great rivers.

သခုဘူ, *n.* a crest, an ornament for the head.

သရီယ, *(Pali,) n.* the body, ကိုယ်.

သရိယံ, *n.* do.

သရိရိ, *(Pali,) n.* rational beings, သတ္တဝါ.

သရီရ, *n.* a relic of Boodh, ဓာတ်တော်.

သရုပ်, *n.* nature, character.

သရူပံ, *(Pali,) n.* nature, character, သရုပ်၊ သဘော.

သရေ, *n.* skin, leather.

သရေအိတ်, *n.* a leathern bucket, bag, or purse.

သရေစာ, *n.* luncheon, any kind of food except rice and curree.

သရေစာစား, *v.* to eat do.

သရဲဘော, *n.* courage, valour.

သရော, (*Pali,*) (1) *n.* a collection of water, a pond, lake, ကန်အိုင်.

သရော, (2) *n.* a sound, an articulate sound.

သရိုင်, (1) *n.* a wild uncultivated field.

သရိုင်, (2) *n.* a large kind of basket.

သရိုင်ရက်, *n.* a wild uncultivated field.

သရော်, *v.* to provoke, excite, stimulate, ပျက်ရယ်ပြုချင်း.

သရွတ်, *n.* mortar, clay.

သရွေ့, *adv.* as much as there is, all, whatsoever, whosoever, whatever, ရှိသမျှ၊ ဟူသည်မျှ.

သလင်း, *a contraction of* တော်သလင်း, *n.* September.

သလ္လ, (*Pali,*) *n.* a thorn, sharp stick, ငြောင့်.

သလ္လပေါ, *(Pali,)* *n.* sociable conversation, ဆန့်ကျင်ခြင်းမှကင်းလျက်အချင်းချင်းပြောဆိုခြင်း.

သလာဋု, *(Pali,)* *n.* unripe fruit, မိန်းသောအသီး.

သလိလံ, *(Pali,)* *n.* water, ရေ.

သလ္လာဝတီ, *n.* the name of a river, a branch of the Irawaddy, also called ခြင်းတွင်းမြစ်.

သလာပွေး, *n.* scurf, a ring-worm, ပွေးသစင်ငွေ.

သလိပ်, *n.* phlegm, ချွဲကန်း.

သလုံး, *n.* the calf of the leg.

သလုံးသား, *n.* do. ခြေသလုံး.

သလေး, *adj.* small, childish, ခလေး ၊ သူငယ်.

သလေးဆံ, *n.* a small sort of rice.

သလဲ, (1) *n.* sand, သဲ.

သလဲ, (2) *n.* a pomegranate.

သလွန်, *n.* a king's bed, a sofa.

သလွဲ, *n.* lead.

သဝ, *n.* being, a state of being.

သဝိညာဏက, *n.* an animate substance, opposed to အဝိညာဏက.

သဝနံ, *(Pali,)* (1) *n.* the ear, နား ; hearing, ကြားခြင်း.

သဝနံ, (2) *v.* to offer sacrifice, worship, ပူဇော်.

သဝင်္ကော, *(Pali,)* *n.* an eel, a kind of fish, ငါးရွှေ.

သသက္ကံ, *(Pali,)* *adv.* verily, truly, certainly, စင်စစ်.

သသနံ, *(Pali,)* *n.* abuse, severity, injury, ညှဉ်းဆဲခြင်း.

သသမိယ, *n.* an ungrateful person.

သဟဂုတ်, (*Pali,*) *n.* the mind.

ထဟန်ပက္ကူ, *n.* flannel, သက္ကလတ်ပက္ကူ.

သဟာဒိယောဂ, (in grammar,) the instrumental case, when ending in နှင့် ; with, together with.

သဟာယ, *n.* an association of people.

သဟဲ, *(Pali,)* *n.* strength, force, means, အား ၊ ခွန်း.

သံ, (1) *v.* to be determined, resolute, have the mind bent upon any thing, ရည်သံ ၊ ရည်မှတ်.

သံ, (2) *n.* sound, a fine gentle sound, အသံ.

သံ, (3) *n.* iron.

သံ, (4) *n.* a musical instrument.

သံဒိုးကင်း, *n.* a frying pan, any flat iron pan.

သံချိတ်, *n.* a hook of any kind, a fish-hook.

သံကပ္ပေါ, *(Pali,)* *n.* a good intention, a good thought.

သံကြပ်, *n.* a gridiron.

သံချေး, *n.* rust, iron rust.

သံကြိုး, *n.* an iron chain.

သံချပ်, *n.* a coat of mail, မိန်ညီ ၊ မိန်ချပ် ၊ ဝတ်လုံ.

သံချေး, *n.* rust, iron rust.

သံချောင်း, *n.* a piece or bar of iron.

သံခြေခြင်း, *n.* fetters, iron bangles.

သံခြေချောင်း, *n.* iron fetters.

သံချွန်, *n.* a pointed iron, a nail.

သံညင်း, *n.* a tonjan, an uncovered palanquin.

သံညောင်း, *n.* a fine gentle sound, သံလွင်.

သံဒါ, *n.* a precious stone.

သံတမန်, *n.* a messenger.

သံတောင်, *n.* a large cubit-measure from 4 to the breadth of 8 fingers.

သံတော်, *n.* a royal mandate or order: the voice of God; eight particulars are mentioned as distinguishing marks of the voice of Deity; viz. it is clear or intelligible, သန့်ရှင်းသည်; agreeable, pleasant, သာယာသည်; easy to be known, သိလွယ်သည်; worthy to be heard, နာခြင်ဘွယ်ရှိသည်; infrequent, မပြားသည်; full, လုံသည်; deep, နက်နဲသည်; and produces an echo, ပဲ့ထင်ထပ်သည်.

သံတော်ဦးတင်, *v.* to petition, address a king or great personage.

သံတော်ချ, *v.* to issue a royal order.

သံတော်ဆင့်, *n.* a register of royal orders.

သံတွေး, *n.* a red-hot iron.

သံပယာသီး, *n.* a lime, or lemon.

သံပိ, *(Chinese,)* *n.* a ship's boat.

သံပုလ္လိတော, *(Pali,)* *n.* a flower-tree or plant, ပွင့်သောသစ်ပင်.

သံပူထိုး, *v.* to cauterize.

သံပြား, *n.* a plate of iron.

သံပတ်, *n.* the day after to-morrow, သဘက်.

သံပန်း, *v.* to entangle, catch in discourse.

သံမဏိ, *n.* steel.

သံမရာသီး, *n.* a lemon or lime, သံပျာသီး.

သံရိ, *n.* a nail.

သံမှို, *n.* do.

သံမျှားကောက်, *n.* a hook, a fish-hook.

သံမျှားချိပ်, *n.* do.

သံယုတ္တ, *n.* one division of the Boodhist scriptures.

သံထော, *v.* to be crazy, insane, ရူး.

သံလုံး, *n.* an iron ball.

သံလိုက်ကျောက်, *n.* a loadstone.

သံလျက်, *n.* a sword, a sabre, a two-edged sword.

သံလျင်, *n.* a tonjan, an uncovered palanquin, sedan chair.

သံလျော့, *v.* to lessen, diminish, become small.

သံလွင်, *n.* cymbals, a fine gentle sound.

သံလွင်, *n.* the olive tree.

သံလွင်သီး, *n.* the fruit of the olive tree.

သံဘော, *n.* a royal despatch boat.

သံဝရ, *(Pali,) n.* using watchfulness, care, attention, affording protection, စောင့်ရှောက်ခြင်း.

သံဝဋ္ဋ, *n.* one of the four grand divisions in an entire revolution of nature; (see မဟာကပ်.) This period, it is said, commences with rain which deluges the four great and all the small islands together with Myenmo mount, and destroys all that exists therein: after this, seven suns successively break forth, dry up the waters, and consume the system.

သံဝဋ္ဋဋ္ဌာယီ, *n.* another of the four grand divisions in မဟာကပ်. This period continues, from the time the general conflagration ceases, through another deluge, whose waters, by continual motion and dashing together, congeal and harden, and thus form the substance of a new system; see သံဝဋ္ဋ.

သံဝဏ္ဏနာ, *(Pali,) n.* an opening, commencement, ဆင့်.

သံဝါသ, (1) *n.* the genitals ; sexual intercourse.

သံဝါသ, (2) *v.* to associate, to have sexual intercourse.

သံဝေဂ, *n.* fear, dread.

သံသရာ, *n.* the world, လောက ; a state of existence.

သံသတ်, *n.* the name of a certain tree.

သံသေဒဇာ, *n.* that which is produced by filth ; see under ဝဋ္ဋသဇ္ဇ.

သံသော့, *n.* sulphur, fire.

သံဟတိ, *n.* a collection, whole, အပေါင်း.

သာ, (1) *v.* to increase, exceed, surpass, မိုး ၊ လွန် ၊ ကဲ ၊ ရှိ.

သာ, (2) *v.* to be agreeable, pleasant, ပြည်းစွင်း ၊ ပျော်.

သာ, (3) *adv.* only, (applied to any part of speech, and in any position ;) as တခုသာ, only one.

သာ၍, *prefixed to adjectives,* the second degree of comparison.

သာကိ, *(Pali,) v.* to be excellent, ဖြတ်.

သာကီဝင်, *n.* a race of kings, မင်းမျိုး.

သာခါ, *(Pali,) n.* the branch of a tree, သစ်ခက်.

သာခီ, *(Pali,) n.* a tree, သစ်ပင်.

သာဂရော, *(Pali,) n.* the sea, ocean, သမုဒ္ဒရာ.

သာဓု, *(Pali,) v.* to be good, righteous, excellent.

သာဓု, *adv. a term of approbation,* well done, that is right.

သာဓုသာဓု, *adv.* do.

သာမ, *n.* one book of the Vedas.

သာမဂ္ဂိ, *(Pali,) n.* an associate, a companion, အပေါင်းအဖော်.

သာမည, *(Pali,) n.* common, middling, not distinguished, နှင်နှင်.

သာမဏေ, *n.* a probationer for the priesthood.

သာမိ, *n.* an owner ; *in grammar,* the name of the possessive case, terminating in ၏.

သာမော, *v.* to be pleasant, agreeable, joyful.

သာယာ, *v.* to be pleasant, agreeable, joyful.

သာရဏ်, *n.* a certain star ; see နက္ခတ်.

သာရကပ္ပ, *n.* a world, in which but one deity makes his appearance.

သာရမဏ္ဍကပ္ပ, *n.* a world, in which four deities make their appearance.

သာရထိ, *(Pali,) n.* a charioteer, coachman, ရထားထိန်း.

သာဒိယာ, (*Pali,*) *n.* an object of love or delight, that which gives pleasure, နှစ်သက်ဖွယ်.

သာဒိ, *v.* see သက်သာ.

သာလိကာ, *n.* the black-bill Mina.

သာဝကဗုဒ္ဓ, *n.* one of the four classes of Boodhs ; the whole assembly or priests of Boodh collectively considered, တပည့် သားတော်သိမ်းပါဒါပေါင်းသည့်သာဝကဗုဒ္ဓမည်၏.

သာသနာ, (1) *n.* power, authority, (applied to deity ;) the time in which the divine power or authority is displayed, သာသနာ တော်.

သာသနာ, (2) *n.* religion, instruction of a religious nature, doctrine, အဆုံးအမတော်.

သာသနာဝ, *n.* the time in which there is no display of the deity ; a time when religion or religious instruction is neglected or forgotten.

သာသနာထွန်း, *v.* to promulgate religious instruction, to advance or promote religion.

သာသနာပိုင်, *n.* the chief or head of the priests appointed by the king.

သာသနာပြုဆရာ, *n.* a religious teacher, one who propagates a religion.

သား, (1) *n.* a son, offspring.

သား, (2) *n.* the inmates or inhabitants of any place, as of a house, town, or country.

သား, (3) *n.* a line, mark.

သား, (4) *v.* to extend or draw a line, ငင် ၊ ချား.

သား, (5) *n.* the name of a certain animal ; see သားခြီးယင်.

သား, (6) *n.* flesh, အသား.

သားနှုပ်, *n.* the young of any thing before weaned, so called from their needing protection.

သားချင်း, *n.* blood relation.

သားစိမ်း, *n.* raw flesh.

သားညှင်း, *n.* long slices of dried flesh.

သားတော်, *n.* the grandson or daughter of a slave ; applied also to young trees, which sprout from the roots of the parent tree.

သားတော်, (1) *n.* a royal son, or the son of a great personage.

သားတော်, (2) *n.* a distant relation.

သားတန့်, *n.* the fœtus in its fourth stage.

သားနီရည်, *n.* the water of a blister or other sore.

သားနံရေ, *n.* do.

သားနှား, *v.* to mark, draw out, as a line, road, or circle.

သားပေါက်, *n.* the son or daughter of a slave.

သားမွေး, *n.* an adopted son.

သားမီး, *n.* a daughter.

သားမြတ်, *n.* a female's breast, နို့ နို့အုံ.

သားမြီးယပ်, *n.* a chowree, or long brush, made of the tail of a wild cow, or the animal called သား; used by the higher classes to drive away flies: that used by the poor is called ရင်ခြောက်.

သားယောက်ျား, *n.* a son, a male child.

သားရင်း, *n.* an own son, in distinction from an adopted son.

သားရေ, *n.* skin, leather.

သားရေအိတ်, *n.* a leathern bottle or bag.

သားရေနယ်သမား, *n.* a dresser of leather, a tanner or shoemaker.

သားရေသမား, *n.* do.

သားရဲ, *n.* any wild or ferocious animal.

သားလတ်, *n.* the middle son, (of three sons.)

သိ, (1) *v. affix*, sign of the imperative or precative mood.

သိ, (2) *v.* to know, perceive, understand, တတ်.

သိ, (3) *v.* to be grateful, have a sense of favour bestowed, ကျေးဇူးကိုအလွန်သိ.

သီလရှင်, *n.* a female who is disposed to become a religious mendicant, and observes the six duties belonging to that class of persons.

သိက္ခာ, (1) *n.* a duty, religious observance, virtue, good work; applied particularly to the priest, သီလ ၊ ဓုတင် ၊ အကျင့်.

သိက္ခာ, (2) *n.* a general term applied to sins of priests, of which two hundred and twenty-seven are enumerated.

သိက္ခာပုဒ်ငါးပါး, *n.* the five general precepts or commands enjoined on priests by the Burman religion.

သိဋ္ဌိတာ, (*Pali,*) *v.* to be wise, cunning, prudent, knowing, လိမ္မာ.

သိကျွမ်း, *v.* to become acquainted or familiar with. Hence အသိအကျွမ်း, *n.* an acquaintance, familiar friend.

သိကြား, (1) *v.* to know, understand, have a knowledge of things.

သိကြား, (2) *n.* one of the higher orders of intellectual beings, of which there are said to be thirty-two classes.

သိကြားပြည်, *n.* the country inhabited by do.

သိကြားမင်း, *n.* the king of Nats. There are however said to be three Nats who excel him in glory, viz. ဗြဟ္မာ့ဒွေနတ် ၊ အနေ့ဝဏ္ဏနတ်, and မဟာဒွေနတ်: they obtained this transcendency on account of certain offerings, made in the time of one of the incarnations of Boodh.

သိကြားမြင်မြှင်, *v.* to know, receive information, အကြားအသိအမျှား အမြှင်.

သိခင်, *n.* see သခင်.

သိခင်ဘုရား, (from သိခင်, lord, master, &c. and ဘုရား, God,) *n.* this term is applied to great personages, particularly to Boodh, or deity; the whole number of absolute or distinct Boodhs is twenty-eight, viz. တဏှင်္ကရာ ၊ မေဓင်္ကရာ ၊ သရဏင်္ကရာ ၊ ဒီပင်္ကရာ ၊ ကောဏ္ဍည ၊ အနောမဒဿီ ၊ ပဒုမ္မုတ္တိုရ ၊ အတ္ထဒဿီ ၊ ဓမ္မဒဿီ ၊ သိဒ္ဓတ် ၊ တိဿ ၊ မင်္ဂလ ၊ သုမန ၊ သောဘိတ ၊ နာရဒ ၊ သုမေဓာ ၊ သုဇာတာ ၊ ပိယဒဿီ ၊ ဖုဿ ၊ ရေဝတ ၊ ဝေဿဘူ ၊ ဝိပဿီ ၊ သိခီ ၊ ကောဏ္ဍသံ ၊ ဂေါဏာဂုဏ် ၊ ကဿပ ၊ ဂေါတမ, and အရိမိတ္တေယျ: only the five last belong to the present system or မဟာကပ်, and the last of these has not yet appeared. The first twenty-three made their appearance in different successive worlds previous to the present world; (for the different worlds, see မဟာကပ်,) တဏှင်္ကရာ, lived eighty thousand years; မေဓင်္ကရာ, ninety thousand; သရဏင်္ကရာ, eighty thousand; ဒီပင်္ကရာ ၊ ကောဏ္ဍည ၊ အနောမဒဿီ ၊ ပဒုမ္မုတ္တိုရ ၊ အတ္ထဒဿီ ၊ ဓမ္မဒဿီ ၊ သိဒ္ဓတ် ၊ and တိဿ, lived each a hundred thousand years; မင်္ဂလ ၊ သုမန ၊ သောဘိတ ၊ နာရဒ ၊ သုမေဓာ ၊ သုဇာတာ ၊ ပိယဒဿီ, and ဖုဿ, lived each ninety thousand years; ရေဝတ, and ဝေဿဘူ, lived each sixty thousand years; ဝိပဿီ, eighty thousand; သိခီ, seventy thousand; ကောဏ္ဍသံ, forty thousand; ဂေါဏာဂုဏ်, thirty thousand; ကဿပ,

twenty thousand ; and ဂေါတမ, the last Boodh, lived only eighty years : ဒီပင်္ကရာ ။ မင်္ဂလ ။ ရေဝတ ။ အတ္ထဒဿီ ။ and ပိယဒဿီ, were each eighty cubits in stature ; ကောဏ္ဍည ။ နာရဒ ။ ပဒုမုတ္တရ ။ သုမေဓ ။ and ဓမ္မဒဿီ, were each eighty-eight cubits; သုမန, ninety cubits ; သိဒ္ဓတ္ထ ။ တိဿ, and ဝေဿဘူ, were each sixty cubits ; သောဘိတ ။ အနောမဒဿီ ။ ပဒုမ ။ and ဖုဿ, were each fifty-eight cubits ; သုဇာတ, fifty cubits ; သိခီ, seventy cubits ; ကကုသန်, forty cubits ; ဂေါဏာဂုဏ်, thirty cubits ; ကဿပ, twenty cubits; and ဂေါတမ, the last Boodh, was eighteen cubits in stature. (A full account of these different Boodhs will be found in a book entitled ဗုဒ္ဓဝံသကျမ်း, 3rd part, from the 51st page.)

သိခီ, *n.* one of the twenty-eight Boodhs ; see the different Boodhs under သိခင်ဘုရား.

သိင်္ဂီနိက္ခ, (1) *n.* a kind of gold, သိင်္ဂီနိက်ရွှေ.

သိင်္ဂီနိက္ခ, (2) *n.* a four-horned antelope.

သိင်္ဂါရ, *(Pali,)* *n.* enjoyment, pleasure ; delight in an object, ပျော်ပါးခြင်း ; amusement and pleasure enjoyed with women, မြူးထူးခြင်း.

သိင်္ဂါလ, *n.* a jackal, မြေခွေး.

သိင်္ဂူ, *(Pali,)* *n.* a kind of fish, ငါးကျဲ.

သိင်္ဃာဋက, (*Pali,*) *n.* the end of a path or road, ခရီးလမ်းဆုံး.

သိင်္ဃာဏိကာ, *(Pali,)* *n.* mucus, the mucus of the nose, နှပ်.

သိဉ္ဇီဝ, *n.* one of the states of punishment ; see ငရဲ.

သိပ်, *v.* to lay down gently, put to rest, as a child upon a couch.

သိပ်ထား, *v.* do.

သတင်း, (1) *n.* news, intelligence of any circumstance or event, စကားသံ.

သီတင်း, (2) *n.* a duty, performance, work, practice of religious duties, သီလ ။ အကျင့်.

သီတင်းငါးပါး, *n.* five general precepts or duties binding on all mankind, ပဉ္စသီလငါးပါး ; see ငါးထငါးပါး.

သီတင်းစောင့်, *v.* to practise religious duties, to observe worship days.

သီတင်းနေ့, *n.* a day which is set apart for the particular observance of religious duties, a worship day. N. B. In each month or moon there are four days devoted to the particular observance of religious duties, viz. the eighth day of the waxing of the moon; the day of the full; the eighth of the wane; and the day of the change.

သီတင်းသုံး, *v.* to meditate upon and observe religious duties, to think upon the three objects of worship, viz. deity, the commands of deity, and assembly; (see under ရတနာ.) Hence those who attend strictly to their devotions are called သီတင်းသုံးဖိုးသူတော်, if men; and သီတင်းသူမ, if women.

သိတ္ထက်, (*Pali,*) *n.* wax, bees wax, ဖယောင်း.

သိတာဂ္ဃာ, (*Pali,*) camphor, ပရုတ်.

သိတံ, (*Pali,*) *n.* smiling, the act of smiling, ပြုံးချင်း.

သိတိက, (*Pali,*) *adv.* fewish, neither few nor many, ကျော့ကျော့၊ နည်းနည်း.

သိဒ္ဓတ္ထ, (*Pali,*) *n.* mustard, the mustard plant, မုန်ညင်း.

သိဒ္ဓန္တ, (*Pali,*) *n.* any thing received, doctrine, opinion, sentiment, အယူ.

သိဒ္ဓိ, (*Pali,*) *n.* fulness, completion, perfection, ပြည့်စုံချင်း.

သိမ်, (1) *n.* a building, in which the ceremony of initiation is passed on those who are received into the priesthood.

သိမ်, (2) *n.* Leo, the fifth sign of the zodiac.

သီဟိုဠ်ကျွန်း, *n.* the island on which the Burman sacred books (ပိဋကတ်သုံးပုံ) were first written, said to be Ceylon. It was four hundred and fifty years after the death of Gaudama, in the reign of Wootetmane, (ဝဋ္ဋဂါမဏိမင်းကြီး,) that these books were first committed to writing, in doing which all the priests were employed. Nine hundred and thirty years after this event, in the reign of the great king Nammah (မဟာနာမမင်း,) they were translated out of the သီဟိုဠ်ကျွန်း language into Magada by Bokedah-Gauthah, a great religious ascetic, and brought to the island of ဇမ္ဗူ, or, as expressed by the Burmans, our island; see the four great islands under ကျွန်း.

သိန်း, (1) *n.* a kind of kite, (different from စွန်.)

သိန်း, (2) *adj.* hundred thousand, as တသိန်း, 100,000 ; နှစ်သိန်း, 200,000, &c.

သိန့်, *v.* to shake, totter, quake, လှုပ်၊ နှိုင့်.

သိန့်နှိန့်, *v.* to shake, tremble, as with weakness.

သိန့်လှုပ်, *v.* see သိန့်.

သိန့်သိန့်, *adv.* tremblingly, totteringly, moving backward and forward.

သိန္ဓု, (*Pali,*) *n.* the ocean, သမုဒ္ဒရာ ; a river, မြစ်; a place of that name, သိန္ဓုမြည်သောအရပ်.

သိန္ဓာ, *n.* a kind of flying horse.

သိနိဒ္ဓါ, (*Pali,*) *adj.* slow, easy, gentle, ဖြေးဖြေးချောင်း ; soft, pleasant, agreeable, သိမ်မွေ့သည်.

သိနေဟော, (*Pali,*) *n.* affection, regard, love, ချစ်ချင်း.

သိနိုင်, *v.* to know, be acquainted with.

သိပ်, (1) *v.* to stuff, cram, pound down or press together, as earth, for the purpose of hardening it, or as a charge in the barrel of a gun.

သိပ်, (2) *v.* to become numerous, thick, close, crowded, ထူ၊ ထပ်၊ များ. Hence အသိပ်အနှက်, any thing close or compact.

သိပ်, (3) *v.* to hunger or thirst, be famished, မွတ်၊ ငတ် ; (seldom used alone.)

သိပ်မွတ်, *v.* do.

သိပ်သိ, *v.* to cram, stuff, squeeze, press down, crush, stop up by stuffing, &c.

သိပ်ထိုး, *v.* do.

သိပ်နယ်, *v.* do. (most commonly used.)

သိပဒ်, *n.* a certain disease, seated in the feet, ခြေထိုင်သောအနာ.

သိဗ္ဗန်, (*Pali,*) *v.* to confine, bind, tie, secure, shut up, cut off, terminate, ချုပ်.

သိပ္ပံ, (*Pali,*) *n.* a knowledge of arts and sciences.

သိမ်, (1) *v.* to be little, diminutive, inferior, ငယ်၊ ညံ့၊ သေး.

သိမ်, (2) *n.* a spot of ground or building devoted to certain religious purposes, a holy place.

သိမ်, (3) *v.* to be gentle, soft, flexible, pleasant, agreeable, ညှာ.

သိမ်နု, *v.* do.

သိမ်မွေ့, *v.* to be suitable, good, excellent, beautiful, mild, pleasant, meek, gentle, နူးညံ့.

သိမ်း, (1) *v.* to seize, snatch up, to take away, carry off.

သိမ်း, (2) *v.* to gather, collect, take, as taxes; take in possession, confiscate, ရုံး.

သိမ်း, (3) *v.* to lay aside, put into a secure place, sheath, as a sword.

သိမ်း, (4) *n.* a bird which seizes its prey as a hawk, or as birds which live on fish.

သိမ်းရု, *v.* to gather, collect, as taxes, &c.

သိမ်းဆည်း, *v.* to gather up, take away, lay up for future purposes.

သိမ်းထား, *v.* to collect, gather up, put into a secure place, lay aside; sheath, as a sword, &c.

သိမ်းပိုက်, *v.* to take a woman on account of debt, and cohabit with her.

သိမ်းယူ, *v.* to gather, as taxes, take in possession, confiscate, &c.

သိမ်းရိတ်, *v.* to reap, cut down, gather, as grain.

သိမ်းရုတ်, *v.* to gather, collect, as taxes; take into possession, confiscate.

သိမ်းသွင်း, *v.* do.

သိမ့်, *v.* to shake, totter, tremble, quake, လှုပ် ၊ နှိုး.

သိမ့်သိမ့်, (2) an intensive to words of motion.

သိမ့်သိမ့်, (1) *adv.* shakingly, totteringly.

သိမန္တာ, (*Pali,*) *n.* a female, a woman, မိန်းမ.

သိမာ, (*Pali,*) *n.* a separation, boundary, division, district, part, section, အပိုင်းအခြား.

သိမြင်, *v.* to know, perceive, understand, be acquainted with. Hence အသိအမြင်, knowledge, information.

သိထင်, *v.* do.

သိရိ, (*Pali,*) *n.* deserved reputation, excellence of character, အသရေ ၊ ကြက်သရေ.

သိသိ, *adv.* small, fine, powder-like.

သိသိညက်ညက်, *adv.* do.

သီ, (1) *v.* to be dim, as the eyes from dazzle or weakness, မြာ ၊ မှိုင်း ၊ မှုန်.

သီ, (2) *v.* to string, put in order as upon a string, place in a continuous row, ကုန်း ၊ ထိုး.

သီချင်း, *n.* a song or hymn; *also,* a particular kind of verse.

သီချင်းဆို, *v.* to sing, as a song.

သီချင်းသီ, *v.* do.

သီတ, (*Pali,*) *n.* cold, အေးခြင်း.

သီတလော, (1) *n.* do.

သီတလော, (2) *v.* to be cold, ချမ်းသည်.

သီတံ, (*Pali,*) *n.* see သီတ.

သီတာ, *n.* a collection of water, or an imaginary river, of which there are seven which run between the mountains around Myenmo mount, မြစ်.

သီရိ, (*Pali,*) (1) *n.* elegance, beauty, တင့်တယ်ခြင်း.

သီရိ, (2) *n.* happiness, enjoyment, စည်းစိမ်.

သီရိဓမ္မာသောက, *n.* an ancient king, who, for his great merit, obtained authority over the whole of ဇမ္ဗူဒိပ်, or the great south island, and to the extent of twelve miles above and below it.

သီလ, *n.* duties, precepts, religious austerities, ဝန်ပိုလ်ိ ၊ သိတင်း.

သီလဂုဏ်, *n.* the praise or reward due to the practice of religious austerities.

သီလငါးပါး, *n.* the five duties binding on all mankind, viz. to refrain from taking the life of another, that is, murder, သူတပါး၏အသက်ကိုမသတ်အပ်; to refrain from stealing the goods of another, သူတပါး၏ဥစ္စာကိုမခိုးမယူအပ်; to refrain from committing adultery, သတပါးမယားသားအမိခံရာကိုမလွန်ကျူးအပ်; to refrain from drinking intoxicating liquors, သေအရက်ကိုမသောက်အပ်; and to refrain from every evil deed, မကြံတိသောအကြင့်ကိုမကြင့်အပ်.

သီလဗ္ဗတုပါဒါန်, (1) *n.* one of the sacred books.

သီလဗ္ဗတုပါဒါန်, (2) *n.* an evil passion or affection.

သီလပျက်, *v.* to act contrary to duty, to break one's word, သစ္စာပျက်.

သီလ; (*Pali*,) *n*. religious observances, အကျင့်သီလ ၊ သိတင်း; good actions or deeds, ကောင်းသောအကျင့်.

သီလ, (2) *n*. disposition, nature, သဘော.

သီလာ, (*Pali*,) *n*. a rock.

သီလာပထဝီ, (from သီလာ, a rock, and ပထဝီ, the earth,) *n*. the great rock on which the lowest state of punishment is said to be situated.

သီကုံး, *v*. to string, arrange on a string, as pearls.

သိဝ, (*Pali*,) *n*. the termination of evil, that is, annihilation or absorption, ဘေးမရှိခြင်းကို ပြုတတ်သောနိဗ္ဗာန်.

သီသွင်း, *v*. to insert, put in, as in stringing beads, &c.

သီဟ, (*Pali*,) (1) *n*. a lion, ချင်သေ့.

သီဟ, (2) *v*. to be good, excellent, မြတ်သည်.

သီဟရာဖြ, *v*. to come in conjunction, as the heavenly bodies; see ဗျေဆြဲရာဖြ.

သီဟိုဠ်, *n*. the island of Ceylon; see သိန်ဆိုဠ်.

သီး, (1) *v*. to bear fruit, တင်း ၊ ဖူး. Hence အသီး, *n*. fruit; also applied to any thing which has the form or appearance of fruit.

သီး, (2) *v*. to divide, separate, put a space between, make different, ခြား. Hence အသီးအခြား, *n*. a division, separating line. Hence also အသီးသီး, *adv*. distinctly, individually.

သီး, (3) *v*. to sneeze, feel an irritation in the throat or nostrils.

သီးပင်, *n*. a fruit-tree.

သီးပွင့်, *v*. to open or appear, as fruit in its first stage, to produce fruit, တင်းဖူး.

သီးမှည့်, *v*. to ripen, as fruit.

သီးရွက်ကျင်, (1) *v*. to fall off, as fruit or leaves, to shed leaves as trees.

သီးရွက်ကျင်, (2) *n*. the time of shedding leaves or fruit.

သူ, (1) *pers. n*. another, (in distinction from one's self.)

သူ, (2) (*Pali*,) *v*. to be good, well, easy, ကောင်း.

သူ, (3) *adv*. very, exceedingly, အလွန်.

သူကတော, (*Pali*,) *n*. a good deed, the merit of good deeds, ကောင်းမှု.

သူခ, (*Pali*,) *n*. bliss, happiness, ချမ်းသာ.

သုခမိန်, *n.* a wise man, a person of understanding, one fit to be of the king's council, ပညာရှိ.

သုဓမျှာ, *adv.* pitifully, distressingly; see ဓမျှာ.

သုခ, (*Pali,*) *n.* the enjoyment derived from pleasurable objects, ချမ်းသာခံစားတတ်ခြင်း.

သုဂတိ, *n.* a good state, state of enjoyment; a happy transition from one state of being to another.

သုဂ္ဂတိ, *n.* do.

သုဂတိအဟိတ်ပုထုဇ္ဇန်, *n.* persons who are deficient in any of their powers or faculties, whether of body or mind; such are said to have စိတ်လေးဆယ်ထဲ.

သုဋ္ဌဒိန်, *n.* an astronomical term, a division of the day and night according to astronomical calculation.

သုစရိုက်, (from စာရိတ္တ, a deed, *Pali,*) a good deed; opposed to ဒုစရိုက်, a bad deed.

သုဇာတာ, *n.* one of the twenty-eight Boodhs; see the different Boodhs under ဆီခင်ဘုရား.

သုညကမ္ဘာ, *n.* a world in which no Boodh makes his appearance, and all existence remains at rest or quiet.

သုတ်, (1) *v.* to rub, rub on, as oil; to wipe, clean.

သုတ်ဆေး, *v.* to clean by washing, &c.

သုတ်ပျင်, *v.* to put in order, or prepare by cleaning.

သုတ်ပွတ်, *v.* to rub, clean, wipe, rub on, as oil.

သုတ်လိမ်း, *v.* to anoint, rub over, as ointment, &c.

သုတ်သင်, *v.* to rub, make clean, &c. လိမ်းကျံ.

သုတ်, (2) *n.* an aphorism or rule in grammar.

သုတ်, (3) *n.* an auditor, one who hears.

သုတ်, (4) *v.* to hear, hearken.

သုတ်, (5) *v.* to seize, snatch away, လု ၊ ဆိုး.

သုတ်ချည်း, *adv.* suddenly, instantly, ရုတ်ချည်း ၊ မြန်မြန်.

သုတ်သုတ်, *adv.* do.

သုတ်, (6) *n.* one grand division of the Boodhist scriptures, containing three books, viz. သုတ်သီလက္ခန် ၊ သုတ်မဟာဝါ ၊ and သုတ်ပါထေယျ.

သုတ်, *n.* (7) semen, ကာမရေ.

သုတ်စဉ်, *n.* an aphorism or rule in grammar.

သုတ္တန်, *n.* one division of the Boodhist scriptures, the same as သုတ်, which see.

သုတ်ပါထေယျ, *n.* a subdivision of the sacred writings; see သုတ်.

သုတ်မဟာဝါ, *n.* a subdivision of the sacred writings; see သုတ်.

သုတ်သီလက္ခံ, *n.* another do. see သုတ်.

သုတဗုဒ္ဓ, *n.* a kind of semi-Boodh, a person of extensive wisdom and knowledge, အကြားအမြင်များ၍ပညာရှိသောသူသည်သုတဗုဒ္ဓမည်၏.

သုဒ္ဓသုဓ်, *n.* the food of Nats; see ဩဇာ.

သုဒ္ဓဒိန်, *n.* a certain division of the day and night, according to astronomical calculation.

သုဒ္ဓါဝါသဘုံ, *n.* one stage of the Bramha country, consisting of five divisions, viz. အဝိဟာ, in which the inhabitants live throughout a thousand complete revolutions of nature, (for a revolution of nature see မဟာကပ်;) အာတပ္ပာ, the inhabitants of this division live through two thousand revolutions of nature; သုဒဿာ, in this they live through four thousand revolutions of nature; သုဒဿီ, in this, through eight thousand; and အကနိဋ္ဌ, in this, they live through sixteen thousand revolutions of nature.

သုဒဿန, (1) *n.* the name of a city in the Nat country, in which the king of Nats resides.

သုဒဿန, (2) *n.* one of the mountains around the lake အနောတတ်; (see the seven lakes under ဟိမဝန္တာ.) This mountain is said to be made of gold, and is above two thousand four hundred miles in height.

သုဒဿာ, *n.* the third division in the highest stage of the Bramha country; see သုဒ္ဓါဝါသဘုံ.

သုဒဿီ, *n.* the fourth division in the highest stage of the Bramha country; see သုဒ္ဓါဝါသဘုံ.

သုန်, *v.* to be discouraged, dejected, နွမ်း ၊ ညှိုး.

သုန်လေး, *v.* do.

သုန်သပ်, *v.* to be smooth, nice; see သပ်.

သုနန္ဒာ, *n.* a famous garden in the first stage of the Nat country, situated east of the city တာဝတိံသာ; it extends above

12,000 miles, and is the scene for recreation and pleasure to the inhabitants of တာဝတိံသာ.

သုပ်သုဝ်, *adv.* quickly, instantly, မြန်မြန်.

သုဘကိဏှ, *n.* the third division in the third stage of the Bramha country; see ဗြဟ္မာဘုံ.

သုဘကိဏှာဘုံ, *n.* do.

သုဘရာဇာ, (from သုဘ, a dead body, *Pali,*) *n.* a person whose employment it is to burn dead bodies, ဒွန်းစဏ္ဍာ. Hence အသုဘ, *n.* short sentences concerning the human body, of which there are ten, (see ကမ္မဋ္ဌါန်း.)

သုံးဆောင်, *v.* to use, make use of, support, as one's life; take nourishment.

သုမေဓါ, *n.* one of the twenty-eight Boodhs; see the different Boodhs under သီခင်ဘုရား.

သုရာ, *n.* spirits, intoxicating liquors, သေ.

သုတ္တန္တ, *n.* a division of the Boodhist scriptures, (marked သု.)

သုသာန်, *n.* a place of burning dead bodies or of interment, a burying-ground, သင်္ချိုင်း.

သုသာန်စောင့်, *n.* a person who has the care of a burying-ground.

သုသမာ, (*Pali,*) *n.* a good appearance, elegance, ဖြစ်တင့်တယ်ခြင်း.

သုဏှာ, (*Pali,*) *n.* a daughter-in-law, a son's wife, ချွေးမ.

ဂုသိ, (*Pali,*) *n.* a summit, top, highest part, chief, အထွဋ်.

သုသိရ်, (*Pali,*) *n.* an instrument of music, any wind instrument, အပေါက်ရှိသောစည်.

သုဟဒ, (*Pali,*) *n.* a friend, associate, ခင်ပွန်း.

သုံ့, (1) *v.* to turn over, turn on one side, ဖော်.

သုံ့, (2) *v.* to be bad, few, little, inferior; to be empty, desolate.

သုညကမ္ဘာ, *n.* a world in which there are no incarnations of Boodh, and the inhabitants are without any religious system.

သုံ့ပြင်း, *v.* to be destitute of proper qualities; be few, bad, little, desolate or empty.

သုံး, (1) *v.* to use, spend, make use of, as money or any article.

သုံး, (2) *v.* to be empty, destroyed or desolate as a city.

သုံး, (3) *adj.* three, (marked ၃.)

သုံး, (4) *v.* to practise virtue, perform duty, သီလသုံး.

သုံးဆောင်, *v.* to use, spend, make use of; to support, as one's life, take nourishment. Hence အသုံးအဆောင်; *n.* any article of use, furniture, provisions, &c.

သုံးပွင်း, or သုံးဖြင်း, *v.* to be empty, desolate or destroyed, as a city.

သုံးလူ့ကထွတ်မြတ်စွာဘုရား, *n.* the supreme or most high God.

သုံးသပ်, (1) *v.* to examine as a book or science previously studied.

သုံးသပ်, (2) *v.* to feel as a mark of affection, particularly when a person is ill or dying; to soothe.

သုံးစေ, *n.* a messenger, person sent.

သုံ့, (1) *v.* to shut up, secure, imprison, လှောင်ထား. N. B. this root is frequently written with the heavy accent.

သုံ့, (2) *n.* a captive, prisoner of war, လက်ရ.

သုံ့ကျွန်, *n.* do.

သုံ့ခပ်, *v.* to attack, go against, take, as prisoners.

သုံ့ပန်း, *n.* a captive, prisoner of war.

သုံ့ပန်းလူ, *n.* do.

သုံ့လူ, *n.* do.

သူ, *pers. n.* a person, he, she, or it.

သူ့ဇနီးရာ, *n.* another's wife, (in distinction from one's own wife.)

သူကောင်း, *n.* a good or respectable person, an excellent man; this term is particularly applied to persons of a religious character, those of high descent, and those who possess wisdom and riches.

သူကြီး, *n.* a chief, head-man, person of consequence, any great personage.

သူကြွယ်, *n.* a rich man, a person in opulent circumstances, of whom there are said to be five different classes, ငါးဆွေး.

သူခပ်သိမ်း, *n.* all mankind, mankind collectively or generally, လူတကာ.

သူခိုး, *n.* a thief, robber.

သူဗြိထ, *n.* proper name.

လူငယ်, *n.* a small person, a person of little consequence, a child. A child when first born is supposed to have its mind deeply impressed with the past: if it came last from hell, or a state of punishment, it reflects upon what it there suffered, and weeps; but if it came last from the Nat country, it reflects upon its late enjoyments, and smiles.

လူငယ်အိမ်, *n.* the pupil of the eye (or the child's house,) so called because the image or form of a small person is always to be seen by a person looking into the eye.

လူဌေး, *n.* a rich man, person in opulent circumstances, လူကြွယ်.

လူတပါး, *n.* another person, (in distinction from one's self, or some particular person named;) a neighbour.

လူတောင်းစား, *n.* a person who obtains support by asking it of others, a beggar.

လူတော်, *n.* a just, upright, or religious person.

လူတော်ကောင်း, *n.* do. (most commonly used.)

လူဘုန်းစား, *n.* one who lives on the good fortune or bounty of others, a beggar.

လူမိုက်, *n.* an ignorant or foolish person; လူမိုက်လက္ခဏာသုံးပါး, three things or signs by which foolish or ignorant persons may be distinguished, viz. though destitute of property, they desire to marry, ဥစ္စာမရှိဘဲလျက်အာဝါဟကိုအလိုရှိခြင်း; though destitute of strength, they delight in fighting and contention, အားခွန်မရှိဘဲလျက်ခိုက်ရန်ဖြစ်ခြင်းကိုအလိုရှိခြင်း; and though destitute of a knowledge of the sacred books, they have a wish to dispute about the subjects which they contain, ကျမ်းဂန်အကြားအမြင်နည်းလျက်အခြင်းအခုံကိုအလိုရှိခြင်း.

လူမြတ်, *n.* an excellent person; chiefly applied to priests.

လူယုတ်, *n.* an inferior or mean person; လူယုတ်လက္ခဏာသုံးပါး, the three marks or signs of an inferior mean person, viz. he goes into the house or place of another without being invited; he has a great many remarks to make when no questions have been asked him; and he boasts of his own fame and importance.

သုရင်ကဲ့, *n.* a glass which collects the rays of the sun into a focus, a focus-glass.

လုရင်း, *n.* a person who is accustomed to receive wages for labour, a hired person.

သုရပထ, (*Pali,*) *n.* open space, the sky, ကောင်းကင်.

လုရိပု, (*Pali,*) *n.* Athooyah, or the enemy of Nats, နတ်တို့အရိရာန်သူ၊ အသူရာအမည်.

လုရာ, (*Pali,*) *n.* pleasure, delight, enjoyment, applied to pleasure derived from sensual objects, as in eating, drinking, ဖြူးထူး.

သုရာ, *n.* a happy Nat, ရွှင်ထူးထက်သောသူ၊ နတ်အမည်.

သုရိယာ, (*Pali,*) *n.* the sun, နေ.

သုရိယာကန်, *n.* a precious stone, said to produce fire from the rays of the sun.

သုရိယာမဏ္ဍလ, (from သုရိယာ, the sun, and မဏ္ဍလ, a circle, *Pali,*) *n.* the circle or circumference of the sun.

သူရဲ, *n.* a soldier, brave man.

သူရဲရိ, *n.* a champion, ယောက်ျားကောင်း.

သူရဲမြေး, *n.* the surface of a wall or fortress.

သူရဲသူခင်, *n.* a soldier, an army, စစ်သည်.

သုလာ, *n.* the pupil of the eye; see သူငယ်အိမ်.

သူလျှို, *n.* a secret messenger, a spy, an informer, တံလျှို.

သေ, (1) *v.* to die; to be extinguished as fire; to depart, pass by, အသက်ထွက်၊ လွန်. Hence သေရပလေသည်, is dead, &c. သေခြင်းအကြောင်းလေးပါး, *n.* the four causes of death; viz. though the influence of good deeds performed in a previous state is not exhausted, yet the period which is the established term of human life being past, the person will die,—this is called အာယုက္ခယ; though the established term of human life is not yet passed, the influence of good deeds performed in a previous state being exhausted, the person will die,—this is called ကမ္မက္ခယ; when the term of human life is past, and the influence of former good deeds exhausted, the person dies,—this is called ဥဘယက္ခယ; in the last case, though the established term of human life is not past, nor the influence of previous good deeds exhausted, yet on account of some evil deed performed in a previous state, the person dies suddenly without previous illness, and without changing his position,—this is called ဥပစ္ဆေဒကကံ.

သေ, (2) *n.* spirituous liquor, သုရာ ၊ အရက်.

သော်, a contraction of သော၏.

သေက္ခ, see အသေက္ခ.

သေက္ခပုဂ္ဂိုလ်, *n.* a general term, embracing seven classes of persons; viz. သောတာပတ္တိမဂ္ဂဋ္ဌာန်ပုဂ္ဂိုလ်, or a person who has performed the duties of the first state of an Areeyah; သကဒါဂါမိမဂ္ဂဋ္ဌာန်ပုဂ္ဂိုလ်, or one who has performed the duties of the second state of an Areeyah; အနာဂါမိမဂ္ဂဋ္ဌာန်ပုဂ္ဂိုလ်, or one who has performed the duties of the third state of an Areeyah; အရဟတ္တမဂ္ဂဋ္ဌာန်ပုဂ္ဂိုလ်, or one who has performed the duties of the fourth state of an Areeyah; သောတာပတ္တိဖလဋ္ဌာန်ပုဂ္ဂိုလ်, or one who has obtained the rewards of the first state of an Areeyah; သကဒါဂါမိဖလဋ္ဌာန်ပုဂ္ဂိုလ်, or one who has obtained the rewards of the second state of an Areeyah; and အနာဂါမိဖလဋ္ဌာန်ပုဂ္ဂိုလ်, or one who has obtained the rewards of the third state of an Areeyah; see အရိယာ.

သေကောင်, *n.* a dead body, အကောင်.

သေကျာ, *v.* see သေချာ, to remain, &c.

သေခင်း, *n.* death, မသာခင်း.

သေခင်းသေနာ, *n.* do.

သေခင်းသေမှု, *n.* the business or act of dying.

သေချ, *v.* to order, put in order, perform minutely or with precision, စေ့ ၊ ဖြေ ၊ သတ်စေ့ ၊ အပိုင်သေ.

သေချာ, (1) *v.* see သေချ.

သေချာ, (2) *v.* to remain unchanged, be permanent, durable, not easily destroyed, မြဲ.

သေငြိမ်, *v.* to remain in quietness, be unruffled, calm, serene.

သေငယ်, *n.* a swoon, fainting fit, or any thing of the kind, when for a short time life seems extinguished.

သေအ, *n.* spirituous liquor.

သေဋ္ဌမာန်, *n.* one kind of pride, or ostentation, viz. that which acknowledges no superior, ငါသာမြတ်သည်၊ ငါထက်မြတ်သောသူမရှိဟူ မာန်မူခြင်း။

သေဏိ, (*Pali,*) (1) *n.* a company of artists, a name applied to artists in general, အတတ်ထူးတို့၏အပေါင်း။

သေဏိ, (2) *n.* a row, a continued series, အစဉ်.

သေတူရှင်ဘက်, *n.* one who will live and die with his partner or companion.

သေဒဇာ, *n.* a term applied to animals or insects which are engendered by dampness.

သေနတ်, or သေန္နတ်, *n.* a musket, small gun.

သေနတ်ပြောင်း, *n.* the barrel of a musket.

သေနတ်ပစ်, or ပြစ်, *v.* to discharge a musket.

သေနတ်မောင်း, *n.* the lock or trigger of a musket.

သေနတ်မောင်းတင်, *v.* to cock a gun.

သေနံ, (*Pali,*) *n.* a bed, mattress, အိပ်ရာ၊ အိပ်ရာနေရာ.

သေနာ, (*Pali,*) *n.* soldiers, an army, စစ်သည်၊ စစ်သည်ရဲထိပ်ပေါ်.

သေနာနီ, (*Pali,*) *n.* a military officer, a general, စစ်သူကြီး.

သေနာပတိ, *n.* do.

သေမင်း, *n.* the king of death, also called ယမနတ်.

သေယျထာပိ, (*Pali,*) a particle of resemblance, ဥပမာနိပါတ်တည်း.

သေရက်, *n.* spirituous or intoxicating liquor.

သေလော, (*Pali,*) *n.* a mountain, တောင်.

သေလွန်, *v.* to be dead, be extinguished, passed away.

သေဝကော, (*Pali,*) *n.* the suite or guards of a king or governor, မင်းခယောက်ျား.

သေဝန, (*Pali,*) *n.* being, a state of being, ဖြစ်ခြင်း.

သေဝဝ်, *v.* to fix, make steadfast or binding, as an agreement, or any thing to prevent its moving.

သေသတ်, *v.* to be proper, be in due order ; to be well finished, well performed, beautiful, သေချာ.

သေသေချာချာ, *adv.* properly, in proper order, completely, minutely.

သေသေဝဝ်ဝဝ်, *adv.* an intensive to words of fixedness, and quietness.

သေသော, (*Pali,*) *v.* to remain, be fixed, steadfast.

သေသောက်, *v.* to drink intoxicating or spirituous liquor; သေသောက်ခြင်းအပြစ်ခြောက်ပါး, the five particulars in which consists the sin of drinking intoxicating liquor; viz. it occasions loss of property, မျက်မှောက်၌ဥစ္စာယုတ်ဆုံးသည်; it occasions a quarrelsome disposition, အငြင်းအခုံရိုက်ခုံပွားသည်; it produces sickness and disorders in the body, အနာဟောင်းအနာသစ်ဖြစ်သည်; it causes a person to do things very discreditable, and to lose his reputation, မအပ်သောအမှုအကျင့်ထိုကျင့်မိ၍မကောင်းသောသတင်း ရှိသည်; it makes a person shameless and impudent, အကြောက်အရှက်မရှိသည်; and it destroys the understanding, ပညာ အဆင်အချင်ကင်းသည်.

သေး, (1) *v. affix,* denoting present continuance, yet, still; as ပြုသေးသည်, he is still doing; မသွားသေး, he is not yet gone.

သေး, (2) *n.* urine, ရေဟောင်း.

သေး, (3) *v.* to be small, fine, slender, လျော့ ၊ သွယ် ၊ ငယ် ၊ သို့.

သေးအိမ်, *n.* the bladder, ကျင်ငယ်အိမ်.

သေးချောင်း, *n.* the urethra, ကျင်ငယ်ချောင်း.

သေးပေါက်, *v.* to evacuate urine, ဆီးသွား.

သေးရေ, *n.* urine.

သေးသေး, *adv.* very small, very minute, &c.

သေးသေးတင်, *n.* the mark ံ, placed over a letter, which has the power of final မ.

သေးသေးနုတ်နုတ်, *adv.* denotes being cut or broken into fine or small particles.

သေးသွယ်, *v.* to taper away, become long and slender; see သွယ်, to branch off, &c.

သဲ, *v.* to make a loud, mixed, or confused sound; to be clamorous, like the sound of a multitude.

သဲသဲ, *adv.* clamorously.

သဲသဲသိန့်သိန့်, *adv.* clamorously, thunderingly; applied to loud confused sounds, တစ်ကြွေးကြော်သောအသံ.

သဲ, (1) *n.* sand, သဲထဲ.

သဲ, (2) *v.* to be unwell, exhausted, faint, out of breath, as a person dying.

သဲခုံ, *n.* a sandbank, သောင်ခုံ.

သဲနာရီ, *n.* a sand or hour-glass.

သဲပုံ, *n.* a heap of sand, a sandbank.

သဲပြင်, *n.* a sandy, barren plain.

သဲလုံး, *n.* sand.

သဲ့, *v.* to skim, take off scum.

သဲ့ငင်, *v.* do.

သဲ့ယူ, *v.* do.

သဲ့လင်, *n.* see သလေး.

သော, (1) *n.* the genitals, whether male or female, လိင်၊ နိမိတ်.

သော, (2) *a connective affix*, nearly equivalent to who, which, and that, as ခိုးသောသူ, a person who steals; ရောက်သောသင်္ဘော, the ship that arrives, or the arriving ship; but frequently it is merely connective; (when contracted, it is သ, ၏, or ေ၏.)

သော, (3) *v. affix*, sign of the assertive or indicative mood; sometimes contracted to သ.

သော, (4) (*Pali,*) *n.* a thing, goods, property, ဥစ္စာ၊ မိမိဥစ္စာ.

သော, (5) (*Pali,*) *n.* a companion, associate, friend, အဆွေခင်ပွန်း.

သောက်, *v.* to drink, smoke; as ရေသောက်, to drink water; ဆေးသောက်, to smoke tobacco; မျိုသောက်.

သောက်ကြာ, *n.* the planet Venus; the sixth day of the week, Friday.

သောက်စုပ်, *v.* to suck, sup up, drink in, စုပ်ယူ.

သောက်ထုပ်, *v.* do.

သောက, (*Pali,*) *n.* distress, sorrow, grief, oppression of mind, anxiety, ဗျာပါ၊ စိုးရိမ်ချင်း.

သောကော, (*Pali,*) *n.* do.

သောင်, (1) *v.* to be shrivelled, withered, သွေ့.

သောင်သွတ်, *v.* do.

သောင်, (2) *n.* a sandbank, a shoal.

သောင်သာ, *v.* to be well, healthy, in a healthy state, ကျန်းမာ၊ ချမ်းသာ.

သောင်း, (1) *v.* to cry aloud, be clamorous, ဟစ်.

သောင်းသဲ, *v.* do.

သောင်း, (2) *v.* to rebel, revolt, ပုန်ကန်.

သောင်းကြွင်း, *v.* do.

သောင်း, (3) *adj.* ten thousand, as လူတသောင်း, ten thousand men; လူနှစ်သောင်း, twenty thousand men, &c.

သောင်းလေးချပ်, (from သောင်း, 10,000; လေး, 4; and ချပ်, a place,) *n.* a term used to designate four distinct places or countries, viz. ဇမ္ဗူဒိပ်ကျွန်း၊ အဝီစိငရဲ၊ အသူရာပြည်, and တာဝတိံသာနတ်ပြည်, because each of these places are just 10,000 ယူဇနာ, or above 120,000 miles, in extent.

သောငှါ, *v. affix*, for, in order to, for the purpose of.

သောစနံ, (*Pali,*) *n.* oppression of mind, anxiety, grief, sorrow, စိုးရိမ်ခြင်း.

သောစိကော, (*Pali,*) *n.* a tailor, အပ်ချုပ်သမား.

သောဏ္ဏံ, (*Pali*, *n.* gold, ရွှေ.

သောဏီ, (*Pali,*) *n.* a row, a continued series, အစဉ်.

သောတ, (*Pali,*) *n.* the ear, နား.

သောတာယတန, *n.* the faculty of hearing.

သောတာပန်, *n.* a person who has attained the first state of an Areeyah, ရဟန္တာ.

သောတာပတ္တိ, *n.* the first state attained by an Areeyah, the state of an Areeyah.

သောတာပတ္တိမဂ်, *n.* the duties of that state.

သောတာပတ္တိဖိုလ်, *n.* the rewards due to a person who has performed those duties.

သောတာပတ္တိမဂ္ဂဋ္ဌာန်, *n.* a person who has already performed the duties of that state.

သောတာပတ္တိဖလဋ္ဌာန်, *n.* a person who has already obtained the rewards of those duties.

သောမနဿ, (*Pali,*) *n.* joy, delight, pleasure, ရွှင်ချင်း၊ ဖြိုးထူးခြင်း.

သောမနဿဖြစ်, *v.* to rejoice, be delighted, pleased, ဝမ်းသာ.

သောဓနိ, (*Pali,*) *n.* a broom, တံမြက်.

သောပ္ပ, (*Pali,*) *n.* sleep, taking rest in sleep, အိပ်ပျော်ချင်း.

သောမနဿိ, (*Pali,*) *n.* comfort, enjoyment, pleasure, သာယာထတော်ချင်း

သောဘိတ, *n.* one of the twenty-eight Boodhs; see the different Boodhs under သခင်ဘုရား.

သောသော, (1) *adv.* all together, all at once.

သောသော, (2) *n.* an intensive to words of sound, as သောသောညံ, a very great noise, a very confused sound.

သောသောဆူ, *adv.* or *adj.* tumultuous, noisy.

သောသောဆူဆူ, *adv.* do.

သောဠသ, (*Pali,*) *adj.* sixteen, တဆယ်ခြောက်.

သော့, (1) *n.* a key, a lock.

သော့, (2) *v.* to be silly, weak, foolish, သွပ် ၊ ပညာမဲ့.

သော့, (3) *v.* to be light, in regard to weight, shrivelled, destroyed, သွတ် ၊ သွန်ပေါ့.

သော့ဆိတ်, *n.* a lock.

သော့ကျင်, *n.* a bolt or spring, used to fasten a door or any thing of the kind, the bolt or spring of a lock.

သော့ကြောင့်, *affix,* because, on account of.

သော့ခတ်, *v.* to lock, fasten with a lock or bolt.

သော့သဖွယ်, *affix,* as, like as, similar to.

သော့ပေါက်, *n.* a key-hole.

သော့ခလောက်, *n.* a padlock.

သော့သော့, *adv.* lightly, of no weight, of little consequence, destitute of proper qualities.

သော့သွပ်, *v.* to be silly, weak, foolish; to be shrivelled, light, decayed, သွတ်.

သော်, (1) *v. affix,* sign of the subjunctive mood.

သော်, (2) *v. affix,* when, as သွားသော်, when he went or had gone, having gone.

သော်တ, *n.* the moon, လ.

သော်လည်း, *affix,* though, although, notwithstanding, as သွားသော် လည်း, though he goes, went, or had gone.

သို, (1) *n.* the penis, လိင် ၊ လီး.

သို, (2) *v.* to secure, keep back, deposit, lay up, take care of, for the purpose of concealment or preservation.

သိုက်, (1) *n.* a nest, place of rest, depository, &c. as ငှက်သိုက်, a bird's nest; မြေသိုက်, an excavation, or place in the ground for depositing treasures, as gold, silver, &c.; သိုက် is also used figuratively to signify any abode or place of rest; see အသိုက်.

သိုက်တွင်း, *n.* an excavation, or place dug out for the purpose of burying or concealing treasures, &c.

သိုက်; (2) *n.* a prophecy, sign, omen.

သိုက်နိမိတ်တဘောင်, *n.* a sign, omen, common saying, proverb.

သိုက်မြိုက်, *v.* to be beautiful, agreeable, suitable, proper.

သိုက်သိုက်မြိုက်မြိုက်, *adv.* delightfully, beautifully, very suitable, ထင်ထယ် ၊ ကျော့ကပ်ပတ် ၊ သိမ်မွေ့.

သိုင်း, *n.* a cudgel, rod, or stick used in a certain play, ကြိမ်.

သိုင်းကစား, *v.* to play at do.

သိုထား, *v.* to lay aside for future or occasional use, take care of, secure, ဆည်းထူး.

သိုမှီး, *v.* do.

သိုသွင်း, *v.* to put into a secure place, treasure up for the purpose of concealment or preservation.

သိုး, (1) *n.* a sheep, ဆိတ်သိုး.

သိုး, (2) *n.* a hat, ခမောက်.

သိုး, (3) *v.* to ferment, rot, become rancid, ပုတ် ၊ နံ ၊ ဟောင်း.

သိုးခမောက်, *n.* a hat.

သိုးမွေး, *n.* wool.

သိုးရေ, *n.* leather made of the skin of a sheep.

သိုးသား, or သိုးအမဲသား, *n.* the flesh of sheep, mutton.

သိုးသိုးသန့်သန့်, *adv.* scarcely audible, particularly applied to distant sound, အနည်းငယ်မျှကြားသောအသံ.

သို့ , *affix,* to, towards, at, unto, according to.

သို့က, or အသို့က, *affix,* hence, from this, applied to place or manner.

သို့ကြောင့်, သို့သောကြောင့်, *affix,* wherefore, on that or this account.

သို့စင်, *affix,* as, as much, about as much.

သို့တမင်, *affix,* therefore, (obsolete.)

သို့တပြီးကား, *affix,* therefore, being thus, though, although.

သို့တမှန်, *affix,* as, as much, about as much.

သို့တမူကား, *affix,* therefore, for the above reason, but.

သို့ပြီး, *affix,* if so, being so.

သို့မချည်း, *affix,* therefore; *adv.* if not so, (used in conversation.)

သို့ရှိ, *affix,* therefore, if so, နို့ရှိ.

သို့မှ, *affix*, whence, applied to manner or place.

သို့မှာ, *affix*, herein, therein ; applied to manner or place.

သို့သော်လည်း, *affix*, though it is thus, notwithstanding that or this.

သွက်, *v.* to be reduced, weak, as paint which has too much oil, spirits too much water, &c. သွက်သွက်မလျှင်.

သွက်ချာပါဒလေ, *n.* a term used for the palsy.

သွင်, *n.* a form, image, likeness ; see အသွင်.

သွင်း, *v.* to put in, cause to enter, insert.

သွင်းထား, *v.* see သွင်း.

သွင်းထိုး, *v.* see သွင်း.

သွတ်, (1) *v.* to be introduced, inserted, put in, as into any vessel, ထည့်.

သွတ်, (2) *n.* pewter, zinc.

သွတ်, (3) *v.* to snatch, seize, carry off, as a bird its prey, သုတ်.

သွတ်, (4) *v.* to be shrivelled, contracted, dried up, သွေ့ ၊ သောင် ၊ သော့.

သွတ်ထည့်, *v.* see သွတ်, to be introduced, &c.

သွတ်လောင်း, *v.* to pour into ; as water, rice, or any thing of the kind into a vessel.

သွတ်သုတ်, *v.* to seize, snatch away.

သွတ်သောင်, (1) *v.* to be shrivelled, dried up, shrunk, &c.

သွတ်သောင်, (2) *v.* to be silly, foolish, out of one's senses, not to know what one is about, စိတ်မကောင်း. .

သွတ်သော့, *v.* to be shrivelled, dried up, shrunk, &c.

သွတ်သွင်း, *v.* see သွတ်, to be introduced, &c.

သွတ်သွေ့, *v.* see သွတ်သော့.

သွန်, *v.* to be bad, corrupt, rotten, decayed, light, of little value, ပေါ့.

သွန်သင်, *v.* to instruct, teach, give instruction, show, point out, ပြ ၊ ထ.

သွန်း, (1) *v.* to be spiral, rise in a spiral form, သွယ် ၊ မြင့်.

သွန်း, (2) *v.* to pour out, upon, or into ; to sprinkle, scatter upon or about, သွန်း ၊ လျှန်း.

သွန်း, (3) *v.* to make, form, lay out, ထု.

သွန်းထု, *v.* to make, form, lay out, ထု.

သွန်းဖြန်း, *v.* to sprinkle upon, scatter about.

သွန်းမြင့်, *v.* to rise in a spiral manner.

သွန်းလောင်း, *v.* to pour out, upon, or into.

သွန်းသွန်းသွယ်သွယ်, *adv.* spirally, in a spiral form.

သွန်းသွယ်, *v.* to rise in the form of a spire.

သွပ်, *v.* to be silly, foolish, out of one's senses, not to know what one is about.

သွပ်နှမ်း, *v.* do.

သွပ်ရူး, *v.* to be insane, crazy, mad.

သွပ်သောင်, *v.* see both definitions of ထွတ်သောင်.

သွမ်, *v.* to be empty, silly, foolish, void of understanding.

သွမ်ပြင်း, *v.* do.

သွမ်မှား, *v.* to err through folly, or want of understanding.

သွမ်းလွယ်, *v.* do.

သွမ်း, *v.* to ridicule, treat with contempt, ကဲ့ရဲ့.

သွမ်းသွေး, *v.* do.

သွန့်, *v.* to be shrivelled, withered, contracted, useless, ဆော့.

သွန့်ပေါ့, *v.* do.

သွန့်သောင်, *v.* do.

သွန့်သွတ်, *v.* do.

သွယ်, (1) *num. affix*, applied to things which are long and slender, as မြစ်နှစ်သွယ်, two rivers; see Gram.

သွယ်, (2) *v.* to string as beads, file on a string.

သွယ်, (3) *v.* to branch off, as a river; to taper, run in a regular course, spin out, သေးသွယ်. Hence အသွယ်, a branch, as of a river.

သွယ်, (4) *n.* a ray or stream, as of light; a branch, as of a river, &c.

သွယ်လျ, *v.* to be long and slender, taper away, spin out.

သွယ်ဝိုက်, *v.* to be long or drawn out in a winding manner, as a meandering stream.

သွယ်ဖြောင်း, *v.* to be long and narrow, run on in a regular course, as a road, a stream, &c.

သွား, (1) *v.* to go, proceed, depart; သွားလေရှင်း, to be going.

သွား, (2) *n.* a tooth, of any description.

သွား, (3) *n.* the edge of a knife or other instrument ; see အသွား.

သွားကျိန်း, *v.* to set on edge, as the teeth.

သွားကြားထိုး, *n.* a tooth-pick.

သွားချည်လာချည်, *adv.* going backward and forward, repeatedly going and coming.

သွားဖြဲ, *v.* to show the teeth, to grin.

သွေ, (1) *v.* to shun, turn off or aside, to avoid, neglect, as the observance of a duty or command, မဖောက်.

သွေ, (2) *v.* to be changed, become different, ဖောက်ပြန်.

သွေရှောင်, *v.* see the first definition of သွေ.

သွေလှန်, *v.* to be repaired, become different, be reproduced.

သွေဖဲ, *v.* see the first definition of သွေ.

သွေး, (1) *v.* to rub, as a knife upon a stone ; to grind, whet, sharpen, ပွတ်၊ တိုက်.

သွေး, (2) *v.* to pulverize, reduce to powder, make fine.

သွေး, (3) *v.* to cause to do, excite to action, whether good or နှိုးဆော်.

သွေး, (4) *n.* blood. Hence အသွေး, *n.* do. အသွေးအသား, *n.* an own child.

သွေးအိမ်, *n.* the placenta.

သွေးကြောင်း, *n.* a blood-vessel, a vein or artery.

သွေးခုတ်, *v.* to let blood.

သွေးခဲ, *n.* clotted blood.

သွေးစိမ်း, *n.* fresh blood.

သွေးဆောင်, *v.* to tempt, entice, draw away by temptation, excite to action, whether good or bad.

သွေးတက်, *v.* expresses the rising of the blood into the face, as through anger or any sudden emotion.

သွေးတုလာ, *n.* one kind of rheumatism.

သွေးတိုက်, *v.* to rub, as any thing upon a stone, to grind, whet, sharpen.

သွေးထိုး, *v.* to let blood.

သွေးလျည်နာ, *n.* a disease, species of dropsy.

သွေးပွတ်, *v.* see သွေးတိုက်.

သွေးရာ, *n.* an excitement, temptation ; the object of do.

သွေ့, *v.* to dry, become dry, evaporate. Hence အသွေ့, *n.* dryness, (opposed to အစွတ်, moisture.)

သွဲ့, *v.* to shove, push, as an elephant.

သွဲ့ငြှို, *v.* do.

သျှဂ္ဂရ, *n.* a chief disciple, အဂ္ဂသာဝက.

သျှာ, *n.* the tongue, (*pron.* ရှာ.)

သျှား, *v.* to be scarce, not plenty, (*pron.* ရှား) ငတ်.

သျှိုထိုးသျှိုတောပတ်, *adv.* uneven, irregular, up and down, မညီမညွတ်.

သျှူ, *v.* to hiss, as a serpent, (*pron.* ရှူ ,) ရှူး.

သျှောင်ပဒ္ဒိ, *n.* charms found on the head or in the hair.

## ဟ.

ဟ, *v.* to open, make wide, as the mouth, ဟိုက် ၊ ပွင့် ၊ လှစ်.

ဟက်, (1) *v.* to roar, as a lion.

ဟက်, (2) *v.* to cut horizontally, or in a slanting direction.

ဟင်း, (1) *v.* to be vacant, open, empty, mere space, မရှိ.

ဟင်း, (2) *n.* curree, vegetable or animal sauce.

ဟင်းခင်း, *n.* a bed or garden of vegetables.

ဟင်းခါး, *n.* a kind of medicine.

ဟင်းချို, *n.* kind of spoon or ladle.

ဟင်းသျှိုး, *n.* food of any kind, victuals.

ဟင်းနုံဖူး, *n.* see ရုပိကာ.

ဟင်းရည်, *n.* broth.

ဟင်းရွက်, *n.* greens, vegetables for curree.

ဟင်းလင်း, (1) *n.* empty space, vacuity, ကောင်းကင်.

ဟင်းလင်း, (2) *v.* to be empty, vacant, be mere space.

ဟင်းလင်း, (3) *adv.* entirely open, as a door, &c. entirely vacant, as space.

ဟင်းလင်းပွင့်, *v.* to be entirely open, as a door, &c.

ဟင်းလျာ, *n.* victuals, food, ဟင်းသျှိုး.

ဟင်းသပဒါး, *n.* a kind of red paint, vermilion, red lead.

ဟင်းသာ, (1) *n.* a kind of fabulous bird, a wild duck.

ဟင်းသာ, (2) *n.* a certain star or constellation ; see တာရာ.

ဟစ်, *v.* to make a loud noice, cry out, halloo, အော် ၊ ကြွေးအော်.

ဟစ်ကြွေး, *v.* do. (most commonly used.)

ဟင်ကျော်း, *v.* see ဟင်.

ဟည်, *adv.* yes, an affirmation.

ဟည်း, *v.* to roar, as an elephant when irritated.

ဟဋ္ဌစိတ္တာ, *(Pali,) v.* to rejoice, be gratified, delighted, ဝမ်းမြောက်သည်.

ဟာသော, *(Pali,) n.* pleasure, delight, satisfaction, ရွှင်ချင်း.

ဟတ္ထံ, *(Pali,) n.* the hand, လက်.

ဟတ္ထိ, *(Pali,)* (1) *n.* an elephant, ဆင်.

ဟတ္ထိ, (2) *n.* a certain star or constellation; see တာရာ.

ဟတ္ထိကန္တ, *n.* a certain harp which by its sound allures and overcomes elephants.

ဟတ္ထိဃဋာ, *n.* a herd of elephants, ဆင်ပေါင်း.

ဟတ္ထိနီ, *n.* a female elephant, ဆင်မ.

ဟတ္ထိမေဏ္ဍာ, *n.* an elephant driver, a person who has the care of elephants, ဆင်စီးဆင်ထိန်း.

ဟဒယ, or ဟဒယံ, *(Pali,) n.* the mind, spirit, soul, စိတ်နှလုံး.

ဟဒယဂါနိထ, *(Pali,) n.* the breath, ဝင်သက်.

ဟန်, *n.* an appearance, pretence, show, a feigned appearance.

ဟန်ပန်, (1) *n.* do.

ဟန်ပန်, (2) *n.* strength, valour.

ဟန်ပြု, *v.* to make an appearance, pretence, show, feign, dissemble.

ဟန့်, *v.* to stop, prevent, interrupt, hinder, ဆီး ၊ မြစ် ၊ တား.

ဟန့်တား, *v.* do.

ဟပ်, *v.* to unite together, join, cement, bring into contact, စပ် ၊ ဂည် ၊ တွဲ.

ဟမ္ဘော, *(Pali,)* a vocative particle, ခေါ်ချင်း.

ဟဗျ, *(Pali,) n.* boiled rice, which is offered as an act of worship or merit, ယဇ်ပူဇော်အပ်သောထမင်း.

ဟယ်, (1) see ဟဲ.

ဟယ်, (2) *v.* to produce a sound, as in yawning, &c.

ဟယ်မြည်, *v.* do.

ဟယော, *(Pali,) n.* a horse, မြင်း.

ဟရိ, *(Pali,) n.* a green colour, စိမ်းသောအဆင်း; also a yellow or gold colour, ရွှေသောအဆင်း.

ဟရိတော, *(Pali,)* *n.* a green colour, စိမ်းသောအဆင်း.

ဟရိ, *n.* a person employed in filthy work, as a mater.

ဟရေ, *(Pali,)* a vocative particle, ခေါ်ခြင်း.

ဟဝေ, *(Pali,)* *adv.* truly, verily, certainly, really, စင်စစ် ၊ အကယ်ထိ ၊ အကယ် ၊ အမှန် ၊ မချွတ်.

ဟဝေါ, *(Pali,)* *n.* worship, making offerings, ပူဇော်ခြင်း.

ဟသ, *(Pali,)* *n.* smiling, laughing, ရယ်ခြင်း.

ဟသန်, *n.* do.

ဟသိတ်, *n.* do.

ဟံ, *n.* an appearance, pretence, deception, feigned appearance; see ဟန်.

ဟံဆောင်, *v.* to assume an appearance, make a false show or pretence; as သီလရှိသည်ဟံဆောင်သည်, he pretends to piety, that is, makes a hypocritical pretence; see ဟန်ပြ.

ဟာ, (1) *n.* a thing, subject, matter.

ဟာ, (2) *v.* to open, be hollow, gape, ဟောင်း ၊ ဟွင်း.

ဟာထီးထီး, *n.* an expression of anger.

ဟိ, *v.* to be, ရှိ, (sometimes used in writing.)

ဟိတ်, (from ဟေတု,) *n.* a cause, reason, origin of action, motive; *also*, one name for the instrumental case, when terminating in ကြောင့်.

ဟိတ်ခြောက်ပါး, *n.* the six universal causes or origins of action, viz. လောဘဟိတ်, riches, worldly pleasures, &c. ဒေါသဟိတ်, malevolence, ill-nature, &c. မောဟဟိတ်, ignorance, folly, want of understanding; these three are called the origin or cause of all sin or demerit. The other three are, အလောဘဟိတ် ၊ အဒေါသဟိတ် ၊ and အမောဟဟိတ်, which are directly the opposites of the former three, and are called the origin or cause of all good works or works of merit.

ဟိတ်စသေလေး, *adv.* little, very little.

ဟိန်း, (1) *v.* to be insupportable, applied to heat.

ဟိန်း, (2) *v.* to be unequalled in glory, power, or authority, တန်ခိုးဘိုး.

ဟိန်းရှိန်, *v.* see both definitions of ဟိန်း. Hence အဟိန်းအရှိန်, *n.* an insupportable heat; an irresistible power, &c.

ဟိန်း, *v.* to snarl, growl.

ဟိန်းဟုံး, *v.* do.

ဟိန်းဟိန်းဟုံးဟုံး, *adv.* in a growling or snarling manner.

ဟိန်းဟိန်းဟဲးဟဲး, *adv.* do.

ဟိန်းဟဲး, *v.* see ဟိန်း.

ဟီန, *(Pali,) adj.* small, mean, insignificant.

ဟီနမာန်, *n.* one description of pride, an envious feeling toward superiors, ထိုသူကားငါထက်သာသေး၏၊ ငါတို့ကားယုတ်ညံ့သသူတည်းဟူ မာန်မူခြင်း.

ဟိမဝန္တ, (from ဟိမ, snow, and ဝန္တ, a forest, *Pali,)* an immense but imaginary forest, in which are seven large lakes, viz. အနောတတ်၊ ကဏ္ဍမုဏ္ဍ၊ ရထကာရ၊ ဆဒ္ဒန်၊ ကုဏာလ၊ မန္ဒာကိနီ၊ သီဟပ္ပပါတ၊ and မူဠလိန္ဒာ; the width of each is about 560 miles, and the depth the same. It is in this forest that most of the wonderful things mentioned in the Boodhist scriptures are said to be.

ဟိမဝန်, *n.* (from ဟိမဝန္တ,) a famous mountain mentioned in the Boodhist scriptures.

ဟီ, *v.* to neigh as a horse, or to make any similar noise.

ဟီးလားလား, *int.* denoting shame in the person uttering it.

ဟိရိ, *(Pali,) n.* modesty, shame, ရှက်ခြင်း. Hence အဟိရိက, *n.* shamelessness, want of modesty, မရှက်ခြင်း.

ဟိရိဗလ, *(Pali,) n.* great shame.

ဟု, a kind of connective, nearly equivalent to the conjunction that, or to the adverb, to wit, namely, &c. as သိသည်ဟုပြောသည်, he says *that* he knows; မင်းရှင်စောဟူဘွဲ့ကိုပေးသည်, he gave (him) the title, *namely*, Menshenzau; sometimes it takes a verbal affix, but ought then to be written ဟူ, and parsed as a verb.

ဟုတ်, (1) *v.* to be distant, far off, ဝေး.

ဟုတ်, (2) *v.* to be true, right, မှန်. အဟုတ်, *n.* truth, အဟုတ်အမှန်.

ဟုတ်က, *adv.* yes, truly, it is so.

ဟုတ်ကဲ့, *adv.* yes, truly.

ဟုတ်ခနဲ, *adv.* immediately, instantly.

ဟုတ်ချည်, *adv.* do.

ဟုတ်ဟုတ်, *adv.* truly, very true, yes yes.

ဟုတ်ဟုတ်ခြိုးခြိုး, *adv.* do.

ဟုန်, *v.* to be quick, vehement. Hence အဟုန်, *n.* swiftness.

ဟုန်ဖြင်း, *v.* do.

ဟုန်ချွန်, *v.* to be exceedingly swift, move with great velocity, pass by with rapidity.

ဟုန်ဟုန်, *adv.* swiftly, rapidly.

ဟုန်း, *v.* to make a sound like a tiger, or like the rush of water, to make any violent or thundering sound. Hence အဟုန်း, any loud thundering noise.

ဟိုဝ်, *pron. adj.* that, (colloquial.)

ဟိုဝ်မာ, see ဟိုဝ်မှာ.

ဟိုဝ်မှ, *adv.* from that, applied to matter or place.

ဟိုဝ်မှာ, there, in that place.

ဟူ, *v.* or *adv.* to say, that is to say, viz. see ဟု.

ဟူရာ, (1) *n.* the Vedas, ဗိဒ်ထဝ်.

ဟူရာ, (2) *n.* astrology, ဗေဒင်.

ဟူရာ, (3) *n.* an astrologer.

ဟူရာဥဒ္ဒိ, *n.* do.

ဟူရာတတ်, *n.* one who is acquainted with the Vedas or astrology.

ဟူရာဖြူ, *n.* do. ပုဏ္ဏာ.

ဟူရာသမား, *n.* an astrologer.

ဟူ၍, and also, likewise, furthermore, &c.

ဟူသည်ရှိ, all there is, all whatsoever, whoever, whatever, ရှိသော၊ သမျှ ၊ သရွေ့.

ဟူသမျှ, see ဟူသည်ရှိ.

ဟူးဟူး, *adv.* the manner of sound expressed by pronouncing the word itself.

ဟေ, *(Pali,)* a vocative particle, ခေါ်ခြင်း.

ဟေတု, *(Pali,)* *n.* a cause, reason, origin, &c. see ဟိတ်.

ဟေတိ, *(Pali,)* *n.* a weapon, လက်နက်.

ဟေမန္တ, *n.* the cold season, ဆောင်းကာလ.

ဟေးဟေ, *n.* a sound uttered to attract the attention of a person at a distance; also used in calling goats.

ဟော့, see ဟဲ.

ဟဲ, *v.* to gape, yawn, သမ်း.

ဟဲး, *v.* to snarl, growl, ဟိန်း.

ဟဲ့, used in commanding persons quite inferior, and in speaking to beasts ; a term of contempt.

ဟော, (1) that, there.

ဟော, (2) *n.* to repeat, utter, or preach, as the priests, ပြော ၊ ဆို.

ဟောပြော, *v.* do.

ဟောမှုန်း, *v.* do.

ဟောက်, (1) *v.* to gape, be hollow, open, ဟိုက် ၊ နွမ်း ; to be sloping, uneven, concave, ဟာ ၊ ပွင့်.

ဟောက်, (2) *v.* to snore, breathe loud, as in sleep, ဝန် ၊ ဟိုက် ၊ မော.

ဟောက်, (3) *v.* to roar, as a lion, ဟက်.

ဟောက်, (4) *pron. adj.* that.

ဟောက်မှာ, there (the object at a distance.)

ဟောင်, (1) *v.* to stink, be fœtid, smell offensive, နံ.

ဟောင်, (2) *v.* to bark or howl, as dogs, &c. ဟစ်.

ဟောင်း, *v.* to be old, not new or recent, decayed, spoiled, ဆွေး ၊ ဆိုး.

ဟောင်းနွမ်း, *v.* to be old, faded; to be worn out, be out of use.

ဟို, *pron. adj.* that.

ဟိုက်, (1) *v.* to be hollow, concave, deep, ချိုင့် ၊ ရှိုင်း ၊ နိမ့်.

ဟိုက်, (2) *n.* a hollow, concavity.

ဟိုက်, (3) *v.* to pant, breathe loud, be exhausted, ဝန် ၊ မော ၊ ဟောက်.

ဟိုက်, (4) *v.* to make wide, gape, as with the mouth, ဟ.

ဟိုင်း, (1) *n.* an elephant without tusks.

ဟိုင်း, (2) *v.* to be destitute of some natural part or member.

ဟိုင်း, (3) *v.* to be destitute of the ability to acquire what is for one's support or comfort.

ဟိုင်း, (4) *n.* a woman who is unable to procure a husband, or a man who cannot obtain a wife.

ဟိုင်းကြီး, *n.* the little Negrais.

## ဠ

ဠကြီး, *n.* the last letter in the Burman alphabet, not used as an initial.

THE END.